A CRITICAL

HISTORY OF FREE THOUGHT

IN REFERENCE TO

THE CHRISTIAN RELIGION.

Eight Lectures

PREACHED BEFORE THE

UNIVERSITY OF OXFORD, IN THE YEAR M.DCCC.LXII., ON THE FOUNDATION OF THE LATE REV. JOHN BAMPTON, M.A. CANON OF SALISBURY.

BY

ADAM STOREY FARRAR, M.A.

MICHEL FELLOW OF QUEEN'S COLLEGE, OXFORD.

NEW YORK:

D. APPLETON AND COMPANY,

443 & 445 BROADWAY.

1863.

EXTRACT

FROM THE LAST WILL AND TESTAMENT

OF THE LATE

REV. JOHN BAMPTON,

CANON OF SALISBURY.

"——I give and bequeath my Lands and Estates to the "Chancellor, Masters, and Scholars of the University of Oxford "for ever, to have and to hold all and singular the said Lands "or Estates upon trust, and to the intents and purposes here-"inafter mentioned; that is to say, I will and appoint that the "Vice-Chancellor of the University of Oxford for the time being "shall take and receive all the rents, issues, and profits thereof, "and (after all taxes, reparations, and necessary deductions made) "that he pay all the remainder to the endowment of eight Divin-"ity Lecture Sermons, to be established for ever in the said Uni-"versity, and to be performed in the manner following:

"I direct and appoint, that, upon the first Tuesday in Easter "Term, a Lecturer be yearly chosen by the Heads of Colleges "only, and by no others, in the room adjoining to the Printing-"House, between the hours of ten in the morning and two in the "afternoon, to preach eight Divinity Lecture Sermons, the year "following, at St. Mary's in Oxford, between the commencement "of the last month in Lent Term, and the end of the third week "in Act Term.

"Also I direct and appoint, that the eight Divinity Lecture "Sermons shall be preached upon either of the following Sub-"jects—to confirm and establish the Christian Faith, and to con-"fute all heretics and schismatics—upon the divine authority of "the holy Scriptures—upon the authority of the writings of the "primitive Fathers, as to the faith and practice of the primitive "Church—upon the Divinity of our Lord and Saviour Jesus "Christ—upon the Divinity of the Holy Ghost—upon the Articles "of the Christian Faith as comprehended in the Apostles' and "Nicene Creeds.

"Also I direct, that thirty copies of the eight Divinity Lecture "Sermons shall be always printed, within two months after they "are preached; and one copy shall be given to the Chancellor of "the University, and one copy to the Head of every College, and "one copy to the Mayor of the city of Oxford, and one copy to "be put into the Bodleian Library; and the expense of printing "them shall be paid out of the revenue of the Land or Estates "given for establishing the Divinity Lecture Sermons; and the "Preacher shall not be paid nor be entitled to the revenue before "they are printed.

"Also I direct and appoint, that no person shall be qualified "to preach the Divinity Lecture Sermons, unless he hath taken "the degree of Master of Arts at least, in one of the two Uni-"versities of Oxford or Cambridge; and that the same person "shall never preach the Divinity Lecture Sermons twice."

PREFACE.

THE object of this Preface is to explain the design of the following Lectures, and to enumerate the sources on which they are founded.

What is the province and mode of inquiry intended in a "Critical History of Free Thought"[1]? What are the causes which led the author into this line of study[2]? What the object proposed by the work[3]? What the sources from which it is drawn[4]?—these probably are the questions which will at once suggest themselves to the reader. The answers to most of them are so fully given in the work[5], that it will only be necessary here to touch upon them briefly.

The word "free thought" is now commonly used, at least in foreign literature[6], to express the result of the revolt of the mind against the pressure of external authority in any department of life or speculation. Information concerning the history of the term is given elsewhere[7]. It will be sufficient now to state, that the cognate term, *free thinking*, was appropriated by Collins early in the last century[8] to express Deism. It differs from the modern term *free thought*, both in being restricted to religion, and in conveying the idea rather of the method than of its result, the freedom of the mode of inquiry rather than the character of the conclusions attained; but the same fundamental idea of independence and freedom from authority is implied in the modern term.

(1) Pref. pp. v.-ix. (2) Id. pp. x, xi. (3) Id. pp. xii, xiii.
(4) Id. p. xiv. (5) Lect. I. : and Lect. VIII. p. 340 seq.
(6) E. g. in the French expression *la libre pensée*. (7) In Note 21. p. 413.
(8) In 1713.

Within the sphere of its application to the Christian religion, free thought is generally used to denote three different systems; viz. Protestantism, scepticism, and unbelief. Its application to the first of these is unfair [9]. It is true that all three agree in resisting the dogmatism of any earthly authority; but Protestantism reposes implicitly on what it believes to be the divine authority of the inspired writers of the books of holy scripture; whereas the other two forms acknowledge no authority external to the mind, no communication superior to reason and science. Thus, though Protestantism by its attitude of independence seems similar to the other two systems, it is really separated by a difference of kind, and not merely of degree [10]. The present history is restricted accordingly to the treatment of the two latter species of free thought,—the resistance of the human mind to the Christian religion as communicated through revelation, either in part or in whole, neither the scepticism which disintegrates it, or the unbelief which rejects it: the former directing itself especially against Christianity, the latter against the idea of revelation, or even of the supernatural generally.

An analogous reason to that which excludes the history of Protestantism, excludes also that of the opposition made to Christianity by heresy, and by rival religions [11]: inasmuch as they repose on authorities, however false, and do not profess to resort to an unassisted study of nature and truth.

This account of the province included under free thought will prepare the way for the explanation of the mode in which the subject is treated.

It is clear that the history, in order to rise above a chronicle, must inquire into the causes which have made freedom of inquiry develope into unbelief. The causes have usually been regarded by theologians to be of two kinds, viz. either superhuman or human; and, if of the latter kind, to be either moral or intellectual. Bishop Van Mildert, in his History of Infidelity, restricted himself entirely to the former [12]. Holding strongly that the existence of evil in the world was attributable, not only indirectly and originally, but directly and perpetually, to the

(9) Many of the modern French protestant critics so employ it; e. g. A, Reville, *Rev. des Deux Mondes*, Parker, Oct. 1861.

(10) Cfr. pp. 9 and 99.

(11) Cfr. p. 12, and Notes 4, 5, and 6, at the end of this volume.

(12) Boyle Lectures (1802-4). See note, p. 345.

operation of the evil spirit, he regarded every form of heresy and unbelief to be the attempt of an invisible evil agent to thwart the truth of God; and viewed the history of infidelity as the study of the results of the operation of this cause in destroying the kingdom of righteousness. Such a view invests human life and history with a very solemn character, and is not without practical value; but it will be obvious that an analysis of this kind must be strictly theological, and removes the inquiry from the province of human science. Even when completed, it leaves unexplored the whole field in which such an evil principle operates, and the agencies which he employs as his instruments.

The majority of writers on unbelief accordingly have treated the subject from a less elevated point of view, and have limited their inquiry to the sphere of the operation of human causes, the *media axiomata* as it were [13], which express the motives and agencies which have been manifested on the theatre of the world, and visible in actual history. It will be clear that within this sphere the causes are specially of two kinds; viz. those which have their source in the will, and arise from the antagonism of feeling, which wishes revelation untrue, and those which manifest themselves in the intellect, and are exhibited under the form of difficulties which beset the mind, or doubts which mislead it, in respect to the evidence on which revelation reposes. The former, it may be feared, are generally the ground of unbelief; the latter the basis of doubt. Christian writers, in the wish to refer unbelief to the source of efficient causation in the human will, with a view of enforcing on the doubter the moral lesson of responsibility, have generally restricted themselves to the former of these two classes; and by doing so have omitted to explore the interesting field of inquiry presented in the natural history of the variety of forms assumed by scepticism, and their relation to the general causes which have operated in particular ages:—a subject most important, if the intellectual antecedents thus discovered be regarded as causes of doubt; and not less interesting, if, instead of being causes, they are merely considered to be instruments and conditions made use of by the emotional powers.

A history of free thought seems to point especially to the study of the latter class. A biographical history of free thinkers

(13) Bacon's Nov. Org. lib. i. Aph. 104.

would imply the former; the investigation of the moral history of the individuals, the play of their will and feelings and character; but the history of free thought points to that which has been the product of their characters, the doctrines which they have taught. Science however no less than piety would decline entirely to separate the two [14]; piety, because, though admitting the possibility that a judgment may be formed in the abstract on free thought, it would feel itself constantly drawn into the inquiry of the moral responsibility of the freethinker in judging of the concrete cases;—science, because, even in an intellectual point of view, the analysis of a work of art is defective if it be studied apart from the personality of the mental and moral character of the artist who produces it. If even the inquiry be restricted to the analysis of intellectual causes, a biographic treatment of the subject, which would allow for the existence of the emotional, would be requisite [15].

The province of the following work accordingly is, the examination of this neglected branch in the analysis of unbelief. While admitting most fully and unhesitatingly the operation of emotional causes, and the absolute necessity, scientific as well as practical, of allowing for their operation, it is proposed to analyse the forms of doubt or unbelief in reference mainly to the intellectual element which has entered into them, and the discovery of the intellectual causes which have produced or modified them. Thus the history, while not ceasing to belong to church history, becomes also a chapter in the history of philosophy, a page in the history of the human mind.

The enumeration of the causes into which the intellectual elements of doubt are resolvable, is furnished in the text of the first Lecture [16]. If the nature of some of them be obscure, and the reader be unaccustomed to the philosophical study necessary for fully understanding them; information must be sought in the books to which references are elsewhere given [17], as the subject is too large to be developed in the limited space of this Preface.

The work however professes to be not merely a narrative, but a "critical history." The idea of criticism in a history imparts to it an ethical aspect. For criticism does not rest content with

(14) Cfr. pp. 14–20.
(15) Pp. 32–34.
(16) Pp. 24–31.
Pp. 22, 24, 25.

ideas, viewed as facts, out as realities. It seeks to pass above the relative, and attain the absolute; to determine either what is right or what is true. It may make this determination by means of two different standards. It may be either independent or dogmatic;—independent if it enters upon a new field candidly and without prepossessions, and rests content with the inferences which the study suggests;—dogmatic, when it approaches a subject with views derived from other sources, and pronounces on right or wrong, truth or falsehood, by reference to them.

It is hoped that the reader will not be unduly prejudiced, if the confession be frankly made, that the criticism in these Lectures is of the latter kind. This indeed might be expected from their very character. The Bampton Lecture is an establishment for producing apologetic treatises. The authors are supposed to assume the truth of Christianity, and to seek to repel attacks upon it. They are defenders, not investigators. The reader has a right to demand fairness, but not independence; truth in the facts, but not hesitation in the inferences. While however the writer of these Lectures takes a definite line in the controversy, and one not adopted professionally, but with cordial assent and heartfelt conviction, he has nevertheless considered that it is due to the cause of scientific truth to intermingle his own opinions as little as possible with the facts of the history. A history without inferences is ethically and religiously worthless: it is a chronicle, not a philosophical narrative. But a history distorted to suit the inferences is not only worthless, but harmful. It is for the reader to judge how far the author has succeeded in the result; but his aim has been not to allow his opinions to warp his view of the facts. History ought to be written with the same spirit of cold analysis which belongs to science. Caricature must not be substituted for portrait, nor vituperation for description [18].

Such a mode of treatment in the present instance was the more possible, from the circumstance that the writer, when studying the subject for his private information, without any design to write upon it, had endeavoured to bring his own principles and views perpetually to the test; and to reconsider them candidly by the light of the new suggestions which were brought before him. Instead of approaching the inquiry with a spirit of hos-

(18) Cfr. p. 346

tility, he had investigated it as a student, not as a partisan. It may perhaps be permitted him without egotism to explain the causes which led him to the study. He had taken holy orders, cordially and heartily believing the truths taught by the church of which he is privileged to be an humble minister. Before doing so, he had read thoughtfully the great works of evidences of the last century, and knew directly or indirectly the character of the deist doubts against which they were directed. His own faith was one of the head as well as the heart; founded on the study of the evidences, as well as on the religious training of early years. But he perceived in the English church earnest men who held a different view; and, on becoming acquainted with contemporary theology, he found the theological literature of a whole people, the Germans, constructed on another basis; a literature which was acknowledged to be so full of learning, that contemporary English writers of theology not only perpetually referred to it, but largely borrowed their materials from German sources. He wished therefore fully to understand the character of these new forms of doubt, and the causes which had produced them. He may confess that, reposing on the affirmative verities of the Christian faith, as gathered from the scriptures and embodied in the immemorial teaching of Christ's church, he did not anticipate that he should discover that which would overthrow or even materially modify his own faith; but he wished, while exploring this field, and gratifying intellectual curiosity, to re-examine his opinions at each point by the light of those with which he might meet in the inquiry. The serious wish also to fulfil his duty in the sphere in which he might move, made him desire to understand these new views; that if false, he might know how to refute them when they came before him, and not be first made aware of their existence from the harsh satire of sceptical critics. His own studies were accordingly conducted in a spirit of fairness—the fairness of the inquirer, not of the doubter; and a habit of mind formed by the study of the history of philosophy, was brought to bear upon the investigation of this chapter in church history: first, of modern forms of doubt, and afterwards the consecutive history of unbelief generally. Accordingly, while he hopes that he has taken care to leave the student in no case unguided, who may accompany him in these pages through the history, he has wished to place him, as he strove to place himself, in the position to see the subject in its true light before drawing the inferences; to understand each topic to a certain extent, as it appears when seen from the opposite point of view, as well as when seen from the Christian. And when this has been effected, he has criticised each by a comparison with those principles which form his standard for testing them, the truth of which the study has confirmed to the writer's own mind. The criticism therefore does not profess to be independent, but dogmatic; but it is hoped that the definite character of the results will not be found to have prevented fairness in the method of inquiry. If the student has the facts correctly, he can form his own judgment on the inferences.

The standard of truth here adopted, as the point of view in criticism, is the teaching of Scripture as expressed in the dogmatic teaching of the creeds of the church; or, if it will facilitate clearness to be more definite, three great truths may be specified, which present themselves to the writer's mind as the very foundation of the Christian religion: (1) the doctrine of the reality of the vicarious atonement provided by the passion of our blessed Lord; (2) the supernatural and miraculous character of the religious revelation in the book of God; and (3) the direct operation of the Holy Ghost in converting and communing with the human soul. Lacking the first of these, Christianity appears to him to be a religion without a system of redemption; lacking the second, a doctrine without authority; lacking the third, a system of ethics without spiritual power. These three principles accordingly are the measure, by agreement with which the truth and falsehood of systems of free thought are ultimately tested [19].

The above remarks, together with those which occur in the text, where fuller explanation is afforded, will illustrate the province of the inquiry, and the spirit in which it is conducted [20].

The explanation also of the further question concerning the object which the writer proposed to effect, by the treatment of such a subject in a course of Bampton Lectures, is given so fully elsewhere, that a few words may here suffice in reference to it [21].

(19) See especially Lect. VIII. p. 357 seq.

(20) Some valuable remarks on the proper balance of the mind in study are contained in a sermon, *The Nemesis of Excess*, recently preached at Oxford, by Bp. Jackson.

(21) pp. 35-37.

Experience of the wants of students in this time of doubt and transition, which those who are practically acquainted with the subject will best understand, as well as observation of the tone of thought expressed in our sceptical literature, led him to believe that a history, natural as well as literary, of doubt; an analysis of the forms and a statement of the intellectual causes of it, would have a value, direct and indirect, in many ways. His desire, he is willing to confess, was to guide the student, rather than to refute the unbeliever. He did not expect to furnish the combatant with ready-made weapons, which would make him omnipotent in conflict; but he hoped to give him some suggestions in reference to the tactics for conducting the contest. The Lectures have a polemical aspect, but they seek to obtain their end by means of the educational. The writer has aimed at assisting the student, in the struggle with his doubts, in the inquiry for truth, in the quiet meditative search for light and knowledge, preparatory to ministering to others. The survey of a new region, which ordinary works on the history of infidelity rarely touch, may lay bare unsuspected or undetected causes of unbelief; and thus indirectly offer a refutation of it; for intellectual error is refuted, when the origin of it is referred to false systems of thought. The anatomy of error is the first step to its cure.

In another point of view, independently of the value of the line of inquiry generally, and the special suitability of it to individual minds, there is a further use, which in the present day belongs to it in common with all inquiries into the history of thought.

It is hard to persuade the students of a past generation that the historic mode of approaching any problem is the first step toward its successful solution. Yet a little reflection may at least make the meaning of the assertion understood. If we view the literary characteristic of the present, in comparison with that of past ages, we are perhaps right in stating, that its peculiar feature is the prevalence of the method of historical criticism. If the four centuries since the Renaissance be considered, the critical peculiarity of the sixteenth and seventeenth will be found to be the investigation of ancient literature; in the former directed to *words*, in the latter to *things*. The eighteenth century broke away from the past, and, emancipating itself from authority, tried to rebuild truth from its foundations from present materials, independent of the judgment formed by past ages. The nineteenth century unites both methods. It ventures not to explore the universe, unguided by the experience of the past; but, while reuniting itself to the past, it does not bow to it. It accepts it as a fact, not as an authority. The seventeenth century worshipped the past; the eighteenth despised it: the nineteenth mediates, by means of criticism. Accordingly, in literary investigations at present, each question is approached from the historic side, with the belief that the historico-critical inquiry not only gratifies curiosity, but actually contributes to the solution of the problem. Some indeed assert [22] this, because they think that the historic study of philosophy is the whole of philosophy; and, believing that all truth is relative to its age, are hopeless of attaining the absolute and unaltering solution of any problem. We, on the other hand, are content to believe that the history of philosophy is only the entrance to philosophy. But in either case, truth is sought by means of a philosophical history of the past; which, tracking the progress of truth and error in any particular department, lays bare the natural as well as the literary history; the causes of the past, as well as its form. Truth and error are thus discovered, not by breaking with the past, and using abstract speculations on original data, but by tracing the growth of thought, gathering the harvest of past investigations, and learning by experience to escape error.

These considerations bear upon the present subject in this manner: they show not only the special adaptation to the passing tastes of the age, of an historic mode of approaching a subject, but exhibit also that the mode of proof and of refutation must be sought, not on abstract grounds, but historic. The position of an enemy is not to be forced, but turned; his premises to be refuted, not his conclusions; the antecedent reasons which led him into his opinion to be exhibited, not merely evidence offered of the fact that he is in error.

This view, that doubt might be refuted by the historic analysis of its operation, by laying bare the antecedent grounds which had produced it, will explain why the author was led to believe that a chapter of mental and moral physiology might be useful,

(22) Cfr. pp. 31 note, 342; and Note 9. pp. 396–8.

which would not merely carry out the anatomy of actual forms of disease, but discover their origin by the study of the preceding natural history of the patients.

These remarks will perhaps suffice for explaining the object which was proposed in writing this history; and may justify the hope that this work, thus adapted to the wants of the time, may offer such a contribution to the subject of the Christian evidences, as not only to possess an intellectual value, but to coincide with the purpose contemplated by the founder of the Lectures.

It remains to state the sources which have been used for the literary materials of the history. Though they are sufficiently indicated in the notes, a general description of them may be useful.

They may be distributed under four classes;

1. The histories which have been professedly devoted to the subject.

2. The notices of the history of unbelief in general histories of the church or of literature.

3. (Which ought indeed to rank first in importance;) the original authorities for the facts, i. e. the works of the sceptical writers themselves; or of the contemporary authors who have refuted them.

4. The monographs, which treat of particular writers, ages, or schools, of sceptical thought.

In approaching the subject, a student would probably commence with the first two classes; and after having thus acquired for himself a *carte du pays*, would then explore it in detail by the aid of the third and fourth.

1. The works which have professedly treated of the history of infidelity, as a whole, are not of great importance.

One of the earliest was the *Historia Univ. Atheismi*, 1725, of Reimannus; and the *De Atheismo*, 1737, of Buddeus. (An explanation of the word *Atheism*, as employed by them, is given in Note 21. p. 413.) They furnish, as the name implies, a history of scepticism, as well as of sceptics; yet, though the labours of such diligent and learned men can never be useless, they afford little information now available. Their date also necessarily precluded them from knowing the more recent forms of unbelief. Perhaps under this head we ought also to name the chapters on polemical theology in the great works of bibliography of the German scholars of the same time, such as Pfaff (*Hist. Litt. Theol.*); Buddeus (*Isagoge*); Fabricius (*Delectus Argum.*); Walch's (*Biblical Theol. Select.*); which contain lists of sceptical works, either directly, or indirectly by naming the apologists who have answered them. The references to these works will be found in Note 39. p. 436.

Among French writers, the only one of importance is Houtteville, who prefixed an Introduction to his work, *La Religion Chrétienne prouvée par des faits*, 1722, containing an account of the writers for and against Christianity from the earliest times. (Translated 1739.) It contains little information concerning the authors or the events, but a clearly and correctly written analysis of their works and thoughts.

Among the English writers who have attempted a consecutive history of the whole subject was Van Mildert, afterwards bishop of Durham, who has been already named. The first volume of his *Boyle Lectures*, in 1802–4, was devoted to the history of infidelity; the second to a general statement of the evidences for Christianity. This work, on account of its date, necessarily stops short before the existence of modern forms of doubt; and indeed evinces no knowledge concerning the contemporary forms of literature in Germany, which had already attracted the attention of Dr. Herbert Marsh. The point of view of the work, as already described, almost entirely precludes the author from entering upon the analysis of the causes, either emotional or intellectual, which have produced unbelief. Its value accordingly is chiefly in the literary materials collected in the notes; in which respect it bears marks of careful study. Though mostly drawn from second-hand sources, it exhibits wide reading and thoughtful judgment.

A portion of the Bampton Lectures for 1852, by the Rev. J. C. Riddle, was devoted to the subject of infidelity. The author's object, as the title [23] implies, was to give the natural history of unbelief, to the neglect of the literary. Psychological rather than historical analysis was used by him for the investigation; and his examination of the moral causes of doubt is better than

(23) *The Natural History of Infidelity and Superstition in Contrast with Christian Faith.*

of the intellectual. The notes contain a collection of valuable quotations, which supplement those of Van Mildert, but are unfortunately given, for the most part, without references.

This completes [24] the enumeration of the histories professedly devoted to infidelity, with the exception of a small but very creditable production published since several of these lectures were written, *Defence of the Faith; Part I. Forms of Unbelief*, by the Rev. S. Robins, forming the first part of a work, of which the second is to treat the evidences; the third to draw the moral. It does not profess to be a very deep work [25]; but it is interesting; drawn generally from the best sources, and written in an eloquent style and devout spirit.

2. The transition is natural from these works, which treat of the history of unbelief or give lists of the works of unbelievers, to the notices of sceptical writers contained in general histories of the church or of literature.

In this, as in the former case, it is only in modern times that important notices occur concerning forms of unbelief. The circumstance that in the early ages unbelief took the form of opposition or persecution on the part of heathens, and that in the middle ages it was so rare, caused the ancient church historians and mediæval church chroniclers to record little respecting actual unbelief, though they give information about heresy. Even in modern times, it is not till the early part of the eighteenth century that any attention is bestowed on the subject. The earlier historians, both Protestant, such as the Magdeburg Centuriators, and Catholic, like Baronius, wrote the history of the past for a controversial purpose in relation to the contests of their own times: and in the next period, in the one church, Arnold confined himself to the history of heresy rather than unbelief; and in the

(24) A work partly on the history of unbelief, *Scepticism a Retrogressive Move in Theology and Philosophy*, has also been lately written (1861) by the accomplished lord Lindsay. Great learning is shown in it. Though written with a special controversial purpose, and though the facts accordingly are briefly stated, without literary references, it contains a useful summary and suggestive reflections.

(25) In a literary point of view it is incorrect, in one chapter, if the author understands Mr. Robins rightly, where he seems to classify together, under the same head of Pantheism, the atheism of the French school of the Encyclopædists in the last century and that of the German philosophers of the present. The two indeed agree in denying or ignoring the existence of a personal God; but in tone, premises, and metaphysical relations, they differ diametrically. (Since this note was written, the sad intelligence of Mr. Robins's death has appeared.)

other, Fleury and Tillemont wrote the history of deeds rather than of ideas, and afford no information, except in a few allusions of the latter writer to the early intellectual opposition of the heathens.

But about the middle of the eighteenth century, in the period of cold orthodoxy and solid learning which immediately preceded the rise of rationalism, as well as in that of incipient free thought, we meet not only with the historians of theological literature already named above, but with historians of thought like Brucker, and of the church like Mosheim, possessed of large taste for inquiry, and wide literary sympathies, who contribute information on the subject: and towards the close of the century we find Schröckh, who, in his lengthy and careful history of the church since the Reformation [26], has taken so extensive a view of the nature of church history, that he has included in it an account of the struggle with freethinkers. Among the same class, with the exception that he differs in being marked by rationalist sympathies, must be ranked Henke [27].

In the present century the spread of the scientific spirit, which counts no facts unworthy of notice, together with the attention bestowed on the history of doctrine, and the special interest in understanding the fortunes of free thought, which sympathy in danger created during the rationalist movement, prevented the historians from passing lightly over so important a series of facts. It may be sufficient to instance, in proof, the notices of unbelief

(26) *Christliche Kirchengeschichte*, &c. 45 vols. 1768–1812. The writer of these lectures has taken occasion elsewhere (p. 466,) to deplore the want of any complete history of the English church. He may here add also the want of a history in English of European Christianity since the Reformation.

(27) It may offer an explanation of subsequent references to some church historians, to name the classification given by Schaff (*Bibliotheca Sacra*, 1850). After treating of the ancient and mediæval histories, and making the obvious subdivision of the modern into Romish and Protestant, and subdividing these again according to their nations, he arranges the Protestant historians of Germany chronologically under five classes: (1) the Polemico-orthodox, such as the Magdeburg centuriators; (2) the Pietistic,—Arnold and Weismann; (3) the Pragmatico-supernatural,—Mosheim, Walch, Planck, Schröckh; (4) the Rationalist,—Semler, Henke, Gieseler (in reference to which latter he is perhaps hardly fair); (5) the Scientific, viz. (α) of the Schleiermacher school,—Neander; (β) of the Hegelian, unchurchlike and heterodox,—Baur; (γ) of the Hegelian, churchlike and orthodox,—Dorner. Concerning older church historians, see the late Rev. J. G. Dowling's excellent work, *Introduction to the Critical Study of Ecclesiastical History*, 1838; and, on the most modern German church historians, see *North British Review*, Nov. 1858.

which occur in Neander's *Church History*. General histories also of literature, like Schlosser's *History of Literature in the Eighteenth Century*, or the more theological one of Hagenbach (*Geschichte des* 18ⁿ *Jahrhunderts*) incidentally afford information.

The various works just named are the chief of this class which furnish assistance.

3. After a general preliminary idea of the history has been obtained from these sources, in order to prevent being confused with details; it is necessary to resort next to the original sources of information, without careful study of which the history must lack a real basis.

In reference to the early unbelievers, the direct materials are lost; but the contemporary replies to these writings remain. In the case of later unbelievers, both the works and the answers to them exist. It will be presumed that in so large a subject the writer cannot have read all the sceptical works which have been written, and are here named. With the exception however of Averroes and of the Paduan school [28], in which cases he has chiefly adopted second-hand information, and merely himself consulted a few passages of the original writers, he has in all other instances read the chief works of the sceptical writers, sufficiently at least to make himself acquainted with their doubts, and in many cases has even made an analysis of their works. The reader will perceive by the foot-notes the instances in which this applies.

It may be due to some of the historians who have made a special study of particular periods from original sources, to state, that so far as his limited experience extends he can bear witness to their exactness. Lechler's work on English deism, for example [29], is a singular example of truthful narrative; and Leland's [30], though controversial, is worthy of nearly the same praise.

4. There remains a fourth source of materials in the separate monographs on particular men, opinions, or schools of thought. We shall enumerate these according to the order of the lectures; dwelling briefly on the majority of them, as being described elsewhere; and describing at greater length those only which relate

(28) Lect. III. pp. 100–103. (29) *Geschichte des Englischen Deismus*, 1841.

(30) *J. Leland's View of the Deistical Writers*, 1754. An edition published in 1837 contains an account of the subsequent history of Deism by Cyrus R. Edmonds. It is edited by Dr. W. L. Brown.

to the history of the theological movements in Germany described in Lectures VI. and VII.; inasmuch as references are there frequently made to these works without a specific description of their respective characters.

In relation to the early struggle of Paganism against Christianity [31], the work of Lardner, *Collection of Ancient Jewish and Heathen Testimonies to the Truth of the Christian Religion* (1764–7) (Works, vols. vii.–ix.), is well known for carefulness of treatment and the value of its references. Portions also of the works of J. A. Fabricius, especially his *Bibliotheca Græca* and *Lux Evangelii* (1732) are useful in reference to the lost works, and for bibliographical knowledge: also a monograph by Kortholt, *Paganus Obtrectator* (1703), on the objections made by Christians in the early ages, gathered from the Apologies.

Among recent works it is only necessary to specify one, viz. the second series of the *Histoire de l'Eglise Chrétienne*, by E. de Pressensé (1861), containing *La Grande Lutte du Christianisme contre le Paganisme*, the account of the struggle both of deeds and ideas on the part of the heathens against Christianity, and of the apology of the Christians in reply. The sketches of the arguments used both by the heathens, as recovered from fragments, and by the Christian apologists, are most ably executed. The frequent references to it in the foot-notes will show the importance which the writer attaches to this work [32].

The long period of the middle ages, together with early modern [33] history, so far as the latter bears upon the present subject, is spanned by the aid of four works; Cousin's Memoir on Abelard (1836); the *La Reforme* of Laurent (1861), a professor at Ghent; the *Averroes* of E. Renan (1851), one of the ablest among the younger writers of France; and the *Essais de Philosophie Religieuse* of E. Saisset (1859). All these works are full of learning; some of them are works of mind as well as of erudition. Cousin's treatise is well known [34], and may be said to have reopened the study of mediæval philosophy. The contents of Laurent's work are specified elsewhere.[35] That of Renan, besides containing a sketch of the life and philosophy of Averroes, studies

(31) Lecture II.

(32) An older work, in some respects similar to Pressensé's, is Tzchirner's *Geschichte der Apologetik*, 1805.

(33) Lecture III. (34) See p. 82, note. (35) P. 76, note.

his influence in the three great spheres where it was felt,—the Spanish Jews, the Scholastic philosophers, and the Peripatetics of Padua. The work of Saisset is a most instructive critical sketch on religious philosophy.

The period of English Deism [36] is treated in two works; the well-known work of Leland above cited, and the one also named above by Lechler, now general superintendent at Leipsic; a work full of information, and exceedingly complete; one of the carefully executed monographs with which many of the younger German scholars first bring their names into notice. Though the interest of the subject is limited, it well merits a translator [37].

There is a deficiency of any similar work on the history of infidelity in France [38], treating it separately and exhaustively. The work which most nearly deserves the description is vol. vi. of Henke's *Kirchengeschichte* [39]. This want however is the less felt, because almost every portion of the period has been treated in detail by French critics of various schools; among which some of the sketches of Bartholmess, *Histoire Critique des Doctrines Religieuses de la Philosophie Moderne*, 1855; and of Damiron, *Mémoires pour servir à l'Histoire de Philosophie au* 18e *siècle;* [40] are perhaps the most useful for our purpose. One portion of Mr. Buckle's *History of Civilisation*, the best written part of his first volume, also affords much information, in the main trustworthy, in reference to the intellectual condition of France of the same period [41].

A description of the events of a period so complex as that of the German theological movement of the last hundred years [42] would have been an object too ambitious to attempt, especially when it must necessarily, from the size of the subject, be grounded on an acquaintance with single writers of a school, or single works of an author used as samples of the remainder; if it were not that abundant guidance is supplied in the memoirs by German theologians of all shades of opinion, who have studied the history of their country, and not only narrated facts, but investigated causes. A few narratives of it also exist by scholars

(36) Lecture IV.

(37) The able French critic C. Remusat has bestowed attention on some of the English deists. A paper on Shaftesbury has appeared since Lecture IV. was printed, in the *Revue des Deux Mondes*, Nov. 1862.

(38) In Lecture V. (39) Edited by Vater. (40) See p. 177, note.

(41) See p. 164, note. (42) Lectures VI. and VII.

of other countries; but these are founded on the former. We shall in the main preserve the order of their publication in enumerating these various works.

The materials for the condition of Germany at the beginning of the last century, antecedently to the introduction of the new influences which created rationalism [43], are conveyed in Weismann, *Introductio in Memorabilia Eccl. Hist.* (1718), and in Schröckh, *Christliche Kirchengeschichte* (1768–1812). The first distinct examination however of the peculiar character of the movement which ensued, called Rationalism, occurred in the discussion as to its meaning and province; in which Tittmann, Röhr, Staüdlin, Bretschneider, Hahn, &c., were engaged; an account of which, with a list of their works [44], is given under the explanation of the word "Rationalism" in Note 21, p. 416. The chief value of these works at present is, partly to enable us to understand how contemporaries viewed the movement while in progress; partly to reproduce the state of belief which existed in the older school of rationalists, and its opponents, before the reaction toward orthodoxy had fully altered theological thought.

Whilst the dispute between rationalism and supernaturalism was still going on, and the latter was gradually gaining the victory, through the reaction under Schleiermacher just alluded to, an English writer, Mr. Hugh James Rose [45], published some sermons preached at Cambridge in 1825, which were the means of directing attention to the subject both at home and abroad, and stimulating investigation into the history. As this work, and especially the reply of one writer to it, are often here quoted, it may be well to narrate the interesting literary controversy, now forgotten, which ensued upon its publication.

Mr. Rose described the havoc made by the rationalist speculations, alike in dogma, in interpretation, and in church history, and attributed the evil chiefly to the absence of an efficient system of internal church government which would have suppressed such a movement. He was answered (1828) by Mr. (now Dr.) Pusey, then a junior Fellow of Oriel, who, having visited Germany, and become acquainted with the forms of

(43) Lecture VI. p. 213.

(44) Some of these works were subsequent to the discussion caused abroad by the sermons of Mr. Rose, described below.

(45) Afterwards Principal of the King's College, London.

German thought, and the circumstances which had marked its development, conceived justly that the reasons of a moral phenomenon like the overthrow of religious faith in Germany must be sought in intrinsic causes, and not merely in an extrinsic cause, such as the absence of efficient means of ecclesiastical repression. In this work [46], marked by great knowledge of the subject, and characterized by just and philosophical reflections, the author pointed out an internal law of development in the events of the history, and traced the ultimate cause of the movement to the divorce between dogma and piety which had characterized the age preceding the rise of rationalism. His motive for entering the contest was, not the wish to defend the movement, for his own position was fixed upon the faith of the creeds; but seems to have been partly a love of truth, which did not like to see an imperfect view of a great question set forth; and partly the wish to prevent attention being diverted by Mr. Rose's explanation, from perceiving the extreme resemblance of the contemporary time in England to that of the age which preceded rationalism.

To this work Mr. Rose replied in a Letter to the Bishop of London, misunderstanding Mr. Pusey's object, and conveying the impression that he had made himself responsible for the rationalism which it had been the object of the sermons to condemn. He felt himself however compelled, in a second edition of the sermons [47], to enter more largely into proofs from German literature of the position which he had assumed; and produced a collection of literary facts, of value in reference to the movement.

Mr. Pusey replied (1830) with a triumphant vindication alike of his own meaning, and the truth of his own position [48]. The work is necessarily less interesting than the former, as it turns more upon personal questions, and is more polemical; but the literary information conveyed is equally valuable.

If we may be permitted to form an opinion concerning the controversy, it may perhaps be true to say, that Mr. Rose's fault (if indeed we may say so of one who so worthily received honour in his generation) was, that he approached the subject from the polemic and practical instead of the historic side. His work is

(46) *Historical Inquiry into the Probable Causes of the Rationalist Character lately predominant in the Theology of Germany.*

(47) 1829. (48) *Historical Inquiry*, &c. part ii. 1830.

like the description of a battle-field, which gives an idea of the mangled remains that strew the field, but does not recount the causes of contest, nor the progress of the action. The work of his opponent describes the mustering of the forces preparatory to the action, and the causes which led to the struggle. Perhaps, in a few matters of detail, the former writer has taken a truer, though a less hopeful, view than his opponent, of certain classes of opinions, or of certain men; but the latter has better preserved the historical perspective. The former saw mainly the old forms of rationalism, the latter descried the partial return toward the faith which had already begun, and has since gone forward so energetically [49].

These works must always afford much information on the topics which they embrace. It is proper however to add, that Dr. Pusey, some years ago, recalled the remaining copies of the edition of his work. On this account the writer of these lectures, when he has had occasion to give references to it, has taken care not to quote it for opinions, but only for facts [50].

The attack of Mr. Rose on German theology caused replies abroad as well as at home. Several German theologians were led to a more careful study of their own history and position, to which references will be found in Mr. Rose's replies [51].

Previously to the publication of Dr. Pusey's treatises, a work had been written with a purpose less directly controversial, by Tholuck: *Abriss Einer Geschichte der umwälzung, welche seit* 1750, *auf dem Gebiete der Theologie in Deutschland statt gefunden*, now contained in his *Vermischte Schriften*, 1839, vol. 2 [52]. It is valuable for the earlier history of Rationalism. The spirit of it is very similar to that of Dr. Pusey's work. Indeed the latter author, though not aware of the publication of Tholuck's work, was cognisant of his views on these questions, through lectures heard from him abroad.

These works however were all previous to the great agitation in German theology, which ensued in consequence of Strauss's

(49) P. 241.

(50) Dr. S. Lee, of Cambridge, also appended a dissertation on some points of German Rationalism to his *Six Sermons on Prophecy*, 1830.

(51) In the Appendix to the second edition of the *State of Protestantism in Germany*, 1829.

(52) A brief sketch of Tholuck's views is given in the *Foreign Quarterly Review*, vol. 25.

Leben Jesu, in 1835. After the first excitement of that event had passed, we meet with three works, two French and one German, in which the history is brought down to a later period. The French ones were, the *Histoire Critique du Rationalisme*, 1841, of Amand Saintes, translated 1849; and the *Etudes Critiques sur le Rationalisme Contemporain*, of the Abbé H. de Valroger, 1846; the latter of which works the writer of these lectures has been unable to see. The German one was, *Der Deutsche Protestantismus*, 1847 [53], and is attributed to Hundeshagen, professor at Heidelberg.

The *Critical History* of Amand Saintes, though thought by the Germans [54] to be defective, in consequence of want of sufficiently separating between the various forms of rationalism, is more replete than any other book with stores of information, and extracts arranged in a very clear form [55]. It is very useful, if the reader first possesses a better scheme into which to arrange the materials. It is written also in a truly evangelical spirit.

The work of Hundeshagen had a political object as well as a religious. It was composed just before the revolution of 1848, when Germany was panting for freedom; and its object was to defend the position of the constitutional party in church and state; and with a view to establish the importance of their moral and doctrinal position, he surveyed the recent history of his country.

Hagenbach's *Dogmengeschichte* (translated), which was published nearly about the same time, also contains a very interesting sketch, with valuable notes, of the chief writers and works in the movement of German theology.

The view of the history given in Tholuck and Hundeshagen

(53) *Der Deutsche Protestantismus, seine Vergangenheit und seine heutigen Lebensfragen in zusammenhang der gesammten rationalentwickelung beleuchtet von einem Deutschen.* A very instructive article was written in the *British Quarterly Review*, No. 26, May 1851, founded chiefly on this work.

(54) Kahnis, *Internal History of German Protestantism* (E. T.), p. 169, note.

(55) An English clergyman, Mr. E. H. Dewar, wrote a small work in 1844, on *German Protestantism;* based chiefly on Amand Saintes, but in tone like that of Mr. Rose. It was considered very unfair, and was answered by Neander in the *Jahrbücher fur Wissenschaftliche Kritik*, October 1844; and when Mr. Dewar replied, was again answered by him in *Antwortschreiben*, 1845. It may be proper to name here, that Mr. B. Hawkins's work, *Germany, Spirit of her History*, &c. 1838, contains miscellaneous information on many points of German life, which illustrate this portion of the history.

is that which is taken by the school called the "Mediation school" in German theology [56]. The general cause assigned by them for scepticism was the separation of dogma and piety; the recovery from the rationalistic state being due to the reunion of these elements, which Hundeshagen shows to have been also the great feature of the German reformation.

After an interval of about ten years, when the tendencies created by Strauss's movement had become definitely manifest, the history was again surveyed in two works, the one, *Geschichte des Deutschen Protestantismus*, by Kahnis (translated 1856), who belongs to the Lutheran reactionary party; the other, *Geschichte der neuesten Theologie*, 1856, by C. Schwarz, whose work is so candid and free from party bias, that it is unimportant to remark the party to which he belongs [57].

The narrative of Kahnis, originally a series of papers in a magazine, is very full of facts, and generally fair; but it wants form. The author's view is, that the sceptical movement arose from abandoning the dogmatic expression of revealed truth, contained in the old Confessions of the Lutheran church; and he considers the reaction of the Mediation school in favour of orthodoxy to be imperfect; the true restoration being only found by returning to the Confessions.

The work of Schwarz is restricted to the latest forms of German theology, and goes back no farther than the circumstances which led to the work of Strauss. It is unequalled in clearness; bearing the mark of German exactness and fulness, and rivalling French histories in didactic power. These two works differ from most of those previously named, in being histories of modern German theology generally, and not merely of the rationalist forms of it.

Such are the chief sources in which a student may learn the view taken by the German critics of different schools, concerning the recent church history of their country at various moments of its progress. The fulness of this account will be excused, if it

(56) P. 279. Neander has also written a work, *Geschichte des Verflossenen halb-Jahrhunderts.* (*Deutsche Zeitschrift*, 1850.)

(57) He belongs to a new form of the historico-critical school; see Note 41, p. 438; but writes without prejudice. An article elsewhere referred to (p. 7) in the *Westminster Review*, may convey an idea of the facts of Schwarz's work; but it expresses a more definite tendency and opinions than his work.

provide information concerning works to which reference is made in the foot-notes of those lectures which treat of this period.

In describing the doubts of the present century in France [58], considerable help has been found in the *Hist. de la Littérature*, &c. written by Nettement [59], and in the *Essais* of Damiron [60], as well as in criticisms by recent French writers; which are cited in the foot-notes to the lecture which treats of the period.

The subject of the contemporary doubt in England [61] has been felt to be a delicate one. It has however been thought better to carry the history down to the present time, and to deal frankly in expressing the writer's own opinion. Delicacy forbade the introduction of the names [62] of writers into the text of this part of the Sermons, but they have been inserted in the foot-notes.

The mention of one additional source of information will complete the examination which was proposed.

It will be observed, that references have been very frequently given in the notes, to the Reviews, English and French, and occasionally German, for papers which treat on the subjects embraced in the history. When the writer studied the subject for publication, he took care to consult these, as affording a kind of commentary by contemporaries on the different portions of the his-

(58) Lect. VII. p. 289 seq. (59) P. 290, note.
(60) Id. (61) Lect. VIII.

(62) As the relation of the present condition of religious belief in England to forms of philosophy may not have been made perfectly clear even by the remarks in Lect. VIII. p. 330 seq., and Note 9 (p. 396), it may be well here to state the sequence intended, even at the risk of repetition. The father of the modern philosophy is Kant. He first gave the impulse to resolve truth, which was supposed to be objective, into subjective forms of thought. Hence, in succeeding systems of philosophy, the idea was thought to be of more importance than the facts; and an *à priori* tendency was created. But in the two philosophers, Schelling and Hegel, this developed in different modes. Both sought to approach facts through ideas; to both the ideal world was the real: but with the former, truth was absolute; with the latter, relative. In the former case the mind was thrown in upon itself, and had a secure ground of truth in the eternal truths of the reason; in the latter it was thrown (ultimately, though not immediately) outward, and taught to trace the transition of the ideas in the world, the growth of truth in history. Hence in theology, while the tendency of both was to find an appeal for truth independent of revelation, the one produced an intuitional religion, the other, proximately, an ideal, but ultimately generates scepticism: for the one clings to the eternal ideas in the mind, the other views the fleeting, changing aspects of truth in the world. The spirit of the former is seen in Carlyle, Coleridge, and Cousin; the spirit of the latter in Renan and Scherer, and is beginning to appear in the younger writers of the English periodical literature. Hence in English theology we have two broadly marked divisions; one doctrinal, and the other literary; the former of which subdivides into the two just named.

tory. It is hoped that the references to those written in the two former languages will be found to be tolerably complete. The enormous number of those which exist in German, together with the absence for the most part of indexes to them, renders it probable that many separate papers of great value, the special studies by different scholars of passages in the literary history of their own nation, have been left unenumerated. The German literary periodicals are indeed the solitary source of information which the writer considers has not been fully worked for these lectures [63].

Among the articles in English Reviews, many bear marks of careful study; and it is a pleasure to have the opportunity of rescuing them from the neglect which is likely to occur to papers written without name, and in periodicals. The freethinking Reviews have discussed the opinions of the friends of free thought more frequently than the others; but those here cited are of all shades of opinion; and the writer has found many to be of great use, even when differing widely from the conclusions drawn. He is glad indeed to take this opportunity of expressing his thanks to the unknown authors of these various productions, which have afforded him so much instruction, and often so much help. He trusts that he has in all cases candidly and fully acknowledged his obligations when he has borrowed their materials, or condensed their thoughts. If he has in any case, through inadvertence, failed to do so, he hopes that this acknowledgment will be allowed to compensate for the unintentional omission.

The reader being now in possession both of the purpose designed in the lectures, and of the sources of the information used in their composition, it only remains to add a few miscellaneous remarks.

In the delivery of the lectures, several portions were omitted, on account of the excessive length to which they would have run. It has not been thought necessary to indicate these passages by brackets; but, as those who heard them may perhaps wish to have an enumeration, a list is here subjoined [64].

(63) Many references to them are given in Smith's (American) Translation of Hagenbach's *Hist. of Doctr.* 1862.

(64) In Lect. I. p. 16 (last par.), 35, 36 : in Lect. II. p. 66 (last par.) : in Lect. III. p. 80 (last half), 81 (first half), 92, 97 ; 98 (last par.), 99 ; 102, 104, 105, 108, 111

The notes, it will be perceived, are placed, some at the foot of the text, others at the end. Those are put as foot-notes which either were very brief, or which supplied information that the reader might be supposed to desire in connection with the text. Most of those which are appended are of the same character as the foot-notes; i. e. sources of information in reference to the subjects discussed in the text. A few however supply information on collateral subjects. The Notes 4, 5, and 49, will be found to contain a history of Apologetic Literature parallel with the history of Free Thought; and Note 21 discusses the history of some technical terms commonly employed in the history of doubt.

The size of the subject has precluded the possibility of giving many extracts from other works; but it may be permitted to remark, that the literary references given are designed to supply sources of real and valuable information on the various points in relation to which they are cited. It can hardly be necessary to state, that the writer must not in any way be held responsible for the sentiments expressed in the works to which he may have given references. In a subject such as that which is here treated, many of the works cited are neutral in character, and many are objectionable. But it is right to supply complete literary materials, as well as references to works which state both sides of the questions considered.

The index appended is brief, and devoted chiefly to Proper Names; the fulness of the Table of Contents seeming to render a longer one unnecessary, which should contain references to subjects.

The writer wishes to express his acknowledgments to the chief Librarian of the Bodleian, the Rev. H. O. Coxe, for his kindness in procuring for his use a few foreign works which were necessary. He avails himself also of this opportunity of expressing publicly his thanks to the same individual, for the perseverance with which he has accomplished the scheme of providing a reading-room in connection with the Bodleian Library, open to students in an evening. Those whose time and strength are spent in college or private tuition during the mornings, are thus enabled

(part): in Lect. IV. p. 120, 122, 124 (part), 141, 143; 145-147; 148: in Lect. V. p. 181, 182; 184; 196-203: in Lect. VI. p. 210, 237; 250-259 (nearly all): in Lect. VII. p. 281 (part); 291-301: in Lect. VIII. p. 307 (part); 310-339 (for which a brief analysis was substituted); p. 344; 355, 359 (part).

to avail themselves of the treasures of a library, which until this recent alteration was in a great degree useless to many of the most active minds and diligent students in the university.

Thanks are also due to a few other persons for their advice and courtesy in the loan of scarce books; also, in some instances, for assistance in the verification of a reference [65]; and in one case, to a distinguished scholar, for his kindness in revising one of the Notes.

The spirit in which the writer has composed the history has been stated elsewhere [66]. His work now goes forth with no extraneous claims on public attention. If it be, by the Divine blessing, the means of affording instruction, guidance, or comfort, to a single mind, the writer's labour will be amply recompensed.

(65) His thanks are especially due to Mr. Macray, the Librarian of the Taylor Institution, for his kindness in the last respect.

(66) pp. 38, 378.

OXFORD, November 28, 1862.

ANALYSIS OF THE LECTURES.

LECTURE I.

On the subject, method, and purpose of the course of Lectures.

THE subject stated to be the struggle of the human mind against the Christian revelation, in whole or in part. (p. 1.) Explanation of the points which form the occasion of the conflict. (pp. 1–3.)

The mode of treatment, being that of a critical history, includes (p. 3) the discovery of (1) the facts, (2) the causes, and (3) the moral.

The main part of this first lecture is occupied in explaining the *second* of these divisions.

Importance, if the investigation were to be fully conducted, of carrying out a comparative study of religions and of the attitude of the mind in reference to all doctrine that rests on authority. (pp. 4–6.)

The idea of causes implies,

I. The law of the operation of the causes.
II. The enumeration of the causes which act according to this assumed law.

The empirical law, or formula descriptive of the action of reason on religion, is explained to be one form of the principle of progress by antagonism, the conservation or discovery of truth by means of inquiry and controversy; a merciful Providence leaving men responsible for their errors, but ultimately overruling evil for good. (p. 7.)

This great fact illustrated in the four Crises of the Christian faith in Europe, viz. In the struggle

(1) With heathen philosophy, about A. D. 160–360. (p. 8.)
(2) With sceptical tendencies in Scholasticism, in the middle ages (1100–1400). (p. 8.)
(3) With literature, at the Renaissance, in Italy (1400–1625). (p. 9.)

(4) With modern philosophy in three forms (p. 11): viz. English Deism in the seventeenth and eighteenth centuries (p. 11); French Infidelity in the eighteenth century; German Rationalism in the eighteenth and nineteenth.

Proposal to study the natural as well as literary history of these forms of doubt.—The investigation separated from inquiries into heresy as distinct from scepticism. (p. 13.)

II. The causes, seen to act according to the law just described, which make free thought develope into unbelief, stated to be twofold. (p. 13.)

1. Emotional causes.—Necessity for showing the relation of the intellectual causes to the emotional, both *per se*, and because the idea of a history of *thought*, together with the comparative rarity of the process here undertaken, implies the restriction of the attention mainly to the intellectual. (p. 13.)

Influence of the emotional causes shown, both from psychology and from the analysis of the nature of the evidence offered in religion (pp. 14, 15).—Historical illustrations of their influence. (pp. 15–17.)

Other instances where the doubt is in origin purely intellectual (p. 17), but where nevertheless opportunity is seen for the latent operation of the emotional. (p. 18.)

Explanation how far religious doubt is sin. (pp. 19, 20.)

2. Intellectual causes, which are the chief subject of these lectures; the conjoint influence however of the emotional being always presupposed.

The intellectual causes shown to be (p. 20):

(α) the new material of knowledge which arises from the advance of the various sciences; viz. Criticism; Physical, Moral, and Ontological science. (p. 21.)

(β) the various metaphysical tests of truth or grounds of certitude employed. (p. 22.)

An illustration of the meaning (pp. 22, 23), drawn from literature, in a brief comparison of the types of thought shown in Milton, Pope, and Tennyson.

Statement of the exact position of this inquiry in the subdivisions of metaphysical science (pp. 24, 25), and detailed explanation of the advantages and disadvantages of applying to religion the tests of Sense, subjective Forms of Thought, Intuition, and Feeling, respectively, as the standard of appeal. (pp. 25–32.)

Advantage of a biographic mode of treatment in the investigation of the operation of these causes in the history of doubt. (pp. 32–34.)

Statement of the utility of the inquiry:

(1) Intellectually, (α) in a didactic and polemical point of view, in that it refers the origin of the intellectual elements in error to false philosophy and faulty modes of judging, and thus refutes error by analysing it into the causes which produce it; and also (β) in an indirect contribution to the Christian evidences by the historic study of former contests. (p. 36.)

(2) Morally, in creating deep pity for the sinner, united with hatred for the sin. (p. 36.)

Concluding remarks on the spirit which has influenced the writer in these lectures. (pp. 37, 38.)

LECTURE II.

The literary opposition of Heathens against Christianity in the early ages.

The first of the four crises of the faith. (pp. 39–74.) Agreement and difference of this crisis with the modern. (p. 40.) Sources for ascertaining its nature, the original writings of unbelievers being lost. (pp. 41, 42.)

Preliminary explanation of four states of belief among the heathens in reference to religion, from which opposition to Christianity would arise: (pp. 43–118) viz.

(1) the tendency to absolute disbelief of religion, as seen in Lucian and the Epicurean school. (p. 43.)

(2) a reactionary attachment to the national creed,—the effect of prejudice in the lower orders, and of policy in the educated. (pp. 45, 46.)

(3) the philosophical tendency, in the Stoics, (p. 44) and Neo-Platonists. (pp. 45, 46.)

(4) the mystic inclination for magic rites. (p. 47.)

Detailed critical history of the successive literary attacks on Christianity. (p. 48 seq.)

1. that of Lucian, about A. D. 170, in the *Peregrinus Proteus.* (pp. 48–50.)
2. that of Celsus, about the same date. (pp. 50–55.)
3. that of Porphyry, about 270. (pp. 56–61.)
4. that of Hierocles about 303, founded on the earlier work of Philostratus respecting the life of Apollonius of Tyana. (pp. 62–64.)
5. that of Julian, A. D. 363; an example of the struggle in deeds as well as in ideas. (pp. 65–68.)

(Account of the *Philopatris* of the Pseudo-Lucian. (p. 67.)

Conclusion; showing the relation of these attacks to the intellectual tendencies before mentioned (p. 69), and to the general intellectual causes sketched in Lect. I. (p. 69.)—Insufficiency of these causes to explain the whole phenomenon of unbelief, unless the conjoint action of emotional causes be supposed. (pp. 71, 72.)

Analogy of this early conflict to the modern. Lessons from consideration of the means by which the early Church repelled it. (pp. 72–74.)

LECTURE III.

Free Thought during the middle ages, and at the Renaissance; together with its rise in modern times.

This period embraces the second and third of the four epochs of doubt, and the commencement of the fourth. Brief outline of the events which it includes. (pp. 75, 76.)

Second crisis, from A. D. 1100–1400. (pp. 76–92.) It is a struggle political as well as intellectual, Ghibellinism as well as scepticism. (p. 76.)

The intellectual tendencies in this period are four:

1. The scepticism developed in the scholastic philosophy, as seen in the Nominalism of Abélard in the twelfth century.
   Account of the scholastic philosophy, pp. 77–80; and of Abélard as a sceptic in his treatise *Sic et Non.* (pp. 81–85.)
2. The *mot* of progress in religion in the Franciscan book called *The Everlasting Gospel* in the thirteenth century. (pp. 86, 87.)
3. The idea of the comparative study of religion, as seen in the legend of the book *De Tribus Impostoribus* in the thirteenth century; and in the poetry of the period. (pp. 88, 89.)
4. The influence of the Mahometan philosophy of Averroes in creating a pantheistic disbelief of immortality. (pp. 90, 91.)

Remarks on the mode used to oppose these movements; and critical estimate of the period. (pp. 91, 92.)

Third crisis, from 1400–1625. (pp. 93–105.) Peculiarity of this period as the era of the Renaissance and of "Humanism," and as the transition from mediæval society to modern. (p. 93.)

Two chief sceptical tendencies in it:

(1) The literary tendency in Tuscany and Rome in the fifteenth century; the dissolution of faith being indicated by
   (*a*) the poetry of the romantic epic. (p. 94.)
   (*b*) the revival of heathen tastes. (p. 95.)

   Estimate of the political and social causes likely to generate doubt, which were then acting. (pp. 97, 98.) The unbelief was confined to Italy.—Reasons why so vast a movement as the Reformation passed without fostering unbelief. (p. 99.)

2. The philosophical tendency in the university of Padua in the sixteenth century. (p. 99 seq.)
   The spirit of it, pantheism (p. 100), in two forms; one arising from the doctrines of Averroes; the other seen in Pomponatius, from Alexander of Aphrodisias. (p. 101.) The relation of other philosophers, such as Bruno and Vanini, to this twofold tendency. (pp. 102–104.)

Remarks on the mode used to oppose doubt (p. 104); and estimate of the crisis. (p. 105.)

Fourth crisis; (pp. 105–339) commencing in the seventeenth century, through the effects of the philosophy of Bacon and Descartes. (p. 106.)
The remainder of the lecture is occupied with the treatment of the influence of Cartesianism, as seen in Spinoza.
Examination of Spinoza's philosophy (pp. 106–110); of his criticism in the *Theologico-Politicus* (pp. 109–113); and of his indirect influence. (p. 113, 114.)
Concluding remarks on the government of Providence, as witnessed in the history of large periods of time, such as that comprised in this lecture. (p. 115.)

LECTURE IV.

Deism in England previous to A. D. 1760.

This lecture contains the first of the three forms which doubt has taken in the fourth crisis. (p. 116.)—Sketch of the chief events, political and intellectual, which influenced the mind of England during the seventeenth century (p. 117); especial mention of the systems of Bacon and Descartes, as exhibiting the peculiarity that they were philosophies of method. (pp. 117, 118.)
The history of Deism studied:

I. Its rise traced, 1640–1700. (pp. 119–125.)
   In this period the religious inquiry has a political aspect, as seen
   (1) in Lord Herbert of Cherbury (*De Veritate* and *Religio Laici*) in the reign of Charles I. (pp. 119, 120.)
   (2) In Hobbes's *Leviathan.* (pp. 121, 122.)
   (3) In Blount (*Oracles of Reason*, and *Life of Apollonius*), in the reign of Charles II., in whom a deeper political antipathy to religion is seen. (pp. 123, 124.)

II. The maturity of Deism (1700–1740), pp. 125–144. This period includes (p. 127):
   1. The examination of the first principles of religion, on its doctrinal side, in Toland's *Christianity not Mysterious*, &c. (pp. 126–130.)
   2. Ditto, on its ethical side, in Lord Shaftesbury. (pp. 130, 131.)
   3. An attack on the external evidences, viz.
      On prophecy, by Collins, *Scheme of Literal Prophecy*, &c. (pp. 132–136.)

On Miracles, by Woolston, *Discourses on Miracles.* (pp. 136–138); and by Arnobius. (p. 143.)

4. The substitution of natural religion for revealed, in Tindal, *Christianity as old as the Creation.* (pp. 138–140.) in Morgan, *Moral Philosopher.* (pp. 140, 141.) and in Chubb, Miscellaneous Works. (pp. 142, 143.)

III. The decline of Deism, 1740–1760. (pp. 144–153):

1. in Bolingbroke, a combined view of deist objections. (pp. 143–147.)
2. in Hume, an assault on the evidence of testimony, which substantiates miracles. (pp. 147–153.)

Remarks on the peculiarities of Deism, the intellectual causes which contributed to produce it (pp. 154, 155); and a comparison of it with the unbelief of other periods. (p. 156.)

Estimate of the whole period; and consideration of the intellectual and spiritual means used for repelling unbelief in it (pp. 157–161); the former in the school of evidences, of which Butler is the type, the mention of whom leads to remarks on his *Analogy* (pp. 157–159); and the latter in spiritual labours like those of Wesley. (pp. 160, 161.)

LECTURE V.

Infidelity in France in the eighteenth century; and unbelief in England subsequent to 1760.

INFIDELITY IN FRANCE (pp. 163–194).—This is the second phase of unbelief in the fourth crisis of faith.

Sketch of the state of France, ecclesiastical, political (pp. 164, 165,) and intellectual (partly through the philosophy of Condillac, pp. 166, 167), which created such a mental and moral condition as to allow unbelief to gain a power there unknown elsewhere.—The unbelief stated to be caused chiefly by the influence of English Deism, transplanted into the soil thus prepared. (p. 203.)

The history studied (1) in its assault on the Church; as seen in Voltaire: the analysis of whose character is necessary, because his influence was mainly due to the teacher, not the doctrine taught. (pp. 169–176.)

(2) in the transition to an assault on the State, in Diderot, (pp. 179, 180); the philosophy of the Encyclopædists (p. 177); Helvetius (p. 180); and D'Holbach. (p. 181.)

(3) in the attack on the State, in Rousseau (pp. 183–187).—Analysis of the *Emile* for his views on religion, (p. 185), and comparison with Voltaire. (p. 188.)

(4) in the Revolution, both the political movement and blasphemous irreligion (pp. 188, 189); and the intellectual movement in Volney (Analysis of the *Ruines*, pp. 191, 192).

Estimate of the period (pp. 193, 194).

UNBELIEF IN ENGLAND, from 1760 to a date a little later than the end of the century (pp. 194–209), continued from Lecture IV.

These later forms of it stated to differ slightly from the former, by being partially influenced by French thought. (p. 195.)

The following instances of it examined:

(1) Gibbon viewed as a writer and a critic on religion (pp. 196–199).
(2) T. Paine: account of his *Age of Reason* (pp. 199–201).
(3) The socialist philosophy of R. Owen (p. 202).
(4) The scepticism in the poetry of Byron and Shelley (pp. 203–207).

The last two forms of unbelief, though occurring in the present century, really embody the spirit of the last.

Statement of the mode used to meet the doubt in England during this period. Office of the Evidences (pp. 207–209).

LECTURE VI.

Free Thought in the Theology of Germany, from 1750–1835.

This is the third phase of free thought in that which was called the fourth crisis of faith.—Importance of the movement, which is called "rationalism," as the theological phase of the literary movement of Germany (p. 210).—Deviation from the plan previously adopted, in that a sketch is here given of German theological inquiry generally, and not merely of unbelief (p. 211).

Brief preliminary sketch of German theology since the Reformation. Two great tendencies shown in it during the seventeenth century (p. 211).

(1) The dogmatic and scholastic, science without earnestness (p. 212).
(2) The pietistic, earnestness without science (p. 213).

In the first half of the eighteenth century, three new influences are introduced (pp. 213, 214), which are the means of creating rationalism in the latter half: viz.

(α) The philosophy of Wolff, explained to be a formal expression of Leibnitz's principles; and the evil effect of it, accidental and indirect (pp. 214–216).
(β) The works of the English deists (p. 216).
(γ) The influence of the colony of French infidels at the court of Frederick II. of Prussia (p. 217).

The subsequent history is studied in three periods (p. 218): viz.

Period I. (1750–1810).—Destructive in character, inaugurated by Semler (pp. 218–234).

Period II. (1810–1835).—Reconstructive in character, inaugurated by Schleiermacher (pp. 235–261).

Period III. (1835 to present time).—Exhibiting definite and final tendencies, inaugurated by Strauss (Lect. vii).

Period I. (1750–1810), is studied under two Sub-periods:

Sub-period I. (1750–1790, pp. 219–228), which includes three movements;

(1) Within the church (p. 219 seq.); dogmatic; literary in Michaelis and Ernesti; and freethinking in Semler (pp. 221–224), the author of the historic method of interpretation.

(2) External to the church (pp. 224–226); literary deism in Lessing, and in the Wolfenbüttel fragments of Reimarus (p. 225).

(3) External to the church; practical deism, in the educational institutions of Basedow (p. 227).

Sub-period II. (1790–1810, pp. 227–234); the difference caused by the introduction of two new influences; viz.

(α) The literary, of the court of Weimar and of the great men gathered there (p. 228).

(β) The philosophy of Kant, (the effect of which is explained, pp. 229, 230); the home of both of which was at Jena.

As the result of these new influences, three movements are visible in the Church (p. 230); viz.

(1) The critical "rationalism" of Eichhorn and Paulus, the intellectual successors of Semler (pp. 231, 232).

(2) The dogmatic, more or less varying from orthodoxy, seen towards the end of this period in Bretschneider, Röhr, and Wegscheider (pp. 233, 234).

(3) The supernaturalism of Reinhardt and Storr (p. 231).

Period II. (1810–1835.)—Introduction of four new influences (p. 235), which completely altered the theological tone; viz.

(α) New systems of speculative philosophy; of Jacobi, who followed out the *material* element of Kant's philosophy (p. 235); and of Fichte, Schelling, and Hegel, who followed out the *formal* (p. 238).

(β) The "romantic" school of poetry (p. 239).

(γ) The moral tone, generated by the liberation wars of 1813. (p. 240.)

(δ) The excitement caused by the theses of Harms at the tercentenary of the Reformation in 1817. (pp. 240, 241.)

The result of these is seen (p. 241) in

(1) An improved doctrinal school under Schleiermacher (pp. 241–250), (description of his *Glaubenslehre*, p. 245 seq.); and under his successors, Neander, &c. (pp. 250–252.)

(2) An improved critical tone (p. 252 seq.), as seen in De Wette and Ewald, which is illustrated by an explanation of the Pentateuch controversy (pp. 254–258).

Concluding notice of two other movements to be treated in the next lecture (p. 259); viz.

(1) an attempt, different from that of Schleiermacher, in the school of Hegel, to find a new philosophical basis for Christianity; and

(2) the return to the biblical orthodoxy of the Lutheran church.

Remarks on the benevolence of Providence in overruling free inquiry to the discovery of truth. (pp. 259–261)

LECTURE VII.

Free Thought in Germany subsequently to 1835; *and in France during the present century.*

FREE THOUGHT IN GERMANY (continued).—History of the transition from Period II. named in the last lecture, to Period III. (pp. 262–274.)

Explanation of the attempt, noticed pp. 242, 259, of the Hegelian school to find a philosophy of Christianity. Critical remarks on Hegel's system, (pp. 263–267); its tendency to create an "ideological" spirit in religion (p. 264):—the school which it at first formed is seen best in Marheinecke. (p. 265.)

The circumstance which created an epoch in German theology was the publication of Strauss's *Leben Jesu* in 1835 (p. 266). Description of it (α) in its critical aspect (pp. 267, 270), which leads to an explanation of the previous discussions in Germany concerning the origin and credibility of the Gospels (pp. 268, 269); and (β) in its philosophical, as related to Hegel (p. 270); together with an analysis of the work (p. 271). Statement of the effects produced by it on the various theological parties. (pp. 272, 273.)

PERIOD III. As the result of the agitation caused by Strauss's work, four theological tendencies are seen; viz.

(1) One external to the church, thoroughly antichristian, as in Bruno Bauer, Feuerbach, and Stirner. (pp. 274–276.)

(2) The historico-critical school of Tübingen, founded by Chr. Bauer. (pp. 277–279.)

(3) The "mediation" school, seen in Dorner and Rothe. (pp. 279–282.)

(4) A return to the Lutheran orthodoxy, (pp. 282–285,) at first partly created by an attempt to unite the Lutheran and Reformed churches, (p. 282); seen in the "Neo-Lutheranism" of Hengstenberg and Hävernick, (p. 282), and the "Hyper-

Lutheranism" of Stahl and the younger members of the school. (pp. 283, 285.)

Mention of the contemporaneous increase of spiritual life in Germany. (p. 285.)

Concluding estimate of the whole movement, (pp. 286, 287); and lessons for students in reference to it. (pp. 288, 289.)

FREE THOUGHT IN FRANCE during the present century (pp. 290–305), (continued from Lect. IV. p. 194.)

In its tone it is constructive of belief, if compared with that of the eighteenth century.

From 1800–1852.

The speculative thought has exhibited four distinct forms. (p. 290.)

(1) The ideology of De Tracy, in the early part of the century.
(2) The theological school of De Maistre, &c. to re-establish the dogmatic authority of the Romish church.
(3) Socialist philosophy, St. Simon, Fourier, Comte.
(4) The Eclectic school (Cousin, &c.)

Remarks on the first school.—The recovery of French philosophy and thought from the ideas of this school, partly due to the literary tone of Chateaubriand. (pp. 290, 291.)

Influence of the Revolution of 1830 in giving a stimulus to thought. (p. 291.)

Remarks on the third school.—Explanation of socialism as taught by St. Simon (pp. 292, 293); as taught by Fourier (pp. 293, 294); and difference from English socialism. (p. 294.)

Positivism, both as an offshoot of the last school, and in itself as a religion and a philosophy. (pp. 295, 296.)

Remarks on the fourth school.—Eclecticism as taught by Cousin, viewed as a philosophy and a religion. (pp. 297–299.)

Remarks on the second school; viewed as an attempt to refute the preceding schools. (p. 300.)

From 1852–1862.

New form of eclecticism under the empire (p. 302), viz. the historic method, based on Hegel, as Cousin's was based on Schelling.—E. Renan the type. (pp. 302–304.)

Free thought in the Protestant church (pp. 304, 305) regarded as an attempt to meet by concession doubts ot contemporaries.

LECTURE VIII.

Free Thought in England in the present century: Summary of the Course of Lectures: and Inferences in reference to present dangers and duties.

MODERN UNBELIEF IN ENGLAND (continued from Lect. V.):—Introductory remarks on the alteration of its tone. (pp. 306, 307.)—The cause of which is stated to be a general one, the subjective tone created (p. 308) by such influences as, (1) the modern poetry (p. 309), and (2) the two great attempts by Bentham and Coleridge to reconstruct philosophy. (pp. 309, 310.)

The doubt and unbelief treated in the following order (p. 311):

(1) That which appeals to Sensational experience and to Physical science as the test of truth; viz.

(α) Positivism among the educated (p. 312).
(β) Secularism or Naturalism among the masses (p. 313); and in a minor degree,
(γ) The doubts created by Physical science (p. 314).

(2) That which appeals to the faculty of Intuition (p. 315);—expressed in literature, by Carlyle, (pp. 316, 317); and by the American, Emerson. (p. 317.)
(Influence also of the modern literature of romance, (p. 318.)

(3) Direct attacks on Christianity, critical rather than philosophical: viz.

(α) The examination of the historic problem of the development of religious ideas among the Hebrews, by R. W. Mackay (pp. 319, 320).
(β) A summary of objections to revelation, by Mr. Greg, *The Creed of Christendom* (p. 321).
(γ) The examination of the psychical origin of religion and Christianity, by Miss S. Hennell, *Thoughts in aid of Faith*, (p. 323.)

(4) The deism, and appeal to the Intuitional consciousness, expressed by Mr. Theodore Parker (pp. 325, 326), and Mr. F. Newman (pp. 326–329).

(5) The traces of free thought within the Christian church (p. 330); viz.:

(α) The philosophical tendency which originates with Coleridge. (pp. 330–333.)
(β) The critical tendency, investigating the facts of revelation. (pp. 334–336.)
(γ) " " " the literature which contains it. (pp. 336, 337.)

This completes the history of the fourth crisis of faith (p. 339), the history of which began near the end of Lect. III. at p. 105.

Summary of the course of lectures. (pp. 339–41.)—Recapitulation of the original purpose, which is stated to have been, while assuming the potency of the moral, to analyse the intellectual causes of doubt, which have been generally left uninvestigated.

Refutation of objections which might be made; such as

(1) One directed against the utility of the inquiry. (p. 342.)
(2) " " against its uncontroversial character.

A critical history shown to be useful in the present age, (1) in an educational point of view for those who are to be clergymen, and to encounter current forms of doubt by word or by writing (pp. 342–345); and (2) in a controversial point of view, by resolving the intellectual element in many cases of unbelief into incorrect metaphysical philosophy; the value of which inquiry is real, even if such intellectual causes be regarded only as the conditions, and not the causes, of unbelief. (p. 345.)

Further objections anticipated and refuted in reference (3) to the candour of the mode of inquiry, and the absence of vituperation which is stated not to be due to indifference to Christian truth, but wholly to the demands of a scientific mode of treatment (p. 346); (4) to the absence of an eager advocacy of any particular metaphysical theory; which is due to the circumstance that the purpose was to exhibit errors as logical corollaries from certain theories, without assuming the necessary existence of these corollaries in actual life (p. 347); (5) to the insufficiency of the causes enumerated to produce doubt without taking account of the moral causes; which objection is not only admitted, but shown to be at once the peculiar property which belongs to the analysis of intellectual phenomena, and also a witness to the instinctive conviction that the ultimate cause of belief and unbelief is moral, not intellectual; which had been constantly assumed. (p. 347.)

The Lessons derived from the whole historical survey. (p. 348 seq.)

I. What has been the office of doubt in history? (p. 348.)

Opposite opinions on this subject stated. (p. 348.) Examination of the ordinary Christian opinion on the one hand, which regards it as a mischief (p. 348), and of Mr. Buckle's on the other, which regards it as a good. (p. 349.)

1. The office is shown to be, to bring all truths to the test. (p. 349.) Historical instances of its value in destroying the Roman catholic errors. (p. 350.)
2. Free inquiry also shown in some cases to be forced on man by the presentation of new knowledge, which demands consideration. (p. 350.) Denial of the statement that the doubts thus created are an entire imitation of older doubt. (p. 352.)
3. The office of it in the hands of Providence to elicit truth by the very controversies which it creates (p. 352); the responsibility of the inquirer not being destroyed, but the overruling providence of God made visible. (p. 353.)

II. What does the history teach, as to the doubts most likely to present themselves at this time, and the best modes of meeting them? (p. 353.)

The materials shown to be presented for a final answer to these questions. (p. 354.)

The probability shown from consideration of the state of the various sciences, mechanical, physiological (p. 355), and mental (p. 355), that no new difficulties can be suggested hereafter, distinct in *kind* from the present; nor any unknown kinds of evidence presented on behalf of Christianity.

Analogy of the present age as a whole, in disintegration of belief, to the declining age of Roman civilization. (p. 356.)

The doubts which beset us in the present age stated to be chiefly three (p. 357), viz.:

1. The relation of the natural to the supernatural.

   This doubt is sometimes expressed in a spirit of utter unbelief; sometimes in a tone of sadness (p. 358), arising from mental struggles, of which some are enumerated (p. 358). The intellectual and moral means of meeting these doubts. (p. 359.)

2. The relation of the atoning work of Christ to the human race. (p. 360.) Explanation of the defective view which would regard it only as reconciling man to God, and would destroy the priestly work of Christ; and statement of the modes in which its advocates reconcile it with Christianity. (p. 361.)

   The importance that such doubts be answered by reason, not merely silenced by force. (p. 362.)

   An answer sought by studying the various modes used in other ages of the church (p. 362); especially by those who have had to encounter the like difficulties, e. g. the Alexandrian fathers in the third century, and the faithful in Germany in the present. (p. 363.)

   This method shown to have been to present the philosophical prior to the historical evidence, in order to create the sense of religious want, before exhibiting Christianity as the divine supply for it. (p. 364.)

   In regard to the historic evidence, three misgivings of the doubter require to be met for his full satisfaction (p. 366); viz.

   (α) The literary question of the trustworthiness of the books of the New Testament.

   The mode of meeting this explained, with the possibility of establishing Christian dogmas, even if the most extravagant rationalism were for argument's sake conceded. (p. 367.)

   (β) The doubt whether the Christian dogmas, and especially the atonement, are really taught in the New Testament. The value of the fathers, and the progress of the doctrine in church history, shown in reference to this question. (p. 368.)

   (γ) The final difficulty which the doubter may put, whether even apostolic and miraculous teaching is to overrule the moral sense. (p. 369.)

   The possibility shown of independent corroboration of the apostolic teaching, in the testimony of the living church, and the experience of religious men. (p. 371.)

   The utter improbability of error in this part of scriptural teaching, even if the existence of error elsewhere were for argument's sake conceded (p. 370.)

   Difference of this appeal from that of Schleiermacher to the Christian consciousness.

3. The relation of the Bible to the church, whether it is a record or an authority. (p. 372.)
   Statement of the modes of viewing the question in different ages. (p. 373.)
   The Bible an authority; but the importance shown of using wisdom in not pressing the difficulties of scripture on an inquirer, so as to quench incipient faith. (p. 374.)

The mention of the emotional causes of doubt conjoined with the intellectual, a warning that, in addition to all arguments, the help of the divine Spirit to hallow the emotions must be sought and expected. (p. 375.)

Final lesson to Christian students, that in all ages of peril, earnest men have found the truth by the method of study united to prayer. (pp. 376–379.)

NOTES APPENDED.

LECTURE I.

LECTURE II.

LECTURE III.

LECTURE IV.

LECTURE V.

LECTURE VI.

LECTURE VII.

LECTURE VIII.

LECTURE I.

ON THE SUBJECT, METHOD, AND PURPOSE OF THE COURSE OF LECTURES.

LUKE vii. 51.

Suppose ye that I am come to give peace on earth? I tell you, nay; but rather division.

THE present course of lectures relates to one of the conflicts exhibited in the history of the Church; viz. the struggle of the human spirit to free itself from the authority of the Christian faith.

Christianity offers occasion for opposition by its inherent claims, independently of accidental causes. For it asserts authority over religious belief in virtue of being a supernatural communication from God, and claims the right to control human thought in virtue of possessing sacred books which are at once the record and the instrument of this communication, written by men endowed with supernatural inspiration. The inspiration of the writers is transferred to the books, the matter of which, so far as it forms the subject of the revelation, is received as true because divine, not merely regarded as divine because perceived to be true. The religion, together with the series of revelations of which it is the consummation, differs in kind from ethnic religions, and from human philosophy; and the sacred literature differs in kind from other books. Each is unique, a solitary miracle of its class in human history.

The contents also of the sacred books bring them into contact with the efforts of speculative thought. Though at first glance they might seem to belong to a different sphere, that of the soul rather than the intellect, and to possess a different function, explaining duties rather than discovering truth; yet in deep problems of physical or moral history, such as Providence, Sin, Reconciliation, they supply materials for limiting belief in the very class of subjects which is embraced in the compass of human philosophy.

A conflict accordingly might naturally be anticipated, between the reasoning faculties of man and a religion which claims the right on superhuman authority to impose limits on the field or manner of their exercise; the intensity of which at various epochs would depend, partly upon the amount of critical activity, and partly on the presence of causes which might create a divergence between the current ideas and those supplied by the sacred literature.

The materials are wanting for detecting traces of this struggle in other parts of the world than Europe; but the progress of it may be fully observed in European history, altering concomitantly with changes in the condition of knowledge, or in the methods of seeking it; at first as an open conflict, philosophical or critical, with the literary pagans, subsiding as Christianity succeeded in introducing its own conceptions into every region of thought; afterwards reviving in the middle ages, and gradually growing more intense in modern times as material has been offered for it through the increase of knowledge or the activity of speculation; varying in name, in form, in degree, but referable to similar causes, and teaching similar lessons.

It is the chief of these movements of free thought in Europe which it is my purpose to describe, in their historic succession and their connection with intellectual causes.

We must ascertain the facts; discover the causes; and read the moral. These three inquiries, though distinct in idea, cannot be disjoined in a critical history.

The facts must first be presented in place and time: the history is thus far a mere chronicle. They must next be combined with a view to interpretation. Yet in making this first combination, taste guides more than hypothesis. The classification is artistic rather than logical, and merely presents the facts with as much individual vividness as is compatible with the preservation of the perspective requisite in the general historic picture. At this point the artistic sphere of history ceases, and the scientific commences as soon as the mind searches for any regularity or periodicity in the occurrence of the facts, such as may be the effect of fixed causes. If an empirical law be by this means ascertained to exist, an explanation of it must then be sought in the higher science which investigates mind. Analysis traces out the ultimate typical forms of thought which are manifested in it; and if it does not aspire to arbitrate on their truth, it explains how they have become grounds on which particular views have been assumed to be true. The intellect is then satisfied, and the science of history ends. But the heart still craves a further investigation. It demands to view the moral and theological aspects of the subject, to harmonize faith and discovery, or at least to introduce the question of human responsibility, and reverently to search for the final cause which the events subserve in the moral purposes of providence. The drama of history must not develope itself without the chorus to interpret its purpose. The artistic,—the scientific,—the ethical,—these are the three phases of history. (1)

The chief portion of the present lecture will be devoted to explain the mode of applying the plan just indicated; more especially to develope the second of these three branches, by stating the law which has marked the struggle of free thought with Christianity, and illustrating the intellectual causes which have been manifested in it.

In searching for such a law, or such causes, we ought not to forget that, if we wished to lay a sound basis for generalization, it would be necessary not to restrict our attention to the history of Christianity, but to institute a comparative study of religions, ethnic or revealed, in order to trace the action of reason in the collective religious history of the race. Whether the religions of nature be regarded as the distortion of primitive traditions, or as the spontaneous creation of the religious faculties, the agreement or contrast suggested by a comparison of them with the Hebrew and Christian religions, which are preternaturally revealed, is most important as a means of discovering the universal laws of the human mind; the exceptional character which belongs to the latter member of the comparison increasing rather than diminishing the value of the study. All alike are adjusted, the one class naturally and accidentally, the other designedly and supernaturally, to the religious elements of human nature. All have a subjective existence as aspirations of the heart, an objective as institutions, and a history which is connected with the revolutions of literature and society. (2)

Comparative observation of this kind gives some approach to the exactness of experiment; for we watch providence as it were executing an experiment for our information, which exhibits the operations of the same law under altered circumstances. If, for example, we should find that Christianity was the only religion, the history of which presented a struggle of reason against authority, we should pronounce that there must be peculiar elements in it which arouse the special opposition; or if the phenomenon be seen to be common to all creeds, but to vary in intensity with the activity of thought and progress of knowledge, this discovery would suggest to us the existence of a law of the human mind.

Such a study would also furnish valuable data for determining precisely the variation of form which alteration of conditions causes in the development of such a struggle. In the East, the history of religion, for which material is supplied by the study of the Zend and Sanskrit literature, (3) would furnish examples of attempts made by philosophers to find a rational solution of the problems of the universe, and to adjust the theories of speculative thought to the national creed deposited in supposed sacred books. And though, in a western nation such as Greece, the separation of religion from philosophy was too wide to admit of much parallel in the speculative aspect of free thought, yet in reference to the critical, many instances of the application of an analogous process to a national creed may be seen in the examination made of the early mythology, the attempt to rationalize it by searching for historical data in it, or to moralize it by allegory.[1] Again, within the sphere of the Hebrew religion which, though supernaturally suggested, developed in connexion with human events so as to admit the possibility of the rise of mental difficulties in the progress of its history, how much hallowed truth, both theoretical and practical, might be learned from the divine breathings of pious inquirers, such as the sacred authors of the seventy-third Psalm, or of the books of Job and Ecclesiastes, which give expression to painful doubts about Providence, not fully solved by religion, but which nevertheless faith was willing to leave unexplained.[2] If in the Oriental sys-

[1] The attitude of the mind towards the national mythology in successive ages of Greek history has been treated by Grote, *History of Greece*, vol I. ch. 16.

[2] See Quinet's *Œuvres*, t. i. c. 5, and especially § 4. On the doubts expressed in the books of Job and Ecclesiastes respectively, see the article *Job* by Hengstenberg in Kitto's *Cyclopædia of Biblical Literature*, (reprinted in a volume of Hengstenberg's miscellaneous works), and the article *Ecclesiastes* by Mr. Plumptre in Smith's *Dictionary of the Bible*. For the free-thinking inquiry into the two books, see the article on Job in the *Westminster Review*, October 1853, founded mainly on Hirzel; and that on Ecclesiastes in the *National Review*, No. 27, for January 1862, founded chiefly on Hitzig. E. Renan, in his work on Job, and others, have studied the doubts expressed in it as an internal evidence for its date. Very full information in reference to both books may be found in Dr. S. Davidson's *Introd. to the Old Testament* (1862), vol. ii. p. 174 seq., 352 seq. It is deeply interesting to observe, not merely that the difficulties concerning Providence felt by Job refer to the very subjects which painfully perplex the modern mind, but also that the friends of Job exhibit the instinctive tendency which is observed in modern times to denounce his doubt as sin, not less than to attribute his trials to evil as the direct cause. These two books of Scripture, together with the seventy-third Psalm, have

tems free thought is seen to operate on a national creed by adjusting it to new ideas through philosophical dogmatism; if in the Greek by explaining it away through scepticism; in the Hebrew it is hushed by the holier logic of the feelings. The two former illustrate steps in the intellectual progress of free thought; the last exhibits the moral lesson of resignation and submission in the soul of the inquirer.

Nor ought this method of comparison to be laid aside even at this point. It would be requisite, for a full discovery of the intellectual causes that the generalization should be carried further, and the operations of free thought watched in reference to other subjects than religion.[3] Reason in its action, first on Christianity both in Europe and elsewhere, secondly on Jewish and heathen religions, lastly on any body of truth which rests on traditional authority,—these would be the scientific steps necessary for eliminating accidental phenomena, and discovering the real laws which have operated in this branch of intellectual history. The suggestion of such a plan of study, though obviously too large to be here pursued, may offer matter of thought to reflective minds, and may at least help to raise the subject out of the narrow sphere to which it is usually supposed to belong. The result of the survey would confirm the view of the struggle now about to be given which is suggested by European history.

When any new material of thought, such as a new religion which interferes with the previous standard of belief, is presented to the human mind; or when conversely any alteration in the state of knowledge on which the human mind forms its judgment, imparts to

an increasing religious importance as the world grows older. "The things written aforetime were written for our learning."

[3] Attention, for example, should be directed to the efforts of the mind in emancipating itself (1) from particular forms of political government, or social arrangements, or artificial laws, in the struggle against the feudal system, and in the development of political liberty in modern times, or (2) from traditional systems of scientific teaching, as the Ptolemaic theory of astronomy, or the Cartesian of vortices. The absence too of such attempts in the stagnation of Eastern life is an instructive negative instance for study.

an old established religion an aspect of opposition which was before unperceived; the religion is subjected to the ordeal of an investigation. Science examines the doctrines taught by it, criticism the evidence on which they profess to rest, and the literature which is their expression. And if such an investigation fail to establish the harmony of the old and the new, the result takes two forms: either the total rejection of the particular religion, and sometimes even of the supernatural generally, or else an eclecticism which seeks by means of philosophy to discover and appropriate the hidden truth to which the religion was an attempt to give expression.

The attack however calls forth the defence. Accordingly the result of this action and reaction is to produce scientific precision, either apologetic or dogmatic, within the religious system, and scepticism outside of it; both reconstructive in purpose, but the former defensive in its method, the latter destructive. The elements of truth which exist on both sides are brought to light by the controversy, and after the struggle has passed become the permanent property of the world.

These statements, which convey a general expression for the influence of free thought in relation to religion, are verified in the history of Christianity.

There are four epochs at which the struggle of reason against the authority of the Christian religion has been especially manifest, each characterized by energy and intensity of speculative thought, and exhibiting on the one hand partial or entire unbelief, or on the other a more systematic expression of Christian doctrine; epochs in fact of temporary peril, of permanent gain.[4]

[4] It is proper to express my obligations for a few hints in this part of the lecture to an able historic sketch of modern German thought, based on the *Geschichte der neuesten Theologie* of C. Schwartz, in the Westminster Review, April 1857 (especially p. 333). The enumeration of the epochs which follows nevertheless occurred to me for the most part independently of those suggestions, and had been previously expressed in public. A classification of a different kind will be found in Reimannus *Historia Atheismi*, 1725, p. 315.

In the first of these periods, extending from the second to the fourth century, Christianity is seen in antagonism with forms of Greek or Eastern philosophy, and the existence is apparent of different forms of scepticism or reason used in attack. The very attempt of the Alexandrian school of theology to adjust the mysteries of Christianity and of the Bible to speculative thought, by a well meant but extravagant use of allegorical interpretation, is itself a witness of the presence or pressure of free thought. The less violent of the two forms of unbelief is seen in the Gnostics, the rationalists of the early Church, who summoned Christianity to the bar of philosophy, and desired to appropriate the portion of its teachings which approved itself to their eclectic tastes; the more violent kind in the rejection of Christianity as an imposture, or in the attempts made to refer its origin to psychological causes, on the part of the early enemies of Christianity, Celsus and Julian, prototypes of the positive unbelievers of later times. The Greek theology, which embodied the dogmatic statements in which the Christian Church under the action of controversy gave explicit expression to its implicit belief, is the example of the stimulus which the pressure of free thought gave to the use of reason in defence.

As we pass down the course of European history, the Pagan literature which had suggested the first attack disappears: but as soon as the elements of civilization, which survived the deluge that overwhelmed the Roman empire, had been sufficiently consolidated to allow of the renewal of speculation, a repetition of the contest may be observed.

The revived study of the Greek philosophers, and of their Arabic commentators introduced from the Moorish universities of Spain, with the consequent rise of the scholastic philosophy in the twelfth and thirteenth centuries, furnished material for a renewal of the struggle of reason against authority, a second crisis in the history of the Church. The history of it becomes complicated by the circumstance that free thought, in the process of disintegrating the body of authoritative teaching, now began to assume on several occasions a new shape, a kind of incipient Protestantism. Doubting neither Christianity nor the Bible, it is seen to challenge merely that part of the actual religion which, as it conceived, had insinuated itself from human sources in the lapse of ages. Accordingly, the critical independence of Nominalism, in a mind like that of Abelard, represents the destructive action of free thought, partly as early Protestantism, partly as scepticism; while the series of noted Realists, of which Aquinas is an example, that tried anew to adjust faith to science, and thus created the Latin theology, represents the defensive action of reason. The imparting scientific definition to the immemorial doctrines of the Church constituted the defence.

In the later middle ages, however, philosophy gradually succeeded in emancipating itself so entirely from theology, that when the Renaissance came, and a large body of heathen thought was introduced into the current of European life by means of ancient literature, a third crisis occurred. The independence passed into open revolt, and, fostered by political confusion and material luxury, expressed itself in a literature of unbelief.

The mental awakening which had commenced in art and extended to literature paved the way for a spiritual awakening. The Reformation itself, though the product of a deep consciousness of spiritual need, an emancipation of soul as well as mind, is nevertheless a special instance of the same dissolution of mediæval life, and must therefore be regarded as belonging to the same general movement of free thought, though not to that sceptical form of it which comes within the field of our investigation. For Protestantism, though it be scepticism in respect of the authority of the traditional teaching of the Church, yet reposes implicitly on an outward authority revealed in the sacred books of holy Scripture, and restricts the exercise of freedom within the limits prescribed by this authority; whereas scepticism proper is an insurrection against the outward authority or truth of the inspired books, and reposes on the unrevealed, either on consciousness or on science. The one is analogous to a school of art which desires to reform itself by the use of ancient models; the other to one which professes to return to an unassisted study of nature. The spiritual earnestness which characterized the Reformation prevented the changes in religious belief from developing into scepticism proper; and the theology of the Reformation is accordingly an example of defence and reconstruction as well as of revulsion.

During the century which followed, mental activity found employment in other channels in connexion with the political struggles which resulted from the religious changes. But the seventeenth age was another of those epochs which form crises in the history of the human mind. The reconstruction at that time of the methods on which science depends, by Bacon from the empirical side, by Descartes from the intellectual, created as great a revolution in knowledge as the Renaissance had produced in literature or the Reformation in religion; and a body of materials was presented from which philosophers ventured to criticise the Bible and the dogmatic teaching of the Church. This fourth great period of free thought, which extends to the present time, has been marked by more striking events than former ones.[5] Though the movement relates to a similar sphere, the history is rendered more complex by union with literature, and connexion as cause or effect with social changes, as well as by the reciprocal operation of its influence in different countries. Language, which is

[5] The author (supposed to be Hundeshagen) of *Der Deutsche Protestantismus* thus expresses himself (§ 6.): "In the history of the world there are four successive periods in which open unbelief and unconcealed enmity to Christianity made the tour in some degree among the chief nations of Europe. Italy made the beginning in the fifteenth and sixteenth century; England and France followed in the seventeenth and eighteenth; the series closed in Germany in the nineteenth." The first of the four crises in our text occurred in the ancient world; the second is mediæval; the third, at the moment of transition into the modern history, is the Italian crisis of the quotation just cited; the three others therein named make up the fourth in our enumeration.

always a record of opinion, popular or scientific,[6] classifies the forms of this last great movement of free thought under three names, viz. Deism in England in the early part of the eighteenth century; Infidelity in France in the latter part of it; and Rationalism in Germany in the nineteenth; movements which exhibit characteristics respectively of the three nations, and of their intellectual and general history. English Deism, the product of the reasoning spirit which was stimulated by political events, directed itself against the special revelation of Christianity from the stand-point of the religion of natural reason, and ran a course parallel with the gradual emancipation of the individual from the power of the state. French infidelity, breathing the spirit of materialist philosophy, halted not till it brought its devotees even to atheism, and mingled itself with the great movements of political revolution, which ultimately reconstituted French society. German Rationalism, empirical or spiritual,[7] in two parallel developments, the philosophical and the literary, neither coldly denied Christianity with the practical doubts of the English deists, nor flippantly denounced it as imposture with the trenchant and undiscriminating logic of the French infidels; but appreciating its beauty with the freshness of a poetical genius, and regarding it as one phase of the religious consciousness, endeavoured, by means of the methods employed in secular learning, to collect the precious ideas of eternal truth to which Christianity seemed to it to give expression, and by means of speculative criticism to exhibit the literary and psychological causes which it supposed had overlaid them with error.

Nor has the activity of reason used in defence been less manifest in these later movements. The great

[6] On the office of language, and the changes to which it is liable, consult the chapter on the "Natural History of the variations in the meaning of terms," in J. S. Mill's *Logic* (vol. ii. b. 4. ch. 5.) An explanation of many of the terms which occur in the history of doubt, viz., Deism, Rationalism, &c. will be found in Note 21. at the end of these Lectures.

[7] "Empirical," as in Lessing and Paulus; "Spiritual," as in the later schools. See Lect. VI. and VII.

works on the Christian evidences are the witness to its presence; and the deeper and truer appreciation of Christianity now shown in every country, and the increasing interest felt in religion, are the indirect effect, under the guidance of divine Providence, of the stirring of the religious apprehension by controversy.[8]

We have thus at once exhibited the province which will be hereafter investigated in detail, and stated the general law observable in the conflict between free thought and Christianity. The type reappears, perpetuated by the fixity of mind, though the form varies under the force of circumstances. Christianity being stationary and authoritative, thought progressive and independent, the causes which stimulate the restlessness of the latter interrupt the harmony which ordinarily exists between belief and knowledge, and produce crises during which religion is re-examined. Disorganization is the temporary result; theological advance the subsequent. Whatever is evil is eliminated in the conflict; whatever is good is retained. Under the overruling of a beneficent Providence, antagonism is made the law of human progress.

The restriction of our inquiry to the consideration of the free action of reason will cause our attention to be almost entirely confined to the operation of reason in its attack on Christianity, to the neglect of the evidences which the other office of it has presented in defence; and will also exclude altogether the study of struggles, where the opposition to Christianity has rested on an appeal to the authority of rival sacred books; such for example as the conflict with rival religions like the Jewish (4) or Mahometan (5); as well as of heresies which, like the Socinian (6), claim, however unjustly, to rest on the authority of the Christian revelation.

The law thus sketched of this struggle needs fuller explanation. We must employ a more exact analysis to gain a conception of the causes which have operated

[8] A brief view of the history of the Christian evidences will be found in Note 49 appended to these Lectures.

at different periods to make free thought develop into unbelief.

It will be obvious that the causes must depend, either upon the nature of the Christian religion, which is the subject, or of the mind of man, which is the agent of attack. The former were touched upon in the opening remarks of this lecture, and may be reconsidered hereafter;[9] but it is necessary to gain a general view of the latter before treating them in their application in future lectures.

These causes, so far as they are spiritual and disconnected from admixture with political circumstances, may be stated to be of two kinds, viz. intellectual and moral; the intellectual explaining the types of thought, the moral the motives which have from time to time existed.[10] The actions, and generally the opinions of a human being, are the complex result arising from the union of both. Yet the two elements, though closely intertwined in a concrete instance, can be apprehended separately as objects of abstract thought; and the forms of manifestation and mode of operation peculiar to each can be separately traced.

In a history of thought, the antagonism created by the intellect rather than by the heart seems the more appropriate subject of study, and will be almost exclusively considered in these lectures. Nevertheless a brief analysis must be here given of the mode in which the moral is united with the intellectual in the formation of opinions. This is the more necessary, lest we should seem to commit the mistake of ignoring the existence

[9] Viz. toward the close of Lect. VIII.

[10] The moral causes of unbelief have been frequently discussed, but the intellectual rarely. Van Mildert has collected, in his *Boyle Lectures* (note to Lect. XXIV.), references to many valuable authors where the moral sins of pride and impiety are discussed; and J. A. Fabricius (*Delect. Argument.* 1725.) has devoted a chapter to the literature of the subject (c. 36. p. 653.) Dr. Ogilvie wrote in 1783 a separate work on the causes of the recent unbelief; but the causes alleged by him, though well treated in the details, are superficial. A satisfactory discussion of this and cognate topics connected with unbelief is given in a popular but instructive book, *Infidelity, its aspects, causes, and agencies*, a Prize Essay (1853) of the Evangelical Alliance, by the Rev. T. Pearson, Eyemouth, N. B.

or importance of the emotional element, if the restriction of our point of view to the intellectual should hereafter prevent frequent references to it.

The influence of the moral causes in generating doubt, though sometimes exaggerated, is nevertheless real. Psychological analysis shows that the emotions operate immediately on the will, and the will on the intellect. Consequently the emotion of dislike is able through the will to prejudice the judgment, and cause disbelief of a doctrine against which it is directed.[11] Nor can we doubt that experience confirms the fact. Though we must not rashly judge our neighbour, nor attempt to measure in any particular mind the precise amount of doubt which is due to moral causes, yet it is evident that where a freethinker is a man of immoral or unspiritual life, whose interests incline him to disbelieve in the reality of Christianity, his arguments may reasonably be suspected to be suggested by sins of character, and by dislike to the moral standard of the Christian religion, and, though not on this account necessarily undeserving of attention, must be watched at every point with caution, in order that the emotional may be eliminated from the intellectual causes.

It is also a peculiarity belonging to the kind of evidence on which religion rests for proof, that it offers an opportunity for the subtle influence of moral causes, where at first sight intellectual might seem alone to act. For the evidence of religion is probable, not demonstrative ; and it is the property of probable evidence that the character and experience determine the comparative weight which the mind assigns in it to the premises.[12] In demonstrative evidence there is no op-

[11] Compare some remarks on this point in Whately's *Rhetoric* (part 2. ch. I. § 2.)

[12] Proof being of two kinds, viz. *antecedent probability*, εἰκός, (Arist. Rhet. i. 2. § 15. which shows the *cause ;* and *evidence*, σημεῖον, which shows the *fact ;* it is clear that the latter, if of the positive kind, τεκμήριον, is demonstrative ; but if merely of the probable kind, or of the nature of circumstantial evidence, ἀνώνυμον σημεῖον, requires the antecedent probability in addition for the purpose of effecting conviction. Otherwise the evidence may seem to be an accidental concatenation of circumstances, unless ex-

portunity for the intrusion of emotion; but in probable reasoning the judgment ultimately formed by the mind depends often as much upon the antecedent presumptions brought to the investigation of the subject, as upon the actual proofs presented; the state of feeling causing a variation in the force with which a proposition commends itself to the mind at different times. The very subtlety of this influence, which requires careful analysis for its detection, causes it to be overlooked. Accordingly, in a subject like religion, the emotions may secretly insinuate themselves in the preliminary step of determining the weight due to the premises, even where the final process of inference is purely intellectual.

We can select illustrations of this view of the subtlety of the operation of prejudice from instances of a kind unlike the one previously named; in which it will be seen that the disinclination of the inquirer to accept Christianity has not arisen primarily from the obstacle caused by the enmity of his own carnal heart, but from antipathy toward the moral character of those who have professed the Christian faith.

Who can doubt, that the corrupt lives of Christians in the later centuries of the middle ages, the avarice of the Avignon popes, the selfishness shown in the great schism, the simony and nepotism of the Roman court of the fifteenth century, excited disgust and hatred toward Christianity in the hearts of the literary men of the Renaissance, which disqualified them for the reception of the Christian evidences; or that the social disaffection in the last century in France incensed the mind against the Church that supported alleged public abuses,[13] until it blinded a Voltaire from seeing any goodness in Christianity; or that the religious intolerance shown within the present century by the ecclesias-

plained by the antecedent probability that existed for the occurrence of the main fact which the accumulation of circumstances is adduced to attest.

[13] See below, the commencement of Lect. V.; and on the influence of social disaffection in causing modern unbelief, see Pearson's *Infidelity*, part 2. ch. 3. p. 373 seq.

tical power in Italy drove a Leopardi[14] and a Bini[15] into doubt; or that the sense of supposed personal wrong and social isolation deepened the unbelief of Shelley[16] and of Heinrich Heine?[17] Whatever other motives may have operated in these respective cases, the prejudices which arose from the causes just named, doubtless created an antecedent impression against religion, which impeded the lending an unbiassed ear to its evidence.

The subtlety of the influence in these instances makes them the more instructive. If, as we contemplate them, our sympathies are so far enlisted on the side of the doubters that it becomes necessary to check ourselves in exculpating them, by the consideration that they were responsible for failing to separate the essential truth of Christianity from the accidental abuse of

[14] Giacomo Leopardi (1798—1837), a native of the trans-Apennine Roman states. His works were published (1845—49), consisting of philological pieces, poems, papers on philosophy, and letters. The Italians consider him to have been a prodigy in philological power that might have rivalled Niebuhr. As a poet he was one of the finest of his country in the present century. His letters are very classical in expression, and have been said to rival the correspondence of the best ages of Italy. His fine mind was darkened with the deepest shades of doubt. Shelley is the nearest English representative. A masterly sketch of his mental and literary character was given in the *Quarterly Review* (No. 172. March 1850), generally supposed to be from the pen of an English statesman well known for his knowledge of the Italian literature and his sympathy with constitutional government.

[15] Carlo Bini (1806—1842), a native of Tuscany of less note, who belonged to the Republican party in politics, and like Leopardi burned with an unquenchable love of *la patria*. A monument with an inscription by his friend Mazzini has been recently erected over his grave at Livorno. The tender pathos shown in his poetry has been compared to that of Jean Paul. One of his poems, *L'Anniversario della Nascita* 1833, expressive of deep and afflicting scepticism and life-weariness, will be found in the Collection of Italian Poetry edited by Arrivabene (1 vol. 12mo. 1855.)

[16] Shelley's mental character is discussed near the close of Lect. V.

[17] Heinrich Heine (1799—1856), a poet who betook himself to Paris, about 1830, in disgust with the political state of Germany. His poetry was chiefly subsequent to this event. He had a mixture of German imagination with French *esprit*. In tone he has been compared to Byron. Vapéreau (*Diction. des Contemp.*) compares his wit to that of Swift or Rabelais. His collected works have been published at Philadelphia; and his poems were translated into English by E. A. Bowring, 1861. In later life Heine laid aside the extreme unbelief of his earlier years. An article respecting him appeared in the *Westminster Review* (Jan. 1856.)

it shown in the lives of its professors, we can imagine so much the more clearly, how great was the danger to these doubters themselves of omitting the introspection of their own characters necessary for detecting the prejudice which actually seemed to have conscience on its side; and can realize more vividly from these instances the secresy and intense subtlety of the influence of the feelings in the formation of doubt, and infer the necessity of most careful attention for its discovery in others, and watchfulness in detecting it in our own hearts.

There are other cases of doubt, however, where the influence of the emotional element, if it operates at all, is reduced to a minimum, and the cause accordingly seems wholly intellectual. This may happen when the previous convictions of the mind are shaken by the knowledge of some fact newly brought before its notice; such as the apparent conflict between the Hebrew record of a universal deluge[18] and the negative evidence of geology as to its non-occurrence; or the historical discrepancies between the books of Kings and Chronicles,[19] or the varying accounts of the genealogy and resurrection of Christ. A doubt purely intellectual in its origin might also arise, as we know was the case with the pious Bengel,[20] in consequence of perceiving the va-

[18] A brief statement of the difficulties raised on this point is given by Professor Baden Powell in the article *Deluge* in Kitto's Cyclopædia (first edition).

[19] These discrepancies formed part of the subject of an early work of De Wette (ueber die glaubwuerdigkeit der buecher der Chronik 1806), and are noticed in his *Einleitung ins Alt. Test.* (See the chapters which refer to these books); also in Dr. S. Davidson's *Introduction to the Old Testament* 1862, vol. ii. *Chronicles* § 6 and 8. Mr. F. Newman, in his work, *The Hebrew Monarchy*, has made great use of these difficulties for destructive criticism. Movers (*Untersuchungen ueber die Chronik* 1834), and C. F. Keil (*Apologetischer Versuch ueber die Chronik* 1833), endeavour to remove them. Also see the translation of the Commentary of Keil and Bertheau on Kings and Chronicles, the former of the two being based on the work of the same author previously named.

[20] J. A. Bengel (1689—1752), author of the *Gnomon of the New Testament* (translated, with Life prefixed to vol. iv.) Cfr. also the article by Hartmann in Herzog's *Real. Encyclopædie* and Burt's *Life* of him (translated 1837.) The labour of his life, to fix the text of the New Testament, was prompted by the alarm which his pious mind felt at the uncertainty thrown on the sacred books, the inspiration of which he believed to extend to the words.

riety of readings in the sacred text; or, as in many of the German critics, from the difficulty created by the long habit of examining the classical legends and myths, in satisfying themselves about the reasons why similar criticism should not be extended to the early national literature of the Hebrews. Causes of doubt like these, which spring from the advance of knowledge, necessarily belong primarily to the intellectual region. The intellect is the cause and not merely the condition of them. But there is room even here for an emotional element; and the state of heart may be tested by noticing whether the mind gladly and proudly grasps at them or thoughtfully weighs them with serious effort to discover the truth. The moral causes may reinforce or may check the intellectual: but the distinctness of the two classes is apparent. Though co-existing and interlocked, they may be made subjects of independent study.

The preceding analysis of the relations of the moral and intellectual faculties in the formation of religious opinions might enable us to criticise the ethical inferences drawn in reference to man's responsibility for his belief. Those who think that our characters, moral and intellectual, are formed for us by circumstances, are consistent in denying or depreciating responsibility.[21] There is a danger however among Christian writers of falling into the opposite error, of dwelling so entirely on the moral causes, in forgetfulness of the intellectual, as to teach not only that unbelief of the Christian religion is sin, (which few would dispute,) but that even

[21] The denial of responsibility for belief may either be a denial of all responsibility whatever, in consequence of the opinion that our characters are formed for us by circumstances, or else a denial of our responsibility for our belief, as distinct from our responsibility for the agreement of our conduct with our belief; the moral responsibility, according to this view, lying in our adherence to a standard, irrespective of the truthfulness of the standard. The former of these views is the fatalism advocated in the system called (English) Socialism (See Morell's *History of Philosophy*, i. 472 seq.); the latter has occasionally been imputed to teachers of the utilitarian school of Ethics, perhaps with less justice; their assertions in reference to it being intended to apply only to political and not to moral responsibility.

transient doubt of it is sinful; and thus to repel unbelievers by imputing to them motives of which their consciences acquit them.

A truth however is contained in this opinion, though obscured by being stated with exaggeration, inasmuch as the fact is overlooked that doubts may be of many different kinds. Sinfulness cannot, for example, be imputed to the mere scepticism of inquiry, the healthy critical investigation of methods or results; nor to the scepticism of despair, which, hopeless of finding truth, takes up a reactionary and mystical attitude;[22] nor to the cases (if such can ever be,) of painful doubt, perhaps occasionally even of partial unbelief, which are produced exclusively by intellectual causes, without admixture of moral ones. This variety of form should create caution in measuring the degree of sinfulness involved in individual cases of doubt. Yet the inclination to condemn in such instances contains the fundamental truth that the moral causes are generally so intertwined with the intellectual in the assumption of data, if not in the process of inference, that there is a ground for fearing that the fault may be one of will, not of intellect, even though undetected by the sceptic himself. And a conscientious mind will learn the practical lesson of exercising the most careful self-examination in reference to its doubts, and especially will use the utmost caution not to communicate them needlessly to others. The Hebrew Psalmist, instead of telling his painful misgivings, harboured them in God's presence until he found the solution.[23] The delicacy exhibited in forbearing unnecessarily to shake the faith of others is a measure of the disinterestedness of the doubter. "If I say, I will speak thus; behold I should offend against the generation of thy children."

[22] Such an attitude of mind, for example, was presented in the seventeenth century by Huet, and in the present by De Maistre. On the former, see Bartholmess' *Le Scepticisme Theologique* (1852); for reference to sources for the study of the latter, see Lect. VII. Consult Morell's *History of Philosophy* (vol. ii. ch. 6. § 2) for the history of this kind of philosophical scepticism.

[23] Psalm lxxiii. 15—17.

These remarks will enable us to estimate the manner and degree in which the emotions may, consciously or unconsciously, influence the operations of the intellect in reference to religion; and will clear the way for the statement of that which is to form the special subject of study in these lectures, the nature and mode of operation of the intellectual causes, and the forms of free thought in religion to which they may give rise. This branch is frequently neglected, because satisfying the intellect rather than the heart, indicating tendencies rather than affording means to pronounce judgment on individuals; yet it admits of greater certainty, and will perhaps in some respects be found to be not less full of instruction, than the other.

We must distinctly apprehend what is here intended by the term "intellectual cause," when applied to a series of phenomena like sceptical opinions. It does not merely denote the antecedent ideas which form previous links in the same chain of thought: these are sufficiently revealed by the chronicle which records the series. Nor does it mean the uniformity of method according to which the mind is observed to act at successive intervals: this is the law or formula, the existence of which has been already indicated.[24] But we intend by "cause" two things; either the sources of knowledge which have from age to age thrown their materials into the stream of thought, and compelled reason to re-investigate religion and try to harmonize the new knowledge with the old beliefs; or else the ultimate intellectual grounds or tests of truth on which the decision in such cases has been based, the most general types of thought into which the forms of doubt can be analysed. The problem is this:—Given, these two terms: on the one hand the series of opinions known as the history of free thought in religion; on the other the uniformity of mode in which reason has operated. Interpolate two steps to connect them together, which will show respectively the materials of

[24] See pp. 7, 12.

knowledge which reason at successive moments brought to bear on religion, and the ultimate standards of truth which it adopted in applying this material to it. It is the attempt to supply the answer to this problem that will give organic unity to these lectures.

A few words will suffice in reference to the former of these two subjects, inasmuch as it has already been described to some extent,[25] and will be made clear in the course of the history. The branches of knowledge with which the movements of free thought in religion are connected, are chiefly literary criticism and science. The one addresses itself to the record of the revelation; the other to the matter contained in the record. Criticism, when it gains canons of evidence for examining secular literature, applies them to the sacred books; directing itself in its lower[26] form to the variations in their text; in its higher[26] to their genuineness and authenticity. Science, physical or metaphysical, addresses itself to the question of the credibility of their contents. In its physical form, when it has reduced the world to its true position in the universe of space, human history in the cycles of time, and the human race in the world of organic life, it compares these discoveries with the view of the universe and of the physical history of the planet contained in the sacred literature; or it examines the Christian doctrine of miraculous interposition and special providence by the light of its gradually increasing conviction of the uniformity of nature. In its moral and metaphysical forms, science examines such subjects as the moral history of the Hebrew theocracy; or ponders reverently over the mystery of the divine scheme of redemption, and the teaching which scripture supplies on the deepest problems of speculation, the relations of Deity to the universe, the act of creation, the nature of evil, and the administration of moral providence.

[25] See pp. 8–12.

[26] These names for the two respective branches into which literary criticism is divisible, are commonly used in all modern German works of criticism.

There is another mode, however, in which speculative philosophy has operated, which needs fuller explanation. It has not merely, like the other sciences, suggested results which have seemed to clash with Christianity, but has supplied the ultimate grounds of proof to which appeal has consciously been made, or which have been unconsciously assumed:—the ultimate types of thought which have manifested themselves in the struggle.[27]

It will be useful, before exhibiting this kind of influence in reference to religion, to illustrate its character by selecting an instance from some region of thought where its effects would be least suspected. The example shall be taken from the history of literature.

If we compare three poets selected from the last three centuries, the contrast will exhibit at once the change which has taken place in the literary spirit and standard of judgment, and the correspondence of the change with fluctuations in the predominant philosophy of the time.—If we commence with the author of the Paradise Lost, we listen to the last echo of the poetry which had belonged to the great outburst of mind of the earlier part of the seventeenth century, and of the faith in the supernatural which had characterized Puritanism. His philosophy is Hebrew: he hesitates not to interpret the divine counsels; but it is by the supposed light of revelation. Doubt is unknown to him. The anthropomorphic conception of Deity prevails. Material nature is the instrument of God's personal providence for the objects of His care.—But if we pass to the author of the Essay on Man, the revolution which has given artistic precision to the form is not more ob-

[27] The work which will most clearly explain my purpose in the following history is Mr. J. D. Morell's *Historical and Critical View of the Speculative Philosophy of Europe in the nineteenth century.* (1847.) It exhibits the influence of metaphysical philosophy on various branches of knowledge. (See sect. 1 and 5 of the introduction to vol. i., and in vol. ii. ch. 9.) Also in his *Lectures on the Philosophical Tendencies of the Age* (1848), he treats the same subject with direct reference to religion. Compare also on the same points Cousin's *Histoire de la Philosophie du* 8e *siècle*, vol. ii. leçon 30; Pearson on *Infidelity*, part ii. ch. 2. p. 340 seq.

servable than the indications of a philosophy which has chilled the spiritual faculties. The supernatural is gone. Nature is a vast machine which moves by fixed laws impressed upon it by a Creator. The soul feels chilled with the desolation of a universe wherein it cannot reach forth by prayer to a loving Father. Scripture is displaced by science. Doubt has passed into unbelief. The universe is viewed by the cold materialism which arraigns spiritual subjects at the bar of sense.—If now we turn to the work consecrated by the great living poet to the memory of his early friend, we find ourselves in contact with a meditative soul, separated from the age just named by a complete intellectual chasm; whose spiritual perceptions reflect a philosophy which expresses the sorrows and doubts of a cultivated mind of the present day, "perplext in faith but not in deeds.[28]" The material has become transfigured into the spiritual. The objective has been replaced by the subjective. Nature is studied, as in Pope, without the assumption of a revelation; but it is no longer regarded as a machine conducted by material laws: it is a motive soul which embodies God's presence; a mystery to be felt, not understood. God is not afar off, so that we cannot reach Him: He is so nigh, that His omnipresence seems to obscure His personality.

These instances will illustrate the difference which philosophy produces in the classes of ideas in which the mind of an age is formed. In Milton, the appeal is made to the revelation of God in the Book; in Pope, to the revelation in Nature; in the living poet, to the revelation in man's soul, the type of the infinite Spirit and interpreter of God's universe and God's book.[29]

It is an analysis of a similar kind which we must conduct in reference to sceptical opinions. The influence of the first of the two classes of intellectual causes above named,[30] viz. the various forms of knowledge

[28] Tennyson's *In Memoriam*, § 94.

[29] An instructive comparison of Milton, Cowper, and Wordsworth, which will further illustrate this subject, may be found in *Macmillan's Magazine* for Jan. 1862.

[30] See p. 21.

there described, could not exist unobserved, for they are present from time to time as rival doctrines in contest with Christianity; but the kind of influence of which we now treat, which relates to the grounds of belief on which a judgment is consciously or unconsciously formed, is more subtle, and requires analysis for its detection.

We must briefly explain its nature, and illustrate its influence on religion.

Metaphysical science is usually divided into two branches; of which one examines the objects known, the other the human mind, that is the organ of knowledledge. (7) When Psychology has finished its study of the structure and functions of the mind, it supplies the means for drawing inferences in reply to a question which admits of a twofold aspect, viz. which of the mental faculties,—sense, reason, feeling, furnishes the origin of knowledge; and which is the supreme test of truth? These two questions form the subjective or Psychological branch of Metaphysics. According to the answer thus obtained we deduce a corollary in reference to the objective side. We ask what information is afforded by these mental faculties in respect to the nature or attributes of the objects known,—matter, mind, God, duty. The answer to this question is the branch commonly called the Ontological. The one inquiry treats of the tests of knowledge, the other of the nature of being. The combination of the two furnishes the answer on its two sides, internally and externally, to the question, What is truth?

The right application of them to the subject of religion would give a philosophy of religion; either objectively by the process of constructing a *theodicée* or theory to reconcile reason and faith; or subjectively, by separating their provinces by means of such an inquiry into the functions of the religious faculty, and the nature of the truths apprehended by it, as might furnish criteria to determine the amount that is to be appropriated respectively from our own consciousness and from external authority.

The influence of the Ontological branch of the inquiry in producing a struggle with Christianity, has been already included under the difficulties previously named, which are created by the growth of the various sciences.[31] It is the influence of the Psychological branch that we are now illustrating, by showing that the various theories in respect of it give their type to various forms of belief and doubt.

The well-known threefold distribution of the faculties that form the ultimate grounds of conviction will suffice for our purpose: viz., sensational consciousness revealing to us the world of matter; intuitive reason that of mind; and feeling that of emotion.[32] These are the forms of consciousness which supply the material from which the reflective powers draw inferences and construct systems.

It is easy to exhibit the mental character which each would have a tendency to generate when applied to a special subject like religion, natural or revealed.

If the eye of sense be the sole guide in looking around on nature, we discover only a universe of brute matter, phenomena linked together in uniform succession of antecedents and consequents. Mind becomes only a higher form of matter. Sin loses its poignancy. Immortality disappears.. God exists not, except as a personification of the Cosmos. Materialism, atheism,

[31] The cause is, that whatever difficulties may be presented by it are the statements of rival teaching opposed to the Christian; conclusions, not premises: whereas those which arise from the psychological branch are rival premises; not difference of belief merely, but causes of such difference. Therefore the difficulties suggested by Ontology belong to those described above in p. 21, 22. Many illustrations of this branch may be found in Bartholmess' *Hist. Crit. des Doctrines Religieuses de la Philosophie Moderne*, 1855.

[32] The classification of faculties here intended, with their respective functions, will be illustrated by referring to Morell's *Hist. of Phil.*, vol. ii. p. 338; and his *Philosophy of Religion*, ch. 1. and 2. The altered scheme given in his subsequent works on *Psychology* (1853 and 1861,) ought also to be compared with the former one. See also Coleridge's *Aids to Reflection*, i. 168 seq. The terms Sensationalist, Idealist, and Mystic, are nearly always used in the present lectures in the sense in which Morell, following Cousin, uses them; viz. to express those who place the ultimate test of truth in sense, innate ideas, or feeling, respectively.

fatalism, are the ultimate results which are proved by logic and history[33] to follow from this extreme view. The idea of spirit cannot be reached by it. For if some other form of experience than the sensitive be regarded as the origin of knowledge; if a nobler view be forced on us by the very inability even to express nature's phenomena without superadding spiritual qualities; if regularity of succession[34] suggest the idea of order and purpose and mind; if adaptation suggest the idea of morality; if movement suggest the idea of form and will; if will suggest the idea of personality; if the idea of the Cosmos suggest unity, and thus we mount up, step by step, to the conception of a God, possessing unity, intelligence, will, character, we really transfer into the sphere of nature ideas taken from another region of being, viz., from our consciousness of ourselves, our consciousness of spirit. It is mental association that links these ideas to those of sense, and gives to a sensational philosophy properties not its own. If however sensational experience can by any means arrive at the notion of natural religion; yet it will find a difficulty, created by its belief of the uniformity of nature,

[33] E. g. in the history of the eighteenth century in France. (See Lect. V.) In estimating the effects of philosophical opinions, care must be used, to distinguish the results which may be thought by opponents to flow from such opinions by logical inference, from those which have been proved by history to flow from them in fact. Some portion of Cousin's brilliant criticism, *in the Hist. de la Phil. Française du* 18e *siècle*, and in the *Ecole Sensualiste*, is thought to be open to exception on this ground. It is from a conviction of the importance of not attributing to a philosopher that which we merely conceive to be a corollary, though a logical one, from his opinions, that the writer has abstained from introducing here into the text examples of the different views sketched, and has treated the subject in this page broadly and without minuteness. The religious results here stated to appertain to particular metaphysical opinions must accordingly be regarded as logical tendencies, not as necessary effects. The truth of opinions must not be tested merely by supposed consequences, though the practical value of such a test ought to be allowed its due weight.

[34] A statement of the steps of proof similar to those described here, by which we ascend to the knowledge of a Deity, is to be found in the Sermons of the late lamented Rev. Shergold Boone (Sermons 2–7; and especially 2 and 3; 1853). Compare also the steps of proof which Rousseau gives in the Confession of the Savoyard Vicar of the *Emile*, analysed in Lect. V.

in taking the further step of admitting the miraculous interference which gives birth to revealed: and even if this difficulty should be surmounted, the disinclination to the supernatural would nevertheless have a tendency to obliterate mystery by empirical rationalism, and to reduce piety to morality, morality to expedience,[35] the church to a political institution, religion to a ritual system, and its evidence to external historic testimony.

The rival system of proof founded in intuitive consciousness is however not free from danger. A difference occurs, according as this endowment is regarded as merely revealing the facts of our own inner experience, or on the other hand as possessing a power to apprehend God positively, and spirit to spirit.[36] The result of the former belief would be indeed an ethical religion, compared with the political one just described. If it did not rise from the law to the law-giver, it would at least present morality as a law obligatory on man by his mental structure, independently of the consideration of reward and punishment. The ideas of God, duty, immortality, would be established as a necessity of thought, if not as matters of objective fact. Yet religion would be rather rational than supernatural; obedience to duty instead of communion with Deity; and unless the mind can find ground for a belief in God and the divine attributes through some other faculty, the idealism must destroy the evidence of revealed religion. Or at least, if the mind admit its truth, it must renounce the right to criticise the material of that which it confesses to be beyond the limits of its own conscious-

[35] These charges are frequently made indiscriminately against all who hold that expedience is a sufficient explanation of the origin of moral ideas. They were true in a great degree against Utilitarians of the last century, together with some of those in the early years of the present. But when applied at the present time, they only indicate a tendency, not a fact; as may be seen in the delicate manner in which Mr. J. S. Mill has explained the doctrine of Utility, in a series of papers in *Fraser's Magazine* for 1861.

[36] The first of these two views is seen in Kant, with whom the forms of thought are only regulatively true; the second in Schelling and Cousin. The references for studying Kant's religious views will be found in a note to Lecture VI.

ness; and thus, by abdicating its natural powers, blindly submit to external authority, and accept belief as the refuge from its own Pyrrhonism.

If, on the other hand, instead of regarding all attempts to pass beyond logical forms of thought to be mental impotence, the mind follows its own instincts, and, relying upon the same natural realism which justifies its belief in the immediate character of its sensitive perceptions, ventures to depend with equal firmness on the reality of its intuitional consciousness, religion, natural or revealed, wears another aspect; and both the advantages and the dangers of such a view are widely different.[37] The soul no longer regards the landscape to be a scene painted on the windows of its prison-house, a subjective limit to its perceptions, but not speculatively true; but it wanders forth from its cell unfettered into the universe around. God is no longer an inference from final causes, nor a principle of thought. He is the living God, a real personal spirit with whom the soul is permitted to hold direct communion. Providence becomes the act of a personal agent. Religion is the worship in spirit. Sin is seen in its heinousness. Prayer is justified as a reality, as the breathing of the human soul for communion with its infinite Parent (8). And by the light of this intuition, God, nature, and man, look changed. Nature is no longer a physical engine; man no longer a moral machine. Material nature becomes the regular expression of a personal fixed will; Miracle the direct interposition of a personal free will. Revelation is probable, as the voice of God's mercy to the child of His love. Inspiration becomes

[37] The dangers of such a view arise from those results which have been pointed out in Sir W. Hamilton's *Dissertations* (Diss. I. on Cousin). In reference to the office of the intuition in science, Dr. Whewell's view, in the *Philosophy of the Inductive Sciences*, may be adduced as one which appears to possess the advantage designed by Schelling's theory, and not be open to those criticisms which have been directed against it. Possibly a true philosophy of the action of the intellectual faculties in reference to religion might be obtained by transferring to it the analysis which Dr. Whewell has given of their action in reference to science. Dr. McCosh, in his work on *the Intentions of the Mind* (1859), has done much towards effecting it.

possible, for the intuitional consciousness seems adapted to be used by divine Providence as its instrument.[38]

But the type of mind created by the use of intuition as a test of truth is rarely alone. It is cognate to, if it is not connected with, that produced by the third of the above-named tests, feeling. The emotions, according to a law of spiritual supply and demand, suggest the reality of the objects toward which they are aspirations. The longing for help, the feeling of dependence, is the justification of prayer; the sense of remorse is the witness to divine judgment; the consciousness of penitence is the ground for hope in God's merciful interference; the ineradicable sense of guilt is the eternal witness to the need of atonement; the instinct for immortality is the pledge of a future life.

Yet the use of these tests of intuition and feeling in religion, though possessing these advantages, has dangers. If the feelings, instead of being used to reinforce or check the other faculties, be relied upon as sole arbiters; especially if they be linked with the imagination instead of the intuition; they may conduct to mysticism and superstition by the very vividness of their perception of the supernatural.[39] Likewise the intuitive

[38] In Morell's *Philosophy of Religion* (c. 5 and 6,) are remarks on the relation of intuition to inspiration, to which attention may be directed, but only in a *psychological* point of view. Pious minds that believe in miraculous inspiration will rightly hesitate before holding any particular psychological theory of the field of its operation; yet it would seem, if we may hazard a conjecture, that it is the intuitive power of the mind which is mostly the organ to which the divine revelation is unveiled, and on which the inspiring influence acts. It is certain that we cannot understand the *modus operandi*, but we may without irreverence humbly seek to discover the field on which God's Spirit condescends to operate. In this view inspiration would be analogous to natural genius *psychologically*, but wholly different *theologically*, inasmuch as all who believe in its miraculous character must hold firmly that it is due to a *supernatural* elevation of this mental power by *immediate* operation of divine agency, whereas the discoveries of ordinary genius are due to the *unassisted* and normal condition of the faculty. Morell, in the passage referred to, will probably be thought to be right in the psychological question, and wrong in the theological.

[39] The mysticism of the Quakers of the seventeenth century, and of Swedenborg in the eighteenth, is of this character. The excessive self-mortification of the Franciscan order in the middle ages may be set down

faculty, if it be regarded as giving a noble grasp over the fact of God as an infinite Spirit, may cause the mind to relax its hold on the idea of the Divine Personality, and fall into Pantheism, and identify God with the universe, not by degrading spirit to matter, but by elevating matter to spirit.[40] Or, instead of allowing experience and revelation to develop into conceptions of the fundamental truth whose existence it perceives, it may attempt to develop a religion wholly *a priori*,[41] and assert its right to create as well as to verify. Also, when applying itself to revealed religion, this type of thought necessarily makes its last appeal to inward insight. It cannot, like sensationalism, or subjective idealism, admit its own impotence, and receive on authority a revelation, the contents of which it ventures not to criticise. It must always appropriate that which it is to believe. Accordingly it will have a tendency to render religion subjective in its character, uncertain in its doctrines, individual in its constitution.

These general remarks, every one of which admits of historic exemplification,[42] will suffice to illustrate the kind of influence exercised by these respective tests of truth in forming the judgment or moulding the character in relation to the belief or disbelief of natural and revealed religion. These effects are not adduced as the

to the influence, perhaps not consciously analysed, of the same standard used for guidance. On Mysticism, see Morell's *History of Philosophy*, ii. 332 seq. and 356 seq.; and his *Lectures on the Philosophical Tendencies of the Age* (Lect. III.); on Swedenborg, see *National Review* No. 12; and on mystics generally, consult the interesting work of the lamented Rev. R. A. Vaughan, *Hours with the Mystics*, 1856.

[40] As in Spinoza, or the school of Schelling.

[41] As in Herbert in the seventeenth century, and Theodore Parker in the nineteenth. On the intuitional theology, see McCosh, *Divine Government*, b. iv. ch. 2. § 4. (note.)

[42] The above are only a very few instances, of which many will occur hereafter; but they will sufficiently indicate that the French infidelity is mostly connected with the appeal to the first test of truth, sensation; German rationalism, the result of an appeal to an intuitive faculty "transcending consciousness;" English deism, and the earlier forms of German rationalism, the appeal to the ordinary reason, as able to create religion for itself. The separate appeal to feeling has generally, it will be perceived, caused too much belief, instead of too little; mysticism instead of scepticism.

necessary results but as the ordinary tendencies of these respective theories. The mind frequently stops short of the conclusions logically deducible from its own principles. To measure precisely the effect of each view would be impossible. In mental science analysis must be qualitative, not quantitative.

It will hardly be expected that we should arbitrate among these theories, inasmuch as our purpose is not to test the comparative truthfulness of metaphysical opinions, but to refer sceptical opinions in religion to their true scientific and metaphysical parentage. Truth is probably to be found in a selection from all; and historical investigation is the chief means of discovering the mode of conducting the process. It is at least certain, that if history be the form which science necessarily takes in the study of that which is subject to laws of life and organic growth, it must be the preliminary inquiry in any investigation in reference to mental phenomena. The history of philosophy must be the approach to philosophy.[43] The great problem of philosophy is method; and if there be a hope that the true method can ever be found it must be by uniting the historical analysis of the development of the universal mind with the psychological analysis of the individual. The history of thought indicates not only fact but truth; not only shows what has been, but, by exhibiting the proportions which different faculties contribute toward the construction of truth, and indicating tendencies as well as results, prepares materials to be collated with the decision previously made by mental and moral science concerning the question of what ought to be (9).

[43] This was the view presented in the teaching of Cousin and the Eclectic school of France. Many of the younger thinkers of Europe now consider that the history of philosophy constitutes the whole of philosophy, and is not merely, as here maintained, the preliminary to it. This new view is probably unconsciously derived from Hegel, and is the residuum left by his philosophy. Two able living French critics, Renan and Scherer, have so very clearly expressed this view of the function of philosophy, that it may be well to quote their words (see Note 9); the more so, as this subject will be named again in Lect. VII. Renan has also expressed the same ideas in the Revue des deux Mondes (Jan. 15, 1860), *De la Metaphysique et de son avenir.*

A definite conviction on this metaphysical inquiry seems perhaps to be involved in the very idea of criticism, and necessary for drawing the moral from the history; yet the independence of our historical inquiry ought to be sacrificed as little as possible to illustrate a foregone conclusion. It will be more satisfactory to present the evidence for a verdict without undue advocacy of a side in the metaphysical controversy.[44]

The execution of this design of analysing the intellectual causes of unbelief will necessarily involve to some extent a biographical treatment of the subject, both for theoretical and practical reasons, to discover truth and to derive instruction. This is so evident in the history of action, that there is a danger at the present time lest history should lose the general in the individual, and descend from the rank of science to mere biography.[45] The deeper insight which is gradually obtained into the complexity of nature, together with the fuller conviction of human freedom, is causing artistic portraiture and ethical analysis to be substituted for historical generalization. The same method however applies to the region of thought as well as will.

[44] It is not from any wish to evade the real question that the writer thus avoids taking a side in the metaphysical dispute. His object is to explain the various effects of metaphysical theories on religious belief; and while considering that the respective evil effects of these systems are a logical corollary from them, as well as an historical result, he is prepared to admit, as previously remarked, that men are sometimes better than their systems, and do not always draw the logical conclusions from their own premises; and therefore he has not thought it right to make these lectures a direct argument on behalf of some favourite metaphysical system, and attack on some rival one. In such case, the history would lose its independent character. While therefore he has never concealed his opinions on the subject of religion, he has thought it more proper not to obtrude, except indirectly, his opinions on that of metaphysics.

[45] This is the question at issue between modern Positivists and their opponents. Comte declared the possibility of discovering the fixed laws on which society depends as really as the physical ones of matter. Mr. Mill, in his account of the logic of history (*Logic*, b. vi. c. 4. (6–10)), lays down more maturely the theory of such a process. On the contrary, Mr. Kingsley, in his inaugural lecture at Cambridge, 1861, asserts the very opposite position; and, in his wish to elevate the influence of individual men on the course of events, almost reduces history to a series of biographies.

Thought, as an intellectual product, can indeed be studied apart from the mind that creates it, and can be treated by history as a material fact subject to the fixed succession of natural laws. But the exclusive use of such a method, at least in any other subject of study than that of the results of physical discovery, must be defective, even independently of the question of the action of free will, unless the thoughts which are the object of study be also connected with the personality of the thinker who produces them. His external biography is generally unimportant, save when the individual character may have impressed itself upon public events; but the internal portraiture, the growth of soul as known by psychological analysis, is the very instrument for understanding the expression of it in life or in literature.[46] It is requisite to know the mental bias of a writer, whether it be practical, imaginative or reflective; to see the *idola specus* which influenced him, the action of circumstances upon his character, and the reaction of his character upon circumstances; before we can gain the clue to the interpretation of his works. But if we wish further to derive moral instruction from him, the biographical mode of study becomes even more necessary. For the notion of freedom as the ground of responsibility is now superadded; and the story of his life is the sole means for such an apprehension of the causes of his heart-struggles as shall enable us to take the gauge of his moral character, and appropriate the lessons derivable from the study of it.

Indeed biographical notices, if they could be extended compatibly with the compass of the subject, would be the most instructive and vivid mode of presenting alike the facts relating to scepticism and their interpretation. Such memoirs are not wanting, and

[46] The kind of analysis here alluded to may be illustrated by referring to one of the *Essays* of Mr. D. Masson, in which he has compared in a very striking manner Shakspeare and Goëthe, by regarding their respective works as reflecting the mental peculiarity of each writer. He considers the meditative melancholy of Shakspeare's youth, as expressed in his Sonnets, to be the clue to the reflective analysis that in later life could depict the doubts of Hamlet.

are among the most touching in literature. The sketch which Strauss has given of his early friend and fellow student Maerklin,[47] gradually surrendering one cherished truth after another, until he doubted all but the law of conscience; then devoting himself in the strength of it with unflinching industry to education; until at last he died in the dark, without belief in God or hope, cheered only by the consciousness of having tried to find truth and do his duty:—the sad tale, told by two remarkable biographers, of Sterling,[48] doubting, renouncing the ministry, yet thirsting for truth, and at last solacing himself in death by the hopes offered by the Bible, to the eternal truths of which his doubting heart had always clung:—the memoir of the adopted son of our own university, Blanco White,[49] a mind in which faith and doubt were perpetually waging war, till the grave closed over his truth-searching and careworn spirit:—the confessions of one of our own sons of the successive "phases of faith"[50] through which his soul passed from evangelical Christianity to a spiritual Deism, a record of heart-struggles which takes its place among the pathetic works of autobiography, where individuals have unveiled their inner life for the instruction of their fellow-men:—all these are instances where

[47] Christian Maerklin (1807–1849), a fellow student of Strauss at Tübingen, whose views were unsettled, partly by a tone like that of the Renaissance derived from the contrast of classic and Christian culture, and partly by the philosophical speculations of the time. He embraced pantheism and the mythical idea of Christianity. For ten years after 1840 he undertook ministerial work, and then left the church, and till his death in 1849 devoted himself with assiduity to the business of education. A short memoir of him was written by Strauss in 1851, *C. Maerklin, ein Lebens-und-Character-Bild aus der Gegenwart;* a brief review of which is given in the *National Review*, No. 7.

[48] Sterling (1806–1844), a clergyman, curate to archdeacon Hare. His works were edited, with a memoir prefixed, by the archdeacon in 1848; and a life written of him by Carlyle (1851.)

[49] Blanco White (1775–1841), a Spanish priest, who became a protestant, and a refugee in England. He was much respected in Oxford, and the University gave him a degree. He afterwards turned unitarian, and perhaps at last deist. His life was published in 1845; and his mental character analysed in the *Quarterly Review* No. 151, and the *Christian Remembrancer* vol. 10.

[50] Mr. F. Newman. See Lect. VIII.

the great moral and spiritual problems that belong to the condition of our race may be seen embodied in the sorrowful experience of individuals. They are instances of rare value for psychological study in reference to the history of doubt; sad beacons of warning and of guidance. Accordingly, in the history of free thought we must not altogether neglect the spiritual biography of the doubter, though only able to indicate it by a few touches; by an etching, not a photograph.

We have now added to the explanation before given of the province of our inquiry, and of the law of the action of free thought on religion, an account of the moral and intellectual causes which operate in the history of unbelief, and have sufficiently explained the mode in which the subject will be treated.

The use of the inquiry will, it is hoped, be apparent both in its theoretical and practical relations. It is designed to have an intellectual value not only as instruction but as argument. The tendency of it will be in some degree polemical as well as didactic, refuting error by analysing it into its causes, repelling present attacks by studying the history of former ones.

It is one peculiar advantage belonging to the philosophical investigation of the history of thought, that even the odious becomes valuable as an object of study, the pathology of the soul as well as its normal action. Philosophy takes cognisance of error as well as of truth, inasmuch as it derives materials from both for discovering a theory of the grounds of belief and disbelief. Hence it follows that the study of the natural history of doubt combined with the literary, if it be the means of affording an explanation of a large class of facts relating to the religious history of man and the sphere of the remedial operations of Christ's church, will have a practical value as well as speculative.

Such an inquiry, if it be directed, as in the present lectures, to the analysis of the intellectual rather than the emotional element of unbelief, as being that which has been less generally and less fully explored, will require to be supplemented by a constant reference to the intermixture of the other element, and the consequent necessity of taking account of the latter in estimating the whole phenomenon of doubt. But within its own sphere it will have a practical and polemical value, if the course of the investigation shall show that the various forms of unbelief, when studied from the intellectual side, are corollaries from certain metaphysical or critical systems. The analysis itself will have indirectly the force of an argument. The discovery of the causes of a disease contains the germ of the cure. Error is refuted when it is referred to the causes which produce it.

Nor will the practical value of the inquiry be restricted to its use as a page in the spiritual history of the human mind, but will belong to it also as a chapter in the history of the church. For even if in the study of the contest our attention be almost wholly restricted to the movements of one of the two belligerents, and only occasionally directed to the evidences on which the faith of the church in various crises reposed, and by which it tried to repel the invader, yet the knowledge of the scheme of attack cannot fail to be a valuable accompaniment to the study of the defence.[51]

Thus the natural history of doubt, viewed as a chapter of human history, like the chapter of physiology which studies a disease, will point indirectly to the cure, or at least to the mode of avoiding the causes which induce the disease; while the literary history of it, viewed as a chapter of church history, will contribute the results of experience to train the Christian combatant.

The subject will however not only have an intellectual value in being at once didactic and polemical, offering an explanation of the causes of unbelief and furnishing hints for their removal; but it cannot fail also to possess a moral value in reference to the conscience and heart of the disputant, in teaching the lesson of mercy towards the unbeliever, and deep pity

[51] See further remarks concerning the purpose of the course of Lectures in Lect. VIII.

for the heart wounded with doubts. An intelligent acquaintance with the many phases of history operates like foreign travel in widening the sympathies; and increase of knowledge creates the moderation which gains the victory through attracting an enemy instead of repelling him. Bigotry is founded on ignorance and fear. True learning is temperate, because discriminating; forbearing, because courageous. If we place ourselves in the position of an opponent, and try candidly to understand the process by which he was led to form his opinions, indignation will subside into pity, and enmity into grief: the hatred will be reserved for the sin, not for the sinner; and the servant of Jesus Christ will thus catch in some humble measure the forbearing love which his divine Master showed to the first doubting disciple.[52] As the sight of suffering in an enemy changes the feeling of anger into pity, so the study of a series of spiritual struggles makes us see in an opponent, not an enemy to be crushed, but a brother to be won. The utility of a historic treatment of doubt is suggested by moral as well as intellectual grounds.

I hope therefore that if I follow the example of some of my predecessors,[53] in giving a course of lectures historical rather than polemical, evincing the critic rather than the advocate, seeking for truth rather than victory, analysing processes of evidence rather than refuting results, my humble contribution toward the knowledge of the argument of the Christian evidences will be considered to come fairly within the design intended by the founder of the lecture.

It may well be believed that in the execution of so large a scheme I have felt almost overwhelmed under a painful sense of its difficulty. If even I may venture to hope that a conscientious study in most cases of the

[52] John xx. 26–29.

[53] E. g. Mr. J. J. Conybeare (1824), on *the History and Limits of the Secondary Interpretation of Scripture;* Dr. Burton (1829), *The Heresies of the Apostolic Age;* Dr. Hampden (1832), *The Scholastic Philosophy in relation to Christian Theology;* as well as several works which investigate doctrines historically, such as the Lectures on the Atonement by Dr. Thomson (1853), by Dr. Hessey on the Sabbath (1860).

original sources of information may save me from literary mistakes, yet there is a danger lest the size of the subject should preclude the possibility of constant clearness; or lest the very analysis of the errors of the systems named, may produce a painful, if not an injurious, impression. In an age too of controversy, those who speak on difficult questions incur a new danger, of being misunderstood from the sensitiveness with which earnest men not unreasonably watch them. The attitude of suspicion may cause impartiality to be regarded as indifference to truth, fairness as sympathy with error. I am not ashamed therefore to confess, that under the oppressive sense of these various feelings I have been wont to go for help to the only source where the burdened heart can find consolation; and have sought, in the communion with the Father of spirits which prayer opens to the humblest, a temper of candour, of reverence, and of the love of truth. In this spirit I have made my studies; and what I have thus learned I shall teach.

LECTURE II.

THE LITERARY OPPOSITION OF HEATHENS AGAINST CHRISTIANITY IN THE EARLY AGES.

---

1 Cor. i. 22–24.

The Greeks seek after wisdom; but we preach Christ crucified; unto the Greeks foolishness; but unto them which are called, Christ the wisdom of God.

IT has been already stated[1], that in the first great struggle of the human mind against the Christian religion the action of reason in criticising its claims assumed two forms, Gnosticism or rationalism within the church, and unbelief without.

The origin and history of the former of these two lines of thought were once discussed in an elaborate course of Bampton Lectures[2]; and though subsequent investigation has added new sources of information[3],

[1] See above, p. 8.

[2] By Dr. Burton in 1829, *An Inquiry into the Heresies of the Apostolic Age.*

[3] Burton was such a careful student, that he hardly omitted anything on the subject which had been published up to his time. Subsequent investigations have added little material directly for the knowledge of Gnosticism, but much for a better appreciation of those sources from which it sprung. The oriental philosophy, as is shown in note 3 to Lect. I, is much better known; in like manner the Neo-Platonic. The Jewish Cabbala has also been made known by A. Franck (*Memoires sur la Cabbale*). The speculations too of the new Tübingen school, of which Baur's work on *Gnosis*, 1835, is an example, have been specially directed to the study of the *origines* of the Christian church and of Gnostic heresy, and however unsatisfactory in results, present much valuable research. Kurtz

and it would be consonant to our general object to trace briefly the speculations of the various schools of Gnostics,—Greek, Oriental, or Egyptian,—the want of space necessitates the omission of these topics. In the present lecture we shall accordingly restrict ourselves to the history of the other line of thought, and trace the grounds alleged by the intelligent heathens who examined Christianity, for declining to admit its claims, from the time of its rise to the final downfall of heathenism.

The truest modern resemblance to this struggle is obviously to be found in the disbelief shown by educated heathens in pagan countries to whom Christianity is proclaimed in the present day. It was not until the establishment of Christianity as the state religion by Constantine had given it political and moral victory, that it was possible for unbelief to assume its modern aspect, of being the attempt of reason to break away from a creed which is an acknowledged part of the national life. The first opponents accordingly whose views we shall study, Lucian, Celsus, Porphyry, Hierocles, are heathen unbelievers. Julian is the earliest that we encounter who rejected Christianity after having been educated in it.

The resemblance however to this struggle is not wholly restricted to heathen lands. There have been moments in the history of nations, or of individuals, when a Christian standard of feeling or of thought has been so far obliterated that a state of public disbelief and philosophical attack similar to the ancient heathen has reappeared, and the tone of the early unbelievers, and sometimes even their specific doubts, have been either borrowed or reproduced.[4]

in his *Kirchengeschichte* § 48–50, and Hase, *Id.* § 75–82, refer to several other monographs of the same kind. See also the discussion on Gnostic sects in Professor Norton's *Evidences of the Genuineness of the Gospels*, vol. ii.

[4] Such instances are seen in the Renaissance, in the state of France during the eighteenth century, and in some of the writings of the English deists and German critics, as will be shown in subsequent lectures. A general view is given, in the introduction to Houtteville's *Le Christianisme*

In this portion of the history we encounter a difficulty peculiar to it, in being compelled to form an estimate of the opinions described, from indirect information. The treatises of the more noted writers that opposed Christianity have perished; some through natural causes, but those of Porphyry and Julian through the special order of a Christian emperor, Theodosius II., in A.D. 435.

In the absence accordingly of the original writings, we must discover the grounds for the rejection of Christianity by the aid of the particular treatises of evidence written by Christian fathers expressly in refutation of them, which occasionally contain quotations of the lost works; and also by means of the general apologies written on behalf of the Christian religion, together with slight notices of it occurring in heathen literature. The latter will inform us concerning the miscellaneous objections current, the former concerning the definite arguments of the writers who expressly gave reasons for disbelieving Christianity.[5]

We possess a large treatise of Origen against Celsus; passages, directed against Porphyry, of Eusebius, Jerome, and Augustin; a tract of Eusebius against Hierocles; and a work of Cyril of Alexandria against Julian. Yet it is never perfectly satisfactory to be obliged to read an opinion through the statement of an opponent of it. The history of philosophical controversy shows that intellectual causes, such as the natural

prouvé par des faits, of "the method of the principal authors for and against Christianity from its beginning," (translated 1739.) Hase also quotes a work of D. Baumgarten-Crusius, De Scriptoribus sæc. II. qui novam relig. impugnarunt, 1845.

[5] There are four sources of information in reference to the opinions of the heathens concerning Christianity; viz. (1) the slight notices which occur in heathen literature, on which see note 12; (2) the works written expressly against Christianity, which are sufficiently analysed in the text and foot-notes; (3) the special replies to these attacks, on which see notes 13, 17, 19; (4) the general treatises on evidence in the early fathers, on which see note 49. The recent publication of Pressensé's work, 2e série, t. 2, where the analysis of the two latter sources is ably executed, renders unnecessary the publication of an analysis of each. Several of them are also analysed in Schramm, *Analysis Patrum*, 1782.

tendency to answer an argument on principles that its author would not concede, to reply to conclusions instead of premises, or to impute the corollaries which are supposed to be deducible from an opinion, may lead to unintentional misrepresentation of a doctrine refuted, even where no moral causes such as bias or sarcasm contribute to the result. Aristotle's well-known criticism of Plato's theory of archetypes is a pertinent illustration.[6]

The slight difficulty thus encountered, in extracting the real opinions of the early unbelievers out of the replies of their Christian opponents, may for the most part be avoided by first realising the state of belief which existed in reference to the heathen religion, which for our present purpose may be treated as homogeneous throughout the whole Roman world. We shall thus be enabled as it were to foresee the line of opinion which would be likely to be adopted in reference to a new religion coming with the claims and character of Christianity. This prefatory inquiry will also coincide with our general purpose of analysing the influence of intellectual causes in the production of unbelief.

Four separate tendencies may be distinguished among heathens in the early centuries in reference to religion:[7] viz. the tendency, (1) to absolute unbelief, (2) to a bigoted attachment to a national creed, (3) to a philosophical, and (4) a mystical theory of religion.

The tendency to total disbelief of the supernatural prevailed in the Epicurean school. A type of the more earnest spirits of this class is seen at a period a little earlier than the Christian era in Lucretius, living mournfully in the moral desert which his doubts had

[6] It has been recently made a matter of dispute whether Plato's own description of the teaching of the Sophists is not rendered untrustworthy by these faults. See Grote's *History of Greece*, vol. viii. ch. 67.

[7] These tendencies are discussed so fully and with such great learning by Neander (*Kirchengeschichte*, vol. i. Introduction), and by Pressensé, *Hist. de l'Eglise Chrétienne*, (2e série, t. ii. ch. 1), to whom I am largely indebted, that it is unnecessary to quote the original sources. Neander exhibits an analogous process in the Jewish religion, in sects of the later times of the nation. See also Döllinger's *Judenthum und Heidenthum* (translated 1862.)

scorched into barrenness.[8] The world is to him a scene unguided by a Providence: death is uncheered by the hope of a future life. An example of the flippant sceptic is found in Lucian in the second century, A. D. The great knowledge of life which travel had afforded him created a universal ridicule for religion; but his unbelief evinced no seriousness, no sadness. His humour itself is a type of the man. Lacking the bitter earnestness which gave sting to the wit of Aristophanes, and the courteous playfulness exhibited in the many-sided genius of Plato, he was a caricaturist rather than a painter: his dialogues are farces of life rather than satires. It has been well remarked, that human society has no worse foe than a universal scoffer. Lacking aspirations sufficiently lofty to appreciate religion, and wisdom to understand the great crises that give birth to it, such a man destroys not superstition only but the very faculty of belief.[9] It is easy to perceive that to such minds Christianity would be a mark for the same jests as other creeds.

A second tendency, most widely opposed in appearance to the sceptical, but which was too often its natural product, showed itself in a bigoted attachment to the national religion.[10] Among the masses such faith was real though unintelligent, but in educated men it had become artificial. When an ethnic religion is young, faith is fresh and gives inspiration to its art and its poetry. In a more critical age, the historic spirit rationalizes the legends, while the philosophic allegorizes the myths; and thoughtful men attempt to rise to a spiritual worship of which rites are symbols.[11] But in the decay of a religion, the supernatural loses its

[8] The mental character of Lucretius has been well analysed by Mr. Sellar, in the volume of *Oxford Essays*, 1855.

[9] Pressensé (ut sup. 2e série, t. ii. 77 seq.) has ably sketched the character of Lucian. His utter scepticism is seen in the Ζεὺς τραγῳδός (47–49).

[10] Instances, with references, may be seen in the introductory chapter in Neander, p. 18 seq.

[11] The Greek literature offers the opportunity for studying the whole process. See Grote, i. ch. 16, previously quoted.

hold of the class of educated minds, and is regarded as imposture, and the support which they lend to worship is political. They fall back on tradition to escape their doubts, or they think it politically expedient to enforce on the masses a creed which they contemn in heart. Such a ground of attachment to paganism is described in the dialogue of the Christian apologist, Minucius Felix.[12] It would not only coincide with the first-named tendency in denying the importance of Christianity, but would join in active opposition. In truth, it marks the commencement of the strong reaction which took place in favour of heathenism at the close of the second century,—twofold in its nature; a popular reaction of prejudice or of mysticism on the part of the lower classes, and a political or philosophical one of the educated.[13] Both were in a great degree produced by Eastern influences. The substitution which was gradually taking place of naturalism for humanism, the adoration of cosmical and mystical powers instead of the human attributes of the deities of the older creed, was the means of re-awakening popular superstition, while at the same time the Alexandrian speculations of Neo-Platonism gave a religious aspect to philosophy.

Accordingly the third, or philosophical tendency in reference to religion, distinct from the two already named, of positive unbelief in the supernatural on the one hand, and devotion sincere or artificial to heathen worship on the other, comprises, in addition to the older schools of Stoics and Platonists, the new eclectic school just spoken of. The three schools agreed in extracting

[12] The character Cæcilius, in the dialogue of Minucius Felix, is made to express this view, (c. 8. and elsewhere.) A useful modern edition of this dialogue is given by H. A. Holden, 1853.

[13] This reaction deserves to be made the subject of special study. Pressensé is one of the few writers who have pointed out its importance, (2e *série*, t. ii. ch. 1.) Also compare the remarks in Benjamin Constant's posthumous work *Du Polytheisme Romain*, 1833. (t. ii. l. 12, 13, 15.) Kurtz refers on this subject to Tzchirner's *der Fall des Heidenthum*, i. 404, (1829.); H. Kritzler's *Helden-zeiten des Christenthum*, vol. i. (1856), and Vogt's *Neo-Platonismus und Christenthum* (1836.) Also Cfr. Tzchirner's *Apologetik* (1804.) c. 2, parts 2 and 3.

a philosophy out of the popular religion, by searching for historic or moral truth veiled in its symbols. The Stoic, as being the least speculative, employed itself less with religion than the others. Its doctrine, ethical rather than metaphysical, concerned with the will rather than the intellect, juridical and formal rather than speculative, seemed especially to give expression to the Roman character, as the Platonic to the Greek, or as the eclectic to the hybrid, half Oriental half European, which marked Alexandria. In the writings of M. Aurelius, one of the emperors most noted for the persecution of the church, it manifests itself rather as a rule of life than a subject for belief, as morality rather than religion.[14] The Stoic opposition to Christianity was the contempt of the Gaul or Roman for what was foreign, or of ethical philosophy for religion.

The Platonic doctrine, so far as it is represented in an impure form in the early centuries, sought, as of old, to explore the connexion between the visible and invisible worlds, and to rise above the phenomenon into the spiritual. Hence in its view of heathen religion it strove to rescue the ideal religion from the actual, and to discover the one revelation of the Divine ideal amid the great variety of religious traditions and modes of worship. But its invincible dualism, separating by an impassable chasm God from the world, and mind from matter, identifying goodness with the one, evil with the other, prevented belief in a religion like Christianity, which was penetrated by the Hebrew conceptions of the universe, so alien both to dualism and pantheism.

[14] The *Meditations* of M. Aurelius were edited by Gataker (1698.) See concerning them Fabricius, *Biblioth. Græc.* v. 500, (ed Harles); Donaldson, *Gr. Lat.* ch. 54, § 2,; and concerning his opinions, Neander's *Kirchengesch.* I. 177. Mr. G. Long has recently translated the Meditations into English. The philosophy of the Roman Stoics, of which M. Aurelius is one of the best types, is briefly but excellently treated by Sir A. Grant in the *Oxford Essays* for 1858. Also consult Ritter's *History of Philosophy*, vol. iv. b. 12, ch. 3, and Neander's paper on the relation of Greek Ethics to Christianity in the *Zeitschrift für Christliche Wissenchaft und Christliches Leben* (1850,) translated in the American *Bibliotheca Sacra* for 1853.

The line is not very marked which separates this philosophy from the professed revival of Plato's teaching, which received the name of Neo-Platonism, which was the philosophy with which Christianity came most frequently into conflict or contact during the third and two following centuries (10). Fastening on the more mystical parts of Plato, to the neglect of the more practical, it probably borrowed something also from Eastern mysticism. The object of the school was to find an explanation of the problem of existence, by tracing the evolution of the absolute cause in the universe through a trinal manifestation, as being, thought, and action. The agency by which the human mind apprehended this process lay in the attainment of a kind of insight wherein the organ of knowledge is one with the object known, a state of mind and feeling whereby the mind gazes on a sphere of being which is closed to the ordinary faculties. Schelling's theory of "intellectual intuition" is the modern parallel to this Neo-Platonic state of ἔκστασις or ἐνθουσιασμός. This philosophy, though frequently described in modern times as bearing a resemblance to Christianity in method, as being the knowledge of the one absolute Being by means of faith, is really most widely opposed in its interior spirit. It is essentially pantheism. Its monotheistic aspect, caught by contact with Semitic thought, is exterior only. Its deity, which seems personal, is really only the personification of an abstraction, a mere instance of mental realism. Man's personality, which Christianity states clearly, was lost in the universe; religious facts in metaphysical ideas.[15] Religion accordingly would be exclusive, confined to an aristocracy of education; and the existing national cultus would be appropriated as a sensuous religion suited for the masses, a visible type

[15] Pressensé even suggests (2e. série, t. ii. p. 62) that the ultimate result was almost the *nirvana* of Budhism. It will be observed, that the view taken in the text concerning the Neo-Platonic philosophy, for which I am largely indebted to Pressensé, is different from that which regards it as monotheism, and which has been made popular by Mr. Kingsley's novel, *Hypatia*, and by his lectures on *the Schools of Alexandria* (Lect. 3), 1854.

of the invisible. The analogy which this philosophy bore to Christianity in aim and office, as well as the rivalry of other schools which is implied in its eclectic aspect, caused it to take up an attitude of opposition to the Christian system to which it claimed to bear affinity.

The mystical element in this philosophy enabled some minds to find a home for the theurgy which had been increased by the importation of eastern ideas.[16] They form as it were the connecting link with the fourth religious tendency, which manifested itself in the craving for a communication from the world invisible, which found its satisfaction in magic and in a spirit of fanaticism. Some of these fanatics were doubtless also impostors;[17] but some were high-minded men struggling after truth, of whom possibly an example is seen at an early period in Apollonius of Tyana; deceived rather than deceivers. This tendency operated in some minds to cause them to reduce Christianity to ordinary magic and prodigies; while among a few it created yearnings for a nobler satisfaction, which drew them toward Christianity, as in the case of the Clemens, whose autobiography professes to be given in the well-known work of the early ages, the Clementines. (11)

Such seem to have been the chief forms of religious thought existing among the heathen to whom Christianity presented itself, on which were founded the preparation of heart which led to the acceptance of its message, or the prejudices which rejected its claims;—viz. among the masses, a sensuous unintelligent belief in polytheism;—among the educated, disorganization of belief; either materialism, the total rejection of the supernatural, and a political attachment on the principle of expedience to existing creeds; or philosophy, ethical, dualistic, pantheistic, despising religions as mere organic products of national thought, and trying

[16] Ritter happily calls this philosophy Neo-Pythagoreanism, as the former was Neo-Platonism.

[17] E. g. the Alexander of Pontus, whom Lucian holds up to ridicule. On Apollonius of Tyana, see a subsequent note.

to seize the central truths of which they were the expression; or a mystical craving after the supernatural, degrading its victims into fanatics. The further analysis of these tendencies would show their connexion with the threefold classification before given of the tests of truth into sense, reason, and feeling.

We have thus prepared the way for interpreting the lines of argument used in opposition to Christianity, and shall now proceed to sketch in chronological succession the history of the chief intellectual attacks made by unbelievers.

It is not until the middle of the second century that we find Christianity becoming the subject of literary investigation. Incidental expressions either of scorn or of misapprehension form the sole allusions in the heathen writers of earlier date (12); but in the reigns of the Antonines, the Christians began to attract notice and to meet with criticism. We read of a work written against Christianity by a Cynic, Crescens, in the reign of Antoninus Pius;[18] and of another by the tutor of Marcus Aurelius, Fronto of Cirta,[19] in which probably the imperial persecution was justified.

It is at this time too that we meet with an attempt to hold the Christians up to ridicule in a satire of Lucian,[20] which well exemplifies the views belonging to

[18] Crescens is named in Justin Martyr (*Apolog.* II. 3), who wrote against his attack; Tatian (*Orat. adv. Græc.* c. 3); Eusebius (*Eccl. Hist.* iv. 16). The last, on the strength of Tatian, accuses him of causing Justin's death.

[19] Cornelius Fronto is referred to by Minucius Felix (*Octav.* ch. 9 and 31), as having charged incestuous banquets on the Christians. Tzchirner (*Opusc. Acad.* 1829. p. 294) conjectures that his work may have been a legal speech against some Christian, which implied a defence of the imperial persecution. Part of Fronto's works have been found during the present century, and edited with a dissertation on his life and writings by Angelo Mai. (On his work against Christianity, see p. 57 of the dissertation.) A brief account of them may be found in Smith's Biographical Dictionary sub *Fronto.*

[20] Lucian probably lived from about A.D. 125 to 200. Consult the account given by Donaldson (*Gr. Lit.* ch. 54, § 3 and 4) of his life, opinions, and works, where a comparison is drawn between him and Voltaire; also Mr. Dyer's article *Lucianus* in Smith's Biographical Dictionary; also Fabricius' *Bibliotheca Græca*, v. 340 (ed. Harles); Lardner's *Collec-*

the sceptical of the four classes into which we have divided the religious opinions of the heathens. His tract, the Peregrinus Proteus, it can hardly be doubted, is intended as a satire on Christian martyrdom (13). Peregrinus[21] is a Cynic philosopher, who after a life of early villany is made by Lucian to play the hypocrite at Antioch and join himself to the Christians, 'miserable men' (as he calls them), 'who, hoping for immortality in soul and body, had a foolish contempt of death, and suffered themselves to be persuaded that they were brethren, because, having abandoned the Greek gods, they worshipped the crucified sophist, living according to his laws.'[22] Peregrinus, when a Christian, soon rises to the dignity of bishop, and is worshipped as a god; and when imprisoned for his religion is visited by Christians from all quarters. Afterwards, expelled the church, he travels over the world; and at last for the sake of glory burns himself publicly at Olympia about A. D. 165. His end is described in a tragico-comic manner, and a legend is recounted that at his death he was seen in white, and that a hawk ascended from his pyre.

Lucian has here used a real name to describe a class, not a person. He has given a caricature painting from historic elements. There seems internal evidence to show that he was slightly acquainted with the books of the early Christians.[23] It has even been conjectured that he might have read and designed to parody the epistles of Ignatius.[24] With more proba-

tion of Jewish and Heathen Testimonies, Works, vol. viii. ch. 19. The satire referred to above is entitled Περὶ τῆς Περεγρίνου τελευτῆς.

[21] We learn from other writers that Peregrinus was a real character; but Aulus Gellius (xii. 11), gives a much more favourable character of him than Lucian.

[22] The passage (of which this is Tzchirner's paraphrase) is: *Πεπείκασι γὰρ αὐτοὺς οἱ κακοδαίμονες τὸ μὲν ὅλον ἀθάνατοι ἔσεσθαι καὶ βιώσεσθαι τὸν ἀεὶ χρόνον, παρ' ὃ καὶ καταφρονοῦσι τοῦ θανάτου καὶ ἑκόντες αὑτοὺς ἐπιδιδόασιν οἱ πολλοί· ἔπειτα δὲ ὁ νομοθέτης ὁ πρῶτος ἔπεισεν αὐτοὺς ὡς ἀδελφοὶ πάντες εἶεν ἀλλήλων, ἐπειδὰν ἅπαξ παραβάντες Θεοὺς μὲν τοὺς Ἑλληνικοὺς ἀπαρνήσωνται, τὸν δὲ ἀνεσκολοπισμένον ἐκεῖνον σοφιστὴν αὐτῶν προσκυνῶσι καὶ κατὰ τοὺς ἐκείνου νόμους βιῶσι.* Pereg. Prot. § 13.

[23] Cfr. Pereg. Prot. § 11 and 12.

[24] Bp. Pearson considered (*Vindic. Ignat.* part. ii. 6,) that an allusion

bility we may believe that he had heard of and misunderstood the heroic bearing of the Christian martyrs in the moment of their last suffering. Pope Alexander VII. in 1664 placed this tract in the index of prohibited books: yet even beneath the satire we rather hail Lucian as an unconscious witness to several beautiful features in the character of the Christians of his time:[25] viz. their worship of "the crucified sophist," who was their adorable Lord; their guilelessness; their brotherly love; their strict discipline; their common meals; their union; their benevolence; their joy in death. The points which he depicts in his satire are, their credulity in giving way to Peregrinus; their unintelligent belief in Christ and in immortality; their factiousness in aiding Peregrinus when in prison; their pompous vanity in martyrdom, and possibly their tendency to believe legends respecting a martyr's death. His satire is contempt, not anger, nor dread. It is the humour of a thorough sceptic, which discharged itself on all religions alike; and indicates one type of opposition to Christianity; viz. the contempt of those who thought it folly.

Very unlike to him was his well-known contemporary Celsus. If the one represents the scoffer, the other represents the philosopher. Not despising Christianity with scorn like Tacitus, nor jeering at it with humour like Lucian, Celsus had the wisdom to apprehend danger to heathenism, measuring Christianity in its mental and not its material relations; and about the reign of Marcus Aurelius wrote against it a work entitled *Λόγος ἀληθής*, which was considered of such importance, that Origen towards the close of his own life[26] wrote a large and elaborate reply to it.

is made to the death of Ignatius, (Cfr. Le Moyne, *Varia Sacra* (pref.) 1694, for a somewhat similar argument in reference to Polycarp.) A. Planck in his *Lucian und Christenthum* (part i.) in *Stud. und Krit.* 1851, the references to which are given in note 12 of these lectures, tries to show that Lucian alludes even to Ignatius's letters. If he does not succeed in establishing this point, he at least (part iii.) makes Lucian's knowledge of Christian literature extremely probable.

[25] These are enumerated by A. Planck, (id. part ii.)

[26] Huet thinks the date was subsequent to A. D. 246. (*Origeniana* i. c. 3, § 11, ed. 1668.)

We know nothing of Celsus's life.[27] There is even an uncertainty as to the school of philosophy to which he belonged. External evidence seems to testify that he was an Epicurean; but internal would lead us to classify him with the Platonic. Unscrupulous in argument, confounding canonical gospels with apocryphal, and Christians with heretical sects, delighting in searching for contradictions, incapable of understanding the deeper aspects of Christianity, he has united in his attack all known objections, making use of minute criticism, philosophical theory, piquant sarcasm, and eloquent invective, as the vehicle of his passionate assault.

It is impossible to recover a continuous account of the work of Celsus from the treatise of his respondent; but a careful study of the fragments embedded in the text of Origen will perhaps restore the framework of the original sufficiently to enable us to perceive the points of his opposition to Christianity, and the manner in which his philosophy stood in the way of the reception of it. (14)

Celsus commences by introducing a Jewish rabbi to attack Christianity from the monotheistic stand-point of the earlier faith.[28] The Jew is first made to direct his criticism against the documents of Christianity, and

[27] There is a doubt whether the Celsus against whom Origen wrote is the friend to whom Lucian has addressed his life of the magician Alexander of Abonoteichus. The arguments on this question are stated and weighed in Neander's *Kirchengeschichte*, vol. i. 169, and Baur's *Geschichte der drei ersten Jahrhunderte*, p. 371. Both conclude that the persons were different. The evidence of their oneness is chiefly Origen's conjecture that they were the same person (Cont. Celsum. iv. 36.) The evidence against it is, (1) that Lucian's friend attacked magical rites; the Celsus of Origen seems to have believed them: (2) that Lucian's friend was probably an Epicurean, the other Celsus a Platonist or Eclectic: (3) that the former is praised for his mildness, the latter shows want of moderation. Pressensé nevertheless (ut sup. vol. ii. p. 105) regards them as the same person.

[28] B. i. c. 28. The references are made to the chapters in the Benedictine edition by De la Rue (Paris, 1733.) The earlier part of b. i. is miscellaneous in nature and seems prefatory; and it is not easy to determine the relation of Origen's remarks in it to the arrangement of Celsus's book.

then the facts narrated.[29] He points out inconsistencies in the gospel narratives of the genealogy of Christ;[30] utters the most blasphemous calumnies concerning the incarnation;[31] turns the narrative of the infancy into ridicule;[32] imputes our Saviour's miracles to magic;[33] attacks his divinity;[34] and concentrates the bitterest raillery on the affecting narrative of our blessed Lord's most holy passion. Each fact of deepening sorrow in that divine tragedy, the betrayal,[35] the mental anguish, the sacred agony,[36] is made the subject of remarks characterized no less by coarseness of taste and unfairness, than to the Christian mind by irreverence. Instead of his heart being touched by the majesty of our Saviour's sorrow, Celsus only finds an argument against the divine character of the adorable sufferer.[37] The wonders accompanying Christ's death are treated as legends;[38] the resurrection regarded as an invention or an optical delusion.[39]

After Celsus has thus made the Jew the means of a ruthless attack on Christianity, he himself directs a similar one against the Jewish religion itself.[40] He goes to the origin of their history; describes the Jews as having left Egypt in a sedition;[41] as being true types of the Christians in their ancient factiousness;[42] considers Moses to be only on a level with the early Greek legislators;[43] regards Jewish rites like circumcision to be borrowed from Egypt; charges anthropomorphism on Jewish theology,[44] and declines allowing the allegorical interpretation in explanation of it;[45] examines Jewish prophecy, parallels it with heathen oracles,[46] and claims that the goodness not the truth of a prophecy ought to be considered;[47] points to the ancient idolatry of the Jews as proof that they were not better than

[29] Speaking generally, B. i. ch. 27, 28, 32, may be taken as the one, and the rest of b. i., together with b. ii. as the other.

[30] B. ii. § 32. [31] B. i. 28, 32–35. [32] B. i. 37, 58, 66.

[33] B. i. 38, 68. [34] B. i. 57; ii. 9, &c. [35] B. ii. 21.

[36] B. ii. 24. [37] B. ii. 16. [38] B. iii. 38.

[39] B. iii. 59, 55, 57, 78. [40] B. iii. § 1 and elsewhere.

[41] B. iii. § 5. [42] B. iii. § 5. [43] B. i. 17, 18; i. 22.

[44] B. iv. 71; vi. 62. [45] B. iv. 48. [46] B. vii. 3; viii. 45.

[47] B. vii. 14.

other nations;[48] and to the destruction of Jerusalem as proof that they were not special favourites of heaven. At last he arrives at their idea of creation,[49] and here reveals the real ground of his antipathy. While he objects to details in the narrative, such as the mention of days before the existence of the sun,[50] his real hatred is against the idea of the unity of God, and the freedom of Deity in the act of creation. It is the struggle of pantheism against theism.

When Celsus has thus made use of the Jew to refute Christianity from the Jewish stand-point, and afterwards refuted the Jew from his own, he proceeds to make his own attack on Christianity; in doing which, he first examines the lives of Christians,[51] and afterwards the Christian doctrine;[52] thus skilfully prejudicing the mind of his readers against the persons before attacking the doctrines. He alludes to the quarrelsomeness shown in the various sects of Christians,[53] and repeats the calumnious suspicion of disloyalty,[54] want of patriotism,[55] and political uselessness;[56] and hence defends the public persecution of them.[57] Filled with the esoteric pride of ancient philosophy, he reproaches the Christians with their carefulness to proselytize the poor,[58] and to convert the vicious;[59] thus unconsciously giving a noble testimony to one of the most divine features in our religion, and testifying to the preaching of the doctrine of a Saviour for sinners.

Having thus defamed the Christians, he passes to the examination of the Christian doctrine, in its form, its method, and its substance. His æsthetic sense, ruined with the idolatry of form, and unable to appreciate the thought, regards the Gospels as defective and rude through simplicity.[60] The method of Christian teaching also seems to him to be defective, as lacking philosophy and dialectic, and as denouncing the use of

[48] B. iv. 22, 23.
[49] B. iv. 74; vi. 49, &c.
[50] B. vi. 60.
[51] B. iii.
[52] B. v. vi. vii.
[53] B. iii. 10.
[54] B. iii. 5, 14.
[55] B. iii. § 55; viii. 73.
[56] B. viii. 69.
[57] B. viii. 69.
[58] B. iii. 44, 50.
[59] B. iii. 59, 62, 74.
[60] B. iii. 55; viii. 37.

reason.[61] Lastly, he turns to the substance of the dogmas themselves. He distinguishes two elements in them, the one of which, as bearing resemblance to philosophy or to heathen religion, he regards as incontestably true, but denies its originality, and endeavours to derive it from Persia or from Platonism;[62] resolving, for example, the worship of a human being into the ordinary phenomenon of apotheosis.[63] The other class of doctrines which he attacks as false, consists of those which relate to creation,[64] the incarnation,[65] the fall,[66] redemption,[67] man's place in creation,[68] moral conversions,[69] and the resurrection of the dead.[70] His point of view for criticising them is derived from the fundamental dualism of the Platonic system; the eternal severance of matter and mind, of God and the world; and the reference of good to the region of mind, evil to that of matter. Thus, not content with his former attack on the idea of creation in discussion with the Jew, he returns to the discussion from the philosophical side. His Platonism will not allow him to admit that the absolute God, the first Cause, can have any contact with matter. It leads him also to give importance to the idea of δαίμονες, or divine mediators, by which the chasm is filled betwen the ideal god and the world;[71] not being able otherwise to imagine the action of the pure ἰδέα of God on a world of matter. Hence he blames Christians for attributing an evil nature to demons, and finds a reasonable interpretation of the heathen worship.[72] The same dualist theory extinguishes the idea of the incarnation, as a degradation of God; and also the doctrine of the fall, inasmuch as psychological deterioration is impossible if the soul be pure, and if evil be a necessary attribute of matter.[73] With the fall, redemption also disappears, because the

[61] B. vii. 9; i. 2; i. 9; iii. 39; vi. 10.
[62] B. vi. 15; vi. 22, 58, 62; v. 63; vi. 1.
[63] B. iii. 22; vii. 28–30. [64] B. iv. 37; vi. 49.
[65] B. iv. 14; v. 2; vii. 36. [66] B. iv. 62, 70.
[67] B. v. 14; vii. 28, 36, vi. 78. [68] B. iv. 74, 76, 23.
[69] B. iii. 65. [70] B. v. 14, 15. [71] B. vii. 68; viii. (2–14) 35, 36.
[72] B. viii. 2. [73] B. iv. 99.

perfect cannot admit of change; Christ's coming could only be to correct what God already knew, or rectify what ought to have been corrected before.[74] Further, Celsus argues, if Divinity did descend, that it would not assume so lowly a form as Jesus. The same rigorous logic charges on Christianity the undue elevation of man, as well as the abasement of God. Celsus can neither admit man more than the brutes to be the final cause of the universe; nor allow the possibility of man's nearness to God.[75] His pantheism, destroying the barrier which separates the material from the moral, obliterates the perception of the fact that a single free responsible being may be of more dignity than the universe.

Such is the type of a philosophical objector against Christianity, a little later than the middle of the second century. We meet here for the first time a remarkable effort of pagan thought, endeavouring to extinguish the new religion; the definite statements of a mind that investigated its claims and rejected it. Most of the objections of Celsus are sophistical; a few are admitted difficulties; but the philosophical class of them will be seen to be the corollary from his general principle before explained.

A century intervenes before we meet with the next literary assailant, Porphyry. In the interval the new reactionary philosophy has fully taken root, and the fresh attack accordingly bears the impress of the new system.

The chief objections made in the intervening period, as we collect them from the apologies, were such as belongs fitly to a transitional time, when Christianity was exciting attention but was not understood;[76] and are chiefly the result of the second of the tendencies before named, viz., either of popular prejudice, or of the political alarm in reference to the social disorganization likely to arise out of a large defection from the

[74] B. iv. 3, 7, 18. [75] B. iv. 74.

[76] On the alteration in the attacks, Cfr. Gerard (of Aberdeen), *Compendium of Evidences*, 1828 (part ii. ch. 1.)

religion of the empire, which expressed itself in overt acts of persecution on the part of the state. (15) Both equally lie beyond our field of investigation; the one because it does not belong to the examination of Christianity made by intelligent thought; the other because it is the struggle of deeds, not of ideas, which only have an interest for us, if, as in Julian's case hereafter, the acts were dictated by the deliberate advice of persons who had attentively examined Christianity.

The apprehensions of prejudice gradually subsided, and objections began to be based on grounds less absurd in character. The political opposition also was henceforth founded on a more subtle policy, and on an appreciation of the nature of Christianity. Soon after the middle of the third century we meet with the next attack of a purely literary kind, viz., by Porphyry, the most distinguished opponent that Christianity has yet encountered.[77] The pupil of Longinus, perhaps of Origen,[78] and the biographer and interpreter of Plotinus, he is best known for his logical writings, and for the development of the theory of predication in his introduction to the Categories, which formed the text on which hung the mediæval speculations of scholasticism.[79] His Syrian origin and oriental culture perhaps prepared him for a fusion of East and West, and for admitting a deeper admixture of mysticism into the Neo-Platonic philosophy, of which he was a disciple. The points of his approximation to Christianity are the result of those elements in which heathen philosophy most nearly approached to Christian truth, the development of which was stimulated in minds essentially anti-christian

[77] Porphyry lived from about A. D. 233 to 305. For his life and writings see Holstenius *de Vit. Porphyr.* (1630); Fabric. *Bibl. Græc.* v. 725. (ed. Harles); Lardner's *Works*, viii. 37; Donaldson's *Gr. Lit.* ch. 53, § 7. For his attack on Christianity consult Neander's *Kirchengesch.* i. 290; Pressensé ii. 156.

[78] His own words, quoted in Eusebius (*Eccl. Hist.* iii. 19), have been thought to imply this, but seem merely to state his acquaintance in youth with Origen. See Holsten. *Vit. Porphyr.* p. 16.

[79] Cousin (Pref. to Edition of Abelard's *Sic et Non*, p. 61, note 46,) considers that a passage which Boethius quoted from Porphyry was the means of reviving philosophical speculation on this point.

by the effort to find a rival to it. Admirably prepared by his serious and spiritual tone to embrace Christianity, he nevertheless lived a disciple of paganism. His feelings rather than his reason led him to defend national creeds. His philosophy and the Christian, which seemed to be aspirations after the same end, being designed to elevate the spirit above the world of sense, were really radically opposed. Understanding therefore the power of the Christian religion, he felt the necessity for supplanting it; and hoped to do so by spiritualizing the old creeds, which he harmonized with philosophy by means of regarding them as symbolic.[80]

His opposition to Christianity was not however based wholly on a prejudice of feeling. He was a man cultivated in all the learning of his age, and of a more generous temper than Celsus, and seems to have exercised much critical sagacity in the investigation of the claims of Christianity. About the year 270, while in retirement in Sicily, he wrote a book against the Christians.[81] This work having been destroyed, we are left to gather its contents and the opinions of its authors from a few criticisms in Eusebius and Jerome. The entire work consisted of fifteen books; and concerning only five of these is information afforded by them. Their remarks lead us to conjecture that it was an assault on Christianity in many relations. The books however of which we know the purpose, seem to have been critical rather than philosophical, directed against

[80] He seems especially to have felt the difficulty which was before noticed as marking one type of religious opinion, the craving for a theology which rested on some divine authority, or revelation from the world invisible, (Cfr. Augustin's criticism on him in *De Civ. Dei*. x. ch. 9, 11, 26, 28); and hence he drew such a system from the real or pretended answers of oracles, in his *περὶ τῆς ἐκ λογίων φιλοσοφίας*, of which fragments exist in Eusebius and Augustin (Fabric. *Bibl. Gr*. v. 744). Heathens, it would seem, had consulted oracles on this very subject of Christianity; and it is these, the genuineness of which may be doubted, that he uses. His aim seems to have been to support the existing religious system; and for this purpose he favoured the alliance with the priestly system, and the institution of religious rites. See Neander *Kirchengesch*. i. 293.

[81] On this work, *κατὰ Χριστιανῶν*, see Holsten. (*Vita Porphyr*. c. x.), who quotes at length from the Fathers the principal passages in which allusion to it is made.

the grounds of the religion rather than its character; being in fact an assault on the Bible. The existence of such a line of argument, of which a trace was already observable in Celsus, is explained by the circumstance that the faith of Christendom was already fixed on the authority of the sacred books. The church had always acknowledged the authority of the Jewish scriptures; and by the middle or close of the second century at the latest, it had come to acknowledge explicitly the co-ordinate authority of a body of Christian literature, historic, and epistolary.[82] Hence, when once the idea of a rule of faith had grown common, the investigation of the contents of the scriptures became necessary on the part of heathen opponents. The growingly critical character of Porphyry's statements, though partly attributable to the literary culture of his mind, is a slight undesigned evidence corroborative of the authoritative nature already attributed to the scriptures in doctrine and truthfulness. Porphyry seems accordingly to have directed his critical powers to show such traces of mistakes and incorrectness as might invalidate the idea of a supernatural origin for the Jewish and Christian scriptures, and shake confidence in their truth as an authority.

The first book of his work[83] dragged to light some of the discrepancies, real or supposed, in scripture; and the examination of the dispute between St. Peter and St. Paul was quoted as an instance of the admixture of

[82] Omitting allusion to the references concerning the canon furnished in older works, e. g. of Cosin, Dupin, Jones, Lardner, Michaelis, some of which were written in reference to the controversy between the Romanists and Reformed, others between the Christians and freethinkers, we may at least name Moses Stuart's work on the *Canon of the Old Testament*, and Credner *Zur Geschichte des Kanons* with reference to the New; (the former is apologetic, the latter independent and slightly rationalistic, but full of learning;) and especially the work on the *Canon of the New Testament* by Mr. B. F. Westcott (1855), and the article on *Canon* by him in Smith's Biblical Dictionary, where references to fuller literary materials are given.

[83] Hieronymi *Opera*, (at the end of the Proem. of the Commentary on Galatians) vol. 4. part i. p. 223, Benedictine edition of Martianay, 1706; also Galat. ii. 11 (id. p. 244); also at the end of book xiv. (Isaiah liii.) vol. iii. p. 388; also Ep. 74 to Augustin (id. iv. part ii. 619, 622.)

human ingredients in the body of apostolic teaching. His third book[84] was directed to the subject of scripture interpretation, especially, with some inconsistency, against the allegorical or mystical tendency which at that time marked the whole church, and especially the Alexandrian fathers. The allegorical method coincided with, if it did not arise from, the oriental instinct of symbolism, the natural poetry of the human mind. But in the minds of Jews and Christians it had been sanctified by its use in the Hebrew religion, and had become associated with the apocryphal literature of the Jewish church. It is traceable to a more limited extent in the inspired writers of the New Testament, and in most of the fathers; but in the school of Alexandria[85] it was adopted as a formal system of interpretation. It is this allegorical system which Porphyry attacked. He assaulted the writings of those who had fancifully allegorised the Old Testament in the pious desire of finding Christianity in every part of it, in spite of historic conditions; and he hastily drew the inference, with something like the feeling of doubt which rash interpretations of prophecy are in danger of producing at this day, that no consistent sense can be put upon the Old Testament. His fourth book[86] was a criticism on the Mosaic history, and on Jewish antiquities. But the most important books in his work were the twelfth[87] and thirteenth,[88] which were devoted to an examination of the prophecies of Daniel, in which he

[84] Euseb. *Eccl. Hist.* vi. c. 19 (ed. Gaisford, p. 414) gives a long extract from Porphyry. Of the second book nothing is known.

[85] On the school of Alexandria see H. E. F. Guericke *Schola quæ Alex. floruit*, 1825 (p. 51–81); Matter's *Essai sur l'école d'Alexandrie*, 1840; Neander's *Kirchengesch.* II. 908 seq. 1196 seq. On the allegorical method of interpretation adopted by Origen, see Huet's *Origeniana* II. quæst. 13 (vol. i. 170); Conybeare's Bampton Lecture for 1824 (Lect. 2–4); R. A. Vaughan's *Essays and Remains* (Essay I); and an article in the *North British Review*, No. 46, August 1855. Also compare a note on systems of interpretation in Lect. VI.

[86] Euseb. Præp. i. 9; x. 9; which passages merely express the hostility of Porphyry.

[87] In Jerome's Proem. to Daniel are four passages. (See Works, vol. iii. p. 1073–4.)

[88] See Jerome. Comm. on Matt. xxiv. 15 (b. iv. vol. iv. p. 115).

detected some of those peculiarities on which modern criticism has employed itself, and arrived at the conclusions in reference to its date, revived by the English deist Collins in the last century, and by many German critics in the present.

It is well known that half of the book of Daniel[89] is historic, half prophetic. Each of these parts is distinguished from similar portions of the Old Testament by some peculiarities. Porphyry is not recorded as noticing any of those which belong to the historic part, unless we may conjecture, from his theory of the book being originally written in Greek, that he detected the presence of those Greek words in Nebuchadnezzar's edicts, which many modern critics have contended could not be introduced into Chaldæa antecedently to the Macedonian conquest.[90] The peculiarity alleged to belong to the prophetical part is its apocalyptic tone.

[89] As early as the time of Spinoza, from whose work, the Theologicus Politicus, Collins may perhaps have indirectly derived hints; doubts of the authenticity of parts were expressed; and the inquiry was pursued by Michaelis and Eichhorn: but the modern criticism on it dates especially from Berthold (1806), who impugned its authenticity. Bleek (1822), De Wette, Von Lengerke of Königsberg (1835), Maurer (1838), more recently Hitzig (1850), and Lücke (1852), followed on the same side. The English theologian, Dr. Arnold, adopted the same view. The contrary opinion has been maintained by Hengstenberg (1831), Hävernich (1832), Keil (1853); Delitzch (in Herzog's Encycl. 1854), Auberlen (1857), by Moses Stuart, and by Dr. S. Davidson (Introduction to the Old Testament, 1856). Hengstenberg, Hävernich, and Auberlen are translated. The first of these three is valuable, especially for the literary and exegetical questions; the second as a controversial commentary; the third for tracing the organic unity of the book.

[90] The importance attached to the occurrence of Greek words is much over-estimated. They can only be shown to be four, which occur in ch. iii. 5, 7, 10; viz., קַיתְרֹם *κιθάρα*, סַבְּכָא *σαμβυκή*, סוּמְפֹּנְיָה *συμφωνία*, פְּסַנְתֵּרִין *ψαλτήριον*; all of which relate to musical instruments, not unlikely to be introduced by commerce, and which would naturally be called by their foreign names. Some of the writers named in a preceding note have examined incidentally the character of the Hebrew and Chaldee of Daniel, and consider that both are similar to those of works confessedly of the age of Daniel; and that the Chaldee is separated by a chasm from that of the earliest Targums. Professor Pusey delivered a lecture on the subject in the university, containing the results of his own recent studies, in the summer of the present year, which will form one of a printed course of lectures on Daniel. See also an article by the Rev. J. McGill in the Journal of Sacred Literature, Jan. 1861.

It looks, it has been said, historical rather than prophetical. Definite events, and a chain of definite events, are predicted with the precision of historical narrative;[91] whereas most prophecy is a moral sermon, in which general moral predictions are given, with specific historic ones interspersed. Nor is this, which is shared in a less degree by occasional prophecies elsewhere, the only peculiarity alleged, but it is affirmed also that the definite character ceases at a particular period of the reign of Antiochus Epiphanes,[92] down to which the very campaigns of the Seleucid and Ptolemaic dynasties are noted, but subsequently to which the prophetic tone becomes more vague and indefinite. Hence the conjecture has been hazarded that it was written in the reign of Antiochus by a Palestinian Jew, who gathered up the traditions of Daniel's life, and wrote the recent history of his country in eloquent language, in an apocalyptic form; which, after the literary fashion of his age, he imputed to an ancient seer, Daniel; definite up to the period at which he composed it, indefinite as he gazed on the future. (16) It was this peculiarity, the supposed ceasing of the prophecies in the book of Daniel at a definite date, which was noticed by Porphyry, and led him to suggest the theory of its authorship just named.[93] These remarks will give an idea of the critical acuteness of Porphyry. His objections are not, it will be observed, founded on quibbles like those of Celsus, but on instructive literary characteristics, many of which are greatly exaggerated or grossly misinterpreted, but still are real, and suggest difficulties or inquiries which the best modern theological critics have honourably felt to demand candid examination and explanation.[94]

[91] E. g. the wars of the kings of the north and of the south, c. xi.

[92] Viz., till about B.C. 164.

[93] He seems also to have entered into some examination of the specific prophecies; for he objects to the application of the words "the abomina tion of desolation" to other objects than that which he considers its original meaning. See Hieronym. on Matt. xxiv. 15, the reference to which is given in a preceding note.

[94] A few other traces of Porphyry's views remain, which are of less

A period of about thirty years brings us to the date of the Diocletian persecution, A. D. 303; during the progress of which another noted attack was made. It was by Hierocles, then president of Bithynia, and afterwards præfect of Alexandria, himself one of the instigators of the persecution and an agent in effecting it.[95] His line of argument was more specific than those previously named, being directed against the evidence which was derived by Christians for the truth of their religion from the character and miraculous works of Christ; and his aim accordingly was to develope the character of Apollonius of Tyana,[96] as a rival to our Saviour in piety and miraculous power.

Apollonius was a Pythagorean philosopher, born in Cappadocia about four years before the Christian era. After being early educated in the circle of philosophy, and in the practice of the ascetic discipline of his predecessor Pythagoras, he imitated that philosopher in spending the next portion of his life in travel. At-

importance, and are levelled against parts of the New Testament: e. g. the change of purpose in our blessed Lord (John vii.) [Hieronym. vol. iv. part ii. p. 521 (*Dial. adv. Pelag.*); *Ep.* (101) *ad Pammach.* Several are given in Holsten. (*Vit. Porphyr.* p. 86)], the reasons why the Old Testament was abrogated if divine, [Augustin. *Epist.* (102, olim 49, Benedict. ed. 1689) vol. ii. p. 274, where six questions are named, some of which come from Porphyry:] the question what became of the generations which lived before Christianity was proclaimed, if Christianity was the only way of salvation; objections to the severity of St. Peter in the death of Ananias; and the inscrutable mystery of an infinite punishment in requital for finite sin. (Aug. *Retract.* b. ii. c. 31. vol. i. p. 53, concerning Matt. vii. 2.)

[95] Hierocles' work was called Λόγοι φιλαλήθεις πρὸς τοὺς Χριστιανούς. Our knowledge of it depends upon the refutation which Eusebius wrote of it; and upon passages in Lactantius (*Instit.* v. 2, and *De Mort. Persecut.* 16.) Concerning Hierocles see Bayle's *Dictionary, sub voc.* (notes); Fabric. *Bibl. Gr.* i. 792. note; Cave's *Hist. Lit.* i. 131. ii. 99; Lardner's Works, vol. viii. ch. 39. § 1–4, and Neander's *Kirchengesch.* i. 296.

[96] On Apollonius of Tyana, see Lardner's Works, vol. viii. ch. 39. § 5, 6. Ritter's *History of Philosophy* (vol. iv. b. xii. ch. 7), and especially the monograph by C. Baur of Tübingen, *Apollonius von Tyana und Christus oder das Verhaeltniss des Pythagoreismus zum Christenthum* (1832); also the Abbé Houtteville's Essay affixed to the *Discourse on the Method of the Principal Authors for and against Christianity*, translated 1739; and the article *Apollonius* by Professor Jowett in Smith's Biographical Dictionary.

tracted by his mysticism to the farthest East as the source of knowledge, he set out for Persia and India; and in Nineveh on his route met Damis, the future chronicler of his actions. Returning from the East instructed in Brahminic lore, he travelled over the Roman world. The remainder of his days was spent in Asia Minor. Statues and temples were erected to his honour. He obtained vast influence, and died with the reputation of sanctity late in the century. Such is the outline of his life, if we omit the numerous legends and prodigies which attach themselves to his name. He was partly a philosopher, partly a magician; half mystic, half impostor.[97] At the distance of a century and a quarter from his death, in the reign of Septimius Severus, at the request of the wife of that emperor, the second of the three Philostrati dressed up Damis's narrative of his life, in a work still remaining, and paved a way for the general reception of the story among the cultivated classes of Rome and Greece.[98] It has been thought that Philostratus had a polemical aim against the Christian faith,[99] as the memoir of Apollonius is in so many points a parody on the life of Christ. The annunciation of his birth to his mother, the chorus of swans which sang for joy on occasion of it, the casting out devils, the raising the dead, the healing the sick, the sudden disappearance and reappearance of Apollonius, the sacred voice which called him at his death, and his claim to be a teacher with authority to reform the world, form some of the points of similarity.

If such was the intention of Philostratus, he was

[97] He was probably midway between Pythagoras and the Alexander named by Lucian.

[98] It was written about A.D. 210, at the request of Julia Domna, and is entitled τὰ ἐς τὸν Τυανέα Ἀπολλώνιον. On this life by Philostratus see Fabric. *Bibl. Gr.* v. 541; the above-named works of Houtteville and Baur; Donaldson's *Gr. Lit.* ch. lii. § 7; Pressensé ii. 144 seq.; and a recent translation of Philostratus with remarks by A. Chassang, "Le Merveilleux dans l'Antiquité" (1862).

[99] Lardner and Ritter think that Philostratus did not write with a polemical reference to Christianity, but Baur concludes otherwise. Dean Trench has made a few remarks in reference to this question (*Notes to Miracles*, p. 62).

really a controversialist under the form of a writer of romance; employed by those who at that time were labouring (as already named) to introduce an eclecticism largely borrowed from the East into the region both of philosophy and religion. Without settling this question, it is at least certain that about the beginning of the next century the heathen writers adopted this line of argument, and sought to exhibit a rival ideal.[1] One instance is the life of Pythagoras by Iamblichus; another that which Hierocles wrote, in part of which he used Philostratus's untrustworthy memoir for the purpose of instituting a comparison between Apollonius and Christ. The sceptic who referred religious phenomena to fanaticism would hence avail himself of the comparison as a satisfactory account of the origin of Christianity; while others would adopt the same view as Hierocles, and deprive the Christian miracles of the force of evidence,—a line of argument which was reproduced by an English deist[2] who translated the work of Philostratus at the end of the seventeenth century. The work of Hierocles is lost, but an outline of its argument, with extracts, remains in a reply which Eusebius wrote to a portion of it (17). Though couched in a seeming spirit of fairness, the tone was such as would be expected from one who ungenerously availed himself of the very moment of a cruel persecution as the occasion of this literary attack.

But the time of the church's sorrow was nearly past. The hour of deliverance was at hand. The emperor Constantine proclaimed toleration,[3] and subsequently established Christianity as the state-religion. Only one moment more of peril was permitted to befall it.

After an interval in which Christian emperors reigned, Julian ascended the throne, and employed his short reign of two years[4] in trying to restore heathen-

[1] On Iamblichus's Life of Pythagoras, see Fabricius's *Bibl. Gr.* v. 764; Lardner viii. 39. § 7, who however concludes in this case, as in that of Philostratus, that the book was not designed against Christianity.

[2] Charles Blount in 1680. See Lect. IV.

[3] A.D. 313.

[4] A.D. 361–3.

ism; and during the last winter of his life, while halting at Antioch in the course of his Eastern war, wrote an elaborate work against Christianity.[5] The book itself has been destroyed, but the reply remains which Cyril of Alexandria thought it necessary to write more than half a century afterwards; and by this means we can gather Julian's opinions, just as from his own letters and the contemporary history we can gather his plans. The material struggle of deeds belongs in this instance to our subject, inasmuch as it is the overt expression of the struggle of ideas.

Julian, as already observed, differed from previous opponents of Christianity, in having been educated a Christian.[6] Associating when a student at the schools of Athens with Gregory of Nazianzum and Basil, he had every opportunity for understanding the Christian religion and measuring its claims. The first cause of his apostasy from it remains uncertain. One tradition states that the shock to his creed arose from some early injury received through the fraud of a professing Christian. Something is probably due to exasperation at the severity endured from Constantius; and perhaps still more is due to the natural peculiarity of his character. He was swayed by the imagination rather than the reason, and was kindled with an enthusiastic admiration of the old heathen literature and the historic glories of the heathen world. His very style exhibits traces of imitation of the old models after which he formed himself.[7] With a spirit which the Italian writers of the Renais-

[5] Κατὰ Χριστιανῶν. See Fabric. *Bibl. Gr.* vii. 738; Lardner viii. 46. § 2, and 4; Donaldson iii. 303. Fragments of it are preserved in Cyril's reply. The Marquis d'Argens, at the court of Frederick the Great of Prussia, translated and tried to unite them. *Défense du Paganisme par l'Empereur Julian*, 1764.

[6] On the life and reign of Julian, see Gibbon (*Decline and Fall*, c. 22–24); Fabricii *Lux Evangelii*, 1721, c. 14, where the edicts which refer to Christianity are collected; Lardner viii. 46; Abbé de la Bletterie's *Vie de Julien;* Neander, *Kirchengesch* iii. 76. and 188, who also wrote in 1812 a monograph on the subject; Wiggers in Illgen's *Hist. Zeitschr.* 1837; Milman's *Hist. of Christianity* iii. 6. On Julian's works see Fabric. *Bibl. Gr.* vi. 719 seq.; Donaldson iii. 57. § 6.

[7] Wyttenbach *Opusc.* i. 6; Donaldson iii. p. 307.

sance enable us to understand, his sympathies clung round heathens until they entwined in their embrace heathenism itself. To a mind of this natural bias sufficient grounds unhappily would easily be found to produce aversion to Christianity, in the quarrels among sections of the church, and in the ambition and inconsistency of the numbers of nominal converts who embraced the religion when its public establishment had rendered it their interest to do so; and prejudice would add arguments for rejecting it.

Accordingly he devoted his short reign to restore the ancient heathenism. Like Constantine, having arrived at the throne through a troublous war, he found the religion of the state opposed to his own convictions, and determined to substitute that which he himself professed. The difference however was great. The religion of Constantine was young and progressive; that of Julian was effete. It is in this respect that Julian has been compared,[8] in his character and acts, to those who in modern times, both in literature and in politics, have devoted their lives to roll back the progress of public opinion, and reproduce the spirit of the past by giving new life to the relics of bygone ages. If Julian had succeeded in his attempt, the victory could not have been permanent.

The steps by which he strove to carry out his views were not unlike those of Constantine.[9] He first proclaimed the establishment of the emperor's religion as the religion of the state, permitting toleration for all others. He next transferred the Christian endowments to heathens, acting on the principle previously established by Constantine. But beyond this point he proceeded to measures which had the nature of persecution. He declared the Christian laity disqualified for office in the state,—a measure which could only be sophistically maintained on the plea of self-defence; and, afraid of

[8] By Strauss, *Der Romantiker auf dem Throne des Caesaren oder Julian der abtruennige* 1847.

[9] There are some good remarks on Julian in Waddington's Church History, ch. viii.

the engine of education, forbade Christian professors to lecture in the public schools of science and literature: and probably he at last imposed a tax on those who did not perform sacrifice. At the same time he saw the necessity of a total reformation in paganism, if it was to revive as the rival of Christianity; and planned, as Pontifex Maximus, a scheme for effecting it, which involved the concealment of the absurdity of its origin by allegorical interpretation, together with the establishment of a discipline and organisation similar to the Christian, and special attention on the part of the priesthood to morality and to public works of mercy.[10] His bitter contempt for Christianity manifested itself in a public edict, which commanded that Christians should be denominated by the opprobrious epithet "Galilæans;" and in some of his extant letters[11] he evinces a bitterness against it which finds its parallel in Voltaire and Shelley.

A work remains, the Philopatris, (18) usually falsely assigned to Lucian, but which internal evidence proves to belong to the reign of Julian, in which the unknown author, imitating the manner but wanting the power of Lucian, holds up to ridicule the sermons and teaching of some Christian preachers. This work probably conveys the creed of the imperial party, which is simply Deism. This however is not the only source for ascertaining the creed of Julian, and the nature of his objections to Christianity. In his letters, and in the reply of Cyril to his now lost work, we possess more exact means for determining his position and sentiments. (19)

He omitted, as we might expect, the grosser and more frivolous charges against Christianity which had

[10] He also made the well-known attempt to rebuild the temple of Jerusalem. On the alleged miracle which prevented the execution of the scheme, see Warburton's works, vol. iv., Lardner, vol. viii. ch. 46. § 3, and Milman's note to Gibbon (c. 23.) Warburton believes the miracle; but Lardner hesitates. The original passages which refer to it are Amm. Marcell. xxiii. ch. 1; Ambr. *Ep.* xi. 2; Chrysost. *adv. Jud. et Gent.*; Greg. Naz. *Orat.* 4. *adv. Jul.*

[11] E. g. Ep. to Ecdidius (Ep. 9, Spanheim's edition, 1696); Decree to the Alexandrians (Ep. 26, 51); Ep. to Arsacius (49).

been formerly expressed by those who were ignorant of its real character. Indeed he seems to have been willing to recognise it as one form of religion, but declined to admit its monopoly of claim to be regarded as the only true form. Though himself a Theist,[12]—his view of Deity being more simply monotheistic than that of his predecessors, derived furtively from the Hebrew idea transmitted through Christianity; he nevertheless considered that discrepancy of national character required corresponding differences in religion.[13] In his work he seems to have repeated some of the objections of the older assailants, Celsus and Porphyry; attacking the credibility of scripture and of the Christian scheme in its doctrines and evidences. He offered in it a criticism on primæval and Hebrew history;[14] attacking the probability of many portions of the book of Genesis;[15] objecting to the Hebrew view of Deity as too appropriating in its character, and as making the divine Being appear cruel.[16] He denied the originality of the Hebrew moral law,[17] and pointed out the supposed defectiveness of the Hebrew polity; comparing unfavourably the type of the Hebrew lawgiver as seen in Moses, and of the king as seen in David, with the great heroes of Greek history.[18] The Hebrew prophecy he tried to weaken by putting it in comparison with oracles. In estimating the character of Christ, he depreciated the importance of his miracles;[19] and noticing the different tone of the fourth Gospel from those of the Synoptists, he asserted that it was St. John who first taught Christ's divinity.[20] He regarded Christianity as composed of borrowed ingredients; considered it to have assumed its shape gradually; and regarded its progress to have been unforeseen by its founder and by St. Paul;[21] attacked its relation to Judaism in superseding it while depending on it;[22] regarded proselytism as absurd; and directed some few charges, which may have been

[12] Cyril, adv. Jul. B. iii. and iv. [13] B. iv. [14] B. ii.
[15] B. iii. [16] B. iii. [17] B. v.
[18] B. v. and vii. [19] B. vi. [20] B. x.
[21] B. vii. and x. [22] B. viii.

more deserved, against practices of his day, such as Staurolatry[23] and Martyrolatry.[24]

With the death of Julian the hopes of heathenism departed; and two eloquent orations of Gregory Nazianzen[25] still convey to us the Christian words of triumph. Christianity progressed, protected by the favour of the sovereigns. Heathenism no longer expressed itself in free examination of Christianity, and lingered only in the prejudices of the people. In the West it is merely seen as it pleads for toleration,[26] or makes itself heard in the murmurs which attributed the woes of the Teutonic invasions to the displeasure of the heathen gods at the neglect of their worship.[27] In the East it disappears altogether. Doubt there expires, because speculation ceases and Christian thought becomes fixed; nor will it be necessary in future to recur to the history of the eastern church.

In this survey we have tried to understand the objections alleged by unbelievers during the first four centuries, successively changing in character, from the calumnies of ignorance in the second century, to the statements of intelligent disbelief in the third and fourth, until they finally subside in the fifth into the murmuring of popular superstition; and have endeavoured to give their natural as well as literary history, by exhibiting them as corollaries from the various views concerning religion enumerated at the commencement of the lecture. The blind prejudices of the uneducated populace, and the attachment, merely political, to heathen creeds, manifested themselves in deeds rather than words; but each of the other lines of thought there indicated gave

[23] B. vi. [24] B. x.

[25] Greg. Naz. Op. i. Orat. 4 and 5.

[26] Q. Aurelius Symmachus was deputed by the senate to remonstrate with Gratian on the removal of the altar of Victory (A.D. 382) from the council hall; and afterwards, when appointed (384) præfect of the city, he addressed a letter to Valentinian requiring the restoration of the pagan deities to their former honours. Both Symmachus's address and St. Ambrose's refutation are given in Cave's *Lives of Fathers* (Life of Ambrose, § 3. p. 576.)

[27] Augustin refutes this objection in several places of the first five books in the *De Civ. Dei.*

expression in literature to its opinion concerning Christianity; the flippant impiety of Epicureanism in Lucian, the debased form then prevalent of Platonism in Celsus, the subtle and mystic philosophy of the neo-Platonists in Porphyry, the oriental Theosophy in Hierocles, the romantic attachment to the old pagan literature in Julian.

If these causes be still further classified for comparison with the enumeration of intellectual causes stated in the previous lecture, we find only the adumbration of some of the forms there named. The attack from physical science, so prevalent since the era of modern discovery, is barely discernible in the passing remarks on the Mosaic cosmogony in Celsus and Julian.[28] The attack from criticism is seen in a trifling form in Celsus; in a superior manner in the perception which Porphyry exhibits of the literary characteristics of the Old Testament, and Julian of the New. The chief ground of the attack was derived from metaphysical science, which acted not so much in its modern form of a subjective inquiry into the tests of truth, as in the shape of rival doctrines concerning the highest problems of life and being, which preoccupied the mind against Christianity. If the eclectic attempts to adjust such speculations to Christianity which marked the progress of Gnosticism could have been embraced in our inquiry, the force of this class of causes would have been made still more apparent.

The obvious insufficiency however of this analysis to afford an entire explanation of the prejudices of these early unbelievers points to the close union before noticed[29] of the emotional with the intellectual causes. While asserting the possibility of the independent action of the intellectual element under peculiar circumstances as a cause of doubt, and while thus vindicating the im-

[28] The work of Cosmas Indicopleustes in the middle of the sixth century is designed to show the falsehood of the Ptolemaic system of astronomy in assuming the world to be a sphere, and proves the continuance of speculation on the harmony of science and revelation. See Donaldson's *Gr. Lit.* III. 59. § 3.

[29] P. 14—17.

portance of investigating the history of free thought from the intellectual side, we admitted the necessity of taking the probability of the action of the moral element into account when we pass from the abstract study of tendencies to form a judgment on concrete instances. Here accordingly, in the mental history of these early unbelievers, we already encounter cases where philosophy as well as piety requires that a very large share in the final product be referred to the influence of emotional causes. Christianity addresses itself to the compound human nature, to the intellect and heart conjoined. Accordingly the excitement of certain forms of moral sensibility is as much presupposed in religion as the sense of colour in beholding a landscape. The means fail for estimating with historic certainty the particular emotional causes which operated in the instances now under consideration. The moral chasm which separates us from heathens is so great that we can hardly realize their feelings.

If however we cannot pronounce on the positive presence of moral causes which produced their disbelief, we may conjecture negatively the nature of those, the absence of which precluded the possibility of faith. Christianity demands a belief in the supernatural, and a serious spirit in the investigation of religion, both of which were wholly lacking in Lucian. It requires a deep consciousness of guilt and of the personality of God, which were wanting in Celsus. It exacts a more delicate moral taste to appreciate the divine ideal of Christ's character than Hierocles manifested. Porphyry and Julian are more difficult cases for moral analysis. Porphyry is so earnest a character, so spiritual in his tastes,[30] that we wonder why he was not a Christian; and except by the reference of his conduct to general causes, such as philosophical pride, we cannot understand his motives without a more intimate knowledge than is now obtainable of his personal history. The

[30] This appears from a letter of Porphyry to his wife Marcella, discovered by Angelo Mai, and edited at Milan, 1816, in which his personal religious aspirations are seen.

difficulty of understanding Julian's character arises from its very complexity. Who can divine the many motives which must have combined with intellectual causes at successive moments of his life, to change the Christian student into the apostate, to convert disbelief into hatred, and to degrade the philosopher into the persecutor? History happily offers so few parallels to enable us to form a conjecture on the answer, that we may be content to leave the problem unsolved.

We have now summed up the causes which operated in the first great intellectual struggle in which Christianity was engaged. No means exist for estimating the amount of harm done by the writings of unbelievers. The retributive destruction of some of them and the indignant alarm of the Christian apologists indicate the probability that these works had excited attention. But under a merciful Providence truth has in the end gained rather than lost by this first conflict of reason against Christianity. The church encountered the unbelievers by apologetic treatises, and met the Gnostics by dogmatic decisions. The truths brought out by the action and reaction, and embodied in the literature stimulated by Gnosticism, in the apologies created by unbelief, and in the creeds suggested as a protest against heresy, are the permanent result which the struggle has contributed to the world.

The contest however is not quite obsolete, and has a practical as well as antiquarian interest. Though the analogy to the attacks of ancient unbelievers must be sought in pagan countries in the objections of modern heathens, yet some resemblance to them may be found in the unbelief of Christian lands. Such parallels are frequently hasty generalizations founded on a superficial perception of agreement, without due recognition of the differences which more exact observation would bring to view; for identity of cause as well as result is necessary in order to establish philosophical affinity. In the present cases however the agreement is moral if not intellectual, in spirit if not in form, generally also in condition if not in cause. The flippant wit of Lucian, which attributes religion to imposture and craft, is repeated in the French criticism of the last century. Some of the doubts of Celsus reappear in the English deists. The delicate criticism of Porphyry is reproduced in the modern exegesis. The disposition to explain Christianity as a psychological phenomenon, as merely one form of the religious consciousness, an organic product of human thought, unsuited for men of superior knowledge, who can attain to the philosophical truth which underlies it, is the modern parallel to Julian.

Accordingly the conduct of the early church during this struggle has a living lesson of instruction for the church in Christian lands, as well as in its missionary operations to the heathen. The victory of the early church was not due wholly to intellectual remedies, such as the answers of apologists, but mainly to moral; to the inward perception generated of the adaptation of Christianity to supply the spiritual wants of human nature.[31] As the heathen realized the sense of sin, they felt intuitively the suitability of salvation through Christ; as they witnessed the transforming power of belief in Him, they felt the inward testimony to the truth of Christianity. The external evidence of religion had its office in the early church, though the belief[32] in magic and in oracles probably prevented the full perception of the demonstrative force due to the two forms of external evidence, miracles and prophecy. But the internal evidences,—Christ, Christianity, Christendom,

[31] See this discussed towards the close of Lect. VIII.

[32] It is obvious that this belief blunted in some degree the force of arguments built upon miracles and prophecy: this circumstance explains the comparative absence of these arguments in the early apologies against the heathens. The reality however both of miracles and prophecy is always implied; and occasionally the direct appeal to them is used. The apologists were thus compelled, even if no other reason founded deeper in the philosophy of evidence had inclined them to do so, to lay stress on what would now be called the argument from internal evidence for the truth of Christianity. The Hulsean Prize Essay for 1852, by Mr. W. J. Bolton, contains a useful account of the apologists, with extracts from their writings. And Mr. H. A. Woodham, in the preface to his edition of Tertullian's Apology (1843), has made some very suggestive remarks. Both writers show that the fathers use the argument from miracles more frequently than had generally been supposed.

were the most potent proofs offered,—the doctrine of an atoning Messiah filling the heart's deepest longings, and the lives of Christians embodying heavenly virtues.

The modern church may therefore take comfort, and may hope for victory. The weak things of the world confounded the strong, not only because the Holy Spirit granted the dew of his blessing, but because the scheme and message of reconciliation which the church was commissioned to announce, were of divine construction. Each Christian who tries, however humbly, to spread the knowledge of Christ by word or by example is helping forward the Redeemer's kingdom. Let each one in Christ's strength do his duty, and he will leave the world better than he found it; and in the present age, as in the times of old, Gnosticism and heathenism will retire before Christianity; the false will be dissipated, the good be absorbed, by the beams of the Sun of righteousness.

LECTURE III.

FREE THOUGHT DURING THE MIDDLE AGES, AND AT THE RENAISSANCE; TOGETHER WITH ITS RISE IN MODERN TIMES.

LUKE xxi. 33.

Heaven and earth shall pass away; but my words shall not pass away.

WE have studied the history of unbelief down to the fall of heathenism. A period of more than seven hundred years elapses before a second crisis of doubt occurs in church history. The interval was a time of social dissolution and reconstruction; and when the traces of the free criticism of religion reappear, the world in which they manifest themselves is new. Fresh races have been introduced, institutions unknown to the ancient civilization have been mingled with or have replaced the old; and the ancient language of the Roman empire has dissolved into the Romance tongues. But Christianity has lived through the deluge, and been the ark of refuge in the storm; and its claims are now tested by the young world which emerged into being when the waters of confusion had retired. The silence of reason in this interval was not the result of the abundance of piety, but of the prevalence of ignorance; a sign of the absence of inquiry, not of the presence of moral and mental satisfaction.[1] Even when speculation

[1] For the intellectual and social condition during this period, consult Guizot's *History of Civilization in France*; Hallam's *History of the Mid-*

revived, and reason re-examined religion, the literary monuments in which expression is given to doubt are so few, that it will be possible in the present lecture not only to include the account of the second and third crises which mark the course of free thought in church history, but even to pass beyond them, and watch the dawn of unbelieving criticism caused by the rise of the modern philosophy which ushers in the fourth of the great crises named in a previous lecture.[2]

The former of these periods which we shall now examine, the second in the general scheme, may be considered to extend from A. D. 1100 to 1400. Its commencement is fixed by the date at which the scholastic philosophy began to influence religion, its close by the revival of classical learning. The history of free thought in it is complicated, by being to some extent the struggle of deeds as well as of ideas, a social as well as a religious struggle. It was the period which witnessed both the dissolution of feudalism and the theocratic centralization in the popedom; and while reason struggled on the one side against the dogmatic system, it struggled on the other to assert the rights of the state against the church, and to put restraints upon the privileges, dominion, and wealth, of the pope and clergy. The social struggle, to vindicate the liberty of the state against the undue power of the church, so far as it is the effect of free thought, appertains to our subject, in the same manner as was the case with the early attempts of a converse character of the Roman emperors to deny due liberty to the church, whenever, as in the case of Julian, they were the result of a deliberate examination of religion. Free thought in the middle ages is at once Protestantism, Scepticism, and Ghibellinism.[3]

dle Ages, ch. ix. part i.; and *History of Literature*, ch. i. Also three works by Laurent, *Les Barbares et le Catholicisme*, *La Papauté et l'Empire*, *La Féodalité et l'Eglise*.

[2] See Lect. I. p. 7.

[3] See Guizot's *History of Civilization in Europe*, ch. vi. and x.; Laurent, *La Reforme*, 1861 (p. 131–271.) The last-named work, to which frequent reference will be made, is an able production by a Professor (probably a freethinker) in the university of Ghent. It is the eighth of a

The intellectual action in this crisis is marked by four forms;—(1) the criticism created by the scholastic philosophy, which has been thought to mark in Abélard the commencement of doubt; (2) the introduction of the idea of progress in religion, in the sense that Christianity is to be replaced by a better religion; (3) the idea of the comparison of Christianity with other religions, so as to obliterate its exceptional character; (4) the traces of disbelief in the doctrine of immortality. The two former are free thought as doubt, the two latter as disbelief.

It will be necessary, for illustrating the first of these forms, to explain the nature of the scholastic philosophy, so far as to show how it might become the means of producing heresy or scepticism, when applied to theology.

Scholasticism is the vague name which describes the system of inquiry common in the middle ages.[4] In truth it marks a period rather than a system; a method rather than a philosophy. In spite of difference of form, it links itself with the speculations of other ages in community of aim, in that it strove to gain a general philosophy of the universe, to reach some few principles which might offer an interpretation of all difficulties.

In the present age the science which attempts this grand problem is denominated Logic, or Metaphysics, according to the different sphere which it covers.[5] But

series of works, entitled, *Etudes de l'Histoire de l'Humanité*, of which three were named in a previous note, and contains a careful examination (1) of the reform, religious and social, of the middle ages; (2) of heterodoxy, both as free thought and incredulity, during the same period; (3) of the Renaissance; (4) of the principles of the Reformation.

[4] It has been conjectured that the name was probably derived from the circumstance that it was the philosophy which arose in the various *Scholæ* which Charlemagne established throughout his empire; and afterwards was that which existed in the scholæ or halls of the mediæval universities. Brucker has discussed the previous history of the word (*History of Critical Philosophy*, iii. 710; and Hauréau, nearly repeating him, *Philosophie Scholastique*, i. 7, with a view to show how it was used before it became changed into the meaning just assigned to it). See also a few remarks by Saisset in the *Revue des Deux Mondes*, 1850, vol. iii. p. 645.

[5] It is called logic, if we denote that part of it which studies the mode

in the middle ages these two fields were not clearly distinguished; in the same manner as in the *Διαλεκτική* of Plato, method and the realities attained by method were not separated.[6] Yet it was mainly in reference to the former that scholasticism wears the aspect of a method, and to the latter the aspect of a philosophy. Adopting deduction as the type of a perfect science, it assumed its data partly on the ground of innate ideas, partly from the truths of revelation, partly from the metaphysical dicta of Aristotle; and from these principles attempted to work out deductively a solution of universal nature. It was the *Σοφία* of Aristotle executed from a Christian point of view. In respect to the logical method there was a general agreement of opinion, but difference of system arose in the metaphysical. The form that the problem of science then assumed was peculiar. Instead of examining the data from which deduction starts, with a view of finding their subjective certainty as thoughts, the inquirers strove to settle the problem of their objective nature as things. The question asked was this: Are the genera and species which the mind contemplates, in its attempts to classify and interpret phenomena, real in nature, or produced only by human thought and speech? A comparison with the modern mode of investigation will explain the importance which the question possessed, and the reason why it monopolized the entire field of inquiry.

The progress of discovery has forced upon us a subdivision of the sciences into two classes, unknown in

of investigation, and the comparative value of evidence in the different fields of inquiry. It is the psychological branch of metaphysics, if it explores the structure and functions of the mind, ascertaining the subjective validity of the data employed in the method which forms the subject matter of contemplation in logic. It is the ontological branch, if it reaches to the still higher problem of searching for the traces of objective reality, independent of the act of human thought, which are involved in the data previously examined.

[6] The Διαλεκτική of Plato, it is well known, was the method of analysis by means of language, and comprised the field which his successor Aristotle separated in two, viz. Διαλεκτική, logic, the inquiry concerning method; and Σοφία, metaphysics, the inquiry concerning being. See Bp. Hampden's article *Aristotle* in the *Encyclopædia Britannica;* Ritter, *History of Philosophy* (English translation), vol. ii. b. 8, c. 2 and 3; and vol. iii. c. 2.

the middle ages; in one of which we discover causes; in the other, in which we are unable to find causes, we rest content with classification by species and genera. In the former we discover antecedents, in the latter types.[7] But in mediæval science, as in Greek, the latter class was regarded as the sole form of all perfect science. Hence the reason will appear why the question as to the true nature of genera and species had a monopoly of the field of inquiry; and also why the theory of predication was exalted into the most important part of logic.[8] Those who thought that genera had a real existence as essences apart from man's mind and from nature, were denominated Realists: those who denied to them any real existence, and considered them to be a common quality labelled by a common name, were Nominalists: those who held the intermediate view, and assumed them to exist, not only as artificial names but also as general classes in the human mind, were Conceptualists. With the realist, classification was not arbitrary, but true and determined for man. With the nominalist and conceptualist it was created by man, and amenable to correction.

The question, though now relegated from metaphysical to physical science, has still sufficient importance to enable us to perceive likewise the reason why these different theories could be the means of dividing men into parties. The bitterness with which a zoological inquiry of analogous character into the perpetuity of natural species[9] has been lately assailed may enable us to realize the earnestness shown on this point in the middle ages. The question, as viewed by the schoolmen, was really the fundamental one as respects knowledge; and

[7] Viz. antecedents in the mechanical class of sciences, types in the zoological and botanical. The distinction is that which is indicated by Mill under the names of "uniformities of causation," and "uniformities of coexistence." See Mill's *Logic*, vol. i. b. i. ch. 7, § 4; vol. ii. b. iii. ch. 22; b. iv. ch. 7. Compare also Whewell's *Philosophy of the Inductive Sciences*, vol. i. b. iii. c. 2. and b. viii.

[8] This is the explanation of the fact already quoted from Cousin, that the mediæval philosophy depended on a quotation made by Boëthius from Porphyry.

[9] Viz. Darwin's Inquiry into the Origin of Species, 1859.

the opinions on it are the counterpart to those which relate to the tests of truth and the nature of being in modern metaphysics. The spirit of realism was essentially the spirit of dogmatism, the disposition to pronounce that truth was already known.[10] Nominalism was essentially the spirit of progress, of inquiry, of criticism. Realism was in spirit deductive, starting from accepted dogmas: Nominalism was in spirit, though not in form, inductive. It tested classifications, and admitted opportunities for the existence of doubt. "Believe that you may know," was the expression of the former: "Know that you may believe," that of the latter.[11]

The two theories were of universal application to every subject of thought. An illustration will explain their relation to theology. In the foolish and almost irreverent attempts to explain by philosophy the nature of the triune existence of the divine Being, the realist assuming the reality of the one genus Deity, was prepared to allow identity of essence in the three species, the three members of the Divine Trinity. The nominalist, allowing only concrete existence, was obliged either to accept unity, only in a verbal sense, and be charged with tritheism, as Roscelin; or diversity only in a verbal sense, and incur the charge of Sabellianism, as Abélard.

Such was Scholasticism, and such its relation to philosophy and theology.[12] Existing for several centuries as an instinct, it became about the end of the

[10] Inasmuch as the realist assumed that the innate ideas of the mind gave a knowledge of real essences in nature.

[11] "Neque enim quæro intelligere ut credam, sed credo ut intelligam," are the words of the realist Anselm (*Proslog.* I. p. 43. ed. Gerberon.) "Dubitando ad inquisitionem venimus; inquirendo veritatem percipimus," are those of the nominalist Abélard. (*Sic et Non*, p. 16. ed. Cousin.)

[12] The best modern work on scholasticism is the *Mémoire Couronné*, by B. Hauréau, 2 vols. 1850, in which the various authors and schools of thought are fully treated. Among older sources, the following are important; Brucker, iii. 709–868; Tennemann's *Manual*, § 237–79; Ritter's *Christliche Philosophie;* Buhle, *Geschichte der Neuern Philosophie*, i. 810 seq.; Hampden's *Bampton Lectures* (I. and II.), and the article by him on *Aquinas* in the *Encyclopædia Metropolitana;* also Maurice's *Mediæval Philosophy.*

eleventh century an intelligent movement.[13] At this period the problem was consciously proposed, and each of the three centuries which are comprised in our present period exhibits a different phase of the controversy. At first the movement was in favour of the nominalism in Roscelin and Abélard, and reason assumed an attitude of alleged scepticism: in the thirteenth century the victory was in the hands of intelligent realists like Aquinas, who used reason in favour of orthodoxy. In the fourteenth, nominalism revived in Occam; the provinces of faith and philosophy were severed, and the final victory on the metaphysical question remained in the hands of the nominalists.

The scientific position of Abélard will thus be clear. We must now study his intellectual character, as embodying the sceptical aspect which belonged to nominalism.

Abélard's character is in many respects one of the most curious in history.[14] The record of his trials, bodily and mental,[15] enlists the romantic sympathy of the sentimentalist, and commands the serious attention of the philosopher. His wonderful reputation at Paris as a public lecturer connects him with the university life of the middle ages, and presents him as the type of the class of great professors created by the absence of books and consequent prevalence of oral instruction. It was his vast influence which made his opinions of importance, and aroused the opposition of St. Bernard. It seems to have been the application of the nominalist philosophy to the doctrine of the Trinity, contained in Abélard's works on dogmatic theology,[16] which excited

[13] Cfr. Tennemann's *Manual of Philosophy*, § 243.

[14] On Abélard's personal character, see Guizot's *Lettres d'Abélard*, 1839; and Remusat's *Abélard*, 1845, vol. i. part x., the latter of which writers has long studied his life, philosophy, and theology; also Taillandier's article *La Libre pensée du moyen age* (*Revue des Deux Mondes*, *Aug.* 1861); Tennemann's *Gesch. der Phil.* viii. 170 seq.; Tennemann's *Manual*, § 251.

[15] In his work *Liber Calamitatum.*

[16] In his *Introductio ad Theologiam*, and *Theologia Christiana.* See Neander's *Kirchengeschichte*, viii. 505 seq.

alarm. The council called at Sens[17] was a theological duel, wherein those two distinguished characters were matched, the most eloquent theologian and preacher against the most influential professor and philosopher; the saint against the critic. Bernard was right in his Theology; Abélard perhaps right in his philosophy.[18] This event however presents the effects of scholasticism in producing heresy rather than scepticism.

The great work which has laid Abélard open to the latter charge merits a brief notice. It was entitled the *Sic et Non*, and remained unpublished in the public documents of France till recent years.[19] It is a collection of alleged contradictions, which exist on a series of topics, which range over the deepest problems of theology, and descend to the confines of casuistry in ethics.[20] In the discussion of them Abélard collects passages from the scriptures and from the fathers in favour of two distinctly opposite solutions. He has however prefixed a prologue to the work, which ought to be taken as the explanation of his object.[21] He insists in it on the difficulty of rightly understanding the scriptures or the fathers, and refers it to eight different causes;[22] ad-

[17] In A. D. 1121.

[18] The nature of this contest is given in Mabillon's edition of Bernard (*Præf.* § 5), and the characters of the two disputants are sketched in Sir J. Stephens's *Lectures on the History of France*, ii. (163–207); also in Neander's *Kirchengesch.*, vol. viii. p. 533 seq.

[19] It was published by Cousin in 1836, with an elaborate preface relating to the literary history of Abélard's works and opinions, as well as the character of the scholastic philosophy generally. An edition of the text, including the passages not printed by Cousin, has subsequently been published by Henke and Lindenkohl, (Marburg, 1851.) See also Neander's *Kirchengesch.*, viii. p. 523 seq.

[20] The following are examples of the questions proposed: No. (5.) Quod non sit Deus singularis et contra; (6) Quod sit Deus tripartitus et contra; (14) Quod sit filius sine principio et contra; (18) Quod æterna generatio filii narrari vel sciri vel intelligi possit et non; (28) Quod nihil fiat casu et contra; (30) Quod peccata etiam placeant Deo et non; (38) Quod omnia sciat Deus et non; (121) Quod liceat habere concubinam et contra; (153) Quod nulla de causa mentiri liceat et contra; (156) Quod liceat hominem occidere et non.

[21] Abélard's Preface is analysed and discussed in Cousin, p. 191 seq., and Stephens, vol. ii. p. 169.

[22] Viz. (1) the peculiarities of their style; (2) their use of popular language on scientific questions; (3) the corruption of the text; (4) the

vising that when these considerations fail to explain the apparent contradictions of scripture, we should abandon the manuscripts as inaccurate, rather than believe in the existence of real discrepancies. He draws also a broad distinction between canonical scripture and other literature, strongly affirming the authority of the former.

Is this work sceptical? Is it designed under a fair show to serve the purpose of unbelief? Or is it merely an instance of the awakening of the spirit of inquiry, the free criticism exercised by nominalism, the desire to prove all dogmas by reason? In other words, was the freethinking of Abélard rationalism, or was it merely Protestantism and theological criticism?

These questions have met with different answers. The Benedictine editors, viewing his condemnation by St. Bernard as parallel to that of the biblical critic R. Simon[23] by Bossuet, declined to publish the manuscript of his work.[24] More recent inquirers, especially the philosophical critic Cousin, have regarded Abélard with a favourable eye. They consider his treatises merely to be a provisional scepticism, fortifying the mind against premature solutions. Some would even claim him as an early protestant, as the first of the line of men whose spirits, while fretting under the dogmatic teaching or the political centralization of the Western church, have unhesitatingly bowed before the authority of scripture.[25]

number of spurious books; (5) the retraction by the fathers of their own previous statements; (6) their careless use of profane learning; (7) the describing things as they appear, not as they are; (8) their ambiguous use of words.

[23] R. Simon had published a work, *Histoire Critique du Vieux Testament*, 1678, in which positions were stated which were new at that time, but which, as Hallam observes, (*Hist. of Lit.* iii. 299,) "now pass without reproof." The history of the controversy connected with Simon is contained in Walch's *Bibliotheca Theologica Selecta*, 1765, vol. iv. (251–9.) See also Bp. Marsh's Lectures, part i. p. 52.

[24] See Martène et Durant in *Thesaur. Nov. Anecdot.* (1717) vol. v. Pref. p. 3.

[25] Cousin thinks him a sceptic. So also Sir J. Stephens, ii. 170. Taillandier (*Rev. des Deux Mondes* quoted above) takes the view given in the text, that his character was complex. See also Laurent's *La Reforme*, pp. 318–331.

Possibly these several views contain elements of truth. Abélard's character was complex, and the purpose of his book equally so. He embodied a movement, and experience had not yet taught men to distinguish in it the boundaries which separated the provinces of free thought. The argument in favour of scepticism drawn from the form of his work seems unfair. The statement of a series of paradoxes is lawful, if a solution of them be offered, or an explanation of the reason why a solution is impossible. The disputative, dialectical tone which assists in the work was the ordinary mode of instruction in the mediæval universities, and finds a parallel in the method of thought observable in other ages. Abélard's statement of paradoxes, of an unsolved mass of contradictions, recalls, for example, the early paradoxes on motion which Zeno presented for the purpose of compelling acquiescence in the Eleatic teaching,[26] or the series of antinomies which Kant has given, as problems insoluble theoretically, but capable of harmony when viewed on the moral side.[27] In truth it is the mark, either, as in one of these cases, of the first awakening of the mind to curiosity; or, as in the other, of the last limit at which curiosity is compelled to pause. Abélard's method is like that which is observable in Socrates, and in those early dialogues of his disciple Plato, in which the pupil is working in his master's manner, wherein difficulties are propounded without being solved. The hearer is cross-questioned, with the view of being made to feel the necessity of possessing knowledge; and a method is offered to him by which he is to find the solution of problems for himself.[28] In this view Abélard's doubt is really the inquiry which is the first step to faith; the criticism which precedes the constructive process, the negation before affirmation.

While its form may be regarded as an embodiment

[26] See Preller's *Hist. Phil. Gr. Rom.* xxxviii. § 158. Bayle's Dictionary, art. *Zeno* (vol. iv. edition 5, p. 539 note).

[27] Kant's *Kritik* (*Transcendent. Dial.* b. ii. div. 2, p. 322, Engl. transl.). The illustration is borrowed from Taillandier, to whose article I am indebted for several other suggestions.

[28] Grote, vol. viii. ch. 68.

of the scholastic method, the manner of handling marks the commencement of modern biblical criticism. The suggestions which he offers[29] in reference to false readings of manuscripts, the spuriousness of books, and the temporary character of the author's sentiments, as elements in determining the reality of a contradiction, or the necessary rejection of a passage on grounds of dogmatic improbability, mark a sagacity which has been perfected into a science by the growth of modern criticism. Thus far we have only the elements of inquiry and criticism which enter into doubt; yet it would be unfair to deny that something of unbelief may have been found in a restless care-worn spirit like that of Abélard; and if any one thinks that he intended in his work to leave the reader with the impression that the solution is impossible, or that the doubter's side is the stronger, then we may consider him to have been an unbeliever, and regard his teaching as an example, often witnessed in later times, of a concealed irony, which, while pretending to accept revelation, has represented its evidence as insufficient, and its doctrines as unprovable. If however he be taken to be a sceptic, it is only the infancy of doubt. It is unlike the bitter disbelief shown by the early antichristian writers, or by the doubters of modern times. Whatever was valuable in the free thought of Abélard outlived his time. The spirit of inquiry which spoke through him, continued to operate in his successors.[30] His method was even adopted by his opponents. His follower, Arnold of Brescia, carried free thought from ideas into acts, and suffered martyrdom in a premature struggle against the papal church.[31] Being dead, Abélard yet spoke, both politically and philosophically; and his character remains as a type of the spirit of mingled doubt and hope and inquiry which is exhibited in the free thought of any of those great epochs, when knowledge is increased, and when earnest minds are standing in doubt whether the new wine can be placed in the old bottles.

[29] In his Prologue [30] See Cousin's Preliminary Dissertation, p. (201–3.)
[31] See Laurent's *La Reforme*, p. 263.

The movement, which was beginning to be felt in every branch of life and thought in the twelfth century, was still more manifest in the course of the thirteenth, an age, which, whether viewed in its great men or great deeds, its movements political, ecclesiastical, or intellectual, is the most remarkable of the middle ages, and one of the most memorable in history.[32] The activity of speculation is evidenced by the increasing alarm which alleged heresy like the Albigensian was causing, and by the establishment of the system of ecclesiastical police[33] which developed into the inquisition. About the middle of the century, the influence of free thought in religion is supposed to have made its appearance, in a work which originated with one of the newly created mendicant orders. A book which had appeared at the beginning of the century, entitled "the Everlasting Gospel," was now edited with an introduction by some person of influence in the Franciscan order.[34] The idea conveyed was, that, as there are three Persons in the Godhead, so there must be three dispensations; that of the Father which ended at the coming of Christ, that of the Son which was then about to conclude, and that of the Spirit, of which the religious ideal of the Franciscans was the embodiment.

The work caused immense alarm, and was condemned by the council of Arles,[35] on the ground that it

[32] It may be sufficient to allude to names like those of Innocent III., Aquinas, Roger Bacon, Frederick II., Cimabue, Dante; and to the great works of law (civil and canon) and philosophy, the great works in Gothic architecture, and the revival of painting, as examples of the intellectual character of the age; and to the commencement of constitutional liberty, the final settlement of Europe, and commencement of the present European kingdoms, as illustrations of its advance in social government.

[33] In 1229.

[34] The work is attributed to Joachim, a Calabrian abbot, about A.D. 1200, whom Dante names (*Paradiso*, xii. 140). It was edited in 1250, with an introduction probably written by John of Parma, general of the Franciscans. Mosheim (*History*, cent. 13, part ii. ch. 2, § 33 note), has carefully investigated the subject. See also Laurent's *La Reforme*, pp. 295–302; F. Spanheim's *Works*, vol. i. p. 1665; Neander's *Kirchengesch.* vol. viii. p. 844 seq.

[35] In 1260. Labbei *Concil.* (1671) vol. xi. part. ii. p. 2361.

assumed that Christianity was imperfect, and was to be replaced by a superior revelation developing from natural causes. It is doubtful whether the book was really intended to be sceptical. More probably it was mystical. Claiming to be founded on an apocalyptic idea,[36] it was a revival of the Chiliasm which haunted the Christians of Asia Minor in the early centuries; perhaps also it was the utterance of the spiritual yearning which marked the rise of the Franciscan order, and a protest against the worldliness of the times. It was connected too with the longings for political deliverance from the temporal dominion of the Popedom which were now beginning to be felt. In these latter aspects the idea, so far from being false, was an advance. Christianity from time to time admits a progress, but from within rather than from without; a deeper spiritual appreciation of old truths rather than a reception of new ones. The demand for progress becomes a ground for alarm only when it implies that the world has bidden farewell to Christianity, either through the mystical expectation of a Millennial reign which is to supersede it, or through the sceptical belief that our religion has only an historic value, and needs remodelling to meet the requirements of advancing civilization. If the latter was the meaning of this utterance of the Franciscan book, the idea was the germ of the modern conception of the function of Christianity in "the education of the race," the first statement of which is usually attributed to Lessing.[37]

The same century which gave birth to this *mot*, expressive of *progress in religion*, created also another which embodied the idea of the *comparative study of religions*. This phrase may have different meanings. It may signify the comparison of Christianity with ethnic creeds in its external and internal character, without

[36] Rev. xiv. 6.

[37] The work so entitled passed under Lessing's name; but its authorship has been recently disputed. In an article in Illgen's *Zeitschrift für die Historische Theologie* for 1839, part iv., on the life of A. Thaer compiled by Koerte, there is evidence given that Lessing was only the editor, Thaer having sent it to him anonymously. See also a remark in a letter of Lessing, *Works*, vol. xii. p. 503, (Lachmann's edition.)

sacrificing the belief that a divinely revealed element exists in it, which caused it to differ from them in kind as well as degree. Or it may mean a comparison of Christianity with other religions, as equally false with them, equally a deliberate and conscious invention of priestcraft which was the shocking view adopted by writers like Volney in the last century,[38] or else a comparison of it as equally true with them, as equally a psychological development of the religious intelligence, which is the view prevalent in many noted works on the philosophy of history in the present.[39] It was the second of these ideas, expressive of actual incredulity, which existed in the thirteenth century. It is traceable in the imputation made by Gregory IX[40] against the celebrated emperor Frederick II, that he had spoken of Moses, Christ, and Mahomet, as the three great impostors who had respectively deceived the Jews, the Christians, and the Arabs.

The very possibility of the existence of such a comparison presupposes intercourse with disciples of foreign creeds. The Christians now no longer possessed a merely vague knowledge of Jews and Mahometans. The crusades were expiring, the danger which evoked them had subsided, and the enmity which supported them was decaying. Europe had entered into relations of commerce, if not of amity, with Mahometan nations; and through contact with them had come to measure them by an altered standard, and to acquire the idea of comparing religions. Frederick II, to whom this expression is imputed, is stated to have manifested admiration of Mahometan literature, and affection for his Mahometan subjects who afforded him aid in carrying out the plans of civilization which his powerful mind

[38] *Les Ruines*, c. 24.

[39] E. g. in Benjamin Constant's work, *De La Religion*, and Laurent's *Etudes de l'Histoire de l'Humanité*; Buckle's *History of Civilization*; Comte's *Philosophie Positive*. It is chargeable in spirit on many others.

[40] The letter of Gregory IX, in which the statement is contained, bears date July 1, 1239. It is quoted in Raynald's Supplement to Baronius. (Annal. Eccles. 1747. vol. ii. p. 218, 13 of Greg. IX. xxvi.)

had formed;[41] and it was his indifference to a crusade, induced probably by other causes, which led the Pope to impute to him the blasphemy just quoted. The contact with the East, half a century later, in like manner afforded the pretext for fastening a charge of unbelief on the Knights Templars.[42] Contact with Mahometans had thus, we have reason to believe, created a latitude of thought in many parts of Christendom.

The same idea of the comparison of Christianity with other creeds reappears in a tale of Boccaccio,[43] in which the three great religions are represented under the allegory of three rings which a father gave to his children, so exactly alike that the judges could not decide which was the genuine one of the three, and which the copies. It is also illustrated by the tradition of the existence of a book, entitled "De Tribus Impostoribus," which has been attributed almost to every great name in the middle ages which was conspicuous for opposition to the claims of the church, or for uneasiness under the pressure of its dogmatic teaching. The existence of the book is legendary: no one ever saw it: and the two distinct works which now bear the title can be shown to have been composed respectively in the sixteenth and seventeenth centuries: but the legend is a witness to the fact of the existence of the idea which the book was said to embody. (20)

It is perhaps in some degree to the influence of the doctrine of absorption in the Mahometan philosophy of Averroes, a commentator on Aristotle, who was the contemporary of Abélard, that we may attribute the disbelief in immortality to which we find a tendency toward the close of the thirteenth and during the fourteenth century.[44] Though it is probable that the indi-

[41] See Renan's *Averroes et l'Averroisme*, pp. 292–300, an admirable work, to which we shall have occasion frequently to refer.

[42] Michelet's *Hist. de France*, iii. 201. The charge of unbelief against the Templars was never satisfactorily established.

[43] *Decameron*, i. 3, "*Le Tre Annella.*"

[44] On Averroes see Ritter's *Geschichte der Christlichen Philosophie*, vol. iv. b. 11, c. 5; Tennemann's *Manual*, § 259; Laurent's *La Reforme*, p. 338–45, 364–85; and especially Renan's *Averroes*, p. 205 seq.

rect influence of the Arabic philosophy was felt earlier, in stimulating a demand for inquiry, a disposition to make dogmas submit to the test of reason, which has been shown to be the earliest form of mediæval doubt; yet it was not until the thirteenth century that the works of Averroes definitely influenced scholasticism, through the teaching of Michael Scot and Alexander Hales, and by means of the rapidity of intellectual communication which forms so singular a feature in mediæval history, spread their influence in Italy as well as in France. It was at this time that the doctrine of Averroes was attacked by Aquinas; and though the amount of its influence can hardly be estimated, we have the means of tracing the growth of dislike to its author in Christian lands, which is an incidental probability of the increasing danger to Christianity arising from it. In the middle of the thirteenth century the Franciscans study him without evincing hatred. About the end of it Dante describes him still without reproaches, though he places him in the Inferno along with other heathen philosophers:[45] but half a century later, in the pictures of the last judgment which exist in several states of Italy, each a little historic satire with its own peculiarities, we find Averroes depicted as the type of incredulity and blasphemy. In a fresco of the Campo Santo of Pisa, executed about 1335, when perhaps the recent canonization of Aquinas as an opponent of Averroes had directed attention to the influence of the Arabic philosopher, Orcagna has placed a separate *bolgia*, the lowest in his hell, for three persons,—Mahomet, Antichrist, and Averroes.[46]

The disbelief of immortality was however too obvious a temptation in a corrupt age, as well as too generally spread, especially in the next century, to be wholly attributable to the subtle influence of the doctrine of absorption of the Arabic philosophy. A mediæval

[45] *Inferno*, iv. 144; "Averrois che il gran comento feo."

[46] Renan enlarges in one chapter of his work in a most interesting manner on "Le rôle d'Averroès dans la peinture Italienne du moyen âge," pp. (301–16). The illustrations above given are borrowed from it.

English poet[47] attributes incredulity to the higher classes of his age; and Dante, in that poem which is a romantic picture of his contemporaries or predecessors, when devoting one circle of the Inferno to the habitation of the "more than a thousand" of those "who make the soul die with the body," attributes the cause of the sin to Epicureanism, a moral and not an intellectual cause.[48] It is a sad and humiliating thought to reflect also that a cause which must have increased incredulity, if it did not create it, was to be found in the vices of the clergy, especially near the papal court of Avignon. Most of the distinguished laymen whom history records as evincing unbelief belonged to the political party, which strove to repress the political centralization and temporal authority of the church; and it is to be feared that the causes just named were the means of repelling more deeply from religion the hearts of such persons whose interests or whose vices already led them to hate its promoters.[49]

We have thus collected the few traces which mark the history of free thought in the second great crisis of church history, and incidentally illustrated its connexion with social movements as well as religious, and shown its relation to intellectual or moral causes. On the intellectual side we have witnessed the scholastic philosophy giving activity to the spirit of change, and contact with Mahometan life and opinion imparting the latitude to Christian thought which passed into incredulity. On the moral we have noticed that the effect of social wants or of actual viciousness gave birth respectively to religious restlessness, or to actual disbelief of the supernatural. The church of the time was not unaware of the movement. In part it tried to repress it by persecution and by the Inquisition; but in part also by the lawful weapon of spiritual contest. The

[47] In the poem Piers Plowman, pp. 179, 180, Wright's edition; the doctrine of the Fall and its consequences is the subject of the scepticism named.

[48] *Inferno*, Canto x; 15, 118.

[49] Compare Dante, *Inferno*, xix. 104, &c. See Laurent's *Reforme*, 364–70, 372–78.

grand works of defence of the thirteenth century, which adjusted scholastic philosophy to dogmatic theology, and the spiritual activity of the mendicant orders, were real and lawful means of victory, appealing respectively to the intellect and heart.

The moral judgment formed on the movement seen in the whole period must vary with the phase of it viewed. The attack is not, like those of the early unbelievers, a struggle with which the sympathies of Christians cannot be enlisted. The darker aspects of it partake indeed of the same character; but it embodies a better element, a nobler form of movement, tainted perhaps with doubt, but not with disbelief; viz. the attempt of the human mind to assert its rights in philosophy, theology, and politics; and as the epoch closes, the great truth has made itself felt in the world as the result of the contest, that Christianity is supreme only within its own sphere, which it is the problem of religious philosophy to discover; that freedom of inquiry is to be used outside the boundary, but that speculation must expire in adoration within it.

A new crisis may be considered to commence in the fifteenth century, in consequence of the introduction of fresh influences through the classical revival. Yet as the two periods are connected in time, the transition is not sudden: the old influences gradually vanish away; the new ones had been slowly preparing before they became distinctly evident. The intellectual and social activity of the past period had been the means of educating the mind of Europe for the reception of the new forces which were now beginning to operate.[50]

The fifteenth century was a remarkable period for Europe, and preeminently for Italy. During several ages Italy had grown great by means of commerce and religion. The crusades, which had impoverished the rest of Europe, had enriched her; and the subjugation of the nations to the court of Rome had made her the

[50] On this subject, see Laurent, b. iii., and J. D. Burchard's *Die Cultur der Renaissance in Italien*, 1860.

treasury of Europe. Material wealth permitted the encouragement of the study of literature, which relations of commerce or of conquest with the Greek empire had been the means of reviving. Manuscripts were collected, and the remains of monuments of classic art were studied. The love of antiquity gave perfection to art, and influenced literature. The work which centuries had slowly prepared now came to perfection. The scholastic philosophy declined; the sources of ecclesiastical education and of the existing religion were weakened; and by the close of the fifteenth century the tone of the age was in all respects changed. The devotion which had expressed itself in the great Gothic works of devotion of early ages was expiring, at least in Italy, and art itself gradually became secular, and expressed ideas more earthly.

When such a moment of material prosperity, combined with intellectual and social change, ensues immediately on the movement previously sketched, we should expect to find religion subjected to re-examination, and placed in temporary peril. The history confirms the supposition. If we regard this crisis as embracing about two centuries and a quarter,[51] comprehending the classical revival, the opening of a new geographical world, and the great religious changes of the Reformation,—a period commencing with the Renaissance, and closed by the creation of modern philosophy;—we shall find two principal movements of unbelief for investigation, the one caused by literature, a return to a spirit of heathenism analogous to that already described in Julian; the second caused by philosophy, a revival of pantheism. The first belonged especially to the close of the fifteenth century, and had its seat for the most part in Tuscany and Rome; the second to the sixteenth, and was represented in the university of Padua. In both these movements, especially in the former, the open expression of unbelief in literature is rare, though the incidental proofs of its existence are abundant. It

[51] 1400–1625.

was a time of the dissolution of faith, not of overt attack. Unbelief was Epicurean indifference, rather than earnestness in destroying the old creed.

Two of the most obvious proofs that we can select for proving the existence of a state of unbelief[52] are, the ridicule of religion expressed in the burlesque poetry of the time, and the antichristian sympathies of several distinguished men.

It would be incorrect however to attribute the satirical allusions in the poetry wholly to the influence of the classical revival; for the romantic epic in which they occur is the offshoot of the old prose romance of mediæval chivalry, which had in earlier ages amused the courts of princes by directing its banter against ecclesiastical persons and institutions.[53] But the tone of the poetry is now changed. The satire is directed against religion itself, not merely against the abuse of it, or the eccentricities of its adherents. Free thought is not merely political dissatisfaction, but religious unbelief. And with the alteration of the tone agrees also the increasing disposition to carry satire into the domain of the supernatural; which thus witnesses to the widespread unbelief in the hearers for whom it was designed. Italian critics have doubted indeed whether these epics are designed to convey a caricature, or pass beyond lawful satire:[54] yet even when allowance is made for the fact that they are an historic reproduction, and for the fund presented for humour by ecclesiastical peculiarities, it seems impossible to overlook the covert satire intended on church beliefs.[55] The intermixture

[52] An Essay of great value, on "the Literature of the Italian Revival," appeared in the *British Quarterly Review*, No. 42, April, 1855, from which most of the illustrations and remarks which follow in the next two pages are taken.

[53] See Laurent, id. p. 364–70.

[54] Among recent critics who think so are Foscolo (*Quarterly Review*, No. 42, p. 521), and Panizzi (*Boiardo* and *Ariosto*, vol. i. 203), and in part also Hallam (*History of Literature*, vol. i. 195, 303–5), and Guinguené (*Hist. Lit. de l'Italie*, vol. iv. c. 3–101).

[55] The view here taken is maintained with great ability by the writer of the Review named above. One joke, which he cites as not uncommon in these epics, is the representation of St. Peter steaming with perspiration

of a comic element would not alone prove this. The miracle plays of the middle ages admitted comedy without intending irreverence; [56] and a gentle humour pervades many of the Autos of Calderon, which were acted on solemn festivals.[57] But there exists in the manner in which the supernatural element is managed by such poets as Pulci, Bello, and Ariosto, such evident purpose to bring into ridicule the existence of belief, that its parallel can only be found in the banter used by their imitator Byron, in his Vision of Judgment, and implies indifference both in author and reader; the expression of contempt, not of anger.[58]

The unbelief which existed in the courts for which this poetry was written, is a specimen of the general incredulity, or indifference to Christianity, which prevailed among the educated classes, and was fostered by classical studies and tastes. It seems strange to us, who have been long accustomed to regard classical culture as the basis of general education, and who are impressed with the conviction of the great assistance ministered by it to theological study, to regard it as the producing cause of unbelief. This result of it however was a transitory one, originating in the shock which arose from the novel thoughts and tastes which mingled themselves with the ancient pursuits, and altered the previous ideal of life. Ever since the earliest times, a chasm had unavoidably separated heathen literature from Christian; and a dislike to heathen studies existed,

with the labour of opening and shutting the gates of Paradise (*Morg. Mag.* 26. 91); and, as a more allowable one, the frequent citation of a certain archbishop Turpin as a witness for any absurdities, (*Berni Orl. Innam.* 18. 26), whose existence and pseudonymous work Pope Calixtus II had pronounced to be real.

[56] The last remnant of these miracle plays, which occurs decennially in a valley in Bavaria, is an actual proof of this statement. An interesting account of the last celebration of it was written by Dr. Stanley in *Macmillan's Magazine* for October, 1860.

[57] See Dean Trench's Introduction (ch. 3) to his *Translations from Calderon.*

[58] The proof of this position must be sought in the Review already indicated. The illustration from Byron is due to it. Pulci lived 1431–87; Bello, about the end of the fifteenth century, the exact date not known; Ariosto, 1474–1533.

which found its full expression in Gregory the Great.[59] The result was, that the Christian civilization did not consciously admit the introduction of heathen thought; and when the mind awoke suddenly to a perception of its beauty and depth, though deeper spirits, like Erasmus, regarded it with the enlightened Christian approbation which Origen had formerly shown, others were led, like Julian of old, from their admiration of it, to look with indifference or hostility on Christianity. Some of the brilliant and elevated minds that adorned the court of the Medicis were suspected of unbelief, or of preferring Platonism to Christianity;[60] and after the woes of the French invasion at the end of the century had deepened the corruption of morals, and stamped out political liberty, the last freshness of artistic creation, which had linked the public mind to Christianity through the deep instincts of the taste, disappeared. The art and literature which succeeded are an index of the tone which prevailed. Gaining perfection in form by the imitation of classic models, they were cold, sensuous, unspiritual.[61] Classical mythology was intermixed with gospel doctrines; and the early years of the sixteenth century represent the semi-heathen tone of thought which was the transition to the perfect fusion which afterwards took place of the old learning and the new. It was an age similar to those of modern times in France and Germany, which have been called periods of humanism, when hope suggests the inauguration of a new moral and social era, and the pride of knowledge produces a general belief in the power of civilization to become the sole remedy for evil.[62]

[59] Eichhorn's *Geschichte der Literatur*, vol. ii. 443; Bayle's *Dictionary*, *sub voc.*; Hallam's *History of Literature*, vol. i. 4. 21.

[60] Roscoe, in his works on the Medicis, is silent about these tendencies. In the fifteenth century, Ficinus, Poggio, Politian, Aretin; and at the beginning of the sixteenth, at the Roman court, Paolo Giovio and Bembo were suspected. See Brucker's *Hist. Philosophiæ*, Period iii. part 1. l. ii. c. 3.

[61] The comparison of the painting of the Roman, or the later Florentine schools of the sixteenth century, with that of the older Florentine, or of the Umbrian of the fifteenth, will establish this fact so far as regards art.

[62] Similar periods will be hereafter described; viz. French "Humanism" in Lect. V. and German in Lect. VI.

The social conditions of the age added moral causes to the intellectual, which tended to increase the unbelief, especially in the literary classes. One of them is perhaps to be found in the fact that the church prizes were the only reward for authorship. By the beginning of the sixteenth century authors became largely appreciated through the press, and received patronage at the courts of the various *Τύραννοι* who had established themselves on the ruins of the old republics. In the absence of any law of copyright there was no protection for them,[63] and consequently no reward except church patronage, which was therefore conferred indiscriminately, and tended to foster disbelief in the very recipients of it. A merely professional hold of religion is the surest road to absolute disbelief. It is inconceivable that the ecclesiastical scandals which history blushes to narrate, could have been perpetrated by believers; and the unbelief imputed to persons in high station, such as Leo X with other popes, and cardinals such as Bembo, was doubtless, if true, partly the result of the degrading effects of professional insincerity.

Such a state of unbelief could not be permanent, whether it was the result of a decaying system, or of the introduction of new influences. Nor would we use unnecessarily a polemical tone in speaking of a period where there is so much cause for Christian humiliation; yet it is worthy of notice that such facts are a refutation of the attack which has frequently been made on Protestantism, as the cause of eclecticism and unbelief. The two great crises in church history, when faith almost entirely died out, and free thought developed into total disbelief of the supernatural, have been in Romish countries; viz., in Italy in this period, and in France during the eighteenth century. In both the experiment of the authoritative system of the catholic religion had a fair trial, and was found wanting.

Other causes besides the classical revival were operating to stimulate activity of mind and freedom of

[63] This fact is also taken from the anonymous reviewer before quoted.

inquiry. It was an age in which the great system of the middle ages was finally dissolving. The discovery of new worlds seemed at once to call to Europe to break connexion with the old centre of ecclesiastical centralization; and to invite to that study of nature which should elevate, and as it were emancipate the mind, by teaching physical truth and the true method of discovery.[64] Political circumstances too, contributed toward the creation of ecclesiastical autonomy. The European nations had gradually grown into united families, and were now ready for coöperation in a system of balance of power.[65] The northern nations, long galled under the power of Rome, were panting for freedom; Germany first reforming her religion, and then throwing off her subjection; England first throwing off her subjection, and then compelled to reform herself. The old systems of thought were at an end. The change, like all social ones, was not abrupt, but it was decisive and final. It was the earthquake which shattered for ever the crust of error which had fettered thought.

It is a matter of wonder that the great revolutions just named passed with so little development of scepticism. In the nations north of the Alps there is hardly a trace. The charge of deism, directed in the fifteenth century against Pecock,[66] bishop of Chichester, appears

[64] It is hardly necessary to point out that physical science has not only made discoveries in its own sphere, but in logic also. By presenting a definite body of verified truth, it has rendered possible the creation of a system of *real* as distinct from *formal* logic. In the scientific discoveries that have been made, we can read the logic of the process by which they were attained, and thus raise "applied logic" to the dignity of a science, and indirectly discover a logic of probable evidence. It is the intellectual, and not merely the material value of physical science to which allusion is made in the text. It shows at once what man can know, and the limits where knowledge must give place to faith, and science to revelation.

[65] See Guizot's *Hist. de la Civilisation de l'Europe*, ch. (9–11.)

[66] Reginald Pecock was a bishop of Chichester about the middle of the fifteenth century; who in his rigour against the Lollards himself incurred the charge of deism. His work which laid him open to it, "The Repressor of overmuch blaming of the Clergy," has lately been edited with an instructive preface by Mr. Churchill Babington. The work appeals to reason, but is not open to the charge of deism. In tone it may be compared to Locke's "Reasonableness of Christianity."

to have been unfounded. The contest which Ulrich von Hütten carried on against the monks and schools of Cologne was literary rather than religious;[67] Hütten being the literary and political reformer rather than the sceptic. Even the most advanced spirits of the reformers,[68] Servetus and the Sozini, came forth from Italy, as from the centre of free thought. Nor were they unbelievers in the reality of a revelation; and they met with no support from the northern reformers. Servetus was martyred at Geneva, and the Sozini were banished into Poland. It was the spiritual earnestness which mingled with the intellectual movement in the Reformation, which prevented free thought from producing rationalism or unbelief. Protestantism was a form of free thought; but only in the sense of a return from human authority to that of scripture. It was equally a reliance on an historic religion, equally an appeal to the immemorial doctrine of the church with Roman Catholicism; but it conceived that the New Testament itself contained a truer source than tradition for ascertaining the apostolic declaration of it.[69]

But Italy was the witness of another sceptical tendency, besides that which resulted from the classic Renaissance, in the last remnant of the influence of

[67] The contest in which Hütten was engaged against the monks, with the *Epistolæ Obscurorum Virorum*, which related to it, is treated in Sir W. Hamilton's *Discussions on Philosophy*, p. 205–240 (reprinted from Edinburgh Review, No. 53, March 1830). Strauss has also published two works on Hütten, the one a memoir, 1858; the other translations from his work, 1861. (See *National Review*, No. 12, April 1858.)

[68] Servetus, though a Spaniard by birth, learned his protestantism in Italy; Castellio, Ochino, and the Sozini were Italians. See Hallam's *History of Literature*, i. 366, 379; 552 seq.: for their views Merle D'Aubigné's "*Three Discourses on the Authority of the Scripture.*" On the Reformation in Italy see Quinet's *Œuvres*, vol. iv. b. iii. ch. 1; and Professor Blunt's *Essays*, p. 89, (Essay reprinted from *Quarterly Review*, January 1828.)

[69] It is important to notice that the question asked by the reformed churches was simply, what did the inspired apostles teach? and the dispute between them and the Roman catholics referred to the question, what source was most suited for supplying information on this point;—whether ecclesiastical tradition or the original documents of the inspired teachers themselves.

mediæval philosophy. Throughout the sixteenth century, pantheism manifested itself in connexion with the philosophical studies of the university of Padua. The form in which it made itself felt was the disbelief of the immortality of the soul on speculative grounds. The cause of the disbelief was the influence of the philosophy of Averroes before noticed.[70]

It will be necessary to explain this system with a little detail. It has been already stated that Averroes was a noted commentator on Aristotle in the twelfth century. The two ground principles of his philosophy were, the eternity of matter and the impersonality of mind. On this high subject there can be only two theories; the one theistic, which declares that God is free, a personal first Cause, and the Creator of matter, and that other minds are free and personal; the other pantheistic, which asserts that matter is eternal, and that individual minds are only the manifestation of the impersonal mind, into which the individual is reabsorbed. Averroes held the latter theory, claiming to derive it from Aristotle. It must be confessed however that Aristotle's views are uncertain on this point: he distinguished between mind, immortal and relative, the latter of which, being connected with body, ceased at death; the former outlived it. But he hardly stated the doctrine that all souls are part of the universal soul, and is silent about their reabsorption into it. These points were added by Averroes.[71]

The influence of the philosophy of Averroes is observable in three classes of thinkers; viz., the Spanish Jews of his own century, the scholastic philosophers of the thirteenth, and the philosophers of the university of Padua in the fourteenth and succeeding ages. The second of these effects has been already traced: we must now notice the third.

Padua was the great medical university of the fif-

[70] See Hallam, *History of Literature*, i. 315. A large portion of Renan's *Averroes*, viz. pp. 322–432, is devoted to this subject, and is the source of much of the following information.

[71] Renan, id. (122–8.)

teenth and sixteenth centuries, and was a type of the tendency which at that time manifested itself in the north-eastern part of Italy toward material and rational studies, as in Tuscany to ideal and humanistic. It was the medical philosophy of Averroes which had first attracted attention to him. But the influence of his teaching was innocuous there until the sixteenth century, during the whole of which this university became the home of free thought.

Strict accuracy would require the separation of two tendencies in the Peripatetic school of Padua, each derived from one of Aristotle's commentators.[72] The one was the Averroist just named, which consisted in the disbelief of immortality on the ground of absorption. Man's soul, being part of the great soul which animates the universe, both emanates from it, and is again reabsorbed. The other was the Alexandrist, so called from following Alexander of Aphrodisias,[73] which consisted in a tendency to pure materialism, an absolute denial of immortality and of religion, which almost reaches the incredulity earlier expressed in the legend of the Three Impostors. Pomponatius is the declared representative of the latter view soon after the beginning of the century.[74] Frequently however the unbelief was secret, and a seeming show of orthodoxy was maintained by drawing a broad distinction between philosophy and theology; and by teaching that these views, though seen to be true in the one, were to be accounted false in obedience to the teaching of the other.

It is customary to class along with the Averroists some philosophers of a more original turn; some of whom were only indirectly connected with Padua, but rather were examples of an attempt to substitute a phi-

[72] Renan, id. (353–67.)

[73] He lived about A.D. 200.

[74] On Pomponatius (1462–1530), see Ritter's *Gesch. der Ch. Phil.* V. pp. 390 seq.; Hallam's *History of Literature*, i. 315; Renan, *Averroes*, 353, &c.; Tennemann, *Manual*, § 293; and the Life in the *Biographie Universelle*. His theological treatise which was chiefly suspected was *De Immortalitate;* but Brucker quotes from his other writings to prove atheism. As early as 1512 a Lateran council took notice of the disbelief of immortality.

losophy in place of that which was expiring. They are said to have manifested the same kind of pantheism, and to have been led by it to similar disbelief. Such are Cesalpini, Cardan,[75] Bruno, and Vanini. The charge is perhaps unfair against the two former, as they seem to have held the separate immortality of souls, which is more compatible with theism. The two latter represent the two schools just noticed, about the end of the sixteenth century.

Bruno[76] belonged mainly to the Averroist school, though his views were probably formed independently, and certainly extended farther. He not only held the existence of a soul pervading the universe, which is the form of Pantheism which has been already considered, but followed the earlier philosophy of the Neo-Platonists in identifying the soul with the matter which it animates; regarding the one as an emanation from the other, in the same manner as an effect is merely cause or force transferred. It is this belief which occurs in Spinoza, which is properly denominated Pantheism,

[75] In place of the scholastic philosophy, which was disappearing, but which lived in Padua nearly a century later than in the rest of Europe, three tendencies manifested themselves; viz., (1) a reconstruction of metaphysical philosophy, on a new, partially Platonic basis; (2) a reconstruction of logic, by P. Ramas in France (see Hallam, *History of Literature*, i. (388–90); (3) attention to experimental science, which led ultimately to the experimental method of Bacon. Telesius and Campanella belong to the first of these classes. The system of the former is briefly explained in Ritter's *Christliche Philosophie*, p. 561 seq.; Renouvier's *Histoire de Philosophie*, t. 2; and in Hallam, *History of Literature*, ii. 7; and of the latter in Hallam, id. (372–6); Tennemann's *Manual*, § 317; and Ritter, id. vi. 3, seq. Both systems are metaphysical rather than theological. That of Cesalpini is also explained in Ritter, id. v. 653, seq.; in Hallam, id. ii. 5; that of Cardan in Brucker, period iii. part ii. lib. 1. c. 3; Buhle, *Gesch. der Neu. Phil.* ii. 857, seq.; and in Morley's *Life of Cardan* (1853).

[76] Giordano Bruno (1550–1600), Ritter's *Chr. Phil.* v. 595. &c. See Hallam's *Hist. of Lit.* ii. (8–14.) Buhle's *Geschichte der Phil.* ii. 703. His life and opinions have been described by Mr. G. H. Lewis in the *Biogr. Hist. of Phil.* p. 314, seq. A list of his works is given in Buhle *Gesch. der Neu. Phil.* ii. 703, seq., and more briefly in Tennemann's *Manual*, § 300. They were collected and published in 1830. One of them, the "*Spaccio della bestia trionfante*," being very scarce, and only known by report, was formerly thought to be a translation of the celebrated work "De Tribus Impostoribus."

where the Creator is forgotten in creation. The former line of Pantheism noticed in Averroes approaches more nearly to theism. Bruno's unbelief was not gay and flippant, but sombre and earnest. With a fantastical conceit which can hardly be explained, he travelled as the missionary to propagate his own views like a knight errant tilting at all opinions, with a soul especially embittered against the Christian priesthood.[77] On his return to Italy from his travels he fell into the hands of the church, and suffered death for his opinions.

Vanini[78] similarly led a wandering life, but is a character of less seriousness: occasionally he manifested the inconsistency of indifference to his own opinions. Reverencing the memory of Pomponatius, he expressed the same disbelief of the spiritual and of immortality. He was possibly an atheist. Certainly his views were tinged with deep bitterness against religion; and after leading a restless life, he suffered a cruel martyrdom for his belief.

Bruno and Vanini were the apostles of a doctrine which the world would no longer hear. The dawn of physical knowledge was turning men to a truer study of the universe, and caused their labours to be in vain. The age of indifference was gone. The alarm caused by the Reformation had kindled a strong ecclesiastical reaction, especially in Italy, and the religious earnestness and intellectual activity of Germany had awoke an intelligent reaction on the part of the Catholic church.[79] Hence these two writers incurred a danger unknown to their predecessors. Martyrs are men who are before their age or behind it. Their sad fate throws an interest around their lives. Unbelief must always have its confessors. It is to be hoped that the inhumanity of

[77] In his travels he reached Oxford, and was admitted to lecture in the university.

[78] Lucilio Vanini (1586–1619.) His chief works were "Amphitheatrum Æternæ Providentiæ," and "De Admirandis Naturæ Arcanis." The latter was condemned by the Sorbonne. Full particulars are given in Brucker's *Hist. Phil.* period iii. part ii. l. i. ch. 6. See also Buhle, *Gesch. der Neu. Phil.* ii. 866, seq.; and the Life in the *Biographie Universelle.*

[79] On this reaction, see Hallam, *Hist. of Lit.* i. (536–44).

Christendom will never again cause it to have its martyrs.

The survey is now complete of the crisis which occurred in the transition from the middle ages to modern history, forming the third of those enumerated in a former lecture. We have witnessed amidst its complexity the manifestation of the same principles as in former epochs; the restlessness of the human mind struggling to be free, intellectually, politically, religiously; and we have endeavoured to trace the operation of the influence of classical literature and metaphysical philosophy in inducing the decay of Christian feeling and belief.

The means adopted for counteracting the movement were similar to those used in former periods, viz. an intellectual argument and a spiritual awakening. In some instances, indeed, in accordance with the spirit of the time, or more truly with the spirit of human nature, material force and cruelty were employed, and the unbeliever was silenced by martyrdom. But neither material power nor the autocratic unity of the Roman church was able to repress the growth of the human mind. Conviction must be directed, not crushed. The revival of books of evidences, as soon as printing became common, about the close of the fifteenth century, which were designed to confirm faith, was a more lawful form of warfare.[80] They were constructed however on a basis unsuited to an age when first principles were being reconsidered, being an attempt to establish the authority of the church and the duty of submission to an external form of faith, and lacked the surer basis adopted in Protestant works of evidence, which is found in the external divine authority of the Bible rather than the church. The creation of the order of the Jesuits, though directed more against Protestantism than against

[80] This revival is at the same time the proof of the existence of doubt. Staüdlin, in Eichhorn's *Geschichte der Lit.* vol. vi. p. 24 seq. enumerates treatises of this kind by Ficinus, Alfonso de Spina, Savonarola, Æneas Sylvius, and Pico di Mirandola. The rare work of Sebonde also, which has been supposed to be deistical, is really a treatise on natural religion as an evidence of revealed. See Hallam's *Hist. of Lit.* i. 139, 40; Tennemann's *Manual*, 277.

unbelief, was a witness, like the previous reactionary movement of the scholastic writers in the thirteenth century, to the wish to wrest the use of learning out of the hands of the opponents of the church, and to employ the weapons of reason in defence of it.

The judgment formed on this epoch of free thought, when we have separated from it the Protestantism which craves other satisfaction for the human mind than that which is implied in submission to human authority, and the scepticism which was merely transitional doubt, must be condemnatory. The unbelief was indeed a phase of the general improvement; but one which is instructive as a warning rather than as an example, illustrating the abuse not the use of free thought. The evil nevertheless was temporary, and belongs to the past; the good was eternal: and the elements of real intellectual improvement contained in the struggle have been taken up into the constitution of modern thought and society.

We have now considered three great epochs in the history of free thought, and watched Christianity in contact or conflict with the old heathen philosophy, with the thought Scholastic or Mahometan of the middle ages, and with the revival of classical learning. It remains to enter upon the consideration of the fourth, and to observe it in relation to modern science.

The seventeenth century introduced as striking a revolution in philosophy as the corresponding ones which the two preceding ages had produced in literature and religion.

Two distinct thinkers, Bacon and Descartes, from different points of view, perceived the necessity for constructing a new method of inquiry. Their position was similar to that of Socrates of old. They saw that if knowledge was to be rendered sound, it must be based on a new method.[81] They both alike sought it in experience; Bacon in sensational, Descartes in intellectual,

[81] On Socrates, see Grote's *History of Greece*, vol. viii. ch. 68.

the instinctive utterance of consciousness.[82] The indirect effects on religion produced by their teaching will be seen more fully hereafter. Our present object is to sketch the influence exercised by Descartes on the theological speculations of Spinoza, before passing in succeeding lectures to the detailed study of those peculiarities which free thought has presented in the different countries in which it has been manifested.[83]

Spinoza's memory has been branded with the stigma which attached to his character during life.[84] Born in Holland, of Jewish origin, his early repudiation of the legends of the Talmud in which he was educated, caused his excommunication by his own people. Finding himself an outcast, he sought society among a few sceptical friends, one of whom was a physician named Van den Ende, whom a sense of injustice united to him by the

[82] On Bacon and Descartes see Ritter, *Christliche Philosophie*, v. 309 seq., and vii. 3 seq., Buhle iii. (1–86), Tennemann's *Geschichte*, x. 200 seq.; and the references given in Tennemann's Manual, § 312 and 333. Among English sources, see Morell's *History of Philosophy*, i. 76, 166; Lewes' *History of Philosophy*, Hallam's *History of Literature*, vol. ii. part 3. ch. 3. On Descartes, see also Bouillet's *Histoire de la Revolution Cartesienne* (1842) p. 95–144; and on Bacon, the monograph by Kuno Fischer of Jena, translated 1857.

[83] In chronological order Herbert and Hobbes ought to come before Spinoza. Indeed their works furnished suggestions to him; but as the forms of scepticism which follow are arranged by nations, it is more convenient to place Spinoza here alone previously to treating the others.

[84] The best means of understanding Spinoza is the perusal of his own works. It is only in modern times that he has been understood. The old works against him, Reimannus (*de Atheismo*), Mansveldt, Cuperus, and Kortholt (*de Trib. Impostoribus*), are chiefly obsolete. A memoir exists by Colerus, 1706. Among the moderns he has been carefully studied by E. Saisset, both in *Essais de Philosophie Religieuse*, 1859, and in a dissertation prefixed to a translation of his works, 1861, and in a learned article in the *Revue des Deux Mondes* for Jan. 1862; also by Damiron, *Essai sur Spinoza.* Among English writers, see Hallam, *History of Literature*, iii. 344 seq., Lewes' *History of Philosophy*, and an article on the Theologico-Politicus in the *British Quarterly Review*, No. 16, for Nov. 1848, referring to Spinoza's theology. In Germany his opinions have been examined by Ritter, *Chr. Phil.* vii. 169 seq.; Buhle iii. 503 seq.; Tennemann's *Geschichte*, x. 462 seq. Schleiermacher in early life expressed his opinion of him in words of extravagant eulogy, (*Reden über die Relig.*, p. 47, quoted in Lewes' *History of Philosophy.*) Consult also the various references given in Tennemann's Manual, § 338. A volume of Spinoza's writings has lately been found and published, which is made interesting by a photograph from a rare portrait of him.

bond of common sympathy. His life was passed in retirement, in hard, griping poverty. Possessing a mind of great originality, and a fondness for demonstrative reasoning never surpassed, he lived a model of chaste submissive virtue, searching for speculative truth; branded as an atheist in philosophy while living, and regarded since his death as the parent of many of the worst forms of rationalism in religion. Yet his character is one that cannot fail to excite a certain kind of pity. Unlike the frivolous selfish atheism, the immoral Epicureanism, of the French unbelief of the following century, his investigations were grave, his tone dignified, his temper gentle, his spirit serious. It is to be feared that he did not worship God; but he at least worshipped, at the cost of social martyrdom, what he thought to be truth. If he did not believe in revealed religion, he at least tried to embody what he believed to be its moral precepts. Though we may shrink with horror from his teaching, we cannot, when we compare him with other unbelievers, withhold our pity from the teacher.

His works are short, but weighty. Of his important treatises, the one, the *Tractatus Theologico-Politicus*, shows him as the Biblical critic; the other, the *Ethica*, exhibits his philosophy. In the former, written in early life, he derives his materials and mode of handling from the Jewish mediæval theologian Maimonides; in the latter, the product of his riper years, from Descartes.[85] But he had undoubtedly come under the influence of Descartes before writing the former work, and it is certain that the effects of it on his own philosophical

[85] In the admirable article in the *Revue*, quoted in the last note, Saisset discusses carefully the sources from which Spinoza derived his theology and philosophy. Cousin in earlier life had regarded his philosophy as borrowed from Descartes (*Fragm. de Phil. Cartes.*, p. 428 seq.), and Ritter coincides in this opinion. More recently, in the new edition (1861) of his *Hist. Gen. de la Philos.*, he regards it as borrowed from Maimonides (p. 457.) See on Maimonides' Philosophy, Adolph. Franck's *Etudes Orientales*, p. 318. Saisset after a careful examination comes to the conclusion that the theology was suggested by Maimonides' *More Nevochim*, but that the philosophy was derived neither from the Kabbala, nor Averroes, nor Maimonides, but from Descartes.

scheme are already discernible in it. We shall therefore commence with the latter, and attempt to understand his philosophy, and its application to religion, before studying his special criticism of Revelation.

Descartes had aimed, like the great thinkers of earlier times, to gain a general view of the universe of being; but had sought it by a different mode. Caring rather for certitude of method, reality in the highest principles, than for results attained, he had seen that a knowledge of being must rest on a knowledge of the consciousness which tells us of being. His principle, "Cogito, ergo sum," is the expression of this conviction. Therefore, carrying analysis into the human mind, he had grasped those ideas which appeal to us with irresistible clearness, and commend themselves as axioms requiring no proof; and from these ideas, or rather from the idea of cause, the primitive of them, regarded by him as innate, he had demonstrated *a priori* the being and attributes of God, and the principles which dominate in the great fields of knowledge.[86]

Spinoza's object was similar; but he sought to attain it in a different manner: rejecting, on the one hand, the dualism by which Descartes had opposed mind and matter, he regarded each as a different mode of the same primitive substance, and, on the other, the limited idea of the divine Being, he conceived that the mind of man realizes the notion of Him as unlimited. There are three different opinions in reference to our capacity of knowing the infinity of God. Either our knowledge of Him is only negative and relative; we know only what He is not, and our positive notions of His nature are drawn from the analogy of human personality; or, secondly, we have an intuition of His infinity, but so bare of attributes, that while it guarantees the reality of our apprehensions of Him, we are dependent on experience for its development into a conception; or, thirdly, the human mind can apprehend His infinity positively, antecedent to the application of limitations

[86] See the references given in a former note.

to it.[87] The last of these three views belonged to Spinoza, along with the ancient Eleatics, the Neo-Platonists of the early ages, and the principal schools of modern German philosophy. Accordingly he tried to work out with mathematical rigour in geometrical form a philosophy of existence, conceiving that the mind grasps the idea of God as infinite substance, and understands its development under two modes; viz. extension and thought: the former the objective act of Deity, the latter the subjective.[88] The universe therefore is nothing but the manifestation of God: God is the sum total of it; the unity in its variety; the infinite comprehending its finity. Cause and effect are identical; the *natura naturans*, and *natura naturata*. Causation is change; but it is nothing but substance assuming attributes, and attributes assuming modes. Phenomena are only the bubbles which arise on the bosom of the ocean and disappear, absorbed in its vastness. The universe is bound in one vast chain of fatalism, one grand and perfect whole. Man's perfection is to know by contemplation the universe in which he has his being.

Such a system has been called atheistic, because it is silent about the presence of a personal first Cause. It might be more truly denominated Pantheistic, not in the vague sense in which that term is applied to denote the belief in a Deity as an *anima mundi*, like that explained in reference to the Averroists,[89] but to imply that the sum total of all things, the universe, is Deity. Its influence on the question of revealed religion will be obvious. It admits that the phenomena which we attribute to miracle in the process of revelation are facts, but it denies their miraculous character.[90] They are the mere manifestation of some previously unknown law, turning up accidentally at the particular moment, some previously unknown mode in which the all-embracing substance manifests itself. In

[87] Compare the Essay on Cousin by Sir W. Hamilton (Dissertations, p. 32).

[88] *Ethica*, part ii. prop. 1 and 2.

[89] P. 100.

[90] *Theol. Polit.* c. vi.

this view all religions become various expressions of the great moral and spiritual truths which they embody, and true piety consists in rising beyond them to the vision of the higher truths which they typify, and the practice of the principles which they enjoin as rules. "Dico," wrote Spinoza, "ad salutem non esse omnino necesse, Christum secundum carnem noscere; sed de æterno illo filio Dei, hoc est, Dei æternâ sapientiâ quæ sese in omnibus rebus, et maxime in mente humana et omnium maxime in Christo Jesu manifestavit, longe aliter sentiendum."[91]

Spinoza, though a Jew, had examined the claims of Christianity. Indeed the discussions, half political, half religious, of the Dutch theology, would have compelled the investigation of it, independently of his own largeness of sympathy with the philosophical history of human religion.[92] His philosophy of revealed religion is contained in his *Tractatus Theologico-Politicus*.[93] This work was called forth by the disputes of the age, and had the political object of defending liberty of thought as necessary to the safety both of the state and of religion. The question of predestination had rent the Dutch church shortly before this time; and when the victory remained with the Calvinistic party, the opinions of the liberal Remonstrants were treated as crimes. Spinoza proposed in this work a plan, perhaps suggested by the perusal of Hobbes, for curing these dissensions. The book is a critical essay, in which he surveys the Jewish and Christian religions, and ends in the conclusion that certainty on the subject of a revelation is impossible; accordingly that the remedy for theological acrimony must be sought in a return to

[91] *Ep.* xxi. vol. iii. p. 195. (Lips. ed. 1846.) It will be hereafter seen how exactly this result is parallel to the religious philosophy and Christology developed in the Hegelian school. See Lect. VII.

[92] A succinct account of the contests in Holland is given in C. Butler's *Life of Grotius*, c. 5, 6, 12. See also Amand Saintes, *Histoire de la Vie Spinoza*, p. 63; Hase's *Church History*, E. T. § 356; Hagenbach, *Dogmengeschichte*, § 235.

[93] A good analysis for an English reader may be found in the article quoted above from the *British Quarterly Review.*

what he regards to be the simple doctrine which Christ taught, the love of God and one's neighbour; that philosophy and theology ought to be severed; the one aiming at truth and resting on universal ideas, the other at obedience and piety and resting on historic authority and special revelation. Hence, while uniformity of religious worship and practice was to be prescribed, he claimed that unlimited liberty of speculation ought to be tolerated.[94]

It is in the survey of Judaism and Christianity in the earlier part of this work that he exhibits the views in which he has anticipated many of the speculations of rationalism. He examines first into the grounds which Revelation puts forward for its claim to authority, viz. prophecy, the Jewish polity, and miracles;[95] next the principles of interpretation, and the canon of the two Testaments;[96] lastly, the nature of the divine teaching;[97] endeavouring to show that the fundamental articles of faith are given in natural religion. In this way he exhibits his views on those branches which are now denominated the evidences, exegesis, and doctrines. In the discussion of prophecy he analyses the nature of prophetic foresight into vividness of imagination; and exhibits the human feeling and sentiment intertwined with it.[98] He regards the Hebrew idea of election as merely the theocratic mode of representing their own good success in that region of circumstances which was not in human power.[99] His explanation of miracles has been already stated: the course of nature seems to him to be fixed and immutable; and he argues that interference with its course is not a greater proof of Providence than a perpetual unchanging administration.[1]

As his philosophy is seen in the treatment of the evidences, so his criticism appears in the discussion of the canon. He examines the several books of scripture, and concludes from supposed marks of editorship that the Pentateuch and historical books were all composed

[94] *Theol. Pol.* ch. 19, 20. The idea here is borrowed from Hobbes.
[95] Ch. (1–6.) [96] Ch. 7–12. [97] Ch. 13–15. [98] Ch. 1, 2.
[99] Ch. 3. [1] Ch. 6.

by one historian, who was, he thinks, probably Ezra, Deuteronomy being the first composed.[2] The prophetic books he resolves into a collection of fragments. His opinions on this department would be rejected as immature by modern rationalist critics; yet they have an historic interest as marking the rise of the searching investigations into the sources and construction of the Hebrew sacred literature, which have been pursued in an instructive manner in modern times. His view respecting the nature of scriptural doctrines,[3] that they can be reduced to the teaching of natural reason, is a corollary from his philosophy, which cannot admit that any religious truth is obligatory which is not self-evident, and is analogous to the doctrine which a short time previously had been stated by Lord Herbert of Cherbury.[4]

These remarks will suffice in explanation of the criticism exhibited in this work. The book marks an epoch, a new era in the critical and philosophical investigation of religion. Spinoza's ideas are as it were the head waters from which flows the current which is afterwards parted into separate streams. If viewed merely as a specimen of criticism, they are in many respects very defective. For this branch was new in Spinoza's time. Learning had been directed since the Renaissance rather to the acquisition of stores of information concerning ancient literature than reflective examination of the authenticity and critical value of the sources. Yet Spinoza's sagacity is so great, that the book is suggestive of information, and fertile in hints of instruction to readers who dissent most widely from his inferences.[5] In Spinoza's own times the work met with unbounded indignation. Indeed hardly any age could have been less prepared for its reception. So rigorous a theory of verbal inspiration was then held, that the

[2] Ch. 8.

[3] Ch. (12–14.)

[4] *De Veritate.* See Lect. IV.

[5] Great critical sagacity is evinced in describing the characteristics of prophecy (ch. i. and ii.), and the historic peculiarities of the Pentateuch (ch. viii.); which however, it would seem, had been observed partially by some of the learned Dutch theologians of the time.

question of the date of the introduction of the Hebrew vowel points was discussed under the idea that inspiration would be overthrown, if the admission was made that they were introduced after the time of the closing of the canon.[6] The tone of fairness in Spinoza's manner, which compels most modern readers to believe in his honesty, and which presents so striking a contrast to the profaneness of subsequent scepticism, was then regarded as latent irony. The work on its appearance was suppressed by public authority; but it was frequently reprinted; and probably no work of free thought has ever had more influence, both on friends and foes, except the memorable work of Strauss in the present age. Not only have freethinkers been moulded by it, but it has produced lasting effects on those who have loved the faith of Christ. For Spinoza's work, if it did not create, gave expression to the tendency of which slight traces are perceptible elsewhere,[7] to recognize a large class of facts relating to the personal peculiarities of the inspired writers, and to the "human element," as it has been frequently called[8] in scripture, for which orthodox criticism has always subsequently had to find a place in a theory of inspiration; facts which first shook the mechanical or verbal theory, which, however piously intended, really had the effect of degrading

[6] This lay at the bottom of the opposition which Buxtorf and Owen offered to the view, now universally adopted, of Capellus and Morinus, that the vowel points were a late introduction in Hebrew, perhaps of the sixth to the tenth centuries A.D. The history of the controversy is given in Walch's *Bibliotheca Theol. Select.* vol. iv. p. 244, 268; and Wolf's *Bibliotheca Hebr.* part iv. p. 7; part ii. p. 25 and 270. The *Formula Consensûs* of the Helvetic church (1675), (on which see Schweizer in Herzog's *Real. Encycl.* xi. 439 seq.; Henke's *Kirchengeschichte*, vol. iv. § 34; Hagenbach's *Dogmengesch.* § 222), was partly designed against the views of Capellus. On the question of the vowel points, consult the *Prolegomena* to Walton's Polyglot, iii. 39; Carpzov. *Crit. Sacr.* 242 seq. Wolf's *Bibliotheca Hebraica*, ii. 475; iv. 214 seq.; and among the moderns, Gesenius's *Gesch. der Hebr. Sprache*, § 48.

[7] E. g. in Le Clerc. See *Sentimens de Quelques Theologiens d'Hollande sur l'Histoire Critique du père Simon*, and his Five Letters on Inspiration; and in the French Roman catholic critic, R. Simon, in reference to whom see note on p. 83.

[8] E. g. by Dr. Lee on *Inspiration*, Lect. I.

the sacred writers almost into automatons, and regarded them as the pens instead of the penmen of the inspiring Spirit.[9] Indirectly the effect of Spinoza's thought was seen even in the English church. The difficulties which, through means of the English deists, it brought before the notice of the great apologetic writers of our own country, created the free, but perhaps not irreverent theory of revelation manifested in the churchmen of the last century,[10] which restricted the miraculous assistance of inspiration to the specific subject of the revealed communication, the religious element of scripture, and did not regard it as comprehending also the allusions, scientific or historic, extraneous to religion.

Nor is it merely in respect of criticism that Spinoza's views have affected subsequent thought. The central principle of his philosophy, the pantheistic disbelief of miraculous interposition which has subsequently entered into so many systems, was first clearly applied to theology by him. Wherever the disbelief in the supernatural has arisen from *a priori* considerations, and expressed itself, not with allegations of conscious fraud against the devotees of religion, nor with attempts to explain it away as merely mental realism, but with assertions that miracles are impossible, and nature an unchanging whole; this disbelief, whether insinuating itself into the defence of Christianity, or marking the attack on it, has been a reproduction of Spinoza.

In taking a retrospect of the long period over which we have travelled in this lecture, embracing the twofold crisis of free thought in the middle ages and the inauguration of the modern era, we cannot fail to be im-

[9] Compare Dr. Lee's learned and valuable work on Inspiration, ch. iv. The writer of this lecture need hardly say, that he cordially and reverently believes in the miraculous character of scripture inspiration; and that the remarks here in the text are only aimed at the extravagant views held in the seventeenth century, such as that, above named, in reference to the Hebrew vowel points. No Christian however ought to fail to appreciate the deep reverence for holy scripture implied in the theory from which dissent is here expressed.

[10] A note, giving proof of the fact here stated, will be found at the end of Lect. VIII.

pressed with the grand idea of the permanent victory of truth, and the exquisite order according to which the fatherly providence of God makes all things conduce together for good. When the course of history is viewed in its true perspective, we perceive that Almighty love ruleth. The period has comprised most of the great movements, political or intellectual, which have occurred in European history since the Christian era. The fall of the Roman empire, the gradual reconstruction of society, the revival of learning, the invention of printing, the discovery of a new geographical world, the creation of modern philosophy, embraced in it, include the mention of almost every great event, with the exception of the French revolution, which has modified the character of the human mind, or affected the destiny of Christianity. At times it seemed as if Christianity was on the point of being extinguished by unbelief; at other times, the church seemed to lend itself to the extermination of all freedom of investigation. Yet Christianity has lasted through all these dangers, throwing off, like a healthy system, the errors which from time to time insinuated themselves into it, and diffusing its blessings of eternal truth into every region of life and thought. The past is the pledge of hope for the future.

Look forth!—that stream behold,
That stream upon whose bosom we have passed
Floating at ease, while nations have effaced
Nations, and death has gathered to his fold
Long lines of mighty kings:—look forth, my soul!
(Nor in this vision be thou slow to trust)
The living waters, less and less by guilt
Stained and polluted, brighten as they roll,
Till they have reached the eternal city—built
For the perfected spirits of the just.[11]

[11] Wordsworth, *Ecclesiastical Sonnets*, part ii. 47.

LECTURE IV.

DEISM IN ENGLAND PREVIOUS TO A. D. 1760.

ISAIAH lix. 19.

When the enemy shall come in like a flood, the Spirit of the Lord shall lift up a standard against him.

THE forms assumed by free thought in the fourth great crisis of the Christian faith, which commenced with the rise of modern philosophy, and has continued with slight intervals to the present time, have been already stated[1] to be chiefly three, corresponding with the three nations in which they have been manifested.

In this lecture we shall sketch the history of one of these forms—English Deism—by which name the form of unbelief is denominated which existed during the close of the seventeenth and the first half of the eighteenth century. If the dates be marked by corresponding political history, its rise may be placed as early as the reign of Charles I; its maturity in the period from the revolution of 1688 to the invasion of the Pretender in 1745; its decay in the close of the reign of George II, and the early part of that of George III.[2]

This long period was marked by those great events in intellectual and social history which were calculated

[1] See above p. 11.

[2] This computation regards lord Herbert of Cherbury as marking the commencement, and Hume the close; the doubters of the latter half of the eighteenth century, such as Gibbon, being excluded, because their writings are marked by the forms of French unbelief.

to awaken the spirit of free inquiry. It witnessed the dethronement of constituted authorities—intellectual, ecclesiastical, and political; the constant struggle of religious factions; and on two occasions civil war and revolution. It was affected by the rise of the philosophy of Bacon, and the positive advances of natural science under Newton and his coadjutors. It comprehended moments marked by the outburst of native genius, and others influenced by contact with the continental literature, both with the speculative theology of Holland and the dramatic and critical literature of France.[3] Above all it was illumined by the presence of such an array of great minds in all departments of intellectual activity as can rarely be matched in a single period. If, when the human mind in the middle ages was warmed into life after the winter of its long torpor, under the genial influence of the revival of literature, the renewal of its power was marked by a disposition to throw off the trammels which had bound it in the night of its darkness, how much more might such a result be expected when it was basking under the sunshine of meridian brightness, and exulting in the consciousness of strength.

A special peculiarity of this period likely to produce effects on religion has been already mentioned. The philosophy of this age compared with former ones was essentially a discussion of method. The two rival philosophies which now arose are generally placed in opposition to each other, as physical and mental respectively, that of Bacon being conversant with nature, that of Descartes with man.[4] But in truth in one respect both were united. Each was analytical; each strove to lay down a general method for investigating the sphere of inquiry which it selected. Both were reactions against

[3] The former in the struggle of Arminians and Calvinists in the Puritan controversy; the latter in the revolution supposed to be caused in our literature by the influence of Dryden.

[4] In addition to the references given in Lect. III. (p. 106) see Cousin's *Hist. de la Phil. au* 18e *siècle* (Leçon 3); and Remusat's *Essai sur Bacon*, 1857; but especially the sketch of the relation of Bacon's philosophy to religion in K. Fischer's monograph on Bacon. (c. x. and xi.)

the dogmatic assumptions of former systems; both assumed the indispensable necessity of an entire revolution in the method of attaining knowledge. Accordingly, though differing widely in appealing to the external senses or the internal intuitions respectively, they both built philosophy in the criticism of first principles. Hence, independently of any particular corollaries from special parts of their systems, the influence of their spirit was to beget a critical, subjective, and analytical study of any topic. When applied to religion, this is the feature which subsequently characterizes alike the unbelief and the discussion of the evidences. Difficulties and the answers to difficulties are found in an appeal to the functions and capacities of the interpreting mind. This appeal to reason was denominated rationalism in the seventeenth century, prior to the present application of the term in a more limited and obnoxious sense. The specific doctrine arrived at by this process, which allows the existence of a Deity, and of the religion of the moral conscience, but denies the specific revelation which Christianity asserts, was called *theism* or *deism*. (21)

In the period which we have mentioned as marking the first stage of deism, extending from its commencement to the close of the seventeenth century, the peculiarity which characterized the inquiry was the political aspect which it bore. The relation of religion to political toleration[5] gave occasion for examining the sphere of truth which may form the subject of political interference.

Two writers of opposite schools are usually regarded as marking the rise of deism, both of whom belonged to this phase of it, Lord Herbert of Cherbury, and Hobbes. Both formed their systems in the reign of Charles I.[6] The one rejected revelation by making religion a matter

[5] This inquiry was called forth in the disputes of the established church against popery and puritanism, and led to works in favour of toleration by Chillingworth, Bp. Jeremy Taylor (*Liberty of Prophesying*), and later by Milton; and towards the close of the century by Locke.

[6] Hobbes's *Leviathan* was not published till 1651; but the thoughts were evidently suggested by the woes of the reign of Charles I.

of individual intuition, the other by making it a matter of political convenience.

Lord Herbert,[7] the elder brother of the saintly poet, if looked at as a philosopher, must be classed with Descartes rather than with Bacon, though chronology forbids the idea that he can have learned anything from Descartes. It is probable that while on his early embassy in France he came under the same intellectual influences which suggested to Descartes his views. Fragments of knowledge and partial solutions derived from older philosophies exist before a great thinker like Descartes embodies them in a system. Herbert may have been led by the indirect effect of such influences to a theory of innate ideas, independently of Descartes; or he may have arrived at it by reaction against the Pyrrhonism of some of the French writers of the preceding age, such as Montaigne, with whose writings he was familiar.

His works furnish his views on knowledge and on religion, both natural, heathen, and Christian. They include a treatise on truth, which suggested another on the cause of errors. The views on religion therein named, further suggested one on the religion which could be expected in a layman, and this again a critique on heathen creeds, written to show the universality of the beliefs so described.[8]

In discussing truth[9] he surveys the powers of the human mind, and places the ultimate test of it in the natural instincts or axiomatic beliefs. These accord-

[7] Herbert (1581–1648). His works were, *De Veritate*, 1624, *De Causis Errorum*, 1645, *De Religione Laici*, *De Religione Gentilium*, 1663. An autobiography was published in 1764. He was answered by Locke (*Reason. of Christianity*), Baxter, Halyburton, Leland (*Deists*, lett. 1 and 2), and Kortholt; and his philosophy was attacked by Gassendi. On Herbert see Ritter's *Christliche Philosophie*, vi. 390 seq.; Tennemann's *Gesch.* x. 113 seq.; Eichhorn's *Gesch. der Lit.* 6, 95 seq.; Hallam's *History of Literature*, ii. 380 seq.; and Lechler's *Geschichte des Englischen Deismus*, p. 36–54; Remusat in *Rev. des Deux Mondes*, 1854, vol. iii. His views in some respects seem to have resembled those of Pecock or Sebonde.

[8] In its mode of treatment it has been compared to Bacon's *Wisdom of the Ancients*.

[9] In the *De Veritate*.

ingly become the test of a religion. The true religion must therefore be a universal one; that is, one of which the evidence commends itself to the universal mind of man, and finds its attestation in truth intuitively perceived. Of such truths he enumerates five:[10]—the existence of one supreme God; the duty of worship; piety and virtue as the means thereof; the efficacy of repentance; the existence of rewards and punishments both here and hereafter. These he regards as the fundamental pillars of universal religion; and distinguishes from these realities the doctrines of what he calls particular religions, one of which is Christianity, as being uncertain, because not self-evident; and accordingly considers that no assent can be expected in a layman, save to the above-named self-evident truths. His view however of revelation is not very clear. Sometimes he seems to admit it, sometimes proscribes it as uncertain. His object seems not to have been primarily destructive, but merely the result of attempts to discover truth amid the jarring opinions of the churches of his day.[11]

The ideas which his writings contributed to deist speculation are two; viz., the examination of the universal principles of religion, and the appeal to an internal illuminating influence superior to revelation, "the inward light," as the test of religious truth. This was a phrase not uncommon in the seventeenth century. It was used by the Puritans to mark the appeal to the spiritual instincts, the heaven-taught feelings; and later by mystics, like the founder of the Quakers, to imply an appeal to an internal sense.[12] But in Herbert it differs from these in being universal, not restricted to a few persons, and in being intellectual rather than emotional or spiritual. It was not analysed so as to separate intuitional from reflective elements, and seems to

[10] *De Relig. Gentil.*, 15. 199. App. to Relig. Laici, 2, 3.

[11] There is a curious record in his journal (*Autobiography*, p. 171–3) of an earnest prayer for guidance on the subject of the publication of his first book *De Veritate*, which he no doubt saw was opposed to popular belief.

[12] Lechler, *Geschichte des E. D.* p. 64.

have been analogous to Descartes' ultimate appeal to the natural reason, the self-evidencing force of the mental axioms.[13]

If it was the anxiety to find certainty in controversies concerning theological dogmas, which suggested Herbert's inquiries, it was the struggle of ecclesiastical parties in connexion with political movements which excited those of Hobbes.[14]

In his philosophical views he belonged to an opposite school to Herbert. A disciple of Bacon, he was the first to apply his master's method to morals, and to place the basis of ethical and political obligation in experience; and in the application of these philosophical principles to religion, he also represented the contrary tendency to Herbert, state interference in contradistinction from private liberty, political religion as opposed to personal. The contest of individualism against multitudinism is the parallel in politics to that of private judgment against authority in religion. While some of the Puritans were urging unlimited license in the matter of religion, Hobbes wrote to prove the necessity of state control, and the importance of a fulcrum on which individual opinion might repose, external to itself; and referring the development of socie-

[13] Because they bear, as he thought, the great test of being self-evident. It will be remembered that the *clearness* of an idea was the test of the innate character of it in Descartes' system (*Principia Philosophiæ*, § 10). Such ideas are those which would be regarded in Kant's system as necessary forms of thinking, and in Cousin's as belonging to the impersonal reason.

[14] Hobbes (1588–1679). The *Leviathan* is a philosophy of society, studied as the development of the individual. He first treats of the individual, book i.; then the commonwealth, book ii.; then the Christian commonwealth, book iii.; and the kingdom of error, book iv.; borrowing the idea from Augustin's *De Civ. Dei.* The brevity of the notice in the text prevents the possibility of doing justice to the grandeur and to the good sense shown in many respects in Hobbes's works. He was answered by Cudworth (*Intellectual System*); Cumberland (*De Leg. Nat.*); Dr. Seth Ward; Bramhall, (1658); Archbp. Tenison, 1760; and Lord Clarendon, in his *Survey of Leviathan* (1676). For an explanation and criticism on his philosophical principles, see Ritter, ch. vi. 453 seq.; Tennemann, b. x. 53 seq.; Lewes' *History of Philosophy;* Morell's Id.; Hallam, b. ii. 463 seq.; and on his religious opinions, Leland (ch. iii.), and Lechler (p. 67–107).

ty to the necessity for restraining the natural selfishness of man, and resolving right into expedience as embodied in the sovereign head, he ended with crushing the rights of the individual spirit, and defending absolute government.

The effect of the application of such a sensational and materialist theory to religion will be anticipated. He traced[15] the genesis of it in the individual, and its expression in society; finding the origin of it in selfish fear of the supernatural. The same reason which led him to assign supremacy to government in other departments induced him to give it supreme control over religion. Society being the check on man's selfishness, and supreme, deciding all questions on grounds of general expedience; the authority of the commonwealth became the authority of the church.[16] Though he had occasion to discuss revelation and the canon[17] as a rule of faith, yet it is hard to fix on any point that was actual unbelief.

The amount of thought contributed by him to deism was small; for his influence on his successors was unimportant. The religious instincts of the heart were too strong to be permanently influenced by the cold materialist tone which reduced religion to state craft. With the exception of Coward,[18] a materialist who doubted immortality about the end of the century, the succeeding deists more generally followed Herbert, in wishing to elevate religion to a spiritual sphere, than Hobbes, who degraded it to political expedience. A slight additional interest however belongs to his speculations, from the circumstance that his ideas, together with

[15] Part i. c. 12.

[16] Part iii. c. 39.

[17] Part iii. c. 33.

[18] Coward (1657–1724 *circ.*) was a physician, who wrote in 1702 *Second Thoughts on Human Souls*, apparently intended to disprove the existence of spirit and natural immortality, but not of immortality itself as a divine gift from God to man, though opponents disbelieved him in this assertion. The list of answers written is given in Chalmers's *Biographical Dictionary* under *Coward.* The house of commons in 1704 condemned the book, and caused it to be burned.

those of Herbert, most probably suggested some parts of the system of Spinoza.[19]

The two writers of whom we have now been treating, lived prior to or during the Commonwealth. From the date of the Restoration the existence of doubt may be accepted as an established fact. During the reaction, political and ecclesiastical, which ensued in the early part of the reign of Charles II, it is not surprising that doubt concealed itself in retirement; but the frequent allusions to it under the name of atheism,[20] in contemporary sermons and theological books, proves its existence. Indeed the reaction contained the very elements which were likely to foster unbelief among undiscerning minds. The court set a sad example of impurity; and the excessive claims of the churchmen, alien to the spirit of political and religious liberty, were calculated to generate an antipathy to the clergy and to religion.

Toward the end of Charles's reign, a feeling of this kind expresses itself in the writings of Charles Blount,[21] who availed himself of the temporary interval in which the press became free, owing to the omission to renew the act which submitted works to the censor,[22] to publish with notes a translation of Philostratus's Life of Apollonius of Tyana, with the same purpose as Hierocles in the fourth century, to disguise the peculiar character of Christ's miracles, and draw an invidious parallel between the Pythagorean philosopher and the divine founder of Christianity. Subsequently to Blount's death, his friend Gildon, who lived to retract his opinions,[23] published a collection of treatises, entitled

[19] Spinoza's view of religion is the part suggested by Herbert, and his view of the relation of the state to religion that suggested by Hobbes.

[20] See Note 21 (p. 413).

[21] C. Blount (1654–93) wrote the *Anima Mundi*, 1679; *Life of Apollonius Tyana*, 1680; *Oracles of Reason*, 1695. (See Macaulay, *History of England*, vol. iv. 352.) He was refuted by Nichols (1723) *Conference with a Theist*. See Lechler (114–124), and Leland, ch. iv.

[22] The Licensing Act of 1662 concerning the press was allowed to expire in 1679. When James II. came to the throne (1685) the censorship was renewed for seven years; and again in 1693 was revived for two years, at which time it finally expired. See *North British Review*, No. 60, (May 1859.)

[23] As proved by his work in 1705, *The Deist's Manual*.

"The Oracles of Reason;" a work which may be considered as expressing the opinions of a little band of unbelievers, of whom Blount was one.[24] The mention of two of the papers in it will explain the views intended. One is on natural religion,[25] in which the ideas of Herbert are reproduced, and exception is taken to revelation as partial and not self-evident, and therefore uncertain; and the objections to the sufficiency and potency of natural religion are refuted. A second is on the deist's religion,[26] in which the deist creed is explained to be the belief in a God who is to be worshipped, not by sacrifice, nor by mediation, but by piety. Punishment in a future world is denied as incompatible with Divine benevolence; and the safety of the deist creed is supported by showing that a moral life is superior to belief in mysteries. It will be seen from these remarks that Blount hardly makes an advance on his deist predecessor Herbert, save that his view is more positive, and his antipathy to Christian worship less concealed.

At the close of the seventeenth century two new influences were in operation, the one political, the other intellectual; viz., the civil and religious liberty which ensued on the revolution, generating free speculation, and compelling each man to form his political creed; and the reconsideration of the first principles of knowledge[27] implied in the philosophy of Locke.[28]

[24] The *Oracles of Reason* (1693) consists of sixteen papers in several letters to Mr. Hobbes and others, by Ch. Blount, Gildon, and others. Papers (No. 1–4) are a defence of T. Burnet's archæology, or on subjects cognate to it. No. 5 is concerning the deist's religion; 6 on immortality; 7 on Arians, Trinitarians, and Councils; 8 that felicity is pleasure; 9 of fate and fortune; 10 of the original of the Jews; 11 of the lawfulness of marrying two sisters successively; 12 of the subversion of Judaism, and the origin of the Millennium; 13 of the auguries of the ancients; 14 of natural religion; 15 that the soul is matter; 16 that the world is eternal.

[25] No. 14. [26] No. 5.

[27] Attention had been called a little earlier to the consideration of the first principles of religion, by the Platonizing Cambridge party of More and Cudworth, followers partly of Descartes. See Burnet's *Mem. of his Times*, i. 187; and the Rev. A. Taylor's able introduction to the edition of *Simon Patrick's Works*, Oxford 1858, (p. 28–42).

[28] On Locke's philosophy see Ritter *Chr. Phil.* vii. 449–534; Cousin's

The effect of these new influences on religion is very marked. Controversies no longer turned upon questions in which the appeal lay to the common ground of scripture, as in the contest which Churchmen had conducted against Puritans or Romanists, but extended to the examination of the first principles of ethics or politics; such as the foundation of government, whether it depends on hereditary right or on compact, as in the controversy against the nonjurors[29] before the close of the century; or the spiritual rights of the church, and the right of every man to religious liberty and private judgment in religion, as in the Convocation and Bangorian[30] controversy, which marked the early years of the next century. The very diminution also of quotations of authorities is a pertinent illustration that the appeal was now being made to deeper standards.

The philosophy of Locke, which attempted to lay a basis for knowledge in psychology, coincided with, where it did not create, this general attempt to appeal on every subject to ultimate principles of reason. This tone in truth marked the age, and acting in every region of thought, affected alike the orthodox and the unbelieving. Accordingly, as we pass away from the speculations which mark the early period of deism to those which belong to its maturity, we find that the attack on Christianity is less suggested by political considerations, and more entirely depends on an appeal to reason, intellectual or moral.

The principal phases belonging to this period of the maturity of deism, which we shall now successively encounter, are four:

Hist. de Philos. au 18e *siècle*, ch. 15–25; Morell's *Hist. of Phil.*, vol. i. p. 100 seq.; Lewes *Id.*; Lechler, 154–179. His work the *Reasonableness of Christianity* typified the tone of the writers on the Christian evidences for the next half century.

[29] For this and the next named controversy, see Lathbury's *Non-Jurors* (1845), ch. iv., and *History of Convocation*, ch. 12–14.

[30] On the Bangorian controversy (1717, 18), see Hallam's *Constitutional History* (vol. ii. 408). A list of the pamphlets which were written during the controversy was made by the antiquarian Thomas Hearne, and is printed in Hoadley's works (3 vols. fol. 1773). See vol. ii. 381, and the continuation in vol. i. 689.

(1) An examination of the first principles of religion, on its dogmatic or theological side, with a view of asserting the supremacy of reason to interpret all mysteries, and defending absolute toleration of free thought. This tendency is seen in Toland and Collins,

(2) An examination of religion on the ethical side occurs, with the object of asserting the supremacy of natural ethics as a rule of conduct, and denying the motive of reward or punishment implied in dependent morality. This is seen in Lord Shaftesbury.

After the attack has thus been opened against revealed religion, by creating prepossessions against mystery in dogma and the existence of religious motives in morals, there follows a direct approach against the outworks of it by an attack on the evidences,

(3) In an examination, critical rather than philosophical, of the prophecies of the Old Testament by Collins, and of the miracles of the New by Woolston.

The deist next approaches as it were within the fortress, and advances against the doctrines of revealed religion; and we find accordingly,

(4) A general view of natural religion, in which the various differences,—speculative, moral, and critical, are combined, as in Tindal; or with a more especial reference to the Old Testament as in Morgan, and the New as in Chubb; the aim of each being constructive as well as destructive; to point out the absolute sufficiency of natural religion and of the moral sense as religious guides, and the impossibility of accepting as obligatory that which adds to or contradicts them; and accordingly they point out the elements in Christianity which they consider can be retained as absolutely true.

The first two of these attacks occur in the first two decades of the century: the two latter in the period from 1720 to 1740, when the public mind not being diverted by foreign war or internal sedition, and other controversies being closed, the deist controversy was at its height. After examining these, other tendencies will meet us, when we trace the decline of deism in Bolingbroke and Hume.

The first of these tendencies just noticed is seen in Toland,[31] who directed his speculations to the ground principles of revealed theology,[32] and slightly to the history of the Canon.[33]

Possessing much originality and learning, at an early age, in 1696, just a year after the censorship had been finally removed and the press of England made permanently free, he published his noted work, "Christianity not Mysterious," to show that "there is nothing in the Gospels contrary to reason, nor above it; and that no Christian doctrine can properly be called a mystery." The speculations of all doubters first originate in some crisis of personal or mental history. In Toland's case it was probably the change of religion from catholic to protestant which first unsettled his religious faith. The work just named, in which he expressed the attempt to bring religious truth under the grasp of the intellect, was one of some merit as a literary production, and written with that clearness which the influence of the French models studied by Dryden had introduced into English literature. Yet it is difficult to understand why a single work of an unknown student should attract so much public notice. The grand jury of Middlesex was induced at once to present it as a nuisance, and the example was followed by the grand jury of Dublin.[34] Two years after its publication the Irish parliament

[31] Toland (1669–1722). He was born an Irish catholic, turned protestant, wrote his first deist book, 1696; fled for refuge to the court of Hanover, and found protection there; wrote political pamphlets, and lived abroad till near the close of his life. His chief theological writings are, *Christianity not Mysterious*, 1696; *Amyntor*, or Defence of the Life of Milton, 1699 (on the Canon); *Nazarenus*, 1718; *Tetradymus*, 1720; *Pantheisticon*, 1720, sive formula celebrandæ sodalitatis Socraticæ, 1720, a parody on the Christian service books. These are collected in his *Miscellaneous Works* (1726). (Vol. i. contains his translation of the *Spaccio* of Bruno.) He was answered by John Norris, Archbp. Synge, and Dr. Peter Browne; by S. Clarke, and by Jones in his work on the Canon. Consult Leland's *View of Deistical Writers*, Lett. iv.; Lechler (180–210), and (463–73), and note on p. 193.

[32] In his *Christianity not Mysterious.*

[33] In his *Amyntor.*

[34] For these facts see the Memoir of Toland prefixed to his *Miscellaneous Works*, and also Chalmers's *Biographical Dictionary.*

deliberated upon it, and, refusing to hear Toland in defence, passed sentence that the book should be burnt, and its author imprisoned—a fate which he escaped only by flight.[35] And in 1701, no less than five years after the publication of his work, a vote for its prosecution passed the lower house of the English convocation, which the legal advisers however denied to be within the power of that assembly.[36] Toland spent most of the remainder of his life abroad, and showed in his subsequent works a character growing gradually worse, lashed into bitterer opposition by the censure which he had received.

His views, developed in his work, *Christianity not Mysterious*, require fuller statement. He opens with an explanation of the province of reason,[37] the means of information, external and internal, which man possesses; a part of his work which is valuable to the philosopher, who watches the influence exercised at that time by psychological speculations; and he proposes to show that the doctrines of the gospel are neither contrary to reason nor above it. He exhibits the impossibility of believing statements which positively contradict reason;[38] and contends that if they do not really contradict it, but are above it, we can form no intelligible idea of them. He tries further to show that reason is neither so weak nor so corrupt as to be an unsafe guide,[39] and that scripture itself only professes to teach what is intelligible.[40] Having shown that the doctrines of the gospel are not contrary to reason, he next proceeds to show that they do not profess to be above it; that they lay claim to no mystery,[41] for that mystery in heathen

[35] This opposition increased Toland's bitterness, for, in the following year, 1698, in publishing a Life of Milton, and taking occasion to disprove that Charles I was the author of the Ikon Basilike, he threw out hints of similar forgeries in works attributed to the apostles. The hatred of churchmen was further increased by this work.

[36] See Wilkins's *Concilia*, vol. iv. 631; Burnet's *History of his own Times*, vol. iv. 521; Lathbury's *History of Convocation* (1842), p. 288 seq.

[37] Sect. I.

[38] Sect. ii. ch. 1. [39] Id. ch. 4. [40] Ch. 1, 2.

[41] Sect. iii. ch. 2.

writers and the New Testament does not mean something inconceivable, but something intelligible in itself, which nevertheless was so veiled that it needed revealing;[42] and that the introduction of the popular idea of mystery was attributable to the analogy of pagan writers, and did not occur till several centuries after the foundation of Christianity.[43]

It is possible that the book may have been a mere paradox,[44] the effort of a young mind going through the process through which all young men of thought pass, and especially in an age like Toland's, of trying to understand and explain what they believe. But students who are thus forming their views ought to pause before they scatter their half-formed opinions in the world. In Toland's case public alarm judged the book to have a most dangerous tendency; and he was an outcast from the sympathy of pious men for ever. If he was misunderstood, as he contended, his fate is a warning against the premature publication of a paradox. The question accordingly which Toland thus suggested for discussion was the prerogative of reason to pronounce on the contents of a revelation, the problem whether the mind must comprehend as well as apprehend all that it believes. The other question which he opened was the validity of the canon.[45] Here too he claimed that his views were misunderstood. It was supposed that the mention made by him concerning spurious works attributed to the apostles, referred to the canonical gospels. Accordingly, if in his former work he has been considered to have anticipated the older school of Ger-

[42] Ch. 3. [43] Ch. 5.

[44] Cfr. his *Apology for Christianity not Mysterious* 1697, and also a letter from Mr. Molyneux to Locke (Locke's Works, ed. 1723, vol. iii. p. 566), quoted in the memoir (p. 17) prefixed to Toland's *Miscellaneous Works.*

[45] In his Life of Milton (1698) pp. 91, 92, he had alluded to works falsely attributed to Christ and the apostles. This was attacked by Blackhall as if intended against the canonical scriptures, and was defended by Toland by the publication of the *Amyntor*, a catalogue of books mentioned by the fathers as truly or falsely ascribed to Jesus Christ, his apostles, &c. The learned Pfaff calls it "insignem Catalogum" (*Diss. Crit. Nov. Test.* ch. i. § 2).

man rationalists, in the present he has been thought to have touched upon the questions discussed in the modern critical school. The controversy which ensued was the means of opening up the discussion of the great question which relates to the New Testament canon, viz., whether our present New Testament books are a selection made in the second century from among early Christian writings, or whether the church from the first regarded them as distinct in kind and not merely in degree from other literature; whether the early respect shown for scripture was reverence directed to apostolic men, or to their inspired teaching.

If Toland is the type of free speculation applied to the theoretical side of religion, lord Shaftesbury[46] is an example of speculations on the practical side of it, and on the questions which come under the province of ethics.

The rise of an ethical school parallel with discussions on the philosophy of religion is one of the most interesting features of that age, whether it be regarded in a scientific or a religious point of view. The age was one in which the reflective reason or understanding was busy in exploring the origin of all knowledge. The department of moral and spiritual truth could not long remain unexamined. In an earlier age the sources of our knowledge concerning the divine attributes and human duty had been supposed to depend upon revelation; but now the disposition to criticise every subject by the light of common sense claimed that philosophy must investigate them. Reason was to work out the system of natural theology, and ethics the problem of the nature and ground of virtue. Hence it will be obvious how close a relation existed between such speculations and theology. The Christian apologist availed himself of the new ethical inquiries as a corroboration of revealed religion; the Deist, as a substitute for it.

[46] A Memoir of Lord Shaftesbury (1671–1713), has been lately published (1860). His chief work was the *Characteristics*. On his religious views see Leland ch. 5 and 6; Lechler 243–265; and on his philosophical views, see Ritter vii. 535 seq.; Eichhorn, *Geschichte der Literatur*, vi. 424 seq.

Lord Shaftesbury is usually adduced as a deist of this class. He has not indeed expressed it definitely in his writings; and an ethical system which formed the basis of Butler's sermons,[47] cannot necessarily be charged with deism. But the charge can be substantiated from his memoirs; and his writings manifest that hatred of clerical influence, the wish to subject the church to the state, which will by some persons be regarded as unbelief, but which was not perhaps altogether surprising in an age when the clergy were almost universally alien to the revolution, and the Convocation manifested opposition to political and religious liberty. The ground on which the charge is generally founded is, that Shaftesbury has cast reflections on the doctrine of future rewards and punishments.[48] It is to be feared that sceptical insinuations were intended; yet his remarks admit of some explanation as a result of his particular point of view.

The ethical schools of his day were already two; the one advocating dependent, the other independent morality; the one grounding obligation on self-love, the other on natural right. Shaftesbury, though a disciple of Locke, belonged to the latter school. His works mark the moment when this ethical school was passing from the objective inquiry into the immutability of right, as seen in Clarke, to the subjective inquiry into the reflex sense which constitutes our obligation to do what is right, as seen in Butler. The depreciation accordingly of the motives of reward, as distinct from the supreme motive of loving duty for duty's sake, was to be expected in his system. The motives of reward and punishment which form the sanctions of religious obligation, would seem to him to be analogous to the employment of expedience as the foundation of moral. His statements however appear to be an exaggeration even in an ethical view, as well as calculated to insinu-

[47] On his moral system, see Mackintosh's *Dissertation on Ethics*, p. 158–166; and on Butler's ethical system, and its relation to Shaftesbury, see the same work, p. 171 seq.

[48] *Works*, vol. ii. *Inquiry concerning Virtue. Charact.* ii. 272 etc.

ate erroneous ideas in a theological. It is possible that his motive was not polemical; but the unchristian character of his tone renders the hypothesis improbable, and explains the reason why his essays called the "Characteristics" have been ranked among deist writings.

We have seen, in Toland and Shaftesbury respectively, a discussion on the metaphysical and ethical basis of religion, together with a few traces of the rise of criticism in reference to the canon. In their successors the inquiry becomes less psychological and more critical, and therefore less elevated by the abstract nature of the speculative above the struggle of theological polemic.

Two branches of criticism were at this time commencing, which were destined to suggest difficulties alike to the deist and to the Christian; the one the discovery of variety of readings in the sacred text, the other the doubts thrown upon the genuineness and authenticity of the books. It was the large collection of various readings on the New Testament, first begun by Mills,[49] which gave the impulse to the former, which has been called the lower criticism, and which so distressed the mind of Bengel, that he spent his life in allaying the alarm of those who like himself felt alarmed at its effect on the question of verbal inspiration. And it was the disproof of the genuineness of the Epistles of Phalaris by the learned Bentley,[50] which first threw solid doubts on the value attaching to traditional titles of books, and showed the irrefragable character belonging to an appeal to internal evidence; a department which has been called the higher criticism. This latter branch, so abundantly developed in German specula-

[49] The readings of the text had been disturbed by Courcelles (1658), and by Walton in his Polyglot, which caused an alarm, on which see Hody (*De Bibl. Text.* 563 seq.), but not widely till Mills, 1707. Mills' readings were attacked by Whitby in 1710, and the arguments of the latter were afterwards turned by Collins against Revelation.

[50] In 1699. Daillé's criticism on the Ignatian Epistles (1666) had shown similar sagacity to that afterwards displayed by Bentley, and bore to his inquiries the same relation which those just named in the text bore to those of Mills.

tion, is only hinted at by the English deists of the eighteenth age, as by Hobbes and Spinoza earlier; but we shall soon see the use which Collins and others made of the former inquiry.

The form, though not the spirit, of Toland and Shaftesbury, might by a latitude of interpretation be made compatible with Christianity; but Collins and Woolston, of whom we next treat, mark a much further advance of free thought. They attack what has always been justly considered to be an integral portion of Christianity, the relation which it bore to Jewish prophecy, and the miracles which were wrought for its establishment.

Collins[51] must be studied under more than one aspect. He not only wrote on the logic of religion, the method of inquiry in theology, but also on the subject of scripture interpretation, and the reality of prophecy.[52]

It was in 1713 that he published "A discourse of free-thinking, occasioned by the rise and growth of a sect called Free-thinkers." This is one of the first times that we find this new name used for Deists; and the object of his book is to defend the propriety of unlimited liberty of inquiry, a proposition by which he designed the unrestrained liberty of belief, not in a political point of view merely, but in a moral. His argument was not unlike more modern ones,[53] which show that civilization and improvement have been caused by free-thinking; and he adduces the growing disbelief in the reality of witchcraft, in proof of the way in which the rejection of dogma had ameliorated politi-

[51] Collins (1676–1729). His works were on *Immortality* (1707, 8) in the Dodwell controversy; *Freethinking*, 1713, refuted entirely by Bentley in the *Phileleutherus Lipsiensis.* (See also Dr. Ibbot's Boyle Lectures, 1713, where the general subject is treated.) On *Necessity*, 1715. The *Grounds of the Christian Religion*, 1724 (occasioned by Whiston's work on Prophecy); answered by bishop Chandler, Samuel Chandler, T. Sherlock, and Moses Lowman; *Scheme of Literal Prophecy*, 1727, in answer to Chandler. See Leland, ch. vii., and Lechler, 217–240. Henke's *Kirchengeschichte*, vi. s. 29.

[52] In the two works named below in the text.

[53] E. g. that of Buckle in *History of Civilization.*

cal science, which until recently had visited the supposed crime with the punishment of death.[54] After thus showing the duty of free-thinking,[55] he argued that the sphere of it ought to comprehend points on which the right is usually denied; such as the divine attributes, the truth of the scriptures, and their meaning;[56] establishing this by laying a number of charges against priests, to show that their dogmatic teaching cannot be trusted, unchallenged by free inquiry, on account of their discrepant[57] opinions, their rendering the canon and text of scripture uncertain,[58] and their pious frauds;[59] concluding by refuting objections against free-thinking derived from its supposed want of safety.[60]

The book met with intelligent and able opponents; the critical part, containing the allegations of uncertainty in the text of scripture, and the charge of altering it, being effectually refuted by Bentley. The work is an exaggeration of a great truth. Undoubtedly free inquiry is right in all departments, but it must be restrained within the proper limits which the particular subject-matter admits of;—limits which are determined partly by the nature of the subject studied, partly by the laws of the thinking mind.

Eleven years afterwards, in 1724, Collins published his "Discourse of the Grounds and Reasons of the Christian religion." This work is chiefly critical. It does not merely contain the incipient doubts on the variety of readings, and the uncertainty of books, but spreads over several provinces of theological inquiry. Under the pretence of establishing Christianity on a more solid foundation, the author argues that our Saviour and his apostles made the whole proof of Christianity to rest solely on the prophecies of the Old Testament;[61] that if these proofs are valid, Christianity is established; if invalid, it is false.[62] Accordingly he examines several of the prophecies cited from the Old

[54] P. 71. [55] P. 5–27. [56] P. 32, &c.
[57] P. 56. [58] P. 86. [59] P. 92.
[60] P. 100, &c.
[61] Part i. § 1–5 [62] Id. § 6, 7.

Testament in the New in favour of the Messiahship of Christ, with a view of showing that they are only allegorical or fanciful proofs, accommodations of the meaning of the prophecies; and anticipates the objections which could be stated to his views.[63] He asserts that the expectation of a Messiah among[64] the Jews arose only a short time before Christ's coming;[65] and that the apostles put a new interpretation on the Hebrew books, which was contrary to the sense accepted by the Jewish nation; that Christianity is not revealed in the Old Testament literally, but mystically and allegorically, and may therefore be considered as mystical Judaism. His inference is accordingly stated as an argument in favour of the figurative or mystical interpretation of scripture; but we can hardly doubt that his real object was an ironical one, to exhibit Christianity as resting on apostolic misinterpretations of Jewish prophecy, and thus to create the impression that it was a mere Jewish sect of men deceived by fanciful interpretations.

The work produced considerable alarm; more from the solemn interest and sacredness of the inquiries which it opened, than from any danger arising from excellence in its form, or ability in the mode of putting. It anticipated subsequent speculations,[66] by regarding Christianity as true ideally, not historically, and by insinuating the incorrectness of the apostolic adoption of the mystical system of interpreting the ancient scripture.

A writer came forward as moderator[67] between Collins and his opponents, who himself afterwards became

[63] Id. 11. [64] Id. (8–10.)

[65] Two other writers, Mandeville and Lyons, have been omitted; Mandeville (*Fables of the Bees*, 1723), because his speculations did not bear directly on religion; Lyons, because his work is not important. In 1723 he published *the Infallibility of Human Judgment*, in which he analysed the mind, and applied the results of his analysis to the first principles of natural religion, and to discredit the evidences and doctrines of revealed. It bears more resemblance to Toland and Chubb than to any other writers, but is a feeble work, interesting only as showing the prevalence of psychological inquiries, and the tendency to examine psychologically the subject of religion.

[66] E. g. Some of those in Germany, see Lect. VI and VII.

[67] In the *Moderator*, or *controversy between the author of the Grounds, &c. and his reverend opponents*, 1727. (Woolston's Works, vol. v.)

still more noted, by directing an attack on miracles, similar to that of Collins on prophecy;—the unhappy Woolston.[68] A fellow of a college[69] at Cambridge, in holy orders, he was for many years a diligent student of the fathers, and imbibed from them an extravagant attachment to the allegorical sense of scripture. Finding that his views met with no support in that reasoning age, he broke out into unmeasured insult and contempt against his brother clergy, as slaves to the letter of scripture.[70] Deprived of his fellowship,[71] and distracted by penury, he extended his hatred from the ministers to the religion which they ministered. And when, in reply to Collins's assertion, that Christianity reposed solely on prophecy, the Christian apologists fell back on miracles, he wrote in 1727 and the two following years his celebrated *Discourses on the Miracles.* (22) They were published as pamphlets; in each one of which he examined a few of the miracles of Christ, trying to show such inconsistencies as to make it appear that they must be regarded as untrustworthy if taken literally; and hence he advocated a figurative interpretation of them; asserting that the history of the life of Jesus is an emblematical representation of his spiritual life in the soul of man.[72] The gospels thus become a system of mystical theology, instead of a literal history. In defence of this method he claimed the example of the ancient church,[73] ignoring the fact that the fathers admitted a literal as well as a figurative meaning. Whether he really retained towards the close of his life the spiritual interpretation,[74] or merely

[68] Woolston, 1669–1733. His works are collected in five volumes, with a life prefixed. His pamphlets on Miracles were refuted by bishops Pierce, 1729, Gibson, and Smabroke, by Lardner, and by Sherlock in the Trial of the Witnesses. On Woolston, see Leland (Let. 8), Lechler (289–311), Henke, vi. 49.

[69] Sydney Sussex.

[70] A *Free Gift to the Clergy, or the Hireling Priests challenged*, 1722, (*Works*, vol. iii.).

[71] See Memoir prefixed to his Works, pp. 5 and 22.

[72] In Discourse iii.

[73] Disc. i. Div. I.

[74] Strauss (*Leb. Jes.* Introd. § 6) thinks that his bitterness manifests that he did not.

used it as an excuse for a more secure advance to the assault of the historic reality of scripture, is very uncertain.

The letters were written with a coarseness and irreverence so singular, even in the attacks of that age, that it were well if they could be attributed to insanity. They contain the most undisguised abuse which had been uttered against Christianity since the days of the early heathens. Occasionally, when wishing to utter grosser blasphemies than were permissible by law, or compatible with his assumed Christian stand-point, he introduced a Jewish rabbi, as Celsus had formerly done, and put the coarser calumnies into his mouth,[75] as difficulties to which no reply could be furnished except by figurative interpretation. The humour which marked these pamphlets was so great, that the sale of them was immense. Voltaire, who was in England at the time, and perhaps imbibed thence part of his own opinions, states the immediate sale to have exceeded thirty thousand copies;[76] and Swift describes them as the food of every politician.[77] The excitement was so great, that Gibson, then bishop of London, thought it necessary to direct five pastorals to his diocese in reference to them,[78] and, not content with this, caused Woolston to be prosecuted; and the unhappy man, not able to pay the fine in which he was condemned, continued in prison till his death.[79]

In classifying Woolston with later writers against miracles, he may be compared in some cases, though with striking differences of tone, with those German rationalists like Paulus who have rationalized the miracles, but in more cases with those who like Strauss have idealized them. His method however is an appeal to general probability rather than to literary criticism.

[75] Disc. iv. and *Defence*, sect. i.

[76] Voltaire, *Œuvres Crit.* vol. xlvii. pp. 346–356.

[7] Swift's Poem on his Death, *Works*, vol. xiv. p. 359.

[78] The latest Pastorals of Gibson are not only against Woolston, but other deists also, such as Tindal.

[79] His friends would have found money for the fine; but Woolston could not find securities for his good behaviour if released.

The next form that Deism assumed has reference more to the internal than the external part of Christianity, the doctrines rather than the evidences. Less critical than the last-named tendency, it differs from the earlier one of Toland in looking at religion less on the speculative side as a revelation of dogma, and more on the practical as a revelation of duties. While it combined into a system the former objections, critical or philosophical, the great weapon which it uses is the authority of the moral reason, by which it both tests revelation and suggests a substitute in natural religion, thus using it both destructively and for construction.

Dr. Tindal,[80] the first writer of this class, had early given offence to the church by his writings; but it was not till 1730, in his extreme old age, that he published his celebrated dialogue, "Christianity as old as the Creation, or, the Gospel a Republication of the Religion of Nature." This was not only the most important work that deism had yet produced, composed with care, and bearing the marks of thoughtful study of the chief contemporary arguments, Christian as well as Deist, but derives an interest from the circumstance that it was the book to which more than to any other single work bishop Butler's Analogy was designed as the reply.

Tindal's object is to show that natural religion is absolutely perfect, and can admit of no increase so as to carry obligation. For this purpose he tries to establish, first, that revelation is unnecessary,[81] and secondly, that obligation to it is impossible. His argument in favour of the first of these two positions is, that if man's perfection be the living according to the constitution of human nature,[82] and God's laws with the penalties at-

[80] Matthew Tindal, (1657–1733), a fellow of All Souls' college, wrote in 1706 *The Rights of the Christian Church asserted*, probably suggested by Spinoza's writings, to show that the absolute subjection of the church to the state was the only safeguard for public happiness; and in 1730, *Christianity as old as the Creation*, which was answered by Conybeare 1732, Leland 1733, and by Waterland. The reply of the latter was attacked by Conyers Middleton. On Tindal, see Lechler, 326–341; Leland, Lett. 9; Henke, vi. 57.

[81] Ch. (i–vi.)

[82] Ch. iii.

tached be for man's good,[83] nothing being required by God for its own sake;[84] then true religion, whether internally or externally revealed, having the one end, human happiness, must be identical in its precepts.[85] Having denied the necessity, he then disputes the possibility, of revelation, on the ground that the inculcation of positive as distinct from moral duties, is inconsistent with the good of man, as creating an independent rule.[86] Assuming the moral faculty to be the foundation of all obligation, he reduces all religious truth to moral. It is in thus showing the impossibility of any revelation save the republication of the law of nature that he notices many of the difficulties in scripture which form the mystery to the theologian, the ground of doubt to the objector. Some of these are of a literary character, such as the assertion of the failure of the fulfilment of prophecies, and of marks of fallibility in the scripture writers, like the mistake which he alleges in respect to the belief in the immediate coming of Christ.[87] Others of them are moral difficulties, points where the revealed system seems to him to contradict our instincts, such as the destruction of the Canaanites.[88] In reference to this last example, which may be quoted as a type of his assertions, he argues against the possibility of a divine commission for the act, on the principle asserted by Clarke,[89] that a miracle can never prove the divine truth of a doctrine which contravenes the moral idea of justice; or, in more modern phrase, that no supposed miracle can be a real one, if it attest a doctrine which bears this character. In the present work Tindal denied the necessity and possibility of a new revelation distinct from natural religion. He did not live to complete the concluding part of his book, wherein he intended to show that all the truths of Christianity were as old as the creation; i. e. were a republication of the religion of nature.

Tindal is an instance of those who have unconsciously kindled their torch at the light of revelation.

[83] Ch. iv. [84] Ch. v. [85] Ch. vi. [86] Ch. ix–xii.
[87] Ch. xiii. p. 258 seq. [88] P. 272 seq. [89] Ch. xiv.

The religion of nature of which he speaks is a logical idea, not an historic fact. The creation of it is analogous to the mention of the idea of compact as the basis of society, a generalization from its present state, not a fact of its original history. It is the residuum of Christianity when the mysterious elements have been subtracted. But in adopting the idea, the Deists were on the same level as the Christians. Both alike travelled together to the end of natural religion.[90] Here the Deist halted, willing to accept so much of Christianity as was a republication of the moral law. The Christian, on the other hand, found in reason the necessity for revelation, and proceeded onward to revealed doctrines and positive precepts.

The works of the two writers Morgan and Chubb in part supply the defect left in Tindal, the omission on the part of deism to show that Christian truths were a republication of natural religion; the former especially attacking the claims of the Jewish religion to be divine, the latter the claims of the Christian.

Morgan's chief work,[91] the "Moral Philosopher," was published in 1737. Starting from the moral point of view, the sole supremacy and sufficiency of the moral law, the writer exhibits the necessity of applying the moral test as the only certain criterion on the questions of religion, and declines admitting the authority of miracles and prophecy to avail against it,[92] an investigation suggested partly by the questions just named of the ground of unbelief, and partly by the circumstance that the Christian writers were beginning to dwell more strongly on the external evidences when unbelievers professed the internal to be unsatisfactory. The adoption of this test of truth prevents the admission of an historic revelation with positive duties. He

[90] See the remarks in *Essays and Reviews*, 1860, p. 272.

[91] Morgan died 1743. His chief work was the *Moral Philosopher*, 1737, with two volumes more in reply to opponents. It was refuted by Leland, and the controversy was carried forward in Tracts which are described in Leland's *Deists*, vol. i. Lett. 11 and 12. See also Lechler, 370–390; Henke, vi. 70.

[92] Vol. i. p. 86, 96. vol. ii. § 1.

thinks with Tindal that natural religion is perfect in itself, but seems to admit that it is so weak as to need republication,[93] which is a greater admission than Tindal made in his extant volume. When however he passes from the decision on the general possibility of revelation to particular historic forms, the Mosaic and Christian, he discredits both. The infallibility of the moral sense is still the canon by which his judgment is determined. On this ground he disbelieves the Jewish religion,[94] selecting successive passages of the national history, such as the sacrifice of Isaac, the oracle of Urim,[95] the ceremonial religious system,[96] as the object of his attack. A degree of interest attaches to his criticism on these points, in that it was the means of calling forth the celebrated work of Warburton on the Divine Legation of Moses.

The same principles of criticism mislead him in his examination of Christianity. The hallowed doctrine of the atonement forms a stumblingblock to him, on the ground of the transfer of merit by imputation.[97] He regards Christianity as a Jewish gospel, until it was altered by the apostles, whose authority he discredits by arguments not unlike the ancient ones of Celsus. The method of Morgan is more constructive than that of his predecessors. Not denying the historic element of Christianity by idealizing it as Collins, he attempts a natural explanation of the historic facts. The central thought which guides him throughout is the supreme authority of the moral reason. His works open up the broad question whether the moral sense is to pronounce on revelation or to submit to it, and thus form a fresh illustration of the intimate dependence of particular sceptical opinions and methods upon metaphysical and ethical theories.

In the period which we are now examining, deism was almost entirely confined to the upper classes. It was in the latter part of the century that it spread to the lower, political antipathy against the church giving

[93] P. 145 seq. [94] Vol. i. [95] Id. p. 272, &c. ii. § 6.
[96] Id. § 7. [97] Id. § 10.

point to religious unbelief. Chubb,[98] whom we next consider, is one of the few exceptions. He was a working man, endowed with strong native sense; who manifested the same inclination to meddle with the deep subject of religion which afterwards marked the character of Thomas Paine and others, who influenced the lower orders later in the century. In his general view of religion, Chubb denied all particular providence, and by necessary consequence the utility of prayer, save for its subjective value as having a reflex benefit on the human heart.[99] He was undecided as to the fact of the existence of a revelation, but seemed to allow its possibility.[1] He examined the three great forms of religion which professed to depend upon a positive revelation, Judaism,[2] Mahometanism, and Christianity. The claims of the first he wholly rejected, on grounds similar to those explained by Morgan, as incompatible with the moral character of God. In reference to the second he anticipated the modern opinions on Mahometanism, by asserting that its victory was impossible, if it had not contained truth which the human spirit needed. In examining the third he attacked, like Morgan, the evidence of miracles[3] and prophecy,[4] and asserted the necessity of moral right and wrong as the ground of the interpretation of scripture.

One of his most celebrated works was an explanation of "the true gospel of Jesus Christ," which is one of the many instances which his works afford of the unfairness produced by the want of moral insight into the

[98] T. Chubb (1679–1747), of whom a brief memoir was published 1747. He was the author of various tracts, of which a list is given in Darling's *Cyclopædia Bibliographica*, 1852. The account of Chubb's views given in the text is brief, partly because of their similarity to others previously named, and partly because the author has been able to see only very few of Chubb's works. But they are explained in Lechler, p. 343–356, and Leland, ch. 13. Chubb's earlier writings seem to be Socinian, his later deistical. His best known works are, *A Discourse concerning Reason*, 1731; *the True Gospel of Jesus Christ*, 1739; and *Posthumous Works*, 2 vols.,1748.

[99] *Posthumous Works*, i. 287.

[1] Id. i. 292.

[2] Id. ii. sect. 6.

[3] *Posthumous Works*, ii. 152.

[4] Id. 177, &c.

woes for which Christianity supplies a remedy, and into the deep adaptation of the scheme of redemption to effect the object proposed by a merciful Providence in its communication.[5] It will be perceived that the three last writers whose systems have been explained, resemble each other so much as to form a class by themselves. They restrict their attack to the internal character of revelation, employ the moral rather than the historical investigation, embody the chief speculations of their predecessors, and offer, as has been already stated, a constructive as well as a destructive system; morality or natural religion in place of revealed.[6]

An anonymous work was published in 1744, which merits notice as indicating a slight alteration in the mode of attack on the part of the deists. It was entitled, *The Resurrection of Jesus considered*, and is attributed to P. Annet, who died in the wretchedness of poverty.[7] It was designed in reply to some of the defences of this subject which the writings of Woolston and others had provoked. Its object was to show that the writings which record the statement of Christ's prediction of his own death are a forgery; that the narrative of the resurrection is incredible on internal grounds, and the variety in the various accounts of it are evidences of fraud. It indicates the commencement of the open allegation of literary imposture as distinct from philosophical error, which subsequently marked the criticism of the French school of infidelity, and affected the English unbelievers of the latter half of the century.

[5] Id. i. 22.

[6] Another work was published anonymously in 1742, entitled *Christianity not founded on Argument*, supposed to be written by the younger Dodwell, son of the learned nonjuror. Its aim is to show that Christianity never propagated itself by argument, but that the evidence of it depends upon a personal illumination of each person who believes it. The work was supposed to be a satire on Christianity. If earnest, it marked the truth that emotional causes are intertwined with intellectual in the formation of belief. See Lechler, pp. 411–421; Leland, Lett. xi. The book of Jasher, published in 1751, is a forgery, written probably by some deist (Horne's *Introduction*, vol. ii. part ii. p. 142. ed. 8).

[7] He was imprisoned in the King's Bench, and kept from starvation by money from the benevolent archbishop Secker. He died in 1768. See Lechler, pp. 313–22; Leland, ch. x.

Deism had now reached its maximum. The attention of the age was turned aside from religion to politics by the political dangers incident to the attempts of the Pretender; and when Hume's scepticism was promulgated in 1749 it was received without interest, and Bolingbroke's posthumous writings published in 1754 fell comparatively dead. These two names mark the period which we called the decline of deism. Bolingbroke's views[8] however depict deistical opinions of the period when it was at its height, and are a transition into the later form seen in Hume, and therefore require to be stated first, though posterior in the date of publication.

Bolingbroke's writings command respect from their mixture of clearness of exposition with power of argument. They form also the transition to the literature of the next age, in turning attention to history. Bolingbroke had great powers of psychological analysis, but he despised the study of it apart from experience. His philosophy was a philosophy of history. In his attacks on revelation we have the traces of the older philosophical school of deists; but in the consciousness that an historical, not a philosophical, solution must be sought to explain the rise of an historical phenomenon such as Christianity, he exemplifies the historic spirit which was rising, and anticipates the theological inquiry found in Gibbon; and, in his examination of the external historic evidence, both the documents by which the Christian religion is attested, and the effects of tradition in weakening historic data, he evinces traces of the influence of the historical criticism which had arisen in France under his friend Pouilly.[9]

His theological writings[10] are in the form of letters,

[8] Bolingbroke (1678–1751). See Schlosser's *History of the Eighteenth Century*, vol. i. ch. i. § 3 (transl.); Lechler, pp. 396–405; Leland, ch. 22–34.

[9] On Pouilly, see Sir C. Lewis, *Inquiry into the Credibility of Roman History*, vol. i. ch. i. p. 5, note. Pouilly published in 1722 his *Dissertation sur l'Incertitude et l'Histoire des quatre premiers siècles de Rome.* (See *Mém. de l'Academ. des Inscr.*, vol. ix.) Beaufort followed out the same line of inquiry in 1738. The two writers are considered to have laid the basis of the modern historical criticism of ancient history.

[10] They are chiefly, *A Letter on one of Tillotson's Sermons* in vol. iii.

or of essays, the common form of didactic writings in that age. We shall briefly state his views on deity, futurity, and revelation.

He teaches the existence of a deity, but was led, by the sensational philosophy which he adopted from Locke, to deny the possibility of an *a priori* proof of the divine existence,[11] and contends strongly that the divine attributes can only be known by observation of nature, and not by the analogy of man's constitution. He considers too that the deity whose existence he has thus allowed, exercises a general but not a special providence;[12] the world being a machine moving by delegated powers without the divine interference. The philosophy expressed in Pope's didactic poetry gives expression to Bolingbroke's opinions[13] on providence.

In his views of human duty Bolingbroke refers conduct to self-love as a cause, and to happiness as an end; and doubts a future state,[14] either on the ground of materialism, or possibly because his favourite principle, that "whatever is, is best," led him to disbelieve the argument for a future life adduced from the inequality of present rewards. Future punishment is rejected, on the ground that it can offer no end compatible with the moral object of punishment, which is correction.

When he passes from natural religion to revealed, he allows the possibility of divine inspiration, but

of his works; the *Essays*, in vols. iii. and iv.; viz. Essay 1 on Human Knowledge, (2) on Philosophy, (3) on the rise of Monotheism, (4) on Authority in Religion; and Fragments in vol. v.

[11] Vol. iii. *Letter on Tillotson*, also *Letter to Pouilly.*

[12] Vol. v. No. 57, 58.

[13] Cfr. Remusat's *Angleterre au* 18e *Siècle* i. 22, for remarks on Bolingbroke's influence on Pope. The following lines of Pope exactly express Bolingbroke's philosophy:

> "The universal Cause
> Acts not by partial, but by general laws,
> And makes what happiness we justly call,
> Subsist not in the good of one, but all."
>
> (*Ep.* iv. 35.)

[14] Instances are to be found in Leland, who discusses his opinions at great length. The reader who compares Leland's quotations with Bolingbroke's works will perhaps think that he has pressed their meaning rather far; but further consideration will show that he has correctly expressed Bolingbroke's spirit and purpose.

doubts the fact; rebuking those however who doubt things merely because they cannot understand them. In criticising the Jewish revelation,[15] he puts no limits to his words of severity. He dares to pronounce the Jewish history to be repugnant to the attributes of a supreme, all-perfect Being. His attack on the records is partly on account of the materials contained in them, such as the narrative of the fall, the numerical statistics, the invasion of the Canaanites, the absence of eternal rewards as sanctions of the Mosaic law; and partly on the ground of the evidence being, as he alleges, not narrated by contemporaries. In giving his opinion of Christianity, he repeats the weak objection already used by Chubb, of a distinction existing between the gospel of Christ and of Paul;[16] and tries to explain the origin of Christianity and of its doctrines, suggesting the derivation of the idea of a Trinity from the triadic notions of other religions. But he is driven to concede some things denied by former deists. He grants, for example, that if the miracles really occurred, they attest the revelation;[17] and he therefore labours to show that they did not occur, by attacking the New Testament canon[18] as he had before attacked the Old; attempting to show that the composition of the gospels was separated by an interval from the alleged occurrence of the events; applying, in fact, Pouilly's incipient criticism on history which has been so freely used in theology by more recent critics.

These remarks will exhibit Bolingbroke's views, both in their cause and their relation to those of former deists. It will be observed that they are for the most part a direct result either of sensational metaphysics or of the incipient science of historical criticism.

The inquiry was now becoming more historical on the part both of deists and Christians. Philosophy was still the cause of religious controversy, but it had changed in character. It was now criticism weighing the evidence of religion rather than ethics or meta-

[15] Letter on *Tillotson*.
[16] Ch. iv. 328. [17] Ch. iv. 227, 8. [18] Ch. iv. 405, 272.

physics testing the materials of it. The question formerly debated had been, how much of the internal characteristics of scripture can be supported by moral philosophy; and when the conviction at length grew up, that the mysteries could not be solved by any analogy, but were unique, it became necessary to rest on the miraculous evidence for the existence of a revelation, and make the fact guarantee the contents of it. Inasmuch however as the revelation is contained in a book, it became necessary to substantiate the historical evidence of its genuineness and authenticity. Bolingbroke's attacks are directed against a portion of this literary evidence.

Historical criticism, in its appreciation of literary evidence, may be of four kinds. It may (1) examine the record from a dogmatic point of view, pronouncing on it by reference to prepossessions directed against the facts; or (2) make use of the same method, but direct the attack against the evidence on which the record rests; or (3) it may examine whether the record is contemporary with the events narrated; or (4) consider its internal agreement with itself or with fact.

We have instances of each of these methods in the examination of the literary evidence on which miracles are believed. The first, the prepossession concerning the philosophical impossibility of miracles, is seen in Spinoza; the second, the impossibility of using testimony as a proof of them, in Hume; the third, the question whether they were attested by eyewitnesses, is the ground which Bolingbroke touches; the fourth, the cross-examination of the witnesses, is seen in Woolston. Of these, the first most nearly resembles the great mass of the deist objections to revelation, being philosophical rather than critical. The second forms a transition to the two latter, being philosophy applied to criticism, and is the form which deism now took. The two latter are those which it subsequently assumed.[19]

[19] The history of Apologetik passes through the same phases, and when it devotes itself to the later forms, becomes of less general interest, and is more simply literary; which illustrates the fact that the later doubts

These remarks will explain Hume's position,[20] and show how he forms the transition between two modes of inquiry; his point of view being critical, the cause of it philosophical. His speculations in reference to religion are chiefly contained in his Essays on the Human Understanding. A brief explanation is necessary to show the dependence of his theology on his philosophy.

The speculations of Locke, as we have before had occasion to notice, gave an impulse to psychological investigations. He clearly saw that knowledge is limited by the faculties which are its source, which he considered to be reducible to sensation and reflection; but while denying the existence of innate ideas, he admitted the existence of innate faculties. Hartley carried the analysis still farther, by introducing the potent instrument offered by the doctrine of the association of ideas. Hume, adopting this principle, applied it, in a manner very like the independent contemporaneous speculations of Condillac in France, to analyse the faculties themselves into sensations, and to furnish a more complete account of the nature of some of our most general ideas, such, for example, as the notion of cause. The intellectual element implied in Locke's account of the process of reflection here drops out. Faculties are regarded as transformed sensations; the nature of knowledge as coextensive with sensation. According to such a theory therefore, the idea of physical cause can mean nothing more than the invariable connexion of antecedent and consequent. The notion of force or power which we attach to causation becomes an unreality; being an idea not given in sensation, which can merely detect sequence.

are of a much less practical and more recondite character than those hitherto named.

[20] Hume (1711–1776). For his philosophy, see Tennemann, *Geschichte*, xi. 425; Ritter, *Christliche Philosophie*, viii. b. 7. ch. ii.; Cousin, *Histoire de la Philosophie Moderne*, *Leçon* xi.; Morell, *History of Philosophy*, i. 338; Lord Brougham's *Preliminary Discourse to Paley's Natural Theology*, p. 248. For his religious opinions, see Leland, *Lett.* 16–21; Lechler, pp. 425–34. His views on miracles were answered by Paley, Bp. John Douglas, Campbell, and Chalmers.

Such was Hume's psychology; an attempt to push analysis to its ultimate limits; valuable in its method, even if defective in its results; a striking example of the acuteness and subtle penetration of its author. There is another branch of his philosophy in which he is regarded as a metaphysical sceptic, in reference to the passage of the mind outwards, by means of its own sensations and ideas, into the knowledge of real being, wherein he takes part with Berkeley, extending to the inner world of soul the scepticism which that philosopher had applied to the outer world of matter. In the psychological branch Hume is a sensationalist, in the ontological a sceptic. The latter however has no relation to our present subject. It is from the former that his views on religion are deduced. In no writer is the logical dependence of religious opinion on metaphysical principles visible in a more instructive manner. For we perceive that the influence adverse to religion in his case was not merely the result of rival metaphysical dogmas opposed to religion, such as were seen in the Pantheists of Padua, or in Spinoza; nor even the opposition caused by the adoption of a different standard of truth for pronouncing on revelation, as in his fellow English deists; but it sprung from the application of the subjective psychological inquiry into the limits of religious knowledge, as a means for criticising not only the logical strength of the evidence of religion, but specially the historic evidence of testimony. We consequently see the influence exercised by the subjective branch of metaphysical inquiries in the discussion not only of the logic of religion, but also of the logic of the historic aspect of it.

Hume's religious speculations[21] relate to three points:—to the argument for the attributes of God, drawn from final causes; to the doctrine of Providence, and future rewards and punishments; and to the evidence of testimony as the proof of miracles. Though he does not conduct an open assault in reference to any

[21] Works, vol. iv. *Inquiry Concerning the Human Understanding;* Essay xi. on Providence and Future Life; Essay x. on Miracles.

of them, but only suggests doubts, yet in each case his insinuations sap so completely the very proof, that it is clear that they are intended as grounds not merely for doubt, but for disbelief. His doctrine of sensation is the clue to his remarks on the two former. He argues that we can draw no sound inferences on the questions, because the subjects lie beyond the range of sensational experience. It is however in consequence of his remarks on the last of the three subjects in his essay on Miracles that his name has become famous in the history of free thought.

The essay consists of two parts. In the first he shows that miracles are incapable of proof by testimony. Belief is in proportion to evidence. Evidence rests on sensational experience. Accordingly the testimony to the uniformity of nature being universal, and that which exists in favour of the occurrence of a miracle, or violation of the laws of nature, being partial, the former must outweigh the latter. In the second he shows, that if this is true, provided the testimony be of the highest kind, much more will it be so in actual cases; inasmuch as no miracle is recorded, the evidence for which reaches to this high standard. He explains the elements of weakness in the evidence; such as the predisposition of mankind to believe prodigies, forged miracles, the decrease of miracles with the progress of civilization, the force of rival testimony in disproof of them, which he illustrates by historic examples, such as the alleged miracles of Vespasian, Apollonius, and the Jansenist Abbé Paris.[22] The conclusion is, that miracles cannot be so shown to occur as to be used as the basis of proof for a revelation; and that a revelation, if believed, must rest on other evidence.

The argument accordingly is briefly, that testimony cannot establish a fact which contradicts a law of na-

[22] The miracles connected with the Abbé Paris were defended in *La Verité des Miracles de M. Paris*, by C. de Montgéron, 1745. See concerning them, C. Butler's *Church of France*, (*Works*, v. pp. 135–142); Bp. John Douglas's "Criterion by which the true miracles contained in the New Testament may be distinguished from those of Pagans and Papists;" Tholuck's *Vermischte Schriften*, i. 183.

ture; the narrower induction cannot disprove the wider. The reasoning has been used in subsequent controversy[23] with only a slight increase of force, or alteration of statement. The great and undeniable discoveries of astronomy had convinced men in the age of Hume of the existence of an order of nature; and modern discovery has not increased the proof of this in kind, though it has heightened it in degree, by showing that as knowledge spreads the range of the operation of fixed law is seen to extend more widely; and apparent exceptions are found to be due to our ignorance of the presence of a law, not to its absence. The statement of the difficulty would accordingly now be altered by the introduction of a slight modification. Instead of urging that testimony cannot prove the historic reality of the fact which we call a miracle, the assertion would be made that it can only attest the existence of it as a wonder, and is unable to prove that it is anything but an accidental result of an unknown cause. A miracle differs from a wonder, in that it is an effect wrought by the direct interposition of the Creator and Governor of nature, for the purpose of revealing a message or attesting a revelation. That testimony can substantiate wonders, but not distinguish the miracle from the wonder, is the modern form of the difficulty.

The connexion of Hume's view with his metaphysical principles will be evident. If nature be known only through the senses, cause is only the material antecedent visible to the senses. Nature is not seen to be the sphere of the operation of God's regular will; and the sole proof of interference with nature must be a balancing of inductions. It will be clear also that the true method of replying to Hume has been rightly perceived by those who consider that the difficulty must be met by philosophy, and not by history.

Suppose the historic evidence sufficient to attest the wonder, it does not prove that the wonder is a miracle. The presumption in favour of this may be indefinitely

[23] E. g. by Professor Powell, in *Essays and Reviews.*

increased by the peculiarity of the circumstances, which frequently forbid the idea of a mere marvel; but the real proof must depend upon the previous conception, which we bring to bear upon the question, in respect to the being and attributes of God, and His relation to nature. The antecedent probability converts the wonder into a miracle. It acts in two ways. It obliterates the cold materialistic view of the regularity of nature which regards material laws to be unalterable, and the world to be a machine; and it adds logical force to the weaker induction, so as to allow it to outweigh the stronger. No testimony can substantiate the interference with a law of nature, unless we first believe on independent grounds that there is a God who has the power and will to interfere.[24] Philosophy must accordingly establish the antecedent possibility of miracles; the attribute of power in God to effect the interruption, and of love in God to prompt him to do it. The condition therefore of attaining this conception must be by holding to a monotheistic conception of God as a being possessing a personal will, and regarding mind and will as the rule by which to interpret nature and law,[25] and not conversely measuring the mental by the material. In this manner law becomes the operation of God's personal fixed will, and miracle the interposition of his personal free will.

It will be perceived that in distinguishing miracle from wonder, we also take into account the final cause of the alleged interposition as a reason weighty enough to call forth divine interposition. As soon as we introduce the idea of a personal intelligent God, we regard Him as acting with a motive, and measure His pur-

[24] This line of thought concerning the necessity of establishing the antecedent probability of the fact, in order that the evidence may be logically convincing, is adopted by two writers of very different opinions, by Mr. Mansel (Essay in the *Aids to Faith*, § 18–23), and Mr. J. S. Mill (*Logic*, vol. ii. b. iii. ch. 25. § 2). The distinction between wonder and miracle is allowed by Dean Lyall (*Propædia Prophetica*); and Mr. Penrose (*The use of Miracles in proving a Revelation*). Cfr. also Doederlin's *Instit. Theol. Christ.* § 9, 10.

[25] See *Aids to Faith*, Mansel's Essay, § 22.

poses, partly by analogy to ourselves, partly by the moral circumstances which demand the interposition.[26]

These remarks may furnish the solution of the puzzle whether the miracle proves the doctrine, or the doctrine the miracle.[27] Undoubtedly the miracle proves the particular doctrine which it claims to attest; but a doctrine of some kind, though not the special one in point, some moral conception of the Almighty's nature and character, must precede, in order to give the criterion for distinguishing miracle from mere wonder. Miracles prove the doctrine which they are intended to attest; but doctrines of a still more general character are required to prove the miracle.

This examination of the doctrine of Hume will not only illustrate our main position, of the influence of intellectual and philosophical causes in generating doubt, or at least in directing free thought into a sceptical tendency, but will illustrate the application made of that special department of metaphysics which relates to the test of truth, to discredit the literary proof of revelation as an historic system.

[26] There follows hence another peculiarity in reference to miracles; viz., that we require an interpreting mind to explain them. This is the reason why so many thoughtful men believe that the outburst of fire when Julian tried to rebuild the Jewish temple, and the wonder of the thorn in the history of Port Royal, were nothing more than natural wonders. If the final cause be considered to have been sufficient in these cases to warrant divine interposition, at least there was no interpreter to explain them, nor any revealed message to be taught. It must be conceded that this trait is wanting in some miracles recorded in scripture, but not in those which are wrought to attest a revelation, those which we use in proof of a special message from the unseen world. Werenfels (*Opusc. Theol.* 1718, *Diss.* v.) has given tests for the discrimination of miracles which are quoted by Van Mildert (Boyle Lect. II. p. 534).

[27] Cfr. Dean Trench's remarks on the apologetic value of miracles, (*Notes on Miracles*, Introd. ch. vi). In the same work will be found an excellent and interesting account of the various assaults made on the argument from miracles. He classifies the assaults as follows: (1) the Jewish, (2) the heathen (Celsus, &c.), (3) the pantheistic (Spinoza), (4) the sceptical (Hume), (5) that which regards miracles as such only subjectively (Schleiermacher), (6) the rationalistic (Paulus), (7) the historico-critical (Woolston, Strauss). With Dean Trench's remarks. Compare also Pascal, *Pensées*, part ii. art. 19. § 9; Lyall, *Prop. Proph.* p. 441; Dr. Arnold's *Lectures on Modern History*, pp. 133, 137.

We have now sketched the natural history of deism, by showing that in this as in former periods the forms which free thought assumed were determined by the philosophy, and, in a slighter degree, by the critical knowledge of the age.

The inquiry into method in the seventeenth century had led men to break with authority, and rebuild from its foundations the temple of truth. Locke, imbibing this spirit, had gauged anew the human understanding, and had sought a new origin for its knowledge, and given expression to the appeal to the reasoning powers, which marked the age. Political circumstances had not only generated free inquiry, but had required each man to form his political creed. In all departments reason was appealed to. Even the province of the imagination was invaded by it, and perfection of form preferred to freshness of conception in art and poetry. The doubt of the age reflected the same spirit. Whether its advocates belonged to the school of Descartes or of Locke, both alike examined religion by the standard of psychology and ethics. That which was to be believed was to be comprehended as well as apprehended. Yet the appeal was not made to reason in its highest form; and, with a show of depth, philosophy nevertheless failed to exhibit the deepest analysis.

We have watched the exhibition of the successive phases of the attack, and have seen reason, first examining the method of theology, protesting against mystery in doctrine or morals; next criticising the historic reality of the evidence offered for its doctrines; then denying the moral utility of revelation, or attacking the doctrines and internal truths; lastly denying the validity of testimony for the supernatural.

In the later steps the influence of the French school of speculation is already observable, mingling itself with English deism. Consequently the subsequent traces of unbelief in England must be deferred till the nature of this movement has been explained.

Deism stands contrasted with the unbelief of other times by certain peculiarities. In its coarse spirit of bitter hostility, and want of real insight into the excellence of the system which it opposed, it recalls in some respects the attack of the ancient heathen Celsus; and the difficulties propounded are frequently not dissimilar to those stated by him, though resulting from a different philosophical school. The tenacious grasp which it maintained of the doctrine of the unity of God would cause it to bear a closer resemblance to the system of Julian, if the deists had not lacked the literary tastes which strengthened his love for heathenism. The monotheism constitutes also a line of demarcation between deism and more modern forms of unbelief. It restrained the deists from falling into the forms of subtle pantheism previously noticed, and the atheism which will hereafter meet us. The character of their doubts too, selected from patent facts of mind and heart, which appealed to common sense, and were not taken from a minute literary criticism, which removes doubt from the sphere of the ordinary understanding into the world of literature, separates them from more modern critical unbelief.

Standing thus apart, characterised by intense attachment to monotheism, and placing its foundation in the great facts of nature, deism errs by defect rather than excess; in that which it denies, not in that which it asserts. It is a system of naturalism or rationalism; the interpretation which reason, without attaining the deepest analysis, offers of the scheme of the world, natural and moral. Its only parallel is the particular species of German thought derived from it which existed at the close of the last century, and sought like it to reduce revealed religion to natural.[28]

Whether emotional causes, personal moral faults coincided with these intellectual causes, and were the obstacle which prevented the attainment of a deeper insight into the mysteries of revelation, and made them to halt in the mysteries of nature, ought to be taken into account in forming a judgment on the concrete cases, but does not so properly belong to the general

[28] E. g. Lessing, &c. Reimarus, &c. See Lect. VI.

consideration in which we are now engaged, of tracing the types of deist thought. Some of the deists were very moral men, a few immoral; but the truth or untruth of opinions may be studied apart from the character of the persons who maintain them.

The movement, if viewed as a whole, is obsolete. If the same doubts are now repeated, they do not recur in the same form, but are connected with new forms of philosophy, and altered by contact with more recent criticism. In the present day sceptics would believe less than the deists, or believe more, both in philosophy and in criticism. In philosophy, the fact that the same difficulties occur in natural religion as well as in revealed, would now throw them back from monotheism into atheism or pantheism; while the mysteries of revelation, which by a rough criticism were then denied, would be now conceded and explained away as psychological peculiarities of races or individuals. In criticism, the delicate examination of the sacred literature would now prevent both the revival of the cold unimaginative want of appreciation of its extreme literary beauty, and the hasty imputation of the charge of literary forgery against the authors of the documents. In the deist controversy the whole question turned upon the differences and respective degrees of obligation of natural and revealed religion, moral and positive duties; the deist conceding the one, denying the other.

The permanent contribution to thought made by the controversy consisted in turning attention from abstract theology to psychological, from metaphysical disquisitions on the nature of God to ethical consideration of the moral scheme of redemption for man. Theology came forth from the conflict, reconsidered from the psychological point of view, and readjusted to meet the doubts which the new form of philosophy—psychology and ethics—might suggest.

The attack of revealed religion by reason awoke the defence; and no period in church history is so remarkable for works on the Christian evidences,—grand monuments of mind and industry. The works of defenders are marked by the adoption of the same basis of reason as their opponents; and hence the topics which they illustrate have a permanent philosophical value, though their special utility as arguments be lessened by the alteration in the point of view now assumed by free thought.

The one writer whose reputation stands out preeminently above the other apologists is bishop Butler.[29] His praise is in all the churches. Though the force of a few illustrations in his great work may perhaps have been slightly weakened by the modern progress of physical science,[30] and though objections have been taken on the ground that the solutions are not ultimate,[31] mere *media axiomata;* yet the work, if regarded as adapted to those who start from a monotheistic position, possesses a permanent power of attractiveness which can only be explained by its grandeur as a work of philosophy, as well as its mere potency as an argument. The width and fulness of knowledge displayed in the former respect, together with the singular candour and dignified forbearance of its tone, go far to explain the secret of its mighty influence. When viewed in reference to the deist writings against which it was designed, or the

[29] Butler (1692–1752). The Analogy was published in 1736. The reader's attention is invited to the excellent edition of it by bishop Fitzgerald (1st ed. 1849), and the able memoir and criticism which precede. Mr. Bartlett has also written a memoir of Butler. Cfr. also Blunt's *Essays*, p. 490 seq.

[30] For example, some of the physical proofs of immortality in part i. ch. i. are weakened by the discoveries of physiology; and those in favour of the miraculous character of creation, in part ii. ch. ii. would be regarded as of small value by those who hold the hypothesis either of the transmutation of species, or of their occurrence according to a law of natural selection. Some things of a different kind in Butler, which need correction, are pointed out in Fitzgerald's edition. See e. g. p. 184, note.

[31] This is the objection taken by Tholuck (*Vermischt. Schrift.* p. 192, 3.) A somewhat similar objection is quoted by Fitzgerald from Mackintosh, Introd. p. 49, upon both of which he offers criticisms. A kindred objection has been stated (probably by Mr. Martineau) in the *National Review*, No. 15. Jan. 1859, (pp. 211–214,) and another by Miss S. Hennell in *the Sceptical Tendency of Butler's Analogy*, 1857, in which she traces doubt in Butler's life as well as teaching. Others may be found stated and examined in bishop Hampden's *Philosophical Evidence of Christianity*, 1827. (pp. 229–291.)

works of contemporary apologists, Butler's carefulness in study is manifest. Though we conjectured that Tindal's work[32] was the one to which he intended chiefly to reply, yet not one difficulty in the philosophy, hardly one in the critical attacks made by the various deists, is omitted; and the best arguments of the various apologists are used. But both the one and the other are so assimilated by his own mind, that the use of them only proves his learning, without diminishing his originality. They are so embodied into his system, that it is difficult even for a student well acquainted with the deist and apologetic literature to point precisely to the doubt or parallel argument which may have suggested to him material of thought. And thus, though his work as an argument ought always to be viewed in relation to his own times, yet the omission of all temporary means of defence, and the restricting himself to the use of those permanent facts which indelibly belong to human nature, and to the scheme of the world, have caused his work to possess an enduring interest, and to be a *κτῆμα ἐς ἀεί*. The persuasive moderation of its tone also proves that Butler had really weighed the evidence. In its absence of arrogant denunciation, and its candid admission that the evidence of religion is probable, not demonstrative; and in the request that the whole evidence may be weighed like a body of circumstantial proofs, we can perceive that Butler had felt the doubts as well as understood them, and evidently meant his works for the doubter rather than for the Christian;

[32] This conjecture is given by Fitzgerald in the life prefixed to his edition of the Analogy (p. 36), where also two passages are quoted, one from Foster, and the other from Berkeley, which certain passages of Butler resemble. It would be interesting to know whether the work of Dr. Peter Browne on *Things Divine and Natural conceived of by Analogy*, 1733, had come under Butler's notice. Many similar passages, as well as references to the sources of the difficulties which Butler answers, are given in the notes to Fitzgerald's edition. Mr. Pattison also (*Essays and Reviews*, p. 286) has expressed an opinion that Butler was much assisted by the works of his predecessors. The probability is, that in all great works their authors assimilate an amount of information current in the age, as well as create new material. This was probably the case even in works like Euclid's Geometry and Aristotle's Natural History and Organum.

to convince foes, or support the hesitating, rather than to win applause from friends.

The real secret of its power however lies not merely in its force as an argument to refute objections against revelation, but in its positive effect as a philosophy,[33] opening up a grand view of the divine government, and giving an explanation of revealed doctrines, by using analogy as the instrument for adjusting them into the scheme of the universe.[34] He seems himself to have taken a broad view of God's dealings in the moral world, analogous to that which the recent physical discoveries of his time had exhibited in the natural. In the same manner as Newton in his Principia had, by an extension of terrestrial mechanics, explained the movements of the celestial orbs, and united under one grand generalization the facts of terrestrial and celestial motion; so Butler aimed at exhibiting as instances of one and the same set of moral laws the moral government of God, which is visible to natural reason, and the spiritual government, which is unveiled by revelation.

Probably no book since the beginning of Christianity has ever been so useful to the church as Butler's Analogy, in solving the doubts of believers or causing them to ignore exceptions, as well as in silencing unbelievers. The office of apologetic is to defend the church, not to build it up. Argument is not the life of the church. It is therefore a proof of the philosophical power and truth of Butler's work that it has ministered so extensively to the latter purpose, by actually reinforcing and promoting the faith of professing Christians. It has acted not only as an argument to the deists, but as a lesson of instruction to the church.

Few efforts of free thought seemed more unpromising in yielding any useful results than deism; yet by its agitation of deep questions, which are not the mere

[33] The value of Butler's argument is fully discussed in the admirable work on Butler by bishop Hampden before quoted, which is the best existing commentary on the author: second to it are Chalmers's *Natural Religion* and *Bridgwater Treatise*.

[34] Hampden's *Phil. Evid.* (131–228.)

phantoms of a morbid mind, but real and solid difficulties and mysteries in revelation, it was the means of creating Butler's noble work, and is a fresh illustration of the beneficent arrangement of the Almighty, that makes knowledge progress by antagonism, and overrules evil for good.

But there is another weapon for repelling unbelief besides the intellectual; just as there are two causes for creating it, the one intellectual, the other emotional. Thus, in the period that we are now considering, though we may believe that many hearts were cheered and many doubts hushed by the Christian apologies, yet the revival of religion[35] which marked the eighteenth century, and which by spreading vital piety prepared an effectual check against unbelief, when the lower orders were afterwards invaded by it, was due to the spiritual yearnings created by the ministrations of men, often rude and unlettered, who told the wondrous story of Christ crucified, heart speaking to heart, with intuitions kindled from on high. The sinful began to feel that God was not afar off, reposing in the solitude of his own blessedness, and abandoning mankind to the government of conscience and to the operation of general laws, but nigh at hand, with a heart of fatherly love to pity and an ear of mercy to listen. The narrative of Christ the Son of God, coming down to seek and to save that which was lost, awoke an echo in the heart which neutralized the doubts infused by the deist. And it is a comfort to every Christian labourer to know that if he cannot wrangle out a controversy with the doubter, he can speak to the doubter's heart.

Few would compare the irregular missionaries of spiritual religion in the last century with the great writers of evidence. The names of the latter are honoured; those of the former are unknown or too often despised. It might seem strange, for example, to insti-

[35] The revival in the early part of the century was due to the agency of Wesley and Whitfield outside the church; in the latter to those of such men as Romaine, Newton, and ultimately Simeon, within it.

tute a comparison between the two contemporaries, bishop Butler and John Wesley. Yet there are points of contrast which are instructive. Each was one of the most marked instruments of movement and influence in the respective fields of the argumentative and the spiritual; the one a philosopher writing for the educated, the other a missionary preaching to the poor. Butler, educated a nonconformist, turned to the church, and in an age of unbelief consecrated his great mental gifts to roll back the flood of infidelity; and died early, when his unblemished example was so much needed in the noble sphere of usefulness which Providence had given him, leaving a name to be honoured in the church for generations. Wesley, nursed in the most exclusive church principles, kindled the flame of his piety by the devout reading of mystic books;[36] when our university was marked by the half-heartedness of the time; and afterwards, when instructed by the Pietists of Germany,[37] devoted a long life to wander over the country, despised, ill-treated, but still untired; teaching with indefatigable energy the faith which he loved, and introducing those irregular agencies of usefulness which are now so largely adopted even in the church. He too was an accomplished scholar, and possessed great gifts of administration; but whatever good he effected, in kindling the spiritual Christianity which checked the spread of infidelity, was not so much by argument as by stating the omnipotent doctrine of the Cross, Christ set forth as the propitiation for sin through faith in his blood. The earnestness of the missionary may be imitated by those who cannot imitate the philosopher's literary labours. Gifts of intellect are not in our own power. But industry to improve the talents that we possess is our own; and the spiritual perception of divine truth, and burning love for Christ which will

[36] E. g., W. Law's *Serious Call*, and *Christian Perfection*.

[37] Viz., by means of the Moravians of Hernnhut, whose founder, Zinzendorf, himself sprang from the pietist movement.

touch the heart, and before which all unhealthy doubts will melt away as frost before the sun, will be given from on high by the Holy Ghost freely to all that ask. "Not by might, nor by power, but by my Spirit, saith the Lord." [38]

[38] Zech. iv. 6.

LECTURE V.

INFIDELITY IN FRANCE IN THE EIGHTEENTH CENTURY, AND UNBELIEF IN ENGLAND SUBSEQUENT TO 1760.

ISAIAH xxvi. 20.

Come, my people, enter thou into thy chambers, and shut thy doors about thee: hide thyself as it were for a little moment, until the indignation be overpast.

WE now approach the study of a period remarkable no less in the history of the world than in that of religious thought, in which unbelief gained the victory in the empire of mind, and obtained the opportunity of reconstructing society and education according to its own views. The history of infidelity in France in the eighteenth century forms a real crisis in history, important by its effects as well as its character. For France has always been the prerogative nation of Europe. When wants intellectual or political have been felt there, the life of other nations has beat sympathetic with it as with the heart of the European body. Ideas have been thrown into form by it for transmission to others. It will be necessary to depict the free religious thought, both intellectually and in its political action; to characterise its principal teachers; to show whence it sprung, and to what result it tended; to point out wherein lay the elements of its power and its wickedness; to show what it has contributed to human woe, or perchance indirectly to human improvement.

The source of its influence cannot be understood

without recalling some facts of the history of French politics and philosophical speculation. What was the cause why English deists wrote and taught their creed in vain, were despised while living and consigned to oblivion when dead, refrained almost entirely from political intermeddling, and left the church in England unhurt by the struggle; while on the other hand deism in France became omnipotent, absorbed the intellect of the country, swept away the church, and remodelled the state? The answer to this question must be sought in the antecedent history. It is a phenomenon political rather than intellectual. It depended upon the soil in which the seed was sown, not on the inherent qualities of the seed itself.[1]

The church and state have hardly ever possessed more despotic power in any country of modern times, or seemed to all appearances to repose on a more secure foundation, than in France at the time when they were first assailed by the free criticism of the infidels of the eighteenth century. Each had escaped the alterations which had been effected in most other countries. The clergy of France had in the sixteenth century successfully resisted the Reformation, and gained strength by the issue of the civil wars which supervened on it. In the seventeenth century, though compelled to admit toleration of their Protestant adversaries, they had contrived before the end of it to obtain a revocation of the edict, even though the act cost France the loss of a million of her industrious population, and though the en-

[1] The most effective sketch of the intellectual and social state of France in the last century is given in Buckle's *History of Civilisation*, vol. i.; especially in ch. 8, 11, 12, and 14. His narrative only sets forth the dark side of the picture, and the Christian reader frequently feels pained at some of his remarks; but it is generally correct so far as it goes, and the references are copious to the original sources which the author used. I have therefore frequently rested content with quoting this work without indicating further sources. An instructive account of the centralization under Louis XIV is given in Sir J. Stephens's *Lectures on the History of France*, Lect. 21–23. The reign of Louis XV is treated in De Tocqueville's *Histoire Philosophie du Règne de Louis XV*. A brief view of the history may be seen in the works of the liberal Roman catholic, C. Butler, vol. v. on *Church of France*.

forcing of it had to be effected by the means of the dragonnades, in which a brutal soldiery was let loose on an innocent population.[1] Thus the church, united with rather than subjected to the state, adorned by great names, asserting its national independence in the pride of conscious strength against the metropolitan see of Christendom,[2] possessed a power which, while it seemed to promise perpetuity, stood as an impediment to proggress and a bar to intellectual development.

Nor was the cause of liberty more hopeful in relation to the state than the church. The crown, in passing through a similar struggle against the feudal nobility to that of other countries, had succeeded in securing its victory without yielding those concessions to the demands of the people which in our own country were extorted from it by the civil war. The strength gained by the defeat of the nobility in the wars of the Fronde, offered the opportunity for an able sovereign like Louis XIV to dry up all sources of independent power, by centralizing all authority in the monarchy. Proud in the consciousness of internal power and foreign victory, surrounded by wealth and talent, with a court and literature which were the glory of the country, he seemed likely to transmit his power to coming generaations. But the inherent weakness of despotism was soon apparent. Unrestrained authority appertains only to the Divine government, because power is there synonymous with goodness; but it is always unsafe in human. The wisdom which partially supplied the place of goodness in Louis XIV being wanting in his successor, unchecked selfishness produced the corruption which brought inevitable ruin.

These remarks on the political state of France will

[2] The passages from Benoit's *Histoire de l'Edict de Nantes*, vol. v. p. 887 seq., and Quick's *Synodicon*, i. p. 130 seq., respecting the cruelties of the dragonnades, are quoted at length in Buckle, i. p. 624, note.

[3] This occurred in the contest concerning the Gallican liberties, and the dispute about the Bull Unigenitus. Concerning the former see C. Butler's *Church of France* (Works, vol. v.) p. 34 seq., and Hase's *Church History*, § 424; and, on the latter, Butler ut sup. 188–149, and Hase, § 420.

sufficiently show why a free criticism directed against either religion or tyranny should assume revolutionary tendencies, and should manifest an antipathy to social and ecclesiastical institutions, as well as to the principles on which they were supposed to depend.

But the forces operating in the world of mind, as well as in society, must also be understood, in order to estimate the influence of unbelief in France. In a previous lecture we have seen that in the middle of the seventeenth century the philosophy of Descartes had created a complete revolution in modes of thought. It was only in the philosophy of Spinoza that it produced theological unbelief; but by its indirect influence it had led generally to an entire reconsideration of the first data of reasoning, and the method of establishing truth; and thus had stimulated the struggle of reason against faith, of inquiry against credulity, of progress against reaction, and of hopefulness in the future against reverence for the past. The activity of mind displayed in the literature of the reign of Louis XIV is its first expression.[4] But thoughts ferment long in society before they fully express themselves in form: they first exist as suggestions; then they become doubts; lastly, they pass into disbelief. It was not until the time of the regency,[5] which ensued after the death of Louis, that the literature became impressed with a thoroughly new tone.[6]

Other causes of a more direct kind cooperated. The English philosophy of Locke, which marked an epoch in speculation, was introduced at that time. This philosophy however could not have resulted in those speculations which arose in France, if it had not been carried farther by the analysis which Condillac employed in that country, analogous to that of Hume in Scotland.

[4] The nature of the literature of the reign of Louis XIV, and the alteration of position of authors in the new reign, are explained in Buckle, i. ch. 11 and 12.

[5] 1715–1723.

[6] Literature really became a political power, and exercised a similar influence to that of the modern newspaper press.

In itself it expressed the reasoning type of mind and thought which reigned throughout the English literature; but the corollaries from it which produced harm were no part of the original system.[7] Condillac, desiring to carry out the analysis of the origin of knowledge, lost sight of the intellectual element in Locke's account of the process of reflection; denied the existence of innate faculties as well as innate ideas; and attempted to show that man's mind is so passive, so dependent on the evidence of the senses for the material of its thoughts, and on language for the power to combine them, that its very faculties are transformed sensations.[8] From these premises it was not hard for his followers to draw the inferences of materialism[9] in philosophy, selfishness in morals, and an entire denial of those religious truths which cannot be proved by sensuous evidence. This philosophy began to leaven the mind of France, and was accepted by nearly the whole of French unbelievers.

Such was the intellectual state of France in reference to the standard of appeal contemporaneously with the political and ecclesiastical condition before described. In the state and church all was authority; all was of the past: in the world of literature and philosophy all was criticism, activity, hope in the future. Into a soil thus prepared the seeds of unbelief on the subject of religion were introduced. We cannot deny that they were imported mainly from England. Doubt had indeed not been wholly wanting in France. In the pre-

[7] Professor Webb of Dublin, in his work, *The Intellectualism of Locke*, has given evidence which establishes this point.

[8] On Condillac see Cousin, *Cours de la Philosophie Morale*, leçon 3; Renouvier, *Philosophie Moderne*, v. 2. § 4; Villemain, *Cours de Literature*, ii. 20; Morell's *History of Philosophy*, i. 148 seq.; Lewes' *History of Philosophy*.

[9] It may prevent ambiguity to state that the term *materialism*, when employed in these lectures, is not used in its modern popular sense of mere animalism, the obedience to the lower side of human nature; but in its technical sense, as the kind of philosophy which so regards spirit to be a property of matter as to produce inferences unfavourable to the belief in immortality or moral obligation.

ceding centuries Montaigne[10] and Charron,[11] and, at the commencement of the one of which we speak, Bayle[12] and Fontenelle,[13] were probably harassed with disbelief, and their influence was certainly productive of doubt. And free thought, in the form of literary criticism of the scriptures, had brought down the denunciation of the French church on Richard Simon.[14] But undoubtedly the direct parent of the French unbelief was English deism.[15] In no age of French history has English literature possessed so powerful an influence.[16] England had recently achieved those liberties of which France felt the need. It had safely outlived civil war and revolution, and had established constitutional liberty and religious toleration. In England the victims of the French oppression found shelter. Being itself free, it became the refuge for the exile, the shelter for the oppressed. It thus became the object of study to the politician, and of love to the philanthropist. Its literature too, in two branches, viz. political inquiry, and, towards the middle of the century, romance, offered subjects for imitation. Montesquieu studied the former; Rousseau and Diderot the latter. But England furnished also a series of fearless inquirers on the subject of religion, whose works became the subject of study and of translation.[17] Voltaire spent three

[10] On the scepticism of Montaigne (1532–1592) see Tennemann's *Geschichte der Philosophie*, ix. 443; Vinet's *Essai de Philosophie Morale;* Sainte-Beuve *Critiques et Portraits Littéraires*, vol. iv.; Hallam's *History of Literature*, ii. 29; Emerson's *Representative Men;* and R. W. Church in *Oxford Essays*, 1857.

[11] On Charron (1541–1603) see Tennemann, Id. ix. 527, Sainte-Beuve, t. xi.; Hallam, i. 570, ii. 362, 511; and the article in the *Biogr. Univ.*

[12] On Bayle (1647–1706) see Tennemann, xi. 268 seq.; Renouvier, *Phil. Mod.* iii. 3. § 6; Sainte-Beuve, iii. 392.

[13] On Fontenelle (1657–1757) see Sainte-Beuve, iii. and the *Biogr. Univ.* Another writer, Dolet (1509–1546), was also suspected, at an earlier period, not only of scepticism but of atheism. See his Life, by J. Boulmier, 1857.

[14] On R. Simon see Lect. III. p. 83.

[15] See Lechler's *Gesch. des Eng. Deismus*, p. 445.

[16] On the great eagerness for English literature in France at that time, see the facts collected by Buckle, i. (658–670).

[17] A list of those that are said to have been translated is given by

years of exile in England,[18] at the time when the ferment existed concerning Woolston's attack on miracles, and both knew Bolingbroke personally, and translated his writings.

Having now explained the sources of doubt in France; we must next direct our attention to the course of its speculations, and to the chief authors.

If we estimate its course by literary works, or by social and political movements, we may distribute the history of it into two periods; one comprising the first half of the century, wherein it attacks the French church and Christianity; the other, the latter half, wherein it mingles itself with the demand for political change, and assaults the state,[19] until its effects are seen in the anarchy of the French revolution. In the former of these periods the unbelief is tentative and suggestive. About the time of the transition to the second, in the pride of supposed victory it becomes dogmatic. Christianity is supposed to be exploded. Philosophy seeks to occupy its place in the social and intellectual world. The early doubters and Voltaire mark the former of these epochs. Diderot and the French encyclopædists, with the ramification of their school at the court of Frederick II of Prussia, form the point of transition. Rousseau marks the opening of the second period, when unbelief was attempting to reconstruct society and remodel education. The selfish philosophy of Helvetius and his friends then carries on the course of the history of unbelief, until in the storm of the revolution it shows itself in the teaching of Volney, and the absurd acts of the theophilanthropists.

The name of Voltaire, which the logical and chronological order introduces first to our notice, is so pre-

Lechler, Id. 446. On the comparison of English and French deism see Henke's *Kirchengeschichte*, vi. s. 131.

[18] 1726–1729. Cfr. Villemain, *Cours de Litt.* i. (168–177). A letter of Fleury, quoted from Schlosser by Lechler (Id. 446), proves that his fears were excited by the influence which English literature was producing.

[19] On this charge of attack about 1750 see Buckle, i. 716–718; and on the origin of the attack on the church, and the causes why it preceded that on the state, Id. 684 seq. Cfr. also De Tocqueville's *Louis XV*, t. ii. ch. 10.

eminent, that his character and teaching may express the history of the early movement in France.

The story of his life, so far as we require now to be made acquainted with it, can be briefly told.[20] Born toward the close of the seventeenth century, he manifested, as a legend assures us, such a doubting spirit, even in boyhood, that his priestly preceptor predicted that he would prove a Coryphæus of deism. His rare precocity of intellect early acquired for him a reputation in the world of letters. Compelled to become an exile in England,[21] he studied its politics, its science, and its scepticism. On his return to France, he endeavoured to introduce among his countrymen the cosmical and mathematical doctrines of Newton; and made himself conspicuous in history, in poetry, in fiction, and above all, in theology, by his attacks on revealed religion and the French church. About the middle of the century, accepting an invitation to the court of Frederick the Great of Prussia, he aided thence the introduction of infidel doctrines in Germany. A few years later he withdrew into retirement at Ferney, but was able from his seclusion to wield an intellectual power throughout Europe.

It was from this retirement that he denounced the acts of tyranny, or supposed injustice, inflicted by the French church. His indignant denunciations in the cases of the Sirven,[22] of La Barre,[23] and above all of the

[20] Voltaire lived 1694–1778. The Life by Lord Brougham, in *Lives of Men of Letters*, is not only very full of facts, but contains some very able criticism, especially on the dramatic works of Voltaire. More biographies have been given in this lecture than in others, in accordance with the reasons explained in Lec. I. p. 33, because in this period the infidel influence was the result of the teachers, as much as of the ideas taught. See concerning Voltaire, Henke's *Kirchengesch.* vi. 166; Schlosser, *Hist. of Eighteenth Century*, i. 2. § 1, iv. § 1. Bartholmess, *Hist. Crit. des Doctr. Relig. de la Phil. Mod.* i. 211 seq.; Bungener's *Voltaire.*

[21] In 1726.

[22] Sirven was condemned in 1762, on an unjust suspicion of causing his daughter's death, to prevent her becoming a protestant.

[23] La Barre was a youth of seventeen, who, on the suspicion of having injured a crucifix on the bridge of Abbeville, was condemned (1763) to be tortured on the rack, to have his tongue cut out, and to be put to death;

Calas,[24] gained for him the commendation and sympathy of Europe, and remain as monuments of the power of the pen.

Such was his life. Let us search in it for the secret of his power, and inquire what were his views in the department which we are studying.

His character has been analysed by so many critics, especially by one of our own countrymen in an essay of rare power, now become classical, that the opportunity of original investigation is impossible, and the attempt undesirable.[25]

In the opinion of this writer, the secret of Voltaire's strength was the tact which he displayed in expressing the wants of his time to his countrymen in the precise mode most suited to them.[26] He belonged to the class of those who exercise their influence in their own lifetime—men of the present, not men of the future; accordingly, whether he be viewed as a man, in his own personal qualities, in the moral and intellectual properties which constituted his character, or as an artist, in the manner in which he conveyed his thoughts to the world, he will be found to be the loftiest exponent and type of the spirit of his age. It was an age without

which sentence was literally executed. See *Biographie Universelle*, sub *Voltaire*, vol. xix. p. 484, and Brougham's Life of him (94–99).

[24] The Calas were a family at Toulouse, the father of which was put to death (1762) by catholic fanaticism. Voltaire investigated the facts with care; and, by instituting legal proceedings at Paris, got the sentence of the Toulouse court reversed, and all the reparation that was possible made to the family. Money to defray the expenses was sent to him from all the reformed parts of Europe. The English queen (Charlotte) and the archbishop of Canterbury (Secker) headed the English subscription list. The facts have lately been reinvestigated by the accomplished A. Coquerel *fils.*, *Jean Calas et sa Famille*, 1858. The narrative is told in the *Westminster Review*, No. 28, for Oct. 1858. See also Henke's *Kirchengeschichte*, vi. 298 seq.

On the tomb of Voltaire, now a cenotaph, in the vaults of the Pantheon, is an inscription, "Il défendit Calas, Sirven, De la Barre, et Montbailly." Since the Pantheon has been converted into a church, the side of the tomb which bears this inscription has been concealed by a screen, so that visitors are only permitted to view one of the other sides.

[25] Carlyle's *Miscellaneous Works*, vol. ii. It will be observed that many of the following remarks are abbreviated from this source.

[26] Carlyle, Id. p. 113.

originality, without spiritual insight, careful of manners rather than morals, corrupted by selfishness, led by ambition, dissatisfied with the present, and anxious for deliverance; but unable to espy the real causes of the mischief, and to escape confusing principles with men; fond of form rather than material; classical rather than Gothic; critical rather than reverent; proud of its own discoveries, without appreciation of the efforts of the past.—Such are the qualities which characterised the times of Voltaire,[27] and in their most striking form marked his mind.

To qualities which were thus in some sense formed in him by circumstances, he added remarkable ones which were Nature's special gift to him. His extraordinary tact and good sense, both in dealing personally with individuals and in literary criticism; his fiery ardour, and vehement spirit of proselytism; his singular penetration of vision, and power to arrange in the clearest mode the thoughts which he wished to transmit; above all, his wit and wonderful power of satire were qualities which, though in some degree shared by his countrymen, cannot be explained by mere circumstances, but are natural gifts. These three intellectual endowments, acuteness, order, and satire,[28] are regarded by the authority that we are taking for our guide, as the qualities which formed the secret of his power as a writer, and at the same time as the sources of intellectual temptation which prevented him from gaining a deeper insight into truth, and deprived him of influence with posterity. For his quickness prevented the exercise of the reflection, the patient meditation, which is the only high road to solve the mysteries of existence. It has been well said,[29] that Voltaire saw so much more deeply at a glance than other men, that no second glance was ever given by him. His power of order assisting his quickness, was

[27] i. e. the age of Louis XV. See Id. pp. 180–185.

[28] On Voltaire's power of ridicule, see Id. 120, 167; and on his power of order, 163 seq.

[29] Id. p. 161.

a still further temptation. Though far inferior in erudition to some of his contemporaries, such as Diderot, and in depth of feeling to Rousseau, lacking originality, and borrowing most of his philosophical thoughts at second hand, he yet surpassed them all by a matchless power of arrangement. The perfection of form diverted attention from the subject matter. He possessed method rather than genius, intellect rather than imagination. But above all his other powers, his most singular gift was his power of satire. When stimulated by a sense of injustice, or of hatred against men or systems, it made him omnipotent in destruction. This satirical power contributed to preclude the possession of depth of reflection. Ridicule has an office in criticism. It is the true punishment of folly. But it has been well observed,[30] that it is dangerous to him who employs it, as being directly opposed to humility. The satirist places himself above that which he ridicules, and makes himself the judge: the humility of the listener is laid aside; the selfish belief of his own infallibility is fostered; forbearance and sympathy are laid aside. The critic argues, the satirist only laughs. Pity may be compatible with humour, but only contempt with satire. Voltaire was by nature a satirist; and when his mockery was applied to a subject like Christianity or religion, his utter want of reverence not only caused him to substitute a caricature for a picture, but prevented him from exercising discrimination in distinguishing Christianity from its counterfeit, religion from the ministers of it. Hence his attacks on Christianity partake of the tone of blasphemy; and he manifests in reference to religion, which to most readers was the most sacred of subjects, a tone of indescribable scurrility, which was not only inexcusable and disgraceful if viewed merely in a literary point of view, but constituted politically a public outrage against the dearest feelings of others which no citizen has a right to perpetrate.[31] This tone too was mainly his own;

[30] Id. p. 119.

[31] The question of Voltaire's blasphemy is treated by lord Brougham (*Life*, p. 7).

and is not to be found, except in rare instances, in the English deists from whom he borrowed.

We have tried to comprehend the mind of Voltaire, to notice his peculiarities and faults, before considering his opinions; because his influence was due to his mental and personal character rather than to the matter of his writings. It remains to state his views on religion, and the grounds of his attack on revelation. The chief materials for ascertaining them are the four volumes in the vast collection of his works, which contain his philosophical and theological writings.[32] They partake of every variety of form,—essays, letters, treatises, pamphlets, translations, commentaries. They include, besides smaller works, a commentary on the Old Testament; translations of parts of Bolingbroke and of Toland; an investigation concerning the establishment of Christianity; deist sermons which he pretends had been delivered; discourses written under false names;[33] and doubts proposed and solved after the manner of preceding philosophers. Yet in these numerous treatises there is no claim to originality. His doubts and his beliefs are taken mainly from the English deists; and chiefly from Bolingbroke, the most French in mind of any of the English school.

A few words therefore will suffice to characterise his opinions. It appears that he believed in a God,[34]

[32] The four volumes are xxxii–xxxv of the *Œuvres Complètes*, 8vo. 1785. Vol. xxxii contains the philosophical works, of which ch. 2, 6, 7, 9, of the *Traité de Metaphysique*, relate to religion; also the *Profession de Foi des Théistes;* the *Homélies prononcées à Londres.* Vol. xxxiii contains the *Examen de Milord Bolingbroke;* and the *Epitre aux Romains.* Vol. xxxiv, *La Bible enfin Expliquée*, where the notes contain Voltaire's views fully. Vol. xxxv, *Histoire de l'Etablissement du Christianisme.*

[33] On the persecutions which fell on literary men, see Buckle, i. (672–684.)

[34] The proof of this assertion is clear in his *Traité de Metaphysique*, c. 2. (*Œuvres*, vol. xxxii); in Letter iii of Memmius to Cicero; in the *Profess. de Foi des Théistes;* and is shown by the fact of his opposition to the Encyclopædists on the ground of their atheism; which is confirmed by the inscription on his tomb, "Il combattit les athées." It is his blasphemous tone which has, not unnaturally, given rise to the idea of his atheism.

but firmly disbelieved the divine origin of the revealed religion, Jewish and Christian. The main purpose of his life however was not affirmation, but denial.[35] Accordingly the sole object of all his efforts was to destroy belief in the plenary inspiration of the scriptures, and the divine origin of revelation which is attested by them. There is hardly a book in scripture that he did not attack. Successively surveying the narrative of Jewish history, the Gospels, and statements of early church history,[36] he tried to show absurdities and contradictions in them all; not so much literary differences in the authors as difficulties of belief in the material revealed. In his views of Judaism and of Christianity he seems to have fluctuated between attributing them to the fraud or mistake of their propagators, and denying their originality. The science of historical criticism was beginning in his day, and was applied to the legends of Roman history. Voltaire embodied the spirit of this inquiry. In his histories he exemplified the cold, worldly, modern mode of looking at events, as opposed to the providential and theocratic view of them which had found expression as recently as in the works of Bossuet.[37] And he transferred this method to the treatment of holy scripture. No new branch of information was left unused by him for contributing to his impious purpose. The numerous works of travels which were affording an acquaintance with the mythology of other nations, were made to furnish him with the materials for hastily applying one solution to all the early Jewish histories, which he failed to invalidate by the application of the historic method just described.

[35] "Ecrasez l'infame" are the words, the initials of which, signed at the end of his letters to infidel friends, baffled the French police. Buckle considers them to have been designed against the French church, but offers no proof. It is to be feared that they were rather intended against the Christian religion, if not against the sacred person of our blessed Lord.

[36] See his *Commentary* (*Œuvres*, vol. xxxiv.), the *Homélies* (vol. xxxii.), and the *Histoire* (vol. xxxiv.).

[37] On the contrast of his historic tone to that of Bossuet, see Buckle, i. 726, and Schlosser, *History of the Eighteenth Century*, (English translation), vol. i. ch. iv. § 2. p. 273.

By an inversion of the argument of the early Christian apologists, he pretended that the early history preserved among the Hebrews was borrowed from the heathens, instead of claiming that the heathen mythology was a trace of Hebrew tradition; and, with a view to sustain this opinion, he discredited the integrity of the Hebrew literature. In nothing is his singular want of poetic taste, and of the power to appreciate the beauties of the literature of young nations, and the ethical value of moral institutions, more visible, than in denying the literary and monumental value of the Bible, and the moral influence of Christianity.[38] Infidels who have hated revealed religion as bitterly as Voltaire, have at least not had the meanness or the want of taste to depreciate the literary and moral interest which attaches to it.

Such was the character of the man, and of the efforts which he directed to the injury of revelation. It has been said[39] that to obliterate his influence from the history of the eighteenth century would be to produce a greater difference than the absence of any other individual in it would occasion; and would be similar to the omission of Luther from the sixteenth. The analogy, though startling, is true in the particulars which it is intended to illustrate. The influence of each was European in his respective century; and the doctrine acted not only on the world of thought, but of action.

We have described Voltaire alone; not because he was isolated by any interval of time from a general movement, but because his attack is more rudimentary, being directed rather to disintegrate Christianity than dogmatically to affirm unbelief. He was perhaps rather logically prior to the others than chronologically; being really connected with two bodies of men, which formed the centres of two infidel movements, the one in Paris, the other at the court of Frederick at Berlin.

Frederick the Great surrounded himself with

[38] Compare Carlyle's remarks *ut sup.* p. 175.
[39] Id. 105.

French literary men.[40] They were mostly persons who were exiles from France to escape persecution for their opinions, who had first found a refuge in Holland, and thence endeavoured by means of the Dutch booksellers to introduce their writings into France. From about 1740–60 several such teachers of infidelity were invited to the Prussian court, and dispersed their influence in Germany; the effects of which we shall subsequently find. One of them was the physician La Mettrie,[41] who wrote works on physiology marked by a low materialism. Such also was De Prades,[42] and more especially D'Argens.[43] The latter, struck with the force of "the Persian Letters" of Montesquieu, threw his doubts into an epistolary form, "the Jewish Letters;" in which the traditional opinions and ruling systems of the time were attacked with great freedom. He translated also some ancient works to serve his purpose, especially the fragments of the abusive work of the emperor Julian against Christianity, written in favour of the state religion of the Greeks and Romans.

While this was the character of some of the Frenchmen at the court of Frederick, whom Voltaire subsequently joined; men who, imbued with the most extravagant form of the philosophy of sensation, verged upon materialism; there were coteries of literary persons in Paris, which were the rallying point of sceptical minds, and centres of irreligious influence.

The existence of them is due in part to the altered position already named which literature assumed in reference to the court during the regency. Instead of being fostered, it was discouraged; and Fleury manifested an almost puritan spirit, and has left on record the

[40] On Frederick's entertainment of these French refugees, see Henke, *Kirchengesch.* vi. 180; Schlosser, vol. i. 2. § 3.

[41] La Mettrie (1709–1751). His views are seen in the *Discours Préliminaire* to his *Hist. Nat. del âme*, and in the *L'homme machiné* (1748). See a criticism on him in Ph. Damiron's *Memoires pour servir à l'Histoire de Philosophie au* 18e *siècle* (vol. i. pp. 1–49), reprinted from the Report of the *Académie des Sciences;* also Henke, vi. 13.

[42] De Prades (1720–1782). See Henke, vi. 201; also the article in the *Biographie Universelle.*

[43] D'Argens (1704–1771). See Damiron, Id. ii. 256–376.

expression of his alarm at the growing sceptical tone of literary works, and the imitation of the English spirit. Owing accordingly to the absence of patronage, and to the lavishment of those favours on extravagance which the elder Louis had bestowed on the fostering of intellect, literature became disjoined from court influences; and hence there grew up small centres of literary influence, analogous to those preceding the times of Louis XIV,[44] and nuclei for intellectual movement, where of old the various bodies had all moved round one central sun.

It would be irrelevant to enter into the details of these coteries. (23) Some were simply of fashion and taste; but others were undoubtedly gatherings of powerful thinkers, imbued with infidel principles, whose character belongs to French literature and the mental and moral culture of the time. One of the most remarkable of these coteries included names noted in French literature, such as Voltaire, Diderot, D'Alembert,[45] D'Holbach, Marmontel,[46] Helvetius, Grimm,[47] St. Lambert,[48] and Raynal.[49] We must notice some of them in detail, in order at once to appreciate the character of their works, and to illustrate the relation of their unbelief to the philosophy which they adopted.[50]

[44] On the old coteries of Rambouillet, &c., see Hallam's *Hist. of Literature*, iii. 137.

[45] D'Alembert (1717–83). For particulars of his life, see Brougham's memoir in *Lives of Men of Letters.* For his philosophy, see Damiron, ii. 1–114; Henke, vi. 218; Schlosser, i. 4. § 7. His infidelity was known to friends, but not openly avowed.

[46] Marmontel (1723–99). See Sainte-Beuve, *Portraits*, vol. iv.; Schlosser, ii. 2. § 1.

[47] Grimm, 1723–1807. See Sainte-Beuve, vol. vii. The *Correspondance Litt. par le Baron Grimm et Diderot* is the great source for the knowledge of his character.

[48] St. Lambert (1717–1803). See Damiron, ii. 144–256.

[49] Abbé Raynal (1711–96). See Schlosser, ii. 2. § 1. Henke, vol. vi. enumerates many more of the same class. Particulars of all are given in the *Biographie Universelle.*

[50] The following refer to places where the tendency and spirit of this whole movement are described, as well as literary information supplied. Henke, vi. 208, &c.; Bartholmess, i. 117–210; Lerminier's *Influence de la Phil. du* 18e *siècle* (1833); Morell's *Hist. of Phil.* i. 158, &c.; Maurice, *Mod. Phil.* p. 527–59; H. Martin's *Hist. de France*, vol. xv. and xvi. liv.

Diderot,[51] next to Voltaire, was the most able of the infidel writers, and greatly superior to the other members of the same class. His history is one of those narratives of struggle and suffering which so often have been the lot of men of letters. Those who have been the teachers of the world have too often been also its martyrs. The great peculiarity of Diderot, as of Johnson, was his encyclopædic knowledge, and his versatility in comprehending a variety of subjects. Less critical than Voltaire, and less philosophical than Rousseau, he exceeded both as the practical teacher. But in unbelief he unhappily advanced farther than either; his temper lacked moral earnestness; and in later life he was an atheist. A growth of unbelief may be traced in him: at first he was a doubter, next he became a deist, lastly an atheist. In the first stage he only translated English works, and even condemned some of the English deists. His views seem gradually to have altered, probably under the influence of Voltaire's writings, and of the infidel books smuggled into France; and he thenceforth assumed a tone bolder and marked by positive disbelief. In 1746 he wrote his *Pensèes Philosophiques*, intended to be placed in opposition to the *Pensées* of Pascal. Pascal, by a series of sceptical propositions, had hoped to establish the necessity of revelation. Diderot tried by the same method to show that this revelation must be untrue.[52] The first portion of the propositions[53] bore upon philosophy and natural

96, 99, 100, 101; Renouvier, *Mod. Phil.* b. v. ch. 2. § 6–8; also Kuno Fischer's *Bacon*, p. 451, and the references above given to Schlosser and to Damiron; Tennemann (*Manual*, § 378, &c.) also gives many literary references.

[51] Diderot (1713–84). His life and character have been sketched by Carlyle, (*Misc. Works*, vol. iv.); also by Damiron, ii. (227–324); St. Beuve, i. 355. Also see Villemain, *Tableau de la Litt. au* 18e *siècle*, lec. xix. 20. His novels are the parent of the impure novel of modern times. See Schlosser, i. 4. § 5, ii. 2. § 1.

[52] In the *Essai sur le Mérite et la Vertu*, pp. 73, 87, he allows deism, the God of moral order. Similarly in the *Pensées Philos.* § 46, but it is the God of nature. But in the Dialogue with D'Alembert he teaches atheism. On his theological views see Damiron, ii. 261 seq

[53] § 25, &c.

religion, but at length he came to weaken the proofs for the truth of Christianity, and controverted miracles, and the truth of any system which reposes on miracles; yet even in this work he did not evince the atheism which he subsequently avowed. It was soon after the imprisonment in which he was involved by this book, that he projected the plan of the magnificent work, the *Encyclopédie*, or universal dictionary of human knowledge. Its object however was not only literary, but also theological; for it was designed to circulate among all classes new modes of thinking, which should be opposed to all that was traditionary. Voltaire's unbelief was merely destructive: this was reconstructive and systematic. The religion of this great work was deism: the philosophy of it was sensationalist and almost materialist; seeming hardly to allow the existence of anything but mechanical beings. Soul was absorbed in body; the inner world in the outer;—a tendency fostered by physics. It was the view of things taken by the scientific mind, and lacks the poetical and feeling elements of nature—a true type of the cold and mechanical age which produced it. Diderot's atheism is a still further development of his unbelief. It is expressed in few of his writings, and presents no subject of interest to us; save that it seeks to invalidate the arguments for the being of a God, drawn from final causes. It has been well observed, that the lesson to be derived from him[54] is, that the mechanical view of the world is essentially atheistic; that whosoever will admit no means of discovering God but common logic, cannot find him. Diderot's unbelief may be considered to embody that which resulted from the abuse at once of erudition, physical science, and the sensational theory in metaphysics.

Among the band of friends who from connexion with the Encyclopædia acquired the name of Encyclopædists, was also Helvetius.[55] He was the moralist of

[54] See Carlyle, *Misc. Works*, iv. 322.

[55] Helvetius (1715–1771). See C. Remusat in *Rev. des Deux Mondes*, Aug. 15, 1858. On the circle of Helvetius see Carlyle *ut sup.* 287 seq.; and on their atheism Buckle, i. 786 seq. Concerning Helvetius himself

the sensational philosophy, one of those who applied the philosophy of Condillac to morals. Each man's tastes are so far affected by circumstances, that it is possible that Helvetius's exclusive association with the selfish circles of the French society, which never lived for the good of others, together with the perception of the hollowness of the respect which persons paid him for his wealth and influence, led him to regard self-love as the sole motive of conduct. His philosophy is expressed in two works;[56] the one on the spirit, the other on man: the former a theoretical view of human nature, the latter a practical view of education and society. His primary position is, that man owes all his superiority over animals to the superior organization of his body. Starting from this point, he argues that all minds are originally equal, and owe their variation to circumstances;[57] that all their faculties and emotions are derivable from sensation; that pleasure is the only good, and self-interest the true ground of morals and the framework of individual and political right.[58]

If in Diderot we have met with atheism, and in Helvetius with the selfish theory of morals; in the author of "the System of Nature" we meet with utter materialism, and the two former evils as corollaries from it. This work, which was published about 1774, though bearing a different author's name on the title, was probably the work of D'Holbach,[59] aided by Diderot and Helvetius,

see Ritter's *Christliche Philos.* viii. b. ix. ch. 2; Cousin's *Hist. de Phil. Morale*, leçon 7; Schlosser, i. 4. § 6.

[56] Viz., *De l'Esprit et de l'Homme* (Œuvres compl. 1818, vol. i. and ii.). Both treatises are excellently analysed in the table of contents prefixed to the work. The allusions in the text here may be thought to fail from their brevity in showing that Helvetius's opinions were a logical corollary from his principles; they cannot at least give any notion of the great power of analysis exhibited by him in expressing his own views.

[57] In Discourse ii. [58] Id.

[59] D'Holbach (1723–89). The *Système de la Nature* bears the name of a Mirabaud, secretary to the Academy. Some have thought it to be written by Robinet, author of a similar work. (His works are discussed in Damiron, ii. 480 seq.) Concerning the work see Villemain, iii. leç. 38; Damiron, i. (93–177); Ritter, *Christ. Philos.* viii. b. 9. ch. 3; Schlosser, i. 4. § 1. On D'Holbach's view of God see Damiron, Id. p. 155, &c.; Buckle, i. 787, note. The *Système de la Nature* is partly analysed and

and other members of the society which met at D'Holbach's house. It is a work of unquestionable talent and eloquence, in which materialism, fatalism, and atheism, combine to form a view of human nature which even Voltaire is said to have denounced.

The grand object of this work being to show that there is no God, the first part is occupied by the most rigorous materialism, and is designed to prove that there is no such thing as mind, nothing beyond the material fabric,[60] which is maintained by simple and invariable laws; and that the soul is a mode of organism,[61] the mere action of the body under different functions. The freedom of the will[62] and immortality[63] are accordingly denied. The first part having been directed to disprove the existence of mind, the second part is designed against religion. The author attributes the idea which man has formed of a first Cause to fear,[64] generated through suffering; and attempts to show the insufficiency of the *à priori* argument in favour of a God,[65] omitting the consideration of the arguments derived from final causes. Nature becomes in his scheme a machine; man an organism; morality self-interest; deity a fiction.

The work we have just named formed the crowning result of infidelity.[66] Voltaire showed philosophy shrinking from the hard materialism, morality from the fatalism, and religion from the atheism, to which they afterwards attained. In these steps, as witnessed in the circle of intellect just sketched, we see the ramification of the French sensational philosophy pushed to its farthest limits.

criticised in Brougham's *Discourse on Natural Theology*, pp. 232–47. It comprised two volumes, and is followed by a volume containing three small treatises relating to the natural principles of morals, and social philosophy. The work was refuted by Bergier (1771).

[60] Partie 1ere ch. iii. and iv.

[61] Part ii. ch. vii.

[62] Part ii. ch. xi.

[63] Part i. ch. xiii.

[64] Part ii. ch. i.

[65] Id. ch. iv. and v.

[66] Damiron discusses, in addition to the writers already named, two or three others, viz., Naigeon, Sylv. Marechal, and De la Lande, whose names are not introduced here into the text.

The writers lately described, though in some degree eminent, do not, like Voltaire, stand in the first rank of the French literary writers. Amid the circle of unbelievers, however, another of the highest rank was found, who, though he must be classed with the others, stood so apart in taste, in sympathy, in purpose, and in belief, that the study of his life and character is an interruption to the series of the materialist writers whom we are describing. Rousseau[67] was not an atheist like Diderot, nor a materialist like D'Holbach, nor a moralist of the selfish school like Helvetius, nor a scoffer like Voltaire. We discover in him a spirit endowed with deep feeling, and trained by much greater experience of life and of internal sorrow. His writings also mark the period when French philosophy ceased to attack the church, and found itself strong enough to act against the state. The greater portion of his works lies out of the range of our inquiry. Even his political writings, which indirectly injured religion in the world of action by stimulating the revolutionary hatred to the church, require notice only so far as they involved principles fundamentally opposed to the teaching of revealed religion.

It was about the middle of the century[68] that Rousseau commenced the "Political Essays" which made his name famous, and unhappily afterwards formed as it were the very bible of the French revolution. Retaining through life the preference for the simple institutions of the republic in which he had been born, he saw in

[67] On Rousseau see Villemain ii. leçon (23–24); Brougham's life of him in *Men of Letters;* Bartholmess, i. 233–270; Henke, vi. 232, especially p. 253, which refers to his theology; Schlosser, i. 4. § 4, and ii. § 2; St. Marc Girardin on the Emile in *Rev. des Deux Mondes*, Dec. 1854; and an article, too favourably written, but full of information, in the *Westminster Review*, Oct. 1859, which has been of much use for this lecture.

[68] The chief facts of Rousseau's life are these:—Born 1712; came to Paris, 1741; wrote *Sur les Sciences et les Arts*, 1750; *L'inegalité parmi les hommes*, 1753; lived in the Paris coteries, 1754–60; wrote *Nouvelle Heloise*, 1760; *Le Contrat Social*, 1761, and *Emile;* an exile in Switzerland 1762, where he wrote *Lettres de la Montagne;* accompanied Hume to England 1776; wrote his *Confessions;* returned to the Continent 1767; died 1770.

French society the abuses which appertain to civilization; and, with somewhat of the same feeling which Tacitus exhibits in his portraiture of the Germans, was led to study the comparative advantages of a primitive and refined age, and to maintain the paradox that the empire of corruption and inequality was to be regarded as the artificial creation of civilization. Ignoring the natural sinfulness and selfishness of the human race, he sought deliverance for mankind in the return to a primeval state, in which all should be free, equal, and independent. The inartificial state of society was the beau-ideal. And from this philosophical origin he traced society in the historical formation of an actual polity, describing how the social contract, while subordinating individual liberty to the collective will of a society, recompensed men by investing them with rights of civilization.

His doctrine was false theologically in its view of human nature; false philosophically in attempting to investigate an historical question by means of abstract metaphysical analysis; and false politically in drawing the attention of men away from practical and possible schemes of reform to visionary ones. It typified the movement of the French revolution in its extravagant hopes and its errors, in its destructive, not its remedial aspect.[69]

It was a few years later than the publication of these speculations that Rousseau wrote his celebrated treatise

[69] There are some good remarks on this theory in the article in the *Westminster Review* before quoted, the substance of which is to show that Rousseau's doctrine was false in its method and in its tendencies. It marked the stage of inquiry, indicative of the last part of the last century, when men, ignoring the teaching of history, strove to solve problems by means of abstract speculations; the attempt to study the origin of phenomena instead of the facts of their progressive manifestation. The social contract is nothing but the description of the collective development to which society tends. The scheme was visionary: but, as a protest against unjust monopolies which existed in that age, it woke up a response in society (cfr. Mill on *Liberty*, p. 47–50); and in its tendency it made Rousseau the precursor of the French revolution; but in typifying that movement it represented only its transient aspect of subversive energy, not its work of political reformation.

on education, *the Emile*,[70] which is the chief source for ascertaining his religious opinions. It has been called the Cyropædia of modern times, an attempt to show the education which a philosopher would give his pupil, in contradistinction to the religious and Jesuit training common in Rousseau's time.

In examining the religious education to be given to the young, he introduces a Savoyard vicar, the original of which his own early travels had suggested to him, to narrate the history of his convictions, and explain the nature of his creed. This creed is deism, and bears a very striking resemblance to that taught by the English deists. Rejecting tradition and philosophy,[71] the vicar grounds his creed on reason, the interior light. Commencing with sensation, he shows how step by step we arrive at the doctrine of the being and attributes of one God. Though he does not reject the argument from final causes, he seems to lay more stress on the metaphysical argument of the necessity of the divine existence. He first proves the existence of personality and will,[72] and uses this idea for the purpose of exploring the outer world; arguing that matter is inert and not self-active, he regards matter in motion as indicating force, and therefore volition; uniformity in its motion as proving a law, and therefore an intelligent will,[73] in which wisdom, power, and goodness combine.[74] This being is God, to whom man is subject. The universe is universal order. The physical evil therein originates in our vices, the moral in our free will.[75]

Having established the being of a God, he next proceeds to give reasons for believing in immortality. He bases it on the fact of the goodness of God, which leads Him to recompense with happiness the suffering

[70] *Emile*, b. iv. (See *Œuvres*, vol. iv. p. 14–119, ed. Paris, 1823, by Musset-Pathay.)

[71] Id. p. 17–20.

[72] Id. p. 22–30.

[73] *Emile*, p. 33: "Si la matière mue me montre une volonté, la matière mue, selon de certaines lois me montre une intelligence. C'est mon second article de foi."

[74] P. 34, 36. [75] P. 40–49.

good; and he disbelieves the eternity of punishment for the bad.[76] Having fixed the objects of belief, he next lays down the rule of duty in conscience, which he regards as an innate and infallible guide.[77] After thus establishing natural religion, he proceeds to criticise revealed, arguing its want of irrefragable evidence,[78] the discrepant[79] opinions in reference to it, the improbability of portions of its history;[80] attacking strongly the external evidence of prophecy and miracles; the former on the alleged want of proof of agreement between prophecy and its fulfilment; the latter on the ground of the alleged circle, that miracles are made to prove doctrine, and doctrine miracles.[81] He accordingly rejects the idea of Christianity being necessary to salvation; but renders a tribute of praise to its moral precepts, and regards the gospels, though partly fictitious, as containing indestructible moral truths; and concludes with the well-known comparison of Socrates to Christ, showing the stupendous superiority of the death and example of the latter. "If the death of Socrates," he says, "was that of a sage, that of Jesus was that of a God."[82]

It would have been thought that such teaching as this would hardly have excited a legal prosecution, in comparison with the more violent attacks that were made on religion: but the wide reputation and fascinating style of the author, the extraordinary ability of the work, above all the fact that many of the previous infidel doctrines had been published without the writers' names, were the means of subjecting him to persecution which they escaped. Voltaire and the infidel party were indignant at Rousseau's partial acceptance of Christianity. The French clergy were angry at his rejection of the remainder. The parliament ordered the book to be burned, and the author to be imprisoned. Rousseau had to seek refuge in Switzer-

[76] P. 50–53.
[77] P. 57–75. [78] P. 83–86. [79] P. 75–119.
[80] P. 86, &c. [81] P. 86.
[82] *Emile*, pp. 105–107.

land, and there defended his views of Christianity and miracles in a series of celebrated letters, which in their political effects have been compared with the letters of Junius. Driven out from Switzerland, he found a shelter in England, with Hume; and, until he could safely return to France, employed his time in writing his *Confessions*;[83]—the celebrated work, a mixture of romance and fact, which takes its place in the first rank of autobiographies,—a sad witness to the desperate wickedness of the human heart, and to the impotence of even a high moral creed, which we know Rousseau elsewhere expressed,[84] in creating morality, without Christian motives to give practical efficacy to it.

Such was Rousseau, an enemy of artificial society, of Roman catholic education, and of supernatural revelation; yet far removed from Voltaire and the other infidels, both in tone and literary character.[85] While Voltaire aimed only to destroy, Rousseau sought to reconstruct. Voltaire was a flippant, hasty reviler of Christianity, without originality in the material of his works, without depth of soul: Rousseau was serious, fresh, full of pathos. Voltaire either had no creed, or thought one unimportant, and was actuated by ma-

[83] The comparison of the statements of the *Confessions* with fragments of Rousseau lately published, shows that many statements which they contain in reference to other persons is false. The statement in the text is made in deference to the opinion latterly stated (e. g. in Heine's *Allemagne*), that there is a general air of romance pervading the work. If the statements in reference to himself are untrue, the narrative is only a greater proof of the immorality of the author. The supposition however seems groundless. The defender of Rousseau, G. H. Morin (*Essai*, 1851), does not exculpate his author by impeaching the historical truthfulness of the Confessions.

[84] The high moral standard is not of course seen in the *Confessions*, which show Rousseau to have been the incarnation of selfishness, and much worse than most of the other unbelievers, but is exhibited in the *Emile*. The fact that the author of the latter work could write the former is a sad example of a man knowing, like the ancient heathens, how to do good and doing it not.

[85] Henke (vi. p. 267 seq.) draws out the comparison of Voltaire with Rousseau in an excellent manner. Coleridge (*Friend*, vol. i. 165–186) has given a comparison of Voltaire with Erasmus, and of Rousseau with Luther.

lignant hatred against Judaism and Christianity: Rousseau had a firm creed, and spoke with decency of the religion which he rejected. Voltaire was devoid of taste for ancient literature, witty under a mask, a selfish sycophant to the ancient political régime: Rousseau never denied the authorship of his writings, was democratic in tastes, and was the means of exciting a love for antiquity. Finally rejecting to a great degree the sensational philosophy; rising above it in heart, if not in thought, Rousseau taught a spiritual philosophy, destined to bear fruit when the dreams of the revolution had passed. He stands alone however at present in this respect, like Montesquieu in politics[86] and Buffon in science; and the course of our history again brings before us men who must be classed with the materialists that preceded him.

We have stated that by the middle of the century the infidel writers turned their attention from the attack on the church to that on the state; and had already made such impression on the government, that it joined them in expelling the Jesuits.[87] For more than a quarter of a century before the revolution the literary writers were infidel. At length the evils of the state grew incurable, and the storm of the revolution burst.

It is possible in the present age to take a much more dispassionate view of that vast event than was taken by contemporaries.[88] It can now be adjusted to its true historic perspective, and its function in the scheme of history can be clearly perceived. The vastness of the movement consisted in this, that it was at once political, social, and religious.[89] It aimed at redressing the grievances under which France had suffered, and reconstructing society with guarantees for future liberty. It sought not merely to destroy

[86] See Villemain, i. 14, 15., ii. 22; Schlosser, i. 2. § 2., 4. § 3, and ii. 2. § 2.

[87] See Buckle, i. (772–783).

[88] Compare Macaulay's remarks in reference to the Revolution, *Essays* (ed. 8vo. 1843), ii. 215, &c.

[89] For the causes of the revolution compare the statements of Alison, *Hist. of Europe*, i. ch. ii. and iii., and Buckle, i. (836–850).

the feudalism which had outlived its time, and to equalize the unfair distribution of the public burdens, as means to accommodate society to modern wants; but it tried to effect these changes among a people whose minds were fully persuaded both that the privileges of particular classes and the existence of an established religion were the chief causes of the public misfortune. When so many movements combined, the catastrophe was intensified. It is indeed possible now to see that in the end the solid advantages of the revolution were reaped, while the mischief was temporary; but the severity of the storm while it lasted was increased by the infidel views with which society had become impregnated. For the revolution attempted to embody in its political aspect those poetical but wild theories of society which sceptical students had taught; and was founded on the false assumption of the perfectibility of man, and the perfect goodness of human nature, except as depraved by human government.

At first, under the National Assembly; the attack was only made on the property of the church; but on the establishment of the Convention, when the nation had become frantic at the alarm of foreign invasion, to which the king and clergy were supposed to be instrumental, the monarchy was overthrown, and religion also was declared obsolete. The municipality and many of the bishops abjured Christianity; the churches were stripped; the images of the Saviour trampled under foot; and a fête was held in November 1793,[91] in which an opera-dancer, impersonating Reason as a goddess, was introduced into the Convention, and then led in procession to the cathedral of Notre Dâme; and there, elevated on the high altar, took the place of deity, and received adoration from the audience. The services of religion were abandoned; the churches were closed; the

[90] On the incipient hostility to religion in the National Assembly, see Alison, vol. ii. ch. v. § 46, Id. § 32–35. On the full development of it in the Convention, see Id. iv. ch. xiv. § (45–48).

[91] Nov. 9.

sabbath was abolished; and the calendar altered. On all the public cemeteries the inscription was placed, "Death is an eternal sleep." Robespierre himself saw the necessity for the public recognition of the being of a God; and after the fall of the Girondists, obtained an edict for that purpose shortly before his death, in 1794; which event marks the return of society from atheism and materialism back to deism.[92] When the horrors of the dictatorship of Robespierre closed, and a regular government was established under the Directory, the priests obtained liberty to reopen the churches provided they maintained them at their own expense.[93] But the great majority of the people lived wholly without God in the world; while some sought refuge in the extravagant creed of a deist sect called the Theophilanthropists.[94] Nor was it till the year 1802 that Napoleon was able, and even then amid much opposition, to reestablish the Sunday.[95] Christianity was then reinaugurated by a public ceremony[96] in the cathedral, polluted eight years before by the blasphemy of the goddess of Reason. But the total cessation of religious instruction snapped asunder a chain of faith which had descended unbroken from the first ages; and to this must be ascribed the irreligious mode of spending the Sunday in French society.

The reign of atheism in religion was fortified by a philosophy; and the works of one infidel writer preserve the expression of the view which it took of Christianity and religion. As soon as the excitement of the revolution allowed leisure to return to the study of mental facts, there arose the extreme form of sensationalism, which was called (in a different meaning from the pres-

[92] Concerning this act of Robespierre, see Alison, iv. ch. xv. § 23, 24, 27.

[93] On the state of religion under the Directory, see Alison, vol. v. ch. xix. § 41, and vol. vi. ch. xxiv. § 19.

[94] See M. Gregoire's *Histoire de la Théophilanthropie*, forming part of his *Histoire des Sectes Relig.*, and the notice of it in the *Quarterly Review*, No. 56. Also the references in Alison, vi. ch. xxiv. § 19; Staüdlin, *Geschichte des Rationalismus und Supernat.* 1826, (44–54.)

[95] On the state under Napoleon, see Alison, viii. ch. xxxv. § 1, and 30–40.

[96] April 11, 1802.

ent popular use of the term) Ideology, (24). Cabanis and Destutt de Tracy are the best exponents of its physiological and psychological aspects; and the well-known Volney of its moral and religious side. Starting from the principles of Condillac and Helvetius, that the very faculties as well as ideas are derived from sensation, and moral rules from self-love, it almost reaches the same point as D'Holbach. Mental science was approached from the physiological side, and so viewed that mind seemed to be made a property of brain.[97]

The chief work in which Volney expresses his unbelief is entitled the "Ruins, or Meditations on the Revolutions of Empires."[98] It is a poem in prose. Volney imagines himself falling into a meditation, amid the ruins of Palmyra, on the fall of empires.[99] The phantom of the ruins appears, and, entering into converse with him, causes him to see the kingdoms of the world, and guides him in the solution of the mysteries which puzzle him.[1] It unveils to him the view of nature as a system of laws, and of man as a being gifted with self-love. It traces the origin of society in a manner not unlike Rousseau,[2] and refers the source of evil to self-love; states the cause of ancient prosperity and decline, and draws the moral lesson from the past.[3] While Volney is despondent at the prospect of the future, a vision is unveiled to him of a new age. It is of a nation ridding itself of privileged classes, and arming itself when its young liberties were threatened by foreign powers.[4] It is an apocalyptic vision of France in his time. Then suddenly the vision changes, and an assembly of the nations of the world is gathered as in one common arena, to ascertain how they may arrive at unity and peace.[5] Their differences are illus-

[97] See Morell, *Hist. of Phil.* vol. i. ch. iv. § 2.

[98] *Les Ruines ou Meditations sur les Revolutions des Empires* (1791.) A similar view of religion is taken in Dupuis, *Origine de tous les Cultes*, 1795.

[99] Ch. ii. [1] Ch. iii. [2] Ch. v.

[3] Ch. vii–xii. [4] Ch. xv. [5] Ch. xix.

trated by the discrepant opinions which they utter on religion; and the origin of each religion on the earth is traced.[6] It is here that Volney makes his speaker convey his own scepticism. He tracks the origin of the religious ideas[7] through the worship prompted by fear of the physical elements[8] and the stars[9] to that of symbols or idols,[10] with its accompanying mysteries and orders of priests; and then onward through dualism[11] to the belief of an unseen world;[12] then through mythology[13] and pantheism[14] to the belief in a Creator;[15] next, to Judaism[6] as the worship of the soul of the world; and lastly, through the Persian[17] and Hindu[18] systems to Christianity,[19] which he attempts to show to be the worship of the sun under the cabalistic names of Christ and Jesus. Availing himself of some of the fragments of mythology which such writers as Eusebius have preserved, and with a faint perception of the nature of mythology, he tries to resolve the narrative of the fall of man into solar mythology; and, pointing to contact with the Persians at the captivity as the source from which the Jews borrowed their ideas of a symbolic system, he regards the incarnation and life of Christ as the mistaken literalization on the part of contemporaries of their preconceived opinions. The conclusions to which Volney makes his interlocutor come[20] is, that nothing can be true, nothing be a ground of peace and union, which is not visible to the senses. Truth is conformity with sensations. The book is interesting as a work of art; but its analysis of Christianity is so shocking, that its absurdity alone prevents its becoming dangerous. It is the most unblushing attempt to resolve the noblest of effects into the most absurd of origins; and embodies in the consideration of religion the school of philosophy which he represented.

[6] Ch. xx. &c.
[7] Ch. xxii. p. 218. [8] P. 226. [9] P. 232.
[10] P. 238. [11] P. 255. [12] P. 262.
[13] P. 268. [14] P. 274. [15] P. 277.
[16] P. 285. [17] P. 286. [18] P. 287.
[19] P. 288. [20] Ch. xxiv. p. 320.

We have now completed the history of unbelief in France during the eighteenth century. We have seen how literature gradually emancipated itself from the power of the court, and, under the influence of a sceptical stimulus received from the importation of English free thought, was changed into political and ecclesiastical antipathy, and acquired a mastery over the public mind, until it involved the state, the church, and Christianity, in a common ruin. History offers no parallel instance of the victory of unbelief, through the power of the pen, nor of the union of the political with the theological movement, and of the intimate connexion of both with the current philosophy of the time.

The theological movement has contributed nothing of permanent literary value. The few apologies written were unimportant; and the thoughts of those who attacked Christianity were neither new nor characterised by depth. Their criticism was shallow, and was marked by the feature of which traces were observed in a few English authors, the disposition to charge imposture on the writers of the holy scriptures; so that they not only failed to appreciate the literary excellence of the works, but scarcely even allowed the possibility of unintentional deception on the part of the writers. The doubts were chiefly the reproduction of the English point of view, with the addition of a few physical difficulties;[21] protests of free thought against dogma in natural science. The view entertained concerning deity was eventually grovelling; the greatness of nature seemed to inspire no reverence. Unbelief gradually lost hold of monotheism; and in doing so never ascended in grandeur to the idea of pantheism, but fell into blank atheism. The theoretical morality of the English deists, even when depending on expedience, was noble; but in place of it the French school presented the lowest form of theory which ethical science has ever stated, and which finds its refutation with the philosophy that gave it birth.

No age exhibits a body of sceptical writers whose

[21] Such as the idea of the plurality of worlds suggested by Fontenelle.

characters are so unattractive as the French unbelievers; whose coarseness of mind in failing to appreciate that which is beautiful in Christianity is so evident, that charity could not forbid us to doubt, even if there were not independent proof, that faults of character contributed very largely to the formation of their unbelief. Nevertheless, the political aspect of the movement carries a solemn warning to the Christian church, not to endanger the everlasting Gospel of the Son of God by making it the buttress to support corrupt political and ecclesiastical institutions. It is true that Christ will not abandon his true church. Whatever is divine and eternally true will always as in this case survive the catastrophe. But this period of history shows that Providence will not work a miracle to save religion from a temporary eclipse, if the church forgets that Christ's kingdom is not of this world; and that the mission which he has given it is to convert souls to him; and that learning and piety are intellectual and moral means for effecting this object.[22] The political faults or shortcomings of the church are no apology for the infidelity of France; but they must be taken into acconnt in explaining its intensity.

A theological movement so vast could not fail to exercise an influence in other lands. Incidental allusions have already been made to its effects at the court of Prussia,[23] and to the traces of its tone in some of the later of the English deists.

The remainder of this lecture will be employed in tracing the history of free thought in England, from the date at which the narrative was interrupted to a little later than the end of the century; especially noticing the mode in which it was influenced by the movement in France.

It will be remembered that we brought down the

[22] The apologetic literature of this period of the French church is not powerful. See Buckle, i. 692, note; and Alison, i. 2. § 62.

[23] The influence on Germany will be seen in Lect. VI.

history of it as far as Hume.[24] We paused there, because deism then ends as a literary movement. Politics and new forms of literature absorbed the mind. Free thought continued to exist; but it was less frequently expressed in literature, and was considerably modified by foreign influences. In Gibbon, about 1776, the ancient spirit of deism, the spirit of Bolingbroke, speaks, but the form is changed. Instead of denying Christianity on *à priori* moral considerations, he feels bound to explain facts. The attack is not so much moral as historic. The inquiry into historical *origines* as well as logical causes has commenced. The mode of attack too has changed, as well as the point from which it is made. The French influence is visible in the satire and irony prevalent. There is no longer the bitter moral indignation of the early English deists, but the sneer that marks the spirit of contempt. Fear and hatred of Christianity have given way to philosophical contempt. (25)

In Thomas Paine, who wrote in France in the midst of the meeting of the French Convention, we meet a nearer reproduction of the spirit of early English deism, but he has even more than Gibbon caught the spirit of the French movement. Gibbon's scepticism is that of high life; Paine's of low. The one writer sneers, the other hates. The one is a philosopher, the other a politician. Paine represents the infidel movement of England when it had spread itself among the lower orders, and mingled itself with the political dissatisfaction for which unhappily there was supposed to be some ground. Paine's spirit is that of English deism animated by the political exasperation which had characterised the French. His doctrines come from English deism; his bitterness from Voltaire; his politics from Rousseau.

Within the limits of the present century two other traces are found of the influence of the French school of infidelity, which therefore ought logically to be comprised with it. The one is political, the other literary;

[24] In Lect. IV.

viz. the socialist schemes of Owen, which in some respects seem to be derived by direct lineage from Paine, and the expression of unbelief in the poetry of Byron and Shelley.

We must briefly notice these writers in succession.

The first in the series is Gibbon.[25] Though he has left an autobiography, he has not fully unveiled the causes which shook his faith, and made him turn deist. We can however collect that the reaction from the doubts suggested by the perusal of Middleton's work on the subject of the cessation of miracles, then recently brought into notoriety, (26) turned him to the church of Rome; and that his residence abroad and familiarity with French literature caused him to drift afterwards into the opposite extreme of scepticism. He did not become an atheist, like some of the French writers whom we have been studying: but he seems to have given up the belief in the divine origin of Christianity; and he manifested the spirit of dislike and insinuation common in the unbelief of the time.

He did not write expressly against Christianity; but the subject came across his path in travelling over the vast space of time which he embraced in his magnificent History of the Decline and Fall of the Roman Empire. It is a subject of regret to be compelled to direct hostile remarks against one who has deserved so well of the world. That work, though in the pageantry of its style[26] it in some sense reflects the art and taste of the age in which it was written, yet in its love of solid information and deep research is the noblest work of history in the English tongue. Grand alike in its subject, its composition, and its perspective, it has a right to a place among the highest works of human conception; and sustains the relation to history which the works of Michael Angelo bear to art. In the fif-

[25] Gibbon (1737–1794). See *Autobiography* (Milman's edition 1839), ch. iii. p. 73, &c.

[26] Cfr. some remarks (p. 27, 28,) in an instructive paper on Gibbon in the *National Review*, No. 3, on the relation of his method and style to his age.

teenth and sixteenth chapters of this work, Gibbon had occasion to discuss the origin of Christianity, and assigned five causes for its spread; viz. its internal doctrine, and organization, miracles, Jewish zeal, and excellence of Christian morals. The chapters were received with denunciations. Yet those[27] who in later times have re-examined Gibbon's statements candidly admit that they can find hardly any errors of fact or intentional mis-statement of circumstances.

The great mistake which he commits is obvious, and the cause hardly less so. The mistake is twofold: first, he attributes to the earliest period of Christianity that which was only true of a later; and secondly, he confounds the circumstances of the spread of Christianity with the cause which gave it force.[28] The powerful influence of the causes which he specifies cannot be doubted;[29] and we may hold it to be not derogatory to our religion that it admits of union with every class of efficient causes; and adapts itself so fully to man's wants, as to accept the support of ordinary sources of influence. But the causes which he alleges operated far less strongly, and some of them not at all, in the primitive age of Christianity. The discussion of this period lay beyond Gibbon's purpose; and as he dwelt wholly on the aspects of a later age, he has left the impression that the earliest age partook of the same characteristics. Nor is he correct in regarding the five causes as solely efficient. There is a subtler force at work, of the operation of which they exhibit only the conditions. They reveal the mechanism, but do not explain the principle. Without judging him as a theologian in omitting the theological cause for an alleged supernatural power, he must be censured as a historian in failing to appreciate the spiritual movement at work in Christianity, the deep excitement of the spiritual faculty, the yearning of the

[27] Milman and Guizot.

[28] The first of these is explained by Dr. Milman, Preface to edition of Gibbon, p. 10, and the article in the *Quarterly Review*, No. 100.

[29] Cfr. Mackintosh (*Life*, i. 244), quoted by Milman in his edition of Gibbon, c. xv. first note.

mind after truth and holiness. The same fault is observable in his appreciation of religion generally, and not merely of Christianity. With the want of spiritual perception common to his age, he had not the ethical sensibility to appreciate the internal part of a religious system; and hence he regards unworldly phenomena in the tone of the political world of his time.

In pointing out his errors, we have hinted at their causes. The coldness which scepticism and sensational philosophy[30] had induced in his mind, which could kindle into warmth in describing the greatness either of men or of events, but not in depicting the moral excellence of Christianity, was but the reflection of the cold hatred of religious enthusiasm common in his day. Nor would the historic views of primitive Christianity commonly entertained in his time tend to dissipate his error. For it was usual in that age of evidences to regard the early converts as cold and cautious inquirers, accustomed to weigh evidences and suggest doubts. In attempting to discover the doctrines and discipline of the English church in apostolic times, there was a danger of transferring the notions of modern decorum to the marvellous outburst of enthusiastic piety and supernatural mystery which attended the communication of the heaven-sent message; and therefore it is some palliation for Gibbon that he too failed to perceive that those were times of excitement, when new ideas fell on untried minds and yearning hearts. And it is a remarkable proof of the improved general conception which men now entertain of Christianity, that no apprehension of danger is now felt from Gibbon's views. The youngest student has imbibed a religious spirit so much deeper, that he cannot fail instinctively to perceive their insufficiency as an explanation of the phenomena.[31]

[30] The remarks which follow are partly taken from the above-named article in the *National Review* (pp. 33–36). Nearly the same thing is said by Miss Hennell in the fifth Baillie Prize Essay on the early Christian anticipation of the end of the world, 1860, a treatise which in other respects is very objectionable.

[31] Bp. Watson's *Apology for Christianity* was a reply to Gibbon,

One of our great poets has celebrated the two literary exiles of the Leman lake.[32] But how different are our feelings in respect of them in relation to this subject! Both were deists; but the one dedicated his life to a crusade against Christianity, the other only insinuated a few slight hints: the one derived his faults from himself, the other from his age: the one, the type of subtlety, acted by his pen on the world political; the other, the type of industry, sought to instruct the student. The writings of Voltaire remain as works of power, but not of information: Gibbon's history will endure as long as the English tongue.

Paine is a character of a very different kind from the freethinker last named.[33] Instead of the polished scholar, the polite man of letters, and the historian, like Gibbon, we see in him an active man of the world, educated by men rather than books, of low tastes and vulgar tone, the apostle alike of political revolution and infidelity. Though a native of England, his earliest life was spent in America at the time of the war of independence. Returning to England with the strong feelings of liberty and freedom which had marked the revolt of the colonies, he wrote at the time of the outbreak of the French revolution a work called the Rights of Man, in reply to Burke's criticism on that event. Prosecuted for this work, he fled to France, and was distinguished by being the only foreigner save one[34] elected to the French Convention. During its session he composed the infidel work called the Age of Reason, by which his name has gained an unenviable notoriety; and after the alteration of political circumstances in France, he returned to America, and there dragged out a miserable existence, indebted in his last

1776. Dean Milman's notes to chapters xv. and xvi. of Gibbon are an excellent comment and criticism.

[32] Byron, *Childe Harold*, iii. 105–108.

[33] Paine (1737–1809), published *Rights of Man*, 1790; *Age of Reason*, 1794. See the life by Cheetham, 1809, and Chalmers's *Biographical Dictionary*. Bp. Watson's *Apology for the Bible* was a reply to Paine (1796).

[34] Anacharsis Clootz.

illness for acts of charity to disciples of the very religion that he had opposed.

The two works, the Rights of Man, and the Age of Reason, being circulated widely in England by the democratic societies of that period, contributed probably more than any other books to stimulate revolutionary feeling in politics and religion.[35] This popularity is owing partly to the character of the language and ideas, partly to the state of public feeling. Manifesting much plebeian simplicity of speech and earnestness of conviction, they gave expression in coarse Saxon words to thoughts which were then passing through many hearts. They were like the address of a mob-orator in writing, and fell upon ground prepared. Political reforms had been steadily resisted; and accordingly, when the success of foreign revolution had raised men's spirits to the highest point of impatience, the middle classes, which wanted a moderate reform, were unfortunately thrown on the side of the wild and anarchical spirits that wished for utter revolution. The church, by holding with the state, was partly involved in the same obloquy. Paine's works, resembling Rousseau's in purpose, though quite opposite in style, were as much adapted to the lower classes of England as his to the polished upper classes of France.

The Age of Reason, was a pamphlet admitting of quick perusal. It was afterwards followed by a second part, in which a defence was offered against the replies made to the former part. The object of the two is to state reasons for rejecting the Bible,[36] and to explain the nature of the religion of deism,[37] which was proposed as a substitute. A portion is devoted to an at-

[35] The danger arising from republican clubs is described in Alison, iv. ch. xvi. § 6; and in W. Hamilton Reed's *Rise and Dissolution of Infidel Societies in the Metropolis*, 1800. See also the Report of the Committee of the House of Lords on them, 1801. The works of Godwin on *Political Justice*, 1793, and of Mary Woolstencraft on the *Rights of Women*, are generally adduced as illustrations of the prevalence of French political principles at that time in England.

[36] Part i. pp. 3–19, and part ii. pp. 8–83.

[37] Part i. pp. 3, 4; 21–50; part ii. pp. 83–93.

tack on the external evidence of revelation, or, as the author blasphemously calls it,[38] "the three principal means of imposture," prophecy, miracles, and mystery; the latter of which he asserts may exist in the physical, but not by the nature of things in the moral world. A larger portion is devoted to a collection of the various internal difficulties of the books of the Old and New Testament, and of the schemes of religion, Jewish and Christian.[39] The great mass of these objections are those which had been suggested by English or French deists, but are stated with extreme bitterness. The most novel part of this work is the use which Paine makes of the discoveries of astronomy[40] in revealing the vastness of the universe and a plurality of globes, to discredit the idea of interference on behalf of this insignificant planet,—an argument which he wields especially against the doctrine of incarnation. But no part of his work manifests such bitterness, and at the same time such a specious mode of argument, as his attack on the doctrine of redemption and substitutional atonement.[41] The work, in its satire and its blasphemous ribaldry, is a fit parallel to those of Voltaire. Every line is fresh from the writer's mind, and written with an acrimony which accounts for much of its influence. The religion which Paine substituted for Christianity was the belief in one God as revealed by science, in immortality as the continuance of conscious existence, in the natural equality of man, and in the obligation of justice and mercy to one's neighbour.[42]

The influence of the spirit of Paine lingered in some strata of our population far into the present century: by means of the views of Owen,[43] the founder of Eng-

[38] P. 44. [39] Part ii. pp. 10–83.

[40] Part i. pp. 37–44. This difficulty, first suggested by Fontenelle, is met in the eloquent *Astronomical Discourses* (1822) of Chalmers. The controversy has been newly opened by the brilliant essay on the *Plurality of Worlds* (1853), supposed to be by Dr. Whewell, and pursued by Dr. Brewster (*More Worlds than One*), Professor Baden Powell (Essays on the *Order of Nature*), and by Professor H. S. Smith in the *Oxford Essays*, 1855. [41] Page 20. [42] Part i. pp. 3, 4; p. 50.

[43] Robert Owen (1771–1858). About the year 1800 he became known

lish socialism, which essentially reproduce the visionary political reforms which belonged to the philosophy and to the doubt of the last century.

Being desirous to improve the condition of the industrial classes, Owen speculated on the causes of evil; and, approaching the subject from the extreme sensational point of view, regarded the power of circumstances to be so great, that he was led to regard action as the obedience to the strongest motive. He thus introduced the idea of physical causation into the human will; and made the rule of right to be each one's own pleasures and pains. Founding political inferences on this ethical theory of circumstantial fatalism, he proposed the system called socialism, which aimed at modifying temptations and removing two great classes of temptations, by facilitating divorce, and proposing equality of property. The system is now obsolete both in idea and in history, yet it has an interest from the circumstance that until recently it deceived the minds and corrupted the religious faith of many of the manufacturing population.

The history of the influence of French infidelity on the course of English thought closes with names of greater note.[44] If Owen, though belonging to the present century, represents the political tone of the past,

in connexion with schemes of industrial reform at the Lanark mills; and from 1813–19 conducted them as a social experiment to carry out his views. He attempted also to spread his opinions in America. After his return to England, by means of lectures and his work, *The New Moral World*, he taught them in the manufacturing towns; and they were widely spread about the time of the Chartist movement (1839–41). His opinions may be learned from his *Essays on the Formation of Character* (1818), which explain his Lanark system; and especially his *New Moral World*, published about 1839. His religious opinions may be gathered from the *Debate on the Evidences and on Society with A. Campbell*, 1839. His autobiography was published in 1857, and a review of his philosophy by W. L. Sargeant, 1860. An article also related to him in the *Westminster Review* for Oct. 1860. See also Morell's *History of Philosophy*, i. 386 seq. Mr. R. Dale Owen, son of the above, published several deist tracts in America, from about 1840–44.

[44] It has been considered unnecessary to name three other unimportant writers, Burgh, Farmer, a writer on the subject of Demoniacs, and Carlisle, who was prosecuted in 1830.

we must also refer to the same period, morally though not chronologically, the spirit of unbelief which animated literature in the poetry of Byron and Shelley.

Saddened by blighted hopes, political and personal, Byron affords a type of the unbelief which is marked by despair.[45] If compared with the two exiles of the Leman lake, whom the sympathy of a common scepticism and common exile commended to his meditation, he stands in many respects widely contrasted with them in tone and spirit. Allied rather to Gibbon in seriousness, he nevertheless wholly lacked his moral purpose and resolute spirit of perseverance. More nearly resembling Voltaire in the nature of his unbelief, he nevertheless differed in the features of gloom by which his mind was characterized. His unbelief was a remnant of the philosophic atheism of France; but it received a tinge in passing through the wounded mind of the poet.

His brother poet, of a still loftier genius, is more widely contrasted with him in mental qualities, than united by similarity in the character of his unbelief. Both were weary of the world; but the one was drawn down by unbelief to earth, the other soared into the ideal: the one was driven to the gloom of despair, the other was excited by the imagination to the madness of enthusiasm: the one was made sad by disappointment, the other was goaded by it into frenzy.

Shelley merits more than a passing notice, both because his poetry is a proof of our main position concerning the influence of certain forms of philosophy in producing unbelief, and because his mental history, as learned by means of his works and memoirs, is a psychological study of the highest value. The infidelity which shows itself in him is an *idolum specûs*, as well as an *idolum theatri*.[46]

[45] Byron (1788–1824). The *Vision of Judgment*, written in 1821, has been already referred to in Lecture III. as a vehicle for sceptical banter. For a brief comparison between the scepticism of Byron and Shelley, see remarks in the *Westminster Review*, April 1841, by Mr. G. H. Lewes.

[46] Bacon, *Nov. Org.* Aph. 52, 53.

His life, his natural character, and his philosophy, all contributed to form his scepticism.[47] His life is a tale of sorrow and ruined hopes, of genius without wisdom: one of the sad stories which will ever excite the sympathy of the heart. Early sent to this university, he seems like Gibbon to have lived alone; and in the solitude of that impulsive and recluse spirit which formed his life-long peculiarity, to have nursed a spirit of atheism and wild schemes of reform. Charged by the authorities of his college with the authorship of an atheistical pamphlet,[48] he was expelled the university. An outcast from his family, he went forth to suffer poverty, to gather his livelihood as he could by the wonderful genius which nature had given him. Wronged as he thought by his university and his country, his wounded spirit imputed the supposed unkindness which he received to the religion which his enemies professed. In a foreign land, brooding over his wrongs, he cherished the bitter antipathy to priestcraft and to monarchy which finds such terrific expression in his poems.[49] His end was a fit close of a tragic life. A friendly hand paid the last office of friendship to his remains; and the urn which contains the ashes of his pyre rests in the solemn and beautiful cemetery of the eternal city, which he himself had described so strikingly in his affecting memorial of his friend, the poet Keats.[50]

His natural character contributed to produce his

[47] Shelley (1792–1822). The materials are abundant for understanding the character and works of Shelley, in biographies both friendly and hostile. The second edition of the *Shelley Memorials*, by lady Shelley, 1859, contains an essay on Christianity by him. Several important articles in Reviews have been published in reference to him, among which it is desirable to call attention to the one in the *National Review*, No. 6, Oct. 1856, which contains a very instructive analysis of his mental and moral character. It has been used in the few remarks which follow.

[48] The pamphlet appears to have been an anonymous statement of the weakness of the argument for the existence of deity; negative rather than positive. See the account of the transaction and its results in T. J. Hogg's *Life of Shelley*, 1858, vol. i. pp. (269–286).

[49] E. g. in the *Ode to Liberty* (§ 15 and 16), written in 1820.

[50] In the *Adonais*, § 49–51. For Shelley's own cremation and burial, see the *Memorials* by lady Shelley, p. 201.

scepticism not less than his life to increase it. He has left us a clear delineation of himself in his writings. If considered on the emotional side, he was a creature of impulses. His predominant passion was an enthusiastic desire to reform the world. Filled with the wildest ideas of the French revolution, his impulsiveness hurried him on to give expression to them. His intellectual nature was analogous to the moral, and itself received a stimulus from it. His mental peculiarity was his power of sustained abstraction. His poems are not lyrics of life, but of an ideal world. His tendency was to insulate qualities or feelings, and hold them up to the mental vision as personalities. The words which he has addressed to his own skylark fitly describe his mind as it soared in the solitude of its abstraction:

Higher still and higher
  From the earth thou springest,
    *   *   *   *   *
And singing still dost soar, and soaring ever singest.

It has been well observed, that this tendency of the mind to personify isolated qualities or impulses, was essentially the mythological tendency[51] which had created the religion and expressed itself in the poetry of the Greeks, and possibly contributed to foster Shelley's sympathies with heathen religion. His mind was peculiarly Greek, simple not complex, imaginative rather than fanciful, abstract not concrete, intellectual not emotional; wanting the many-sidedness of modern taste, partaking of the unity of science rather than the multiformity of nature, like sculpture rather than painting. This mental peculiarity contributed to scepticism by inclining his mind to the pantheistic philosophy, which can never be held save by those whose minds can give being to an abstraction, and is revolting to those who are deeply touched with the Hebrew consciousness of personality and of duty. His philosophy was at

[51] This is well put in the Review above quoted, (p. 356).

first a form of naturalism, which identified God with nature, and made body and spirit co-essential. In this stage he oscillated between the belief of half personified self-moved atoms, or a general pervading spirit of nature. From this stage he passed into a new one, by contact with the philosophy of Hume; and, while admitting the diversity of matter and spirit, yet denied the substantial reality of both. In this state of mind he studied the philosophy of Plato, which was originally designed for doubters somewhat analogous to him; and he readily imbibed the theory that the passing phenomena are types of eternal archetypes, embodiments of eternal realities. But it was Plato's view of the universe that he accepted, not his view of man; his metaphysics, not his ethics. In none of these three theories is the rule of the universe ascribed to a character, but in each to animated abstractions. They are a pantheistic or mythological view of things.[52] Nor was the effect of this philosophy merely theoretical, for the distorted view of the physical and moral cosmos led him to believe that both should be regulated by the same conditions; that men should have the unconstrained liberty which he thought he saw in material things. Like Rousseau, ascribing moral evil to the artificial laws of society, Shelley proposed to substitute a new order of things, in which man should be emancipated from kings and priests. This philosophy also increased his hatred against the moral order of the world, and especially against Christianity; and led him to regard it as the offshoot of superstition and the impediment to progress. Yet even here, while echoing the irreverent doctrines of the French revolution, he bore an unconscious witness to the majesty of the Christian virtues, in that he could find no nobler type with which to invest his ideal race of men.

[52] The Reviewer thinks that the first stage was in tone like Lucretius, i. e. Epicureanism. The second and third are described here in the text. The Queen Mab (end of first division) expressed the first stage; the first speech of Ahasuerus in the Hellas is a specimen of the second; and the Adonais (43 and 52) of the third.

We have dwelt long on Shelley, as a most instructive example for observing the various influences, personal and social, intellectual and moral, philosophical and political, combining to form unbelief. His thoughts are the last echo of the unbelief of the last century. The great movement of Germany has completely changed the scepticism of the present. The instances that we have found of unbelief in England were indications of a tendency rather than a movement. They were however of sufficient importance to call forth the voices of the church in reply or in protest.

It has been remarked, that in the former half of the eighteenth century the attack was chiefly directed against the internal doctrines and narratives of revelation, on the assumption that they clashed with the judgment of common sense, or of the moral faculty. And therefore the writers on the evidences, adapting their defence to the attack, employed themselves chiefly in establishing the internal evidences, the moral need of a revelation generally, and the suitability of the Christian in particular, before producing the divine testimony which authenticates it. But about the middle of this century the historic spirit arose, and the point of attack shifted to an assault on the historic value of the literature which contains the revelation. The question thenceforth became a literary one, whether there was documentary proof that a revelation had been given. The defence accordingly ceased to be philosophical, and became historical.[53]

Opinions have changed with regard to the value of evidences in general, and the historic form of them in particular. When Boyle[54] at the end of the seventeenth century, and Bampton and Hulse in the latter

[53] This contrast however in the evidences, though true in a general way, must not be pressed so as to imply an absolutely defined line of chronological separation between the two classes of evidence.

[54] Robert Boyle died in 1692, and founded the lecture by his last will. The lectures commenced in the same year. Bampton's were founded in 1751; but none delivered till 1780. Hulse died in 1790; but the lectures did not commence till 1820. A list of the lectures delivered in each series may be found in Darling's *Cyclopædia Bibliographica*.

half of the eighteenth, established their respective lectures, they looked forward to the probability of the occurrence of new forms of doubt, and to the importance of reasoning as the weapon for meeting them. In more recent times evidences have been undervalued, through the two opposite tendencies of the present age, the churchly and corporate tendency on the one hand, which rests on church authority, and the individualising tendency on the other, which rests on intuitive consciousness.[55] Evidences essentially belong to a theory, which places the test of truth objectively in a revealed book, and subjectively in the reason, as the organ for discovering morality and interpreting the book.[56] While evidences in general have been undervalued for these reasons, the historic branch of them has been regarded as obsolete, because having reference only to an age which doubts the documents and charges the authors with being deceivers or deceived, and unavailing, like an old fortification, against a new mode of assault. This latter statement is in substance correct. It lessens the value of this argument as a practical weapon against the doubts which now assail us, but does not detract from the literary value of the works in the special branch to which they apply. If the progress of knowledge be the exciting cause of free thought, a similar alteration in the evidences would be expected to occur from causes similar to those which produce an alteration in the attack, independently of the change which occurs from the necessity of adjusting the one to the other.

Abstract questions like this concerning the value of evidences find their solution independently of the human will. The human mind cannot be chained. New knowledge will suggest new doubts; and if so,

[55] The remarks on evidence in Nos. 73 and 84 of the *Tracts for the Times*, and the tone assumed by the ultramontane writers of France, are instances of the undervaluing evidences from the former causes. The deist literature of the last century, and the writings of Carlyle in the present, are instances of that which arises from the latter.

[56] i. e. They belong essentially to the protestant stand-point in theology.

spirit must be combated by spirit. Defences of Christianity, attempts to readjust it to new discoveries, must therefore continue to the end of time. In reference to the minor question of the value of the historic evidences, it is important to remember that these grand works are not simply refutative; they are indirectly instructive and didactic. Just as miracles are a part of Christianity, as well as evidences for its truth, so apologetic is a lesson in Christianity, as well as a reply to doubt.[57] It happens also that the most modern doubt of Germany has assumed the historic line, has become critical instead of philosophical; and, though the criticism is primarily of a different kind, it ultimately becomes capable of refutation by the very line of argument used in the eighteenth century.[58] We cherish therefore with devout reverence the memory of those writers who employed the power of the pen to defend the religion that they loved. They joined their intellectual labours to the spiritual earnestness which was the other weapon for opposing unbelief. Providence blessed their work. They sowed the seed of the intellectual and spiritual harvest which this century is reaping. "And herein is that saying true, One soweth and another reapeth. I sent you to reap that whereon ye bestowed no labour: other men laboured, and ye are entered into their labours. And he that reapeth receiveth wages, and gathereth fruit unto life eternal; that both he that soweth and he that reapeth may rejoice together."[59]

[57] See above, p. 160. The view which Blunt took of the evidences is given in his *Essays*, p. 183, reprinted from the *Quarterly Review*, April 1828.

[58] The controversy raised by the Tübingen school refers to the date of books of the New Testament which testify to facts and doctrines. Supposing this primary question settled in favour of our commonly received view, then the further question follows concerning the honesty and opportunity of information of the narrators; and it is here that the arguments of Lyttleton, Lardner, and Paley, in the last century, find their proper place. See below, Lect. VIII.

[59] John iv. 37, 38, 36.

LECTURE VI.

FREE THOUGHT IN THE THEOLOGY OF GERMANY FROM 1750–1835.

PHIL. iv. 8.

Whatsoever things are true, whatsoever things are honest, whatsoever things are just, whatsoever things are pure, whatsoever things are lovely, whatsoever things are of good report; if there be any virtue, and if there be any praise, think on these things.

WE are about to study the history of the movement in German theology, which is usually described by the vague name of Rationalism,[1]—a movement which, whether viewed specially in its relation to theology, or to literature generally, must be regarded as one of the most memorable efforts of human thought. It was one aspect of the great outburst of mental activity in Germany, which within the last hundred years has created a literature, which not only vies with the most renowned of those which have added to the stock of human knowledge, but holds a foremost rank among those which are characterised by originality and depth. The permanent contribution made by it to the thought of the world is the creation of a science of criticism,—a method of analysis, in which philosophy and history are jointly employed in the investigation of every branch of knowledge. If however it be viewed apart from the question of utility, the works produced during

[1] On Rationalism see Note 21 at the end of this volume.

this period, in poetry, speculation, criticism, and theology, must ever make it memorable for monuments of mental power, even when they shall have become obsolete as sources of information.

The theological aspect of this great period of mental activity, which we are about to sketch, has now probably so far assumed its final shape, and given indications of the tendencies permanently created by it for good or for evil, that it admits of being viewed as a whole, and its purpose and meaning observed.[2]

We shall deviate slightly from the plan hitherto pursued, of selecting only the sceptical form of free thought, and shall give an outline of German theology generally; partly because the limits that sever orthodoxy from heresy are a matter of dispute, partly in order that the movement may be judged of as a whole. The size of the subject will preclude the possibility of entering so fully into biographical notices of the writers, or into the analysis of their writings, as in former lectures. We must select such typical minds as will enable us to observe the chief tendencies of thought.

As the stages of history are not arbitrarily severed, but grow out of each other, we must briefly notice the mental conditions of the period in Germany which preceded the rise of rationalism; next indicate the new forces, the introduction of which was the means of generating the movement; and then explain the movement itself in its chief phases and present results.

We have previously had occasion to imply, that the Protestant reformation of the sixteenth century contained both an intellectual and a spiritual element.[3] The attempt to reconcile these has been the problem of protestant theology in Germany ever since. The intellectual element, so far as it was literary, soon

[2] The sources for the knowledge of this period are briefly stated in the Preface to these lectures.

[3] See p. 9, 99. Hundeshagen (*Der Deutsche Prot.* § 13) insists on the prime importance of the spiritual element as the moving force in the Reformation.

passed into thé hands of lay scholars:[4] the spiritual became a life rather than a doctrine, and the polemic or dogmatic aspect of the intellectual movement alone was left. The time from the passing of the Formula of Concord and the Synod of Dort[5] to the beginning of the eighteenth century, a period nearly corresponding with the seventeenth century, was in Germany an age of dogmatic theology. It was scholasticism revived, with the difference that the only source for the data of argument was the Scripture, not philosophy. But there was an equal absence of inquiry into first principles, an equal appeal to authority for the grounds of belief, and equal activity within these prescribed limits. It was marked, as among the contemporary puritans in England, by the most extreme view of biblical inspiration.[6] Not only was the distinction of law and gospel overlooked, and the historic and providential development in revelation forgotten; but Scripture was supposed to be in all respects a guide for the present, as

[4] Melancthon and Camerarius, Calvin and Beza, represent the union of learning with theology; the second Scaliger, the Stephenses, Casaubon, and others, are instances of the great lay scholars.

[5] The date of the former is 1577; of the latter 1618. These are named as the events from which the theology in the Lutheran and Calvinistic churches respectively became fixed. Buddeus (*Isagoge*, p. 239) dates it rather from the confession of Ratisbon, 1601. On this dogmatic period see *Der Deutsche Prot.* § 9; Hagenbach's *Dogmengesch.* § 216–18; Amand Saintes' *Critical History of Rationalism* (transl.) ch. v. and vi; Pusey's *Historical Inquiry*, part i. pp. (1–52), part ii. ch. viii. and ix. (1830). It was this period which produced the various books of Loci Communes Theologici. The only exception to this scholastic spirit was Calixt. and the school of Helmstadt, which in tone was like the school of Saumur, (Cameron, Amyrauld, and Placæus,) or like Baxter, the controversies connected with which prove the rule. On it see Schröckh, *Christliche Kirchengeschichte seit der Reformation* (1804), viii. 243 seq. On the theologians of this period see Weismann, *Introd. in Memorabilia Eccles. Hist.* (1718), p. 919 seq.

[6] This view of inspiration is stated in Quenstedt's *Syst. Theol.*, and Calov's *Syst. Theol.* i. 554 seq., about the end of the seventeenth century. Dr. Pusey (part i. 140) refers to passages of Semler's *Lebens-Beschreibung* illustrative of these opinions in the German church of that period. On the similar controversy which existed in the French protestant church see note above, p. 113. This is only one instance among many of the close analogy which exists in the development of thought between the reformed churches in different lands.

well as a record of the past. Infallible inspiration was attributed to the authors of the sacred books, not merely in reference to the religious instruction which formed the appropriate matter of the supernatural revelation, but in reference also to the allusions to collateral subjects, such as natural science, or politics; and not merely to the matter, but to the smallest details of the language of the books.

Contemporary with this scholastic spirit was an outburst of the living spiritual feeling which had formed the other element in the Reformation. This religious movement is denominated Pietism. (27) Its centre was at Halle; and the best known name among the band of saints, of whom the world was not worthy, was Spener. Soon after the time when the miseries of the thirty years' war were closing, he established schools for orphans, and a system of teaching and of religious living which stirred up religious life in Germany. These two tendencies—the dogmatic and the pietistic—marked the religious life of Germany at the opening of the eighteenth century. The inference has been frequently drawn by the German writers, that they ministered indirectly to the production of scepticism; the dogmatic strictness stimulating a reaction towards latitude of opinion, and the unchurchlike and isolating character of pietism fostering individuality of belief. This inference is however hardly correct. Dogmatic truth in the corporate church, and piety in the individual members, are ordinarily the safeguard of Christian faith and life. The danger arose in this case from the circumstance that the dogmas were emptied of life, and so became unreal; and that the piety, being separated from theological science, became insecure.

During the first half of the century, certain new influences were introduced, which in the latter half caused these tendencies to develope into rationalism. They may be classed as three;[7]—the spread of the

[7] These are the chief influences which the German writers enumerate. See Tholuck, ii. § 2–5, Kahnis, *History of German Protest.* (transl. 1856) i. 1.

speculative philosophy of Wolff; the introduction of the works of the English deists; and the influence of the colony of French infidels established by Frederick the Great in Prussia. We shall explain these in detail.

The philosophy of Wolff was an offshoot directly from Leibnitz, indirectly from the Cartesian school. It is hardly necessary to reiterate the remark that the revolution in thought wrought by Descartes was nothing less than a protest of the human mind against any external authority for the first principles of its belief. Two great philosophers followed out his method in an independent manner; Spinoza, who attempted to exhibit with the rigour of deduction the necessary development of the idea of substance into the various modes which it assumes; and Leibnitz,[8] who, with less attempt at formal precision of method, starting with the idea of power, endeavoured, by means of the monadic theory, which it is unnecessary here to explain, to exhibit the nature of the universe in itself, and the connexion of the world of matter and of spirit. Wolff was a disciple of Leibnitz; great as a teacher rather than an inventor, who invested the system of his master slightly modified, with the precision of form which raised it to rivalry with the perfect symmetry of Spinoza's system. Adopting his master's two great canons of truth, the law of contradiction as regulative of thoughts, and the law of the sufficient reason as regulative of things,[9] he attempted in his theoretic philosophy to work out a regular system on each of the great branches of metaphysic,—nature, the mind, and God; by deducing them from the abstract ideas of the human mind.[10] The true method of conducting

[8] On Leibnitz and his system see Tennemann, *Geschichte* xi. 93 seq.; Ritter's *Christliche Phil.* viii. 47 seq.; Renouvier, *Phil. Mod.* (278–90); and especially Maine de Biran's *Life of Leibnitz* in the *Biographie Universelle.* Also Morell's *History of Philosophy*, i. 220, and H. Rogers's *Essays* (Essay on Leibnitz,) reprinted from the *Edinburgh Review*, July 1846.

[9] On these canons see Sir W. Hamilton's *Lectures on Logic*, vol. i. lect. vi.; Mansel's *Prolegomena*, ch. vi.; and Mills's *Logic*, vol. ii. b. v. ch. iii. § 5.

[10] Wolff, 1679–1754. Professor of Philosophy at Halle; in 1723 expelled; restored in 1741; Lange and Buddeus were his great opponents

this inquiry would be strictly an *à posteriori* one, an analytical examination of our own consciousness, to ascertain what data the facts of the thinking mind furnish with respect to things thought of. But without any such examination Wolff, assuming in reference to these subjects the abstract ideas of the human mind as his data, proceeded to reason from them with the same confidence as the realists of the middle ages, or as mathematicians when they commence with the real intuitions of magnitude on which their science is founded. Thus his whole philosophy was form without matter; a magnificent idea, but not a fact. Yet though really baseless, it was not necessarily harmful.

This philosophy at first met with much opposition from the pietistic party of Halle.[11] The opposition was not due to any theological incorrectness, for Wolff was an orthodox Christian; but arose from the narrow and unnecessary suspicions which religious men too often have of philosophy, and the sensibility to any attempt to suggest a reconsideration of the grounds of belief, even if the conclusion adopted be the same. But the system soon became universally dominant. Its orderly method possessed the fascination which belongs to any encyclopædic view of human knowledge. It coincided too with the tone of the age. Really opposed, as Cartesianism had been in France, to the scholasticism which still reigned, its dogmatic form nevertheless bore such external similarity to it, that it fell in with

(see Hagenbach's *Dogmengesch.* § 274). His philosophy consisted of an attempt to deduce *à priori* a system of (1) cosmology, (2) psychology, (3) natural theology. The latter relates to God, His attributes in Himself and in creation. See some remarks by Mr. Mansel on his scheme (art. *Metaphysic. Encycl. Brit.*, 8vo. ed. p. 603). On his philosophy see Ritter, *Christ. Phil.* viii. b. x. ch. i.; Tennemann's *Manual*, § (363-5); Morell, i. 228; Rosenkrantz, *Gesch. der Kantischen Schule*, b. i. part iii. ch. i. His religious opinions are found in the *Theol. Nat.* 1736, and *Philos. Moralis*, 1750, and in his *Vernuenftige Gedanken von Gott.* 1747 (p. 604). See on them Henke, *Kirchengesch.* viii. § 3; Mansel's *Bampton Lectures*, note 3. And on the effects of his philosophy, and the state of theology in Germany at the time of its influence, see Tholuck's *Vermischte Schriften*, ii. § 2 and 1.

[11] In 1723, in consequence of the petition from the pietist professors, Frederick I. deposed Wolff. See Kahnis (Engl. Transl.) p. 114.

the old literary tastes. The evil effects which it subsequently produced in reference to religion were due only to the point of view which it ultimately induced. Like Locke's work on the reasonableness of Christianity, it stimulated intellectual speculation concerning revelation. By suggesting attempts to deduce *à priori* the necessary character of religious truths, it turned men's attention more than ever away from spiritual religion to theology. The attempt to demonstrate everything caused dogmas to be viewed apart from their practical aspect; and men being compelled to discard the previous method of drawing philosophy out of scripture, an independent philosophy was created, and scripture compared with its discoveries.[12] Philosophy no longer relied on scripture, but scripture rested on philosophy. Dogmatic theology was made a part of metaphysical philosophy. This was the mode in which Wolff's philosophy ministered indirectly to the creation of the disposition to make scriptural dogmas submit to reason, which was denominated rationalism. The empire of it was undisputed during the whole of the middle part of the century, until it was expelled towards the close by the partial introduction of Locke's philosophy,[13] and of the system of Kant, as well as by the growth of classical erudition, and of a native literature.

The second cause which ministered to generate rationalism was English deism. The connexion of England with Hanover had caused several of the works of the English deists to be translated in Germany,[14] and the

[12] In reference to the introduction of Wolff's philosophy, the reference to Tholuck has been already given. See also Schröch's *Gesch.* viii. 26; Lechler, 448; Amand Saintes' *Critical History of Rationalism*, i. ch. ix.; Hagenbach's *Dogmengesch.* § 274; Kahnis, p. 110. Kahnis (115) names Baumgarten, Canz, and Toellner, as Wolff's pupils. Mosheim and the Walches were too exclusively literary to be affected by the new philosophy. Canz of Tübingen was the first to apply the system to doctrinal theology (1728). See Pusey, part i. 116.

[13] Locke's philosophy in a distorted form was introduced by the French philosophers who lived at the court of Frederick II.

[14] On the introduction of English deism, see Tholuck, § 3. A few only of the deist writings were translated, (e. g. Tindal by Schmidt in 1741,) but

general doctrines of natural religion, expressed by Herbert and Toland, were soon reproduced, together with the difficulties put forth by Tindal. But the direct effect of this cause has probably been exaggerated by the eagerness of those who, in the wish to identify German rationalism with English deism, have ignorantly overlooked the wide differences in premises, if not in results, which separated them, and the regular internal law of logical development which has presided over the German movement.

A more direct cause was found about the middle of the century in the influence of the French refugees and others, whom Frederick the Great invited to his court. Not only were Voltaire and Diderot visitors, but several writers of worse fame, La Mettrie, D'Argens, Maupertuis,[15] who possessed their faults without their mental power, were constant residents. Their philosophy and unbelief were the miniature of that which we have detailed in France. They created an antichristian atmosphere about the court, and in the upper classes of Berlin; and even minds that were attempting to create a native literature, and to improve the critical standard of literary taste, were partially influenced by means of it.[16]

We have now seen the state of the German mind in reference to theology at the beginning of the eighteenth century, and the three new influences which were introduced into it in the interval between 1720 and 1760. The dogmatic tendency became transformed by the Wolffian philosophy; the pietistic retired from a public movement into the privacy of life; while the minds of

very many of the replies; which proves how much attention they excited. See the list in Lechler, p. 447. Up to 1760 no fewer than 106 answers had been written to Tindal alone. Kortholt, in his work *De Tribus Impostoribus*, (viz. Herbert, Hobbes, Spinoza,) 1680, was the first to notice English deism. The appeal to reason in these replies had the same effect as that noticed in the philosophy of Wolff.

[15] For Maupertuis see *Biographie Universelle.* The others have been named in the notes to Lect. V.

[16] See Tholuck, § 4 and 5. He considers that the French literature, with the exception of Bayle, did not affect the Germans, on account of its shallowness; but doubtless it did so indirectly.

men were awakened to inquiry by the suggestions of the English deists, or the restless and hopeful tone of the French mind. It was a moment of transition; the streaks of twilight before the dawn. Yet the signs of a change were so slight, that few could as yet discern the coming of a crisis, none predict its form.

We may now proceed to give the history of the theological movement which sprang up, commonly called Rationalism. It admits of natural division into three parts. The first, a period destructive in its tendency, extending to a little later than the end of the century, exhibits the gradual growth of the system, and its spread over every department of theology. The second, reconstructive in character, the re-establishment of harmony between faith and reason, extends till the publication of Strauss's celebrated work on the Life of Christ in 1835; the third, containing the divergent tendencies which have created permanent schools, reaches to the present time.[17] In all alike the harmony of faith and reason was sought: but in the first it was attained by sacrificing faith to reason; in the second and third, by seeking for their unity, or by separating their spheres. A distinguished name stands at the commencement of each period, representing the mind whose speculations were most influential in giving form to the movements. Semler inaugurated the destructive movement; Schleiermacher, the constructive; and Strauss precipitated the final forms which theological parties have assumed. In the present lecture we shall treat only of the first two of these movements.

The first of these periods, extending from about 1750 to 1810,[18] contains two sub-periods. Till about 1790[19] we find the growth of rationalism. In the last decade of the century we shall meet with its full devel-

[17] This division does not essentially differ from the threefold one adopted by Kahnis, into the illumination period, that of the renovation, and of the church renovating itself.

[18] We place the limit at 1810, because it is the date of the foundation of the university of Berlin, which was the home of the reaction.

[19] This date marks the spread of the Kantian philosophy, as will be shown below.

opment; but at the same time the growth of new causes will be perceived, which prepared the way for a total alteration after the commencement of the present century.

The sub-period extending to 1790 is one of transition, in which we can trace three broadly marked tendencies in religion; one within the church, two outside of it. Such classes indeed slide away into each other; nature is more complex than man; but the use of them may be excused as facilitating instruction.

The movement within the church verged from a literary and dogmatic orthodoxy, which existed chiefly at the Saxon university of Leipsic, through the purely literary tendency, of which Michaelis may be taken as a type in the newly formed university of Göttingen, to the freethinking method typified by Semler, orthodox in doctrine, but in criticism adopting free views of inspiration, which mingled itself with the old pietism of the university of Halle.[20]

The two movements outside the church were, a literary one, indicated by Lessing, which found its chief utterance in the periodical literature, then in its infancy;[21] and a thoroughly deist one, connected with the court of Berlin, embodied in the educational institutions of Basedow.[22]

The movement which we have just named as existing within the church, differed from the older dogmatic one, in being a tendency toward an historical and critical study of the scriptures, instead of a philosophical study of doctrines. It embraced those whose teaching was not at variance with Christianity, and also those

[20] There was thus three chief phases within the church; the dogmatic at Leipsic, the critical at Göttingen, the pietistic eclecticism of Semler at Halle. If to this we add the pietism which still reigned at Tübingen, as seen in Pfaff, &c., we have the condition of the four universities which were at that time the chief centres of intellectual activity in Germany.

[21] Lessing, along with Nicholai, conducted the *Allgemeine Deutsche Bibliothek* from 1765.

[22] On the purpose and nature of these institutions, which arose at Dessau about 1774, see Schlosser, i. 5, 3; ii. 3, 2; Kahnis, p. 47. On Basedow (1724–1790), see Rose on *Rationalism*, p. 66, note (second edition), and Schröch, viii. 52.

who manifested incipient scepticism. Two names, Ernesti[23] at Leipsic, and Michaelis[24] at Göttingen, represent the first class; the former applying criticism chiefly to the New Testament, the latter to the Old. The endeavour of both, especially of Ernesti, was to revive the grammatical and literary mode of interpreting scripture, as opposed to the dogmatic previously in use. Their spirit was not sceptical, but was that of men who felt the sceptical opinions round them; ethical and cold, like that of the Arminians of the preceding century.

Their system developed into rationalism in the hands of two of their pupils. Eichhorn was the pupil of Michaelis, Semler of Ernesti. The name of Eichhorn will recur later; Semler[25] must be considered now.

Semler was one of those minds which fall short of the highest order of originality, but by their erudition and appreciation of the wants of their time institute a movement by giving form to the current feeling of

[23] J. A. Ernesti (1707–1781), was author of *Inst. Interpret. Nov. Test.* 1761 (translated by bishop Terrot). His chief labours were the editions of several classical authors, among which the most valuable was Cicero. See Schlosser, ii. 187; Kahnis, 120; Pusey, 132; Am. Saintes, part ii. ch. ii. The Rosenmüllers (the father, J. G. Rosenmüller, on the New Testament; the son, E. F. Rosenmüller the antiquarian on the Old,) manifest much the same spirit as Ernesti.

[24] Joh. Dav. Michaelis (1716–1791). His chief works were, *Gruendliche Erklaerung des Mosaischen Rechts*, and the *Einleitung in die Schrift, des Neuen Bundes*. The former handled the Hebrew legislation in a free spirit. The latter work was translated by bishop Marsh, and led to the controversy about the composition of the Gospels, to which allusion will be made in the notes of Lecture VII. See Kahnis, p. 121; Henke, viii. part ii. § 2. Jerusalem and Spalding manifest the same spirit as Michaelis.

[25] Semler (1725–1791), Professor at Halle. His *Lebens-beschreibung*, published 1781, is the great source for studying his mental development and the history of his times. His works are numerous, consisting chiefly of Commentaries and Ecclesiastical History. He was one of the first to open up the study of the history of doctrine (*dogmengeschichte*). The works which exhibit his rationalism are chiefly the *Frei Untersuchen des Canons*, 1771; *Versuch einer freiern lehrart*, 1777; *Introduction to Baumgarten's Dogmatik; Institutiones ad Doctrinam Christianam liberaliter docendam*, 1774. His character is discussed at length in Tholuck, § 6; Pusey, 138, &c.; Schlosser, ii. 187; Am. Saintes, b. ii. ch. ii. and iii. On the successors of the writers recently named, see Am. Saintes, b. ii. ch. iv.

their day. Nurtured in pietism, he always retained signs of personal excellence; and his Christian earnestness is said not to have been destroyed by his speculations. His autobiography furnishes us with the means for the full comprehension of his character, and shows him to have been keenly alive to the difficulties which the English literature had suggested. His labours related to criticism, to exegesis, and to doctrine. As a critic he did not restrict himself to the examination of texts, but investigated the canonicity of the books of Scripture.[26] It is probable that the criticism commenced by R. Simon and Spinoza furnished hints for his views. He was one of the first to undervalue external evidence in the formation of the canon. The determination of the canon, i. e. of the list of books which are to be considered scripture, is a question of fact. What did the early church pronounce to be such; and does internal evidence bear out the idea? Semler undervalued the historical evidence of the church's judgment, and replaced it, not by careful study of internal critical evidence, like later rationalism, but by an *à priori* subjective decision, that only such books were to be received as conduced to a religious object. But it is in exegesis that he enunciated the principles which have left a permanent effect. He established what is called the historical method of interpretation.[27]

In the course of Christian history, three great methods for the interpretation of scripture have been used; the allegorical, the dogmatic, and the grammatical.[28] In the early church the tendency in the main

[26] In the work on the Canon named in the last note.

[27] See the historic sketch of interpretation given in Planck's *Introduction to Sacred Philology*, (English translation, 168–186). Interesting information is supplied in Credner's article *Interpretation* in Kitto's *Biblical Encyclopædia;* J. J. Conybeare's *Bampton Lecture* for 1824 on the *Secondary Interpretation of Scripture;* Dr. S. Davidson's *Sacred Hermeneutics* (5–7); and an article in the *North British Review* for August 1855 on the Alexandrian school.

[28] These tendencies must be considered only to express the average. Thus the school of Antioch, of which Theodore of Mopsuestia is a type, leaned to the grammatical mode; (see some remarks on it in Neander's *Church History*, vol. iv. *init.* Germ. ed.; vol. iii. *fin.* Engl. Tr.) In the

was to the allegorical; in the middle ages to the dogmatic; at the Renaissance and Reformation to the grammatical, which however in the seventeenth century was displaced by the allegorical[29] and dogmatic; and it was the work of Ernesti to restore it. Semler added the historic; by which is meant the method, which, after discovering the grammatical sense of the words, rests content exactly with the meaning which the circumstances of society could permit scripture to have at that age. It declines to search for mystical senses, or to use dogma as a clue to interpretation. This principle, so valuable in itself, yet, when abused, so fruitful in producing rationalism, was the discovery of Semler.

The application of this method of interpretation led him to the theory generally known by the name of "accommodation."[30] He felt a strong reaction against the forgetfulness shown by the old dogmatic orthodoxy, which had regarded the Bible as one book, instead of a collection or historic series of books, and had confounded together the Jewish and Christian dispensations, and taken no cognizance of the development of religious knowledge in scripture. Accordingly he desired to remove the deist difficulty by separating the eternal truth in scripture from what he considered to be local and temporary. Our Lord's own declaration,[31] that the Mosaic law of divorce was an adaptation to the par-

middle ages the Franciscans showed an inclination to the mystical or allegorical; and the typical system of the Miracle Plays and of the Biblia Pauperum illustrates the allegorical spirit of those times.

[29] The allegorical is seen in the school of Cocceius (1603–1669) in the Dutch church. The dogmatic has been alluded to above.

[30] The system is called variously, in works of Hermeneutics, συγκατάβασις, condescensio, demissio, obsequium. It is developed in Semler's *Prolegomena* to some of St. Paul's Epistles; in the *Vorbereitung zur Theol. Hermeneutik*, 1762; and in the *Apparatus ad lib. Nov. Test. interpr.* 1767. Tholuck quotes many instances of it in reference to him (ii. 61). Concerning the subject see Planck's *Introduction to Sacred Philology*, (E. T.) 152–168; Wegscheider, *Inst. Theol.* § 25; Bretschneider, *Hist.-Dogm. Auslegung des N. T.* 1806. A list of foreign works in reference to it is given at the end of the article *Accommodation*, in Kitto's *Biblical Encyclopædia.* For a criticism on it see J. J. Conybeare's Bampton Lecture for 1824. (Lect. VII.)

[31] Mark x. 5.

ticular needs of the age, seemed to establish the validity of the principle that revelation was an accommodation to be judged of by the historic circumstances of the age for which it was intended. The principle had been applied by English theologians:[32] but it needed a delicate insight to apply it safely. Semler introduced it indiscriminately into prophecy, miracle, and doctrine; and stated his views in a form which, though well meant, is certainly most repulsive. We may cite an instance in the case of his view of the demoniacal possessions of the New Testament.[33] Not denying them, Semler probably considered them to be nothing but the diseases of epilepsy and madness. But he did not ridicule the narrative as a deist would, nor explain the facts away as legends or myths, as is the plan of the later schools, nor account for them by the supposition that the apostles were left in ignorance about physical science, and inspired only in religious knowledge; but he regarded the narrative as an intentional accommodation on the part of the teachers to their hearers, and consequently stated his views in a form which is the more repulsive as seeming to impute dishonesty.[34] He went so far as to consider some of the doctrines of the New Testament to be an accommodation on the part of our Lord to the Jewish notions; and regarded Christ's work as the compromise between the Mosaic and philosophical parties in the Jewish church, which afterwards were represented in the Christian by St. Peter and St. Paul respectively.[35] Though he himself held the apostles' creed, and was shocked at some later developments of

[32] E. g. By Kidder in his *Testimony of the Messias*, 1694; Nicholls, *Conference with a Theist*, 1733; and by Sykes, in several works from about 1720–40.

[33] Dr. Pusey speaks (*Inquiry*, p. 139, n.) of two works by Semler on Demons, (of which I have seen only the second, 1779,) the first directed against the belief in the occurrence of possessions in the present day; the second to show that some of the Greek words descriptive of such phenomena in the New Testament need not necessarily imply superhuman agency.

[34] Because it seemed to involve the notion of dissimulation on the part of the scripture writers, or even of the divine Being.

[35] *Introd. ad Doctr. Christianam*, b. i. See Am. Saintes, p. 107.

unbelief,[36] yet he seems to have considered practical morality to be at once the sole aim of Christianity, and the supreme rule of doctrine.[37] He founded no school; but his influence decidedly initiated the rationalist movement within the church; one peculiarity of which will be found to be, that it was professedly designed in defence of the church, not as an attack upon it.

The tendency which we have just studied was within the church. The two now about to be named were external to it. The one, earnest and scholarlike, formed chiefly on the model of English deism, is represented by Lessing. The other, modelled after Rousseau, was practical rather than intellectual, and aimed at remodelling education as well as altering belief.

Lessing,[38] a name honoured in the history of literature, is little known in England, save by his exquisite comparison of art and poetry, called the Laocoon.[39] He was one of those whose labours remain for the benefit of other ages, like that of the coral worms, which die, but leave their work. That a native German literature exists, is the work of Lessing as pioneer; that it is worth studying, is the result of his criticism and influence. Finding literature just arising, and the dispute still raging between the Saxon and Swiss schools, whether it should model itself after reason and form like the French literature, or after nature and the soul like the English, (28) he showed the true mode of uniting the two by turning attention to Greek models;

[36] E. g. The Wolfenbüttel Fragments. See Am. Saintes, p. 86, and Niemeyer's *Letzte Aeusserungen ueber religioese Gegenstaende zwei Tage vor seinem Tode*, which he quotes.

[37] His doctrinal views are seen in the *Lebens-beschreibung*, part ii. p. 220, &c.

[38] Lessing (1729–1781). In 1754 he joined Nicholai and Mendelssohn in literary criticism; in 1757, in the *Bibliothek der Schönen Wissenschaften;* and in 1765, in the *Allgem. Deutsche Biblioth.* An account of his life and literary character may be seen in the *Foreign Quarterly Review* (No. 50) for 1840, and an able criticism on him by C. Dollfus in the *Revue Germanique* for 1860 (vol. ix.). Consult also Menzel's *Deutsch. Litt.* iii. 291, &c.; Metcalfe's work based on Vilmar, p. 400 seq. A separate study of his theological opinions was made by C. Schwartz in 1854, entitled *Lessing als Theolog*, especially c. iv.; see also Bartholmess, b. ii. ch. ii

[39] Published in 1766.

and, in conjunction with Nicholai and the Jewish philosopher Mendelssohn, established a critical periodical, which became the agency for a literary reformation. But the point of interest, in relation to our present subject, is his influence on religion. Availing himself of the right which his position as librarian of Wolfenbüttel, a small town near Brunswick, gave him to publish manuscripts found in the library, he edited, in 1774 and the four following years, several fragments of a larger work, which he professed to have found. They are usually called the Wolfenbüttel fragments. (29) Till recently their authorship remained a secret. They are now known to have been written by the learned Hamburg philosopher, Reimarus.[40] They treated very nearly the same subjects, and in much the same tone, but with consummate skill, as the English deists. Reimarus, as is now known, in the introduction[41] to the larger unprinted work from which they were extracted, gave his own intellectual history, his early doubts on the doctrines of the Trinity, and the destruction of the heathen; and also on the history of the Old and New Testaments; and ends, like the English deists, with resting in natural religion.

The first two[42] fragments, published by Lessing, touched only upon the question of tolerating deists, and on the custom of declaiming against human reason in the pulpits. The third referred to the impossibility that all men should be brought to believe revelation on rational evidence. The fourth and fifth attacked the Old Testament history, such as the passage of the Red Sea. The sixth directed an assault against the New Testament; pointing out with unsparing severity the discrepancies in the accounts of the resurrection. The concluding one was on the object of Christianity, in

[40] H. S. Reimarus (1694–1768). See Schlosser, ii. 26, &c., and the article *Reimarus* in the Conversations-Lexicon.

[41] See Note 29 at the end of this volume.

[42] The Fragments are here named according to the order of their original publication; not that in which they are usually printed, as, e. g. in the Berlin edition, 1835.

which our blessed Lord's life and work were represented as a defeated political reform.

These views however were not professedly sanctioned by Lessing, for he added notes in refutation of them, and stated his object to be merely to stimulate free inquiry.[43] His wish was gratified in the tremendous effect which the publication produced. In the literary controversy which ensued, and which embittered his few remaining days,[44] he explained himself to be a doubter rather than a disbeliever; and defended himself by urging the distinctness of the religious element in scripture from the scientific; asserting that, as Christianity existed before the New Testament, so it could exist after it. The Christian religion is not true, he said, merely because evangelists and apostles taught it; but they taught it because it is true. And in order to restore Christianity to its true place in the estimation of thinking men, he composed or edited a well-known work[45] on the Education of the World,[46] which became a fertile source of thought for the philosophy of history, and was designed to explain the function of the Jewish religion in reference to the Christian, and to the world. The theology of Lessing's coadjutors however, if not also that of Lessing himself, did not rise higher than that of the more serious among the English deists.[47]

The other tendency, more decidedly sceptical even than that of Lessing, gave definite form to the extreme

[43] Compare Strauss's description of them in his *Leben Jesu*, Introd. § 5. Lessing's own object in their publication is expressed in the concluding pages of his edition of them.

[44] The chief opposition arose from Göze, a pastor of Hamburg, who attacked Lessing even before the last and most obnoxious fragment was published; but both Semler and Jerusalem also wrote against him. See Boden's *Lessing und Göze, Ein Beitrag zur Lit. und Kirchengesch. des 18 Jahrh.* 1862; also the references given at the end of Note 29 (p. 427); especially Hagenbach's *Dogmengesch.* § 275, note.

[45] See the note on p. 87.

[46] *Die Erziehung des menschlichen Geschlechts*, lately partially translated into English. It conveyed the thoughts suggested by the perusal of some apologies for religion.

[47] The theologians Steinbart and Teller represented a similar spirit.

sceptical opinions excited by French philosophy, which had been fermenting in German society, and had earlier expressed themselves. It is best represented by Edelmann,[48] and by the unhappy Bahrdt, who passed gradually from Semler's school into this. Its religious tenets were simple naturalism, moral as distinct from positive religion; and it was connected with the attempt by Basedow,[49] patronised by Frederick, to establish educational institutions on the model proposed in Rousseau's Emile. The name which it gave to the movement was, the Period of Enlightenment (Aufklärung-zeit),[50] which expressed the consciousness of illumination, and the yearning for deliverance which was finding its expression in France; and this name therefore has been usually adopted among foreign writers to describe this period of the history.

Such are the historical tendencies from about 1750 till about 1790—cold but learned orthodoxy; the commencement of critical rationalism, and open deism. About that time new influences came into operation, the effects of which are at once evident. Without taking account of the excitement caused by the political events of the French revolution, we may name two such new causes of movement—the literary influence of the court of Weimar, and the philosophy of Kant.

The centres of intellectual activity in Germany now changed. We are so apt to forget that Germany, especially at the end of the last century, formed a set of

[48] On Edelmann, who died 1767, see Kahnis, p. 126; and on Bahrdt (1741–92), Id. pp. 136–145; and Schlosser, ii. 211. The life of Bahrdt is a sad subject for study. Kahnis (p. 125 seq.) enumerates other deists, some of them earlier than those whom we are now considering, e. g. Knuzen, Dippel (1673–1734).

[49] See the reference above, p. 219.

[50] The contrast of the English, French, and German periods of illuminism is well drawn out by Kuno Fischer (*Bacon*, ch. xi. 2, 3, and xiii. 3). I have been unable to discover positively whether the term in its first use meant merely *Renaissance* (cfr. the Italian term *illuminati*), or whether it meant the philosophy which makes its appeal to common sense, being connected with the Cartesian principle, *wahr ist, was klar ist*. The former appears almost certain; but some of the German writers seem to favour the latter. On its nature, see Kahnis, p. 61–63.

independent principalities, which varied in taste, in belief, and in literary tone, that we fail to realise the individuality of the scenes of literary activity. At the end of the last century there was one spot which became the very focus of intellectual life. The court of Karl August at Weimar, insignificant in political importance, was great in the history of the human mind.[51] There were gathered there most of the mighty spirits of the golden age of German literature,—Herder, Wieland, Goethe, Schiller, Jean Paul; a constellation of intellect unequalled since the court of Ferrara in the days of Alphonso.[52] The influence made itself felt in the adjacent university of Jena; and this little seminary became from that time for about twenty years,[53] until the foundation of Berlin, the first university in Germany. In it alone the philosophy of Kant became naturalized.[54] Some of the ablest men in Germany were its Professors; and about this time Jena and Weimar became the stronghold of free thought.

Except in the case of Herder,[55] the literary influence was not directly influential on theology. But it gave moral support to theological movement; though ultimately, by introducing a truer and more subjective appreciation of human nature, it was the means of gen-

[51] A very interesting article on Weimar and its celebrities appeared in the *Westminster Review* for April 1859. The illustration about the court of Ferrara, just below, is taken from it. Mr. G. H. Lewes, in his *Life of Goethe*, gives incidentally sketches of the intellectual and moral influence of the court of Weimar.

[52] Alfonso d'Este reigned from 1505–34. He was the husband of Lucrezia Borgia.

[53] i. e. from about 1790 to 1810.

[54] Kant's great work, *Kritik der reinen Vernunft*, appeared in 1781, but was not known out of Königsberg until one of his disciples, Schulze in 1784, elucidated it in a separate work. The *Jenaische Literatur-Zeitung* also favoured it. In 1786 Reinhold became Professor at Jena, and began to teach Kant's system. See Schlosser, vol. ii. p. 182–4.

[55] Herder did not adopt the new philosophy of Kant. His theological writings were rather earlier than 1790. They created a love for the literature of young nations, and for the Hebrew religion, in a literary rather than a spiritual point of view. On Herder's religious influence, see Schlosser, ii. 278, &c.; and the article by Hagenbach in Herzog's *Real. Encyclop.*; also Hagenbach's *Gesch. des* 18 *Jahrh.* § 4 and 5; and Quinet's *Œuvres*, vol. ii.

erating the deep insight in the critical taste of thinking men which furnished the death-blow to rationalism. The same remark is true of the effects of the philosophy of Kant.[56] Its ultimate result was valuable in removing the eudæmonism common in ethics, and turning men's attention to the moral law within. But its immediate effects were to reinforce the appeal to reason, and to destroy revelation by leaving nothing to be revealed.

The nature of this system, so far as is necessary for our purpose, may be soon told. Kant, dissatisfied with the distrust in the human faculties induced by the scepticism of Hume, and the one-sided sensationalism of Condillac, carried a penetrating analysis into the human faculties;[57] attempting to perform with more exactness the work of Locke, to measure the human mind, which is the sounding-line, before fathoming the ocean of knowledge. Like Copernicus inverting astronomy, he reversed metaphysics, by referring classes of ideas to inward causes which before had been referred to outer.

He detected, as he supposed, innate forms of thought[58] in the mental structure, which form the conditions under which knowledge is possible. When he applied his system to give a philosophy of ethics and religion, he asserted nobly the law of duty written

[56] Kant lived 1724–1804. On his philosophy see Chalybaus, *Hist. of Speculative Philosophy* (translated 1854); Am. Saintes' *Philos. de Kant*, 1844; Cousin, *Leçons de la Phil. de Kant*, 1843. A good account of it also is given in Morell's *Hist. of Philosophy*, i. 233–63, in R. Vaughan's (sen.) Essays, and in a Lecture by Professor Mansel on the *Philosophy of Kant*, 1860. See also the references in Tennemann's *Manual*, § 387–94. In reference to its theological effects, see Am. Saintes' *Critical History of Rationalism*, ii. 5 and 6; Bartholmess, b. v. and vi. The parts of Kant's writings which are of special importance for ascertaining his theological views are, his work *Die Religion innerhalb der Grenzen der blossen Vernunft*, 1793, and his criticism on natural theology in the *Kritik der reinen Vernunft*, b. ii. div. 3. See Strauss, *Leben Jesu*, introd. § 7. Staüdlin, Ammon, and Tieftrunk, were Kantist theologians.

[57] In the *Kritik der reinen Vernunft* above named, which was so called because he strove to analyse the *pure* reason, before it is defiled by contact with the world through experience.

[58] The categories, the test of the existence of which is necessity and universality.

in the heart,[59] but identified it with religion. Religious ideas were regarded as true regulatively, not speculatively. Revelation was reunited with reason, by being resolved into the natural religion of the heart. Accordingly, the moral effect of this philosophy was to expel the French materialism and illuminism,[60] and to give depth to the moral perceptions: its religious effect was to strengthen the appeal to reason and the moral judgment as the test of religious truth; to render miraculous communication of moral instruction useless, if not absurd; and to reawaken the attempt, which had been laid aside since the Wolffian philosophy, of endeavouring to find a philosophy of religion.[61] From this time in German theology we shall find the existence of the twofold movement; the critical one, the lawful descendant of Semler, examining the historic revelation; and the philosophical one, the offshoot of the system of Kant, seeking for a philosophy of religion.

During the next twenty years, from 1790 to 1810, when so many influences were operating in common, it is not easy to measure the effect of the speculative philosophy upon particular minds with such exactness as to ascertain which ought properly to be classed in the destructive tendency, and which gave signs of the reaction. We must however be careful to exclude those younger minds[62] that were already appearing on the field, to become the heroes of the subsequent history, whose tone was so decidedly affected by new influences as to belong to the age of reaction.

In this sub-period we may name three tendencies: (1) the continuation of the Exegesis inaugurated in the last epoch by Semler, until about the end of the century it found its utmost limit in Paulus,[63]—the result of the

[59] This appears in his *Kritik der practischen Vernunft.*

[60] Illuminism is used as the translation of *Aufklaerungs-Zeit.*

[61] The difference between Wolff and Kant is, that while the former sought a philosophy of religion *ontologically*, the latter sought it *psychologically*, by first ascertaining the functions of the mind in reference to religion.

[62] Such as Schleiermacher.

[63] Paulus, 1761–1851; Professor at Jena, and from 1811 at Heidelberg. Some of his works are named below.

age of illumination; (2) a dogmatic tendency, more or less the growth of new influences introduced by the new philosophy, which attempted to reconcile reason with the supernatural, and may be represented in its nearest approach to orthodoxy, at the end of this period, by Bretschneider;[64] and (3) the awakening of a distinct expression of the appeal to the supernatural which had never quite died out in the church, in the Arminianism of Reinhardt in the north, and of Storr in the south.[65] The last needs no further investigation; but we shall consider briefly the other two.

The exegetical method which formed the first was that which is now usually called the old or common-sense rationalism.[66] This form of rationalism differed from the English deism and French naturalism, in not regarding the Bible as fabulous in character, and the device of priestcraft;[67] but only denied the supernatural. By them the apostles had been regarded as impostors; and scripture was not only not received as divine, but not even respected as an ordinary historical record; whereas rationalism was intended as a defence against this view. It denied only the revealed character of scripture, and treated it as an ordinary history; and, distinguishing broadly between the fact related

[64] K. G. Bretschneider, 1776–1848; General Superintendent at Gotha. A short autobiography was published after his death, which is translated in the *Bibliotheca Sacra* for 1852–3. His best work is the *Handbuch der Dogmatik*, 1814, 1838. He was the writer of the *Probabilia* concerning St. John's Gospel, named in Lect. VII.

[65] F. Reinhardt (1753–1812) of Saxony. His supernaturalism was perhaps rather ethical than biblical. (See Kahnis, 187, Am. Saintes, c. viii.) Storr (1746–1805) was Professor at Tübingen. The belief in the supernatural had never died out. A philosophical supernaturalism was seen in Flatt, Planck, Schröch and a truly biblical kind in Knapp. Along with Reinhardt ought perhaps to be reckoned Morus and Döderlein; at a little earlier period Seiler, and a little later Steudel: on this school see Am. Saintes, ch. iv.

[66] i.e. *Rationalismus Vulgaris.* On Rationalism, see Note 21 (p. 413.) On this particular kind see Kahnis, p. 169. It is distinguished from naturalism chiefly by being connected with the church, and by the opinion that it is the very essence of Christianity. It was represented by Paulus in criticism, Wegscheider in dogma, and Röhr in preaching.

[67] As Woolston, Bolingbroke, and Voltaire. Cfr. Strauss, *Leb. Jes.* Introd. § 5.

and the judgment on the fact, sought to separate the two, and explained away the supernatural element, such as miracles, as being orientalisms in the narrative, adapted to an infant age, which an enlightened age must translate into the language of ordinary events.

Eichhorn at Göttingen[68] applied this view to the Old Testament. Deeming miracles impossible, he did not regard them as fraud, but admitted on the contrary that the agents or narrators honestly believed them. The supernatural was not imparted to deceive, but was the result of oriental modes of speech, such as hyperbole, parable, or ellipsis, in which the steps by which the process was performed were omitted. The smoke of Sinai was considered a thunderstorm; the shining of Moses's face a natural phenomenon.

The principles which Eichhorn applied to the Old Testament, Paulus of Jena extended to the New.[69] The miraculous cures were explained by an ellipsis in the omission of the natural remedies; the casting out of devils as the power of a wise man over the insane; the transfiguration as the confused recollection of sleeping men, who saw Jesus with two unknown friends, in the beautiful light of the morning among the mountains: nay, trespassing on still more holy ground, he dared impiously to explain away the resurrection of our blessed Lord by the hypothesis that his death was only apparent. These are a specimen of the mode of exegesis adopted in this school, which is usually specifically called Rationalism. In this mode Jesus appeared to

[68] Eichhorn (1752–1827), one of the most learned men of his age. For illustrations see his *Einleitung*, § 435, and cfr. § 421. The instances cited in the text, from one of his works which the writer could not consult, are quoted from the *British Quarterly Review*, No. 26; cfr. also Strauss, *Leben Jesu*, § 6.

[69] In his *Exeget. Handb. des Neuen Test.* The account will be found by referring to the respective narratives. See also his commentary on the miracle of the tribute money, and of the feeding the multitudes. See Kahnis, pp. (171–6). Eichhornstopped short when he came to apply his principles to the New Testament. L. Bauer (*Hebr. Mythol.*), Gabler, Vater, Bertholdt, Von Lengerke, and Von Böhlen, though some of them were affected by later influences, belonged in the main to this rationalist critical school.

be merely a wise and virtuous man; and his miracles were merely acts of skill or accident. Paulus presented this as the original Christianity. The theory did not last long, save in the mind of its author, who lived until a recent period, to see the entire change of critical belief. Attributing the supernatural to ignorance, it did not even propose, like the later schools, to explain the marvellousness of the phenomena, objectively by so plausible a theory as legends, nor subjectively by myths:[70] it was too clumsy, not to say irreverent, an explanation of the facts to satisfy a people of deep and poetical soul like the Germans.

While this is a specimen of the critical side of rationalism, its dogmatic side varied from natural ethics to a kind of Socinianism. But in all alike, as its name would imply, it not only asserted that there is only one universal revelation, which takes place through observation of nature and man's reason; but that Christianity was not designed to teach any mysterious truths, but only to confirm the religious teaching of reason; and that no one ought to recognise as true that which cannot be proved to him rationally. The doctrine of a Trinity was necessarily disbelieved; the death of Christ regarded as an historic event, or a symbol that sacrifices were abolished. Holiness was reduced to morality. Extreme veneration for the Bible was called Bibliolatry.[71] Religion was represented as acting by natural motives: the ethical superseded the historic. The early theologians of this dogmatic branch of the

[70] The difference of legend and myth is now well known. "Myth is the creation of a fact out of an idea; legend the seeing an idea in a fact." Strauss, *Leb. Jes. Einl.* § 10. The myth is purely the work of imagination, the legend has a nucleus of fact.

[71] Henke, 1752–1809, Professor at Helmstädt, is said to have been the first who made use of the term "Bibliolatry" in the preface to his *Lineamenta Instit. Fidei Christianæ.* He probably however only brought it into use. (The writer remembers to have seen it occur somewhere earlier, but cannot recall the reference.) He was a church historian of great learning, whose works have been frequently used for reference in Lect. V. Kahnis speaks with great respect (p. 177) of his earnestness. For Henke's position as a church historian see a note in the Preface to these Lectures.

school are now little known; but we may name Bretschneider[72] as the type of the least heretical portion of it at the close of this period, who believed Christianity to be a republication of natural religion, supernatural but reasonable: and, as the literary tendency of this school continued to exist in Röhr,[73] after the movement had become extinct in other minds, so Wegscheider,[74] until a recent period, was the solitary instance of the dogmatic position slightly modified.

This completes the history of the first of the three movements, the destructive action of rationalism. The most flourishing period of this form of it was about the beginning of the present century. We have seen it originating in the rational tone of Wolff's philosophy, and the well-meant but ill-judged exegesis which Semler exhibited under the pressure of sceptical difficulties. Stimulated by critical investigations, and by the strong wish which operated on our own theologians, to find the cause of everything, its adherents were led into a

[72] Concerning Bretschneider see a preceding note on p. 231. Bretschneider shows in his reply to Mr. Rose, and in his *Autobiography*, that he was much hurt at being classed with the rationalists. In truth the dogmatic tendency which we are here describing admits, as is shown more fully in Note 21, (p. 413), of a twofold subdivision. (1) "Rationalists" proper, who are pure Socinians, but hardly believe in the supernatural element of revelation: such were Wegscheider and Röhr; also Echermann and C. F. A. Fritsche may be reckoned with the same school (see Kahnis, 177 seq.; Am. Saintes, ch. vii.); and (2) "Rational Supernaturalists," like Bretschneider, Schott of Jena (1780–1835), and Tzchirner of Leipsic (1778–1828), who believed in a supernatural revelation, but held to the supremacy of reason;—a position not very unlike Locke's in the *Reasonableness of Christianity*. The tone of opinion changed so much in Germany after 1830, that Bretschneider, who in earlier life had been considered to lean towards orthodoxy as opposed to rationalism, appeared in later life, though really standing still, to side with the rationalists against the reaction which took place in favour of supernaturalism. A volume of sermons, translated by Baker in 1829, called *The German Pulpit*, contains, along with a few sermons of more spiritual tone, many sermons by preachers of this school. See on this school Am. Saintes, ch. viii. Mr. Rose also has collected many facts in reference to this part of the subject; also Staüdlin in his *Gesch. des Rat. und Supernat.*, and P. A. Stapfer (*Arch. du Christianisme*, 1824), quoted by Rose (second edition).

[73] J. F. Röhr (1777–1848), Superintendent at Weimar; noted as a preacher. His Historical Geography of Palestine has been translated.

[74] Wegscheider (1771–1848); Professor at Halle. His chief work is *Inst. Theol. Chr. Dogmat.* 1813.

disbelief of the supernatural, and ended in explaining away the miraculous, and reducing Christianity to natural religion. The movement, it will be observed, was professedly not intended to be destructive of Christianity. Instead of being inimical, it originated with the clergy, and aimed at harmonizing Christianity with reason. But it contained its own death. The negative criticism is essentially temporary.

The activity of thought was already producing change. We have previously stated that even the Kantian philosophy itself, though at first stimulating the appeal to reason, fostered a deeper perception of duty, and thus prepared the way for a moral reawakening.[75]

We shall accordingly now proceed to state the causes which introduced new elements into the current of public thought; and then describe the gradual progress of the reactionary movement which ensued from them.

Four causes are usually assigned. The first of them was the introduction of new systems of speculative philosophy.

It is not unusual, in those who have no taste for speculation, and who understand only the prosaic, though in some respects the truer, philosophy of Scotland, to despise the great systems of German speculation. Yet, if the series be measured as an example of the power of the human mind, whatever may be the opinion formed in respect to its correctness, it stands among the most interesting efforts of thought. Though the writers can be matched by isolated examples in former ages, perhaps no series of writers exists, hardly even the Greek, certainly not the Neo-Platonist nor the Cartesian, which, in far-reaching penetration, in minuteness of analysis, in brilliancy of imagination, in loftiness of genius, in poetry of expression, in grasp of intellect, in influence on every branch of thought or life, approximates to the series of illustrious thinkers which

[75] Hundeshagen calls Kant a second Moses, on account of the moral revolution which his teaching effected.

commenced with Kant and ended with Hegel.[76] The two philosophers at this time whose teaching formed a new influence, were Fichte[77] and Jacobi.[78] Details in reference to their systems must be sought elsewhere.[79] It is only possible here to indicate their central thought, in order to notice their effects on theological inquiry.

We have seen that Kant had reconsidered the great problem, commenced by Descartes and Locke, concerning the ground of certitude, and the nature of knowledge; and had revolutionised philosophy, by attributing to the natural structure of the mind many of those ideas which had usually been supposed to be derived from experience. In his system he had left two elements, a formal and a material; the formal, or innate forms, through which the mind gains knowledge, and the material, presented from external sources. It was the former or ideal element which was examined by Fichte; the latter by Jacobi.

Fichte began to teach at Jena soon after 1790. Grasping firmly Descartes' principle, "Cogito, ergo sum," he conceived that, as we can only know ourselves, there is no proof that the datum supposed to be external is anything but a form of our own consciousness; and thus he arrived at a subjective idealism not unlike that of bishop Berkeley.[80] Under his view God was only an idea or form of thought; a regulative principle of human belief, the moral order of which the

[76] i. e. Kant, Jacobi, Fichte, Schelling, Hegel; on whom see Morell, ii. ch. v. § 2, and Chalybaüs, *History of Speculative Philosophy*.

[77] J. G. Fichte (1762–1814); Professor at Jena; deprived for the supposed atheistic tendency of his philosophy (1799); afterwards Professor at Berlin. His great work is his *Wissenschafts-lehre*, 1794. He was the author of the celebrated patriotic addresses to the German people. The educational institutions of Pestalozzi were founded on Fichte's philosophy, as Basedow's on Rousseau. See Kahnis, p. 216.

[78] Jacobi (1743–1819); President of the academy of sciences at Munich.

[79] On Fichte see Chalybaüs, ch, vi. and vii.; Tennemann, Manual § 400–5; Morell, ii. p. 89–122; Lewes, *History of Philosophy;* Mansel's art. on *Metaphysics* in *Encycl. Britan.* p. 607. On Jacobi see Chalybaüs, ch. iii.; Tennemann, § 415; Morell, ii. 402; Am. Saintes, part ii. ch. xiii.

[80] This atheistic corollary is not deducible from Berkeley's system, and was not designed by Fichte.

mind was conscious in the universe; and, as atheism was suspected to follow as an inference from his views, he became the subject of persecution. But the instincts of the heart, as well as the arguments of the understanding, were too potent for him; and when he had thus as it were shut up man within the circle of his own finite self, he strove to find a logical passage into a knowledge of the infinite by a principle analogous to that of Spinoza; viz. by regarding both self and the outer world, the subjective and objective, to be identified in some absolute self-existence, of which they were respectively phases.[81]

This aim was only partially effected by Fichte, and was completed by his distinguished successor, Schelling.[82] Schelling saw that the subjective tendency had been pushed too far; and, relying on the spiritual sense through which men of all ages have conceived that they saw the infinite, the reality of which accordingly seems to be attested by a universal induction, he tried to grasp the idea of the self-existent One, who is the one absolute Reality, the one eternal Being, the eternal Source from which all other light is derived, and from which all things develope. "Intellectual intuition" he thought to be the means by which we have this knowledge of the infinite, and are able to trace the development of it into its limitations in nature and in the mind. The method is analogous to that of Spinoza, save that the infinite is studied dynamically instead of mechanically, as a movement not a substance, in time not in space.

The roll of these great thinkers, whose speculations were suggested by the formal side of Kant's philosophy, is not yet full. But the two which have been named wrote and affected thought, the one before, the other soon after, the commencement of the present century. Hegel followed in the same track, but influenced

[81] See Chalybaüs, ch. viii.; and Morell, ii. 118.

[82] Schelling (1774–1854), Professor at Munich and Berlin. See Chalybaüs, ch. ix–xii.; Tennemann, § 406–11; Morell, ii. 122–161; Bartholmess, *Hist. Crit. des Doctr. Relig.* b. ix.

thought at a later period.[83] He too aimed at solving the same problem as Schelling: he too sought to transcend the conditions of object and subject which limit thought; but it was by assuming a representative or mediate faculty that transcends consciousness, and not, as Schelling, an intuitional or presentative.[84]

Such were the philosophers who aimed at solving the problem of knowledge and being from the intellectual side. Jacobi on the other hand attempted it from the emotional. Perceiving the necessity of finding some justification for the material element which Kant had assumed in his philosophy, he sought it in faith, in intuition, in the direct inward revelation of truth to the human mind. He thought that, as sensation gives us an immediate knowledge of the world, so there is an inward sense by which we have a direct and immediate revelation of supernatural truth. It is this inward revelation which gives us access to the material of truth. His position was analogous to that of Schelling, but he asserted the element of feeling as well as intuition.

These philosophies, of Fichte, Schelling, and Jacobi, formed one class of influences, which were operating about the beginning of the century, and were the means of redeeming alike German literature and theology. Their first effect was to produce examination of the primary principles of belief, to excite inquiry; and, though at first only reinforcing the idea of morality, they ultimately drew men out of themselves into aspirations after the infinite spirit, and developed the sense of dependence, of humility, of unselfishness, of spirituality. They produced indeed evil effects in pantheism and ideology;[85] but the results were partial, the good was general. The problem, What is truth?—was through their means remitted to men for reconsideration; and the answers to it elicited, from the one

[83] 1770–1831. See Lect. VII.
[84] See some remarks on this point in Mr. Mansel's *Lecture on the Philosophy of Kant.*
[85] Lect. VII.

school,—It is that which I can know:—from the other, —It is that which I can intuitively feel:—threw men upon those unalterable and infallible instincts which God has set in the human breast as the everlasting landmarks of truth, the study of which lifts men ultimately out of error.

These systems had even a still more direct effect on the public mind. They were the means of creating a literature, which insinuated itself into public thought, and familiarised society with spiritual apprehensions long obliterated. The school of literature commonly called the Romantic,[86] commencing with such writers as Schlegel and Novalis, fanciful as it may in some respects seem to be, created the same change in the belief and tastes of the German mind as the contemporary school of Lake Poets in England. The German literature bore the marks either of the old scholasticism, or of the materialism introduced from France, or of the classic culture introduced by Lessing and his coadjutors. The element now revived was the mediæval element of chivalry, the high and lofty courage, the delicate æsthetic taste, which had marked the middle ages. Herder,[87] to whom Germany owes much, disgusted with the stoical and analytic spirit of the Kantian philosophy, had already attempted, and not in vain, to throw the mind back to an appreciation of old history, and especially had manifested an enthusiastic admiration of Hebrew literature; but now, as if by one general movement, the public taste was turned to an appreciation of the freshness of feeling, and fine elements of character, which existed in the Christianity of the middle ages.[88]

[86] The Romantic school included L. F. Stolberg, the Schlegels, Tieck, Novalis (Hardenberg), Fouqué. See Kahnis, p. 202; Morell, ii. 421; Vilmar. (English translation), p. 500 seq.; Carlyle's *Essay on Novalis* (Misc. Works, vol. ii.); and Bartholmess, ii. b. xi.

[87] Herder, 1744–1803. See a previous note. His most interesting works were, the *Spirit of Hebrew Poetry* (translated 1802), and the *Philosophy of History* (translated 1800).

[88] The influence of the movement extended into the Roman catholic church; and Hermes, Moehler, and Goerres, were affected by it. Hermes (1775–1831) was Professor at Bonn; and, endeavouring to find a philoso-

This literary movement prepared the way for and accompanied another, which, though occurring a little later, may be reckoned as the third influence which caused a religious reaction. Indeed it is the one to which the Germans attribute the chief effect. It is found in the outburst of national patriotism which took place in the liberation wars of 1813;[89] the spontaneous chivalry which made the heart of Germany beat as the heart of one man, to endeavour to hurl back Napoleon beyond the limits of the common fatherland. In that moment of deep public suffering, the poetry and piety of the human heart brought back the idea of God, and a spirit of moral earnestness. The national patriotism,[90] which still lives in the poetry of the time, expelled selfishness: sorrow impressed men with a sense of the vanity of material things, and made their hearts yearn after the immaterial, the spiritual, the immortal: the sense of terror threw them upon the God of battles. It was the age of Marathon and Salamis revived; and the effect was not less wonderful.[91]

A fourth influence remains to be noticed, which was in its nature more strictly theological, and limited to the church. When after the return of peace the tercentenary of the Reformation was celebrated in 1817, an obscure theologian at Kiel, named Harms,[92]

phy for Romish doctrines, was opposed by his own church. Moehler, 1796–1838, author of the *Symbolik*, which revived the controversy with Protestantism, and was answered by the most learned Protestant theologians, has been pronounced (by Schaff) to be the ablest Romish theologian since Bellarmine and Bossuet. Goerres (1776–1848), a mystic writer in Bavaria. See Am. Saintes, c. xx.; and on Goerres see Quinet, *Œuvr.* vi. ch. vii.

[89] See Hundeshagen, *Der Deutsch Prot.* § 12; Kahnis, p. 223.

[90] This patriotism still lives in the poetry of Koerner.

[91] This allusion is used by Kahnis (p. 220). He also (p. 221) refers the great outburst of historic study which followed, to the historic sense then awakened.

[92] Harms (1778–1855). See Am. Saintes, part ii. ch. ix; Kahnis, p. 223 seq., where some of Harms's Theses are given. They are founded on the doctrinal spirit of the sixteenth century, and are full of force and humour. Some of them are directed against rationalism; others are the asseveration of high Lutheran tenets. The following are specimens: No. 3. "With the idea of a progressive reformation, in the manner in which it is at present understood, Lutheranism will be reformed back into hea-

published a set of theses as supplements to the celebrated theses of Luther, which, by the excitement and controversy unexpectedly occasioned by them, turned attention anew to the study of the reformational and biblical theology, and created a revival of the spiritual element which was too much forgotten.

Such were the four influences—the philosophical, the literary, the political, the spiritual,—which entered into German life, and produced or increased the reaction that took place in German theology in the period which we are about to sketch.

We placed the limits of this second period from about 1810 till the literary revolution caused by alarm at Strauss's work in 1835.[93] It was in 1810, in the depth of Prussian humiliation, when Halle had passed into one of the kingdoms dependent on France, that the university of Berlin was founded. Schleiermacher, Neander, and De Wette, were its teachers. The first was the soul of its theological teaching; and through his agency it became the great source of a religious reaction. It is around these names that our studies most centre. The signs indeed of some other movements are traceable. The deistic rationalism is not dead, but it is dying: it is a thing of the past: a return to strict dogmatic orthodoxy is also visible in the Lutheran clergy rather than in the university; but it is as yet in its infancy: and a new form of gnosticism is observable in the philosophy of Hegel, but the full development of it belongs to the next period. The field is now occupied by the partial reaction to orthodoxy, which aimed at a reconciliation of science and piety, of criticism and faith.[94] Schleiermacher, with his follower Neander, will typify the philosophical and

thenism." No. 21. "In the sixteenth century the pardon of sins cost money after all; in the nineteenth it may be had without money, for people help themselves to it." See Pelt in Herzog's *Real. Encyclop.* sub *voc.*

[93] On this second period, see Schwarz's *Geschichte der Neuesten Theologie*, b. i.; and for brief notices of the whole of the German movement, see Hagenbach's *Dogmengeschichte* (period 5).

[94] It has been more recently, for this reason, called the Mediation-Theology (*Vermittellungs-Theologie*).

more orthodox side of it; perhaps De Wette, and at the end of the period Ewald, the critical.

Schleiermacher[95] was by education and sympathy eminently fitted to attempt the harmony of science and faith, to which he devoted his life. Gifted with an acute and penetrating intellect, capable of grappling with the highest problems of philosophy and the minutest details of criticism, he could sympathise with the intellectual movement of the old rationalism; while his fine moral sensibility, the depth and passionateness of his sympathy, the exquisite delicacy of his taste and brilliancy of imagination, were in perfect harmony with the literary and æsthetic revival which was commencing. German to the very soul, he possessed an enthusiastic sympathy with the great literary movements of his age, philosophical, classical, or romantic. The diligent student and translator of Plato,[96] his soul was enchanted with the mixture at once of genius, poetry, feeling, and dialectic, which marks that prince of thinkers, and he was prepared by it for understanding the speculations of his time. The dialectical process through which Plato's mind had passed (30) represents not improbably, in some degree, the history of Schleiermacher's own mental development as traceable in his works. The conviction derived from Plato's early dialogues, that the mind, in travelling outward to study the objective, could not prove the highest realities, but must have faith in its own faculties, prepared him for imbibing the philosophy of Jacobi. The looking in-

[95] Schleiermacher (1768–1834). His *Leben in Briefen* (1858) has been recently translated. His philosophical and religious stand-point is well discussed, and some portions of his works analysed, in the Rev. R. A. Vaughan's *Essays and Remains* (reprinted from the *British Quarterly Review*, No. 18). A brief explanation of his philosophy is seen in Morell's *History of Philosophy*, ii. 433, and Julius Scheller's *Vorlesungen über Schleiermacher*, 1844. His religious views are criticised, with extracts, in Amand Saintes, part ii. ch. xiv–xvi; Kahnis, 204 seq.; Lücke, *Stud. und Krit.* 1834, H. 4. The facts of his life are given in the *Westm. Rev.* for July, 1861.

[96] He joined F. Schlegel in the plan of translation, and continued it after Schlegel had retired from it. He did not however complete the whole of Plato. The parts finished were published at intervals from 1804–27. The introductions to the dialogues are valuable.

ward to the deep utterances of the soul, the interpretation of the objective world by means of the internal, prepared him for Fichte. The mystical attempt to understand the ideas themselves, to use the archetype for creating an ontology from the objective side, observable in Plato's latest works, found its parallel in Schelling. Schleiermacher had large sympathies with these three processes, but mainly with the first; which was to be expected from his purpose. Aiming at gaining spiritual certitude rather than speculating for intellectual gratification, Jacobi's philosophy appeared to combine the excellences of the other two systems, the subjective character of the one, and the intuitional of the other; with the additional advantage of seeming to give expression to the instincts of the heart, as well as the intuitions of the mind. Beyond all these qualities, Schleiermacher inherited from his Moravian education the spirit of pietism, which, almost extinguished by the recent activity of mind, had retired to the quiet sphere where a Stilling[97] or an Oberlin[98] communed with God and laboured for man.

Possessing therefore the two great elements which had been united in the Reformation,—endowed on the one hand with the largest sympathy with every department of the intellectual movement, and the mastery of its ripest erudition, and at the same time with a soul kindled with a hearty love for Christianity,—he was fitted to become the Coryphæus of a new reformation, to attempt again a final reconciliation of knowledge and faith. Whether we view him in his own natural gifts and susceptibilities; in the aim of his life; in his mixture of reason and love, of philosophy and criticism, of

[97] J. H. Jung Stilling (1740–1817), a distinguished oculist in Westphalia, who employed himself in acts of religious usefulness. His works were published in 1835. His Autobiography, written by desire of Goethe, has been translated. See an article on him in the *Foreign Quarterly Review*, vol. xxi.

[98] Oberlin (1740–1826), the interesting pastor of the Vosges mountains, who united efforts for civilization with piety, and the temporal improvement of his people with the spiritual. His memoir has been written in English. To the same class of saintly men about the end of the last century belonged Hamann, Lavater, and Claudius. See Kahnis, p. 80 seq.

enthusiasm and wisdom, of orthodoxy and heresy; or regard the transitory character of his work, the permanence of his influence; church history offers no parallel to him since the days of Origen.[99]

His early education was received in the university of Halle; an institution which had long been the home of pietism, and has continued with but few intervals[1] to evince much of the same Christian spirit. He became professor there early in the century,[2] until the town passed, as already stated, into the power of the French. He removed to Berlin when that university was founded,[3] and continued to exercise his influence there, from the pulpit and the professor's chair, for a quarter of a century, until his death.[4]

Before the conclusion of the last century, while still the literary influence of Weimar was at its height, he wrote Discourses on Religion,[5] to arouse the German mind to self-consciousness; which produced as stirring an effect in religion[6] as Fichte's patriotic addresses to the German nation subsequently in politics; and from them may be dated the first movement of spiritual renovation, as from the latter the first of German liberation from foreign control. In successive works his views on ethics and religion were gradually developed, until, in his *Glaubenslehre* (31) he produced one of the most important theological systems ever conceived. We can give no idea of the compass exhibited in that work, nor spare time to trace the growth in Schleiermacher's own mind as new influences like that of

[99] Mr. R. A. Vaughan, in the Essay above cited, compares Schleiermacher with Hugo St. Victor (on whom see Ritter, *Chr. Phil.* viii. 9. 2). The analogy with Origen is close. Speaking technically, the difference would be, that the Neo-Platonic school, to which Origen belonged, was rather one of "Objective Idealism" like Schelling; Schleiermacher's of "Subjective Idealism" like Fichte.

[1] The Rationalist and Socinian element was taught by Wegscheider.

[2] In 1802.

[3] Halle was taken by the French in 1806; the university of Berlin was founded in 1810.

[4] He died in 1834. [5] See note 31 (p. 428.)

[6] Neander's witness to the effect produced by them is quoted in Kahnis, p. 208.

Harms, which he rejected, indirectly influenced him; but we must be content to define his general position in its destructive and constructive aspects.

The fundamental principles[7] were, that truth in theology was not to be attained by reason, but by an insight, which he called the Christian consciousness,[8] which we should call Christian experience; and that piety consists in spiritual feeling, not in morality. Both were corollaries from his philosophical principles.

There are two parts, both in the intellectual and emotional branches of our nature;—in the emotional, a feeling of dependence in the presence of the Infinite, which is the seat of religion; and a consciousness of power, which is the source of action and seat of morality;—and in the intellectual, a faith or intuition which apprehends God and truth; and critical faculties, which act upon the matter presented and form science.[9] In making these distinctions, Schleiermacher struck a blow at the old rationalism, which had identified on the one hand religion and morality, and on the other intuition and reason. Hence from this point of view he was led to explain Christianity, when contrasted with other religions, subjectively on the emotional side, as the most perfect state of the feeling of dependence; and on the intellectual, as the intuition of Christianity and Christ's work: and the organ for truth in Christianity was regarded to be the special form of insight which apprehends Christ, just as natural intuition apprehends God; which insight was called the Christian consciousness.[10] Thus far many will agree

[7] Cfr. *Glaubenslehre*, § 3–6.

[8] Selbst-bewuszt-seyn.

[9] Schleiermacher's views are rarely put with sharpness of form; and as they varied in the manner shown in Note 31, it is hardly possible to lay down a fixed account of his system. The following remarks are rather the spirit of his Glaubenslehre than an analysis of it. His psychological views are seen in § 1–4 of that treatise (ed. 1842); but the *Reden*, pp. 58, 59, and the introduction by his pupil Schweizer to the *Entwurf eines systems der sittenlehre*, 1835, besides his posthumous philosophical works, ought also to be consulted. His psychological views are nearly reproduced in Morell's *Philosophy of Religion*, ch. iii.

[10] § 7–10; and also § 11–14.

with him. Perhaps no nobler analysis of the religious faculties has ever been given. Religion was placed on a new basis: a home was found for it in the human mind distinct from reason. The old rationalism was shown to be untrue in its psychology. The distinctness of religion was asserted; and the necessity of spiritual insight and of sympathy with Christian life asserted to be as necessary for appreciating Christianity, as æsthetic insight for art.

In its reconstruction of Christian truth, however, fewer will coincide. Following out the same principles; in the same manner as he regarded the intuitions of human nature to be the last appeal of truth in art or morals, so he made the collective Christian consciousness the last standard of appeal in Christianity. The dependence therefore on apostolic teaching was not the appeal to an external authority, but merely to that which was the best exponent of the early religious consciousness of Christendom in its purest age.[11] The Christian church existed before the Christian scriptures. The New Testament was written for believers, appealing to their religious consciousness, not dictating to it. Inspiration is not indeed thus reduced to genius, but to the religious consciousness, and is different only in degree, and not in kind, from the pious intuitions of saintly men. The Bible becomes the record of religious truth, not its vehicle; a witness to the Christian consciousness of apostolic times, not an external standard for all time. In this respect Schleiermacher was not repeating the teaching of the reformation of the sixteenth age, but was passing beyond it, and abandoning its reverence for scripture.

From this point we may see how his views of doctrine as well as his criticism of scripture were affected by this theory. For in his view of fundamental doctrines, such as sin, and the redeeming work of Christ, inasmuch as his appeal was made to the collective consciousness, those aspects of doctrine only were regarded

[11] § 129–131.

as important, or even real, which were appropriated by the consciousness, or understood by it.[12] Sin was accordingly presented rather as unholiness than as guilt before God;[13] redemption, rather as sanctification than as justification; Christ's death as a mere subordinate act in his life of self-sacrifice, not the one oblation for the world's sin;[14] atonement regarded to be the setting forth of the union of God with man; and the mode of arriving at a state of salvation,[15] to be a realisation of the union of man with God, through a kind of mystical conception of the brotherhood of Christ.[16]

Hence, as might be expected, the dogmatic reality of such doctrines as the Trinity was weakened.[17] The deity of the Son, as distinct from his superhuman character, became unimportant, save as the historical embodiment of the ideal union of God with humanity.[18] The Spirit was viewed, not as a personal agent, but as a living activity, having its seat in the Christian consciousness of the church.[19] The objective in each case was absorbed in the spiritual, as formerly in the old rationalism it had been degraded into the natural. It followed also that the Christian consciousness, thus able to find as it were a philosophy of religion, and of the material apprehended by the consciousness of inspired men, possessed an instinct to distinguish the unimportant from the important in scripture, and valued more highly the eternal ideas intended than the historic garb under which they were presented.

The ideological tendency, as it is now called,[20] the natural longing of the philosophical mind that tries to

[12] His views on sin are given § 65–85; and on the work of Christ, § 100–105.

[13] § 68.

[14] § 104.

[15] The mode of reconciliation is treated in § 106–112, and indirectly in the *Weihnachtsfeier*. Mr. Vaughan compares it with Osiander's view in the sixteenth century.

[16] His views may be seen in § 50–56, especially § 54. His system in earlier life almost resembled pantheism, as in his praise of Spinoza. See Reden, p. 471.

[17] § 170–172.

[18] The person of Christ is discussed § 93–99. Vaughan compares the view with that of Justin Martyr. See also Strauss's *Leben Jesu*, § 148.

[19] § 121–125.

[20] See Note 24 (p. 421).

rise beyond facts into their causes, to penetrate behind phenomena into ideas, grows up in a country, as is seen by the example of ancient Greece, when the popular creed and the scientific have become discordant. Suggested in Germany by the old rationalism, it had been especially stimulated by the subjective philosophy of Kant and Fichte. Historic facts were the expression of subjective forms of thought. The Non-ego was a form, in which the Ego was expressing itself. This theory, suggested to Schleiermacher from without, fell in with his own views as above developed, and affected his critical inquiries. When he involved himself in the great questions of the higher criticism, which have been already treated in connexion with Semler, subjective criticism[21] was used in an exaggerated manner, not merely to suggest hypotheses, or to check deductions by Christian appreciation, but as a substitute *à priori* for historic investigation. In the controversy as to the composition of the Gospels, which will be hereafter explained, he was led, by his ideological theory and his instinctive perception of the relative importance of doctrines in theological perspective, to abandon the historical importance of miracles as compared with doctrine, and also the verity of the early history of Christ's life, considered to have been communicated by tradition; while he held fast to the moral and historical reality of the latter.[22]

[21] His critical is much less important than his philosophical position. The same spirit of seriousness marks his writings in this department. Two of his chief critical works are, his *Ueber den sogenannten ersten Brief des Paulus an den Timotheus*, 1807, and *Ueber die Schriften des Lukes, ein Kritischer Versuch*, 1817, translated into English 1825. The reasons given for his appreciation of the Gospel of St. John in the *Weihnachtsfeier*, also his posthumous work, *Hermeneutik und Kritik*, 1838, and his *Einleitung ins Neue Test.* 1845, ought also to be taken into account in estimating his exegetical views.

[22] The above remarks on Schleiermacher will perhaps be considered severe by those who know his works, and will be regarded as putting the worst face on his system. The criticism however of the late Mr. Vaughan, who deeply appreciated Schleiermacher, and had devoted much patient study to his works, and who viewed him from the stand-point of English orthodoxy, coincides with the above estimate of him. A criticism on Schleiermacher from Bretschneider's point of view may be seen in his *Dogmatik*, i. p. 93–115.

These remarks must suffice to point out the position of Schleiermacher. We have seen how completely he caught the influences of his time, absorbed them, and transmitted them. If his teaching was defective in its constructive side; if he did not attain the firm grasp of objective verity which is implied in perfect doctrinal, not to say critical, orthodoxy; he at least gave the death-blow to the old rationalism, which, either from an empirical or a rational point of view, proposed to gain such a philosophy of religion as reduced it to morality. He rekindled spiritual apprehensions; he above all drew attention to the peculiar character of Christianity, as something more than the republication of natural religion, in the same manner that the Christian consciousness offered something more than merely moral experience. He set forth, however imperfectly, the idea of redemption, and the personality of the Redeemer; and awakened religious aspirations, which led his successors to a deeper appreciation of the truth as it is in Jesus. Much of his theology, and some part of his philosophy, had only a temporary interest relatively to his times; but his influence was perpetual. The faults were those of his age; the excellencies were his own. Men caught his deep love to a personal Christ, without imbibing his doctrinal opinions. His own views became more evangelical as his life went on, and the views of his disciples more deeply scriptural than those of their master. Thus the light kindled by him waxed purer and purer. The mantle remained after the prophet's spirit had ascended to the God that gave it.

In strict truth he did not found a school. Though his mind was dialectical, he had too much poetry to do this. Genius, as has been often observed, does not create a school, but kindles an influence. The university of Berlin, the very centre of intellectual greatness in every department from its foundation, was the first seat of Schleiermacher's influence; and the political importance of the capital added impulse to the movement. The reaction extended to other universities,[23] and not only marked the chief theologians of an orthodox tendency which are commonly known to us,[24] —Tholuck, Twesten, Nitzch, Julius Müller, Olshausen, —but even modified the extreme rationalist party, and diffused its influence among theologians of the church of Rome.[25]

It is impossible to specify the views of those who were the chief representatives of the effects of Schleiermacher's teaching. One however, his friend and colleague, deserves mention, the well-known church historian Neander.[26] Brought up a Jew, he passed into Christianity, like some of the early fathers, through the gate of Platonism; and, knowing by experience that free inquiry had been the means of his own conversion, he ever stood forth with a noble courage as the advo-

[23] Especially at Bonn, which was founded in 1818.

[24] The following theologians were influenced chiefly by the spirit of Schleiermacher: Tholuck, professor at Halle, author of various well-known works, (see the expression of his views in the tract, the *Guido and Julius, or true Consecration of the Doubter*, in reply to De Wette's *Theodor*); Twesten, successor of Schleiermacher at Berlin, author of the well-known *Dogmatik;* H. Olshausen, the commentator; Nitzch, author of the *Handbook of Doctrine* (translated); Julius Müller, writer of the able work on the *Nature of Sin;* Ullmann, editor of the *Studien und Kritiken*, the organ of the party. Also Sach, Stier, Tittmann, Umbreit, Ebrart, Hagenbach, Baumgarten-Crusius, Hundeshagen, Bleek, Lücke, Lange, belong to the same party; and Gieseler also in the main. Their doctrine is called the *Deutsche Theologie.* Bunsen must also perhaps be classed with them, though much freer and less biblical than the others. The writings of the late archdeacon Hare are perhaps no inapt English parallel to the tone of these teachers.

[25] More especially Moehler, named above (p. 239, note), was influenced. The modern Catholic theologians are to be treated in the forthcoming (3rd) edition of C. Schwarz's *Gesch. der Neuesten Theologie.*

[26] For Neander's life and character as a theologian and church historian, see the interesting particulars gathered in the *British Quarterly Review*, No. 24, for Nov. 1850, and in the *Bibliotheca Sacra*, vol. viii. Neander (1789–1850) was a Jew by birth. About 1805 he embraced Christianity (his life at this period is seen in his letters to Chamisso); studied at Halle under Schleiermacher 1806; at Göttingen under Planck; was made Professor at Berlin 1812; author of various early monographs; of the *Church History*, 1825; *History of the Planting of the Church*, 1832; *Life of Christ*, 1837. His opinions may be learned from the Preface to the third edition of his Life of Christ, and the Preface to his Church History. On his position as a church historian, see Hagenbach in *Studien und Kritiken* for 1851.

cate of full and fair investigation, feeling confidence that Christianity could endure the test. More meditative and less dialectical than Schleiermacher, and too original to be an imitator, he surpassed him in the deeper appreciation of sin and of redemption; placing sin rather in alienation of will than in the sense of discordance, and holding more firmly the existence of some objective reality in the anthropopathic expression of the wrath of God removed by Christ's death.[27] His great employment in life was history; not, like his master, philosophy and criticism. Viewing human nature from the subjective stand-point, the central thought of his historical works was, that Christianity is a life resting on a person, rather than a system resting on a dogma. Hence he was able to find the harmony of reason and faith from the human side instead of the divine, by noticing the adaptation of the divine work to human wants. The inspiration of the scriptural writers was viewed as dynamical not mechanical, spiritual not literal;[28] and Christianity as the great element of human progress, being the divine life on earth which God had kindled through the gift of his Son.[29] The great aim accordingly of Neander in his historical sketches was to exhibit the Christian church as the philosophy of history, and God's work in Christ, realised in the piety of the faithful, as the philosophy of the Christian church. The history of the church in his view is the record of the Christian consciousness in the world. The subjective and mystical spirit engendered by such a conception, was in danger of converting history into a series of biographies; but the deep influence which it possessed in contributing to foster the reaction against the old rationalism will be obvious. It becomes us to speak with reverence of the writings of a man whose labours have been the means of turn-

[27] His views on sin and redemption are chiefly to be gathered from criticisms on the Pauline doctrine in the *History of the Planting of the Church* (vol. ii.); and on the Christian doctrine in vol. ii. of his Church History.

[28] Introduction to the Life of Christ, § 6.

[29] Preface to *Church History* (first edition).

ing many to Christ. Though lacking form as works of art, yet, if they be compared with works of grander type, where church history has been treated as an epic, we cannot help feeling that the depth of spiritual perception and of psychological analysis compensates for the artistic defects. We are conducted by them from the outside to the inside; from things to thoughts; from institutions to doctrines; from the accidents of Christianity to the essence.

Neander's teaching, while an offshoot from Schleiermacher, marks the highest point to which the principles of the master could be carried. It advances farther in the hearty love for Christ and for revelation, and bears fewer traces of the ancient spirit of rationalism; being allied to it in few respects, save in the wish constantly exhibited to appropriate that which is believed; but the wants of the heart, not the conceptions of the understanding, are made the gauge of divine truth, and the interpreter of the divine volume.

We pointed out that the great reaction in the present century was marked not only by the philosophical and doctrinal school just described, but by a contemporaneous one, which employed itself on literary and critical inquiries in reference to the Bible, and was the continuation of the earlier rationalist criticism on improved principles. The most important name representing this critical movement in the beginning of the period was De Wette. (32) Perhaps too we may without injustice mention, as a type of it at the close of the period, a theologian who is almost too original to admit of being classified—the learned Ewald. (32)

De Wette was nurtured amid the old rationalism of Jena, at the time of its greatest power, about the beginning of the present century; and imbibed the peculiar modification of the doctrines of Kant and Jacobi which was presented in the philosophy of Fries.[30] It was the appeal to subjective feeling thence

[30] On Fries' philosophy see Morell, ii. 418; Tennemann's *Manual*, § 122. Accepting Kant's categories, he held the existence of an inward faith-principle, which gives an insight into the real nature of things; but

derived which preserved him from the coldness of older critics, and caused his labours to contribute to the reaction. His works were very various; but the earlier of them were especially devoted to the examination of the Old Testament, and the later to the New.

The peculiarity of this school generally may be said to be, a disposition to investigate both Testaments for their own sake as literature, not for the further purpose of discovering doctrine. These writers are primarily literary critics, not dogmatic theologians. Like the older rationalists, they are occupied largely with biblical interpretation; but, perceiving the hollowness of their attempt to explain away moral and spiritual mysteries by reference to material events, they transfer to the Bible the theories used in the contemporary investigations in classical history, and explain the Biblical wonders by the hypothesis of legends or of myths. Though they ignore the miraculous and supernatural equally with the older rationalists, they allow the spiritual in addition to the moral and natural, and thus take a more scholarlike and elevated view of the Hebrew history and literature. The system of interpretation adopted is the transition from the previous one, which admitted the facts but explained them away, to the succeeding one of Strauss, which denies the facts, and accounts for the belief in them by psychological causes.

The wish to give a possible basis for the existence of legend, by interposing a chasm between the events and the record of them, stimulated the pursuit of the branch of criticism slightly touched on by their predecessors, which investigates the origin and date of scripture books. They transferred to the Hebrew literature the critical method by which Wolf had destroyed the unity of Homer, and Niebuhr the credibility of Livy. Not a single book,—history, poetry, or prophecy,—was left unexamined. The inquiries of this kind, instituted with reference to the book of Daniel, were alluded to

only as subjective truths, and as tests of truth. The church historian Hase (see Kahnis, p. 236) is moulded by this philosophy.

in a former lecture;[32] and those which relate to the Gospels will occur hereafter.[33] At present it will only be possible to specify a single instance in illustration of these inquiries—the celebrated one which relates to the authorship and composition of the Pentateuch. It is the one to which most labour has been devoted, and is an excellent instance for exhibiting the slow but progressive improvement and growing caution shown in the mode of exercising them.[34]

As early as the time of Hobbes and Spinoza it was perceived that the Pentateuch contains a few allusions which seem to have been inserted after the time of Moses; a circumstance which they, as well as R. Simon, explained, by referring them to the sacred editor Ezra, who is thought to have arranged the canon: but about the middle of the last century a French physician, Astruc,[35] pointed out a circumstance which has introduced an entirely new element into the discussion of the question; viz. the distinction in the use of the two Hebrew names for God,—Elohim and Jehovah. It will be necessary to offer a brief explanation of this distinction, in order that we may be able to perceive the line at which fact ends and hypothesis commences, and understand the character of the criticism which we are describing.

It is now generally admitted that the word *Elohim*

[32] Lect. II. p. 61. Similar discussions have arisen with regard to the integrity and purpose of the books of Job, Zechariah, and Isaiah. Particulars of these literary questions will be found in Hengstenberg's articles *Job* and *Isaiah* in Kitto's *Bibl. Cycl.*, and in Davidson's *Introduction to the Old Testament*, in the chapters concerning these books. The classical student need hardly be reminded of the close analogy between these literary investigations in the Hebrew literature and those which were conducted by F. A. Wolf in respect to Homer, and by other scholars in reference to various classical authors.

[33] Lect. VII.

[34] Perhaps the clearest account of the controversy will be found in Michel Nicholas, *Etudes Critiques sur la Bible*, Essay i. 1862. See also Hengstenberg's *Authentie des Pentateuches* (Die Gottesnamen im Pentat. i. 181 seq.; Hävernick's *Introd. to the Pentateuch* (English translation), p. 56, &c.; Keil's *Lehrbuch*, p. 82, &c.; and Dr. S. Davidson's *Introduction to the Old Testament* (1862), pp. 1–135.

[35] *Conjectures sur les Memoires Originaux du livre de la Genèse*, 1753.

is the name for Deity, as worshipped by the Hebrew patriarchs; *Jehovah*, the conception of Deity which is at the root of the Mosaic theocracy.[36] El, or the plural Elohim, means literally "the powers," (the plural form being either, as some unreasonably think, a trace of early polytheism, or more probably merely emphatic,[37]) and is connected with the name for God commonly used in the Semitic nations. Jehovah[38] means "self-existent," and is the name specially communicated to the Israelites. The idea of power or superiority in the object of worship was conveyed by Elohim; that of self-existence, spirituality, by Jehovah. Elohim was generic, and could be applied to the gods of the heathen; Jehovah was specific, the covenant God of Moses. (33)

In this age, when words are separated from things, we are apt to lose sight of the importance of the difference of names in an early age of the world. The modern investigations however of comparative mythology enable us to realize the fact, that in the childhood of the world words implied real differences in things; not merely in our conceptions, but in the thing conceived.[39] But the explanations above offered will show that, independently of the general law of mind just noticed, a really different moral conception was offered by Providence to the Hebrew mind through the employment of these two words.

Nor was the difference unknown or forgotten in later ages of Jewish history. The fifty-third Psalm, for example, is a repetition of the fourteenth with the

[36] See Exodus vi. 3.

[37] The older critics however think that the plural form relates to the plurality of persons in the divine Being.

[38] Jehovah is translated in the English version, the LORD.

[39] Independently of comparative mythology, which is still an hypothesis, there is evidence of the fact in the very derivations constantly offered of words in the Old Testament, as well as in the modern investigations concerning language. Ewald has shown in an interesting manner the means afforded by the Hebrew proper names for gaining a conception of Hebrew life (see his article on *Names* in Kitto's *Bibl. Encycl.*); and a similar analysis has recently been applied to the Indo-Germanic languages in Pictet's *Les Origines Indo-Européennes*, 1859.

name Elohim altered into Jehovah. In the two first of the five books into which the Psalms are divided, the arrangement has been thought to be not unconnected with the distinction of these names.[40] In the book of Job also the name Jehovah is used in the headings of the speeches of the dialogues; but in the speeches of Job's friends, as not being Israelites, the name Elohim is used.[41] In the book of Nehemiah the name Elohim is almost always used, and in Ezra, Jehovah; and in the composition of proper names, which in ancient times were not merely, as now, symbolical, the names El and Jah respectively are employed in all ages of the Hebrew nation: and, though no exact law can be detected, it seems probable that in the great regal and prophetic age the name Jehovah was especially used. (34)

These remarks will both explain the difference of conception existing in the Hebrew names of Deity, and show that the Jews were aware of the distinction to a late period. When we advance farther, we pass from the region of fact into conjecture.

The distinctness of conception implied in the two names has been made the basis of an hypothesis, in which they are used for discovering different elements in the Pentateuch. Throughout the book of Genesis especially, and slightly elsewhere,[42] the critics that we

[40] It is well known that the book of Psalms is divided, in the Hebrew and the Septuagint, into five books; viz. Psalms i–xli; xlii–lxxii; lxxiii–lxxxix; xc–cvi; cvii–cl; each of them ending with a doxology, which is now inserted in the text of the psalm. In the first book the name *Elohim* occurs 15 times, and *Jehovah* 272 times; in the second, *Elohim* 164 times, and *Jehovah* 30 times. This computation is stated on the authority of Dr. Donaldson, *Christian Orthodoxy*.

[41] There are two exceptions, viz. i. 21, xii. 9, which Hengstenberg considers to prove the rule. On this subject see Hengstenberg's *Dissertation on Job* in Kitto's *Bibl. Cyclop.* ii. 122, now reprinted in a volume of his Miscellaneous Essays.

[42] De Wette tries to exhibit traces in other books than Genesis, but unsuccessfully. It is in Genesis alone that the difference can be so clearly seen, that, even if the peculiar use had no theological meaning, which not even Hengstenberg denies, it must remain as a literary peculiarity. A list of the passages in Genesis which have been considered by these critics to represent the respective uses of the two names, is given in the learned and

are describing have supposed that they detect at least two distinct narratives, with peculiarities of style, and differences or repetitions of statement; which they have therefore regarded as proofs of the existence of different documents in the composition of the Pentateuch; an Elohistic, in which the name Elohim, and a Jehovistic, in which the name Jehovah was used; upon the respective dates of which they have formed conjectures.

Though we may object to these hazardous speculations, we shall perceive the alteration and increasing caution displayed in the criticism, if we trace briefly the successive opinions held on this particular subject.

Astruc, who first dwelt on the distinction, regarded the separate works to be anterior to Moses, and to have been used by him in the construction of the Pentateuch.[43] Eichhorn took the same view, but advanced the inquiry by a careful discrimination of the peculiarities which he thought to belong to each. Vater followed, and allowed the possibility of one collector of the narratives, but denied that it could be Moses. Thus far was the work of the older critical school of rationalists. It was purely anatomical and negative. It is at this point that we perceive the alteration effected by the school which we are now contemplating.

De Wette strove to penetrate more deeply into the question of the origin, and to attain a positive result. His discussion was marked by minute study; and he changed the test for distinguishing the documents from the simple use of the names to more uncertain characteristics, which depended upon internal peculiarities of style and manner. The conclusion to which he came was, that the mass of the Pentateuch is based on the Elohistic document, with passages supplemented from the Jehovistic; and he referred the age of both to a rather late part of the regal period. Ewald, with great learning and delicacy of handling, has reconsidered the question[44] and, though arriving at a most extraordinary

reverently written article *Genesis*, in Smith's *Biblical Dictionary*, by Mr. J. J. S. Perowne.

[43] The references to these various authors will be found in M. Nicholas, Essay i.

[44] *Geschichte des Hebr. Volk.* i. 75 seq.

theory as to the manifold documents which have supplied the materials for the work, has thrown to a much earlier period the authorship of the main portion; and the views of later critics are gradually tending in the same direction. Both study the Pentateuch as uninspired literature; but De Wette absurdly regarded it as an epic created by the priests, in the same manner as the Homeric epic by the rhapsodes: Ewald on the contrary considers it to be largely historic.[45]

This statement of mere results, too brief to exhibit the critical acumen shown at different points of the inquiry even where it is most full of peril, will show the increasing learning displayed, and the appreciation of valuable literary characteristics. It will be perceived that prepossessions still predominate over this criticism; but they are of a different kind from those which existed earlier. They are not the result of moral objections to the narratives, but of the contemporary critical spirit in secular literature. The discrepancy of result obtained by the process is a fair practical argument which proves its uncertainty; but its adherents allow that both in art and literature internal evidence admits of few canons, and consequently that the result of criticism could only admit of probability.

The general summary of the movement shows a steady advance in criticism, as was before shown in doctrine, toward a higher and more spiritual standard.

[45] In writing the history of this dispute, as being here viewed only in its literary aspect, it will be seen that my object has been simply to select it, for the purpose of exhibiting the gradual increase of taste as well as of learning shown by the German critics in reference to questions of the "higher criticism." Concerning the theological aspect of it we can all form an opinion, which would probably be in a great degree condemnatory; but concerning the literary, none but a few eminent Hebrew scholars. Some of the greatest of them, Gesenius, De Wette, Ewald, Hupfeld, Knobel, have given in their adherence to some form of the theory above described. The references to the works of Hengstenberg, Hävernick, and Keil, who have written on the other side, are given above. The rashness of some forms of criticism must not make us abandon a wholesome use of it; and a literary peculiarity such as that described, if it really exist, demands the reverent study of those who wish to learn the mind of the divine Spirit, as it was communicated to the ancient chosen people, or expressed in the written word. Compare McCaul's Essay, *Aids to Faith*, p. 195.

It is not the recognition of the inspired authority of scripture, but it is some approach to it. Instead of the hasty denunciation of narratives or of books as imposture, seen in the Wolfenbüttel Fragments, or the merely rationalist view of Eichhorn and Paulus, we perceive the recognition of spiritual and psychological mysteries as subjects of examination; and even when the result established is altogether unsatisfactory, valuable materials have been collected for future students. If we were to abandon our position of traditional orthodoxy, and accept that of Schleiermacher in doctrine, or of De Wette in criticism, it would be a retrogression; but for the Germans of their time it was a progress from doubt towards faith. It was not orthodoxy, but it was the first approach to it.

This double aspect, philosophical and critical, of the reaction, brings us to the end of the second period in the history of German theological thought.

It has already been stated that the elements of other movements existed, which were hereafter to develope; and that one of these was an attempt, originating in the philosophy of Hegel, to reconstruct the harmony of reason and faith from the intellectual, as distinct from the emotional side. It bore some analogy to the gnosticism of the early church; and the critical side of it gave birth to Strauss.

We have traced the antecedent causes which produced rationalism, and two out of the three periods into which we divided the history of it. We are halting before reaching the final act of the drama; but we already begin to see the direction in which the plot is developing.

It is when a great movement of mind or of society can be thus viewed as a whole, in its antecedents and its consequents, that we can form a judgment on its real nature, and estimate its purpose and use. As in viewing works of art, so in order to observe correctly the great works of God's natural providence, we must reduce them to their true perspective. It is the peculiarity of great movements of mind, that when so viewed they do not appear to be all shadow and formless, nor acts of meaningless impiety. They are products of intellectual antecedents, and perform their function in history. In nothing is the Divine image stamped on humanity, or the moral providence of God in the world, more visible, than in the circumstance, of which we have already had frequent proofs, that thought and honest inquiry, if allowed to act freely, without being repressed by material or political interference, but checked only by spiritual and moral influences, gradually attain to truth, appropriating goodness, and rejecting evil. Thought seems to run on unrestrained, stimulated by human caprice, sometimes by sinful wilfulness; yet it is seen really to be restrained by limits that are not of its own creation. In the world of conscious mind, as in unconscious matter, God hath set a law that shall not be broken. Reason, which creates the doubts, also allays them. It rebukes the unbelief of impiety, making the wrath of man to praise God; and guides the honest inquirer to truth.

A period of doubt is always sad; but it would be an unmixed woe for an individual or a nation, if it were not made, in the order of a merciful Providence, the transition to a more deeply-seated faith. It is a means, not an end.

> You tell me, doubt is devil-born.
>
> I know not; one indeed I knew
> In many a subtle question versed,
> Who touch'd a jarring lyre at first,
> But ever strove to make it true:
>
> Perplext in faith, but not in deeds,
> At last he beat his music out.
> There lives more faith in honest doubt,
> Believe me, than in half the creeds.
>
> He fought his doubts, and gathered strength,
> He would not make his judgment blind,
> He faced the spectres of the mind
> And laid them: thus he came at length
>
> To find a stronger faith his own.[46]

[46] Tennyson's *In Memoriam*, § 95.

Religious truth is open to those who will seek it with humility and prayer.

In addition to the natural action of reason, the fatherly pity of God is nigh, to give help to all that ask it, and that endeavour to sanctify their studies to His honour. Even though the search be long, and a large portion of life be spent in the agony of baffled effort, the mind reaps improvement from its heart-sorrows, and at last receives the reward of its patient faith. "Blessed are they which hunger and thirst after righteousness, for they shall be filled."[47] If we are thankful to be spared the sorrows of the doubter, let us admire the wisdom and mercy shown in the process by which Providence rescues men or nations from the state of doubt. "The Lord God omnipotent reigneth;"[48] and He shall reign for ever and ever.

[47] Matt. v. 6. [48] Rev. xix. 6

LECTURE VII.

FREE THOUGHT: IN GERMANY SUBSEQUENTLY TO 1835; AND IN FRANCE DURING THE PRESENT CENTURY.

MATT. xiii. 52.

Every scribe which is instructed unto the kingdom of heaven is like unto a man that is an householder, which bringeth forth out of his treasure things new and old.

THE last lecture was brought to a close before we reached the final forms assumed by German theology. In the present one we must complete the narrative; and afterwards carry on the history of free thought in France, as affected by the influence of German literature, from the period at which the narrative was previously interrupted to the present time.

We have noticed the traces of the reaction in favour of orthodoxy, which was produced in Germany by the influence of Schleiermacher. We treated the philosophical side of the movement, the vindication of the distinctness of religion and ethics; and also witnessed the improved tone in the critical, tending, if not to the recognition of a supernatural character in the holy scriptures, yet to a more spiritual appreciation of their literary characteristics, and of the psychological peculiarity of the facts recorded. We adverted also, in conclusion, to a rival philosophical influence, springing from the teaching of Hegel, which assisted the reaction by seeking a philosophical reconstruction of religion, though from a different point of view from Schleiermacher.

It was this school which gave origin to the subsequent movements in Germany. The sudden alteration in German thought induced by Strauss, which ushers in the modern period, arose from the union of the philosophical principles of this school with the criticism of that of De Wette. We must therefore endeavour to understand this movement, which forms the turning point between the reaction before described, which is the second of the three general divisions made of this portion of history,[1] and the forms which succeed constituting the third division. Hegel,[2] a name almost as important in its influence on the German mind as that of Goethe, has been already mentioned[3] as the last of that band of philosophers which strove to develop the mental as distinct from the material principle, presented in Kant's philosophy. Kant had completed the process of turning man's search inward, which Descartes had begun. Philosophy became psychology; the discovery of the limits of knowledge, rather than of the nature of the thing known. We have seen that Fichte and Schelling, not content with this result, had sought, though by opposite processes, to escape from this limited knowledge; to attain an ontology as well as a psychology. All philosophy aims at attaining a knowledge of reality, either *à posteriori* by means of generalisation, or *à priori* from the data of mind. These two philosophers strove to attain it by the latter mode; but their method either lacked system, or failed in its results: their philosophy was poetry rather than logic. Hegel followed in their steps, but adopted a basis which admitted of being developed in a formal system. The logical rigour of his method, and the encyclopædic

[1] Lect. VI. p. 218.

[2] Hegel, 1770–1831, Professor at Berlin after 1818. The rudiments of his system are in the *Phenomenology*, written about 1806; the *Logic* gives the mature form of it about 1816; the *Encyclopædia* its completion; the two former works being embodied in the latter. For the sources for the study of his system, &c. see Note 35 at the end of this book.

[3] See p. 237.

grasp which it gave over knowledge, partly accounted, as in the case of Spinoza or of Wolff, for its popularity. The universe was to be interpreted from the mind; the laws of thought were the laws of things. The microcosm and the macrocosm were one; thought, and the mind that thinks; or, more truly, both were phases of the universal mind which was unfolding. The mind of man could transcend the limits of the finite and phenomenal; and, being able to apprehend the idea, the *νοούμενον*, absolutely, without condition, thus possessed the solution of any branch of universal knowledge by an *à priori* process. The problem of philosophy was, to find the laws of this evolution in thought, to catch the ideal when it strives to become immanent and to manifest itself in the actual.

Without attempting here to explain the kind of threefold process, (35) according to which this evolution takes place, it is better, as in the case of the former philosophies named, to exhibit the influence of the general method rather than the effects of particular theories inculcated by it.

The method had many advantages, in displacing a low materialism, in stimulating loftiness of conception, and generating an historic study of every subject, by its view of the universe as a development; and also created a largeness of sympathy with differing views, by regarding all things as in transition, relative, true only in reference to their contradictory; and by considering all hypotheses to contain a germ of right, and to be the result of partial views of truth; but it will also be obvious, that the method had its evil effects. For, when applied to any department, it produced a disposition to seize the principle, the idea, of which the concrete is the embodiment; to descend from the type upon the individual. Its method was deductive and idealistic; giving being to abstractions, like the realism of the middle ages. It lost the fact in the principle; it personified the genus. Philosophy became a vast mythology.

When applied to Christianity, for example, it did

not attempt to find a philosophic ground for it psychologically in the human aspirations, as Schleiermacher had done,[4] but objectively in the dogma. It discovered the ideal truth in religion, and regarded Christianity and Christ as being the manifestation of the effort of the great Spirit of the universe to convert the idea into act; the symbol which expressed the speculative truth of the essential unity of the ideal and the real, of the divine and the human. Like the ancient Gnosticism, it believed in dogmatic Christianity, because it descended upon it from an *à priori* principle, in which it found the explanation of it. Religion and philosophy were reconciled, because religion was made a phase of philosophy.

This system was taught by its founder at Berlin from about 1820 to 1830, contemporary with that of Schleiermacher; and the learned theologian Marheinecke[5] is the name best known of those who applied it to theology. It was regarded at that time as an instrument of orthodoxy.[6] It had the advantage over

[4] Schleiermacher sought it in the consciousness of dependence, craving for an infinite object; and regarded Christianity as supplying the means for the perfect harmony of this principle with the opposing one of voluntary power. Hence, the solution of difficulties in religion would be sought in such a system by seeing the adaptation of the Christian scheme to human needs, not in the solution of the mysteries themselves.

[5] Marheinecke (1780–1846), Professor of Theology at Berlin, the author of many works, chiefly on dogmatic theology, of which his *Symbolik*, 1810, and *Dogmatik*, 1827, are the most important. See Bretschneider's explanation and criticism on his system (*Dogmatik*, i. 115–140). Perhaps the name of K. Daub (1765–1836), Professor at Heidelberg, ought also to be added. Originally Hegel's teacher, he adopted his pupil's system. See Kahnis's remarks, p. 244 seq., and Amand Saintes, part ii. ch. xvii. It has been usual to classify the followers of Hegel under the analogy of political parties in foreign parliaments, thus:—in the extreme right, Heinrichs and Goeschel; in the right, Schaller, Erdmann, and Gabler; in the centre, Rosenkranz and Marheinecke; in the left centre, Vatke, Snellmann, and Michelet; in the left, Strauss, Bruno Bauer, and Feuerbach. See Morell, *Hist. of Philosophy*, ii. 199, 203. Several of these however are philosophers rather than theologians. A simpler classification of the Hegelian theologians is into three parties: the first, Daub and Marheinecke, and more recently Dorner; the second, Chr. Baur and the Tübingen school; the third, Strauss, B. Bauer, and Feuerbach.

[6] See the article by Scherer in the *Revue des Deux Mondes*, Feb. 1861, p. 841; and on the influence of Hegel see Kahnis, p. 244 seq., and Am. Saintes, P. II. ch. 17; and Bartholmess, b. xii.

the old rationalism, in that while using similarity of method in seeking to explain mysteries, it did not pare them down, but absorbed them in principles of philosophy; and over the school of Schleiermacher, in that it was less subjective, less a matter of feeling, supplying a doctrine and not merely a spirit; and therefore it satisfied the longing of the mind for dogmatic truth, and at the same time more readily linked itself, ecclesiastically with churchlike and corporate tendencies, and politically with conservative and autocratic ones. Yet it is easy to see that its spirit was really far less Christian than Schleiermacher's. For it not only confused again philosophy and religion, which his system had severed, but it proudly claimed to explain doctrines rationally where his had only sought to appropriate them intuitionally. It verged towards pantheism. It was in danger of losing the historic fact in the idea; of encouraging, as it is now sometimes called, the "ideological tendency;"[7] whereas with Schleiermacher, the historic belief had only been regarded as less important than the emotional apprehension. Its *à priori* spirit created also a depreciation of the investigations which had been pursued by the critical school. It gave encouragement to the study of history; but it was to the history of philosophy, not to the investigations conducted by historical criticism.

Such was the system which, along with those described in the last lecture, was regarded as contributing to favour orthodox reaction, and was disputing theological preeminence with that of Schleiermacher, when a work was published by one of its disciples, which was the means, through the ferment produced, of altering completely the whole tone and course of German thought. It was the celebrated *Life of Jesus* by Strauss,[8] a criticism on the four biographies given in the gospels; a work in which the whole destructive movement was concentrated, with such singular ability and clearness, that hardly any work of theology has

[7] See Note 24 (p. 412).

[8] *Leben Jesu*, 1835.

subsequently been written without some notice of the propositions there maintained.

It presented a double aspect: it was both philosophical and critical. Strauss added to a general admission of the Hegelian point of view a love for the critical studies so much neglected by that party. Brought up in the moderate orthodoxy of Tübingen, he had studied at Berlin under Schleiermacher, but caught the critical rather than the philosophical side of that master's teaching, and especially interested himself in the solution of the question relating to the origin and credibility of the Gospels, already partially considered in the critical inquiries of the old rationalism, and of the school of De Wette. It was an investigation which in its nature, in the spirit in which it was decided, and in its similarity to the contemporaneous discussions of classical criticism, bore a close resemblance to that before described in reference to the Pentateuch. A few words of explanation concerning it are necessary, previous to the statement of the nature of Strauss's work.[9]

As early as the last century the resemblance between the three "synoptical" Evangelists had excited attention; and examination was directed to discover the cause. Some, as Wetstein,[10] supposed that one or two of the Gospels were borrowed from the third; others, as Michaelis[11] and Eichhorn, that the three were all de-

[9] The account of this controversy may be seen in bishop Marsh's *Dissertation*, 1807; and a continuation of the history subsequently to his work in the introduction to the *Translation of Schleiermacher's Essay on St. Luke*, 1825 (by the present Bp. Thirlwall). The controversy is also treated with great learning and reverence by Dr. S. Davidson, *Introd. to New Test.* i. (373–425). Important references and quotations in regard to it are given in the Appendix to Tregelles' edition of *Horne's Introd.* 10th ed. vol. iv.; also see Amand Saintes, *Hist.* p. ii. 12; Renan's *Etudes de l'Hist. Relig.* (Ess. 3); Hase's *Leben Jesu;* Quinet's review of Strauss (*Œuvres*, vol. iii). A series of studies on the subject is in course of publication in the *Revue Germ.* 1862, by Michel Nicholas.

[10] Wetstein, with Mill, Calmet, and others, regarded St. Mark's Gospel to be the epitome of St. Matthew's. Griesbach and Dr. Townson thought that St. Luke as well as St. Mark had seen the one by St. Matthew. A further list may be seen in Tregelles (as above), p. 642; and Davidson (as above).

[11] Michaelis regarded the Greek translator of St. Matthew to have had

rived from one common original, now lost; others, as Schleiermacher, that they were composed from many detached written narratives; others, as Herder, and subsequently Gieseler, that they were the committal to writing of the oral tradition common in the church. Thus, whether the Gospels were regarded as copies, or as being composed from earlier documents, or from primitive tradition, the effect was, that they were reduced to the level of natural testimony, and instead of being three witnesses they became one. The fourth Gospel also was involved in uncertainty. Bretschneider added the full examination of it, and provoked a discussion concerning the alleged disagreement of its tone and statements with those of the synoptists.[12] Thus a chasm was introduced between the events and the record of them; and the testimony was reduced to traditional evidence.

This alteration in the critical attempt to shake the evidence of independent authorship had been accompanied by a corresponding change in the interpretation, as seen in the assaults made on the credibility of the facts narrated. In the hands of the English deists and of Reimarus this attack had been an allegation against the moral character of the writer. In Eichhorn and Paulus the imputation of collusion had been superseded by the rationalistic interpretation, which, without denying the historical recital, denied the supernatural, and explained it away by reference to the peculiarities

access to the same Greek document as St. Mark and St. Luke. Semler and Lessing advocated a Hebrew or Syriac original. Eichhorn adopted the theory of an Aramaic original, which was adopted with slight alterations by bishop Marsh. (It was criticised by bishop Randolph, by Mr. Veysie, and in Falconer's *Bampton Lectures*, 1810.) Schleiermacher regarded the Gospels to be pieced together out of separate documents. Gieseler's hypothesis was put forward in 1818.

[12] *Probabilia de Evangel. et Epist. Joannis origine et indole*, 1820. The theory suggested was, that it was written in the second century. It was well answered by Schott, Stein, and others. The controversy has been revived in more modern times; the Tübingen school denying the authorship to St. John, Ewald and others, asserting it. The subject is discussed in Davidson's *Introduction to the New Testament*, i. 233–313. See also two articles in the *National Review*, No. 1. July 1855, and No. 9. July 1857.

of time at which the events were described. The next step was to transfer the doubt to the recital itself, and to find, in the absence of contemporary evidence for the events, the possibility for legend, and, in the antecedent expectation of them, the possibility for myth.

This was the state of the critical question with regard to the Gospels when the work of Strauss appeared. The Hegelian philosophy gave him the constructive side of his work, and criticism the destructive. Setting out with the preconception which had lain at the basis of German philosophy and theology since Kant, that the idea was more important than the fact,[13] the mythical interpretation of history furnished to him the medium for applying this conception as an engine of criticism.

The mythical system of interpretation, though slightly suggested by his predecessors in criticism, was Strauss's great work. The difference between allegory, legend, and myth, is well known. Our blessed Lord's miracles would be allegories, if they were, as Woolston claimed, parables intentionally invented for purposes of moral instruction, or facts which had a mystical as well as literal meaning: they would be legends if, while containing a basis of fact, they were exaggerated by tradition: they would be myths if, without really occurring, they were the result of a general preconception that the Messiah ought to do mighty works, which thus gradually became translated into fact. A legend is a group of ideas round a nucleus of fact: a myth is an idea translated by mental realism into fact. A legend proceeds upwards into the past; a myth downwards into the future.[14] Strauss's peculiarity consisted in trying to show that if a small basis of fact, height-

[13] On the spirit of Kant's philosophy in this respect, see Strauss's own remarks, *Leben Jesu*, Introd. § 7.

[14] On the contrast of myth and legend there are some good remarks in Strauss, who quotes George's *Mythus und Sage* for the explanation; also in the *Westminster Review* for April 1847 (p. 149), an article which, though written in favour of Strauss, gives an instructive account of the object and position of his work. The history of Strauss's work, with its antecedents and consequents, mainly based on Schwarz (b. ii.) and on Scherer, but bearing marks of independent study, is given in Mr. F. C. Cook's Essay on Ideology in the *Aids to Faith*, 1862. Theodore Parker

ened by legend, be allowed in the gospel history, the influence of myth is a psychological cause sufficient to explain the remainder. The idea is regarded as prior to the fact: the need of a deliverer, he pretends, created the idea of a saviour: the misinterpretation of old prophecy presented conditions which in the popular mind must be fulfilled by the Messiah. The gospel history is regarded as the attempt of the idea to realise itself in fact.

The fundamental fallacy of the inquiry is apparent from one consideration. Legends are possible in any age; myths, strictly so called, only in the earliest ages of a nation. Comparative philology has lately shown that mythology is connected with the formation of language, and restricted to an early period of the world's history.[15] But the encouragement offered to the mythic interpretation by Hegel's philosophy will be apparent. The mythus embodying itself in the facts of the gospel was the miniature of the process of universal nature. Everywhere the idea strives for realisation.

The scheme of Strauss formed the link between philosophy and criticism. Philosophy had explained the doctrines of Christianity, but not the facts of Christian history. Criticism had explained the facts by historical examination, but not by philosophy. Strauss attempted, for the first time, to present the philosophical explanation of facts as well as doctrines. He explained them, neither by charge of fraud, nor by historical causes, but by reference to the operation of a psychological law, the same which the Hegelian philosophy regarded as exemplified universally. Early Christian fiction was resolved into a psychological law, regulated by a definite law of suggestion, of which plausible instances were traced. The gospel history was regarded to be partly a creation out of nothing,

has given an accurate analysis, and of course a defence, of Strauss (*Miscellaneous Writings*, p. 231).

15 The new view of the nature of myths is developed in Max Müller's Essay on *Comparative Mythology*, *Oxford Essays*, 1856. See also Note 47 (p. 450).

partly an adaptation of real facts to preconceived ideas. This same philosophy, which thus contributed to the critical or destructive side of the theory, also furnished the reconstructive. The facts in Christianity were temporary, the ideas eternal. Christ was the type of humanity. (36) His life and death and resurrection were the symbol of the life, death, and resurrection, of humanity. The former were unimportant, the latter eternal. An exoteric religion for the people might exhibit the one: the esoteric for the philosopher might retain the other.[16]

This is Strauss's system and position. The book itself comprises three parts;—first, an historic introduction, in which the history of previous criticism and of Hermeneutics, and of the formation of the mythical theory is most ably presented:[17]—secondly, the main body of the work, which consists of a critical examination of the life of Christ,[18] subdivided into three parts; viz. an examination of the birth and childhood of Jesus,[19] of his public life,[20] and of his death;[21] the object of which is to point out in the narrative the historic or mythic elements:—and thirdly, a philosophical conclusion,[22] in which the doctrinal significance of the life is given. As a specimen of didactic and critical writing it is perhaps unrivalled in the German literature. The second part is the embodiment of all the difficulties which destructive criticism had presented. If the historic sketches captivate by their clearness, the critical do so by their surprising acuteness and dialectical power;

[16] Strauss, *Leben Jesu*, § 152. (ii. p. 713.)

[17] § 1–16. It contains a history of the different explanations of sacred legends among the Greeks; the allegorical systems of the Hebrews (Philo,) and Christians (Origen); the system of the Deists; and the Wolfenbüttel Fragmentist; the naturalist mode of Eichhorn and Paulus, and the moral of Kant; lastly, the rise of the mythic, both in reference to the Old and New Testaments. Then the discussion of the possibility of myths in the Gospels, and a description of the evangelical mythus.

[18] § 1–142. [19] § 17–43. [20] § 44–110. [21] § 111–142.

[22] § 143–152. The author gives the dogmatic import of the life of Jesus, criticising the Christology of Orthodoxy, of Rationalism, of Schleiermacher, the Symbolic of Kant and De Wette, the Hegelian; and draws his own conclusions.

and the philosophical by the appreciation of the ideal beauty of the very doctrines, the historic embodiment of which is denied.. It is the work of a mind endowed with remarkable analytical power; in which the force of reflective theory has overwhelmed the intuitional perception of the personality and originality of the sacred character which is the subject of his study.[23]

The effect of the publication of the work was astonishing. It produced a religious panic unequalled since the Wolfenbüttel fragments. The first impulse of the Prussian government was to prevent the introduction of the book into the Prussian kingdom; but Neander stood up to resist the proposal, with a courage which showed his firm confidence in the permanent victory of truth; saying that it must be answered by argument, not suppressed by force; and forthwith wrote his own beautiful work on the life of Christ in reply to it. Yet neither the peculiarity of Strauss's theory nor the nature of the work gave ground for the panic. For the book was in truth not a novelty, but merely a fuller development of principles already existing in Germany; and Schleiermacher, before his death, when contemplating the tendency of religious criticism, had predicted[24] the probability of such an attempt being made. Nor was the work irreligious and blasphemous in its spirit, like the attacks of the last century. It professed to be executed solely in the interests of science; and, though subversive of historic religion, to be conservative of ideal. The critical part was only a means to an end; its real basis was speculative. But the literary aspect of the question was lost sight of in the religious. The heart spoke forth its terror at the idea of losing its most sacred hope, the object of its deepest trust, an historic Saviour. The alarm had not been anticipated by the author of the attack. He is

[23] This idea is well brought out in Renan's critique on Strauss. (*Etudes Relig.* Essai iii.)

[24] One passage of this kind is quoted by Amand Saintes (p. 263) from Lücke in *Stud. und Krit.* vol. ii. p. 489.

described by a hostile critic[25] as a 'young man full of candour, of sweetness, and modesty, of a spirit almost mystical, and as it were saddened by the disturbance which had been occasioned.' But he became a martyr for his act, and an outcast from the sympathy of religious men. Unable to exercise his singular gifts of teaching in any professorship, he has continued to write from time to time literary monographs of more defiant tone; proofs of his ability, but vehicles for the expression of his opinions. (37)

The effect on the different theological critics throughout Germany, both friendly and hostile, was so remarkable, that the year 1835, in which the book was published, is as memorable in theology as the year 1848 in politics. The work carried criticism and philosophy to its farthest limits, and demanded from theologians of all classes a thorough reconsideration of the subject of the *origines* of Christianity.[26] The ablest theologians either wrote in refutation of it, or reconsidered their own opinions by the light of its criticisms. (38) The alarm at the loss of the historic basis of Christianity created a strong reaction in favour of the Lutheran orthodoxy, the commencement of which has already been named;[27] and gave the death-blow, not only to the Hegelian

[25] Edgar Quinet (*Œuvres*, iii. 316, reprinted from *Revue des Deux Mondes*, Sept. 1838). His words are, "Un jeune homme plein de candeur, de douceur, de modestie, une âme presque mystique et comme attristée du bruit qu'elle a causé." The unaltered view which Strauss now takes of his own work, after the interval of twenty-five years, is given in the Vorrede to his *Gespräche von Hütten übersetzt und erlaütert*, 1860. It is quoted in the *National Review*, No. 23, art. 7.

[26] The effect which it produced is described, with details of the answers written, in book ii. of the excellent little work of C. Schwarz already named, *Geschichte der Neuesten Theologie*, 1856. This part of the work is translated into French, with some useful notes, in the *Rev. Germ.* vol. ix. parts ii. and iii. See Note 38 (p. 000). The most useful replies are those of Neander and Dorner. Dr. Beard also published a valuable series of papers called *Voices of the Church* (1845), containing translations of the Essay by Quinet above quoted, of one by A. Cocquerel (père), and others. Dr. Mill's work on *The Application of Pantheistic Principles to the Gospels* (1840) is intended also as a reply. The Life of Christ, contained in vol. i. of Dean Milman's *History of Christianity*, also contains important remarks on Strauss's scheme.

[27] P. 241.

school, but almost to the passion for ontological speculation in Germany. While some thus assumed a churchly and conservative aspect, others outstripped Strauss, and, uniting with French positivism, advanced into utter pantheism and materialism.

The Hegelian party, to which Strauss belonged, and which would fain have been excused from this *reductio ad absurdum* of its principles,[28] became split into sections through the various attempts made to parry the blow, and reconstruct their system on the philosophical side. The critical tendency had now too found a home, by means of Strauss's work, among the Hegelians; and this led to the creation of a new school of historical criticism to be hereafter described, which arose in Strauss's own university of Tübingen.[29]

We have now explained the circumstances attending the change which closed the second and introduced the third period in German theology.

In this third period, which is that of contemporary thought, we may distinguish four broadly marked tendencies; three within the church, and one directly infidel in character outside of it.[30]

The last named, which we shall describe first, started from Strauss's position, and advanced still farther. It sprang from the destructive side of the Hegelian philosophy, and has sometimes been named the young Hegelian school. From the first it lacked the air of respect toward religion which Strauss did not throw aside in his work; and it also extended itself from theology to politics.

[28] Scherer clearly brings out this relation of Strauss's work, in § 5 of the article before quoted.

[29] Accordingly it will be understood that the mention of "the old Tübingen school" of the last century denotes a Pietist school like that of Bengel or Pfaff; the mention of "the new Tübingen school" means one of ultra-rationalism.

[30] The materials for the following sketch have been largely supplied by the work of Schwarz, and partly by an article before cited in the *Westminster Review* for April 1857. Schwarz, after devoting the first chapter of book ii. to the Straussian contests, devotes the second and first three chapters of book iii. to the history of these four movements.

Bruno Bauer,[31] a Professor at Berlin, by turning suddenly round from the most orthodox to the most heterodox position in his school, may be classed with Strauss in his method, though not in his spirit. He carried out Strauss's critical examination of the Gospels with a coarse ridicule; and extended it by denying the historic basis of fact, and imputing the myth to the personal creation of the individual writer. But his successors advanced even farther. As Bauer developed the critical side of Strauss, Feuerbach[32] and Ruge[33] developed the philosophical, and destroyed the very idea of religion itself, by showing that the idea of God or of religion is of human construction, the giving objective existence to an idea. The aspiration, instead of guaranteeing the existence of an object toward which it is directed, is represented as creating it. This was the final result of the subjective point of view of the Kantian philosophy, and of the idealism of Hegel. Reason

[31] See Amand Saintes, book ii. ch. 18; Hase, § 450; Hundeshagen, *Der Deut. Prot.* § 17. Bruno Bauer, born 1809, was once Professor at Bonn, and teacher at Berlin. In his first manner he showed himself to be a disciple of Hegel, in works published from 1835 to 1839, such as a criticism on Strauss, and also on the Old Testament. From 1839 to 1842 he exhibited a destructive tendency directed against the sacred books; e. g. a work on the Prussian church and science, and a criticism on St. John's Gospel. The persecution which he encountered stimulating his opposition, he showed in his next works (in 1842 and 1843) a spirit of defiance in his *Das Eklekte Christenthum.* From 1843 to 1849 he connected himself with questions of politics, and wrote largely on social science. Since that period he has again written, both in theology, criticisms of the Gospels and Epistles, and on politics. A list of his works and a sketch of his mental character may be found in Vapereau, *Dict. des Contemp.* 1858.

[32] On this movement see Schwarz, b. iii. ch. i.; and on the German political socialism see the *North British Review*, No. 22, for Aug. 1848. Feuerbach (see Vapereau) was author of many works on the history of philosophy about 1833 to 1845. His chief works on religion were *Das Wesen des Christenthums* (1851), and *Das Wesen der Religion*, 1845. The former work was translated in 1854, and contains a discussion (1) of the true or anthropological essence of religion; (2) of the false or theological. His collected works have been published. The *Hallische Jahrbücher* was his organ. Criticisms on his school are given by Bartholmess (*Hist. Crit. des Doctr. de la Phil. Mod.* b. xiii. ch. ii.), and by E. Renan (*Etudes de l'Hist. Relig.* p. 405).

[33] Ruge, once a teacher at Halle; went into voluntary exile at Paris, like Heine, in 1843; was mixed in the revolutionary schemes of 1848; and in 1850 became an exile in England. See Vapereau.

must, it was pretended, be followed, to whatever extent it contradicts the feelings. Theology becomes anthropology; religion, mythology; pantheism, atheism; man, collective humanity, becomes the sole object of the belief and respect which had been previously given to Deity; religion vanishes in morality. The love of man becomes the substitute for the love of God. This was a position analogous to that which positivism reached in France, but from a mental instead of a physical point of view. This form of thought found expression in literature through the poetry of Heine,[34] and linked itself with political theories of communism more extreme than the contemporary ones in France.

Still the lowest point was not reached: religion was treated as a psychological peculiarity, and the virtue of benevolence recognised. But when religion was felt to be only an idea, and the belief of the supernatural to be the great obstacle to political reform, an intense feeling of antipathy was aroused; and Schmidt,[35] under the pseudonym of Stirner, reached the naturalistic point of view held by Volney, the worship of self-love. This new school, which had arisen in the few years subsequent to Strauss's work, mingled itself with the revolutionary movements of Germany in 1848, and was the means of exciting the alarm which caused the suppression of them. Since that date the school has been extinct as a literary movement.

The tendency just described was entirely destructive. The three others, which remain for consideration, exist within the church, and are in their nature reconstructive, and aim at repelling the attacks of Strauss and

[34] See above, note on p. 16. Gutskow and Mundt belonged to the same school. The former a dramatic poet, whose works against religion were about 1835, in the Prefaces to Letters of F. Schlegel, &c.; the latter, librarian at Berlin, was noted for his political connexion with the party of young Germany, rather than for any assault on religion. See Vapereau for an account of his works. The spirit of this school was tinged with bitterness against existing institutions.

[35] Gaspard Schmidt (1806–1856) wrote in 1845, under the pseudonym of Max Stirner, *Der einzige und sein Eigenthum.* His later works were on political economy.

of other previous critics. The one that we shall describe first is that which is most rationalistic, and approaches most nearly to Strauss's views; and is frequently called, from the Swabian university which has been its stronghold, the Tübingen school.[36] It is a lineal offshoot in some slight degree from the school of Hegel, and more decidedly from the critical school of De Wette, before named. But it stands contrasted with the latter by caution, as marked as that which separates recent critics[37] of Roman history from earlier ones, like Niebuhr. Like Strauss, it restricts its attention to the New Testament; but it is a direct reaction against his inclination to undervalue the historical element. The great problem presented to it is, to reconstruct the history of early Christianity, to reinvestigate the genesis of the gospel biographies and doctrine. Declining to approach the books of the New Testament with dogmatic preconceptions, it breaks with the past, and interprets them by the historic method; proposing for its fundamental principle to interpret scripture exactly like any other literary work. Pretending that after the ravages of criticism, the Gospels cannot be regarded as true history, but only as miscellaneous materials for true history, it takes its stand on four of the

[36] As schools of thought have been occasionally named in this narrative in connexion with universities, it may facilitate clearness to collect together the few hints which have been given concerning the subject. In the first period previous to 1790, we showed the theological tendencies of the four universities, Göttingen, Leipsic, Halle, and Tübingen: next, in the period after 1790, the state of Jena as the home of rationalism and of the Kantian philosophy. In our second period we pointed out the condition of Berlin as the seat of philosophical reaction under Schleiermacher and Hegel; and indirectly of the universities which represented the school of De Wette. In the third period, the school of Lutheran reaction has specially existed in Berlin, Leipsic, Erlangen, Rostock, and the Russian university of Dorpat; the school of "Mediation" chiefly at Berlin, Heidelberg, Halle, and Bonn; and the historico-critical at Tübingen. It may be useful to add, for the completion of the account, that the Tübingen school is now almost extinct in its original home; and that the two universities which at the present time represent the freest criticism are supposed to be Giessen and Jena. The latter is marked by the realistic school of philosophy described in Note 41. Hilgenfeld, the best representative of the Tübingen school, is Professor there; see Note 39, at the end of this volume.

[37] E. g. Th. Mommsen.

Epistles of St. Paul, the genuineness of which it cannot doubt, and finds in the struggle of Jew and Gentile its theory of Christianity.[38] Christianity is not regarded as miraculous, but as an offshoot of Judaism, which received its final form by the contest of the Petrine or Judæo-Christian party, and the Pauline or Gentile; which contest is considered by it not to have been decided till late in the second century. By the aid of this theory, constructed from the few books which it admits to be of undoubted genuineness, it guides itself in the examination of the remainder, tracing them to party interests which determined their aim, pronouncing on their object and date by reference to it.[39] In this way it arrives at most extraordinary conclusions in reference to some of them. Not one single book, except four of St. Paul's Epistles, is regarded to be authentic. The Gospel called that of St. John is considered as a treatise of Alexandrian philosophy, written late in the second century to support the theory of the *Λόγος*. It will thus be perceived that the inquiry, though it professes to be objective, yet has a subjective cast.

The leader of this school was Christian Baur, (39) lately deceased; a man of large erudition; a wonder of acuteness even in Germany; distinguished for the extraordinary ability displayed in his reply to the attacks made on Protestantism by the celebrated Roman catholic theologian Moehler: and though the doctrinal result of the school is ethics or pure Socinianism and naturalism, and the critical opinions obviously are most extravagant, the sagacity and learning shown in the monographs published by it make them some of the most instructive, as sources of information, in modern theology, to those who know how to use them aright. From an orthodox point of view the effect of the school is most destructive; but, if viewed in reference to the preceding schools, it manifests a tenacious hold over the

[38] Viz. the Epistles to the Romans and Galatians, and the two to Corinth.

[39] An explanation and criticism of some of these opinions are given in Davidson's *Introduction to the New Testament.*

historic side of Christianity, and has affected in a literary way the schools formerly described, which claim lineage from the older critics.

As the tendency just described is the modern representative of the older critical schools; so the next holds a similar position to the philosophical.

The school is frequently on this account described by the same name, of "Mediation theology,"[40] originally applied to Schleiermacher, because it attempts to unite science with faith, a true use of reason with a belief in scripture. It comprises the chief theological names of Germany, some of whom were disciples of Schleiermacher, others of the orthodox portion of the Hegelian party. Their object is not simply, like the revivers of Lutheran orthodoxy, to surrender the judgment to an external authority in the church, nor to give unbounded liberty to it like the critical school: not going back like the one to the ancient faith of the church, nor progressing like the other to new discoveries in religion, they seek to understand that which they believe, to find a philosophy for religion and Christianity.

Two theologians stand out above the others, as evincing vitality of thought, and boldly attempting to grapple with the philosophical problems;—Dorner[41] and Rothe,[42] both very original, but bearing traces of the influence of their predecessors. The former, moulded by the Hegelian school, investigates the Christologi-

[40] *Vermittellungs-Theologie*, and sometimes called *Deutsche Theologie.* See Schwarz, book iii. ch. ii. The organs of this party are the *Studien und Kritiken* and the *Neue Evangel. Kirchenzeitung.*

[41] Dorner, born in 1809; successively Professor in several universities: he has recently gone to Berlin. It is a matter of gratification that his great work, described in the text, is now in course of translation. The account of the successive steps through which it passed may be seen in the American *Bibliotheca Sacra* for 1849. Also an account of it is given in Theodore Parker's *Miscellaneous Works*, p. 287. Lange, author of the *Leben Jesu*, ought perhaps to be named along with the two in the text, as belonging to this school.

[42] Perhaps these two theologians ought to be regarded apart from the average of the members of the Mediation school, as being of a grander type. They approach the subject from a higher stand-point, and also are more largely moulded by philosophy. On Rothe, see Note 40 (p. 437).

cal problem which lies at the basis of Christianity; the latter, moulded rather by the school of Schleiermacher, has attempted the cosmological, which lies at the basis of religion and providence.

The work of Dorner on "the Person of Christ" formed an epoch in German theology, by its fulness of learning, its orthodoxy of tone, and its union of speculative powers with historic erudition. The Christian doctrine of the incarnation is, that God and man have been united in an historic person as the essential condition for effecting human salvation. If the doctrine be viewed on the speculative side, the problem is to show *à priori* that this historic union ought to exist; if viewed on the historic, to prove that it has existed as a fact. The great aim of the Christology of the Hegelian system was to effect the former; the aim of Strauss was to destroy the latter. Dorner strove to reconstruct the doctrine, by making the historical study of its progress the means of supplying the elements of information for doing so. He commences by an examination of other religions,[43] in order at once to show the existence in them of blind attempts to realise that truth which the incarnation supplied, and to prove the impossibility that the Christian doctrine can have been borrowed from human sources, as the critical and mythical interpreters would assume. He discovers in all religions the desire to unite man to God; but shows[44] that the Christian doctrine cannot have been derived from the oriental, which humanised God; nor from the Greek, which deified man; nor from the Hebrew in its Palestinian form, which degraded the idea of the incarnate God into a temporal Messiah; nor in its Alexandrian form, which never reached, in its theory of the *Λόγος*, the idea of the distinction of person of the Son from the Father. Thus establishing the originality of the idea in Christianity, and exhibiting it as the fulfilment of the world's yearnings, he traces it in the teaching of the apostles, and of the apostolic age,[45] next as marking

[43] In the *Einleitung*. [44] Id. [45] Vol. i. period i. ch. i.

the different heretical sects,[46] which respectively lost sight of one of the two elements, till he finds the church's explicit statement of the doctrine in its fulness;[47] and then pursues it onwards through the course of history to the present time.[48] Though the work is to an English mind difficult, through the air of speculation which pervades it, and perhaps open to exception in some of its positions; yet, viewed as a whole, it is a magnificent argument in favour of Christianity; exhibiting the incarnation as the satisfaction for the world's wants, as the original and independent treasure in Christianity; and showing the process through which Providence in history has caused the doctrine to be evolved and preserved.

The other great problem, the origin of things, and the relation of God to the world, which is at the basis of religion, as the incarnation is at the basis of Christianity, has been less frequently handled. Originally discussed, like the latter, in controversy with the early unbelievers, it had been touched upon in the speculations of Averroes and Spinoza, in the materialism of French infidelity, and in the earlier systems of speculative philosophy in Germany itself. It was this problem which was attempted by Rothe. (10) Advancing beyond this first question, he has considered the scheme of Providence in the development of religion, and the theory of the Christian church in relation to political society. It is unnecessary here to explain his system: his mind is too original to admit of comparison without injustice; yet the speculations of our own Coleridge, who on philosophical principles makes the state to be the realisation of the church, will perhaps give some imperfect conception of the character of his attempts.

This second school that we have been considering, though approximating extremely nearly to orthodoxy, and furnishing the works of most value in the modern theology, yet seeks to approach religion from the psychological or philosophical side. It speculates freely,

[46] Id. ch. ii. and iii. [47] Epoche, Abth. 2. [48] Vol. ii.

and believes revelation because it finds it to coincide with the discoveries of free thought. But there is a third tendency, which believes revelation without professing to understand it; which rests on the revelation in scripture as an objective verity, and believes the Bible on the ground of evidence, without questioning its material.[49]

The first germ of this reaction in favour of rigid orthodoxy was observable in the feeling aroused by the theses of Harms, in 1817, already named, on occasion of the celebration of the tricentenary of the Reformation; but it was quickened by the attempts, initiated by the Prussian king, between the years 1821 and 1830, to unite the Lutheran and Calvinistic branches of the Protestant church.[50]

The time seemed then to thoughtful men a fitting one, when doctrines were either regarded as unimportant or superseded by the religious consciousness, to unite these two churches under the bond of a common nationality, and the practice of a common liturgy. But the old Lutheran spirit, which still survived in the retirement of country parishes, was aroused, and some pastors underwent deprivation and persecution rather than submit to the union.[51] This new movement at first caught the spirit of pietism, just as had been the case with that of Schleiermacher; but gradually abandoned it for a dogmatic and churchlike aspect, as he for a scientific expression. Its aim was to return to the Lutheranism of the sixteenth century, and to rally round the confessions of faith of that period. Heng-

[49] If the reader follows out the pedantic but useful mode before named, of arranging the actual schools of theology after the fashion of foreign assemblies, he will place in the right, the friends of the confessional theology; in the centre, those of the mediation theology; in the left, the old critical school of De Wette; and in the extreme left, the school of Tübingen. The first has its chief seat in Prussia, and the third probably in Thuringia and central Germany.

[50] See Kahnis, p. 262, &c.; Am. Saintes, part ii. ch. x; Hase, § 453; Schwarz, book iii. ch. iii.

[51] The dissenters from the union were not recognised legally by the state till 1845. (See the references given in the last note.) The principal of those who dissented were Kellner, Scheibel, and Huschke.

stenberg[52] at Berlin, and Hävernick,[53] are the names best known as representing this party at the period of which we speak. Their efforts were directed to criticism rather than to doctrine, to reconstruct the basis for Christianity in Judaism by defending the authenticity and credibility of the ancient scriptures. In doctrine and the canon, they reverted to the position of the Reformation. But the alarm ensuing upon the work of Strauss, in 1835, invested this movement with a more reactionary character; and the journal[54] which gave expression to Hengstenberg's views, gradually assumed the character of an ecclesiastical censorship, frequently marked by defiance and severity, like the tone of Luther of old.

The panic caused by the revolutions of 1848 gave increased stimulus, by adding a political reaction to the religious. The extreme rationalist party had favoured the Revolution, and the school of Schleiermacher had supported the schemes for constitutional government. In the suppression of liberty which ensued for about ten years, the orthodox movement in theology united itself with the reaction in political. Absolute government was not merely a fact, but a doctrine. The theological reaction was no longer the spiritual aspiration of Germany seeking repose after doubt, but a political movement veiled under an ecclesiastical colour. The result has been, the creation of a Lutheran party far more extreme in its opinions than the one just described;—the political leader of which in the Prussian parliament was the jurist Stahl;[55]—intolerant towards

[52] Hengstenberg, born in 1802; professor at Berlin. His works are well known. His work on Christology (1829), Introduction to the Pentateuch (1831), Commentary on the Psalms (1842), and several others, are translated.

[53] Hävernick, Professor at Königsberg; died a few years since. His chief works are, a Commentary on Daniel (1838); and an Introduction to the Old Testament, which is translated.

[54] The *Evangelische Kirchenzeitung*, the organ of his opinions, was Pietist till about 1838; after which it favoured the reaction; especially since the theological disputes of 1845 and the political revolution of 1848. See Hase, § 451; Schwarz, book i.

[55] Stahl, who died in 1861, was eminent for piety as well as learning. His views may be learned from an address, *Ueber Christliche Toleranz*, 1855. The *Kreuz Zeitung* is the journal which has supported this political reaction.

other churches, suspicious of any independent associations for religious usefulness in its own, disowning pietism because of its unchurchlike character, and in its principles going back beyond the Reformation, discarding the subjective inward principle, and reposing on the objective authority of the church. Taking a political view of religion, it does not so much ask what is truth, but what the church asserts to be true. Though not offending popular prejudices by the introduction of Romish doctrines or rites, it really reposes on the Romish principle of a visible authoritative church with mystical powers, upholding a rigid sacramental theory and the doctrine of consubstantiation. Extending the sacramental efficacy to the ministerial office, and denying communion between God and the individual soul independently of the church as the element of communication.[56] Yet it contains many honoured names, and has produced many instructive works. The movement in English theology, which originated a generation ago in the panic caused by the liberal acts of the

The "Theology of the Confessions" (i. e. of Augsburg, &c.) is the name which is given to the movement by its friends. See Kahnis, p. 311 seq. Much interesting information in reference to it, though occasionally expressed in a rude manner, together with references to the German authors from which it is drawn, will be found in the *North British Review*, No. 47, Feb. 1856, and *British Quarterly Review*, No. 46, April 1856. The extracts there quoted are the authority for several of the statements here made. See also Schwarz, iii. 3; Hundeshagen, *Der Deutsche Protestantismus*, § 22.

[56] In enumerating a few names among those that belong to this reactionary party, it is fair to state that some of them have not taken open part in the political aspects of it, and do not teach all that is described in the last few lines, which rather express the teaching of the more violent, and mark the tendencies to which the others only approximate. Some of the best known are, Harless, Delitzch, Keil, as biblical investigators; Rudelbach, Guericke, Schmid, Kurtz, and Kahnis, as historical; and Kliefoth in practical doctrine. (Kahnis has however lately adopted free views in criticism. See Colani's *Nouvelle Revue de la Theologie*, July 1862.) Vilmar in Hesse Cassel, and Leo at Halle, belong to the most ultra section of the school. The universities where it predominates are named at p. 277. Those however who dissent from the views of the theologians here described ought not to forget to render a tribute to the reverent piety and high motives of many of them. They are men who know and love Christ, and are striving to lead men to love him.

government which was introduced by the reform act,[57] offers a parallel; with the exception that the ecclesiastical principles then advocated had always had supporters in the English church, whereas they were nearly new in the Lutheran. The Lutheran movement too, only proposes to go back to the Reformation, the English ecclesiastical movement professed to go back to the early fathers. (41).

While the church has thus attempted a renovation of itself in doctrine, the value of which some will dispute, all will allow thankfully that there has been a deep increase of spiritual life throughout the German churches. Religion indeed had never died out; but in the retirement of country districts[58] the flame of divine love still burned with unextinguished glory. This spiritual fire has now spread, and expressed itself in acts of earnest life. Foreign missions have been promoted;[59] an inner or home mission established for schools, and other religious agency;[60] and an annual ecclesiastical diet[61] constituted, for promoting co-operation and ecclesiastical improvement.[62]

[57] It is a remarkable circumstance that the Oxford movement in the church of England was at first an anticatholic movement. The Catholic Emancipation Bill and the liberality of the parliament after the Reform Bill created an alarm, which led to the study of the non-juring divines and Anglo-catholics who had asserted the rights of the church, and to the reproduction of their opinions. Deeper causes were however at work; among which was the wish to find a more solid groundwork for church belief: but the political circumstances contributed the stimulus, though they were not truly the cause.

[58] The names of Stilling and Oberlin have been already cited, as instances of devoted Christians who realised the truth and tried to spread it. A writer in the *Foreign Quarterly Review*, vol. xxv. p. 132, attests from personal experience his knowledge of the existence of earnest faith in parishes at the time when the universities were nurseries of doubt.

[59] The missions existed previously, having been commenced by the Moravians in the last century, and carried on by several detached missionary associations in the present. On the recent improvement in Germany, see articles in the *North British Review*, No. 31 for Nov. 1851, and No. 40 for Feb. 1854.

[60] *Die Innere Mission*, founded by Dr. Wichern.

[61] The Kirchentag arose out of the Kirchenbund, and met first at Wittenberg, in the church which contains the bones of Luther and Melancthon, in 1848, while war and revolution were raging around.

[62] In addition to those named in the text, mention ought to be made

These three separate movements of the present age, even when incorrect, have contributed something to form a perfect theology. In the orthodox school we see the attempt to return to the Bible, as interpreted by the Reformation; in the mediation school, as interpreted by the religious consciousness; in the critical school, as interpreted by historic and critical methods.

We have now completed the history of the great movement in German theology, in its two elements, doctrinal and critical. Commencing in the first period, —in doctrine, with the disbelief of positive religion, replacing dogma by ethics; and in criticism, supplying a rationalistic interpretation: in the second, it was improved on the doctrinal side by the separation of religion and ethics; and on the critical by a spiritual acknowledgment of the literary characteristics and psychological peculiarities of revelation: in the third, by a total reconstruction of both inquiries, in a more historic and orthodox spirit; and by the creation of a traditionalist position in reference to each. The solution of the problem how to reconcile faith and reason, was attempted in the first by obliterating faith; in the second by uniting them; in the third by separating them. The whole movement stands remarkable, not only as being the most singular instance in history, where the action of free thought can be watched in its intellectual stages, disconnected in a great degree from emotional causes, and where the effort was exercised by the friends of religion, not by foes; but also in the circumstance that though referable to the influence of similar intellectual causes as former epochs of free

of the association of the "Friends of Light," founded by Uhlich, which represents the individual principle like the Quakers, and has resulted in forming some free congregations in Königsberg and Magdeburg. (Consult *Die Deutsche Theologie*, p. 26; Hase's *Church History*, § 456.) The movement was accused of rationalism by its opponents. Also the Gustavus Adolphus Association, begun in 1832 for the relief of all classes of protestants, was one of the first means of promoting Christian union, and indirectly produced the Kirchentag. An account of these two last associations may be found in a pamphlet (1849) by C. H. Cottrell, *Religious Movements of Germany in the Nineteenth Century*. Kahnis notices the great facts of this revival, but with a slight sneer (p. 276, &c.).

thought, it is characterised by wholly different forms of them.

We have found, on nearer inspection, as might be anticipated in any great movement of mind, that instead of being without purpose, and a mere heap of ruins, there was a plan and method in it. It is a history which offers much cause for sorrow and much for joy. Though, as has been before remarked, a period of harrowing doubt in the life of an individual or a nation is a melancholy subject for consideration, yet when it is not induced by immorality, but produced, as in this instance, by the operation of regular causes, and is the result of the attractiveness of new modes of inquiry which invited application to the criticism of old truths, to be accepted or rejected after being fully tested; there is something to relieve the dreariness of the prospect. And when we look to the result, there is abundant cause for thankfulness. The agitation of free thought has produced permanent contributions to theology. Extravagant and shocking as some of the inquiries have been, and injurious in a pastoral point of view, being the utterance of men who had made shipwreck of faith; yet in a scientific, hardly one has been wholly lost, and few could be spared in building up the temple of truth. In criticism, in exegesis, in doctrine, in history alike, how much more is known than before the movement commenced: and what light has been thrown on that which is the very foundation problem, the just limits of inquiry in religion. Each earnest writer has contributed some fragment of information. At each point error was met by an apologetic literature, rivalling it in learning and depth; reason was conquered by reason; and though we cannot help rejoicing that we are able to reap the results of the experience, without undergoing the peril of acquiring it, yet we must acknowledge that the free and full discussion has in the end resulted in truth: the very error has stimulated discovery. So far from being a warning against having confidence in the exercise of inquiry, it is an unanswerable ground for reposing confidence in it.

Christianity is not a religion that need shrink from investigation. Christians need not tremble at every onset. Our religion is vital, because true; and we may place trust in the providence of God in history, which overrules human errors and struggles for the permanent good of men; and, extricating the human race from the follies of particular individuals, makes the antagonism of free discussion the means to conserve or to promote intellectual truth.

In concluding this sketch however it is proper to make a few remarks, as hints to theological students, in reference to the study of works of German theology. Many such works are translated, and many more exist in the original, which are of the highest value,[63] and are likely to be read, and indeed may justly be read, by all students of large cultivation. The works of Schleiermacher or Dorner in doctrine, of De Wette or Ewald in criticism, of Neander or Baur in history, are works of power as well as erudition, and contain a treasure-house of information and suggestion for those who know how to use them wisely, and separate the precious from the untrue. While I have endeavoured to present a fair history of the whole movement, I should feel inexpressible pain if these remarks were the means of leading unwary students to plunge unguardedly into the study of many parts of it. Its original connexion with the deist and ethical points of view, and the constant sense of living in an atmosphere of controversy, have impressed even some of the more orthodox writers with a few peculiarities, of which a student ought to be made aware:—for example, with a slight tendency to a kind of Christian pantheism; a disposition to reduce miracle to a minimum; and in the department of Christian doctrine to consider Christ's life as more important than his death, and to regard the atonement as an effect of the incarnation, instead of the incarnation being the means to the atonement.

[63] It is enough to mention Schleiermacher's *Glausbenslehre*, and the works of Ewald; e. g. the prefaces to the poetical and prophetical books, and his work, the *Geschichte des Hebr. Volkes.*

If then a young student would avoid a chaos of belief, and pursue a healthy study of the German writers, there are two conditions which he ought to observe. First, care should be taken to understand the precise school of thought which his author represents, in order to be able to allow for the possibility of prepossession in him;—a remark true in reference to all literature, but especially important in that which marks a particular phase of controversy. (42) Secondly, a student's duty to English society, and to the church of which he is a member—as also, I humbly venture to think, to his own soul—requires that he shall first listen thoughtfully to the vernacular theology of England. Let him learn the chief affirmative verities of the Christian faith before meddling with the negative side. Let him master the grand thoughts or solid erudition of Hooker and Pearson; of Bull, and Bingham, and Waterland; of Butler and Paley;—the seven most valuable writers probably in the English church;—and then reconsider his opinions by the light of foreign literature. Each one of us is on his intellectual as well as moral trial. None whom duty calls need be afraid to encounter it in God's strength, and with prayer to Christ for light and truth and love.

It remains to mark the influence produced by German theology on free thought in other countries. (43)

In the remainder of this lecture we shall carry on the history of free thought in France, from the point at which we left it[64] down to the present time. We shall find that the open attacks on Christianity of former times have ceased. There, as elsewhere, the present century has been constructive of belief in spiritual realities, not destructive; but the reconstruction has in some cases been so connected with an abnegation of revelation, that it merits some notice in a history of free thought.

The speculative thought in France during the present century has manifested itself chiefly under four

[64] In Lecture V. (p. 194.)

forms:[65] (1) a sensational school, called in the early part of the century Ideology, in the latter Positivism: (2) a theological school, which has attempted to re-establish a ground for reposing on dogmatic authority: (3) a social philosophy, which has directed itself to the study of society and labour: and (4) the eclectic philosophy, created by German thought, which has sought to reconstruct truth on the basis of psychology. The chronological sequence of these schools connects itself with the political sequence of events, and has altered with their change. We must trace them briefly in succession, in order to understand their religious influence and tendencies. The first has tended directly to atheism, the second to superstition, the two last indirectly to pantheism.

When treating of Volney in a former lecture, we noticed the philosophy which took its rise amid the ruins caused by the revolution. Christianity was replaced by materialism, theism by atheism, ethics by selfishness. The philosophy of Cabanis, of Volney, and of De Tracy,[66] was founded so entirely on a physical view of human nature, that it could hardly aid in any way in instilling nobler conceptions. Society grew up without the belief of God or immortality; but in this very poverty the system met its downfall. The deep yearnings of the human heart craved satisfaction. The inextinguishable poetry of the soul yearned for the spiritual; the devotional instincts of human nature caught the first notes of that heavenly melody to which they were naturally fitted to be attuned.

Literature rather than religion was the source from which the mind of France began to imbibe the deep and spiritual conceptions which obliterated the mate-

[65] See Damiron, *Essai sur l'Histoire de la Philosophie en France au 19me siècle*, 1828; and Nettement's *Hist. de la Litt. Franc. sous la Restoration*, 1853, and *Hist. de la Litt. Franc. sous le Gouvernement de Juillet*, especially b. v, vi, vii, xi; and a review of Nettement in the *British Quarterly Review*, No. 37; also H. J. Rose's *Christian Advocate's Publication* for 1832.

[66] See Morell's *Hist. of Philosophy*, i. 543–72, and Damiron, pp. (1–105).

rialism of the revolution. The spiritual tone of such a writer as Chateaubriand,[67] similar to that of the Romantic literature of Germany, awakened in France early in the century the conceptions of a world of spirit, of chivalrous honour, of immortal hope, of divine Providence; and led mankind to feel that there was something in them nobler than mere material organism; even a spirit that yearned for the world invisible. Chateaubriand showed,[68] in answer to the school of Voltaire, that Christianity was not merely suited to a rude age, but was the friend of art, of intellect, of improvement. The church as yet possessed only little influence. Beginning to revive under the fostering influence of Napoleon, who saw clearly the necessity of cultivating religion, its moral usefulness was lessened by falling under the suspicion of opposing the public liberty, when patronised by the government after the re-establishment of the monarchy.

The nobler conceptions just described, whether they arose from literature or from religion, gradually penetrated into the minds of thoughtful men; and, the ground being thus prepared, several rival systems of thought gradually sprang up in the fifteen years (1815–1830) of the restoration of the Bourbon dynasty. Accordingly, when the revolution of 1830 gave freedom to France, there was a universal activity of mind, and free thought assumed a bolder attitude; sceptical, if compared with the Christian standard, but embodying deep moral convictions, if compared with the unbelief of the last century. Among the definite schemes of philosophy, theoretical or practical, which were proposed for acceptance, the first which we shall notice was Socialism.[69]

[67] Chateaubriand (1768–1848) wrote his *Génie du Christianisme* in 1802. See Nettement, first work, quoted above, vol. i. b. x.; and, second work, vol. ii. p. 330; and the criticism by Villemain, *La Tribune Moderne*, ch. v.; and Sainte-Beuve's *Portraits*, vol. x.

[68] In his *Génie du Christianisme.*

[69] The sources for understanding the systems of Socialism, besides the works of its founders, are Alfred Sudre's *Histoire et Refutation du Communisme*, 1850, (especially ch. xvi–xx,) which obtained the Monthyon

It originated with St. Simon.[70] The stirring events of the great revolutionary era, together with the social philosophy of Rousseau which preceded it, had directed attention to the philosophy of social life. St. Simon had lived through this period, and early in the present century devoted himself to the study of schemes of social reform; and shortly before his death in 1825, announced his ideas as a new religion, a new Christianity. In the ferment which followed the revolution of 1830, the opinions of this dreamer became suddenly popular, and, enlisting around them some distinguished minds, forced themselves on the attention of the public during the two following years; and as the political schemes which resulted from them have left their mark on the theological literature of the time, they merit some attention.

St. Simonism offered itself as a system of religion, of philosophy, and of government, which should be the perfect cure of all the evils which existed. The source of these evils St. Simon conceived to be the want of social unity; individualism, selfishness, to be the cause of virtual anarchy. He considered that philosophy and religion had striven in vain to remedy the evil, because they had not made the spiritual to bear upon the material interests of mankind. This, which was the true remedy, he proposed to discover historically.

Borrowing the thought of the German philosophers, he sought it in the elements which are to operate on human nature in the progress of its development. The mode of development by which society advances to perfection he found in a supposed law, that society shows two great epochs, which in long cycles alternate,—the or-

prize, and gives a history of communism in all ages; also Nettement, second work, ii. b. vii.; Morell's *Hist. of Philosophy*, ch. vii. § 2; an article in the *Quarterly Review*, No. 90, July 1831; and in the *Westminster Review*, 1832; and two very valuable articles in the *North British Review*, No. 18, May 1848, and No. 20, Feb. 1849. Those who are aware how much Socialism has influenced French philosophy and literature, as well as politics, will see that it is at once the index of certain forms of religious thought and the cause of subsequent ones, and will pardon the space bestowed in the text upon these visionary schools.

[70] 1760–1825. See Morell, as above.

ganic and the critical; the former, where the individual is obedient to the purpose of the society; the second, where the individual rises against it. He found two instances of them in the ancient and modern world respectively, viz. in the ancient pagan period and its disruption; and again in the Catholic centralization of the middle ages, and the disorganization which succeeded from the time of the Reformation to the French revolution. He considered himself to be raised up to announce the dawn of the third organic period, the world's millennium, a new epoch, and a new religion. It was to be the realisation of the fraternity, which the great moral teachers of the world had promised and prepared. This religion consisted in raising the industrial classes, by a scheme which it is irrelevant to our purpose to explain.

Contemporaneously with this socialist system was that of Fourier,[71] which, though presented more as a scheme of social amelioration, and less as a religion, implied the same abnegation of Christianity. Starting from an avowedly pantheistic view of philosophy, the author of it gradually passed through the sciences, until he arrived at man, and reached the study of human history and constitutions. Exaggerating the good elements of human nature, and ignoring the necessity for any other than a social power to amend the heart, he traced the source of evil to social competition, and proposed to rearrange society on the principle of substituting co-partnership for competition.[72] The two ideas accordingly which these speculations introduced were; —first, that European society was approaching a crisis, the peculiarity of which, as distinct from former ones, would be, that it would be an industrial revolution; and the industrial mind would obtain the mastery of the administration; and, secondly, that the accompani-

[71] Fourier, 1768–1818. See the same sources for information, and Nettement's second work, ii. 30. One of the chief Fourierists was Considérant.

[72] It was a system in fact which has been tried in the mode of working the Cornish mines.

ment would be a new organization of industry on the principle of co-operation. We cannot track these schools into their ramifications[73] and their indirect expression in lighter literature,[74] nor notice the levelling system of communism or co-operative socialism which completed the cycle;[75] but it will be remembered, that when the revolution of 1848 ensued, the schemes for organization of labour were one of its peculiarities; the social republic of those who regarded the democracy as a means, mixed with the political republicans, who thought it to be an end.

It will be noticed that the schemes of these socialist philosophers, though analogous as political theories, in proposing organization of labour and consequent monopoly, to the English socialism of Owen before named, are unlike it in philosophical origin and religious tendency. In philosophical origin his system rests on sensation, theirs on feeling; his degrades human nature, theirs elevates it. His denounces priestcraft as imposture, and religion as obsolete; theirs, though identifying religion and industry, regards religion as the highest

[73] The St. Simonians separated about 1831 into two parties; one led by Bazard, showing a logical tendency, and including Leyroux; and the other led by Enfantin at Menilmontant, showing an emotional, among whose adherents was Michel Chevalier. The source of dispute was the emancipation of the working classes and of woman; Enfantin going beyond the other school in reference to these points. In 1832 the government interfered, and dispersed his supporters. On the relation of French journalism to the political movements, see two articles in the *British Quarterly Review*, vols. iii. and ix.

[74] The novels of such writers as George Sand, Victor Hugo, &c. give expression to these aspirations for social improvement, and the disposition to attribute all evil to social disarrangement.

[75] The systems of St. Simon and Fourier did not demand the abrogation of social inequality between man and man. Both would revolutionise the present state of things; but the one would replace it by a graduated scale of functionaries, the other by a more democratic and less federal system of corporations. But communism is founded on the idea of entire social equality as regards the material advantages of life. The old schemes of Babœuf and the first French revolution hardly existed in 1848, but were replaced by two forms of communism; the theoretic or "Icarian" of Cabet, and the practical of Louis Blanc. On these systems, with that of Proudhon, see the sources before described, especially Sudre and the *North British Review*, No. 20, where this new phase is well described. Also Hase's *Church History*, § 493.

expression of humanity, the great goal to which nature is developing: his leads to deism or atheism, theirs to pantheism. Yet theirs is not less hurtful, for they reject with contempt the dogmatic teaching of revelation, though they appropriate the Christian virtues; like the German philosophy they resolve the Deity into a law; according to which the universe evolves.

One of the minds however which was trained in the school of St. Simon, viz. Comte,[76] has developed a system known by the name of Positivism, which in its effects is not merely thus negative, but amounts to positive and dogmatic unbelief. He showed traces of the school from which he sprang, both in considering politics to be the highest science, in regarding humanity as a progress, and in adducing individualism as the sole cause of social evil and anarchy. He commenced similarly by taking an estimate of the present state of knowledge, and seizing the law which presides over the progress of knowledge.[77] This law he stated as consisting of three stages, through which each science passes as it grows to perfection; the first, the theological or imaginative stage, wherein the mind inquires into final causes, and refers phenomena to special providence; the second, the metaphysical, wherein the idea of supernatural or personal causes being discarded, it seeks for abstract essences; the third, the positive, wherein it rests content with generalized facts, and does not ask for causes.[78] The first in its religious phase is theistic; the second pantheistic; the third atheistic. The perfection of science consists in reaching the third stage, wherein the knowledge is strictly generalized from sensation. Having thus seized the law which presides

[76] Comte's chief work, the *Philosophie Positive*, has been well translated in an abridged form by Miss Martineau, 1853. In reference to him see Morell, *History of Philosophy*, i. 577, &c. and important criticisms on his system in the following reviews, *Revue des Deux Mondes*, by E. Saisset, 1850, vol. iii; *North British Review*, No. 30, Aug. 1851; No. 41, May 1854; *British Quarterly Review*, No. 38, April 1854. Comte's later religious views are given in the *Catéchisme Positiviste*, 1852, and the *Culte Systématique de l'Humanité ou Calendrier Positiviste* (1853).

[77] Introduction, ch. i. (English translation.)

[78] Id. ch. ii. and books i–v.

over intellectual development, and settled the limits of the human reason to be confined to phenomena, agreeing in this respect with the ideologists, and opposed to Cousin, he next offered a classification of the sciences, commencing with the simplest, and showing that, as the mind passes from the simple to the complex, the methods of investigation multiply; accompanying his account by a delineation of the steps in each case by which science attains perfection; and thus gradually ascending to the science of man[79] and society, to which the preliminary investigation had been the preface, designed to prepare the way for showing how the science of society may be similarly brought into the positive stage.

Such is the scheme of Comte. The very breadth of it possesses an attraction; and if viewed merely as a logic of the sciences, it may justly command attention. Many of the analyses which he supplies of the methods and history of science are masterly; and his generalisations, even when hasty, are fertile in suggestion. He was a most original and powerful thinker; scientific rather than artistic. But his philosophy, viewed as a whole, is a grand system of materialism which is silent about God, spirit, personal immortality; diametrically opposed to Christianity, in that it makes man's social duty higher than his individual, science the only revelation, demonstration the only authority, nature's laws the only providence, and obedience to them the only piety; and destroys Christianity by destroying the possibility of its proof. In later life this distinguished man, feeling the unutterable yearnings of the religious sentiment, and the necessity that his philosophy should afford satisfaction to them, invented the system of religion developed in his catechism;[80] in which, in a manner analogous to that employed by Feuerbach or St. Simon, he regarded the collective humanity as the true God, the proper object of worship and reverence; and marked out a church and a cult,

[79] Book vi.

[80] See note on the subject in Lecture VIII.

the caricature of the Catholic church, in which the world's heroes should receive canonization. The probability of mental derangement palliates the absurdity of this system in the originator, but throws the burden of responsibility from the master upon those who are insane enough to adopt it.

We have traced two of the schools which flourished in the second quarter of this century. Another remains, which has incurred from opponents the charge of pantheism, viz. the idealist school, commonly called the Eclectic; (44) which was especially dominant in France, and in the university of Paris, during the rule of the Orleans dynasty. Viewed as a philosophy it is a very noble one. Implying, as its name denotes, an attempt to reap the harvest of the industry of all preceding schools of philosophy, it was the chief means of restoring intellectual and spiritual belief to France, and of creating the great movement of historical study which marks that period of French literature. Commencing with a reaction against the materialist and sensationalist school, it sought, by imitating the mode by which Reid had refuted the philosophical scepticism of Hume, to find a method for restoring belief in spiritual realities; and afterwards, when its chief leader Cousin[81] had been exiled to Germany, he brought back an acquaintance with the successive speculative schools which existed there.

The results of the preceding efforts are expressed in him. His system consisted in a psychological analysis of the human consciousness, which led him to believe, that spiritual truth is revealed to the reason, or intuitional and impersonal power, apart from the limitations of sense, or of the ordinary critical faculties; that the true, the beautiful, and the good, are perceived by it in their absolute, unlimited essence; and that the revelation of the infinite is the basis of all intellectual truth, of all moral obligation, and offers the clue to the criticism of religion, the solution of the problems of history,

[81] On Cousin, see Morell's *History of Philosophy*, ii. 478 seq.

and the construction of a philosophy of the universe. Its chief effect on literature, the permanent contribution which it has made to human improvement, is to encourage the historic study of every branch of phenomena, and especially to exemplify it in the history of thought. Asserting that human society is a gradual progress of development and of improvement, it regards every age as manifesting some phase of truth, or of error, and contributing its portion of knowledge to the student. Humanity is regarded as a divine revelation: its social and intellectual changes as manifestations of the Eternal.

From this account, brief though it be, the relation will be evident which such a philosophy and the historic method of eclectic discovery would have towards religion.

As a system of psychology it is potent, as a means of reasserting the dignity of human nature against the material and selfish ethics of a preceding age, and of reconstructing the basis of ethics and natural religion: but as an ontology, it is in danger of unconscious pantheism; of identifying God with the universe, and regarding Him merely as a name to describe a process, instead of a person. As a philosophy of humanity, it identifies the natural revelation in history with the supernatural; finds in the psychological faculty of intuition, not merely the basis for, but the explanation of, the phenomenon of inspiration;[82] and in its view of religion is essentially antidogmatic, regarding religion as imperfect and progressive; the idea universal, the symbol transient; and allows the psychological truthfulness of all creeds; and regards Christianity as only the most refined species of them, as one of the transient forms that the religious sentiment has adopted, and as destined to give place to philosophy; beneficial to humanity, but not constituting it.

This philosophy therefore, though containing so many noble elements, ended in the view which we

[82] Mr. Morell, who was formerly a disciple of this school, has brought out this thought in his work on the *Philosophy of Religion*, 1849, ch. vi.

have already seen to exist in the Gnostic and German rationalism, that Christianity was not to be final, the one solitary and final religious utterance of God to man.[83]

The three schools illustrate the principal tendencies in which unbelief manifested itself in France previous to the establishment of the empire;[84] and show clearly the intimate relation of particular kinds of sceptical views to particular systems of metaphysical philosophy.[85]

In the latter years of Napoleon I. the struggle first commenced between the Voltairian party and the church; a middle course being taken by the eclectics. The constitutional tendency of this last school gave

[83] During the reign of Louis Philippe an attack was made on the university of Paris by the Jesuits, on the ground that the views taught there were pantheistic. The same view was adopted in an article in *Fraser's Magazine*, No. 170, Feb. 1844, which is valuable in giving quotations of passages which indicate the tendency of this philosophy, though the writer fails to appreciate the value of it as a reaction against the old Voltairism. The same charge is expressed in the sketch which H. L. C. Maret gives of the philosophy of the nineteenth century (in *Essai sur le Panthéisme*, 1845). See also Nettement's second work, vol. i. book vi; Saisset, *Revue des Deux Mondes*, 1850, vol. iii; and Damiron's *Essai*, pp. 105–197.

[84] It has not been thought necessary to name Salvador the Jew, author of *Hist. des Institutions de Moses*, 1828; *Jésus Christ et sa Doctrine*, 1839; *Paris, Rome, et Jerusalem.* His writings were criticised by Mr. H. J. Rose's *Christian Advocate's Publication*, 1831, and have been lately reviewed by the Semitic scholar A. Franck, in a series of papers in the *Journal des Débats*, Jan. 24, Feb. 12, May 29, June 4 and 6, 1862; and by Renan in the *Etudes de l'Hist. Relig.* p. 189, &c. Salvador's view is both Jewish and sceptical. Magnifying the Jewish system, he regards Christianity as an offshoot of it, imperfect in its kind; and looks to the spirit of Judaism as the future hope for the world. He professes a creed which is called by Franck *Infinitheism.* Whatever in his opposition to Christianity is not derived from the eclectic school is the result of his Jewish prejudices.

[85] No mention has been made of several aggressive writers who publish in the French language, mostly in Belgium, works on infidelity resembling in tone those of the last century, such as Volney. There are two such works by P. Larroque, viz. a destructive one, *Examen Critique des Doctrines de la Religion Chrétienne*, first, as they are stated in the dogmas of the church, and secondly, in the scriptures; in which he makes a collection of difficulties in the Bible, book by book: and another work, constructive in tone, *Renovation Religieuse*, 1860. A work of similar intention by P. Rénand, *Christianisme et Paganisme, identité de leurs origines ou nouvelle symbolique*, 1861, is a kind of reproduction of Dupuis and Volney, modified by Feuerbach. In the preface to the last-named work, the writer refers to works by Eenen and Proudhon, similarly directed against Christianity.

them the moral victory during the restoration, over the democratic tendency of the one and the reactionist of the other. After the revolution of 1830, the socialist struggle was superadded; which, when mixed with the old ideology, produced Positivism.

The catholic church had sought to restore faith in Christianity, partly by the establishment of *Conférences*,[86] lectures to reply to the systems now described; and partly by trying to satisfy the reason by establishing a rival philosophy, and stating philosophically the grounds of faith. (45) This philosophy, though noble in its aim, and taught by many pious minds, is visionary. It was based on the principle first evolved by Huet; the weakness of human reason, and the supposed necessity of submission to authority. In De Maistre, its founder, who carried out in philosophy what Chateaubriand did in literature, it was the suggestion of an abject submission to the papacy, as the living authority on earth; accompanied by a sceptical disbelief of the value of inductive science. It has expressed itself in different forms; but in all it has been an attempt to find a solution for difficulties by means of religion instead of philosophy; an attempt analogous to that in other lands, not merely to restrain the human reason in matters of religion, but to inculcate distrust of it; falling into the very error which Plato made his master describe, of those who, baffled in the search for truth, blame not their own unskilfulness, but reason itself; and pass the rest of their lives in contempt of it; and thus are deprived of the knowledge that they seek.

[86] The *Conférences* originated with Frayssinous in a kind of public catechising about 1802. Being changed into sermons in 1807, they were transferred from the Carmes to St. Sulpice, but closed by the government in 1809. They were resumed in 1815, and were transferred about 1830, through Ozanam's intercession with the archbishop of Paris, De Quelen, to Nôtre Dame; where Lacordaire opened his course in 1836. He, Ravignan, and Felix, respectively made themselves distinguished. A. Pontmartin has pointed out the adaptation of each teacher to the phase of public thought. (*Père Félix*, 1861, pp. 26–32, quoted in the *Christian Remembrancer*, Jan. 1862). These particulars are partly taken from Nettement's works above cited.

The history of thought in France, thus studied, exhibits a general resemblance to that of Germany in its forms and tendency. In both alike there has been a contest, between the school which seeks to absorb Christianity in philosophy, and that which extinguishes philosophy by Christianity. There is an absence indeed in France of the spiritual return to a living Christian faith, the union of science and piety, which is observable in the latter country. But within the sphere of natural religion, in reference to the belief in a spiritual world, an advance is perceptible, if the present condition of France be measured against that which was observable at the period when the philosophic unbelief of the last century predominated.

Since the re-establishment of the empire, some of the forms of philosophy which have been described have almost disappeared. The socialist philosophy has become extinct as a direct movement; the eclectic school has gradually passed from philosophy to literature; and the chief tendencies, so far as mere materialism does not, as in most reactions, extinguish thought, are toward a modification of eclecticism on the one hand, and to ultramontism on the other.[87]

The difference of this new eclecticism from the former kind seen in Cousin, lies in the fact that while that was chiefly derived from Schelling's philosophy, this is an offshoot from Hegel. The one considered that the mind, by its intuitions, can find absolute truth, and by the light of these absolute ideas can criticise history, and prejudge the end toward which society is moving. This denies the possibility of attaining absolute truth. All being is a state of flux: all knowledge is relative to its age. Philosophy expires in historical criticism; in the history of the soul of man under its various manifestations. It rests in what is; it judges only from fact. The absolute is displaced by the rela-

[87] The church during the Bourbon restoration was more Gallican than Ultramontane. See Nettement's first work, t. ii. book vii. For a survey of French literature during the present reign, see Reymond's *Etudes du second Empire.*

tive; being by becoming.[88] Though not positivism in its aspects, this system is so in its scientific results.[89]

The unbelief is critical, not aggressive. The grand idea of an historical progress, of tracing especially the historic growth of ideas, of culture, of the great unfolding of humanity, presides over religious speculations, and lends its fascinating power and its danger. The necessity is recognised for solving the nature of the religious consciousness, and satisfying its wants; but the remedy is sought in other means than in Christianity. While this is the condition of the philosophy just described, positivism, so far as it prevails, is wholly antichristian, and regards religion as the product of an unscientific age, for which a belief in nature's laws and science is a sufficient substitute. Christianity, though the ripest of religious forms, is only symbolical of a higher truth towards which humanity is tending.

We may select the name of a writer who stands pre-eminent in critical investigations connected with religion, as the best representative of the tone assumed in reference to the Christian faith by the most highly educated younger spirits of the French nation, of whose literature he is one of the brightest living ornaments,—Ernest Renan.[90] Exhibiting a mind of the rarest delicacy, and bearing traces of the collective cultivation

[88] This idea is well expressed in the passages quoted in Note 9.

[89] One of the modern young French writers most distinguished for power of analysis, is H. Taine, who deserves mention in connexion with the tendency which is in a different manner represented by Renan. Taine's literary character was sketched, but not with the praise which he deserves, in the *Westminster Review*, July 1861; and also with a special reference to his religious opinions in Scherer, *Mélanges*, ch. xi. He was supposed to be a positivist, but now declares himself to favour Spinoza.

[90] E. Renan, born 1823. His chief works are, *Histoire Générale et Systèmes Comparés des Langues Sémitiques*, 1845; *De l'Origine du Langage*, 1849; *Averroes*, 1851; *Job*, 1859; *Cantique des Cantiques*, 1860; and Essays collected, viz. *Essais de Critique et de Morale*, 1859; and especially *Etudes de l'Histoire Religieuse*, 1859, which contains a remarkable preface on the office of modern criticism. A true criticism on the last two works may be seen in *Blackwood's Magazine*, Nov. 1861, used in these remarks; and another by Scherer, *Mélanges de la Critique Religieuse*, ch. xv. He is now writing on *Les Origines du Christianisme*. See *Fraser's Magazine*, October 1862.

which arises from detailed acquaintance with most varied branches of human culture, he has brought his vast acquaintance with the Semitic tongues to bear on the historical criticism of portions of the Hebrew literature; and has sketched with the hand of a master the great passages in the history of religion,—the symbolism of mythology; the monotheistic systems, Jewish, Christian, and Mahometan; the four chief phases of Christianity, the Catholic, the Protestant, the Socinian, the rationalist;[91] and has speculated on the future religious tendencies of the age, in essays, which those who feel most deeply pained with the views presented must acknowledge to be marked by rare power and freshness. Possessing a delicate appreciation of the past, and a cheerful confidence in the future; loving the advance of the knowledge of physical nature, yet protesting against the tendency to materialism; dreading the democracy of opinion, which threatens to suppress independence of inquiry by a power analogous to centralization in the state; the artist no less than the critic, imaginative as well as reflective, he may be studied as in all respects the contrast to the French philosopher of the last century, and as the type of the cultivated minds on whom Christianity has made its impression. His view of philosophy is the one recently explained: his view of religion and of Christianity, so far as we can gather it indirectly from his criticisms, seems to mark a belief in the religious sentiment as a subjective feeling, rather than in the reality of its external object of worship. Its objective side seems to him to be a symbolism, and Christian dogma to be an obsolete form of religious philosophy; inspiration a form of natural consciousness; and even its highest expression to be but the poetry, the art, of the imagin-

[91] This will be seen to be the enumeration of the essays in the *Etudes de l'Histoire Relig.* The essay on the future prospects of Christian churches alluded to is in the *Revue des Deux Mondes* for Oct. 15, 1860, where Renan examines the prospects of the centralised system of papacy, of the national system of the English and Russian churches, and of the individual system of free churches; and argues that the tendency of society is to adopt the latter, both in freedom of creed and of constitution.

ative faculties. There is audible at times an undertone of despondency, as the sigh of one who has searched for truth and not found it;[92] and who, in despair of discovering it on the intellectual side, has taken refuge in the moral. Religion, vain speculatively, is resolved by him into ethics. Faith expires in conscience; dogma in morality. And this interesting writer closes his speculations with the regret, that he feels himself isolated from those Christian saints whose characters he regards as the purest in the world.[93] Such may probably be regarded as the type of thought of the most educated thinkers of France; a feeling of partial belief, partial doubt; a keen appreciation of the beauty of the character of the great Founder of Christianity, and of the type of Christian morality, yet mixed with an entire distrust in the reality of all doctrines respecting the object of faith, from belief in which alone, as we contend, this morality is the product.

Doubts always suggest replies; and there are not wanting minds in the Protestant church of France (46) that fully appreciate the doubts of educated minds such as these, and try to meet them by a more persuasive method than that by which the Catholic school sought to meet the doubters of the earlier part of the century. By the improper concessions however which they have made to save the vital part of religion, they have themselves incurred the charge of sharing the rationalism of the country with whose literature they are acquainted. Assuming a position somewhat like Schleiermacher's, they are careful to distinguish between critical theology and doctrinal, and endeavour to propagate the latter rather than the former. Yet in the branch of doctrinal

[92] At the close of *La Chaire d'Hébreu*, 1862, he has however assumed a view of the world and of nature, less negative and more definite.

[93] See the preface to *Etudes Relig.* especially pp. 14, 15. It is hoped that injustice is not done to M. Renan by these statements. Perhaps they interpret his thoughts more pointedly than he himself would do, and attribute to him as positive conclusions what rather are incipient tendencies. They are the result however of a careful study of his various works, and were written before his recent *Discours d'Ouverture; De la part des Peuples Sémitiques*, which seems to confirm them.

theology,' it must be feared that they have either conceded some of the mysteries of Christianity as obsolete, or at least have improperly concealed them as likely to repel doubters. Though we must indeed be careful wisely to divide the word of life, and not to quench the quivering flame of faith by creating an unnecessary repugnance; yet, if Christianity be a supernatural revelation from God, our plain course is to present the truth as it is in Jesus, unmutilated in the mystery of its difficulties, and leave the result with God.

There is one feature however, in which these writers are a pattern worthy of imitation by all Christian apologists. They preach to doubters not Christian dogmas, but Christ. If the doubters can be brought to appreciate Christ; to meditate on his life; to think of him as one who tasted of human suffering, and knew the poignancy of human temptation; and whose heart of tender pity was ever open to the petition of the needy; they will first admire, then believe, then trust: and when they have learned to love him as a Man of pity, it is to be hoped that they may be brought, by the drawings of the Holy Spirit, to worship and adore him as a God of love. Beginning, not with history, but with feeling; starting with a religion based on the intuitive consciousness of needing Divine help; we may hope to prepare them for receiving the historic testimony which tells of the Divine plan for human redemption: leading them from the sense of sin to Him who saves from sin; from the inward to the outward; from Christ to Christianity; from Christian doctrine to the perfectness of Christian faith.

LECTURE VIII.

FREE THOUGHT IN ENGLAND IN THE PRESENT CENTURY: SUMMARY OF THE COURSE OF LECTURES: INFERENCES IN REFERENCE TO PRESENT DANGERS AND DUTIES.

ECCLES. xii, 13.

Let us hear the conclusion of the whole matter: Fear God, and keep his commandments; for this is the whole duty of man.

IN the last lecture we brought the history of unbelief on the continent down to the present time. In this, the concluding one of the series, we shall complete the history of it in our own country or language during this century; and afterwards deduce the moral of our whole historical sketch, and suggest practical inferences.

In the account of unbelief in England, given in a previous lecture,[1] we hardly entered upon the present century, except so far as to observe the influence of the philosophy of the last on works of literature, such as those of Shelley; or on political speculations, such as those of Owen. Yet even here we were already made to feel the presence of the new influences, which have completely altered the tone of unbelief. Even Shelley's later works, though marked by the outbursts of bitter passion against religion, contain more of the spiritual perception which is the characteristic of present thought:[2]

[1] In Lect. V.

[2] Some remarks will be found a few pages farther, in reference to the subjective spirit and stronger consciousness of the ethical element in human nature, which are evinced in the lite·ature of the present century.

and the oblivion into which Owen's system soon fell, save as it has been resuscitated in moments of political disaffection, together with its failure to leave a permanent impression, like the socialist systems of France, arose from the circumstance that the one-sided survey of man's nature, on which it was based, could not deceive an age which was characterised by an increasing depth in its moral perceptions.

The unbelief of the present day differs from that of the last century in tone and character; and in many respects shares the traits already noticed in the modern intellectualism of Germany, and the eclecticism of France. It is not disgraced by ribaldry; hardly at all by political agitation against the religion which it disbelieves: it is marked by a show of fairness, and professes a wish not to ignore facts, nor to leave them unexplained. Conceding the existence of spiritual and religious elements in human nature, it admits that their subjective existence as facts of consciousness, no less than their objective expression in the history of religion, demands explanation, and cannot be hastily set aside, as was thought in the last century in France, by the vulgar theory that the one is factitious, and the other the result of priestly contrivance. The writers are men whose characters and lives forbid the idea that their unbelief is intended as an excuse for licentiousness. Denying revealed religion, they cling the more tenaciously to the moral instincts: their tone is one of earnestness; their inquiries are marked by a profound conviction of the possibility of finding truth: not content with destroying, their aim is to reconstruct. Their opinions are variously manifested. Some of them appear in treatises of philosophy; others insinuate themselves indirectly in literature: some of them relate to Christian doctrines; others to the criticism of scripture documents: but in all cases their authors either leave a residuum which they profess will satisfy the longings of human nature, or confess with deep pain that their conclusions are in direct conflict with human aspirations; and, instead of revelling in the ruin which they have made, deplore with a tone of sadness the impossibility of solving the great enigma.

It is clear that writers like these offer a wholly different appearance from those of the last century. The deeper appreciation manifested by them of the systems which they disbelieve, and the more delicate learning of which they are able to avail themselves, constitute features formerly lacking in the works of even the most serious-minded deists,[3] and require a difference in the spirit, if not in the mode, in which Christians must seek to refute them.

The solution of this remarkable phenomenon is to be found in the universal change which has passed over every department of mental activity in England in the present century. The peculiar feature of it may be described by the word *spirituality*, if that word be used to imply, in contrast to the utilitarian and materialist tendencies of the last century, the consciousness in ourselves, and appreciation in others, of the operation of the human spirit, its rights, its powers, and its effects. This conviction stimulates in one the vivid consciousness of duty and moral earnestness; in another it hallows human labour, and throws a blessedness around the struggles of industry; in another it kindles the inspiration of art, breaking up conventionalities of style, or expresses itself in poetry, in soliloquies on the inner feelings or in meditations on life, as a set of problems to be explained by the heart. Elsewhere it lifts the man of science above the grovelling idea that discoveries must be sought solely for the purpose of utility. Again, transferring its perception of the operation of spirit to the world of nature, it not unfrequently attributes a soul thereto, and induces a subtle pantheism. Sometimes too by a singular reaction it has a tendency, by the moral earnestness which it stimulates, to depress intellectual speculation, and to wear the appearance of fostering the utilitarianism which it combats.

Such is the central principle which characterises our literature, and which, through the diffusion of

[3] Such as Herbert and Morgan.

reading, has moulded the public judgment, and, operating in every department of educated thought, has even altered the form in which unbelief expresses itself.

Probably the successive steps of the growth of this subjective tendency in literature might admit of easy statement. The meditative school of poetry, which flourished early in the century[4] among a few refined minds at the English lakes; which loved to ponder mystically on nature or on the spiritual world, or to catch the thought excited in the mind by nature, and follow the series of thoughts which the law of mental association suggested,[5] was one means of creating a subjective and spiritual taste among the youth of the generation which succeeded.

Another cause was found in the philosophy which arose. The years following the general declaration of peace, while the public attention was directed to the political reforms which were consummated in the Reform act, were marked by the thorough investigation of the first principles of every branch of knowledge. Two minds of that period have, more than any other, affected the succeeding generation; the one a utilitarian philosopher, the other an intuitional.

Both alike carried out the system which Descartes and Bacon had inaugurated, of finding the standard of truth in the analysis of the powers of the human understanding. But Bentham criticised to destroy the past; Coleridge to rebuild it. The one asked, Is a doctrine

[4] On the influence of the Lake school of poetry, see D. M. Moir's *Sketches of the Poetical Literature of the past half century*, 1851, ch. i. and ii. The Lake school being a reaction against the materialist school, which almost degraded spirit to matter, traced a soul in nature, and was in danger of elevating matter to spirit. Other branches of art besides poetry exhibit a similar change of tone. This is remarkably manifest in the modern landscape art of England, and is developed incidentally in Mr. Ruskin's work, *The Modern Painters*. We have already had occasion, in Lecture VI, to advert to the similarity in result of the Lake school of English poetry to the Romantic school of Germany. Both were spiritual schools; but the former strove to learn from the freshness of nature, the latter from the freshness of an earlier stage of civilization.

[5] A very able analysis of the mental character of Wordsworth, to whom the words in the text allude, was given in the *National Review*, No. 7, Jan. 1857.

true? The other asked, what men had meant by it who had thought it so?[6] The one overlooked the truth previously known; the other too boldly strove to rebuild it from his own consciousness, after surrendering the old proofs of it. The one, with the practical spirit of the Englishman, looked upon an opposing opinion only as an object suited for attack; the other, with a spirit caught from Germany, felt that there was some truth everywhere latent. But both were reformers; both stimulated the revolt against the cold spirit of the last century; both contributed to create, the one indirectly, the other intentionally, a subjective spirit by their psychological analysis.

Even movements which at first sight seem most alien to this spirit in character, have really been affected unconsciously by it.[7] The ecclesiastical reaction which sprang up about a quarter of a century ago, though seemingly most objective in its nature, witnessed not less than the very opposite, or rationalistic tendency, to the presence of this influence. For both alike were founded on the idea that religion lacked a philosophical groundwork: both sought a new ground of faith different from that of the last century; the one in those utterances of consciousness which created a reverence for historic tradition; the other in those intuitions which were supposed to rise above scripture and tradition, and to form the basis and measure of both.

The causes just named in literature and philosophy respectively, are some of those which have contributed to create or to foster the change in the character of the literature, and in the spirit of the age, which has produced the alteration of tone which exists in the modern sceptical literature.

[6] Two very valuable essays occur, on Bentham and Coleridge respectively, in Mr. J. S. Mill's *Essays and Dissertations*, vol. i. (reprinted from the *Westminster Review*, Aug. 1838 and March 1840). See especially the comparison of these two philosophers at p. 395 seq.

[7] This is shown in a very striking manner in the *National Review*, Oct. 1856, in which a comparison is instituted of the effects on the English mind of the three teachers, J. H. Newman, Coleridge, and Carlyle.

In passing from these remarks on the peculiarly subjective tone of modern unbelief, and the literary influences which have produced the general change in the public taste, of which it is only one example, to an enumeration of the authors who have given expression to doubt, and of the specific forms of doubt now existing, we encounter a difficulty of classification.

The most obvious arrangement would be to place the writers in groups, according as they manifest a tendency toward atheism, pantheism, deism, or rationalism,[8] respectively; but the mode which more nearly accords with our general purpose would be to adopt a philosophical rather than a theological classification, and arrange them according to the variety in the tests of truth employed by them, and the sources from which their arguments start, rather than the conclusions at which they arrive. Perhaps the advantage of both plans will be in a great degree combined, if we classify them according to the branch of science, physical, mental, or critical, from which the doubts take their rise.

We shall commence with those writers who make sensation to be the last appeal in belief, or whose doubts arise either from the methods or the results of physical science. This class of opinions varies from positive disbelief of the supernatural, generated by the fixed belief in the stability of nature and disbelief of miraculous interference, to merely isolated objections suggested by the conflict between the discoveries of natural science and the statements of holy scripture.

The name which most fitly describes the extreme form of unbelief is Positivism.[9] This system of philoso-

[8] This is the arrangement adopted in Mr. Pearson's work on Infidelity, named on p. 13, note.

[9] Concerning Comte's philosophy see the note on p. 295. The *Westminster Review* is the periodical which at present embodies its spirit. The works of Mr. G. H. Lewes, his *History of Philosophy*, and his exposition of Comte (Bohn 1853), may be noticed as books in which the philosophical, and, to some extent, the theological spirit of positivism prevails. The mind of Mr. J. S. Mill has been largely influenced by this philosophy, to which his tastes for natural science disposed him; though the influence on

phy, already stated to have been invented by Comte, is silent about the existence of a Deity. It inculcates the belief in general laws, and acknowledges the order in Nature, which we are accustomed to regard as the result of mind; but declines to argue to the existence of a designing mind, where the evidence cannot be verified by proof referable to sensation. Nature's laws are in its view the only Providence; obedience to them the only piety. A few minds may be found, which not only accept the positive philosophy, but even receive the religion taught in the positivist catechism.[10] Unable to satisfy the longings of their heart by this system of Cosmism, they receive the extravagant idea of the worship of humanity, which Comte invented in his later days.

Such a creed cannot hold the masses. But Positivism in another shape, called Secularism,[11] is actively

him of the philosophy of his father, James Mill, and of Bentham, as well as his own originality of mind, prevents him from being a mere disciple of Comte. These writers however have almost abstained from touching directly on the subject of religion. The character of Positivism, as an intellectual tendency, has been sketched by Mr. Morell, in the Lectures on *the Philosophical tendencies of the Age*, 1848.

[10] The view of religion as a worship of the ideal of humanity, in the form of practical ethics and social study, which is taken by the better class of Positivists, is stated at length in the *Westminster Review* for April 1858, together with an explanation of the extravagant views of Comte, in the *Catéchisme Positiviste*, which has been translated by one who was formerly highly respected as an indefatigable teacher, in one of the public schools, and afterwards in one of the universities.

[11] Secularism is the name adopted a few years ago by Mr. G. J. Holyoake. See *Christianity and Secularism; Report of the Public Discussion between the Rev. B. Grant and Mr. Holyoake;* also, *Modern Atheism, or the Pretensions of Secularism examined; a course of Four Lectures, delivered in the Athenæum, Bradford*, by the Rev. J. Gregory, &c. 1852; *Secular Tracts*, by the Rev. J. H. Hinton; *The Outcast and the Poor of London*, Whitehall Sermons, by the Rev. F. Meyrick, p. 91 seq. In its social aspect it is the form of naturalism which has been borrowed from Owen and Combe; in its religious, from Comte. The political tone of this system is expressed in a poem, *The Purgatory of Suicides; a Prison Rhyme, by Thomas Cooper the Chartist*, 1858; and the religious in *the Confessions of Joseph Barker, a Convert from Christianity*, 1858. Also in the tracts of Mr. Holyoake, e. g. *The Logic of Death*, written in 1849, during the cholera. These last two writers are the chief teachers of the system. Some small magazines are devoted to its propagation. A criticism on these tendencies among the working classes will be found, from

propagated among the lower orders. Replacing the sensuous philosophy and political antipathies of Owen, it is taught, unconnected with the political agitation which marked his views, as a philosophy of life, and a substitute for religion. It asserts three great principles:—first, that nature is the only subject of knowledge; the existence of a personal God being regarded as uncertain: secondly, that science is the only Providence: and thirdly, that the great business of man is, as the name, secularism, implies, to attend to the affairs of the present world, which is certain, rather than of a future, which is uncertain. Not content however with this negative position, the writers of this class, as was to be expected, have directed positive attacks against the special doctrines of Christianity, and regard the Bible to be the enemy of progress.[12]

It is impossible to estimate the extent to which these views are diffused. The statistics of the sale of secularist tracts would doubtless give an exaggerated idea of it. The high standard of morality advocated in them, so likely to attract rather than repel, the clear writing, and the agreement of the views with the experience afforded by the daily life of working men, give them power among the lower orders. The absorbing character of labour has a tendency, especially in an advanced state of civilization, to depress the sense of the super-

the Unitarian point of view, in the *National Review*, No. 15, Jan. 1859, where this class of political and religious obstacles, encountered in dealing with the working classes, is contrasted with the mere animalism described in Miss Marsh's *English Hearts and Hands;* and from a more sceptical point of view, in the *Westminster Review* for Jan. 1862, where an extract is given (p. 83) concerning Holyoake's view of Deity. The following terrible utterance, taken from his *Discussion with Townley* (p. 68), will give an idea of his tone: "Science has shown us that we are under the dominion of general laws, and that there is no special Providence. Nature acts with fearful uniformity: stern as fate, absolute as tyranny, merciless as death; too vast to praise, too inexplicable to worship, too inexorable to propitiate; it has no ear for prayer, no heart for sympathy, no arm to save."

[12] The chief points against which the objections have been taken are, the scriptural account of the character of Christ, the doctrine of atonement, and the necessity of faith to salvation. See the Report of the discussion which is referred to at the commencement of the last note.

natural in man, and fix his thoughts on the present world: and it is generally the sense of trouble alone which can lift men out of themselves, and recall to their remembrance the presence of a God on whom the sorrowing heart may lean for help.

Opinions derived from positivism, or at least from physical science, enter into other spheres of thought than those just named; and both affect writers who hardly touch upon the subject of religion; and create difficulties in the minds of Christians themselves, either in reference to prime doctrines of religion, or the particular teaching on physical questions implied in the sacred books.

The diffusion of the fundamental conception of the perpetuity of nature's laws, has a tendency to create in literature a mode of viewing the world alien to the providential view of the divine government implied in religion. The application of statistics in social philosophy for the discovery of the general laws which regulate society and create civilization, not unfrequently leaves an impression that man as well as matter depends upon fixed laws; which is irreconcileable with belief in human freedom or in divine interference, and sometimes causes religion to be regarded as a conservative force, which in its nature is alien to civilization.[13]

Nor is the danger confined to the various branches of secular literature: the views of even religious men are not unfrequently modified by it, or painful doubts are created where the head contradicts the heart. In proportion as phenomena are shown not to depend on chance, the misgiving is felt as to the reality of special providence and the value of prayer, in reference to temporal affairs. The sphere for confiding petitions is felt to be narrowed; and miracles, instead of becoming an evidence for religion, become a difficulty. Even where fundamental difficulties, such as these, do not sap the religious life, the belief that the inspiration of the sacred books guarantees the truth of the views of physical

[13] Mr. Buckle's work on the History of Civilization is an instance to which these statements apply.

science, the cosmogony, physiology, ethnology, and chronology, contained therein, creates a further body of difficulties,[14] less fundamental but more painful, because founded on the apparent want of harmony of scripture with the progressive discoveries of natural science.

While these are the species of temptations to unbelief which appertain to one source of opinions, viz. that which relies upon sensation as the ultimate test of truth; doubts similar in character, though different in cause, manifest themselves in that portion of our literature which appeals for its proof to the faculty of insight, and which believes in mental sources of information which are independent of sensation. If the one tends towards atheism, or to a deism in which the world is viewed as a machine; the other tends towards pantheism or to naturalism, wherein no opportunity for interposition by miraculous revelation is retained, but the inner consciousness of man is regarded as able to create a religion. The former class of views belongs to minds accustomed to experimental science; this to those which are conversant with spiritual or æsthetic subjects: the former expresses itself in the region of science, and tempts men of thought; the latter expresses itself rather in the region of literature, and tempts men of sentiment.

One writer, a prince in the region of letters,[15] may be adduced, many of whose works imply, directly or indirectly, a mode of viewing the world and society contrary to that which is taught in Christianity. He is the highest type of the antagonist position which literature now assumes in reference to the Christian faith,

[14] The difficulties alluded to are, those suggested by geology, concerning the narrative of creation, the deluge, and the date of the creation of man; or by physiology, concerning the longevity of the patriarchs; or by ethnology, concerning the unity of mankind.

[15] T. Carlyle. The character of his writings and philosophy is explained and criticised in Morell's *History of Philosophy*, ii. 249 seq.; and in an able manner in the *Westminster Review*, Oct. 1839; both which sources have been much used in the following brief account. The latter article would be considered probably to need a slight alteration, in consequence of the slight change of character in Carlyle's more recent works.

and which finds some parallel in the contest which occurred in Julian's time, and at the Renaissance.

Though possessing too much originality to borrow consciously from the literature of Germany, yet it is easy to discover that the fire of his imagination has been kindled in contact with the marvellous insight of Goethe, the pathos of Jean Paul, and the faith in eternal truth which marked Jacobi. Their rival rather than disciple, he hails the philosophy of his own country as a first approximation to truth; but regards the German mind as having seen more deeply than any other of modern times into the mysteries of existence. Though not formal enough to throw his philosophy into a system, he has left an impress on the English literature of this century. In every branch of literature which he has surveyed, he has made it his mission to expose the hollow formalism, the cold materialism, which he considers that utilitarian philosophy had produced. "Self in the sense of selfishness, and God as the artificial property of a party;" these have been said to be the two faults which he sees in politics, in science, in law, in literature, in religion: and, to oppose this inrush of objective knowledge; to call man to a recognition of his better self, to the unaltering spiritual laws stamped in the structure of the human consciousness, and to God as the eternal, infinite Divinity, whose presence fills creation; this is the mission which he has striven to effect.

Yet can there be no doubt that the victory of this great truth is won at the sacrifice of others; and that in the general tone of his writings, and above all in his memoir of the doubter Sterling,[16] he occupies a position opposed to the particular forms of religious truth taught by Christianity, and one which a philosopher of tastes cognate to his own, Coleridge, forming himself under the psychological rather than the literary influence of German thought, strove to retain. In elevating the doctrine of the revelation in the soul, he regards as unnecessary the revelation in the book:[17] his

[16] Cfr. his *Life of Sterling*, 1850, pp. 126, 7.

[17] It may be enough to refer to such a passage as *Past and Present*, pp. 305-9.

teaching tends to inculcate a worship of earnestness, and to ignore all consideration of the object toward which the earnestness is directed. In asserting the reality of spiritual laws in the soul, he has implied the veracity of all religions, caring only for the subjective zeal of the believer, not for the objects of his belief.[18] In opposing the mechanical view of the universe, he is so overwhelmed with the mystery which belongs to it, that the soul recoils in the hopelessness of speculation, to rest content with work rather than belief. And his readers, attracted by his power of satire and depth of insight, expressed in a style full of force by reason of its peculiarity, return to their daily life after imbibing his teaching, excited to greater earnestness and faithfulness, but filled, it is to be feared, with a contempt for objective systems, for dogmatic truth, and for the Christian creed.[19]

In the master the strong and deep sense of personality and of freedom obliterates the tendency to absorb human individuality in the overpowering mystery of the universe; but this tendency is developed in the early works of an American writer,[20] who has drawn from some of the same sources as the author just described, but who also owes much directly to him. In him philosophy seems to degenerate into pantheism. Nature is a vast whole, in which we are parts, vibrations of a chord, radiations of the eternal light.[21] Starting from a unitarian point of view, Christianity appears to be resolved into natural religion; and the historic view of Christianity, and the habit of considering the revelation as something long ago given, are regarded

[18] *Past and Present*, pp. 193, 4.

[19] Id. pp. 271, 2.

[20] Mr. Emerson: it ought to be noticed however that the following remarks are applicable mainly, if not wholly, to his earlier works; on which there is a criticism, similar to that cited in reference to Carlyle, in the *Westminster Review*, March 1840.

[21] I am nothing—I see all—the currents of the universal being circulate through me—I am part or particle of God."—*Nature*, p. 13. These were the words which this author formerly used. The same tendency can probably be traced in the characters of Plato and Goethe in his *Representative Men*. See also the *Oration on the Christian Teacher*.

as being at the bottom of the decay of religion. In his admiration of genius, he seems to imply an idolatry of mere intellect; and developes that tendency which has been always observable in pantheism to unite the worlds of good and evil, and teach that evil is "good in the making." The universe is God; evil and good are equally essential parts of it.

This peculiar tendency to narrow the barrier between the two worlds is observable, not merely in direct admissions of writers like the one just adduced, but lurks as a peculiar danger in the modern literature of fiction. The danger in fiction, as in all art, can arise only from the character of the subject portrayed, or the manner employed in producing the copy. In the present day the evil arises specially from the latter cause. The subjective spirit, causing a perception of the duty of exactness, has contributed to foster a realistic taste in art, which requires such minuteness of treatment, that a work of fiction so constructed, while preserving the freshness of nature, may violate moral perspective, and leave the impression that good and evil are inseparably intermixed in each character or in nature itself. The very photographic exactness of the modern novel copies the features without selection or discrimination, and presents each moral character as a mixed one, and makes evil pass into good, and good into evil. Though it is quite true that no character is unmixed, yet it ought not to be forgotten that the evil is present as a disease, the good as the normal state. If approached from the philosophical side, the presence of evil as well as its origin is inexplicable, save by the pantheistic hypothesis; if approached however from the moral, our own instincts tell us that it is diametrically opposed to good; and it is important to be on our guard against the influence of modern literature, which in any way implies the contrary.

We have hitherto exhibited the systems in the present day, which by their influence, direct or indirect, assume a position antagonistic to Christianity. Commencing with positivism, we explained the doubts which, being built on a sensationalist basis, reject the possibility of revelation; or, on an ideal, reject its necessity. We now proceed to describe the works written as direct attacks upon Christianity, founded indeed on an idealist basis, but in which the philosophy is in the main subordinate to the critical investigation. Marked by the improved tone which was before described, and enriched with the fruits of the researches of German theologians, they form at once the books which are likely to meet us in daily life; and equal those of past generations in subtlety and danger. We shall commence with those which are most openly infidel, and gradually pass onward to those which shade off almost into unitarianism, until we reach the critical difficulties which in the writings of avowedly Christian professors have given ground for the charge of rationalism.

The first writer to be named[22] is one who in two works, the one "a Comparison of the Intellectual Progress of Hebrews and Greeks in their religious development," the other on "the Origin of Christianity," has made a daring attempt, not to refute Christianity directly, but to grapple with the historic problem of the origin of revealed religions; and endeavoured to explain them by regular historic and psychical considerations. In making this attempt he has availed himself of the modern investigations into mythology, and the relation which it bears at once to the soul, to philosophy, and to religion. In the last century mythology was either derided in a Lucian-like spirit, or else regarded as the relic of primitive traditions. In the present these views have mostly disappeared; and the theories which exist in reference to it are chiefly two, in the one of which myths are explained by nature-worship, and sacred mysteries, and are regarded as parables descriptive of natural processes; in the other they

[22] R. W. Mackay, whose two works are, *The Progress of the Intellect as exemplified in the Religious Development of the Greeks and Hebrews*, 2 vols. 1850, and *The Rise and Progress of Christianity*, 1854. (No. 7 of *Chapman's Quarterly Series*.)

are regarded as being connected with the origin of language, and the transfer of names from one object to another. (47) It is the former view which this writer has employed. Commencing with the Hebrew Cosmogony,[23] he traces the origin of the metaphysical notion of God[24] through personification and polytheism, up to theism; and next the origin of the moral notion of God,[25] regarding the notion of a fall to be a hypothesis to account for sin; and explains away the idea of mediation by the absurd theory of supposing it to be made up of the two notions, of emanation, and of a waning deity derived from the personification of natural processes.[26] Having thus used mythology, in the manner of Volney, to illustrate the rise of these conceptions among the Greeks and Hebrews respectively, he enters[27] upon the religious history of the Hebrew people, and attempts to show that the idea of the theocracy with temporary rewards suggested the two correlative ideas of temporary reverse, and eventual restoration; and thus, by the personification of the people's suffering, led to the idea of a suffering Messiah.[28] Discussing the complex Messianic conception, he tries to explain its origin by natural causes, by resolving it[29] into a combination of the different types of thought, presented in the earlier history. Approaching the subject of Christianity, he considers it to be one of the Jewish sects, a lawful continuation of the prophetic reforms;[30] therein anticipating the idea which he has developed in the second work above named, concerning the rise and progress of Christianity; in which he has adopted the views of the historical criticism of the school of Tübingen. Regarding Christianity to be a reform of Juda-

[23] *Progress of Intellect*, vol. i. ch. ii. on "Mythical Geography and Cosmogony."

[24] Ch. iii.

[25] Ch. iv.

[26] Vol. ii. ch. v. § 3 and 9. He illustrates from natural processes; such as the decay of nature.

[27] Ch. vi.

[28] Ch. vii.

[29] Ch. viii. The types of thought which he traces in it are, the conception of prophet as taught by Moses; the idea of a supernatural incarnation; the Davidic conception of a temporal sovereign; and the suffering Messiah of the book of Daniel.

[30] Ch. ix. and x.

ism mixed with Greek dogmas,[31] he attributes to St. Paul, in contrast to the Jewish apostles, the idea of giving it universality; and to the early Roman church the idea of giving it unity;[32] illustrating by natural causes the gradual origin of the church,[33] and the pretended concretion of dogmas[34] by mixture with Alexandrian philosophy.

These works, too recondite to be popular, and too unsatisfactory to be dangerous, do not appear likely to affect largely the English inquirer; but the case is different with the work which next meets us by another author, "the Creed of Christendom,"[35] which, on account of its clearness of statement and variety of material, is the most dangerous work of unbelief of this age.

In the first part of the work the writer attacks the idea of inspiration,[36] with all modifications of the notion, as a gratuitous assumption; and tries to disprove it by recapitulating the controversy respecting the authorship of the Pentateuch, and the authority of the Old Testament canon,[37] as well as by the pretended non-fulfilment of the prophetic writings,[38] and the gradually progressive development of the Theism of the Jews.[39] Applying a similar process to the Gospels, he states the difficulties which attend the literary question of their origin[40] and fidelity of the narrative;[41] trying to show that the apostles differed from each other, and held views differing from those taught by the Saviour, as recorded in the first three Gospels.[42] Approaching the subject of the use of miracles as an evidence, he contends that

[31] *Rise of Christianity*, parts i. and ii.

[32] Part iii. [33] Part iv. [34] Parts v. and vii.

[35] *The Creed of Christendom, its Foundation and Superstructure*, by W. Rathbone Greg, 1851. A review of it by Mr. Martineau may be seen in *Studies on Christianity* (reprinted from the *Westminster Review*), and by Remusat in *Revue des Deux Mondes*, Jan. 1859.

[36] Ch. i. and ii. [37] Ch. iii. [38] Ch. iv.

[39] Ch. v. [40] Ch. vi. [41] Ch. vii.

[42] Ch. viii–xii. He adopts the view of the new Tübingen school, in exaggerating the contrast between the description of the character and teaching of Christ in the "Synoptical" evangelists, and in the fourth Gospel.

they cannot prove a doctrine, and that their existence cannot be proved by documents.[43] In the examination of Christianity he holds only the humanity of Christ,[44] and regards Christianity not to be superhuman, but an eclecticism from the Jewish religion; a conception, not a revelation.[45] Successively attacking[46] the most sacred doctrines of our faith,—prayer, pardon, sin,—he is at last landed in the doubt of a future life, save so far as the intuitions seem to suggest it;[47] and in conclusion he contents himself with the religion which consists in obedience to the physical, moral, intellectual, and social laws; confessing however that the heart dictates to prayer and religion, but maintaining that the idea of general laws forbids the possibility of their reality.[48]

The next writer whom we must name,[49] has not rested content with a literary examination of existing religious forms, but has shown the consummation to which the modern criticism of religion leads. The work, "Thoughts in aid of Faith," that is, hints to advise those who have given up all other faith, is too characteristic of a certain type of thought to be omitted. It is an instance where the final result, to which philosophical investigation has conducted, bears a resemblance to that reached by Feuerbach in Germany.[50] In

[43] Ch. xiii. [44] Ch. xiv.
[45] Ch. xv. [46] Ch. xvi.
[47] Ch. xvii. He quotes the beautiful lines of Wordsworth, (*Ode on Intimations of Immortality*, § 5,) "Heaven lies about us in our infancy," &c. as illustrative of the instinctive feeling of man in reference to immortality. [48] Page 303.
[49] Miss S. Hennell, whose chief writings are, *Christianity and Infidelity*, a prize essay, an exposition of the arguments on both sides, 1857; *The Sceptical Tendency of Butler's Analogy*, 1859; *The Early Christian Anticipation of the End of the World*, 1860; *Thoughts in Aid of Faith, gathered chiefly from recent works in Theology and Philosophy*, 1860. Her views originally were the same as those of her brother, a deceased unitarian minister, author of a work on Theism (1852), in which the use of miracles as an evidence was depreciated. It is hoped that it will not be considered improper to have named a writer, whose sex might be expected to shelter her from remark; but her writings are too able to be unproductive of influence.
[50] *Thoughts in Aid of Faith*, ch. i. This work was reviewed in the *Westminster Review*, July 1860, and the *North British Review* for Nov. 1860.

the treatment of the subject, the tenderness of human character has not disappeared; and belief in the teaching of religion is surrendered with painful sadness. Starting at first from the unitarian point of view, this writer has gradually advanced, by the aid of the modern philosophy, to the very pantheism at which philosophy stood in the early ages of oriental speculation. In a review of the historical and psychical[51] origin of religion and Christianity, the idea of a divine Being is regarded as merely the giving existence to an abstraction, the objectifying of the subjective; and Christianity, as the form in which the notion of a personal God necessarily clothes itself: so that the idea of God becomes a fiction created by the mind; Christianity a fiction created by the heart. Though an appreciation is shown of ancient forms of religion,[52] all are regarded as visionary; and, in looking forward to the future, philosophy affords no cheering hope: nothing remains, save the annihilation taught by the ancient Buddhists.[53]

The course of the history now brings before us two writers, who stand distinguished from the last group by their firm theism, and strong protest against pantheism in every form. One of them was an American;[54] the other an alumnus of this university.[55]

The life and work of the former, so far as they relate to our inquiries, may soon be told.[56] In early life a

[51] Ch. ii. [52] E. g. ch. v.

[53] Ch. vi. and vii. It is a result not unlike that of positivism, but reached from the ontological instead of the physical side.

[54] Mr. Theodore Parker of Boston.

[55] Mr. F. Newman. The wide spread of the works of these two writers, especially of the latter, is the reason why it is thought desirable to exhibit their views at some length. The pathos and eloquence which belong to their writings impart to them a fascination which makes it the more necessary that readers should be on their guard, by understanding the position which these authors hold in relation to faith and to unbelief.

[56] The particulars are obtained from the account of Mr. Parker's ministry, prefixed to his *Sermons on Theism.* He was at first a unitarian minister; but, changing from unitarianism into deism, he left that body, and became a preacher in Boston, until he was compelled to visit Europe on account of enfeebled health. He died at Florence, 1860. His doctrinal views may be learned from the *Discourse on Matters pertaining to Religion*, written in 1846, and the *Sermons on Theism, Atheism, and the*

unitarian minister, he caught the spirit of intellectual inquiry and reconsideration which Channing had excited; and devoted himself with indefatigable industry to study the modern philosophy and criticism of Germany, until he became one of the most learned men of the American continent. In his own country his fearless and uncompromising denunciation of slavery, as well as of political and commercial hollowness, caused him to be viewed as a social reformer rather than a theological teacher. In ours he is viewed as a teacher of deism. The cause of his power is obvious. Feeling that his mission was not merely to pull down, but to build up, he spoke with the vigour of a dogmatist, not with the coldness of a critic. To a burning eloquence and native wit he united the picturesque power of the novelist or the artist. But his vigour of style was deformed by a power of sarcasm which often invested the most sacred subjects with caricature and vulgarity; a boundless malignity against supposed errors. How different is the tone of his satire from the delicate touches of the modern French critic[57] who was named in the last lecture! and yet, on the other hand, how changed from that of the infidel writers of the last century. Though he equals Paine in vulgarity, and Voltaire in sarcasm, his spirit and moral tone are higher. They wrote, actuated by a bitter spirit against the Christian religion, without earnestness, without religious aspirations, with the coldness of unbelievers: he, with the earnestness of a preacher touched with the deepest feelings; and though the Christian writer will shudder at his remarks as much as at theirs, yet he sees them modified by passages of pathetic sentiment, in which, in words unrivalled in sceptical literature, ad-

Popular Theology, 1853; and his critical and literary views, from the *Introduction to the Old Testament*, based on De Wette; and from his *Miscellaneous Writings*, 1848. A comparison of him with Strauss, which has been here used, was given in the *Westm. Rev.* for April 1847. His character and life have also been sketched in the *Nat. Rev.* Jan. 1860, and especially by A. Reville in the *Revue des Deux Mondes*, Oct. 1861.

[57] E. Renan. See p. 303.

miration is expressed of Christ, of Christianity, and of scripture.[58]

Such was the man as a teacher. What was his doctrine? He sought and found in the human faculties the test of truth, not dwelling, like Strauss, on their tendency to deceive; but, like Schelling, on their certitude. He placed the ground of religion on the emotional side of the soul, in the feeling of dependence;[59] and correlatively, on the intellectual side, in the intuitions of God, the moral law, and immortal life.

Assuming, on the principle of spiritual supply and demand, that capacity proves object, (the natural realism which we attribute to the senses being thus applied to the intellectual instincts,) he regarded the intuitions to be real, and traced the mode in which reasoning and experience develope them into conceptions.[60] But, afraid of giving too anthropomorphic a form to his conception of deity, he fell almost into the abstract conception of the English deists; and in the notion of God's general providence, lost the fatherlike conception of the divine Being with which the human analogy invests Him. Few nobler attacks however on atheism,[61] or defences of the benevolent character of the divine Being,[62] exist, than those which he has supplied. But at this point the Christian must altogether part company with him; for he next proceeded to argue against the possibility of miracle or special providence; identifying inspiration[63] with the utterance of human genius, and regarding Christianity merely as the best exponent of man's moral nature; as one form of religion, but not the final one. The Bible, which as a collection of literary works,

[58] In the *Discourse pertaining to Matters of Religion*, books ii, iii, iv. The writer is unable to put the exact references to this work in the remarks which follow; having omitted to note them down when he had the book at hand.

[59] *Discourse*, book i.

[60] The steps through which he considers that the idea of God is developed into a conception are, Fetishism, Polytheism, and Monotheism; Dualism and Pantheism being errors which lead astray from Monotheism.

[61] *Sermons on Theism*, sermons i. and ii.

[62] Id. sermons ix. and x.

[63] *Discourse on Religion*, books ii. and iv.

the religious literature of a Semitic people, he appreciated with enthusiastic admiration,[64] was degraded from its position of a final authoritative utterance of religious truth, and was regarded as the embodiment of the thoughts of spiritual men of old time who were striving after truth, and spoke according to the light which they possessed. The religion which he taught was called by him "the absolute religion." It was merely deism, built on a sounder basis, and spiritualized by contact with a truer philosophy.

The other writer[65] to whom allusion has been made, though superior to the one just described in refinement and acuteness, resembles him in possessing deep aspirations and serious research, and in standing apart from the unbelief of the last century, which manifested no loftiness of aim, nor earnest conviction. He stands forth too in a more interesting position, from the circumstance that his starting-point was not unitarianism, but the creed of our own church; and that he has given a psychological autobiography, a painful and thrilling self-portraiture;[66] in which he traces step by step his surrender of his early opinions, from the time of his first doubts, when he was a student in this university, to his fully developed deism.

The destructive side of his teaching is conveyed in the narrative of the "Phases" of his faith. Educated in the tenets of the more spiritual section of the church, he gradually began, as he has stated, to reconsider his opinions as his mind was awakened by study. The moral identity of Sabbath and Sunday; the practice of infant baptism; the connexion of a spiritual effect with what he considered to be a material cause implied in baptismal regeneration; the reasons for the superior efficacy of Christ's sacrifice over the Mosaic; the discovery of gradual development in scripture; these were the first thoughts that agitated him.[67] Unable to solve them to his satisfaction, he hesitated not to abandon,

[64] E. g. in *Discourse*, book iii. and several passages in the *Introduction to the Old Testament.*

[65] Mr. F. W. Newman. [66] *The Phases of Faith*, 1850. [67] Ch. i.

with noble and manly self-sacrifice, the friends that he held dear; and to wander forth from the established church, to seek a primitive Christianity elsewhere. Puzzled by the difficulty of the supposed mistake of the apostolic church, in expecting the sudden return of Christianity, he adopted the chiliastic hypothesis; and, unable to join in ministerial work in England, went as a missionary into the East.[68] On his return, alienated from the friends of his youth and from the new instructors with whom he had consorted, he sought truth in the solitude of his own heart; and was led to throw off Calvinism and adopt Unitarianism.[69] His fourth phase of faith led him, while clinging to Christianity, to renounce the religion of the Book. It consisted in an examination of many of the difficulties which criticism has discovered; from which he was unhappily led to conclude that the Bible was not free from error, nor above moral criticism;[70] believing nevertheless that the Bible was made for man, though not man for the Bible. The two concluding phases of his faith[71] consisted in appreciating the great law of progress which he considers to mark religion; and discovering that faith at second hand is vain, and that the historical truthfulness of Christianity is unimportant, the ideas embodied in it constituting its truth.[72]

In reading this painful record, we feel ourselves in contact with a mind cultivated in miscellaneous science and in the Semitic languages, disciplined as well as informed; which lays bare with transparent sincerity the history of the stages through which he has successively passed. Hitherto we have seen only the destructive side of his teaching; but he also strove to attain a defi-

[68] Ch. ii. [69] Ch. iii.

[70] Ch. iv. [71] Ch. v. and vi.

[72] To complete this account it is necessary to add, that Mr. Newman has developed some portion of the critical investigations of his studies of Jewish history in the *History of the Hebrew Monarchy*, 1847. It is a treatment of the Old Testament analogous to that to which we are accustomed in classical history; the answer to which would be by denying that the records of the Hebrew history are amenable to criticism, inasmuch as they do not partake of the ordinary conditions which appertain to human literature.

nite dogma: his truth-searching spirit, touched by deep longings for the presence of God, could not rest in the blank of unbelief. The nature of this attempt is developed in a work on "the Soul,"[73] in which the author lays bare at once his psychology, his ethics, and his religion; which in substance are not unlike those of the writer last named. He lays the foundation of religion in the spiritual faculty, the sense of the infinite personality; showing the generation of the various complex feelings which make up religion—awe, wonder, admiration, reverence—as the attributes of this divine Personality successively discover themselves.[74] Holding strongly the doctrine of human freedom and the natural existence of a moral sense, he allows fully the existence of the consciousness of sin,[75] and the necessity of spiritual regeneration; asserting the belief in God's sympathy and communion with the soul, the efficacy of prayer, and the duty of encouraging holy aspirations.[76]

Few more suggestive, and in many respects few truer, specimens exist of the analysis of those facts of human nature which concern the basis of natural religion and of the spiritual life,[77] than that which he has offered in order to find a psychological basis for religion. The deep spiritual longing for communion with God, the belief in prayer and in moral renewal, are evidences of a creed which separate him utterly from the naturalism and pantheism before described, and place him almost on the frontier line between Christianity and deism.[78] And we may be permitted to express the belief, that philosophy could not have raised

[73] *The Soul, her Sorrows and her Aspirations*, 1849. In the date of publication this preceded the *Phases*. Mr. Newman has subsequently published, *Theism, Doctrinal, Practical, or Didactic*, 1858. The most complete view of his scheme, but of course wholly favourable to him, is in the *Westminster Review*, Oct. 1858.

[74] Ch. i. [75] Ch. ii. [76] Ch. iii. and iv.

[77] Ch. i. The scheme much resembles that of Schleiermacher.

[78] Deism and Unitarianism are both monotheistic; but the latter allows the existence of a revelation, the former denies it. The modern school of Unitarians, however, nearly approach to the position of Mr. Newman. See end of Note 6, at the close of this book.

him to his present moral standard. His spirituality is due to the fragments of Christianity which he has retained in his system. It has been truly said, that the defenders of natural religion furtively kindle their torches by the light of revealed.

In the course of this sketch of contemporary unbelief, we have gradually advanced from the forms most alien to faith, till we have reached the threshold of the Christian church. The necessity for making the narrative complete compels us to pass within its limits, and to indicate, though it be by a brief notice and with a delicate hand, the forms of the movement of free thought therein which have given rise to the charge of rationalism. This movement of thought is separated from those just described, in that it loyally holds that God has revealed His will to man; but it varies from the general view of the church of Christ in reference to the extent and manner in which He has been pleased to reveal Himself; and, under the pressure of the difficulties, doctrinal or literary, which the progress of knowledge or of speculation has suggested, proposes to separate in the holy scripture, or in the immemorial teaching of the church, that which it regards to be the eternal element of revealed truth from that which it ventures to conceive to be temporary; the heavenly treasure from the earthen vessels in which it is contained. The literary parallel to this tendency is not to be found in the deism of the last century, but in some of the schools of free thought in Germany and France in the present. Like them it professes to be conservative of revelation, desiring to surrender a part in order to save the remainder.[79]

The movement is characterised by two forms; the one philosophical, the other critical. We shall indicate their general character, without specifying individual writings.[80]

[79] In many respects it resembles the "Mediation school" of Germany, described in Lectures VI and VII, and the modern school of the French protestant church, described in p. 304, and in Note 46, p. 448.

[80] It would be more delicate perhaps to leave to the reader the application of these tendencies, and to omit the mention of names; but as the

It is perhaps to the influence of Coleridge, more than to that of any other single person, that the origin of this philosophical movement can be traced.[81] We have already[82] had occasion to mention the general design of his philosophy. At a time when the world was wishing to break with the past, in politics, in literature, and in religion, his spirit was conservative of older truth, while sympathetic with that which was new. In looking backwards, he sought to discover what mankind had meant by their beliefs; in looking around, he asked what were the elements which the present generation disapproved: and, wishing to eliminate the error of the past and appropriate the truth of the present, he

practice in this work has been to give the names even in contemporary history, fairness requires the enumeration. The tendencies in the text however are rather a combination from the views of different modern authors, and cannot be definitely referred as a whole to any one single writer. Probably the reader will himself conjecture that the first tendency is meant in the main to describe the teaching of Mr. Maurice and Mr. Kingsley; the second, of Professor Jowett; the third, of some of the writers in *Essays and Reviews*. But if this be approximately true, it must not be supposed that every specific statement in the following account is intended to be charged upon these respective authors. The description is meant to indicate certain tendencies of free thought, of which their writings among others seem to exhibit instances. It is always hard to judge of a movement which is in progress, and of which we are ourselves spectators. The view here taken is the result of the attempt which the writer of these lectures has made in his own studies, to adjust the existing forms of free thought into their true position in the history of speculation. If injustice is done, it is at least not intended.

[81] It may be useful to draw attention to a book on the relation of Coleridge to recent theological thought, *Modern Anglican Theology, by the Rev. J. H. Rigg*, 1857. The book is by a Wesleyan minister, and is written from that point of view. The tone of censure on the writers criticised is in some parts severe, and has, it is understood, caused pain to some of them. Apart from its tone, objection may perhaps be taken to it, as discovering in their works as positive teaching, doctrines which probably only exist as incipient tendencies. Nevertheless it contains material suggestive of serious thought; and certainly gives the clue to the interpretation of many points which are usually felt to be obscure in the systems of several of the writers described. The author does not however appear to have distinguished sufficiently between the two forms of modern historical inquiry (see Note 9 of these lectures, at the end of the book). He consequently makes the last of the list of writers whom he criticises (ch. xiii.) to be a disciple of Coleridge; whereas he rather belongs to the other form of the historico-philosophical school.

[82] Page 310.

looked inwards into the human heart, and thought that he perceived a faculty there which unveiled to man the eternal, absolute truth,—the true, the beautiful, and the good; which had been the object of search in all systems, the end for which all earnest spirits had ever yearned. This faculty, "the reason" or intuition, thus became the guide, by the light of which he was able to thread his way through the manifold systems of thought of past times.[83] Not content with applying it to other subjects, he carried it also into the domain of revealed religion. It was the engine by which he hoped to get a view of the truth which the ancient writers of holy scripture intended to convey. It would become the means of interpreting their thoughts, by raising the student to a perception of the same objects, similar in kind to that which they possessed. Their inspiration was regarded as only an elevated form of this faculty. When accordingly this method was applied by him to the study of Christianity, it did not lead him to pare down the supernatural by the cold interpretation of the older rationalism, but gave the explanation of the mysteries by raising men to a state where mysteries ceased to be such any longer. It did not pull down revelation to the level of the mind, but strove vainly[84] to raise the mind to a level with revelation.

If viewed in reference to cognate schools of Christian philosophy, it bears similitude in many respects to some of the schools of Germany. In the analysis offered of the human faculties, it has much akin to Kant: in the deep conviction that the highest truth is revealed to

[83] The reference to Mr. J. S. Mill's dissertation on Coleridge has been already given (p. 310.) See also the Essay by Mr. Hort in the *Cambridge Essays*, 1856; the *British Quarterly Review*, Jan. 1854; Morell's *History of Philosophy*, ii. 343 seq.; and Remusat in *Revue des Deux Mondes*, Oct. 1856. Coleridge's philosophy of religion is especially to be found in his *Aids to Reflection;* and his critical views of inspiration in the *Confessions of an Inquiring Spirit.*

[84] The distinctness of the "reason" (*νοῦς*) from the "understanding" (*λόγος* or *διάνοια*) has been allowed in these lectures; but only as guaranteeing the reality of the objects of intuition, not as allowing the mind to create a religion *à priori*. The objection in the text is accordingly not so much directed against the psychological theory as its theological application.

a faculty of faith, and in the undoubting belief in our own intuitions and the conviction of their reality, it resembles Jacobi and Schelling: in regarding the human reason to be the impersonal reason, the divinity in man, it resembles Schelling or Cousin. But it also has an element akin to the ancient Neo-Platonic philosophy of Alexandria.[85] This is seen both in the view taken of the organ of knowledge, and in the scheme of philosophy evolved by it. The intuitive reason, the divine faculty above described, which reveals eternal truth, is viewed as the divine *Λόγος* in man, as was taught by the Neo-Platonists.[86] Inspiration is the action of the same *Λόγος*. This branch of human intellect is absorbed in divinity: a divine teacher is considered to exist in the human mind.[87] And as the view of the faculty is parallel with the teaching of this ancient school, so the explanations suggested of divine mysteries[88] like the Trinity or Redemption are similar. These explanations are the mystical expressions of the thoughts apprehended by this faculty, when it strives to raise itself to oneness with the infinite object which it contemplates.

These remarks will explain the philosophical system taught by Coleridge, and will furnish the clue to interpret the form of theological thought which has originated from him. The parallel between his system and

[85] The sources for studying Neo-Platonism have been given in Note 10 (p. 399). Among writers influenced by Coleridge, the element of thought which is derived from Neo-Platonism is stronger in the writings of Mr. Kingsley than in those of Mr. Maurice; but it is sufficiently observable in both to form a separation, by marked philosophical features, between their teaching and the system of Schleiermacher.

[86] The *Λόγος* of Philo and of the Neo-Platonists is not to be contrasted with the faculty called *reason* by Coleridge, and *νοῦς* by other authors, but to be identified with it. For Philo's views, see Gfrörer, *Philo*, and Dähne's article *Philo* in Ersch and Grueber's *Encyclopædia:* see also Jowett's *Commentary on St. Paul's Epistles*, vol. i. (*Essay on Philo*, § 1).

[87] The existence of a divine teacher in the human mind in the faculty of conscience would be generally allowed; especially by those who adopt the theory of the distinctness of the faculty of *reason* from that of *understanding;* but the idea implied in the hypothesis referred to in the text is the existence of a faculty which is supreme over revelation.

[88] Cfr. *Biogr. Lit.* p. 321, and *Aids to Reflection*, vol. i. 204 seq.

those with which it has now been compared, will be no less obvious in noticing the results of it. The system of Schleiermacher was the theological corollary from the theories of German philosophy above named; and the school of the Alexandrian fathers was the corresponding one which resulted from the Neo-Platonic.[89] We should therefore expect that, if the philosophy of Coleridge was a mixture of the two schools above described, the teaching of his disciples would combine the two theological schools which flowed from those systems. Attentive consideration of the philosophical side of the modern movement of free thought in English theology will confirm this anticipation, and show that its chief elements are a union of these two theological schools. The tendency to require that the human soul shall apprehend divine mysteries intellectually, as well as feel their saving power emotionally; the reduction of inspiration theologically, as well as psychologically, to an elevated but natural state[90] of the human consciousness; the inclination to regard the work of Christ as the office of the divine teacher to humanity, and human history as the longing for such a divine voice; the description of the work of Christ as a divine manifestation of a reconciliation which previously existed, instead of being the mode of effecting it; the tendency to view the death of Christ by the light of the incarnation, instead of regarding the incarnation by the light of the atonement, the death of Christ as the solution of the enigma of God becoming flesh;—these seem all to be corollaries from the philosophy of the Neo-Platonists, and find their parallel in the school of the Alexandrian fathers: they express too, though with some differences, which will be apparent by recalling the remarks in a preceding lecture,[91] the fundamental religious conceptions

[89] On the school of the Alexandrian fathers, see note on p. 59.

[90] Cfr. the note on p. 29, where we have conceded the probability that inspiration is, if analysed psychologically, a form of the "reason;" but considered it, if viewed theologically, to be an elevated state of this faculty, brought about by the miraculous and direct operation of God's Spirit: so that in this view it differs in kind, and not merely in degree, from human genius.

[91] Lect. VI, pp. 245–48.

of Schleiermacher, to which we before had occasion to object as inverting the gospel scheme, and falling short of the dogmatic teaching of the revelation of God.

The causes and character of the philosophical movement of free thought in the church will now be clear. We stated that there had been also a critical tendency. A stricter analysis would probably subdivide the critical movement into two; viz. a philosophical form of it which examines facts,[92] and a literary one which examines documents.

This philosophical movement differs from the former, in that it neither approaches the subject of inquiry from a lofty speculative point of view, which is intended to furnish a solution of the mysteries of nature and revelation; nor seeks by means of the intuitive reason to penetrate beneath the doctrines of ancient teachers, and discover the absolute truth after which they were striving. It rather disbelieves in the possibility of the attainment of absolute truth by the human mind, and regards all truth to be relative to the age in which it was expressed.[93] Like the former movement it possesses a method; but one which is tentative and critical, not speculative; empirical, not *à priori;* founding its knowledge on history, not on philosophy. The mode of investigation is probably indirectly a result of the teaching of Hegel, as that which was before described was the result of the rival schools contemporary with him; but it is the adoption of Hegel's method, and not of his philosophy. In this respect it may be regarded as a critical tendency rather than a philosophical; but one which is critical of the truths and religious facts of revelation, and of its doctrinal teaching, and not merely of the documents which record it.

Hence, when applied to revealed religion, in examining the teaching of the scripture writers, it does not attempt, as the former school, to raise the mind to a level with that of the writers, in order to apprehend the

[92] Cfr. note (80) on p. 329.

[93] Cfr. Note 9, at the end of the book, and the remarks in the Preface on the historic method of study.

eternal truth which was revealed alike to their intuition and to ours; but it throws itself into the circumstances of their age, so as to understand their meaning; and tests it by the altered conceptions which the progress of ages has given to the world. Thus the inquirer not only asks what the writers meant, but views the truth which they taught as relative to their own age; and regards the office of criticism to be, to discriminate in it that which is conceived to have been temporary and local, and that which applies to all time. This school thus resembles the last, in asking what the scripture writers meant in their own time, and what their meaning is to us; but it seeks the answer, by using the same methods for the investigation which would be applied in ordinary literature; not by abstract speculation, apart from literary study of actual documents. It makes the conceptions which civilization and history have created, to be the test for comparison, not the eternal truths of reason which are supposed to exist irrespective of civilization and history.

We may select one illustration. In surveying the doctrine of the atoning work of Christ, the former school seeks to apprehend the absolute meaning of the atonement as the manifestation of an act previously wrought out; and, starting with the notion of the divine teacher of humanity, the *Λόγος* of God in Christ teaching the world, and the *Λόγος* in the soul of man apprehending this teaching, it construes the atoning work of Christ from its didactic side, as teaching man concerning God's love by means of a majestic example of self-sacrifice. The second school treats the doctrine historically; and, when it has separated the apostolic teaching from all subsequent additions, compares this doctrine with the age in which it was expressed, in order to separate what it conceives to be the permanent from the temporary; and hence comes to view the atonement, apart from all the hallowed associations of propitiatory sacrifice which in the minds of the early converts were inseparably united with it. These ideas, which the doctrine of the church regards as integral portions of revealed verity, it considers to be the peculiarity of the age in which the revelation was communicated. The revealed doctrines are handled in the same manner as corresponding doctrines of philosophy.

The minuteness of this method, its disposition to seek for truth in the investigation of details rather than by approaching a subject from some general principle, connects it with the other form of the critical tendency above named, which employs itself in the literary criticism of the sacred records. The main object of this movement consists in examining the questions, first, of the origin of the canon, its grounds and contents; next, the authenticity and genuineness of the books; lastly, the credibility of their contents. It is plain that, however objectionable may be the conclusions arrived at on questions such as these, they are too recondite and literary in character to possess the same doctrinal and pastoral importance as those of the former kind; though the alarm which they may cause will often be greater, because the variation from ordinary belief is more easily apprehended by the mind, and, being a variation in fact, and not only in idea, cannot be concealed by any ambiguity in the use of theological terms, as may be the case in the former instances. Yet in the third of these three questions, this species of criticism may have a very intimate relation to practice; for it may so affect the rule of faith as to overthrow the standard on which we repose for the proof of revealed doctrines. In truth, in this branch it becomes identical with the critical method before described, save so far as that examined the credibility of doctrines, this of facts. But in spirit they are identical. It proceeds upon the assumption, that the same critical process is applicable in the investigation of the sacred history, as the former assumed in the investigation of the sacred philosophy. The attitude of both is independent: both teach that the sacred books are not to be approached with a preconceived definition of their character or meaning: prepossessions are not to bar the way to the exercise of criticism. The difference from the first method above described will be equally obvious. We may adopt the doctrine of inspiration as an illustration. The first view would approach the contents of scripture with a psychological theory of inspiration, as being a form of the intuition, which may furnish an instrument for eclecticism: the second and third would investigate the question empirically, and, declining on the one hand to accept the psychological definition just described, and on the other to approach Scripture with the preconceived notion of the nature of inspiration, as held by the Church, would seek to determine the notion of inspiration from the contents of scripture.[94]

The relation to holy scripture of the critical modes of inquiry will obviously be as intimate in reference to the standard of faith, as that of the philosophical in reference to doctrine. If the first of the three methods which we enumerated[95] overlays doctrine with philosophy; the second is in danger of subtracting from it integral elements of its system; and the third of disintegrating it by criticism, and introducing uncertainty with regard to the sacred books, which are the basis of doctrine. In questions relating to literary criticism, like those which are made the subject of investigation in the last-named method, it is impossible to lay down, so absolutely as in the two former cases, the tests to distinguish truth from error. The creeds are a practical gauge in the former instances which is partly wanting in the latter. The greater difficulty however which thus appertains to the latter, of placing the limits to which reverent criticism may extend without endangering faith, ought to generate the more solemn caution in its application.

[94] It is a truth indeed to which all will assent, that we must learn from scripture what is meant by inspiration: but the difference between the view here described and the view of the church of Christ is this: the Church discovers in scripture the statements of the writers concerning the reality and nature and authority of their own inspiration; and considers henceforth that the character of the revelation is in its substance removed beyond the limits of critical investigation; and can only admit that an empirical inquiry can be useful in settling the limits to which inspiration extends, and determining the question as to the writings to be accounted the subject of it.

[95] Pages 330 and 334.

We have dwelt long upon the modern forms of free thought which exist within the church of Christ, because they have a living interest for us. They meet us in life as well as in literature; and we must daily form our judgment upon their truth and falsehood. They are not indeed peculiar to one church, nor to one country;[96] but form the theological question which is presented to the Christian church in this age.

The result of our inquiries in reference to the free thought of the present time has been especially to exhibit three main tendencies; one, arising from Positivism, a tendency to deny the possibility of revelation;[97] a second, from an opposite philosophy, to deny

[96] The existence of this movement in foreign churches is stated in Lect. VII, and also in Notes 43 and 46, pp. 444, 448. In America, besides those instances which have occurred in this lecture, the writings of Mr. Bushnell are thought to exhibit a free spirit. They however deviate very slightly from traditional dogmas, and may be compared with the writings of the late archdeacon Hare. In England, in the established church, there have been several works, besides those referred to in p. 330. They chiefly belong to the first and third classes of the three named in the text. The sermons of the late F. W. Robertson of Brighton, matchless in freshness, but most unsound in questions of vital doctrine; the sermons, &c. of the Rev. J. L. Davies; bishop Colenso's Commentary on the Epistle to the Romans (1861); and the *Tracts for Priests and People* (1861, 62), may be considered to be examples of the first type of thought; but, if breathing the same spirit as Coleridge, they express his thoughts with a clearness which was wanting in him. The doubts of Blanco White and Sterling; and of Mr. Macnaught, in his work on Inspiration (1856); Mr. Foxton's *Popular Christianity* (1849); bishop Colenso's work on the Pentateuch (1862); and the *Christian Orthodoxy* (1857) of Dr. Donaldson, a name honoured by the philological student; are instances of the third tendency named in the text. A tribute of acknowledgment is nevertheless due to many of these writers, for the earnest and truth-seeking tone which pervades their works. The movement of free thought exists also outside the national church. The recent work of Dr. S. Davidson, *Introduction to the Old Testament* (second edition) is an instance. The views however of this eminent biblical scholar met with so little sympathy in his own denomination, that he was made to suffer for an earlier edition (1856) of the same work, which deviated in a much slighter degree from received opinions. In the Unitarian body also free thought has wrought a change. (See Note 7, at the end of this book.) The influence of Cousin has expelled the old utilitarianism. Mr. Martineau and Mr. W. J. Fox (see his *Religious Ideas*, 1849,) are illustrations of the new spirit.

[97] Cfr. p. 312, and the note to it. Positivism only differs from Naturalism (see Note 21, at the end of this book), in that it expresses a particular theory concerning the limits and method of science, as well as the disbelief in the supernatural implied by the latter term.

its necessity;[98] and a third, to accept it only in part.[99] These are the three tendencies by which the world and church of the coming generation are likely to be influenced. Our path in life will be in a world where they are operating; and we shall have need to be armed with the whole armour of God. If we have in our personal history so investigated the evidences of our faith, as to feel that we have a well-grounded hope, unassailable by these doubts, we may be thankful: if we have gone safely through the perilous test of a careful examination of them, sometimes staggering perhaps in our faith, yet struggling after truth in prayerful trust that the Lord would himself be our teacher, until we now are able to feel that we have our faith grounded on a Rock,—a faith which is the result of inquiry, not of ignorance,—let us be still more thankful, and exemplify our thankfulness by trying to assist the doubter with our tender sympathy, and to aid him in finding the truth and peace which Christ has given to us. Our attitude in moments of peril must be that of solemn reliance on God's help; and our behaviour towards others ought to exhibit Christian firmness, mingled with candour and tenderness; evincing the moderation of true learning, joined to the uncompromising adherence to the Christian faith.

The history now given, of the doubt which is expressed at present through the English language, completes the account of the fourth great crisis of belief in church history;[1] and with it we bring to an end our long survey of the history of free thought.

Since the commencement of the second lecture, we have been so involved in the details of the investigation, that, to those who have lost sight of the plan proposed in the commencement, the lectures may have

[98] Cfr. p. 317.

[99] An instructive sketch of the tendencies of modern thought was given by principal Tullock, in his Inaugural Lecture at St. Andrew's, 1845.

[1] See p. 10. This crisis has occupied our attention since the middle of Lecture III, p. 105.

appeared historical rather than controversial, and hardly compatible with the purpose of the founder of the Lecture. We have been like travellers moving in a tangled plain, where the path at times seems lost. Before entering upon it, we took our stand, as it were, on an eminence; and indicated the plan of the route; pointed to the kind of territory through which it would conduct us, and the direction to which it would tend. Now, that we have at last extricated ourselves from its windings, and rest after our journey, let us cast a glance backward over its course, and see how far the result has verified our anticipations. Let us reconsider the purpose designed by this course of inquiry; notice how far the promises in respect to it have been fulfilled; show its relation to controversial purpose; and collect the moral lessons which are derivable.

It will be remembered that we stated[2] the topic to be, a critical history of free thought in Europe in relation to the Christian religion. Our criticism started from a Christian point of view, and assumed alike the miraculous character of Christianity, the exceptional character of the religious inspiration of the first teachers of it, and the reality of its chief doctrines. From this point of view we proposed to consider the attempts of the human mind to get free from the authority of the Christian religion, either by rejecting it in whole or in part.[3] Four great crises of faith were enumerated in church history;[4] the first, the struggle, literary and philosophical, of early heathenism against Christianity;[5] the second, the reawakening of free thought in the middle ages;[6] the third, that which appertained to the revival of classical literature;[7] the fourth, to the growth of modern philosophy;[8]—a series of epochs which exhibit the struggle of Christianity in the great centres of thought and civilization, ancient or modern; and it was proposed that our investigation should not

[2] Lect. I. page 1.
[3] Page 7.
[4] Page 7.
[5] This was treated in Lecture II.
[6] Lecture III. page 76 seq.
[7] Lecture III. page 92 seq.
[8] Lectures IV. to VIII.

only contain a chronicle of the facts, but explain the causes, and teach the moral.[9] We considered that the causes which make thought develope into unbelief are chiefly two,—the emotional and the intellectual;[10] and, while vindicating distinctness of operation for the intellectual under certain circumstances,[11] yet we allowed the union of them with the moral to be so intimate,[12] that not only must account always be taken of the latter in estimating the unbelief of individuals, but the exclusive study of the former, without allowing for the existence of the latter, must be regarded as likely to lead to an imperfect and injurious idea of unbelief.

The intellectual causes were however selected as the special subject of our study;[13] partly because they have been much neglected by Christian writers, partly because they are the forms which for the most part create the doubts which Christians encounter in the present age. The principal intellectual causes were considered[14] to be, either the new material of knowledge, such as the physical or metaphysical sciences, which may present truth antagonistic to the teaching of the sacred literature; or new methods of criticism, the application of which creates opinions differing from those of the traditionary belief; and, above all, the effects of the application of particular tests of truth,—sense, reason, intuition, feeling,—to the doctrines of revealed religion.

This was our plan; and we have been employed in tracing the influence of these causes in generating doubt in the four great crises, with a minuteness which may almost have been tedious; endeavouring to supply the natural as well as the literary history; analysing each successive step of thought into the causes which produced it; searching for them when necessary in the intellectual biography of individuals; and, if not refuting results, at least laying bare by criticism the processes through which they were attained. At the same time we have attempted to show the grounds on which

[9] Page 2.
[10] Page 13.
[11] Pages 16, 17.
[12] Pages 14–17.
[13] Page 20.
[14] Page 21.

the faith of the church has reposed in the various ages of history. A defence, itself also twofold in its character—emotional and intellectual—has been generated by the attack in each of the crises, and an example thus furnished of the law which governs human society,—progress by antagonism. Permanent gain to truth was seen to be the result of the various controversies; quiet and refreshment after the discharge of the storm had cleared the atmosphere from the intellectual and moral ills with which it was charged.

The utility of the inquiry will now, it is hoped, be apparent. Though these lectures must be regarded as instructive for the believer, rather than polemic against the unbeliever, yet they are intended to serve also a controversial purpose.

There are times indeed when the mere instructiveness of a history, independently of practical use, is a sufficient justification for writing it;—times when it is important to take the gauge of past knowledge as the condition of a step forward in the future. Those who are accustomed to meditate on the present age, on the multifarious elements which in a time of great peace are quietly laying the basis of great changes, and on the unity of intellectual condition which the international intercourse is creating in the world of letters, as really as in that of industry, will perhaps think that the present is such a period, when the knowledge of the history of the former perils of the Christian faith, the nature of the attack and of the defence, is itself of value in regard to the prospects of the future.[15] Those again also, who are accustomed to look at the contemporary works of evidence in our own country, will deplore the fact that in many cases, however well meant in spirit, they are essentially deficient in a due appreciation of the precise origin and character of present forms of doubt, and the natural and literary history of doubt in general;[16] reproducing arguments unanswer-

[15] Cfr. remarks in Note 9, at the end of this volume.

[16] This remark does not apply to the principal writers (named in Note 49), nor to the literature called out by the "Essays and Reviews" contro-

able against older kinds of doubt, but unavailing against the modern, like wooden walls against modern weapons of war. We stand in the presence of forms of doubt, which press us more nearly than those of former times, because they do not supersede Christianity by disbelief, but disintegrate it by eclecticism; which come in the guise of erudition, unknown in former times, appealing to new canons of truth, reposing on new methods, invested with a new air. In such a moment a reconsideration of the struggles of past ages becomes indirectly a contribution to the evidences, by supplying the knowledge of similarity and contrast, which is necessary, as a preliminary, before entering on a new conflict.

The dangers to faith in the present day are sometimes exaggerated; but there cannot be a doubt that we live in a time when old creeds are in peril; when the doubt is the result not of ignorance, but of knowledge, and acts in the minds that are pre-eminent for intellectual influence, and advances with a firmness that is not to be repelled by force but by argument. It is not the duty of Christians to shut their eyes to the danger, like the ostrich, which supposes by burying her eyes in the sand to avoid the huntsman's arrow. There seems accordingly special reason why in such an age an acquaintance with the forms of doubt is requisite on the part of those who have to minister the religion which is the subject of attack.

If accordingly a clergy is to be trained up likely to supply the intellectual cravings of the present day, they must be placed on a level with its ripest knowledge, and be acquainted with the nature and origin of the forms of doubt which they will encounter. The church has indeed a large field, where work and not thought is to be the engine which the clergy must use in their labours; truly a home mission, where men and women for whom Christ died, require to be lifted out of their mere animalism, and taught the simplest truths

versy; but it applies to many of the popular manuals which are directed against old deist literature. and are not adapted to modern critical doubts.

of Christ, and prayer, and immortality: and noble are the efforts that Christians have made, and are making, for an object so religious and philanthropic; but there is a danger lest this very energy of work, which accords so naturally with the utilitarianism of the English character, should lead us to forget that there is an opposite stratum of society, to which also Christianity has its message, which is only to be reached by the delicate gifts of intellect and by the ripest learning.

If Christianity is to be presented to this class, adapted tó the demands of the age so far as they are reasonable, but unmutilated and unaltered in its body of revealed doctrine, preserving in its integrity the faith delivered to the saints; so that apostles might recognize it as being that which they themselves taught, and for which they laid down their lives; it is necessary that Christian students should be trained specially for the work, by a learned and intelligent appreciation of truth, such as will create orthodoxy without bigotry, and charity without latitude. If we have to dread their going forth with hesitating opinions, teaching, through their very silence concerning the mysterious realities which constitute the very essence of Christianity, another gospel than that which was once for all miraculously revealed; there is almost equal ground for alarm if they go forth, able only to repeat the shibboleths of a professional creed, and unable to give a reason of the glorious hope that is in them. In the former case they will fail to teach historic and dogmatic Christianity, because they do not believe it; in the latter because they do not understand its meaning and evidence. If they need piety as the first requisite, they need knowledge as the second. In certain conditions of the church, study is second only to prayer itself as an instrument for the Christian evangelist.

It is hoped, therefore, that a sketch of a department not previously treated as a whole, may indirectly be an aid to the Christian faith, if it shall perform the humble office of supplying some elements of instruction to the Christian student.

Such a purpose however would hardly have justified the introduction of the subject here. The motive which dictated its consideration was much more practical. It was hoped that the answer to many species of doubt would be found by referring them to the forms of thought or of philosophy from which they had sprung; that it would be possible to perceive how they might be refuted, by understanding why and how men have come to believe them.[17] This is a study of mental pathology seldom undertaken. The practical aim of Christian writers has generally suggested to them a readier mode of treating the history of unbelief, by referring its origin to intellectual pride; and, if any margin remained unaccounted for by this explanation, to refer it to an invisible agent, the direct operation of Satan.[18] Such a method, however true, commits the error, against which Bacon utters a warning, of ascending at once to the most general causes without interpolating the intermediate. It ignores the intellectual class of causes, and omits to trace the subtlety of their mode of manifestation;—a problem equally interesting, whether they be regarded as original causes of doubt, or only as secondary instruments obeying the impulse of the emotional causes. It would have been possible to investigate the subject, by selecting a few leading instances to illustrate the natural history of doubt; but the most likely mode for exhausting the subject, as well as for presenting it in a manner which would fall in with the historic tastes of the age, seemed to be, to treat it by means of a critical history, presenting the antidote by a running criticism; and to ask, frankly and fully, what have been the grounds on which Christianity has been doubted; and what have been those on which the faith of Christians in their hour of peril has reposed; and then finally to gather up the lessons which the history itself teaches.

[17] See note on p. 22.

[18] Van Mildert so exclusively adopted this latter view in his Boyle Lectures, that his opponents charged him with Manichæism. See remarks on him in the Preface to this volume.

The inquiry has been analogous to the study of the history of a disease; and scientific rigour required that it should be conducted with a similar spirit of fairness towards those that manifest its symptoms. As the physiologist, who wishes to learn the laws of a disease, watches patiently the symptoms in the subject of it, not reproaching the sufferer, even if the malady be self-caused; so in moral diagnosis, the student of mental and religious error must carry out his inquiries in the spirit of cold analysis, if he would arrive at the real character of the intricate facts which he studies. The candour of our examination has not been prompted by any spirit of indifference to truth, nor by sympathy with error; but partly by the demands of historical accuracy, partly by deep pity for those who are the subject of spiritual doubts, even when the doubts are of their own fault.

This view of the inquiry, as an analysis of the intellectual causes of doubt, will also explain one or two peculiarities in it, which, if left unnoticed, might leave an impression of its inutility.

It will be seen, for example, that in the investigation of the natural history of doubt, and in the explanation of the antecedent metaphysical or critical questions which have produced it, we have indicated the schools of thought which have created it, but have abstained from insisting on the inherent necessity of the relation which subsists between the metaphysical tests of truth and the religious conclusions discussed. The reason is, that it seemed unfit to assume a side eagerly in the metaphysical controversy; and therefore, while showing that the use of certain grounds of belief and methods of inquiry has produced, both as a matter of history and logic, certain species of doubt or disbelief; we have not attempted to condemn the particular metaphysical theories on the ground of the logical consequences which are supposed to flow from them, nor to deny that they could be so amended, as either to avoid the sceptical conclusions to which our objections are taken, or be rendered innocuous by the co-existence of other causes. Science only shows the general tendency or law of logical connection between intellectual causes and effects. The production of the results in particular cases is subject to exception from the introduction of interfering causes.[19]

Another peculiarity which appertains to the analysis of the intellectual sources of doubt, besides the seeming absence of invariable necessity in their operation, might be thought to destroy the practical value of the inquiry; viz. the feeling of disappointment excited when it is perceived that they do not wholly explain the phenomenon, and are merely antecedents or elements, not causes. This arises from the very nature of mental analysis. Being in nature like chemical, it aims only at the detection of the elements that make up the compound, and furnishes the material or formal causes, not the efficient. This longing of the mind to find causes, and to discover the original motive power, is however a witness to the ineffaceable connection of the idea of power with that of will. And while it does not destroy the completeness of the analysis, as the solution of the intellectual problem proposed, it nevertheless points to the instinctive wish of the heart to resolve the causes of doubt into some ultimate source in the will; and is thus a witness to the truth of the position which we have always asserted,[20] that the intellectual causes selected for our special study are only one branch, and must be united to the emotional in order to attain a full explanation of the phenomenon of doubt.

Thus the analysis offered will have, it is hoped, a utility in the limited sphere which was claimed for it, in supplying the account of the tangled and subtle processes through which doubt has insinuated itself.

What then are the lessons which the whole history teaches? To discover these was part of our original purpose,[21] as well as to learn the facts and find the

[19] Cfr. the notes on pp. 26 and 32.

[20] Pages 14, 71, &c.

[21] Page 3.

causes; to satisfy the longings of the heart, no less than the curiosity of the understanding.

First, What has been the office of doubt in history? Has it been wholly an injury, a chronic disease? or simply a gain? or has it operated in both ways? Let us find the answer, by testing each of these theories of its office by means of the facts.

The first of the three is that which has generally been held within the Christian church. It dates from the first ages of the church, and witnesses to a valuable truth. The sacred care with which the Christians treasured the doctrine, and spurned the attempts of heretics to explain it away, proves the strength of the conviction that they possessed a definite treasure of divine truth, introduced at a definite period. Their very want of toleration,[22] the tenacity of their attachment to the faith, is a proof of their undoubting conviction concerning the historic verity of the facts connected with redemption, and the definite character of the dogmas which interpreted the facts. In later ages however, the same idea of sacredness has been extended by the Romish church to the mass of error which Christianity has taken up into itself in the progress of ages; and in Protestant countries has led to the attempt to restrain the thoughts of men even on the secular subjects most remote from religion, where the ancient sacred literature seemed to suggest any indirect information. The doubt on the part of religious men, of any progress being made by free thought, has often expressed itself too in the affirmation, that the history of unbelief shows an exact recurrence of the same doubts, without progress from age to age, and an intimation that new suggestions of doubt are only old foes under new faces.

While Christians have thus generally regarded free inquiry in religion as wholly a loss; freethinkers have taken the very opposite view, and regarded it as an

[22] This is seen in their scrupulous care against heresy, and is attested by the very complaint of their opponent Celsus. (Orig. *Contr. Cels.* i. 9, iii. 44.)

unmixed gain. The distinguished writer[23] of our own time on the history of civilisation, whose premature death will prevent the fulfilment of his large design, has illustrated, with the clearness and grasp over facts which constitute some of his excellences, the office of scepticism, in securing for the human mind the political liberty and toleration which he prized so dearly. His central thought was, that civilisation depended upon the progress of intellect,[24] the emancipation of the human mind from all authority save that of inductive science: he pointed out with triumphant enthusiasm, the services which he conceived that unbelief had performed, in rescuing Europe from degrading beliefs like witchcraft, and from the introduction of supernatural causes for natural events, and in securing in France, in the eighteenth century, the political rights of the lower orders against the claims of the church. Accordingly in his opinion scepticism was an almost unmixed boon.

Those who recall the outline of the history will probably think that each of these views, taken alone, is one-sided, and contains a partial truth. The review of facts shows that free thought has had an office in the world; and, like most human agencies permitted under the administration of a benevolent Providence, its influence has neither been unmixed evil nor unmixed good. It has been an evil, so far as in the conflict of opinions it has invaded the body of essential truth which forms the treasure given to the world, in the miraculous revelation of our Lord Jesus Christ; but it has been a good, so far as it has contributed, either directly to further human progress intellectually and socially, or indirectly to bring out into higher relief these very truths by the progress of discussion.

When, for example, Christian doctrine has been overlaid from age to age by concretions which had gathered round it, as was the case previously to the

[23] H. T. Buckle, the news of whose death, at the end of May 1862, had just reached England when this lecture was delivered.

[24] *History of Civilisation*, vol. i. ch. iv.

Reformation,[25] it has been free thought which has attacked the system, and, piercing the error, has removed those elements which had been superadded. Or, when the church has attempted to fetter human thought in other departments than its own proper domain of religion, as when the ecclesiastical authorities disgraced themselves by vetoing the discoveries of Galileo,[26] it has been to free thought that we owe the emancipation of the human mind. Or, when the church linked itself in alliance with a decaying political system, as in the last century in France, it was free thought that recalled to it the lesson to render to Cæsar the things that were Cæsar's, and to God the things that were God's. It is instances like these, where free thought has been the means of making undoubted contributions to human improvement, or of asserting toleration, which have led writers to describe it as almost innocuous, and hastily to regard the ratio of the emancipation of the human mind from the teaching of the priesthood to be the sole measure of human improvement.

In many instances also, free thought has indirectly contributed to intellectual good, in points where it has run a greater risk, than in those just cited, of trespassing upon the sacred truths of religion; instances, in fact, where the benefit resulting has been owing to the overruling Providence which brings good out of evil, rather than to any direct intention on the part of those who have exercised it. Examples are to be found in those epochs, when some sudden outburst of knowledge compelled a reconsideration of old truths by the light of new discoveries. The awakening of the mind in the middle age, the Renaissance, the advance of modern science, the birth of literary criticism, are instances of such moments, wherein free inquiry has been a necessity forced on the mind by outward circumstances, not self-prompted. This attitude of inquiry, this exercise

[25] *History of Civilisation*, ch. xii and xiii.

[26] An article by a distinguished scientific writer appeared in the *North British Review* for Nov. 1860; in which the question of Galileo's trial was discussed in reference to the recent re-examination of the subject.

of a provisional doubt, was not, like that described, called forth merely by the circumstance that religion had received additions from error, but must have arisen even if the faith once delivered had been preserved uncorrupted. For religion being a fixed truth, while truth in other departments is progressive, it would have been impossible to avoid the necessity of comparison of it with them from time to time, in those spheres where it intersected the field occupied by them.

Such examples, indeed, are not restricted to Christian history, but are general facts of the history of the human mind. The fifth century B.C. was such an epoch in Greece;[27] when various causes, social and intellectual, created a sudden awakening of the human mind to reconsider its old beliefs, and find a home for the new views of nature and of the world which were opening. The free thought of the Sophists was the scepticism of doubt, of distrust; the proposal to surrender, to destroy the old: the free thought of Socrates was the scepticism of inquiry, the attempt to reconsider first principles, to rebuild truth anew. In all such moments, investigation is indirectly the means of stimulating knowledge. The history of the progress of it, in reference to the difficulties which have beset the Christian church, shows us that the epochs of doubt have not generally been produced by unbelief taking the initiative in attacking old truths without some fresh stimulus, and repeating old objections so as to exhibit perpetually recurring cycles of unbelief. We have rather seen that doubt is reawakened by the introduction of new forms of knowledge; and though old doubts recur, yet that they come arrayed in a new garb, suggested by different motives, deduced from fresh premises, and accompanied by doubts of a new kind before unknown. In a practical point of view, frequently they may be thought not to differ widely in appearance from old ones, and to present similar effects as well as forms; but in a scientific one, they ought not to be confounded, inasmuch as they

[27] Cfr. Grote's *History of Greece*, vol. viii. ch. lxvii; Lewes, *History of Philosophy* (chapter on Sophists); Grant, *Aristotle's Ethics*, vol. i; essay ii.

do not present identity of cause. There has been a slow but real progress in knowledge, and a slow but real change in the modes of applying it to Christian religion. The effect of the defence offered for Christianity is equally powerful in leaving its impress on subsequent doubt, as the progress of knowledge is in suggesting novelty of form. The sphere is narrowed, or the direction changed. If thought seems to have come round in its revolution to the same spot in its orbit, it will be found to be moving not on a circle, but on a spiral; slowly but surely approaching a little nearer to the great central truth, toward which it is unconsciously attracted.

The value of the free inquiry in this latter class of cases is not in the process, but in the results; in producing the branch of theology which sets forth the evidences of revealed truth. We have previously had occasion to imply that the Christian evidences are too often regarded as mere weapons of defence; like the battle-fields of history, monuments of the struggle of evil. Being a form of truth which would never have been called forth if the church had not been attacked, the apologetic literature is usually regarded, either as obsolete because controversial, or as useless for believers. Yet truths brought to light by it, though dearly purchased, are a real contribution to Christian knowledge. As miracles are a part of Christianity as well as an evidence, so apologetic literature, while useful in argument, serves the purpose of instruction as well as of defence.[28] The controversy with heresy or unbelief has caused truths to be perceived explicitly, which otherwise would have been only implicit; and has illustrated features of the Christian doctrine which might otherwise have remained hidden. Though these good results have not been designed by unbelievers, and cannot therefore warrant the claim asserted for scepticism, that it is always innocuous, nor be set down to the credit of free thought as a spirit; yet they evidence the value

[28] See above, Lecture IV. p. 159.

of it as a method; the free thought, that is, which is inquiry and consideration, not that which is disbelief.

While therefore fully appreciating the reverent wish of Christian men to defend the truth with sacred tenacity, which leads them to regard all doubt with alarm; we can frankly allow the function and use of the phenomenon of doubt in history, when viewed as an intellectual fact. The use of it is to test all beliefs, with the view of bringing out their truth and error. But the good result has often, we perceive, been undesigned. It has frequently too been dearly bought, attained at an incalculable spiritual loss to the souls of those who have doubted. The result accordingly leaves untouched the responsibility of the doubter, and only shows the use which an allwise Providence makes free thought subserve in the general progress of the world.

But the heart asks a further moral. Though it derives satisfaction from perceiving that even features of history which seem the darkest, and moments the most perilous, bear witness to the presence of a benevolent Creator, who overrules all for the improvement of man and the progress of the church; it still claims to know what those limits are, where doubt must expire in awe, and speculation in adoration. It longs to exercise inquiry, and yet retain the Christian faith. It asks earnestly what does the history teach us concerning the doubts that are most likely to meet us in our lifetime, and what lessons are supplied by it in reference to the best mode at once of maintaining our own faith, and of leading those who doubt to the faith which we receive. The materials are supplied for an answer to these questions; probably even the materials for the final answer which the church can give to them.

We venture not to utter predictions in reference to the future; but the thought is interesting and solemn, that there seems some reason to believe that the weapons which doubt on the one hand, and religion on the other, must use in the final adjudication of their claims, at least in reference to all fundamental questions, are already in men's hands. Though our express denial that doubt perpetually recurs in cycles might cause it to be supposed that we should be inclined to anticipate the existence of future crises of faith; yet we have remarked that such crises are always produced by the opening of some unexplored field of knowledge, the introduction of a collection of new ideas or of a new spirit excited by new ideas, on subjects traversed either by the Christian religion, or by the Christian inspired books. A survey of the present state of knowledge would probably lead us to think that no field lies unexamined from which such new material can hereafter come. The physical sciences which, by the discovery of an order of nature and general laws of causation, have heretofore suggested difficulties in reference to miraculous interposition, and, by means of the discoveries in astronomy and geology, have come into conflict with the ancient Hebrew cosmogony, are not likely to suggest fresh ones distinct in kind from the past. If there be not ground for discouragement in science, nor for doubting that the present state of it, which seems to offer employment for originality of mind rather in tracking old principles into details than in ascending to new ones,[29] is merely a temporary one, destined to pass away when some happy guess shall reveal the highest laws which now baffle inquiry; yet it is not probable that such an advance will traverse the province of religion. The survey of those regions where discovery seems most hopeful, will explain the reason of this assumption.

If the present examination of some of the subtler forms of matter or of force,[30] and of their existence in other globes of the solar system than our own, should hereafter lead to a generalization which shall extend

[29] Cfr. Mill's *Logic*, vol. i. book iii. ch. xiii. § 7.

[30] The allusion is to the discoveries, such as that of Kirchoff, of the existence of some of the material elements in the solar atmosphere, which exist in our own; also of the connexion between the periodic recurrence of the solar spots, and terrestrial magnetism; and especially to the discussion on "the correlation of physical forces," contained in Mr. Grove's work, and in Sir H. Holland's *Essays* (essays i. and ii.), reprinted from the *Edinburgh Review*, July 1858 and Jan. 1859.

natural philosophy as widely beyond its present limits as the discovery made by Newton beyond those of his predecessors, yet these discoveries can have no bearing, favourable or unfavourable to religion, distinct in kind from that of present ones. If even a still mightier stride should be taken, and physiology be able to lay bare the subtle processes through which mind acts on body;[31] yet the difficulty would only be an enhanced form of that which is already used to discredit the spirituality and immortality of the soul.

If we pass from the physical to the moral or metaphysical sciences, there is still less ground for expecting progress. True so far as they go, they offer no opportunity for enlargement, unless perhaps a more careful analysis, by means of the fertile principle of mental association,[32] should cast light on the sensational source of ideas and the physiological side of mind; and even this would leave the independent evidence of the mental data, moral and intellectual, of religion, on the same basis as at present. Critical science again has attained such perfection, that there is no possibility of an entirely new range of critical thought springing up in reference to religion, such as arose when the German mind was creating the science of historical criticism.

Thus, though each branch of science,—physical, metaphysical, and critical,—offers grounds of hope to the labourer, there is no reason to fear that sceptical difficulties will be generated by any of them, distinct in

[31] The discoveries of the distinction between the sensational and motor nerves, by Sir C. Bell; of the phenomena of reflex action, by Dr. M. Hall; of the connexion of the same phenomena with those of sensation, by Dr. Carpenter; and the identification of the centres of conscious activity with separate departments of the cerebral organism, by Dr. Laycock; are instances of hints toward the solution of this problem. Many continental physiologists, such as Müller, Carus, Wagner, and Brown-Séquard, have worked toward the same end. J. F. Herbart in Germany, and Mr. H. Spencer in England, are writers who have approached the psychological problem from the physiological side.

[32] Bayn's *Senses and Intellect*, 1855; *Emotions and Will*, 1859; and Spencer's *Principles of Psychology*, 1855; are works in which analysis of this character is carried farther than in former works. A popular view of past attempts of this kind is given in an article on *Mental Association*, in the *Edinburgh Review* for Oct. 1859.

kind from those which now exist. And a similar line of argument will suggest, that there is little reason to hope, on the other hand, for enlargement of the grounds of the evidence of natural and revealed religion. If this be the case, the materials are accordingly supplied, from which thoughtful students must make up their minds finally on the questions at issue. Indeed the survey of modern thought which we have already made, will have shown that men are already taking their place in hostile array; and will have revealed differences so fundamental in reference to religion, on subjects where no further evidence can be offered, that there can be little reason to hope for the alteration of the state of parties to the end of time. Never was there an age wherein Christianity had so real, so potent an effect as the present; yet never was there one which, while so largely moulded by it, was so really hostile to it.[33] It is the hostility, not of opposition which regards Christianity as false, but of the criticism which views it as obsolete, and considers it to be one phase of the world's religious thought, the eternal truths of which may be assimilated without the historic and dogmatic basis under which its originators conceived it. Though the special forms of doubt that now exist derive their lineage, philosophical and historical, from the modern German and French sources, which we have studied in the last two lectures; yet it is in an older age of European history that the nearest general parallel to the present state of feeling may perhaps be found; and there is a deep truth in the analogy which the learned and excellent critic,[34] who has recently made a special study of the struggle of classical heathenism against Christianity, has pointed out, between the feeling of philosophers in the second and third centuries of the Christian era and in the present time.

[33] An example is seen in Strauss. No one can be more inimical to the dogmatic and historical Christianity of the church than he; yet he asserts firmly that Christ and Christianity is the highest moral ideal to which the world can ever expect to attain. (*Soliloquies*, E. T. 1845, part ii. § 27–30.)

[34] E. de Pressensé. *Histoire* 2e Série, ii. 524.

Amid very wide differences in tone and learning, there is this fundamental agreement between the age which was enriched with the accumulated learning of the old civilization, and the present, enriched with that of the new. There is the same spirit of naturalism; the same indisposition to rise to the belief of the interference of Deity; the same feeling of contempt for positive religions; the same sensation of heart-weariness,—the utterance as it were of the desponding feeling, "Who will show us any good?" the same lofty theory of stoic morality, and disposition to find perfection in obedience to nature's laws, physical and moral; the same approximation to the Christian ideal of perfection, while destroying the very proof of the means by which it is to be acquired. And if it be true that the state of intellectual men presents so marked a parallel, so in like manner the study of the arguments by which the early fathers in their apologetic treatises met the doubts of such minds, becomes a question of great practical as well as literary interest.[35]

What then are the doubts which are most likely to meet us, either insinuating themselves into our own minds, or offering their difficulty to those who intend to become ministers of Christ? and what are the means by which they may be most effectually repelled?

The main difficulties may be summed up as three:—

(1) The question of the relation of religion, and more particularly of Christianity, to the human soul; whether religion is anything but morality, and Christianity its highest type.

(2) The question of the relation of the work of Christ to the human race, whether it involves a secret mystery of redemption known only to God, and hidden from the ken of man, except so far as revealed; or whether it is to be measured by the human mind, and reduced to the proportions which can be appropriated or understood by man.

(3) The question of the relation of the Bible to the human mind, whether it is to be that of a friend or a

[35] Pressensé has devoted attention to this point. (vol. iv. book iv.)

master; and its religious teaching to be a record or an oracular authority.

The history of recent doubt has brought before us some whose minds doubt wholly of the supernatural. In the case of a few of these, but only of a few, the doubt has passed into positive unbelief; their convictions have become so fixed that they manifest a fierce spirit of proselytism, and can dare to point the finger of scorn at those who still believe in the unseen and supernatural relations of God to the human soul. Between these and religious men the struggle is internecine. We can have no sympathy with them: we can rejoice that they retain a moral standard, where they have rejected many of the most potent motives which support it; but must tremble lest their unbelief end in thorough animalism; lest Epicureanism be their final philosophy. But there are many more whose tone is that of sadness, not of scorn; the temper of Heracleitus, not Democritus; whose souls feel the longing want which nothing but communion with a Father in heaven can supply, but who are so clouded with doubt, and retain so faint a hold on the thought of God's interference, and on the reality of the supernatural, that they are unable to soar on the wings of faith beyond the natural, either material or spiritual, up to the throne of God.

The history of such men generally tells of some mighty mental convulsion, which has driven them from their anchor-ground of belief. Sometimes the study of science, as it is seen gradually to absorb successive ranges of phenomena into the regular operation of universal law, until it removes God far away, and creation seems to move on without His interference, has been the cause:—in other cases philanthropic pity, musing on the sad catastrophes which daily occur, when the happiness and lives of innocent human beings are for ever destroyed by the stern unyielding action of nature's laws, leading the heart to doubt God's nearness, and the fact of a special Providence:—in other cases again, the study of the human mind in history, and the perception of the manner in which the gradual growth of knowledge seems to lessen the region of the supernatural, until the mind doubts whether the supernatural itself is not the mere *idolum tribûs*, a mere giving objective being to a subjective idea, a truth relative merely to a particular stage of civilization. Such causes as these, producing a convulsion of feeling, may form the sad occasion from which the soul dates its loss of the grasp which it has heretofore had over the belief of God's nearness, and of religion; and mark the moment from which it has gradually doubted whether anything exists save eternal law; or whether a personal Deity, if he exist, really communes with man; whether, in short, religion be anything but duty, and Christianity anything but the noble type of it to which one branch of the Semitic people was happy enough to attain.

Doubts like these, where they exist in a high-principled and delicate mind, are the saddest sight in nature. The spirit that feels them does not try to proselytise; they are his sorrow: he wishes not others to taste their bitterness. Any one of us who may have ever felt chilled, as the thought insinuated itself, of the remote possibility of the perception of the machine-like sweep of universal law removing our belief of the guardian care of Him to whom alone we can fly for refuge when heart or flesh faileth, as to a Father as infinite in tenderness as in condescension, the friend of the friendless:—whoever has known the bitterness of the thought of a universe unguided by a God of justice, and without an eternity wherein the cry of an afflicted creation shall no longer remain unavenged, has known the first taste of the cup of sorrow which is mournfully drunk by spirits such as we are describing. And who that has known it would grudge the labour of a life, if by example, by exhortation, by prayer, he might be the means of rescuing one such soul?

Yet no task is so hard; argument well nigh fails, because the doubts refer to those very ultimate facts which are usually required as data for argument. If intellectual means are sought for remedy, it is philosophy to which we must look to supply it;—the philosophy which recalls man to the natural realism of the heart, to the simple unsophisticated trust in the reality of the spiritual intuitions, not as derived from sense only, nor merely as necessary forms of thought, but as the vision of a personal God by the human soul.

If however there is any field which requires the presence of moral means, it is this: and we who believe in a God who careth so much for man that He spared not His own Son for our sakes, may well look upwards for help in such instances; in hope that the infinite Father, whose love overlooks not one single solitary case of sorrowing doubt, will condescend to reveal himself to all such hearts which are groping after Him, if haply they may find Him. The soul of such doubters is like the clouded sky: the warming beams of the Sun of righteousness can alone absorb the mist, and restore the unclouded brightness of a believing heart.

The instances however are rare, where we meet with a chaos of faith, half pantheism, half atheism, such as that which we have just described. The great majority of doubters are persons who not only retain a tenacious grasp over monotheism, but even possess a love for Christianity. Their love is however for a modified form of it, different from that which the apostles taught. They cordially believe that God cares for man, and that He has spoken to man through His Son. They accept the superhuman, perhaps the divine, character of Christ; but they consider his life to be a mere example of unrivalled teaching, and of marvellous self-sacrifice; his death the mere martyrdom that formed the crowning act of majestic self-devotion. God's gift of His son is accordingly, in their view, to reconcile man to God; to remove the obstacle of distrust which prevented man from coming to God, by showing forth the love which God already bore to the world; not to remove obstacles, known or unknown, which prevented God from showing mercy to man. Christ is accepted as a teacher, and as a king, but not as a priest. His work is viewed as having for its purpose, to inculcate and embody a higher type of morality, not to work out a scheme of redemption. The ethical element of Christianity becomes elevated above the dogmatic. The sermon on the mount is regarded as the very soul of Christ's teaching. And in looking forward to the future of Christianity, the Christian religion is considered likely to become the religion of the world, merely because it will have ceased to be the religion of form and dogma, and become the highest type of ethics.

Views like these are common, and their compatibility with Christianity is defended in different ways:—sometimes by the bold attempt, as in the speculations of the Tübingen school, to prove that primitive Christianity was such a religion as that just described; that the dogmatic Christianity of the early fathers was the addition made by philosophy to the first doctrine, the *idola theatri*, which haunted the minds of the early teachers; and that the books of the New Testament, to which we appeal to prove the contrary, belong to a later date than that usually assigned:—sometimes, with less consistency, admitting the antiquity of the dogmas, by representing that we can penetrate into the philosophy of the apostolic doctrine, and express in modern phrase, more clearly than in the ancient, the meaning which was intended to be conveyed:—at other times, by regarding all truth as relative to its age, and supposing that Christ's work was seen by the light of the sacrificial and Messianic ideas common in the apostolic times.

Connected with this fundamental disagreement with the ordinary teaching of the Christian church, on the central question of Christ's work and the nature of Christianity, is the cognate question concerning the relation of the Bible as a rule of faith. Its superiority to ordinary books is admitted, as cordially as the superiority of Christ's work to that of ordinary beings; but the religious contents of it, not to speak of the literary, are criticised, not indeed in a polemical, but in an independent spirit; and are measured in the manner just described, and approved or rejected in accordance with it.

Thus these two questions,—the atoning work of Christ, and the authority of the scriptures,—are the two forms of doubt which are most likely to meet us in the present age.

The expression of them in the clergy of any particular church may of course, if it be deemed necessary, be prevented by political means. A church, if regarded merely in a worldly point of view, is a political as well as a spiritual institution, where the members cede somewhat of individual freedom for the good of the whole; a compact where certain privileges and remunerations are granted, in return for the communication of certain kinds of instruction, and the performance of certain offices: and no one can object that the terms of a treaty be maintained; but the prevention of the expression of doubt is not the extinction of the feeling. And such acts of repression cannot reach the laity of the church, even if they touch the clergy. The inquiry accordingly here intended, as to the means for repressing such doubts, does not descend to the political question, but is a spiritual one; viz. if these doctrines are contrary to Christ, how can such thinkers be directed by moral means to the truth which we believe? or what reason can we give for the hope that is in us, which leads us to decline yielding up one iota of dogmatic Christianity to them?

The history of evidences offers a series of experiments, in which we may find an answer to these questions, by studying the different methods adopted in various centuries for spreading Christianity.

In the earliest age of the church, previous to the establishment of Christianity as the state religion, we observe the unaided appeal to argument, and especially the abundant use made of the internal evidence, or philosophical argument concerning the excellence of Christianity, as a means for arresting attention, preparatory to the presentation of the external and historic proof.[36] In the long interval of the middle ages, the church was able to supplement or supersede argument by force; yet it must be admitted that the political and

[36] Cfr. Pressensé, vol. iv. book iv, 161, 521

intellectual condition of the European mind was then, to a large extent, such as to receive benefit from the imposition of an external rule of religious authority and doctrine, in the same manner that individuals, when in a state of childhood, need a rule, not a principle; a law, not a reason.[37] This method however was unsuited when the mind of Europe awoke, and when free thought could no longer be suppressed by force.

The history of evidences since the spread of modern unbelief exhibits not only the return to the ancient Christian weapon of argument instead of force; but not unfrequently to the ancient mode of presenting the philosophical proof prior to the historical.

An attempt of this kind was intermingled with the English school of evidences of the last century; and the argument of analogy used by Butler, if viewed as constructive, and not refutative, may be considered to have for its object to prepare the mind for accepting revealed religion, by first showing the probability of it on the ground of its similarity to nature. (48) And in the German movement, where the doubt thrown by criticism over the historical evidences even still more compelled the resort to the philosophical argument on the part of those who strove to defend the faith, we have seen various attempts to reconstruct Christianity from the philosophical side.[38] Both methods, the philosophical and the historical, have had their place; but their use has varied with the wants of the age. In proportion as the pressure of doubt left less opportunity for the constraining force of the latter, the persuasiveness of the *à priori* moral argument has been used.

The history of the means which have been successful in removing doubts lends little support to the opinion which would save the faith by the sacrifice of the reason, or would imperil the truth of religion by throwing discredit on the immutability of moral distinctions,

[37] This is the view at which Guizot arrives; *Hist. de la Civil.* leçon v, vi, x.

[38] E. g. in Kant, Jacobi, Fichte, Schelling, and Hegel. See Lectures VI. and VII.

perceived by the conscience which Providence has placed in the human mind; to which the great writers on evidence have been wont to make their appeal; and which they have justly perceived must lie at the basis of the evidences themselves. "If the light that is in thee be darkness, how great is that darkness!"

The two periods in church history among those here named, which offer most instruction to us in consequence of affording examples of the same class of difficulties as those which we encounter, are, the struggle in the early centuries, and that in Germany during the present. The line of argument which was used in the former of these crises is seen in the Alexandrian school of the fathers in the third century, and that used in the latter, in the school of Schleiermacher. The study of the life and mental development of Schleiermacher's disciple, Neander, would be in this view one of the most valuable in history.[39] He was himself led by the mercy and providence of God to the knowledge of Christ; his own spirit was rescued from doubts such as we describe; his life was spent in trying to save others from the like difficulties, and to plant their feet upon the rock upon which he himself stood: and it is only the secrets of the great day that will declare the number of the souls that were led by his teaching to find Christ and salvation.

In both these periods the method adopted for recommending Christianity was, to carry out the plan used by St. Paul at Athens,[40] to lay a basis for the proof of it by developing the moral and philosophical argument.

In the Alexandrian period the method used was, to show that all former religions, all former philosophies, were not unmixed error, but contained the germ of truth, which Christianity gathered into itself; to exhibit Christianity as the fulfilment in the field of history of the world's yearnings, and thus to awaken the

[39] References for the study of Neander's life are given in a note on page 250.

[40] See Acts xvii. 22–31.

response of the heart to the narrative of its message.[41] Reasons, to which allusion has before been made,[42] may have lessened the utility at that period of the positive evidence, which proves the fact that a Redeemer had been given; but we cannot doubt that, independently of this circumstance, a deep philosophical reason suggested the stress which was laid on the moral argument, on account of its suitability for convincing the opponent;—a reason indeed to which the history of some of the fathers gave a personal force in the fact that it was by this manner that they had themselves been led to accept of Christianity.[43]

In the German period the same method has been adopted, with the corresponding alterations suggested by modern philosophy. Not to mention the instructive attempts of the school of Kant to find a philosophy from the subjective side of religion, in the denial of its possibility if attempted on the objective, and to exhibit the limitations of the human mind in speculating on the subject of religious method; nor again to mention the bold attempt of Hegel, to which we have previously taken exception as opposing the simplicity that is in Christ, to work out this forbidden problem, and find a philosophy for Christianity on the objective side: we allude to that which has marked the disciples of Schleiermacher to find it on the subjective as a life, and fact, and doctrine, which fulfils the yearnings of the individual heart.

In pursuing a method of this kind, the appeal must be made to the inextinguishable feeling of guilt; to our personal consciousness of a personal judge; our terror at the sense of justice; our penitence for our own ill deserts; the deep consciousness of the load of sin as an insupportable burden from which we cannot rescue ourselves; and to the guilt of it which separates

[41] Cfr. Pressensé on Clement and Origen, *Hist.* iv. pp. 203, 360, and the references there given.

[42] Page 73.

[43] E. g. Justin Martyr, who gives the account of his own conversion to Christianity in the introduction to the Dialogue with Trypho; and Clement of Alexandria.

between us and God, as a bitter memory that we are powerless to wipe away.[44] When these facts are not only established as psychological realities, but appropriated as personal convictions, then the way is prepared for the reception of Christianity. The heart, by realising the personality of God, is at once elevated above naturalism or pantheism. It feels that in Christ's incarnation it finds God near, the infinite become finite, God linked to the heart of a man; and in his atonement it finds God merciful. Its deep instinct leads it to reject the theories which would pare down the marvel of that mystery. Its consciousness of guilt tells it of an obstacle which it cannot believe to lie merely in itself, but attributes to the mind of the infinite Spirit which it wants a method for removing. No mere example of majestic self-sacrifice proclaiming God's love to man suffices to solace its sorrows. Some mighty process, wrought out between the Son and the almighty Father, is instinctively felt to be necessary, as the means by which God can be just and yet the justifier of the sinful. And when philosophy has thus prepared the heart by its appeal to the yearnings of the soul, and brought it to long for the very remedy which Christianity supplies; then the historic argument can be properly introduced, to afford the solid comforting assurance that the remedy wanted has really been given; that miracles and prophecy are divine evidences, attesting the truth of the claim that certain teachers at a particular period received superhuman aid to reveal certain religious truths. (49)

The work of persuasion however is not yet completed; for, ere the heart can fully trust with adoring thankfulness, there are no less than three questions which must still be answered, if the object be to direct doubt instead of suppressing it, and to lead a sinner to Christ by the bands of love.

The first will be the literary one, as to the trust-

[44] Cfr. Lect. I. p. 28. Suggestions on this point are given in Miller's *Bampton Lectures*, 1817. "The Divine Authority of Holy Scripture asserted from its adaptation to Human Nature."

worthiness of the books of the New Testament, which are the record of this teaching.

The second, the inquiry into the fact whether the books teach, and whether the early church taught, dogmatic Christianity as the church now presents it.

The third, though of such a nature as in a great degree to be suppressed by the claim of authority already conceded to the apostolic teachers, may still rise up to harass the mind if a further answer be not supplied: it refers to the reason that we possess for believing, that if these teachers asserted such truths as dogmatic Christianity, and especially vicarious atonement, these doctrines were a real verity, and not merely a passing form under which the truth presented itself to their minds, to be explained away by after ages into less mysterious and more self-evident truths.

The first of these questions, which concerns the trustworthiness of the books, has been most thoroughly tested by the historical criticism of Germany. The data are thus presented for forming a final decision, which in the opinion of most persons will probably be widely different from that which has been arrived at by critics in that country. Yet, supposing we should meet with a doubter who accepted all the views of the Tübingen school,[45] there are nevertheless four books of the New Testament, the genuineness of which the most extravagant criticism fully admits; viz. the Epistles of St. Paul to the Romans, to the Galatians, and the two to the Corinthians. These four would be sufficient to establish the main articles of dogmatic teaching as presented in the creeds of the Christian church, and the main outline of Gospel and Jewish history as facts on the reality of which St. Paul and his converts relied, and for which he was staking his life. Suppose the Gospels and the Acts[46] involved in the historic uncer-

[45] See above, p. 277.

[46] The question of the attacks made on the historic character of the Acts was not noticed in Lecture VII. The statement of the difficulties which have given rise to them may be seen in Baur's *Paulus, der Apostel Jesu Christi*, 1845, and in an article in the *National Review*, No. 20, for

tainty which these critics have attributed to them; yet we possess in the Galatians the outline of the life of Paul, the statement of the reason why Paul accepted a religion which he detested. The incomparable argument of Lyttleton[47] irrefragably proves his honesty. He cannot have been a deceiver. Let the reader of the Galatians say if he was deceived. The two Epistles to Corinth attest the history of the early church; the Epistle to the Romans its dogmatic beliefs. If there is a doubting heart, thoroughly imbued with the most destructive criticism, unable to find historical standing-ground in scripture, he may surely find it in the study of these four works of St. Paul.

The second question, whether the great features of the dogmatic teaching which we receive, and especially the doctrine of vicarious atonement, are taught in the New Testament, admits of satisfactory settlement. The negative of this position has been asserted, in consequence of the alleged fact that this particular doctrine is rather expressed implicitly than explicitly in the earliest fathers; which is to be accounted for by the tendency, while contending against Jewish monotheism, or heathen theism, to put forward the messiahship and incarnation of Christ, in comparison with other religions, rather than his atoning work.[48] Careful study will soon decide a question of this kind, if directed first

April 1860; and a refutation of them in Dr. S. Davidson's *Introduction to the New Testament*, vol. ii.

[47] *Observations on the Conversion and Apostleship of St. Paul*, by Lord Lyttleton, 1747. Cfr. also the note above, on p. 209.

[48] The history of the doctrine of the atonement is given in Bp. Thomson's *Bampton Lectures*, 1853 (lectures vi. and vii.), and in the essay on the Atonement in *Aids to Faith*, 1862; also in Hagenbach's *Dogmengeschichte*, § 68, 134, 180, 268, and 300. The two chief works on the subject are, Chr. Baur's *Lehre von der Versöhnung*, 1838, and Dorner's *Lehre von der Person Christi*. The fair conclusion in respect to the doctrine of the early church on the subject seems to be the one stated in the text. The doctrine of the atonement was believed and taught; but for the reason here named it was not drawn out into such explicit statement as in modern times. Anselm developed it by eliciting what was already contained in it, not by superadding any human elements which did not exist there before. It is Baur, to whom allusion is made in the text, who implies the contrary; and some English writers have followed him.

to the text of scripture; and secondly, as is most important in all questions of the history of doctrine, to the fathers, as the historic witnesses at once to the teaching of their day, and to the traditions of the teaching of an older age than their own.[49]

Supposing however that the authenticity of the books be granted, and the existence in them of dogmatic teaching, as we now hold it, be conceded; how are we to answer the final misgiving which might arise, that a doctrine like the atonement was not merely truth relatively to the age in which it was taught, to be surrendered if it conflict with the moral sense? If indeed miraculous attestation, the authority of supernatural assistance, be conceded, this doubt will be extinguished in most minds by such an admission; but how is it to be fully met, consistently with our object to point out how a doubter may be directed, who desires not to have the natural revelation in his heart crushed, and yet who does not claim, like the deists, that he must comprehend that which he believes, but only that at least he must apprehend it?[50]

We concede the authority of the moral sense to check all dogmas that are not shown to be part of the teaching of men supernaturally inspired; and we should feel surprised if there were a direct conflict between God's voice through the apostles and God's voice through the human conscience. Probably it could be shown that no such conflict exists; but if it did, we should be inclined to ask whether the moral sense, infallible in what it forbids, is equally so in what it asserts:[51] whether it cannot possibly admit of such improvement as would cause the difficulty not to be

[49] The work of the late Professor Blunt on the right use of the Fathers may be consulted for a true and right view of their value.

[50] We *apprehend* a fact when we recognise its existence; we *comprehend* it when we can refer it to the cause which produces it.

[51] Cfr. the remarks in Dr. Whewell's preface to his edition of Butler's first three sermons for some suggestions on the nature of conscience. His object is to show that Butler taught only its psychological supremacy, not its moral infallibility. Cfr. also his *Lecture on Moral Philosophy in England*, p. 129 seq.

felt; or, if felt, to be cancelled by one of those mental antinomies,[52] the existence of which is undeniable: or whether there is not still independent and contemporary evidence, to which appeal can be made, to corroborate the apostles' teaching.

Let us, for example, suppose that we have come to the conclusion, that the apostles taught the doctrine of the atonement; and that our moral sense is puzzled with the justice of the system, of the transfer of merit implied in those analogies under which the mysterious verity is unveiled to us, and with its apparent incompatibility with a corrective theory of punishment: the thought of error, or of merely relative truth, in the apostles' teaching in such a matter, is forbidden to the mind of any one who admits the least divine inspiration in them, from the fact that this is the innermost and most sacred truth of their creed. We could imagine the early teachers left unaided in all matters irrelevant to religion; nay, by a stretch of supposition, possibly even in some unimportant things appertaining to religion itself: but a mistake on the work and office of Christ,—the very point which, of all others, they were commissioned to teach;—an ingredient of error insinuating itself here, is utterly improbable. If even the inspired authority were denied, the improbability would be hardly less apparent. For this was not a doctrine of the head, but of the feelings; not a fact coldly believed, but appropriated; the voice of the inmost consciousness. If the story of the apostles be true, that the belief of this doctrine, and the prayers founded upon it, had made them changed men; if too their history testifies to the reality of their professions of extraordinary holiness; we could not, even if we did not know from their writings that they were men who were accustomed to the careful analysis of their own feelings, conceive a fatal falsehood to lurk here, in a point where the mixture of inference with consciousness must have been reduced to a minimum.

[52] Page 84. Cfr. also bishop Thomson's *Bampton Lectures* (lect. v. p. 125).

In this particular case of the atonement, there is however an independent proof of the correctness of the apostles' teaching, through the corroboration of it which is offered by the Christian consciousness of the church. We have before had occasion[53] to explain the introduction of this idea in the teaching of Schleiermacher, and to protest against the use which he proposed to make of it as a source of truth, independently of the Christian consciousness of the apostles and first teachers; as the gradual source of doctrinal progress, the oracular utterance to this age, as the apostolic consciousness was to the first age.

But there is a deep truth in it, if we use the Christian consciousness, not to supersede scripture, but as the living corroboration and interpreter of it. The Spirit of God still works on the hearts of men morally, as upon the apostles of old; not by conferring the intellectual gift of inspiration, but in the moral gifts of penitence, of conversion, of pardon, of holiness. Holy men now feel the Spirit of God striving with them as the apostles did, and appropriate the excellence of Christianity, and feel its renovating power now as then. Therefore the attestation of these men, such as is collected by an induction founded on their biographies, to the fact that when they analyse their secret feelings with the most exact care, they recognise that the pardon which they receive is through the mercy of Christ; that their moments of most hallowed communion with the Father-spirit are when they approach the throne of mercy through the mediation and intercession of another, Christ Jesus; that the victory vouchsafed to them over temptation, is by His merits; that their heart finds no Father for one moment except through him;—this evidence, if it can be accepted, is an independent corroboration of dogmatic truth. It may be explained away, by denying the truth of their analysis, or by referring their feeling to mental association; but it cannot fail to have a persuasive force for those who have faith in the instinctive utterances of the human

[53] Page 245 seq.

soul: and the reliance upon it is not more extraordinary than that on which we depend in cognate subjects like æsthetics, where the taste of practical skill is trusted. Christian consciousness thus becomes a new source of facts in theological study; the living voice of the church for illustrating and confirming in some degree the utterance of men of old, who spake that which was revealed to their souls by the inspiring Spirit.

Such are the chief steps which the history of evidences, in the contest with early heathenism, as well as in the recent struggle in Germany, seems to point out as the most likely to lead a doubter to Christ; and such the order in which the philosophical and historical evidences ought to be respectively presented, if our object be to give due heed to the desire which an inquirer evinces to appropriate the truth which he believes. Such too, if the opinion already advanced concerning the future of modern doubt be correct, seems to be the final answer which the church can give. Without undue compromise, commencing with the internal evidence, we thus lead men to the external, and make philosophy as it were the schoolmaster to lead to Christ.

The third question of those which we enumerated as likely to press upon us, viz. that which refers to the inspiration of the scriptures, requires only a few words; inasmuch as the treatment of it has already, to some extent, been implied.

This question has been elevated, since the Reformation, to an importance which it hardly possessed before. Since the authority of the Bible has been substituted for the authority of the church, it has been usual to regard the scriptures as the mode of leading men to Christ, instead of considering the knowledge of Christ received through the ministrations of the church as the clue to interpret scripture. Logically, the scripture is the rule of faith, the ground of the church's teaching; but chronologically, the teaching of the church is the means of our knowing the scripture.[54]

[54] Similarly, an innate law of thought is *logically* prior as a condition in attaining knowledge; but experience is *chronologically* prior.

A caution hence arises, that we should not be willing to allow preliminary difficulties, which a doubter may have in reference to the scriptures, to deter us from leading him straight to Christ, and then allowing him by the light of this teaching to reconsider the question of the scripture. The difficulties will generally be found to have reference to the historical and literary portions, rather than the doctrinal, or those portions of the literature which contain the doctrinal. If indeed they refer to the doctrinal, they must be answered at the outset in the manner already shown. If however to the literary, they will be viewed in a different light, if the doubter has been brought to appreciate the central truths of Christianity, from that which they will bear if wrangled out on the threshold of his approach. In the last century indeed, the comparative importance of the doctrinal parts of scripture over the literary was so perceived, when doubts were pressed on the attention of the clergy by the pertinacity of the deist controversialists, that many of the eminent writers restricted the plenary inspiration of the scripture writers to the appropriate matter of the revelation, the supernatural communication of the miraculous system of redemption; and conceived that it was no derogation from the supreme religious authority of the sacred writers, but rather compatible with the loftiest idea of the providential adaptation of means to ends, to suppose them unassisted in literary matters, such as the transcription of genealogies, the reference to natural phenomena, or the literal exactitude of quotations. The jewel of divine truth did not, in their opinion, sparkle less brilliantly because it was handed down in a frame of antique setting. (50) In the present day there is a strong reaction in religious minds in favour of the opposite view, identical with the one held in the seventeenth century by the Puritans. The reaction is only a special instance of the general movement in favour of authority, political and ecclesiastical, which has taken a sudden advance throughout the religious part of Europe, in opposition to the subjective tendency already noticed in secular literature.[55] This special view however is dictated by a noble motive, a watchful fear lest the loss of a single atom may weaken the whole structure. Whether it be true or not is not at present under consideration, but merely the caution which ought to be used in pressing it upon doubters at the outset of an approach to the subject of religion. If the object be really to draw them to Christ, we must become all things to all men; and, while not mutilating the heavenly message, take heed not to repel the weak believer from coming to the Saviour, by interposing unnecessary literary obstacles.

It is very common to hear or to read the dilemma put before the doubter, that he must accept everything or nothing in Christianity and the Bible.[56] Such an alternative, though dictated by a commendable motive, is likely to prove ineffectual. The Dilemma is a form of reasoning which rarely persuades. Its object is rather to silence than to convince. It is more a trick of rhetoric than an argument of logic. It may make a person pause by showing him his apparent position; but the heart, if not the head, can always find means to escape from an alternative which it dislikes. And in this particular case the use of it involves the risk of overlooking the different degrees of importance which belong to different portions of religion, and the very different degrees of evidence on which different portions of it rest. Though the smallest circumstances in reference to it are of importance, yet it were less vital to doubt the miraculous inspiration of a genealogy than the authoritative teaching of an epistle; or to doubt the date of a book than its contents. No doubt is unimportant; but it were merely repeating the sophistry of the Stoics, in making all sins equal, to deny gradations of importance in doubts; gradations which however are not here put forward to defend eclecticism, but to enforce the lesson,

[55] It has been shown above (p. 310) that this very reaction is itself indirectly a result of the subjective tendency.

[56] E. g. in R. E. H. Greyson (H. Rogers) *Correspondence*. Cfr. the remarks on it in the *National Review* for Oct. 1857.

that, in dealing with a doubter, the consideration of this fact must guide us in the order in which we present the evidence of different parts to his mind. It not unfrequently happens that the perusal of the holy scripture is the means of drawing a soul to Christ; the volume in its solitary majesty telling its own tale: or, to speak more reverently, applied to the heart by the Spirit of God: but generally, if a doubter's heart be filled with historical and critical doubts, he must be led through Christ to the Bible, rather than conversely, and through the New Testament to the Old. If once he can be brought to the perception of a Saviour for sinful man, his doubts will assume a new aspect, and will adjust themselves into their true place, or perhaps find their own solution.

Yet, when we have used all methods of argument which the survey of the history has given us reason to believe may prove useful, it were affectation to conceal our belief in the perpetual operation, secret and unobserved, of an invisible monitor and persuader, the blessed Spirit of God. Though we may look to philosophy to prepare the way, by exciting an appreciation of the wants which Christianity supplies, and an apprehension of the suitability of Christianity as the perfection of our spiritual nature; we must confess that it is to the unseen leadings of the Spirit of God that we trust, to make the heart feel the truth as well as perceive it, and love as well as appreciate it. If we accept the fact of God's interference to effect man's salvation, and regard it as His special will to bring men to the knowledge of Christ, and trust His promise of assistance to the church,[57] it is not enthusiasm, but the most rational faith, to expect divine assistance to attend constantly on the efforts made to spread the truth which He has been pleased to reveal; not to interfere indeed with the fixed laws of the rational faculties, but to remove prejudices of the heart which might blind the apprehension, and to hallow the soul into a temple for the enshrinement of His truth.

More especially if it be true, as we have perpetually

[57] Matt. xxviii. 20.

insisted, that there is a large region for the influence of emotional causes of doubt, in addition to the intellectual, which have been the subject of our special study, we may well believe that here is a field where the Holy Spirit alone can enter, and in which He only has the power to operate. Evidence, as evidence, is apprehended and tested by the intellectual faculties; but whatever is the subtle influence, consciously or unconsciously exercised by the emotions, in a matter where the evidence is probable, not demonstrative, this offers a sphere where the help of an all-loving God may be hoped for to dissipate the alienation of prejudice or indifference. Paul may plant, and Apollos may water; but it is God that giveth the increase.

We have now considered the lessons taught by the history, both as to the moral function of free thought, the forms of it which are most likely to meet Christians in the present day, and the means which seem most useful for guiding a doubter into truth.

The history may teach a final lesson to us as Christian students, not so much in reference to leading others to truth, as in relation to the means by which we can attain it ourselves.

In all the days of peril through which the church has passed, the means used by those who have striven to find the truth, and become a blessing to the world, have been,—study and prayer. In the solitude of their own hearts, by quiet meditation, they have sought to understand the utterance of the inspired volume; and to secure by prayer the illuminating influence of the divine Spirit, to cause them to behold wondrous things in God's law.[58] And thus in an age of coldness they have kept the flame of divine love burning with unextinguished glory on the altar of their hearts; and in an age of questioning have been able to burst forth from their prison-house of doubt, and gaze with the clearness of unclouded faith on the truth once for all

[58] E. g. Augustin, Anselm, and in modern times such men as Bengel and Neander.

delivered to the saints. If, in the dark night of doubt or sin which has spread its veil over the world, there have been stars that have shown to the pilgrim steadier and clearer light than the other luminaries of the heavens, the cause has been that they have reflected some rays of the Divine glory, which had been concentrated in the sunlike brightness of the apostolic inspiration.

If we have found that the present age offers its peculiar intellectual trials; and if we feel ourselves set in the midst of so many and great dangers; let us not be paralysed by the consciousness of them, so as to deem the search for truth unimportant, or anticipate that it will be unsuccessful; but rather be led to increased energy in striving to follow the example of those who have overcome by the blood of the Lamb, and by the word of their testimony.[59] Let us realise the solemnity of our position as responsible and immortal beings. We are creatures of a day, soon to pass into eternity; placed here to prepare ourselves for that unknown world into which we shall carry the moral character that has been stamped upon us here; and capable, whilst we are here, of doing untold good by a godly example, or of contributing to the ruin of the souls of our fellow men. How important, both for ourselves and others, that we should learn and appropriate that truth which is to be the means of our salvation! how important for ourselves, lest we be castaway! how important for others, lest we help them to build a structure of wood, hay, stubble,[60] which shall be consumed in the day of the Lord!

Let us strive to use the two methods of finding truth,—study and prayer. Let us gain more knowledge, and consecrate it to the investigation of the highest problems of life and of religion; especially applying ourselves, by the help of the ripest aid which miscellaneous literature or church history can afford us, to the study of the sacred scriptures. But above all these intellectual instruments, let us add the further one of prayer. For prayer not only has a reflex value on our-

[59] Rev. xii. 11. [60] 1 Cor. iii. 12.

selves, purifying our hearts, dispersing our prejudices, hushing our troubled spirits into peace; but it acts really, though mysteriously, on God. It ascends far away from earth to the spot where He has His dwelling-place. The infinite God condescends to enter into communion with our spirits, as really as a man that talketh with a friend. The Saviour of pity will Himself look down upon us, and condescend to become our teacher, and give us the purity of heart which will lead us into truth. Our own trials, our own struggles for truth and holiness, the desire to know Christ and to be known by Him, will excite our deep pity for those who endure the like temptations, and prepare us for effectually ministering to the good of others. And if the struggle in our own hearts be long, and there be moments when we seem to have our Gethsemane; let us cleave the closer, with the more simple trust, to our heavenly Father; still imploring Him to grant us in this world knowledge of his truth, and in the world to come life everlasting; assured that the clouds shall one day disperse, and the vision of truth be unveiled to us in the bright light of the eternal morning.

I shall be well content that all that I have said to you be forgotten; and when these lectures take their humble place in the series of which they form a part, deriving an honour, not their own, from the great names with which they are associated, I shall be willing that they be consigned to neglect; if I can only hope that this final exhortation to prayerful study may remain fixed in the memory of any one of those that now hear these words, or may impress the mind of any chance student who, in traversing the same ground, may hereafter have occasion to peruse them, at a time perhaps when the voice that now speaks shall be hushed in the tomb, and the spirit shall have gone to its account.

The lectures are now ended. May God forgive the errors, and sanctify any truth that has been uttered to His honour! The faults are mine: the truth is His, not mine. To Him be the glory.

NOTES.

LECTURE I.

Note 1. p. 3.

SUBDIVISIONS OF HISTORICAL INQUIRY.

A FEW words may explain the distinctions intended in the text.

History has been properly distinguished by Macaulay into two branches, the artistic or descriptive, and the scientific or analytic. (*Essays*, vol. i. 2, on Hallam.) If viewed in the former aspect, history aims as far as possible to reproduce what has been, to recover a picture of the past. Hence it is obedient to the two conditions which rule all art,—precise outline in details, and preservation of perspective in the combination. In the latter, theory in some slight degree steps in, but theory dictated by the instinct of taste rather than by reflection. It is in this branch, in which the historian is the critic, that the border line lies between art and science. For it is hard to measure the precise amount which is due in the appreciation of facts respectively to artistic intuition and to reflective analysis.[1]

Supposing the facts to be thus given, it is the province of the science of history to ascertain their causes. Two living writers, Mr. Mill (*System of Logic*), and Dr. Whewell (*Philosophy of Inductive Sciences*), have given an account of the logic of science. That of the latter is more suitable to the conception which we are here forming of history; for history is exactly one of the class of sciences which he calls "Palætiological." (vol. i. b. x.) It requires first, that we recover the record of the successive stages of facts, the narrative of the past, before searching for the causes. The causes are then to be sought by transferring backward for the explanation of the past those which are at present operating. The search will probably exhibit three successive stages in the process

[1] In the able work on *Tite Live* by H. Taine, (Couronné, 1856,) will be found a study of Livy as a critic and as a philosopher; which illustrates not only the scientific aspect of history, but the influence of science in the special determination of the facts, which has frequently been attributed to art.

of examination. First, causes will be found which are the mere antecedents of the events, the mere links which connect the phenomena. Next, a cyclical law of the recurrence of the facts is perceived, such e. g. as Vico's well-known law concerning the development of political society. Such a law as this, supposing it to hold good without exception within the limits of experience, is what Mr. Mill calls an "empirical law." (*Logic*, vol. ii. b. iii. ch. xvi.) Next, this law must be analysed into its causes. Mr. Mill gives three forms which this third stage of analysis may assume in science. (*Id.* vol. i. b. iii. ch. xii.) Probably in history it will generally assume the one of the three in which the complex result is analysed into its simpler component elements. (*Id.* § 2.)

This inquiry would complete the study of history as a science. But when we deal with moral as distinct from material relations, we feel that there is a question of philosophy as well as science, one of ethics and metaphysics, which rises above all lower ones. We instinctively wish to measure the responsibility of the moral agents who have contributed to work out the results which have been studied. We turn to the personal and biographical question for the purpose of the ethical lesson. The theist also asks another question. Believing that nature and man are the work, direct or indirect, of a personal Creator and Governor, of infinite power and goodness, he strives to search out the purposes of Providence, hoping to find in the drama of universal history the solution of the plot which he could not expect to attain by the study of a portion of it.

Such are the ideas which are intended in the text.

Note 2. p. 4.

THE COMPARATIVE STUDY OF RELIGIONS.

The comparison of Christianity with other religions was necessarily forced upon the Christian church by contact with the heathen world.

We meet in the early fathers with two distinct opinions; the one held in the Alexandrian school, that the heathen religions were imperfect but had a germ of truth, and that philosophy was a schoolmaster to bring men to Christ; the other chiefly in the African school, that they were entire errors, and an obstacle to the conversion of mankind.

In the middle ages, contact with Mahometan life (see Lect. III. p. 88) created a sceptical mode of comparing Christianity with other creeds; circumstances compelling toleration, and toleration passing into indifference. A similar spirit is also seen in the hasty attempt of the French philosophers of the last century to resolve all religion into priestcraft.

It is only in still more recent times that the first scientific conception of a comparative study of religion arose. Even in Herder the comparison is æsthetical more than scientific, and relates to the comparison of literatures more than of religious ideas. Benjamin Constant (*De la Religion Considérée dans sa source, ses formes et ses développements*, 1824) seems to have been the first who really suggested a serious psychological examination; and hence there soon arose the idea of comparative theology analogous to comparative anatomy. His spirit has pervaded French literature subsequently. The religious speculations of the eclectic school give expression to it; e. g. Quinet (*Le Génie des Religions*, vol. i.); and the mode of contemplating religion in Renan (*Etudes de l'Histoire Religieuse*) is based upon it. Caution in using the method is necessary on the part of those who believe in the unique and miraculous character of the Jewish and Christian revelations. In Lect. III. (p. 87) we have given an enumeration of three modes; the one true, the others false; in which Christianity may be put into comparison with other creeds.

Mr. Maurice's *Boyle Lectures on the Religions of the World* refer to this subject; and some useful remarks exist in Morell's *Philosophy of Religion*, (c. iii. and iv.) But the book most full of information is the interesting *Christian Advocate's Publication*, of the late archdeacon Hardwick, *Christ and other Masters;* a work full of learning and piety, unfortunately left unfinished by the tragedy of his premature death in August 1859. In the parts published he has compared Christianity with the Egyptian and Persian religions (part iv.), with the Hindoo (part ii.), and the Chinese (part iii.); and he was preparing materials for its comparison with the Teutonic, and with those of the classic nations.

Note 3. p. 4.

ZEND AND SANSKRIT LITERATURE.

The purpose of this note is to indicate the sources of information in reference to (1) the Zend and (2) the Sanskrit literature, for illustrating the comparative history of religion.

1. It was about the middle of the last century (1762) that Anquetil du Perron brought manuscripts to Europe from Guzerat, written in the Zend or ancient Persian tongue. For some time the relation of the language to the Sanskrit was not understood. The great scholar to whom are due both the study of the tongue and the editing of the *Yaçna*, was Eugene Burnouf. The work just named is the first of the three works which make up the *Vendidad Sadé;* parts of which possibly go back to a period almost coeval with Zoroaster, i. e. perhaps the sixth century B. C. Two other works exist for the study of the Persian theology, though much more modern in date,—the *Desatir* of the ninth century A.D., and the *Dabistan* of the seventeenth,—which both contain fragments of ancient traditions embedded in their texts. The

Avesta, of which the *Vendidad* is one of the oldest parts, has been edited by Spiegel. References to the older literature concerning it may be found in Heeren's *History of the Asiatic Nations*, vol. i. ch. ii.

An account of the present results of comparative philology in reference to Persian is given by professor Max Müller in Bunsen's *Philosophy of History*, vol. i. p. 110. E. T. The Persian theology brought to light by these investigations is discussed by A. Franck, in a paper, *Les Doctrines Religieuses et Philosophiques de la Perse*, in his *Etudes Orientales*, 1861; also in Dr. John Wilson's *Parsi Religion*, 1843; Martin Haug's *Essays on the Parsis*, 1861, founded on Burnouf's researches; and in archdeacon Hardwick's *Christ and other Masters*, part iv. ch. iii. (Hyde's *Hist. Relig. Vet. Pers.* 1700, is obsolete.)

2. The Sanskrit literature has been the subject of still more careful study by a series of learned men. See Donaldson's *Cratylus*, b. i. ch. ii. § 36. 3d ed. Nearly the whole of the literature indirectly offers materials for a history of the alteration and deterioration of religious and ethical ideas, and of the relation of schools of philosophy to a national creed preserved by the priesthood and deposited in books esteemed sacred. The literary works can be placed in their relative order, though the absence of all chronological dates from the time of the contact of the Indians with the Greeks (third century B. C.), down to the visits of the Chinese Buddhist pilgrims in the fourth and seventh centuries A. D., whose works have been translated into French by A. Remusat and Stanislas Julien,[2] and the Mahometan histories, renders the determination of absolute dates impossible. The following are the dates approximately given for the chief works of Sanskrit literature. The *Vedas*, especially the oldest, date from B. C. 1200 to 600. The *Epic Poems*, the *Rámáyana* and *Mahábhárata*, are perhaps of the third century B. C.; the laws of *Manu*, or more truly of the family which claimed descent from the mythical *Manu*, contain materials dating from several centuries B. C., but were put into their present form probably several centuries A. D.; the *Bhagavat Gitá*, an episode in the *Mahábhárata* bearing traces of a Christian influence, dates some centuries A. D. The Hindu drama is perhaps subsequent to 500 A. D. The *Puránas* carry on the literature to mediæval times. Several of the systems of philosophy were probably constructed anterior to the Christian era; but the date at which they were put into their present form is undetermined.

The earlier literature is regarded as the most valuable for the study of the growth of religious ideas and institutions. The development or deterioration may be traced from the simple nature-worship of the *Vedas*, to the accumulation of legends which dis-

[2] *Voyage dans l'Inde par C. Fakian, traduit par A. Remusat*, 1837, and *Hist. de la Vie de Hiouen Thsang*, being vol. i. of *Mémoires sur les Contrées Occidentales*, 1858, by Stan. Julien. The former travelled about A. D. 400; the latter in the seventh century.

grace the modern creed. The causes which gave birth to mythology are no longer a matter of conjecture; the study of the Sanskrit language and literature having exhibited an historical instance of it. In this way the early Sanskrit literature becomes one of the most precious treasures to the mental philosopher who approaches his subject from the historical side.

The earliest *Veda* is in course of publication by professor Max Müller. It has been partly translated by the late professor H. H. Wilson, and wholly by Langlois. Mr. M. Müller has given the results of his studies of this early literature in his admirable work, the *History of Ancient Sanskrit Literature*, 1859; which is full of instruction for the philosopher who is inquiring concerning intellectual and religious history. Most of the other works named above have also been translated into European languages, viz. the *Epic Poems*,—the *Rámáyana*, in Italian by Gorresio, and in French by H. Fauche, 1854; and *Episodes* from the *Mahábhárata* by P. E. Foucaux, 1862;—also the *Laws of Manu*,[3] in English by Sir W. Jones, and in French by A. Loiseleur Des-Lonchamps; the *Bhagavat Gitá* by Wilkins, 1809, the text of which was edited by Schlegel, 1823; the 2d ed. by C. Lassen, 1846. One of the *Puránas* (the *Vishnu*) has been translated by Wilson; and part of the *Bhagavat* by Burnouf, who has also edited the text.

Concerning the systems of Hindu philosophy; see Ritter's *History of Philosophy*, E. T. vol. iv. b. xii. ch. v; Archer Butler's *Lectures on Philosophy*, vol. i. p. 243 seq.; Colebrooke's *Essays on the Philosophy of the Hindus*, 1837; *Aphorisms of Hindu Philosophy*, printed under the care of Dr. Ballantyne for the Benares government college; and Dr. R. Williams's *Christianity and Hinduism*, 1856. The work of the late archdeacon Hardwick, *Christ and other Masters*, also contains a brief account of three of the systems of philosophy, the *Vedánta*, founded on the sacred books, the *Sánkhya* or atheistic, and the *Yoga* or mystic, together with a comparison of them with Christianity (part ii.). An explanation of a part of the *Nyáya* or Logical Philosophy, is given by Max Müller in the Appendix to Dr. Thomson's *Outlines of the Laws of Thought*, 3d ed.

On the system of thought in Buddhism, on which the study of the Páli has thrown light, consult E. Burnouf's *Introduction à l'Histoire du Buddhisme Indien;* and Spence Hardy's *Manual of Budhism*, 1853. Also archdeacon Hardwick's work above named. The Hindu history, exhibiting its double movement, of philosophy on the one hand and of the Buddhist reformation on the other, has been thought to offer a distant analogy to the mental history of Europe in the double movement of the scholastic philosophy and the reformation.

The celebrated works of C. Lassen, *Indische Alterthumskunde*, 1844–47, and A. Weber, *Indische Studien*, 1850, are well known

[3] The abbé Migne is publishing in French, *Livres Sacrés de toutes les Religions sauf la Religion Chrétienne.*

as sources of information in reference to the general subject. Also Dr. J. Muir has lately published (1858) *Sanskrit Texts on the Origin and Progress of the Religion and Institutions of India.* Several articles in reviews have appeared which contain much popular information; e. g. in the *North British Review*, Nov. 1858; *Westminster Review*, April 1860; *Edinburgh Review*, Oct. 1860. On the general subject of this note compare also Quinet, *Œuvres*, t. i. l. 2, 3.

Note 4. p. 12.

THE CONTROVERSY BETWEEN CHRISTIANS AND JEWS.

The history of the controversy of Christianity with Judaism is so connected in the writings of the early apologists with the contemporaneous one directed against Paganism, and in recent times so related in one of its aspects to rationalism, that these reasons seem sufficient, independently of the literary interest, to justify the insertion of a brief notice of it, and of the sources of information with respect to it.

The controversy with the Jew varies in different ages. We can distinguish three separate phases; (1) that which is seen in the early centuries, (2) in the middle ages, and early modern times, (3) the position which is taken up by the educated Jew at the present day. The sources for understanding the contest are, partly the Jewish writings, and partly those of Christians who have written against them.

1. In the early ages the controversy merely turned upon the question whether Jesus was the Christ. The Jews did not deny the fact of the Christian miracles, but explained them away; and the controversy accordingly turned on the interpretation of Jewish prophecy. This phase of the contest is seen in the New Testament, in the Apology of Justin Martyr against Trypho, to which a new kind of objection expressive of prejudice is added in the discourse which Celsus, as preserved in Origen (*Contr. Cels.* b. i. and ii.), puts into the mouth of the Jew whom he introduces. In reference to it, the commentators on these fathers, and especially Semisch's work on Justin Martyr (translated), and the works on the Jewish Talmudic literature and philosophy, may be consulted. The contest is continued at intervals in treatises by inferior writers; an account of which may be found in the sources of information hereafter given, and in *Hagenbach's Dogmengesch.* § 144.

2. The second phase of the contest is seen in the middle ages, and in modern times till about 1700 A. D. It is marked by two lines of thought on the part of the Jewish writers; a system of defence of their own tenets by a method of scriptural interpretation; and the attack of calumny or of argument against Christianity. The former existed especially in Moorish Spain about the twelfth century, the golden age of Jewish literature. For a brief account of

the theological literature of the Jewish nation at that time, and in the period which had intervened since the early ages, the writer may be permitted to refer to one of his own Sermons, and the references there given (*Science in Theology*, 1859, Sermon IV.); to which references add Beugnot's *Les Juifs d'Occident*, 1820, and the new work of De Los Rios on *Spanish Literature*. The movement included both a philosophical side in Maimonides, and a critical in Jarchi, Aben Ezra, Kimchi, &c.

The other movement, which was hostile to Christianity, was marked by a series of works, written by Jews for their own nation, and carefully hidden from the sight of Christians, probably for fear of persecution and suffering; which were given to the world by the learning of the foreign Hebrew scholars of the seventeenth century. The chief of these works are, the *Nizzachon Vetus* of the twelfth century, first published in Wagenseil's *Tela Ignea Satanæ*, 1681. In the thirteenth, the *Disputatio Jechielis cum Nicholao*, *Disputatio Nachmanidis cum fratre Paolo*, and the celebrated *Toldos Jeschu* or Jewish view of Christ's life. About 1399 the Rabbin Lipmann wrote the second book *Nizzachon*, which was published by Hackspan, 1644; and also the *Carmen Memoriale;* and about 1580[4] the Rabbin Isaac wrote the noted *Chissuk Emuna*, or *Munimen Fidei*. All these (with the exception of the second *Nizzachon*) are contained in Wagenseil. During the period one important defence of Christianity against the Jews appeared, the *Pugio Fidei* by Raymund Martin, in Arragon, about 1278, which has been edited with an introduction by De Voisin 1651, and by Carpzov. Another defence was by Alphonso de Spina. *Fortalitium Fidei contra Judæos, Saracenos*, 1487. In Eichhorn's *Geschichte*

[4] In the work quoted above, *Science in Theology*, the date of this Rabbin was erroneously given as the seventeenth century (p. 123). This was the date when Wagenseil by great good fortune obtained a copy of his work, and first made it public. The writer avails himself of this opportunity, in which he has occasion to name his own volume, to correct a few mistakes, and make a few alterations where subsequent study has convinced him that he was in error. E. g. In Sermon IV. the illustration from Indian history (p. 111) is based on the view, now known to be wrong, that Buddhism preceded Brahminism in origin. Also the view (p. 109) of the date of the introduction of the Chaldee character has been rendered doubtful by the arguments which Hupfeld has directed to the subject (*Ausführliche Hebraische Grammatik*), in which he shows that the corruption of the language was gradual, and that the adoption of the square Chaldee character did not take place till after Christ. (See a brief account of his views in Davidson's *Introd. to Old Test.* 1856, ch. ii.) Also, p. 121, the use of the word 'surnamed' for Jarchi disguises the origin of the name. In Sermon I. (2d div.) the order of chronology is not sufficiently observed in the quotations from the Old Testament. In Serm. VIII. (p. 244) the apologetic worth of miracles (suggested by a remarkable speech of Bp. Wilberforce in the Town Hall, Oxford, Nov. 28, 1846. See *Oxford Herald* of Dec. 5) is perhaps hardly sufficient. In Serm. VI. the view that the early church held the doctrine of atonement implicitly rather than explicitly, in life rather than dogma, till Anselm's time, is insufficient and liable to convey an erroneous impression. (See Bp. Thomson's restatement of the historic question in *Aids to Faith*, pp. 339–352.) The revelation of God in the New Testament is most express on the subject of substitutional atonement. Of this the writer of these Sermons never had any doubt; but he now thinks that there are clearer evidences of it in the fathers than he had stated. Reasons are perceivable in the circumstance of the constant struggle against heathen religions, in which the fathers were involved, which led them to dwell on the incarnation rather than on the atonement. Anselm only gave expression to the doctrine which the apostles had clearly taught.

der Literatur, vol. vi. 26, another treatise is named by a writer called Hieronymus, 1552.

During the period just considered the contest with the Jews was carried on chiefly in Spain, or the few Jewish settlements of Lithuania. Henceforth it is chiefly seen in Germany and Holland, where the learned Dutch and German theologians of the seventeenth century were brought into contact with them, or were attracted to the study of the controversy by an interest in the newly awakened taste for Hebrew learning. This age supplies works of great value in gaining a knowledge of Jewish literature, some of which will be named below, and a few treatises, such as, one by Micrælius (*De Messiâ*, 1647); a brief notice by Hoornbeek, *Summa Controv.* 1653 (p. 65); an unfinished treatise by Hulsius, *Theologia Judaica*, 1653; and one by Cocceius, *Jud. Respons. Consid.* 1662. The activity of the Jews is seen in the fact that an unfair attack by Bentz, 1614, was answered in the *Theriaca Judaica* of the Jew Salomo Zebi, Hanover 1615, which again met with a Christian respondent in Wulferus, 1681. Also Limborch had a dispute with a Jew in his *Amica Collatio cum Erudito Judæo* (Dr. Orobius), 1687. The controversy continued through the eighteenth century, probably outlasting its cause; for defences on the side of the Jews ceased. We meet with two works by Difenbach, *Judæus Convertendus*, 1696, and *Judæus Conversus*, 1709; Calvoer's *Gloria Christi*, 1710; Mornæus' *De Verit. Relig. Christianæ*, 1707; and, in England, Bp. Kidder's and Dr. Stanhope's *Boyle Lectures*, the former of which was the basis of the treatise, *The Demonstration of the Messias*, 1700; and C. Leslie's *Short Method with the Jews*. Catalogues of the writings, of which the above are the best known, may be found in J. A. Fabricius's *Biblioth. Græc.* (ed. 1715), vii. 125; and *De Verit. Relig. Christianæ*, 1725, ch. xxxi; and *Blasphemia Judæorum*, Id. ch. xxxvii; Walch's *Biblioth. Theol. Selecta*, vol. i. c. v. sect. 8. (1757); also in Bartollocci's *Dictionary of Jewish Authors*, 1678, and Imbonati's *Dictionary of Christian Writers concerning the Jews*, 1694; and especially in Wolff's *Biblioth. Hebr.* 1715, and De Rossi's *Dizionario degli Autori Ebrei*, 1802. For information concerning sources of Jewish theology and literature, it is enough to cite Hottinger's *Historia Orientalis*, Carpzov's *Introductio*, and Owen's *Prelim. Exercitationes*.

3. In the third phase of the controversy, viz. that which exists with the modern Jew, the controversy is a little changed. The old prejudices against Christianity are in a great degree made obsolete by the freedom of commercial intercourse, and the enjoyment of protection and civil liberty; and hence the contest takes two forms; either the continuation of the argument concerning the meaning of Jewish prophecy, or a discussion on the function of the Jewish religion in history. Sources for the former are found in the older books of evidence. A digest of the arguments concerning it is given in J. Fabricius (not the celebrated Fabricius),

Consideratio Variarum Controversiarum, 1704, p. 41, and in Stapfer's *Institut. Theolog. Polemic*, vol. iii. 1–288, 1752; or in the modern works, Greville Ewing's *Essays addressed to the Jews*, and Dr. McCaul's *Old Paths*, 1837, and his *Warburton Lectures*, 1846. The condition of Jewish life and thought may be seen in Allen's *Modern Judaism*. The system of interpretation on which the controversy is conducted is either the ancient Messianic and allegorical of the Targums and Talmud, or the literal and grammatical introduced by the Spanish mediæval commentators.[5]

The other form of Jewish argument which Christians have to encounter is more novel, and, being confined to educated Jews, its influence is less wide, and does not actuate the stratum of Jewish life with which missionaries generally come into contact. It is based on modern rationalist speculations, and is seen in a work of Dr. Philippsohn, late rabbin at Magdeburg, *Development of the Religious Idea in Judaism, Christianity, and Mahometanism*, (translated both into English 1855, and also into French,) and in the writings of Salvador. Dr. Philippsohn regards the mission of Judaism to be, from first to last, to teach to the world the lesson of monotheism. He traces the struggle in the Jewish church between priestism and prophetism; and regards Christianity as an abnormal form of the latter, which has led the world away to Tritheism: and, so far from regarding the office of Judaism to be extinct, he considers that its mission is still to restore monotheism to the world. A comparison with the statement of the views of the Tübingen school in Lect. VII. or the speculations of Mr. Mackay in Lect. VIII. will show how completely this argument is borrowed from the later forms of German historical criticism.

The views of Salvador in France (see p. 299) are too original to be regarded as typical of the views of a party. They reproduce the critical difficulties of Maimonides and Spinoza, which seem never to have found favour with the Jews; but the general similarity of the doctrinal part of Salvador's system to that just described is very observable.

Note 5, p. 12.

THE CONTEST OF CHRISTIANITY WITH MAHOMETANISM.

The contest of Christianity with Mahometanism, so far as it has been a struggle of argument and not of the sword, offers few remarkable points. In the first sweep of the Mahometan conquest, when the Christian nations succumbed both in the east and west, there was no field for a question of truth. It was only in Christian

[5] There are congregations of reformed Jews in some countries who reject the Talmud as a system of interpretation. They are Jewish protestants. Their standpoint only differs from that of the old Jews in laying stress on the ethical aspect of religion. Sermons by one of them, the Rabbin Marks, have lately been published in England. It will be understood from the above account that the modern Jews include three parties; the orthodox Jews, the reformed, and the rationalistic.

nations which were removed from peril, and yet sufficiently in contact to entertain the question of the claims of the Mahometan religion, that a consideration of its nature, regarded as a system of doctrine, could arise. Accordingly it is in Constantinople, or in Spain and the other parts of western Europe which came into connexion with the Moors, that works of this character appear.

The history may be conveniently arranged in three periods, each of which is marked by works of defence, some called forth by danger, a real demand, but subsiding into or connected with inquiries prompted only by literary tastes. The first is from the twelfth to the middle of the sixteenth century; the second during the seventeenth and eighteenth; the third during the present century.

1. A notice of the Mahometan religion exists in a work of J. Damascenus, in the eighth century; and Euthymius Zigabenus, a Byzantine writer of the twelfth: but the first important treatise written directly against it was in 1210, *Richardi Confutatio*, edited in 1543 by Bibliander from a Greek copy. The refutation of Averroes by Aquinas, about 1250, can hardly be quoted as an instance of a work against the Mahometan religion, being rather against its philosophy. A treatise exists by John Cantacuzene, written a little after 1350; which is to be explained probably by the circumstance that the danger from Mahometan powers in the east directed the attention of a literary man to the religion and institutions which they professed. Thus far the works were called forth by a real demand.

A series of treatises however commences about the time of the expulsion of the Moors from Spain, the cause of the existence of which is not so easy of explanation. Such are those in Spain by Alphonso de Spina, 1487, and by Turrecremata (see Eichhorn's *Gesch. der Lit.* vi.); by Nicholas de Cuza, published in 1543; in Italy about 1500 by Ludovicus Vives, and Volterranus; one by Philip Melancthon in reference to the reading of the Koran; and a collection of treatises, including those of Richardus, Cantacuzene, Vives, and Melancthon, published by Bibliander in 1543. Probably the first two of this list may have been the relic of the crusade of Christianity against the Moorish religion; the next two possibly were called forth by the interest excited in reference to Mahometans by reason of their conquests, or less probably by the influence of their philosophy at Padua (see Lect. III. p. 100 seq.). The two last are hardly to be explained, except by supposing them to be an offshoot of the Renaissance, and called forth by the largeness of literary taste and inquiry excited by that event.

2. When we pass into the seventeenth century, we find a series of treatises on the same subject, which must be explained by the cause just named, the newly acquired interest in Arabic and other eastern tongues. We meet however with others, called forth by the missionary exertions which had brought the Christians into contact with Mahometans in the east.

The treatise by Bleda, *Defensio Fidei Christianæ*, 1610, stands alone, unconnected with any cause. It was partly a defence of the conduct of Christians towards the Mahometans. A real interest however belongs to the work of Guadagnoli in 1631. A catholic missionary, Hieronymo Xavier, had composed in 1596 a treatise in Persian against Mahometanism, in which the general principle of theism was laid down as opposed to the Mahometan doctrine of absorption; next the peculiar doctrines of Christianity stated; and lastly, a contrast drawn between the two religions. See Lee's *Tracts on Christianity and Mahometanism* (below, *pref.* p. 5 seq.).

This work was answered in 1621 by a Persian nobleman named Ahmed Ibn Zain Elébidín. The line adopted by him was, (1) to show that the coming of Mahomet was predicted in the Old Testament (Hab. iii. 3); (2) to argue that Mahomet's teaching was not more opposed to Christ's than his was to that of Moses, and that therefore both ought to be admitted, or both rejected; (3) to point out critically the discrepancies in the Gospels; (4) to attack the doctrines of the Trinity and Christ's deity. (Lee, *pref.* 41 seq.)

This work was answered (1631) by a treatise in Latin by P. Guadagnoli, dedicated to Pope Urban VIII. It is divided into four parts; (1) respecting the objections about the Trinity; (2) the Incarnation; (3) the authority of Scripture; (4) the claims of the Koran and of Mahomet. (Lee, *pref.* 108 seq. who also gives references (p. 113) to a few other writers, chiefly in the seventeenth century.)

The further works of defence produced in this century arose as it were accidentally. The lengthy summary of the Mahometan controversy in Hoornbeek's *Summa Controversiarum*, 1653, p. 75 seq. was either introduced merely to give completeness to the work as a treatise on polemic, or was called forth by considerations connected with missions, as is made probable by his work *De Conversione Gentilium et Indorum*. Le Moyne's publication on the subject in the *Varia Sacra*, vol. i. 1685, arose from the accidental discovery of an old treatise, *Bartholomæi Edess. Confutatio Hagareni*. A third work of this kind, Maracci's *Criticism on the Koran*, 1698, arose from the circumstance that the pope would not allow the publication of an edition of the Koran, without an accompanying refutation of each part of it. The work of Hottinger (*Hist. Orient.* b. i.), Pfeiffer's *Theol. Judaica et Mahom.* and Kortholt's *De Relig. Mahom.* 1663, form the transition into an independent literary investigation; which is seen in the literary inquiries concerning the life of Mahomet, as well as his doctrine, in Pocock, Prideaux 1697, Reland 1707, Boulainvilliers 1730, and the translation of the Koran by Sale 1734. A slightly controversial tone pervades some of them. The materials collected by them were occasionally used by deist and infidel writers (e. g. by Chubb), for instituting an unfavourable comparison between Christ and Mahomet.

The great literary historians of that period give lists of the previous writers connected with the investigation. See J. A. Fabricius, *Biblioth. Græc.* ed. 1715, vol. vii. p. 136; Walch, *Biblioth. Theol. Sel.* vol. i. chap. v. sect. 9. A summary of the arguments used in the controversy is given in J. Fabricius, *Delectus Argumentorum*, p. 41, &c. and Stapfer's *Inst. Theol. Polem.* iii. p. 289, &c.

3. In the present century the literature in reference to Mahometanism is, as in the former instances, twofold in kind. Part of it has been called forth by missionary contests in the east; part by literary or historic tastes, and the modern love of carrying the comparative method of study into every branch of history.

The first class is illustrated by the discussions at Shiraz in 1811, between the saintly Henry Martyn and some Persian Moollas. The controversy was opened by a tract, sophistical but acute, written by Mirza Ibrahim; (Lee, pp. 1–39); the object of which was to show the superiority of the standing miracle seen in the excellence of the Koran, over the ancient miracles of Christianity. Martyn replied to this in a series of tracts (Lee, p. 80 seq.), and was again met by Mohammed Ruza of Hamadan, in a much more elaborate work, in which, among other arguments, the writer attempts to show predictions of Mahomet in the Old Testament, and in the New applying to him the promise of the Paraclete (Lee, pp. 161–450). These tracts were translated in 1824, with an elaborate preface containing an account of the preceding controversy of Guadagnoli, by Professor S. Lee of Cambridge, *Controversial Tracts on Christianity and Mahometanism*, which is the work so frequently cited above. To complete the history it is necessary to add, that a discussion was held a few years ago between an accomplished Mahometan and Mr. French, a learned missionary at Agra.

The literary aspect of the subject, not however wholly free from controversy, was opened by White, in the *Bampton Lectures* for 1784; and abundant sources have lately been furnished. Among them are, Sprenger's *Life of Mahomet*, 1851, and Muir's, 1858. Also a new translation of the Koran by the Rev. J. M. Rodwell, where the Suras are arranged chronologically. The following ought also to be added, Dr. Macbride's *Mahometan Religion Explained*, 1857; Arnold on Mahometanism, 1859; Tholuck's *Vermischte Schriften*, i. (1–27); *Die Wunder Mohammed's und der Character des Religionstifters;* Dr. Stanley's *Lectures on the History of the Eastern Church*, lect. viii. and the references there given; Maurice's *Religions of the World;* and Renan's *Etudes d'Histoire Religieuse.* (Ess. iv.) The modern study has been directed more especially to attain a greater knowledge of Mahomet's life, character, and writings; the antecedent religious condition of Arabia;[6] and the characteristics of Mahometanism,

[6] Cfr. Hävernick's *Introd. to Old Test.* (E. T.) § 23, 24.

when put into comparison with other creeds, and when viewed psychologically in relation to the human mind.

The materials also for a study of the Mahometan form of philosophy, both in itself and in its relation to the religion, have been furnished by Aug. Schmoelders, *Essai sur les Ecoles Philosophiques chez les Arabes*, 1842. See also Ritter's *Chr. Phil.* iii. 665 seq.; iv. 1–181.

Note 6. p. 12.

UNITARIANISM.

It may be useful to indicate the chief stages of the history of Unitarianism, and the sources of information with regard to it, as it bears a close analogy to some forms of free thought, such as deism,[7] and connects itself more or less nearly with forms of rationalism which occur in the course of the history.

The first instance of it is in the early ages, either as a Jewish Gnostic sect, Ebionitism, or in some of the other forms of Gnosticism; passing in the east into Arianism, which lowered God, and in the west into Pelagianism, which elevated man. For this period see F. Lange, *Geschichte und Lehrbegriff d. Unitarier vor d. Nicaenischen Synode*, 1831; Hagenbach's *Dogmengeschichte*, § 23; and the church histories which treat of this period.

In the middle ages the tendency may be considered to be mainly represented by Mahometanism, and hardly exists at all in the Christian church.

Its modern form arises at the time of the Reformation.

1. Originating in Italy, it exists as a doctrine in Switzerland and Germany from 1525–1560. See F. Trechsel's *Die Protest. Antitrinitarier vor Faustus Socinus*, 1844. The best known names are Servetus, Lelio Sozini, and Ochino.

2. It exists as a church at Racow in Poland, where the exiles found a refuge. Here Faustus Sozinus (1539–1603), nephew of Lelio, and J. Crellius, are the best known names. In 1609 Schmelz drew up the Socinian Formula, the Racovian Catechism. It was also here that the collection of Socinian writers, the *Bibliotheca Fratrum Polonorum*, 1626, was published. The history of the sect up to this point may be found in the Introduction to *Rees's Translation of the Racovian Catechism*, 1818. Also see Hallam's *History of Literature*, i. 554. ii. 335; Mosheim's *Church History*, sixteenth century, § 2. P. ii. ch. iv; Hase's *Church History* (Engl. Transl.), § 371, 2. The Socinians were driven out of Poland in 1658, by the influence of the Jesuits; and, passing into Holland, became absorbed in the church of the Remonstrants or Arminians.

3. The next stage of Socinianism is, as a doctrine, in England in the seventeenth century. In 1611 two persons, Hammont and Lewis, suffered martyrdom for it; and it spread widely during the

[7] Cfr. Bp. Horsley's *Letters against Priestley*, Lett. xvi, p. 264.

Long Parliament. (See Dr. Owen's *Vind. Evangel.* pref.) The chief teacher was J. Biddle (1615–1662). The interest of it arises from its supposed parallelism to the Arminianism of Hales in the time of Charles I, and to the latitudinarian party of Whichcote and More in that of Charles II. But the parallel is not quite correct. The study of Arminius's writings (see J. Nicholls's translation, 1825,) shows that he was not a Pelagian,[8] if even his successors were. But even Episcopius and Limborch hardly reached this point. Hales resembled Episcopius. Nor is the parallel much nearer with "the latitude men;" for Socinianism lacked their Platonizing tendency. The Arian tendency, which commenced at the end of the century, both in the church, in such writers as Whiston and Clarke, and among the presbyterians, offers a nearer parallel, in being, like Socinianism, Unitarian in tendency. On this period see Hagenbach's *Dogmengesch.* (Notes to § 234.)

4. Its next form, was as a set of congregations in England in the eighteenth century, chiefly arising out of the presbyterians; marked by great names, such as Lardner, Lowman, Priestley.[9] Shortly before the close of the century, it was introduced into America.

5. Its last form is a modification of the old Socinian view, formed under the pressure of evangelical religion on the one side and rationalist criticism on the other. The accomplished writers, Channing in America and Mr. J. Martineau in England, are the best types of this form. Priestley, Channing, and Martineau, are the examples of the successive phases of modern Unitarianism: Priestley, of the old Socinianism building itself upon a sensational philosophy; Channing, of the attempt to gain a larger development of the spiritual element; Martineau, of the elevation of view induced by the philosophy of Cousin, and the introduction of the idea of historical progress in religious ideas. In reference to this part of the history see E. Renan's Essay on Channing, *Etudes de l'Hist. Relig.* p. 357; E. Ellis's *Half Century of Unitarian Controversy* (in America), 1858; J. J. Taylor's *Retrospect of Religious Life in England*, 1845; Dr. Beard's *Unitarianism in its Actual State;* and other references given in the notes to H. B. Smith's translation of Hagenbach's *Dogmengesch.* New York, 1862. ii. p. 441.

In addition to the above references, materials for the history will be found in Sandius, *Biblioth. Antitrin.* 1684; Bock's *Hist. Antitrin.* 1774; Otto Foch's *Der Socinianismus*, &c. 1847; and an article in the *North British Review*, No. 60, for May 1859. The history of the controversial literature on the subject is given in Pfaff's *Introd. in Hist. Theol. Lit.* vol. ii. p. 320 seq.; and more fully in Walch's *Biblioth. Theol. Select.* vol. i. p. 902 seq. For a

[8] The nearest English parallel to the teaching of Arminius personally (as distinct from that of his successors), on the quinquarticular controversy, is the doctrine of John Wesley. The nearest parallel to the general views of Episcopius and Limborch was Hey of Cambridge at the close of the last century.

[9] A sketch of Priestley is given in Mr. Martineau's *Miscellanies.*

digest of the arguments used in the controversy, see Hoornbeek's *Summa Controv.* 1653, p. 440; J Fabricius, *Consid. Var. Controv.* pp. 99–208; and Stapfer's *Inst. Theol. Polem.* vol. iii. c. 12.

Note 7. p. 24.

CLASSIFICATION OF METAPHYSICAL INQUIRIES.

The scheme on the following page will perhaps facilitate the reading of the text. The writer is perfectly aware of the many objections which may be directed against particular parts of this scheme. It is merely introduced here that the reader may be put in possession of his meaning. The following notes may further contribute to the same end.

(*a*) This first subdivision of Metaphysics into Psychology and Ontology is very neatly stated by Professor Mansel (art. *Metaphysics* in *Encycl. Britann.* 8th ed. p. 555, and p. 23 in the reprint of the article, 1860); Cfr. also Archer Butler's *Lect. on Phil.* vol. i. lect. i–iii.

(*b*) It must be understood, that when we pass here from a division of the inquiries concerning the mind to a supposed division of the mind itself, we imply only a division of states of consciousness or mental functions, not an absolute and real division of the mind itself. Distinctness of structure is only the inference; distinctness of function is a fact, given in the act of consciousness.

(*c*) The distinctness of the Will, as a faculty, from the emotions will be disputed by many. It is maintained by Maine de Biran, and the Eclectic school of France. Mr. Mill, *Logic*, vol. ii. b. vi. ch. ii, implies the contrary, and regards Will to be a particular state of feeling.

(*d*) The difference of the presentative from the representative consciousness is now generally understood, since the arguments of Sir W. Hamilton have been commonly known. See his edition of Reid, note B. p. 804; *Discussions*, Ess. ii. and *Lect. on Metaphysics*; Mansel's work above cited, p. 560, 584; Morell's *Phil. of Relig.* ch. ii.

(*e*) The separation of Intuition from Perception is a point much disputed. It is maintained by Schelling and by Cousin, and made familiar by Coleridge, *Aids to Reflection*, i. p. 168 seq. See also Morell's *Philos. of Relig.* ch. ii; *Hist. of Phil.* ii. p. 487 seq. Among English psychologists however, intuition is identified with perception; or if slightly distinguished, as by Mr. Mansel, it is made synonymous with every "pre-

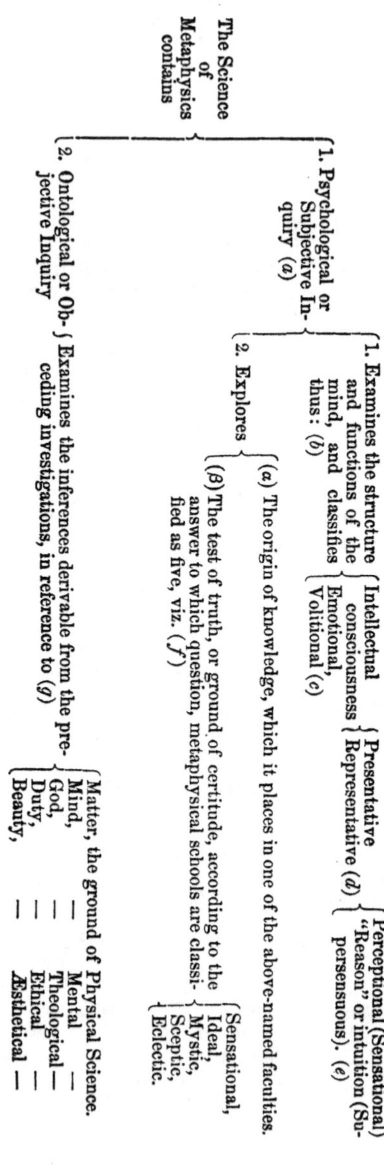
The Science of Metaphysics contains
1. Psychological or Subjective Inquiry (a)
1. Examines the structure and functions of the mind, and classifies thus: (b)
Intellectual consciousness
Presentative
Representative (d)
Perceptional (Sensational)
"Reason" or intuition (Supersensuous). (e)
Emotional,
Volitional (c)
2. Explores
(α) The origin of knowledge, which it places in one of the above-named faculties.
(β) The test of truth, or ground of certitude, according to the answer to which question, metaphysical schools are classified as five, viz. (f)
Sensational,
Ideal,
Mystic,
Sceptic,
Eclectic.
2. Ontological or Objective Inquiry
Examines the inferences derivable from the preceding investigations, in reference to (g)
Matter, the ground of Physical Science.
Mind, — Mental —
God, — Theological —
Duty, — Ethical —
Beauty, — Æsthetical —

sentative" act of consciousness, and thus includes the consciousness of our own minds, as well as the sensational consciousness usually denoted by the word "perception." With reference to the view intended on this subject in these lectures, see a note on p. 28.

(*f*) With reference to these schools, see Morell's *Hist. of Philosophy* (vol. i. Introduction); and Cousin's *Cours de la Philosophie* du 18me Siècle.

(*g*) This subdivision of the subject matter of Ontology is well stated by Mansel in the *Encyc. Britann.* above cited, 603, 613 seq. This work of Mr. Mansel is on the whole the clearest exposition of Psychology, studied from the side of consciousness, which has appeared. Mr. Morell's recent work on Psychology presents a view different from his former ones, and unites the physiological treatment of the inquiry; being borrowed partly from the recent speculations which the teaching of Herbert has induced in Germany. See Note 41.

Note 8. p. 28.

QUOTATION FROM GUIZOT ON PRAYER.

The following eloquent remarks seem worth quoting, as illustrative of the instinct in the soul of man to perform the act of prayer; the natural outgoing of the human soul after the infinite Being. They are taken from Guizot, *L'Eglise et la Société Chrétienne*, 1861.

"Seul entre tous les êtres ici-bas l'homme prie. Parmi ses instincts moraux, il n'y en a point de plus naturel, de plus universel, de plus invincible que la prière. L'enfant s'y porte avec une docilité empressée. Le vieillard s'y replie comme dans un refuge contre la décadence et l'isolement. La prière monte d'elle-même sur les jeunes lèvres qui balbutient à peine le nom de Dieu et sur les lèvres mourantes qui n'ont plus la force de le prononcer. Chez tous les peuples, célèbres ou obscurs, civilisés ou barbares, on rencontre à chaque pas des actes et des formules d'invocation. Partout où vivent des hommes, dans certaines circonstances, à certaines heures, sous l'empire de certaines impressions de l'âme, les yeux s'élèvent, les mains se joignent, les genoux fléchissent, pour implorer ou pour rendre grâces, pour adorer ou pour apaiser. Avec transport ou avec tremblement, publiquement ou dans le secret de son cœur, c'est à la prière que l'homme s'adresse, en dernier recours, pour combler les vides de son âme ou porter les fardeaux de sa destinée; c'est dans la prière qu'il cherche, quand tout lui manque, de l'appui pour sa faiblesse, de la consolation dans ses douleurs, de l'espérance pour sa vertu." (p. 22.)

"Il y a, dans l'acte naturel et universel de la prière, une foi naturelle et universelle dans cette action permanente, et toujours libre, de Dieu sur l'homme et sur sa destinée." (p. 24.)

"'Les voies de Dieu ne sont pas nos voies:' nous y marchons sans les connaître; croire sans voir et prier sans prévoir, c'est la condition que Dieu a faite à l'homme en ce monde, pour tout ce qui en dépasse les limites." (p. 25.)

Note 9. p. 31.

ON THE MODERN VIEW OF THE HISTORICAL METHOD IN PHILOSOPHY.

It has been implied in the text, at this place, and also in the preface, that the "historic method of study" is the great feature of this century. The term is ambiguous. The meaning of it however is, that each problem ought to be approached from the historic side. Whether the problem be a fact of society, or of thought, or of morals, in each case the questions are asked—What are its antecedents? how did it happen? How came it that men accepted it?—This is a method exactly the reverse of that which was common in the last century. The question then was, Is a thing true? The question now is a preliminary one, How came it that it was thought to be true? It is probable that in many minds there is a slight tendency to pantheism in this method of study. The universe is looked at as ever in course of development; evil as "good in the making;" no fact as wholly bad; no thought as wholly false. But, without involving such a tendency, whatever is true in the method may be appropriated. It starts only with the assumption that the human race is in a state of movement; and that Providence has lessons to teach us if we watch this movement. It is the method of learning by experience of the past, a lesson for conduct in the future.

The method thus explained, however, is used for two different purposes. Either it is intended to be the preliminary process preparatory to discovery, or it is designed to take the place of discovery. In the former case, we ask why men have thought a thing true, for the purpose of afterwards discovering, by the use of other methods, what is true; in the latter we rest content with the historical investigation, and consider the attempt to discover absolute truth to be impossible; and regard the problem of philosophy to be, to gather up the elements of truth in the past. In the former case truth is absolute, though particular ages may have blindly groped after it; in the latter it is relative. In the former, the history of philosophy is the preliminary to philosophy; in the latter it is philosophy. In the former, philosophy is a science; in the latter it is a form of criticism. The former view is held by the school of Schelling and Cousin; the latter is an offshoot of that of Hegel. The former marked French literature until recent years; the latter is expressed in it at the present time; and is stated by no one so clearly as by Renan and Scherer. Most English writers will justly prefer the former view; but the explanation of the latter, given in the two passages which follow, is expressed with such clearness, and will be of so much use in explaining subsequent allusions in these lectures (especially Lect. VII. and VIII.), that it is desirable to print it here.

"Le trait caractéristique du 19e siècle est d'avoir substitué la méthode historique à la méthode dogmatique, dans toutes les études relatives à l'esprit humain. La critique littéraire n'est plus que l'exposé des formes diverses de la beauté, c'est à dire des manières dont les différentes familles et les différentes âges de l'humanité ont résolu le problème esthétique. La philosophie n'est que le tableau des solutions proposées pour résoudre le problème philosophique. La théologie ne doit plus être que l'histoire des efforts spontanés tentés pour résoudre le problème divin. L'histoire, en effet, est la forme nécessaire de la science de tout ce qui est soumis aux lois de la vie changeante et successive. La science des langues, c'est l'histoire des langues; la science des littératures et des philosophies, c'est l'histoire des littératures et des philosophies; la science de l'esprit humain c'est, de même, l'histoire de l'esprit humain, et non pas seulement l'analyse des rouages de l'âme individuelle. La psychologie n'envisage que l'individu, et elle l'envisage d'une manière abstraite, absolue, comme un sujet permanent et toujours identique à lui-même; aux yeux de la critique la conscience se fait dans l'humanité comme l'individu; elle a son histoire. Le grand progrès de la critique a été de substituer la catégorie du *devenir* à la catégorie de *l'être*, la conception du relatif à la conception de l'absolu, le mouvement à l'immobilité. Autrefois, tout était considéré comme étant; on parlait de philosophie, de droit, de politique, d'art, de poésie, d'une manière absolue; maintenant tout est considéré comme en voie de se faire. . . . . . A ce point de vue de la science critique, ce qu'on recherche dans l'histoire de la philosophie, c'est beaucoup moins de la philosophie proprement dite que de l'histoire."—(E. Renan, Pref. to *Averroes*, p. vi.)

"Tout n'est que relatif, disions-nous tout à l'heure; il faut ajouter maintenant: tout n'est que relation. Vérité importune pour l'homme qui, dans le fatal courant où il est plongé, voudrait trouver un point fixé s'arrêter un instant, se faire illusion sur la vanité des choses! Vérité féconde pour la science qui lui doit une intelligence nouvelle de la réalité, une intuition infiniment plus pénétrante du jeu des forces qui composent le monde. C'est ce principe qui a fait de l'histoire une science et de toutes les sciences une histoire. C'est en vertu de ce principe qu'il n'y a plus de philosophie mais des philosophies qui se succèdent, qui se complétent en se succèdant, et dont chacune représenté avec un élément du vrai, une phase du développement de la pensée universelle. Ainsi la science s'organise elle-même et porte en soi sa critique. La classification rationnelle des systèmes est leur succession, et le seul jugement équitable et utile qu'on puisse passer sur eux est celui qu'ils passent sur eux-mêmes en se transformant. Le vrai n'est plus vrai en soi. Ce n'est plus une quantité fixe qu'il s'agit de dégager, un objet rond ou carré qu'on puisse tenir dans la main. Le vrai, le beau, le juste même se font perpétuellement ; ils sont à jamais en train de se constituer, parce qu'ils ne sont autre chose que l'esprit humain, qui, en se déployant, se retrouve et se reconnait."—E. Scherer, (article on Hegel in *Revue des Deux Mondes*, Feb. 15, 1861.)

LECTURE II.

Note 10, p. 46.

NEO-PLATONISM.

On the nature and history of Neo-Platonism, see Ritter's *History of Philosophy*, E. T. vol. iv. b. xiii; Creuzer's *Prolegomena to Plotinus;* Tennemann's *Manual of Philosophy*, § 200–222; Hase's *Church History*, § 50, with the references which the two latter supply; Jules Simon's and Vacherot's works on the *Ecole d'Alexandrie;* B. Constant's *Du Polytheisme*, b. xv. Among English works, see Archer Butler's *Lectures on Philosophy*, vol. ii. 348 seq.; Lewes' *History of Philosophy;* Maurice's *History of Philosophy* (part ii.); Donaldson's *History of Greek Literature*, ch. 53 and 57; and an essay in R. A. Vaughan's *Essays and Remains*, 1858.

The mystic and oriental tendency which Neo-Platonism embodied is seen as early as Philo in the middle of the first century; but it was Ammonius Saccus (A. D. 163 243) who developed the new system about A. D. 200. The chief teachers of it were Plotinus (born 203), who introduced it at Rome; Porphyry (233–305), who however manifested more of the mystic Pythagorean spirit and less of the dialectical Platonic; Iamblichus, a generation later, who also inclined to theurgy; and in the fifth century Hypatia, killed 415; and Proclus (412–485), who taught at Athens. A growth of thought is perceptible in the successive members of the school. The skétches of several of the above-named writers in Smith's *Biographical Dictionary* are full of information, and furnished with useful references.

Note 11. p. 47.

THE PSEUDO-CLEMENTINE LITERATURE.

The Pseudo-Clementine literature consists of Homilies and Recognitions; the latter being in a Latin translation by Rufinus. It is published in Cotelerius's *Sancti Patres*, 1698, vol i.

A noble Roman, harassed by his doubts and eager for truth, travels to the east, and there learns Christian truth, which makes him happy. It is the former part of the narrative, viz. the doubts of Clemens before becoming a Christian, which is alluded to in the text, and is adduced by Neander, *Kirchengeschichte*, i. pp. 54–56, as an instance of the preparation for the reception of Christianity made by a sense of want in many hearts. But it is the latter part which is valuable in a literary point of view, on account of the light which the exposition of Christian doctrine contained in it throws upon the Judaizing Gnostics, being an attempt to reconcile Ebionitism with the teaching of St. Paul. Its interest in this point of view has caused it to be made the subject of several monographs by German theologians. A list of them, with an account of the phases of doctrine described, is given in Kurtz's *Church History*, E. T. § 48, and in Hase's *Church History*, § 35, 75, and 80. One of the most important of them is Schliemann's *Die Clementinen*, 1844.

Note 12. p. 48.

THE ABSENCE OF REFERENCES TO CHRISTIANITY IN HEATHEN WRITERS OF THE SECOND CENTURY.

Tzchirner has investigated this subject in an interesting dissertation, *Græci et Romani Scriptores cur rerum Christianarum raro meminerint;* Opusc. Acad. p. 283. Lips. 1829, (translated in the *Journal of Sacred Literature*, Jan. 1853;) and has discussed the passages where mention is made of Christianity. The following is the substance of his inquiries.

Though the notices concerning Christianity in heathen writers are scanty, the silence of Eusebius gives good ground for inferring, that not many further notices existed concerning it in the works which are lost, than have been preserved to us. Perhaps a few passages may have been erased in which Christianity was blasphemed, even in that which is preserved.

The silence concerning Christianity during the first century is not surprising; because the Christians, if known at all, would be regarded as a Jewish sect, as in Acts xviii. 15; xxiii. 29; xxv. 19. In the third century they are both noticed and attacked. The inquiry therefore with regard to the silence about them, refers only to the period from about A. D. 80–180.

During this period, among the Greek writers who omit all mention of Christianity, are Dio Chrysostom; Plutarch (for the passage, *Quæst.* iv. 4. § 3, about happiness consisting in hope, probably does not refer to them); Œnomaus, who wrote expressly to ridicule religion; Maximus Tyrius; and Pausanias: and among Latin ones, Juvenal, who several times mentions the Jews, but only indirectly refers to the Christians (*Sat.* i. 185–7), Aulus Gellius, and Apuleius; (for the opinion of Warburton, *Div. Leg.*

b. ii. § 4, that an allusion is intended, is now rejected,[10] unless one perhaps exists in *Met.* ix. ed. Panck. ii. 195.)

Among those who name Christians we find,—

In Trajan's reign, Tacitus, who describes their persecution by Nero (*Ann.* xv. 44); Suetonius, who names them, *Vit. Neron.* ch. 16, and describes them as seditious, *Vit. Claud.* 25, if indeed the word *Chresto* in the paragraph is intended for *Christo;* and Pliny the younger, in the well-known letter to Trajan (*Ep.* x. 96).

In the reign of Hadrian we find, in a fragment of Hadrian's works in Vopiscus's Life of Saturninus (ch. viii.) a mention of them, comparing them with Serapid worshippers; and one quoted by Eusebius, *Eccl. Hist.* iv. 9, addressed to a proconsul of Asia. Also Arrian names them in two passages, in one describing them as obstinate, *Diss. Epictet.* b. iv. ch. vii. and in the other speaking either of them or of the Jews as *βαπτισταί* (b. ii. ch. ii.)

In the reign of the Antonines we find Galen stigmatising them for obstinacy (*De Pulsuum Diff.* b. iii. ch. iii.), and for believing without proof (b. ii. ch. iv.); and Marcus Aurelius himself inquires (*Comment.* b. xi. ch. iii), what can be the cause of their inflexibility. His two epistles which contain allusions to Christianity, one of them attributing his victory over the Marcomanni to the thundering legion, and the other stating that it is the business of the gods and not men to punish, are rejected as spurious.

In the same reign we find Crescens and Fronto, who are treated of elsewhere, Lect. II. p. 48; and Lucian (p. 49). Tzchirner denies the allusions supposed to lurk in many passages of Lucian examined by Krebsius and Eichstadt; but, independently of those in the Peregrinus, ch. xi–xiv, on which see Lect. II and Note 13, there remains one where Alexander the magician is said to exclude Christians and Epicureans from his magical rites. In the same reign we meet with Celsus; after which time the notices of Christianity are frequent; the account of which will be found in Lardner's Works, vol. viii.

If now we pass from the facts to the cause, and ask why the notices are so few, Tzchirner very properly answers, that the silence in the first century is explained, partly by the general poverty and retirement of the Christians, and partly by the circumstance named above, that they were included among Jews. But in the second century, when Christianity was so far known that several learned men abandoned heathenism for it, such as Quadratus, Melito, Justin, Tatian, Athenagoras, Theophilus, Minucius Felix; Tzchirner refers the silence chiefly to the fact that the opinions and position of the Christians prevented them from being considered worthy of attention by members of any of those schools of philosophy whose probable opinions in reference to it have been already explained in Lect. II. Celsus alone had the far-sightedness to apprehend danger from them, both philosophically and politically.

[10] But see Pressensé, *Hist. de l'Eglise,* 2e Ser. t. ii. p. 154.

Note 13. p. 49.

THE PEREGRINUS PROTEUS OF LUCIAN.

The question of Lucian's intention to injure Christianity has been discussed and maintained by Krebsius in a Dissertation, *De Malitioso Luciani Consilio Religionem Christianam scurrili dicacitate vanam et ridiculam reddendi*, Opusc. Acad. p. 308 seq. The contrary view is maintained by Eichstadt in a dissertation, *Lucianus num scriptis suis adjuvare voluerit Religionem Christianam*, Jena, 1822. Krebsius is extravagant in interpreting many unimportant references in Lucian as relating to Christianity. See Tzchirner, *Opusc. Acad.* p. 296. Neander also states his opinion on the question, *Kirchengesch.* i. 269 seq.

The same subject has been discussed with great care and learning by Adolph Planck, dean of Heidenheim in Würtemburg, *Lucian und Christenthum*, a contribution to the church history of the second century; originally published in the *Studien und Kritiken*, 1851, and translated in the American *Bibliotheca Sacra*, April and July, 1853. He there studies Lucian's tract, *the Peregrinus*, (1) in the character which it offers of Peregrinus as a Cynic, for the purpose of examining the probability of his death being a parody on Christian martyrdom; (2) in his character as a Christian, in order to exhibit Lucian's opinion of Christianity and of the traits of Christian life brought out; (3) with a view to ascertain the sources and amount of Lucian's knowledge of Christianity; discussing fully, by means of quotations, the evidence of Lucian's acquaintance with the early Christian literature.

The analysis of the Peregrinus Proteus is as follows: It professes to be a letter from Lucian to Cromius narrating Peregrinus's death. Peregrinus had gone to Olympia, with the pompous design of displaying his death before the assembly at the games. Lucian lets us hear the speeches, descriptive of Peregrinus's life, delivered before the decisive act. A certain Theagenes, an admirer of Peregrinus, delivers a bombastic eulogy, § 3–7, repelling the charge of vanity imputed to him, and comparing his proposed death with that of Hercules, &c. Lucian opposes to this some invectives delivered by another, whose name he professes to have forgotten, which refer, § 7–30, to the history of Peregrinus to which Theagenes had alluded; tracing his crimes, his journeys from land to land, his turning Christian in Syria, his expulsion for disobedience, his subsequent wanderings and crimes, and the universal contempt which he had brought upon himself. Theagenes replies to this speech; but Lucian preferred to go to see the wrestling-match. Afterwards however he heard Peregrinus pronounce his own eulogy, and boast of his sufferings on behalf of philosophy. Then, after most of the guests had left Elis, § 35, &c, Peregrinus proceeded to erect his own funeral pile, and consumed himself on it. Lucian after seeing the end went away, and added a legend about the appearance of a hawk; which story he soon afterwards found had already gained credence. The moral which he draws is, that Cromius ought to despise such people, and impute their conduct to love of fame.

The passages of the work which have specific reference to Christianity are, § 11-13, which describe Peregrinus's intercourse with the Christians; and § 35–41, which describe his martyrdom. The references are to Dindorf's ed. Paris 1840.

Note 14. p. 51.

THE WORK OF CELSUS.

It is difficult to obtain an exact conception of the work of Celsus. This is due partly perhaps to its original form; for Origen himself complains (Cont. Cels. i. 40) of the want of order in Celsus; and partly to the fact that a mind like that of Origen did not follow his opponent step by step, but frequently grasped a general principle which enabled him to meet a group of objections dispersed through different parts of Celsus's work.

As it was desirable for the object of the lecture to present Celsus's views rather than analyse Origen's treatise, the writer endeavoured, when preparing it, to select materials from Origen for drawing out a sketch in systematic form, somewhat in the manner of Neander's remarks (*Church History*, i. 274), of Celsus's views, concerning (1) God and creation; (2) man's moral state; (3) the Hebrew and Christian religions in their sacred books and doctrines. But on the publication of Pressensé's work (*Hist. de l'Eglise*, 2ᵉ série, ii. pp. 104–142), he perceived the plan of arrangement there suggested to possess so much more life, that he adopted it in the text. Pressensé considers that, by a careful study of the fragments of Celsus quoted by Origen, he is able to reproduce a picture of the whole work, as well as to gather his opinions. Such an arrangement must necessarily be hypothetical, like Niebuhr's treatment of Roman history, though extremely probable. It will be observed however, by noticing the references to Origen's work in the foot-notes of Pressensé's text, and of Lecture II. in this volume, that the arrangement suggested for Celsus's treatise does not always coincide with the order in which Origen has quoted the parts of it. Also the references to the later books of Origen will be seen to be fewer than to the earlier; a circumstance which arises from the quotations from Celsus's work being fewer in those books, and from the thoughts of Origen in them being a continuation of those presented earlier. Pressensé's arrangement has the disadvantage too of leaving out many of the critical difficulties which Celsus alleges in the scriptures; but he rightly points out that they are all corollaries from a philosophical principle. The reader may accordingly consult Neander for a systematic view of Celsus's opinions, and Pressensé for a theory of the arrangement of his work.

It may be useful to give a brief statement of the order in which Celsus's objections occur in Origen's treatise, so as to show the manner in which the subject is there developed.

The first half of book i. is prefatory (ch. i–xl.); the second half, together with b. ii, contains the attack by the Jew on Christianity given in Lect. II. The early part of b. iii. (1–9) contains Origen's refutation of the Jew. The subsequent parts and remaining books give Origen's refutation of Celsus's own attack on Christianity. First, Celsus attacks the character of Christians in the remainder of b. iii. In b. iv. he returns to his attack on Judaism, and on the scriptures of the Old Testament, especially on many of the narratives; either regarding them as false, or as borrowed; and objecting to their anthropomorphic character; also objecting to the account of man's place in creation, and of divine interference. In b. v. he continues his attack on the doctrines of both religions, chiefly so far as he considers them to be untrue; and in b. vi. so far as he considers them to be borrowed, dragging to light the difference which existed between Judaism and Christianity. In b. vii. the subject of prophecy and some other doctrines, as well as the ethics of Christianity, are examined; and in b. viii, when the attack on Christianity is mainly over, a defence of paganism is offered by Celsus.

A detailed analysis of Origen's treatise, which is intricate, will be found in Schramm's *Analysis Patrum*, vol. iv. 1782. Pressensé's view of Origen's arguments is given, *Hist.* 2e Série, t. ii. pp. 281–361. See also Lardner's Works, viii. 19. Hase (*Church History*, § 51) refers to several German works which relate to Celsus.

Note 15. p. 56.

THE CHARGES AGAINST CHRISTIANS, AND CAUSES OF PERSECUTION, IN THE SECOND CENTURY.

The learned Kortholt, Professor at Kiel, in his work, the *Paganus Obtrectator, sive Liber de Calumniis Gentilium in Veteres Christianos* (1703), has carefully collected references to the objections raised by the Pagans against Christianity. He has arranged them according to the subjects, irrespective of the chronological order in which they were respectively suggested; viz. (1) those which relate to the origin and nature of Christianity, such as its novelty, its alleged want of originality, &c.; (2) false charges about public worship; (3) false charges about life and morals. If we exclude on the one hand those charges which are gathered out of Celsus (in Origen), and on the other those from apologists later than the date of Porphyry, the charges between these limits, which are learned from the apologists Minucius Felix, Theophilus (ad Autolycum), and Tertullian, exhibit the objections which were encountered in Rome, Syria, and North Africa, respectively. They chiefly belong to the prejudices adduced in the second and third of the classes made by Kortholt. Among the more intelligible objections which belong to his first class, are found the charges of the novelty of Christianity (ch. i. in his book), the superstitious character of it (ix. and x.), and the want of cultivation in its supporters (xi.). Among the prejudices about public worship (class 2) in his work, we meet with the charge of ass-worship (in Tertullian and Minucius Felix, ch. xi.); sky and sun worship (ii. and iii.); priest and cross worship (iv. and vi.); and secret sacred rites (ix.). Among the false charges about life and morals (which form class 3), we meet with that of private and nocturnal meetings forbidden by law, and the Agapæ (v.); Thyestean banquets (Theoph. and Tertull. ix.); secret insignia (xvi.); treason (vii.); and hatred of humanity (viii.).

All these charges will be seen to be such as mark the transition from a state of indifference to Christianity to that more distinct comprehension of its nature which afterwards existed. Their character indicates a moment when the new religion was forcing itself on public attention as a secret organization ramifying through the Roman world. In the main they resolved themselves into two heads; (1) the vulgar prejudices arising from ignorance; and (2) the alarm at the political danger arising from a vast secret society. The latter charges reappear in the works of later apologists; but the former are peculiar to this special period, between the time of Celsus and of Porphyry.

Among the vulgar prejudices thus named, the only two that need further mention are the charges of priest-worship and ass-worship. The former charge, named by Minucius Felix, ch. ix, and thus described here by a euphemism, may be seen in Kortholt, b. ii. ch. iv. p. 319; it probably arose from the homage paid to the bishop on bended knee at ordination. The latter, taken out of Minucius Felix (ch. ii.), and Tertullian (Apol. 16), is more singular and puzzling even after the discussions by older authors which Kortholt cites, b. ii. ch. i. p. 256, &c. But the fact of the charge has been corroborated by the recent discovery in excavations made in some substructions on the Palatine hill, of a *graffito* or pencil-scratching, in which a person is worshipping toward a cross, on which hangs suspended a human figure with the head of a horse, or perhaps wild ass, and underneath is the inscription "Alexamenus is worshipping God," Αλεξαμενος σεβετε [sic for σεβεται] Θεον. It can hardly be doubted that it is a pagan caricature of Christian worship, embodying the absurd prejudice which Minucius names. A brief account of it may be seen in the *Edinburgh Review*, No. 224, for October, 1859, p. 436, and more fully in *Un Graffito Blasfemo nel Palazzo dei Cesari* (*Civiltà Cattolica*, serie iii. vol. iv. Roma, 1856). The difficulty that the inscription is in Greek, will be explained by the fact that the church of Rome was Greek as late as the time of the writings of the so-called Hippolytus.

The other great class of objections to Christianity, which consisted in imputing the charge of treason, expressed itself in deeds as well as words, and was made the ground of the public persecution of them.

We cannot wonder that the profession of Christianity exposed persons to the suspicion of treason. When we add the fact that Christians declined obstinately to conform to the practice which had grown up, of performing sacrifice to the honour of the reigning emperors as the impersonation of the dignity of the state; and when we consider the organization among Christians, the league of purpose which was evident among them, we can understand how fully they laid themselves open to the charge of treason, the "crimen læsæ majestatis." Perhaps too at particular moments they were in danger of giving real ground for suspicion in reference to this point. The warnings of St. Paul and St. Peter give ground for inferring that there was danger of this even in their times. (Rom. xiii. 1 seq.; 1 Pet. ii. 13 seq.)

A greater difficulty than discovering plausible grounds which may have created the suspicion of treason is, to find the causes why a people so tolerant as the Romans should exhibit so persecuting a spirit against Christianity; but we must remember, first, that the idea as distinct from the practice of toleration was unknown; and secondly, that the practice of toleration was only supposed to be obligatory when the particular religion had been licensed.

The idea of man's universal rights, of universal religious freedom and liberty of conscience, was alien to the views of the whole ancient world. Indeed it is of quite modern introduction. It was not known even in Christendom, not even in the protestant part of it, till the seventeenth century. It was Milton who first enunciated the principle in its breadth. The idea of individualism, though long in spreading, was created in germ by two causes; viz. the free spirit of independence introduced by the Teutonic system; and the idea of the sacredness of the individual soul introduced through Christianity. If the highest end of man be to live for eternity, not to live for society, the individual is invested with a new dignity; and we feel the impropriety of trespassing upon the sphere for which each man is personally responsible. In the ancient world however, where this idea was unknown, all the elements of life, religion, and morals, were made subordinate to the political. The state was supreme. Looked at accordingly from the ancient point of view, a defection from the religion of the state could not appear otherwise than as a crime against the state. The Romans did certainly exercise religious toleration to the religions of nations which they conquered; and in this way the religion of the Jews was a tolerated creed, a *religio licita;* but it was such for the Jews alone; and deviation from the state religion was, as we know from the great lawyers, unlawful. Though doubtless from the abundance of foreigners who crowded to Rome, many foreign religious practices became common, yet a special decree of the senate was necessary before any Roman citizen could be allowed to join in the observance of any such foreign rites. When we consider the free use made by the Christians, for the purposes of worship and burial, of the catacombs, by which the plain in the neighbourhood of Rome is honeycombed, we may conjecture that the vigilance of the imperial police cannot have been strictly exercised; yet occasionally severe laws were passed to repress the evil of the introduction of foreign sacred rites. We may thus accordingly understand the causes of the persecution of Christians, as we before understood the grounds of the prejudice against them.

Note 16. p. 61.

MODERN CRITICISM ON THE BOOK OF DANIEL.

Some account of the modern criticism on the book of Daniel has been introduced into the text of Lect. II. (see pp. 60, 61,) and the chief recent writers on it have been enumerated (p. 60, note[89]). Also the refutation of one argument used against the authenticity of the book, viz. that drawn from the occurrence of Greek words in it, was given in a note on p. 60.

The other arguments which have been advanced against it, in addition to those there named, are, (1) that the angelology and ascetic doctrines are too recent to be of the time of Daniel; (2) that the miracles are of a "grotesque" character, like those which belong to the apocryphal books; (3) that the measure of the golden statue of Dura, sixty cubits by six, is irreconcileable with any theory of proportion suited to the human figure, and still more so with the canon of Assyrian art, as seen in their sculpture, and can apply only to an obelisk; (4) that Daniel has made honourable mention of himself; (5) that the position of the book in the third part of the Jewish canon, the Cethubim or Hagiographa, shows that it was written later than the captivity.

The replies made to these objections are as follows: In reference to No. (1), it is denied that the angelology and asceticism necessarily prove a late period, by referring to traces of them in earlier Hebrew literature: No. (2) that the difficulty which has reference to the character of the miracles is only one of degree; and that the greatness of a miracle is no absolute ground for disbelief if miracles be once admitted: (3) the inferences about the statue are conceded, but reconciled with the text. As the word צֶלֶם (iii. 1) does not necessarily mean a statue (see Buxtorf's *Lexicon*, *sub voc.*), it is possible to conceive it to apply to an obelisk, the existence of which in Assyria is confirmed by recent excavations. (4) Daniel's honourable mention of himself is not improper when taken in its connexion. (5) The argument which relates to the third division of the canon is a difficulty common to several other books, and depends on the theory that the principle of arrangement of the three parts of the canon was founded on the date of composition, and not on the subject matter, which is disputed.

In reference to the definite character of the predictions in the book of Daniel, the difficulty stated in the text (p. 61), reply is easy. If the miraculous character of prophecy be admitted, the definite character, though a peculiarity, cannot be a difficulty. The definiteness too in this instance does not differ in kind, hardly even in degree, from the case of other prophecies, but must be admitted to be paralleled elsewhere, if the objector does not assail those equally by the same process. The pretence that the definite character ends at the reign of Antiochus is shown to be incorrect, by proving (1) that the prophecy about the Messiah (ix. 24–26) cannot refer to the Maccabean deliverers; and (2) that the fourth empire predicted is the Roman, which thus would be equally future even to a writer of the Maccabean era.

The further argument used in defence of the book, that the New Testament authenticates the authorship of Daniel, is necessarily only of value to those who admit, first, the authority of the New Testament, and who, secondly, allow that the New Testament writers never accommodate themselves on questions of criticism to the mental state of their hearers. The opponents of this view on the contrary assert, that the quotations in the New Testament only affirm the predicate, not the subject; the truth of the theological sentiment quoted, not the literary question of the authorship of the book from which it is quoted.

An instructive paper on the book of Daniel by Mr. Westcott appeared in Smith's *Biblical Dictionary*, from which a few of the references to authors on Daniel (p. 60, note [89]) were taken; and another in Kitto's *Biblical Encyclopædia* by the lamented Hävernick.

Note 17. p. 64.

THE REPLY OF EUSEBIUS TO HIEROCLES.

In his book against Hierocles, Eusebius states (b. i.), that he refutes only that portion of the work which related to Apollonius of Tyana; referring to Origen's answer to Celsus for a reply to the remainder of it; and discusses only the parallel of Apollonius and Jesus Christ. In b. i. he gives an outline of the argument of his opponent, with quotations, and states his own opinion about Apollonius; throwing discredit on the veracity of the sources of the memoirs; and proceeds to criticise the prodigies attributed to him, arguing that the statements are incredible, or borrowed, or materially contradictory. Discussing each book in succession, he replies in b. i. to the statements respecting the early part of Apollonius's life; in b. ii. to that which concerned the journey into India; in b. iii. to that which related to his intercourse with the Brahmins; in b. iv. to his journey in Greece; in b. v. to his introduction to Vespasian in Egypt; in b. vi. and vii. to his miracles; and in b. viii. to his pretence to foreknowledge. He adds remarks on his death, and on the necessity of faith; and repeats his opinion respecting the character of Apollonius.

Note 18. p. 67.

THE PHILOPATRIS OF THE PSEUDO-LUCIAN.

This dialogue was held to be genuine by Fabricius; but Gesner disproved it, *De Philopatride Lucianeo Dialogo Dissertatio*, 1730. See also Neander's *Church History*, E. T. (Bohn) iii. 127, note.

The work hardly merits an analysis. Critias, looking ill, is met by Triepho. After a little banter, in which Triepho makes fun of the gods by whom Critias swears, and of their history (§ 2–18), Critias confesses that the cause that has made him pale is the hearing bad news at an assembly of Christians. Having first heard two Christian sermons, the one by a coughing preacher, who was proclaiming release from debt, the other by a threadbare mountaineer preaching a golden age, he had afterwards been persuaded to go to a private Christian meeting; and it was the prediction which he there heard of woes to the state which had so much frightened him, § 20–27. Triepho has not patience to hear him narrate the particulars. Another person enters, and the curtain falls.

The theology of the dialogue is, if viewed on its negative side, the ridicule of heathen mythology and of Christian doctrines and habits; and on its positive, the proclamation of one God as the object of worship. The work exhibits internal evidence of a knowledge of Christian practices, § 20, &c., and Christian doctrines, such as the Trinity, § 12; uses Christian phraseology, § 18; and calls Christians by the name given by Julian, Galilæan, § 12.

Note 19. p. 67.

THE WORK OF JULIAN AGAINST CHRISTIANITY.

It has been already stated that our knowledge of the contents of Julian's lost book is obtained from Cyril's reply to it; the text of which is accordingly given in Spanheim's edition of Julian. It is supposed to have consisted of seven books; but Cyril replies only to three.

In the brief account given in the text of Lect. II. no attempt was made to form a hypothetical restoration of Julian's work from the fragments, such as that which Pressensé has attempted with regard to Celsus; but only a few of Julian's principles were presented concerning the following subjects: (1) on God; (2) on the Hebrew, and (3) the Christian religion. A few hints however toward such a scheme may not be uninteresting. If, as seems probable, Cyril took the statements of Julian in the order in which they stood in the now lost work, the plan of Julian's work may have been somewhat as follows.

He proposed to institute a comparison between the Hebrew and Christian religions and literature on the one hand, and the Greek on the other. If we may judge from the purport of b. i. of Cyril's work, Julian laid himself open to an attack by maintaining the superior antiquity of heathenism, forgetting that the Hebrew system was older than the Greek. At least Cyril establishes this elaborately, and argues the direct derivation of many parts of the heathen system from the Jews. The argument on Julian's part seems to have been conducted by an examination of successive points in the Hebrew history and system. In the beginning the Hebrew cosmogony suggested an argument for the superiority of the Platonic theory over the Mosaic. (*Cyril.* b. ii.) Next he successively attacked the account of Paradise as a fable; entering upon both the probability of the story (*Id.* b. iii.) and the moral features of the Deity brought out in the narrative. He seems also to have passed from the idea of creation to that of providence, and to have dwelt on the inferiority of the Hebrew scheme as a theory of providence, in having an absence of inferior deities beneath the supreme one; and resists the idea of the obligation of all men to embrace one creed, inasmuch as they do not possess one character. (*Id.* b. iv.) Next, turning to the Mosaic moral law, he argued against its originality, except in relation to the sabbath; and passing through several of the narratives of Jewish history, he pointed out characteristics of anger in the Jewish conception of Deity; and compared by instances the Greek legislators and kings with Jewish. (*Id.* b. v.) Next he seems to have passed from Judaism to Christianity, and attacked the miracles, and the Christian morals and practices; challenged the reasons for prophecy; and rallied the Christians on accepting a religion derived from so insignificant a nation as the Jews. (*Id.* b. vi.) He seems next to have returned to the comparison of Greek and Hebrew warriors, and of Greek and Jewish science, and the educational value of the two literatures; and reverted to the subject of Christianity, by representing it as a deviation from the very religion on which it depended. (*Id.* b. vii.) He continued this argument by the special example of prophecy, examining several instances wherein he contended that Christians had abandoned the Jewish sense of them. (*Id.* b. viii.) Next he seems to have continued a similar argument with regard to the Jewish typical system, and the utter dissimilarity of the Christian ideas from its purpose (*Id.* b. ix.); next to have assailed Christianity, by trying to show that there had been a similar development in Christianity itself, and a departure from its primitive form analogous to that which Christianity bore to Judaism, alleging, incorrectly, that St. John was the first to teach the divinity of Christ; and instanced examples, objectionable in practice, such as the worship of martyrs' tombs; and alleged against Christianity an eclectic spirit which had appropriated parts of the Jewish system but not the whole. (*Id.* b. x.)

The reader must however be apprised that the above scheme is entirely hypothetical. The objections of Julian are facts; the *lacunæ* are filled up by conjecture.

The general spirit of Cyril's answer is the *argumentum ad hominem;* showing that the same faults, even if true, are equally true of the Greek scheme of religion.

LECTURE III.

Note 20. p. 89.

ON THE LEGENDARY WORK, ENTITLED "DE TRIBUS IMPOSTORIBUS."

FULL particulars concerning the chapter in literary history which relates to this work, will be found in Prosper Marchand's *Dictionnaire Historique*, 1758 (vol. i. pp. 312–319), and more briefly in F. W. Genthe's *De Imposturis Religionum breve Compendium*, 1833. Both give lists of the earlier writers who have treated of the subject; among which the most useful will be found to be B. G. Struve, *Dissertatio de Doctis Impostoribus*, 1703 (§ 9–23); De La Monnaie, *Lettre sur le Prêtendu Livre;* and Calmet, *Dictionnaire*, article *Imposteur*.

The rumours concerning the existence of a book with the title "De Tribus Impostoribus" commence in the thirteenth century. About the sixteenth, more definite but still unsatisfactory statements appear respecting its existence. Its authorship has been attributed to above twenty distinguished persons; such as Frederick II, Boccaccio, Pomponatius, Bruno, Vanini, &c.; the reasons for which in each case are explained in Marchand. De La Monnaie however wrote, questioning the existence of the book. A reply to his letter respecting it was published in French at the Hague in 1716, which pretended to offer an analysis of the ancient work; the falsehood of which however is shown by the Spinozist philosophy contained in it. Genthe in his tract, besides a literary introduction in German, republishes the French tract just named; and also a second tract in Latin, equally a fabrication, bearing a slightly different title, *De Imposturis Religionum*, Lucianlike in its tone, which, by an allusion to Loyola (§ 20), cannot be older than the sixteenth century, and is probably of German origin. Both writers conclude that the existence of the book in the middle ages was legendary. Renan (*Averroes*, pp. 280, and 272–300), and Laurent (*La Reforme*, pp. 345–8), coincide in this conclusion. The title was a *mot*, not a fact.

It is hardly necessary to state that the numerous writers who, like Kortholt, have adopted the title "De Tribus Impostoribus" for their books, have merely used the name in irony, and do not profess to give transcripts of the old work.

LECTURE IV.

Note 21. p. 118.

ON SOME TECHNICAL TERMS IN THE HISTORY OF UNBELIEF.

THERE are a few terms, which are frequently used in reference to unbelief, of which it would be interesting to trace the meaning and history. A few notes in reference to this subject may both prevent ambiguity and throw some light on a chapter in the history of language. The words alluded to are the following: 1. INFIDEL; 2. ATHEIST; 3. PANTHEIST; 4. DEIST; 5. NATURALIST; 6. FREETHINKER; 7. RATIONALIST; 8. SCEPTIC.

1. INFIDEL.—This word began to be restricted as a technical term, about the time of the Crusades and throughout the middle ages, to denote Mahometan; as being *par excellence* the kind of unbelievers with which Christians were brought into contact. Perhaps the first instance of its use in the more modern sense, of disbeliever generally, is in the Collect for Good Friday, "all Jews, Turks, *infidels*, heretics;" which words were apparently inserted by the Reformers in the first Prayer Book (1547); the rest of the prayer, except these words, existing in the Latin Collect of the ancient Service-book from which it is translated. Ordinarily however, during the sixteenth century, it is found in the popular sense of *unfaithful;* a meaning which the increasing prevalence of Latin words was likely to bring into use. In writers of the seventeenth, the use of it in the sense of *unbeliever* becomes more common: an instance from Milton is cited in Richardson's Dictionary. In the beginning of the eighteenth century it becomes quite common in theological writers in its modern sense; and toward the end of the century was frequently appropriated to express the form of unbelief which existed in France; a use which probably arose from the circumstance that the French unbelievers did not adopt a special name for their tenets, as the English did, who had a positive creed, (Deism,) and not merely, like the French, a disintegration of belief.

2. ATHEIST.—This word needs little discussion. In modern times it is first applied by the theological writers of the sixteenth century, to describe the unbelief of such persons as Pomponatius; and in the seventeenth it is used, by Bacon (Essay on Atheism),

Milton, (Paradise lost, b. vi.), and Bunyan (Pilgrim), to imply general unbelief, of which the disbelief in a Deity is the principal sign. Toward the end of the same century it is not unfrequently found, e. g. in Kortholt's *De Tribus Impostoribus*, 1680, to include Deism such as that of Hobbes, as well as blank Pantheism like Spinoza's, which more justly deserves the name. The same use is seen in Colerus's work against Spinoza, *Arcana Atheismi Revelata.* Tillotson (serm. i. on Atheism); and Bentley (Boyle Lectures) use the word more exactly; and the invention of the term Deism induced, in the writers of the eighteenth century, a more limited and exact use of the former term. But in Germany, Reimannus (*Historia Univ. Atheismi*, 1725, p. 437 seq.) and Buddeus (*De Atheismo et Superstitione*, 1723, ch. iii. § 2), use it most widely, and especially make it include disbelief of immortality. Also Walch, *Bibliotheca Theol. Selecta*, 1757, uses it to include the Pantheism of Spinoza, (vol. i. p. 676, &c.) This transference of the term to embrace all kinds of unbelief has been well compared with the extension of the term βάρβαρος by the Greeks.[11] The wide use of the term is partly to be attributed to the doubt which Christian men had whether any one could really disbelieve the being of a God,—an opinion increased by the Cartesian notions then common concerning innate ideas; and whether accordingly the term Atheist could mean anything different from Deist. Compare Buddeus's *Isagoge*, p. 1203, and the chapter "An dentur Athei" in his work *De Atheismo.* (ch. i.) By the time of Stapfer's work, *Instit. Theol. Polem.* 1744, the two terms were distinguished; see vol. ii. ch. vi. and vii. and cfr. p. 587.

The term was subsequently applied to describe the views of the French writers, such as D'Holbach, who did not see the necessity for believing in a personal first Cause. In more modern times it is frequently applied to such writers as Comte; whose view is indeed atheism, but differs from that of former times, in that it is the refusal to entertain the question of a Deity as not being discoverable by the evidence of sense and science, rather than the absolute denial of his existence. The Comtists also hold firmly the marks of order, law, mind, in nature, and not the fortuitous concurrence of atoms, as was the case with the atheists of France.

3. PANTHEIST.—One of the first uses of this word is by Toland in the *Pantheisticon*, 1720, where however it has its ancient polytheistic sense. It is a little later that it passes from the idea of the worship of the whole of the gods to the worship of the entire universe looked at as God.

This exacter application of it is more modern. It is now used to denote the disbelief of a personal first Cause: but a distinction

[11] The transition of the word *miscreant* from its original meaning of misbeliever (mécroyant, miscredente), to its modern use as a mark of opprobrium, is a similar instance. This change is a proof of the instinctive association of the dependence of right conduct on right belief. It is about the time of Shakspeare that the change of meaning begins to appear. See *Richardson's Dictionary*, *sub voc.*

ought to be made between the Pantheism like that of Averroes, which regards the world as an emanation, and sustained by an *anima mundi;* and that which, like the view of Spinoza, regards the sum total of all things to be Deity. This distinction was noticed and illustrated in p. 107. The account of the word in Krug's *Philosoph. Lexicon* is worth consulting.

4. DEIST.—One of the first instances of the use of this word occurs in Viret, *Epistr. Dedicat. du 2. vol de l'Instruction Chrétienne*, 1563, quoted by Bayle, *Dictionnaire*, (note under the word *Viret.*) It is appropriated in the middle of the seventeenth century by Herbert to his scheme, and afterwards by Blount (*Oracles of Reason*, p. 99), to distinguish themselves from Atheists. In strict truth, Herbert calls himself a *Theist;* which slightly differs from the subsequent term *Deist*, in so far as it is intended to convey the idea of that which he thought to be the true worship of God. It is theism as opposed to error, rather than natural religion as opposed to revealed: whereas deism always implies a position antagonistic to revealed religion. But the distinction is soon lost sight of; and Nichols (1696) entitles his work against the deists, *Conference with a Theist.* Towards the close of the seventeenth century, and in the beginning of the eighteenth, the Christian writers sometimes even use Deist as interchangeable with Atheist, as shown above. It is also used as synonymous with one of the senses of the word *Naturalist.* See below, under the latter word; and cfr. Stapfer, *Inst. Polem.* vol. ii. p. 742, with p. 883.

5. NATURALIST.—This word is used in two senses; an objective and a subjective. Naturalism, in the former, is the belief which identifies God with nature; in the latter, the belief in the sufficiency of natural as distinct from revealed religion. The former is Pantheism, the latter Deism. In the former sense it is applied to Spinoza and others; e. g. in Walch's *Biblioth. Theol. Select.* i. 745 seq. In the latter sense it occurs as early as 1588 in France, in the writings of J. Bodin (*Colloq. Heptapl.* 31. Rem. 2); and towards the end of the seventeenth century both in Germany and England, e. g. in Kortholt's *De Trib. Impost.* 1680; and the Quaker, Barclay's *Apologia*, 1679, p. 28. At the end of the seventeenth century, and in the eighteenth, the name was applied in England to deists, e. g. in Nichols's *Conference with a Theist*, pref. § 15); and in Germany it became a commonly known word, owing to the spread of the Wolffian philosophy. Stapfer (*Instit. Theol. Polem.* 1744, vol. ii. p. 881), using Wolffian phraseology, divides this latter kind of naturalism into two kinds, viz. philosophical and theological. The philosophical kind maintains the sufficiency of natural religion, and disbelieves revealed; the theological kind holds the truth of revelation, but regards it as unnecessary, as being only a republication of natural religion. The

adherent of the former is the "Naturalist" of Kant; the latter his "pure Rationalist" (*Verg. Religion Innerhalb, &c.*); the former the Deist, the latter the Rationalist, of a school like that of Wegscheider, &c. (See Lect. VI.)

Cfr. Bretschneider's *Handbuch der Dogmatik*, i. 72. note. Hahn, *De Rationalismi Indole* (quoted by Rose on Rationalism, 2d ed. Introd. p. 20) names writers who make a third kind of naturalism, viz. Pelagianism; but this is rare.

6. FREETHINKER.—This term first appears toward the close of the seventeenth century. It is used of Toland, "a candid Freethinker," by Molyneux, in a letter to Locke 1697 (*Locke's Works*, fol. ed. iii. 624); and Shaftesbury in 1709 speaks of "our modern free-writers," *Works*, vol. i. p. 65. But it was Collins in 1713, in his *Discourse of Freethinking*, who first appropriated the name to express the independence of inquiry which was claimed by the deists. The use of the word expressed the spirit of a nation like the English, in which, subsequently to the change of dynasty, freedom to think and speak was held to be every man's charter. Lechler has remarked the absence of a parallel word in other languages. The French expression *Esprit fort*, the title of a work of La Bruyère, does not convey quite the same idea as *Freethinker*. *Esprit* expresses the French liveliness, not the reflective self-consciousness of the English mind of the eighteenth century: the *fort* is a relic of the pride of feudalism; whilst the *free* of the English Freethinker implies the reaction against it. The English term smacks of democracy; the French carries with it the notion of aristocracy. (Lechler, *Gesch. des Engl. Deismus*, p. 458.) There is no word to express the English idea in foreign languages, except the literal translation of the English term. Even then, in French the expression *la libre pensée* has changed its meaning; since it is now frequently used to describe the struggle, good as well as evil, of the human mind against authority. It thus loses the unfavourable sense which originally belonged to the corresponding English expression.

7. RATIONALIST.—The history of the term is hard to trace. The first technical use of the adjective *rational* seems to have been about the seventeenth century, to express a school of philosophy. It had probably passed out of the old sense of *dialectical* (cfr. Brucker's *Hist. Phil.* iii. 60.), into the use just named; which we find in Bacon, to express rational philosophy, as opposed to empirical, (see a quotation from Bacon's *Apophthegms* in Richardson's *Dictionary*, *sub voc.*); or, as in North's *Plutarch*, 1657, p. 984, for intellectual philosophy as opposed to mathematical and moral. The word Rationalist occurs in Clarendon, 1646 (*State Papers*, vol. ii. p. 40), to describe a party of presbyterians who appealed only to "what their reason dictates them in church and state." Hahn (*De Rationalismi Indole*) states that Amos Come-

nius similarly used the term in 1661 in a depreciatory sense. The treatise of Locke on the *Reasonableness of Christianity* caused Christians and Deists to appropriate the term, and to restrict it to religion. Thus, by Waterland's time, it had got the meaning of false reasoning on religion. (*Works*, viii. 67.) And, passing into Germany, it appears to have become the common name to express philosophical views of religion, as opposed to supernatural. In this sense it occurs as early as 1708 in Sucro, quoted by Tholuck, *Vermischt. Schriften*, ii. pp. 25, 26, and in Buddeus, *Isagoge*, 1730, pp. 213 and 1151. It is also used often as equivalent to naturalism, or adherence to natural religion; with the slight difference that it rather points to mental than physical truth.

The name has often been appropriated to the Kantian or critical philosophy, in which rationalism was distinguished from naturalism in the mode explained under the latter word. (See Kant's *Religion Innerhalb der Grenzen der Blossen Vernunft*, pp. 216, 17.) During the period when Rationalism was predominant as a method in German theology, the meaning and limits of the term were freely discussed. The period referred to is that which we have called in Lect. VI. p. 230 the second subdivision of the first of the three periods, into which the history of German theology is there divided; viz. from 1790–1810; occupying the interval when the Wolffian philosophy had given place to the Kantian, and the philosophy of Fichte and Jacobi had not yet produced the revival under Schleiermacher. This form of rationalism also continued to exist during the lifetime of its adherents, contemporaneously with the new influence created by Schleiermacher. (See Lect. VI.) The discussion was not a verbal one only, but was intimately connected with facts. The rationalist theologians wished to define clearly their own position, as opposed on the one hand to deists and naturalists, and on the other to supernaturalists. The result of the discussion seemed to show the following parties: (1) two kinds of Supernaturalists, (*a*) the Biblical, such as Reinhardt, resembling the English divines of the eighteenth century;[12] (*β*) the Philosophical, sometimes called Rational Supernaturalists, as the Kantian theologian Staüdlin: (2) two kinds of Rationalists, (*a*) the Supernatural Rationalists, like Bretschneider, who held on the evidence of reason the necessity of a revelation, but required its accordance with reason, when communicated; (*β*) the pure Rationalists, like Wegscheider, Röhr, and Paulus, who held the sufficiency of reason; and, while admitting revelation as a fact, regarded it as the republication of the religion of nature. It is this last kind which answers to the "theological naturalist," named above, under the word *Naturalist*. It is also the form which is called *Rationalismus vulgaris* (as being opposed to the later *scientific*), though the term is not admitted by its adherents. This

[12] It is hardly necessary to state, that when the tone of the English theological writers of the eighteenth century is described as rationalism, it is used in a good sense. (E. g. *Essays and Reviews*, Ess. vi.) The writers of that century would be classified under the school of supernaturalists here named.

rationalism stands distinguished from naturalism, i. e. from "philosophical naturalism" or deism, by having reference to the Christian religion and church; but it differs from supernaturalism, in that reason, not scripture, is its formal principle, or test of truth; and virtue, instead of "faith working by love," is its material principle, or fundamental doctrine. A further subdivision might be made of this last into the dogmatic (Wegscheider), and the critical (Paulus). Cfr. Bretschneider's *Dogmatik*, i. 81, and see Lect. VI. Also consult on the above account Kahnis, p. 168, and Lechler's *Deismus*, p. 193, note; Hagenbach's *Dogmengesch.* § 279, note.

This account of the term being the result of the controversy as to the meaning of the words, it only remains to name some of the works which treated of it.

The dispute on the word *Rationalism* is especially seen at two periods, (1) about the close of the last century, when the supernaturalists, such as Reinhardt and Storr, were maintaining their position against rationalism. One treatise, which may perhaps be considered to belong to this earlier period, is J. A. H. Tittmann's *Ueber Supernaturalismus, Rationalismus, und Atheismus*, 1816; (2) in the disputes against the school of Schleiermacher, when supernaturalism was no longer thrown on the defensive. This was marked by several treatises on the subject, such as Staüdlin's *Geschichte des Rationalismus und Supernaturalismus* 1826, (see the definitions given in it, pp. 3 and 4;) Bretschneider's remarks in his *Dogmatik* (i. pp. 14, 71, 80 ed. 1838); and *Historische Bemerkungen Ueber den Gebrauch der Ausdrücke Rational. und Supernat.* (*Oppositions-Schrift.* 1829. 7. 1); A. Hahn, *De Rationalismi qui dicitur Verâ Indole*, 1827, in which he reviews the attempts of Bretschneider and Staüdlin to give the historic use of the word; Röhr's *Briefe Ueber Rationalismus*, pp. 14–16; Paulus's *Resultate aus den Neuesten Versuch des Supernat. Gegen den Rationalismus*, 1830; Wegscheider's *Inst. Theol. Christianæ Dogmaticæ* (7th ed. 1833. §§ 11, 12, pp. 49–67), which is full of references to the literature of the subject. The controversy was aggravated and in part was due to the translation of Mr. H. J. Rose's *Sermons on Rationalism.* He was answered by Bretschneider in a tract, in which that theologian entered upon the defence of the rationalist position. Mr. Rose (*Introd.* to 2d ed. 1829, p. 17) enters briefly upon the history of the name. Krug (*Philos. Lexicon*) also gives many instances of its use in German theology.

To complete the account it is only necessary to add, that it is made clear by Lectures VI. and VII. that if subsequent theological thought in Germany to the schools now described, be called Rationalism for convenience by English writers, the term is then used in a different sense from that in which it is applied in speaking of the older forms.

8. SCEPTIC.—This term was first applied specifically to one school

of Greek philosophers, about B. C. 300, followers of Pyrrho of Elis (see Ritter's *Hist. of Phil.* E. T. iii. 372–398; Staüdlin's *Geschichte des Scepticismus*, vol. i; Tafel's *Geschichte und Kritik des Skepticismus*, 1836; Donaldson's *Greek Lit.* ch. xlvii. § 5); and also to a revival of this school about A. D. 200. (See Ritter. Id. iii. 258–357; Donaldson, ch. lvi. § 3.) The tenet was a general disbelief of the possibility of knowing realities as distinct from appearances. The term thus introduced, gradually became used in the specific sense of theological as distinct from philosophical scepticism, often with an indirect implication that the two are united. Walch restricts the name Sceptic to the latter kind. Writing about those who are called Indifferentists (*Bibl. Theol. Select.* i. 976), he subdivides them into two classes; viz. those who are indifferent through liberality, and those who are so through unbelief. The former are the "Latitudinarians," the latter the Sceptics above named. Cfr. also Buddeus, *Isagoge*, pp. 1208–10. In more recent times the term has gained a still more generic sense in theology, to express all kinds of religious doubt. But its use to express philosophical scepticism as distinct from religious has not died out. In this sense Montaigne, Bayle (cfr. Staüdlin's *Gesch. des Scept.* p. 204), Huet, Berkeley, Hume, and De Maistre, were Sceptics; i. e. sceptical of the certitude of one or more branches of the human faculties. Sometimes also it is used to express systems of philosophy which teach disbelief in the reality of metaphysical science; e. g. the positive school of Comte; but this is an ambiguous use of the term. For philosophical scepticism may be of two kinds; viz. the disbelief in the possibility of the attainment of truth by means of the natural faculties of man; and the disbelief of the possibility of its attainment by means of metaphysical, as distinct from physical, methods. The former is properly called Philosophical Scepticism, the latter not so. Pyrrho in ancient times, and Hume in modern, represent the former; the Positivists of modern times, and perhaps the Sophists of the fifth century B. C., represent the latter. It is hardly necessary to repeat that the philosophical scepticism proper of Berkeley and Hume must not be confounded with religious. They may be connected, as in Hume, or disconnected, as in Berkeley or De Maistre. See on this subject Morell's *Hist. of Philos.* i. p. 68, ii. ch. vi.

On the subject of the words explained in this note see, besides the works referred to, Walch's *Bibl. Theol. Select.* i. ch. v. sect. 5, 6, 7, 11, and iii. ch. vii. sect. 10. § 4. 1757: Pfaff's *Introd. in Hist. Theol.* lib. ii. b. iii. § 2. 1725: Stapfer's *Inst. Theol. Polem.* ii. ch. vi, vii, x; iv. ch. xiii. 1744: Reimannus' *Hist. Univ. Ath.* sectio i. 1725: J. F. Buddeus's *De Atheismo*, 1737, ch. i. and ii: J. F. Buddeus's *Isagoge*, 1730, pp. 1203–1211: Lechler's *Gesch. des Deismus*, 1841; *Schlussbemerkungen*, p. 453 seq.: J. Fabricius, 1704, *Consid. Var. Controv.* p. 1: Staüdlin's *Gesch. des Skepticismus vorzüglich in Rücksicht auf. Moral. und Religion.* 1794: J. F.

Tafel's *Gesch. und Kritik des Skepticismus und Irrationalismus*, with reference to Philosophy, 1834.

Note 22. p. 136.

WOOLSTON'S DISCOURSES ON MIRACLES.

In addition to the notice of these Discourses given in the text, it may be well to give a brief account of their contents.

In Discourse I. Woolston aims at showing (α) that healing is not a proper miracle for a Messiah to perform, and that the fathers of the church understood the miracles allegorically: (β) that a literal interpretation of miracles involves incredibility, as shown in the miracle of the expulsion of the buyers and sellers from the temple, the casting out devils from the possessed man of the tombs, the transfiguration, the marriage of Cana, the feeding the multitudes: (γ) the meaning of Jesus when he appeals to miracles. In Discourse II. he selects for examination the miracle of the woman with the issue of blood, and also her with the spirit of infirmity; also the narrative of the Samaritan woman, the triumphal entry into Jerusalem, the temptation, the appearance of the spirits of the dead at the resurrection. In Discourse III. he selects the cursing of the fig-tree, and the miracle of the pool of Bethesda. It may be allowable to give one illustration of the coarse humour with which he rationalizes the sacred narrative in his explanation of this last miracle. He says of the healed man, "The man's infirmity was more laziness than lameness; and Jesus only shamed him out of his pretended idleness by bidding him to take up his stool and walk off, and not lie any longer like a lubbard and dissemble among the diseased." It will be perceived, that if the coarseness be omitted, the system of interpretation is the naturalist system afterwards adopted by the old rationalism (*rationalismus vulgaris*). In Discourse IV. he selects the healing with eye-salve of the blind man, the water made into wine at Cana; where he introduces a Jewish rabbi to utter blasphemy, after the manner of Celsus; and the healing of the paralytic who was let down through the roof, which, as being one of the most characteristic passages of Woolston, Dean Trench has selected for analysis. (*Notes on Miracles*, Introduction, p. 81.) In Discourse V. he discusses the three miracles of the raising of the dead; and in Discourse VI. the miracle of Christ's own resurrection.

His conclusion (in Disc. I.) is, that "the history of Jesus, as recorded in the evangelists, is an emblematical representation of his spiritual life in the soul of man; and his miracles figurative of his mysterious operations;" that the four Gospels are in no part a literal story, but a system of mystical philosophy or theology.

LECTURE V.

Note 23. p. 178.

THE LITERARY COTERIES OF PARIS IN THE EIGHTEENTH CENTURY.

An account of these coteries may be seen in Schlosser's *Hist. of Eighteenth Century*, (E. T.) vol. i. ch. ii. § 4; the particulars of which chapter he has gathered largely from the Autobiography of Marmontel, and from Grimm's Correspondence. See also Sainte-Beuve's Papers (*Portraits*, vol. ii.) on Espinasse and Geoffrin. These coteries were specially four: viz. (1) that of Madame De Tencin, mother of D'Alembert, which included Fontenelle, Montesquieu, Mairan, Helvetius, Marivaux, and Astruc; (2) of Madame Geoffrin, who took the place of De Tencin. It included, besides some of the above, Poniatowsky, Frederick the Great when in France, the Swedish Creutz, and Kaunitz, the whole of the Voltaire school, and at first Rousseau; (3) of Madame Du Deffant, contemporary with Geoffrin. This was less a coterie of fashion, and more entirely of intellect; and included Voltaire, D'Alembert, Hénault, and Horace Walpole when in Paris. Later Mlle. Espinasse took the place of Deffant, and this became the union-point for all the philosophical reformers, D'Alembert, Diderot, Turgot, and the Encyclopædists; (4) of D'Holbach, consisting of the most advanced infidels.

Note 24. p. 198.

THE TERM IDEOLOGY.

As the term *Ideology* has lately been employed in a novel theological sense, (e. g. *Essays and Reviews*, Ess. iv.), and as it is employed in these lectures in its ordinary sense, as known in metaphysical science, it may prevent ambiguity to state briefly the history of the term.

The word *Ideology*, as denoting the term to express metaphysical science, seems to have arisen in the French school of De Tracy at the close of the last century. Cfr. Krug's *Philos. Lexicon*, sub voc.

As early as Plato's time metaphysics was the science of ἰδέαι, i. e. of *forms;* but the word ἰδέα implied the objective form in the thing, not the subjective conception in the mind. It was Descartes who first appropriated the word Idea in the subjective sense of *notion.* This arose from the circumstance that in his philosophy he sought for the idea in the mind, instead of the essence in the thing contemplated, as had been the case in mediæval philosophy. In the following century Locke's inquiries, together with Berkeley's speculations, caused metaphysics to become *the science of ideas.* The representative theory of perception which was held, increased, if it did not cause, the confusion: all knowledge was restricted to ideas. The subsequent attempts of Condillac and others to carry forward the analysis of the formation of our ideas still farther, caused metaphysics to be restricted to them alone. This apparently was the reason why De Tracy gave the name of Ideology to the science of metaphysics in the *Elémens d'Idéologie.*[13]

It was the sceptical notion of the unreality of the objects as distinct from the ideas, partly the offshoot of a sensational philosophy, like that of De Tracy, partly of the spiritual philosophy of Germany, which farther caused the term Ideological to slide into the sense of *ideal;* a meaning of the term which the employment of it in English in recent theological controversy seems likely to make common.

Note 25. p. 195.

THE WORKS OF DR. GEDDES.

Towards the end of the eighteenth century, free thought began to manifest itself in England under a rationalistic form, in a Roman catholic, Dr. Geddes, who lived 1737–1802. (See Life by Mason Good, 1804.) Vol. i. of his *Translation* of the Bible appeared in 1792; vol. ii. in 1797; and his *Critical Remarks* (vol. i.) in 1800. His free criticism is seen in discussing the character of Moses (pref. to vol. i. of *Transl.*); the slaughter of the Canaanites (pref. to vol. ii.); Paradise (*Crit. Rem.* p. 35); the remarks on Genesis xlix. (Id. p. 142); on the Egyptian plagues (p. 182); on the passage of the Red sea (p. 200). As soon as the first volume was published the Catholic bishops silenced him. Geddes was a believer in Christianity; but felt so strongly the deist difficulties, that he sought to defend revelation by explaining away the supernatural from the Jewish history, and inspiration from the Jewish literature. His views, so far as they were not original, were probably derived from the incipient rationalistic

[13] In the time of Napoleon I. the circumstance that the ideological philosophers sympathised with the Revolution, in opposition to his régime, led to an application of the term as synonymous with Republican.

speculations of Germany, though he quoted almost none of the German except Michaelis and Herder. His position in the history of doubt is with the early rationalists, not with the deists. A writer of somewhat similar character, Mr. Evanson, a unitarian, wrote a critical attack on the Gospels, *The Dissonance of the Four generally received Evangelists*, in 1805.

Note 26. p. 196.

THE WORKS OF CONYERS MIDDLETON.

Dr. Conyers Middleton lived from 1683 to 1750. In 1749 he published *A Free Inquiry into the Miraculous Powers of the Early Church;* "by which it is shown that we have no sufficient reason to believe, upon the authority of the primitive fathers, that any such powers were continued to the church after the days of the apostles." He was attacked by Dodwell, Church, and Chapman, who described the work as discrediting miracles. The object of it was to place the church in the predicament of denying altogether the authority of the fathers, or else of admitting the truth of the Romish doctrine of miracles. Gibbon, when young, chose the latter horn of the dilemma. A list of Middleton's works in chronological order will be found in vol. i. of his *Miscellaneous Works* (1752). The one which created disputes in theology besides the above was, *An Anonymous Letter to Waterland*, 1731, in reference to his reply to Tindal's work; which was answered by Bishop Pearce. His posthumous work on *The Variations or Inconsistencies which are found among the Four Evangelists*, (Works, vol. ii. p. 22); his essay on *The Allegorical Interpretation of the Creation and Fall* (ii. 122); and his criticism in 1750 on bishop Sherlock's *Discourses on Prophecy*, may cause Middleton to be regarded as a rationalist. See his Works, ii. 24, 131, and iii. 183.

LECTURE VI.

Note 27. p. 213.

ON PIETISM IN GERMANY IN THE SEVENTEENTH CENTURY.

THE person who commenced the religious movement afterwards called Pietism, was John Arndt (1555–1621), who wrote *The True Christian*, a work as useful religiously, as Bunyan's *Pilgrim's Progress*, or Doddridge's *Religion in the Soul.*

Spener followed (1635–1705). The private religious meetings which he established about 1675, *Collegia Pietatis*, were the origin of the application of the name Pietism to the movement. One of his pupils was the saintly A. H. Francke, whose memoir was translated 1837. Paul Gerhardt, the well known author of the German hymns, also belonged to the same party. The university of Halle became the home of Pietism; and the orphan-house established in that town was renowned over Europe. The opposition of the old Lutheran party of other parts of Germany produced controversies which continued till about 1720; for an account of which, see Weismann, *Mem. Eccl. Hist. Sacr.* 1745, p. 1018 seq.

Pietism propagated its influence by means of Bengel in Würtemburg and the university of Tübingen, and in Moravia through Zinzendorf. Arnold and Thomasius belonged to this party at the beginning of the eighteenth century. Œtinger at Tübingen, Crusius at Leipsic, and, to a certain extent, Buddeus also, partook of the spirit of Pietism. It manifested a tendency to religious isolation; and in its nature combined the analogous movements subsequently carried out in England by Wesley and by Simeon respectively.

A brief account of it is given in Hase's *Church History*, § 409: and for a fuller account, see Schröckh, *Chr. Kirchengesch.* vol. viii. pp. 255–91; Pusey on *German Theology*, part i. (67–113); part. ii. ch. x; Amand Saintes, *Crit. Hist. of Rationalism*, E. T. ch. vii. Spener's character and life may be seen in Canstein's memoir of him; and in Weismann, pp. 966–72. A philosophical view of Pietism, as a necessary stage in the development of German religious life, is given by Dorner in the *Studien und Kritiken*, 1840, part ii. 137, *Ueber den Pietismus.* Kahnis, who himself quotes it,

(*Hist. of Germ. Prot.*) E. T. p. 102, regards Pietism as ministering indirectly to rationalism; much in the same way as bishop Fitzgerald criticised the similar evangelical movement of England, *Aids to Faith*, p. 49, &c.

Note 28. p. 224.

CLASSIFICATION OF SCHOOLS OF POETRY IN GERMANY.

The materials for understanding the awakening of literary tastes in the last century in Germany, through Lessing's influence, are furnished by Schlosser, *History of the Eighteenth Century.* See vol. i. ch. iii. E. T. for the period from the Pietists to Lessing; and ch. v. in reference to the Deutsche Bibliothek, and also vol. ii. ch. ii. § 3. See also Vilmar's *History of German Literature* (translated and abridged by Metcalfe).

It may facilitate clearness to name the classification of schools of German poetry and taste, which is given in the last-named work. They are divided into five classes: viz. I. that which was antecedent to Lessing, which is subdivided into (1) the Saxon school of Gottsched; and (2) the Swiss school of Bodmer, and of Wieland in his early manner; which was connected with the Gottingen school of Haller, Hagedorn, and Klopstock, together with the Stolbergs and Voss. II. Lessing, and writers influenced by him, such as (1) Kleist and the Prussian group; (2) Wieland in his second manner, and J. Paul Richter; (3) Kotzebue, who was a mixture of Wieland and Lessing. In these two periods Klopstock, Wieland, and Lessing, were the intellectual triumvirs. III. The "Sturm und Drang" period; the Weimar school with its second literary triumvirate, Herder, Goethe, Schiller. IV. The later schools: (1) the romantic, viz. the two Schlegels, Novalis, Tieck, Uhland, Fouqué; (2) the patriotic of the liberation wars, Arndt and Koerner. V. The modern school of disappointment and uneasy reaction against the absolute government, H. Heine and Grün.

It is an interesting psychological problem to trace the close analogy between the schools of poetical taste and the corresponding character in the contemporary criticism of ancient literature, the speculative philosophy, and the theology.

Note 29. p. 225.

THE WOLFENBÜTTEL FRAGMENTS.

It has been stated in the text that these were Fragments, which Lessing published in 1774 and the following years, of a larger work which he professed to have found in the library of Wolfenbüttel, where he was librarian. They were published in the third of the series of works, *Beiträge zur Geschichte und Literatur aus den Schätzen der Herzoglichen Bibliothek zu Wolfenbüttel*, under the title, *Fragmente Eines Ungenannten Herausgegeben von G. E. Lessing.*

After Lessing's death, C. A. E. Schmidt published further Fragments, under the title *Uebrige noch Ungedruckte Werke des Wolfenbüttelschen Fragmentisten. Ein Nachlass von G. E. Lessing.*

The authorship of the Fragments was suspected at the time by Hamann; but it remained generally unknown, and became as great a secret as the authorship of the Letters of Junius, until 1827, when the question was discussed by Gurlitt in the *Leipziger Literatur-Zeitung*, No. 55, and proof was offered that the author was Reimarus of Hamburg.

The result of this and subsequent investigations is as follows. The original work of Reimarus, from which the Fragments were taken, remains in MS. in the public library of Hamburg. It was entitled *Apologie oder Schutz-Schrift für die vernünftigen Verehrer Gottes.* When written, it was shown only to intimate friends. Lessing was allowed to take a copy, and showed the MS. to Mendelssohn in 1771. Lessing wished to publish it entire; but the censorship would not give the imprimatur. Consequently it came out in fragments among the series of contributions from the Wolfenbüttel library, which were free from the censorship. The pretended discovery of them in the library was a mere excuse; and there is proof in Lessing's remains that he admitted the fact. See the statement of these facts in *Lessing's Leben*, by Guhrauer, (of which, vol. i. is by Danzel; vol. ii. by Guhrauer,) vol. ii. b. iii. ch. iv. p. 133, note 3, and b. iv. p. 141.[14]

Several writers, subsequently to Gurlitt's examination of the question of authorship, have written, either on the question of the authorship of the Fragments, or on the contents of the larger work from which they are selections. In the *Zeitschrift für die Historische Theologie for* 1839, part iv. is an article composed from W. Körte's life of Thaer, in reference to the former question. Also Dr. W. Klose examined the original MS. in the Hamburg library, and published an account of it, with considerable extracts, in several of the numbers of the same journal, Niedner's *Zeitschrift*, 1850, (part iv; 1851, part iv; 1852, part iii.) It is in the preface (*Vorbericht*) to the first of these parts that the account of Reimarus's own mental history is given, to which allusion was made in the text of Lecture VI. (p. 225.)

During the last year the question has been made the subject of a monograph by the celebrated Strauss. He had heard of the existence of a copy of the original MS. in private hands at Hamburg, and proceeded to collate it with the view of publication.

[14] These references to Guhrauer were kindly suggested by the Rev. E. H. Hansell, Prælector of Theology in Magdalen College, who studied the Fragments a few years ago for lectures which he delivered on Lessing.

He found it to differ in some respects from the Fragments published by Lessing and Schmidt. He did not consider the hitherto unpublished parts of the work sufficiently important, either in a literary or historical point of view, to merit publication *in extenso;* but contented himself with stating the results of his study of it in a small work, *H. S. Reimarus und seine Schutz-Schrift, &c.* 1861. It contains a brief account of the literary question of the Fragments, and of Reimarus's life and stand-point; also an analysis of the unpublished parts of the work, written with the clearness which characterises all Strauss's didactic works. It would appear from the analysis that the pieces printed by Lessing were not only some of the ablest, but some of the least offensive of the whole work. The concluding pages contain some very interesting remarks, in which Strauss contrasts the criticism of the eighteenth century with that of the present day; the characteristics of the former being, that it charges imposture on the scripture writers; that of the latter, that it admits their honesty, but explains away their statements and opinions by reference to psychological and historical phenomena.

In addition to the sources given above, information is contained in the following works: Schröckh's *Christ Kirchengesch.* vi. 275; Schlosser's *History of the Eighteenth Century*, E. T. vol. ii. 266 seq.; Hagenbach's *Dogmengeschichte*, § 275 *notes*, (where reference is made to Guhrauer's *Bodin's Heptaplomeres*, 1841, p. 257 seq.;) *Conversations-Lexicon*, art. *Reimarus;* Amand Saintes' *History of Rationalism*, E. T. p. 84; Kahnis, *Id.* p. 145 seq.; K. Schwarz, *Lessing als Theolog*, of which ch. iv. is on the *Fragmenten-streit;* Strauss's *Kleine Schriften*, 1861; Lessing's *Werke*, xii. 503. (ed. Lachmann.)

Note 30. p. 242.

SCHLEIERMACHER'S EARLY STUDIES.

It may be interesting to trace more fully the parallel noticed in the text between the development of Plato's thoughts and Schleiermacher's early studies.

Though it is impossible to arrange the dialogues of Plato in the chronological order in which they were composed, so as to be able to study the master in his successive styles, yet several systems of arrangement, founded on different principles, seem to coincide so far as to render it probable that Plato's great theory of ideas or forms grew upon him through these stages: viz. (1) it was viewed as a fact of mind, an innate conception of forms (e. g. in Meno); (2) as useful in guiding perplexed minds to truth, and sifting philosophical doctrines by means of the dialectical process, e. g. in the Theætetus and Parmenides; (3) as representing an objective reality, a true cause in nature external to the mind, as well as an hypothesis in science (e. g. in the Republic); (4) as having a mystical connexion with divinity, and furnishing a cosmogony. Whether this passage, from the subjective conception to the objective reality, be really or only logically the order of development in Plato's ideal theory, it is clear that the growth of Schleiermacher's mind admits of comparison with this supposed order of development in Plato; though there is a slight variation in the steps of the process. Schleiermacher went through three stages, (1) the philosophy of Jacobi, (2) of Fichte, and probably (3) of Schelling; from which he learned respectively, (1) to have faith in our intuitions, (2) to construe the outward by the inward, (3) to believe in the power of the mind to pass beyond the inward, and apprehend absolute truth. If the resemblance to the above account of Plato were exactly perfect, the love of a philosophy like Fichte's ought to have preceded that of Jacobi. Schelling's influence, it ought to be noted, is very slight on Schleiermacher, compared with that of the others. The traces of it which appear are perhaps resolvable into a similarity to Jacobi's system.

Note 31. p. 244.

SCHLEIERMACHER'S THEOLOGICAL WORKS.

The theological works of Schleiermacher are doctrinal, critical, and pastoral. The latter consist chiefly of the sermons which he delivered in Berlin. The critical works are mentioned in a footnote to p. 248; but it may be useful to give a brief notice of his doctrinal works, of which some are referred to in the text.

The earliest was the *Reden über die Religion an die Gebildeten unter ihren Verächtern*, 1799, (Discourses on Religion addressed to the educated among its despisers,) which ought not to be read in earlier editions than the fourth (1829), the notes of which contain explanations. The object of these discourses was to direct attention away from the study of religion in its outward manifestations, to its inward essence; which he showed to lie neither in knowledge nor in action, but in feeling. See especially Discourse II. *Über das Wesen der Religion.* For the effect which the discourses created, see Neanders testimony, quoted by Kahnis, *Hist. of Prot.* E. T. p. 208.

The works which succeeded the *Reden* were the following: in 1800, the *Monologen* (Soliloquies); in 1803, *Grundlinien einer Kritik der bisherigen Sittenlehre* (Critique on previous Ethical teaching); in 1806, *Die Weinachtsfeier* (Christmas Eve); in 1811, the *Kurze Darstellung des Theologischen Studiums* (Plan of Theological Study;—lately translated), which gave rise to the branch now common in German universities, called *Theologische Encyclo-*

pädie[15]; in 1821, *Der Christliche Glaube nach den Grundsätzen der Evangelischen Kirche* (the Christian Faith on the principles of the Evangelical Church), which was improved in the subsequent editions.

As the *Reden* breathed the spirit of Jacobi, the *Monologen* breathed that of Fichte. They study the ethical, as the former the religious side of man; the action of the personal will as distinct from the feelings of dependence. The dialogue of the *Weihnachtsfeier* showed Christ as the means of effecting that oneness with the absolute which the two former works had shown to be necessary.

In the *Glaubens-lehre*, Schleiermacher gives a general view of dogmatic theology, viewed from the psychological side, i. e. its appropriation by the Christian consciousness. He studies (1) man's consciousness of God, prior to experience of the opposition of sin and grace; next, after being aware of such an opposition, as (2) the subject of sin, and (3) the subject of grace; or, in theological language, the states of innocence, of sin, and of grace. Each of these is subdivided in spirit, even when not in form, in a threefold manner; describing respectively the condition of man, the attributes of God, and the constitution of the world, as they relate to the above three named states. The subjective and psychological character of the inquiry is seen in the fact, that when treating the second of these subdivisions,—the Divine attributes,—he does not study them as peculiarities of God's nature, but as modifications of the mode in which we refer to God our own feeling of dependence. This subjective tendency illustrates the influence of Fichte and Jacobi on Schleiermacher.

The contrast is an interesting one between a dogmatic treatise of the schoolmen, of the reformers, and of Schleiermacher. The first commences with the Deity and his attributes, and passes to man: the second generally begins with the rule of faith, the Bible; and then, passing to the Deity, proceeds mainly after the scholastic fashion: the third begins and ends with the human consciousness, and its contents.

Note 32. p. 252.

ON SOME GERMAN CRITICAL THEOLOGIANS. (DE WETTE, EWALD, ETC.)

Some of the theologians of the critical school which is described in the text, deserve a more full notice than was possible in the foot-notes to the Lecture.

De Wette (1780–1849) was educated at Jena, under Griesbach.

[15] For a description of the division of Theological study implied by this term, see Credner's Introduction to Kitto's *Bibl. Cyclop.*; and the translation of Tholuck's Lectures, given in the American *Biblioth. Sacra*, 1844.

He was made Professor at Berlin in 1810, but was deprived in 1819, in consequence of the Prussian government having opened a letter of condolence written by him to the mother of Sand, the assassin of the dramatist Kotzebue. (For the history of the excited state of the German students at this time, see K. Raumer's *Pädagogik*, vol. iv. translated.) In 1826 he was made Professor at Basle. An interesting life of him is given in the *Bibliotheca Sacra* for 1850. His most important works are, his *Einleitung ins Alt. und Neu. Test.; Lehrbuch der Dogmatik*, 1819; his New Translation of the Bible (1839); and Commentaries on several parts of Scripture. On his doctrinal views see Kahnis, p. 231 seq. He is said to have been a man of sweet and amiable character; and indeed he appears to be so in his writings. It has been remarked, as a proof of his singular fairness, that he not only candidly states the opinions of an opponent, but even sometimes confesses his inability fully to refute them.

Along with De Wette ought to be classed a great number of distinguished men, most of whom wrote parts of the Commentary which he designed under the name of *Exegetisches Handbuch*. They were mostly critics rather than writers on doctrine, and represent the modified state of thought of his later life; but still maintain, for the most part, his critical stand-point in reference to the scriptures; and therefore, though contemporary with the new Tübingen and other schools described in Lecture VII, which have arisen since Strauss's criticism, in that which we called the third period of our sketch, they really belong to the school of critics of the older or second period. Such are, or were, Gesenius, Knobel, Hirzel, Hitzig, Credner, Tuch, E. Meier, Hupfeld, and Stähelin. See Am. Saintes, part ii. ch. xi.

H. Ewald, born 1803, became Professor at Göttingen 1831. In 1837 he was one of the seven professors who sacrificed their position when the new king of Hanover, Ernest, interfered with the constitution. From 1838 to 1848 he was professor at Tübingen: since 1848 at Göttingen. His works are partly on the oriental languages, and partly on theology. Among the latter the chief are, *Die Poetischen Bücher des Alten Test.* 1835; *Die Propheten des Alten Bundes*, 1840; and the *Geschichte des Volkes Israel*, 1842–50; a work which, whatever may be thought of the theological aspects of it, if regarded in respect of scholarship, poetic appreciation, and grandeur of generalization, is one of the most remarkable books ever produced even in Germany. (Renan has based upon it the most brilliant of his essays, ess. ii. in the *Etudes d'Hist. Religieuse.*) His works on the New Testament are partly directed against the views of the new Tübingen school. He differs from the older critical school of De Wette, in applying himself more exclusively to the Semitic literature; and cannot be classed with them in any other way than that he represents the effort of independent criticism, linguistic and historic; removed from the dogmatic school, and also from the later forms of critical.

Note 33. p. 255.

THE NAME JEHOVAH.

The name יהוה is written *Jehovah*, by transferring to it the vowel points of the word *Adonai*, אֲדֹנָי, which the pious scruples of the Jews led them to substitute for it. It was probably read *Yahveh*. In reference to the meaning of *El*, and *Jehovah*, see Gesenius's *Lexicon* on the words אֵל (p. 45. Engl. Transl.), and יְהוָה (p. 337); also the word *hajah*, הָיָה, (p. 221.) See likewise Hengstenberg's *Authentie. des Pentateuches*, i. 222 seq.; especially p. 230, where he shows that *jahveh*, יהוה, is derived by regular analogy from the future of the verb *hajah*, הָיָה (= *havah*, הָוָה). See also M. Nicholas's *Etudes Crit. sur la Bible*, pp. 115, 163; and the article *Jehovah* in Smith's *Biblical Dictionary*.

Note 34. p. 256.

THE USE OF THE NAMES OF DEITY IN THE COMPOSITION OF HEBREW PROPER NAMES.

A curious list of these is given by Dr. Donaldson. (*Christian Orthodoxy*, pp. 235, 6.)

Examples of names before the age of Saul, compounded with *El*, are seen in *El*-kanah, *El*-i, Samu-*el*, Abi-*el*. When Saul reigns we find the name Jah or Jehovah appear, in *Jeho*-nathan, Ahi-*jah*, Jedid-*iah*; and during the regal period in the list of kings, Jos-*iah*, *Jeho*-ahaz, *Jeho*-i-akim, Zedek-*iah*; and among the prophets, Isa-*iah*, Jerem-*iah*, Mica-*iah*, *Jeho*-sheah. After the fall of Judah we find the name El reappear; e. g. Ezeki-*el* (= Hezek-*iah*), Dani-*el*, Micha-*el*, Gabri-*el*, *El*-iashib, Shealti-*el*. After the captivity the name Jah recurs; e. g. Nehem-*iah*, Zephan-*iah*, Zechar-*iah*, Malach-*iah*. The name *El*-i-*jah* (= my God is Jah) is an instance of a word compounded with both names.

Donaldson tries to generalize from the above to the effect, that, previously to the age of the early kings, proper names compounded with *El* were prevalent; and in the regal and prophetic age, those compounded with *Jah*; again, after the fall of Judah, and in the captivity, those with *El*; and after the captivity, with *Jah*. But the selection is too limited to admit of such a generalization being satisfactory. It does however prove the knowledge of the twofold conception implied by the use of the names.

LECTURE VII.

Note 35. p. 264.

THE HEGELIAN PHILOSOPHY.

The purpose of this note is to supply references to sources for the study of Hegel's philosophy; and also to point out the parallel and contrast in the central thought and tendency of the philosophies of Schelling and Hegel.

The most intelligible account of Hegel's system is given by Morell, *History of Philosophy*, ii. 161–196; and the best general view of its tendencies, especially in reference to theology, is contained in an instructive article by E. Scherer, in the *Rev. des Deux Mondes* for Feb. 15, 1861, from which assistance has been derived in this lecture. The student will also find great help in Chalybaüs's *Hist. of Spec. Philos.* ch. xi–xvii (translated 1854); and A. Véra's *Introduction à la Phil. de Hegel*, 1855; together with his French translation of Hegel's *Logic*. (Véra is one of the few Italians who understand Hegel.) The *Philosophie der Geschichte*, and *Geschichte der Philosophie* are the two most intelligible of Hegel's works; the former of which is translated into English; but the study of his *Logic* is indispensable, for seeing the applications of his method, as well as for appreciating his metaphysical ability and real position.

Schelling and Hegel both seek to solve the problems of philosophy, by starting *à priori* with the idea of the absolute; but in Schelling's case it is perceived by a *presentative* power (intellectual intuition), and in Hegel's by a *representative.* The former faculty perceives the absolute object; the latter the absolute relation, if such a term be not a contradiction. In each case the percipient power is supposed to be "above consciousness;" i. e. not trammelled by those limitations of object and subject which are the conditions of ordinary consciousness. In both systems a kind of threefold process is depicted, as the law or movement according to which the absolute manifests itself.[16] Sir W. Hamilton has shown

[16] Hegel used to claim that his doctrine was merely giving expression to the ancient speculations of Heracleitus concerning the union of opposites. It is probable that the fundamental idea was the same; but Hegel supplied an interpretation and application of the principle which the ancient philosopher could not contemplate. Both in truth committed the same fundamental mistake, of making the mind the measure of things. The union of opposites is an act of thought, not a fact relating to things.

the inconsistencies of Schelling's system, in criticising that of Cousin, who was his great exponent; see *Dissertations*, ess. i. (reprinted from the *Edinburgh Review*, 1829); and Mr. Mansel has extended a similar analysis to Fichte and Hegel. (*Bampton Lectures*, ii. and iii; and article *Metaphysic* in *Encyclop. Britann.* 10th ed. p. 607, &c.) See also Rémusat *De la Philosophie Allemande*, Introduction.) Yet a grand thought, even though, psychologically speaking, it be an unreal one, lies beneath the awkward terminology of the systems of Schelling and Hegel; and their *method* has influenced many who do not consciously embrace their philosophy. The effect produced by Schelling is the desire to seize the prime idea, the *beau idéal* of any subject, and trace its manifestations in the field of history; a method which is seen in the French historic and critical literature of the followers of Cousin in the reign of Louis Philippe. (See Note 9, and the references given in Note 44.) The spirit produced by Hegel, is the desire to realise the truth contained in opposite views of the same subject; to view each as a half truth, and error itself as a part of the struggle toward truth. This spirit and method are seen in such a writer as Renan, and is clearly described in the passages quoted from Scherer and others in Note 9.

Note 36. p. 271.

THE CHRISTOLOGY OF STRAUSS.

The following extract from Strauss's work conveys his Christology.

"This is the key to the whole of Christology, that, as subject of the predicate which the church assigns to Christ, we place, instead of an individual, an idea; but an idea which has an existence in reality, not in the mind only, like that of Kant. In an individual, a God-man, the properties and functions which the church ascribes to Christ contradict themselves; in the idea of the race they perfectly agree. Humanity is the union of the two natures;—God become man; the infinite manifesting itself in the finite, and the finite spirit remembering its infinitude: it is the child of the visible mother and the invisible father, Nature and Spirit: it is the worker of miracles, in so far as in the course of human history the spirit more and more completely subjugates nature, both within and around man, until it lies before him as the inert matter on which he exercises his active power: it is the sinless existence, for the course of its development is a blameless one, pollution cleaves to the individual only, and does not touch the race or its history. It is Humanity that dies, rises, and ascends to heaven; for, from the negation of its phenomenal life, there ever proceeds a higher spiritual life; from the suppression of its mortality as a personal, rational, and terrestrial spirit, arises its union with the infinite spirit of the heavens. By faith in this Christ, especially in his death and resurrection, man is justified before God; that is, by the kindling within him of the idea of humanity, the individual man participates in the divinely human life of the species. Now the main element of that idea is, that the negation of the merely natural and sensual life, which is itself the negation of the spirit, is the sole way to true spiritual life. This alone is the absolute sense of Christology. That it is annexed to the person and history of one individual is a necessary result of the historical form which Christology has taken." *Leben Jesu*, vol. ii. § 151. (pp. 709, 10. 4th ed. 1840); in the English translation, vol. iii. p. 433.

Note 37. p. 273.

STRAUSS.

A few facts concerning the life and writings of Strauss may be interesting.

He was born in 1808, and was educated at Tübingen and Berlin. He was *Repetiteur* at Tübingen in 1835, when he published his *Leben Jesu*, described in the text of Lect. VII. In 1837 he published his *Streit-schriften*, or replies to his critics. In 1839 he was elected Professor of theology at Zurich, an appointment which produced such popular indignation that it was cancelled, and a change of government was caused by it. In 1840 he published *Die Christliche Glaubenslehre im Kampfe mit der modernen Wissenschaft dargestellt;* in which, after an introduction concerning the history of opinions on the relation of the two, he discussed the principles of Christian doctrine, such as the Bible, Canon, Evidences, &c. and next the doctrines themselves; viz. (part i.) on the divine Being and His attributes, as an abstract conception; (part ii.) on the same, as the object of empirical conceptions in its manifestation in creation, &c. See *Foreign Quart. Rev.* No. 54. 1841; and C. Schwarz's *Gesch. der n. Theol.* b. ii. ch. i. He published also *Monologen in dem Freihafen*, translated 1848; *Soliloquies on the Christian Religion, its Errors, and Everlasting Truth.*

In 1848, the revolutionary year, he was elected to the Wurtemburg Parliament; and took the conservative side, to the surprise of his constituents. He has subsequently lived chiefly at Heilbronn, engaged in literary labours; mostly writing the lives of sceptics, or persons connected with free thought whose fate has been like his own. Among these have been, a sketch of Julian, 1847, intended probably as a satire on the romantic reaction conducted by the late king of Prussia; a Life of Schubart, 1849, a Swabian poet of the last century; one of Maerklin 1851, his own early friend; one of N. Frischlin, 1856, a learned German of the sixteenth century; a life of Ulric von Hütten, 1858; and *Gespräche von Hütten*, 1861; also *Kleine Schriften*, 1861; and a work on *Reimarus*, 1862, concerning which see Note 29. Some of these works are reviewed in the *Nat. Rev.* Nos. 7 and 12.

Note 38. p. 273.

THE REPLIES TO STRAUSS.

Schwarz gives an interesting account of the various replies to Strauss, and of the works written by various theologians to support their own point of view against his criticisms. *Gesch. der n. Theol.* p. 113 seq.

The work was criticised,—

I. From the old school of orthodoxy, (α) by Steudel, Strauss's own teacher, in a work called *Vorlaüfig zu Beherzigenden zur Beruhigung der Gemüthen.* (β) From the new orthodoxy, by Hengstenberg, in the *Evangelische Kirchenzeitung.* (γ) From the school which formed the transition between this and that of Schleiermacher by Tholuck, in *Glaubwürdigkeit der Evangelischen Geschichte*, 1837.

II. From the school of Schleiermacher, (α) in Neander's *Leben Jesu*, (β) in Ullmann's *Studien und Kritiken*, 1836. part iii. reprinted as *Historisch oder Mythisch.*

III. By the Hegelians; 1. from the "right" of the party (using the illustration drawn from the distribution of political parties in the foreign parliaments), (α) by Göschel in the work *Von Gott, dem Menschen und dem Gottmenschen*, 1838; (β) by Dorner in the *Geschichte der Person Christi*, 1839. (γ) by Gabler and Bruno Bauer, who at that time was on the side of orthodoxy: 2. from the Hegelian "centre" in Schaller's *Der Historischer Christus und die Philosophie*, 1838; 3. from the "left," (α) by Weisse, *Die Evangelische Geschichte kritisch und philosophisch bearbeitet*, 1838: (β) by Wilke, *Der Ur-evangelist;* both of whom regard St. Mark's as the primitive evangile; and (γ) by Bruno Bauer, *Kritik der Synoptiker*, 1842, when he had changed to the opposite side of the Hegelian school: (δ) by Luetzelberger; (ε) by A. Schweizer; both of whom wrote on St. John's Gospel. Several of the latter were not intended to be replies to Strauss, but attempts to reconsider their own position in relation to him. This was particularly the case in reference to the works which were written by the Tübingen school, (see next note,) of which Schwarz gives a description, p. 153 seq.

Note 39. p. 278.

THE TUBINGEN SCHOOL.

The leader of the historico-critical school which bears this name, was C. Baur (1792-1860), author of various works on the history of doctrine, and on church history both doctrinal and critical. His work against the Roman catholic theologian Moehler, which first made him noted, was *Gegensatz des Protestantismus und Katholicismus nach den principien und Haupt-dogmen der beiden Lehrbegriffe*, 1833. An account of his works is given in C. Schwarz's *Gesch. der neuest. Theol.* p. 165. The following may be here specified: his work on the history of the doctrine of the atonement, *Die Lehre von der Versöhnung*, 1838; also *Lehrbuch der Christlichen Dogmengeschichte*, 1845, and *Die Christliche Kirche der drei ersten Jahrhunderte*, 1853; the last part of which has been published since his death. Some interesting remarks, comparing him with Strauss and Schleiermacher, (though hardly fair to the last,) appeared in the *National Rev.* Jan. 1861. See also the sketch by Nefftzer in the *Revue Germanique*, vol. xiii. parts 1 and 2.

The other members of the school besides Baur have been Schwegler, the commentator on Aristotle's Metaphysics, and author of a Roman History (died 1857); Zeller, also a writer on Greek philosophy, now Professor of philosophy at Marburg; whose appointment to Berne in 1847 has been elsewhere stated (Note 42) to have caused a similar excitement to that of Strauss to Zurich; Koestlin, Professor of æsthetics at Tübingen; and Hilgenfeld, Professor of theology at Jena, who is the best living representative of the modified form which the school has now assumed. Respecting these theologians, see the notes which Stap has affixed, in the *Revue Germanique*, vol. ix. p. 560, &c. to a French translation of a part of Schwarz's *Geschichte*.

Concerning this school see Baur's *Die Tübinger Schule*, 1859. The organ of it from 1842–57 was the *Theologische Jahrbücher*, edited by Baur. Since it ceased to be published, Hilgenfeld has created a new journal, the *Zeitschrift für Wissenschaftliche Theologie*, which receives the support of critics not directly of the Tübingen school, such as Hitzig and Knobel. Perhaps Schneckenbürger ought to be ranked with the same school; and Gfrörer also, author of a work on Philo, 1831; but he differed in holding the authenticity of St. John's Gospel; and in 1846 became a Roman catholic, and Professor at Freiberg. See also a paper in Von Sybel's *Hist. Zeitschr.* for 1860, part iv. translated in *Biblioth. Sacr.* Jan. 1862. The Tübingen school has met with able opponents, e. g. Thiersch, Dorner, Ewald, Bleek, Reuss, and Hase.

Note 40. p. 281.

THE GERMAN THEOLOGIAN ROTHE.

Concerning this theologian, now Professor at Heidelberg, see C. Schwarz's *Geschichte der neuesten Theologie*, p. 279 seq. The cause why the remarks in the text are so brief in regard to Rothe is, that the writer has not been able to see his more important works, which are out of print; and accordingly he derives his knowledge of him at second hand.

Rothe's two most important works are, *Die Anfänge der Christlichen Kirche*, 1837, and *Theologische Ethic*, 1845. An account of the former is given in the often-quoted article by Scherer (*Rev. des Deux Mondes*, Feb. 15, 1861), pp. 848–860. It appears to view the Christian church from its ideal side, to absorb the individual in the constitution, to show that Christendom is the object of Christianity, an institution the great means of embodying the doctrines; but that, as society becomes fermented by its spirit, the office of Christianity is fulfilled by the state, and the beau ideal would be a society where the church is the state. It is a view similar to that of Coleridge in his *Church and State*, or of Dr. Arnold in his work on *the Church*. Mr. F. C. Cook, in *Aids to Faith* (p. 159), has given some interesting illustrations of this point.

The second of Rothe's works, the *Ethic*, is briefly described in a previously-cited article in the *Westminster Review* for April, 1857. Like the former it starts with the idea of the identity of ethics and religion. Regarding personality or the moral relations as the central fact of existence, it surveys material creation under this aspect. Next it discusses the moral and religious history of man, as means of enabling the personal being to subordinate to himself all the forces without or within him. The object apparently is to show, that the spiritual element is not an intrusion, but the normal development of nature or providence; and the moral society, the State, the normal development of the religious society, the Church. Rothe's later views have hardly been developed in system. According to him theology is theosophy; philosophy can work out a theology from the consciousness.

It is probable that the writer of these lines is unintentionally doing injustice, through having to trust to secondhand information, to one who is regarded in Germany as belonging to the highest order of scientific theologians; though perhaps the interesting account of C. Schwarz leaves little to be desired.

Rothe, in accordance with his wish to strengthen orthodox theology by an independent philosophy, and not to support it by material agency, has lately taken part politically on the liberal side, in some questions connected with the church constitution of Baden. (See Colani's *Nouvelle Revue de la Theologie*, Aug. 1862.)

Note 41. p. 285.

THE MOST MODERN SCHOOLS OF PHILOSOPHY AND THEOLOGY IN GERMANY.

The object of this note is to carry on the history of philosophy and theology to a more recent date than was necessary in the text.

The idealist school of philosophy reached its highest point with Hegel; and subsequently there has been as great a reaction against this mode of speculation, as the contemporaneous theological one in religion.

The philosopher who was directly or indirectly the cause of the realist tendency was Herbart (1776–1841), who succeeded Kant at Königsberg, and afterwards was Professor at Göttingen. Concerning his system, see Morell's *History of Philosophy*, ii. 206, &c. Chalybaüs, ch. iv. and v. He followed out the *material*, as distinct from the *formal*, system of the Kantian philosophy, and strove to develope it.

The schools of modern Germany may be reckoned as four:—

(1). The young Hegelian school; e. g. of the younger Fichte, which, though professedly idealistic, and adopting Hegel's method, is really affected largely by realistic tendencies, and seeks for a philosophy of matter as well as form. See Taillandier in *Revue des Deux Mondes* for 1853, vol. iii. p. 633; and also Oct. 1858; Morell's *History of Philosophy*, ii. 216, &c. Kahnis, p. 252. This school manifests decidedly realistic tendencies in Kuno Fischer, Weisse, and Branis.

(2.) That which shows a tendency to approach the subject of mental phenomena from the physiological side, in Drobisch, Waitz, and Volkmann, somewhat in the manner of the English writer Herbert Spencer.

(3.) A school decidedly materialist, e. g. Vogt, Moleschott, and Büchner. See Taillandier, *Rev. des Deux Mondes*, Oct. 1858.

These three tendencies form a gradation from the ideal, and approach the real, until at last the ideal itself is destroyed. The other tendency, if such it may be called, stands apart, and is akin to the older ideal ones. It is (4.) that of Schopenhauer (1788–1860), and tries to solve the problem of existence from the side of the will, instead of the intellect, and bears a remote resemblance to that of Maine de Biran. His system has long been before the public, but since his death has been much discussed. It has been explained by Frauenstädt. It is also well described in the *Westminster Review*, April, 1853.

We now pass from the schools of philosophy to theology.

We have implied that there are three great schools of it in Germany; the Neo-Lutheran, the Mediation school, and the Tübingen; and have seen that they are each in course of transition into slightly new forms in younger hands. The "Neo-Lutheranism" has assumed a more ecclesiastical position, which has been called "Hyper-Lutheranism." The "Mediation" school of Schleiermacher is replaced by a newer form, modified by Hegelianism in Dorner. It remains to add, that the Tübingen school is giving place to another, of which C. Schwarz himself is a representative —a kind of derivation from the Tübingen school and that of De Wette. Its organ is the *Protestantische Kirchenzeitung;* and to it are said[17] to belong Dr. Dittenberger, court preacher at Weimar, C. Schwarz, who holds the same position at Gotha; Ellester of Potsdam, Sydow of Berlin, and Schweizer of Zurich. Their position seems to be more ethical and less evangelical than the members of the party of free thought in the protestant church of France.

Note 42. p. 289.

TABLE EXHIBITING A CLASSIFICATION OF GERMAN THEOLOGIANS.

The following classification of the tendencies of German theological thought, and of the chief theological writers, is merely a tabular arrangement of the statements already made in the text and notes of Lectures VI. and VII. A systematic view, in addition to the description given in the Table of Contents, is likely to be useful to the student; and this must be the excuse for the apparent boldness shown in attempting such a scheme. The list is not offered as a complete arrangement; but it is hoped that it includes nearly all the important writers. It is based mainly on the account which German writers themselves have given of their fellow-countrymen; the references to which were given in the Preface, and in the notes to Lectures VI. and VII. Particulars respecting the lives and works of the various theologians may be found also in Hagenbach's *Dogmengeschichte*, part v. *notes;* in Vapéreau's *Dict. des Contemp.;* and some notices of the older ones are given in Mr. Rose's work on *German Protestantism*, 2d ed.; and in Winer's *Handbuch der Theologischen Literatur.*

[17] This statement is taken from a paper on the history of German Theology, in the *Spectator*, May 24, 1862.

Pneliminary Condition of German Theology. 1600–1750.

1600–1730.

1. The Dogmatic Tendency.		2. The Pietstic.
Old Lutheran School.	Helmstadt School.	J. Arndt.
Calov.	Calixt, &c.	Spener.
Quenstedt, &c.		A. H. Francke.
		Paul Gerhardt.
		Thomasius.
		Arnold.
		Bengel.
Mosheim.		Weismann.
		Buddeus.
		Lange.
		Pfaff.

1730–1750.

[New influences introduced; viz.	1. Wolff's Philosophy; which influenced,	2. English Deism.	3. French Infidelity at the court of Fred. II.]
	Baumgarten.		La Mettrie.
	Canz.		D'Argens.
	Toellner.		Maupertuis.

PERIOD I. 1750-1810.

Sub-period I. 1750–1790.

In the Church.			Outside the Church.	
Dogmatic.	Literary.	Freethinking.	Illuminism, like the English Deism.	Illuminism, like the French.
Crusius.	Michaelis. Ernesti. The Rosenmüllers. Jerusalem. Spalding.	Semler.	Lessing. (Wolfenbüttel Fr.) Nicholai. Mendelssohn. Reimarus. Steinbart. Teller.	Knuzen. Dippel. Basedow. Edelmann. Bahrdt.

Sub-period II. 1790–1810.

[New Influences introduced; viz. 1. The Literary Influence of Weimar. 2. The Kantian Philosophy.]

1. Supernaturalism.			2. Rationalism. (Dogmatic and Critical.)	
Biblical.	Philosophical.	Kantist.	Supernatural Rationalism.	Rationalism (proper).
Knapp. Storr. Stilling. Oberlin.	Reinhardt. Seiler. Flatt. Planch. Schröckh. Morus. Döderlin. Steudel.	Staüdlin. Tieftrunk. Ammon.	Bretschneider. Tzchirner.	Eichhorn. Paulus. Wegscheider. Röhr. Eckermann. C. F. A. Fritsche. Vater. L. Bauer. Von Lengerke. Von Bohlen. Henke.

PERIOD II. 1810–1835.

[New influences introduced:

1. New Systems of Speculative Philosophy; Jacobi, Fichte, Fries, Schelling, and Hegel.
2. The Romantic School of Poetry; L. F. Stolberg, the Schlegels, Tieck, Novalis, Fouqué.
3. The Moral Tone of the Liberation War.
4. The Lutheran and Biblical feeling indicated by Harm's Theses.]

Doctrinal School.							Critical School.	
1. Revival of Biblical and Lutheran Theology.	2. Influenced by Fichte and Jacobi.		3. Derived from Hegel. Developed chiefly in next Period.				Influenced by Fries.	Gesenius.
	Schleiermacher.							Knobel.
								Hirzel.
	Neander	and Tholuck	Right.	Centre.	Left.	Extreme Left.	De Wette.	Hitzig.
	Twesten	" Nitzch					Hase.	Credner.
Developed in the next period.	H. Olshausen	" Ullmann	Goeschel, &c.	Daub.	Vatke.			
	Sack	" Hundeshagen	Gabler.	Marheinecke.	Weisse.			Tuch.
	Tittmann	" Umbreit		Schaller.	Wilke.	Strauss.		Stähelin.
	Ebrard	" Stier			Lützelberger.			
	Jul. Müller	" Hagenbach						———
	Lange	" Baumgarten-Crusius						Ewald.
	Lücke	" Gieseler						
		Bleek.						

Roman Catholic Theologians during the same period: Alber, Jahn, Liebner; Hug, Sailer, Staudenmeier; Hermes, Goerres, Moehler; Döllinger.

PERIOD III. 1835–1862.

Prior to 1848.

Within the Church.			External to the Church.
1. Neo-Lutheranism.	2. The Mediation School.	3. The Tübingen School.	4. Unbelief.
Hengstenberg. Hävernick.	Dorner. Rothe.	C. Baur. Schwegler. Zeller. Hilgenfeld. Koestlin.	Strauss. B. Bauer. Feuerbach and Ruge. Stirner (Schmid).

Subsequent to 1848.

[New Influences:—1. The Political Reaction.
2. The New Hegelian Philosophy.
3. The Empirical Philosophy resulting from Herbart.]

1. "Hyper-Lutheranism."	2. The Mediation School continues.	3. New Eclectic School.	4. Materialist Philosophy. (See Note 41, p. 620.)
Stahl and Guericke. Harless " Rudelbach. Delitzch " Keil. Kurtz " Schmid. Kliefoth " Kahnis.		Dittenberger. C. Schwarz. Ellester. Sydow. A. Schweizer.	

Note 43. p. 289.

THE MODERN THEOLOGY OF SWITZERLAND AND HOLLAND.

It will be observed, that no notice has been taken in the text, of the modern theology of Switzerland and Holland. It may be desirable therefore to suggest an outline here.

THE THEOLOGY OF SWITZERLAND.—The materials for the account of it are scanty and disjointed. Since the reform of the Swiss universities during the present century, theological thought has chiefly taken the colour of the adjacent countries, Germany or France, in the respective universities where those languages are spoken. In the church of Geneva, about a quarter of a century ago, there seem to have been two parties, similar to those in the French protestant church: one professing the old Calvinistic orthodoxy, which had degenerated into semi-Socinianism; the other, the result of a revival of biblical truth and spiritual religion, under such pastors as D'Aubigné, the historian of the Reformation, and recently Gaussen, the writer on *Théopneustie*. A movement was commenced under Vinet of Lausanne, which may be considered to be the only native school which Switzerland has produced. It was a mixture of science and earnestness, founded chiefly on a combination of Pascal and Schleiermacher. Concerning Vinet, see a very just article in the *North British Review*, No. 42, August 1854; and see below, Note 46. Scherer was a friend of Vinet, but has since changed his views, or, as some would think, developed logically their results, and has long left his professorship at Geneva, and acts with the new liberal school in the French protestant church. See Note 46.

German Switzerland has been connected with Germany rather than France. The teaching at the university of Basle was moulded by De Wette, who was made professor there in 1826, a few years after his removal from Berlin. Its character, however, expressed the more orthodox and moderate views of his later years. The instructive writer Hagenbach, professor there, belongs to the "mediation school" of theology, and is a worthy representative of its learned and devout spirit. Zurich possessed a teacher, Usteri, belonging to the school of Schleiermacher; and others, whose tone rather resembled that of the critical school of De Wette, or of the Tübingen school. The well-known critics Hitzig and Knobel, were formerly its professors; and at present Schweizer is there, concerning whom see Note 41. A few years after Strauss had published his noted work, he was elected, as stated before, theological professor at Zurich, but the appointment was cancelled by a revolution of the people. See the Address of Orelli (translated 1844). The appointment of Zeller of the Tübingen school to Berne, created a similar excitement. In the proceedings of the Evangelical Alliance at Geneva, 1861, professor Riggenbach, of

Basle, stated that some of the journals of eastern Switzerland adopt sceptical principles. (*News of the Churches*, Oct. 1861.) He named the *Zeit-stimmen aus der Reformirten Kirche der Schweiz*, which is edited at Winterthur by Lang, a pupil of Baur. In German Switzerland, however, as well as French, there exists a biblical school of theology; of which professor Riggenbach of Basle is an example.

THE THEOLOGY OF HOLLAND.—The sources were given above (p. 110.) for the study of Arminianism and Calvinism in the seventeenth century. The subsequent history is soon told. We omit, of course, the history of the Romish church in Holland, and of the Jansenist secession from it, which took place in 1705.

The Protestant church continued to exist in two branches; viz. the Calvinists, or established church, who professed the creed of the synod of Dort; and the Remonstrants, who professed the moderate Arminianism of Episcopius; similar to that which was taught by our own Hales and Chillingworth. The studies in the established church were specially devoted to exegesis, in reference to which the name of Schultens of Leyden, in the last century, is well known; manifesting a slight inclination to free inquiry in Van der Palm (1763–1838).

About 1830, the condition of the church was a cold orthodoxy, much like that of the "moderate" party in the church of Scotland before the rupture of 1843. The stronghold of this party was the university of Utrecht. Living isolated, and resembling the English in not easily admitting foreign influences, the Dutch read little of German literature. A periodical existed, the *Theological Contributions*, which used to bestow praises on the school of Bretschneider.

A little before 1830, a movement of evangelical piety had been kindled in the church, through the influence of the poet Bilderdyk (who died 1831), and of his two disciples, the Portuguese Jew of Amsterdam, Da Costa (who died in 1860), and Cappadose. Their position however was, a return to the rigid decrees of the synod of Dort and the theology of Calvin. They resembled very nearly the party in the church of Scotland which formed the free church. They acquainted themselves with German theology for the purpose of refuting it; and Da Costa wrote a work, *The Four Witnesses*, on the four Evangelists, in reply to Strauss; which has been translated. In 1834 they separated from the national church under two pastors, De Cock and Scholte, and endured much persecution. The *Voices of the Netherlands* was the periodical which expressed their views. Van Oosterze, pastor at Rotterdam, belonged to them. This party has been represented in the Dutch parliament by Groen van Printsterer. It has lost its political influence in some degree in recent years, by opposing political reforms.

Almost simultaneously with this Calvinistic revival, a school arose in the university of Groningen, a "mediation" school, modelled upon Schleiermacher, under the influence of the Platonist Van Heusde (1778–1839), led by Hofstede de Groot, Pareau, and Muurling. Its organ was *Truth in Charity*. The views held were a spiritual Arianism. They may be seen in a novel published recently (1861) at Cape Town, for the Dutch colonists, entitled, *The Pastor of Vliethuizen, or Conversations about the Groningen School*, translated by Dr. Lorgian.

These three parties were the chief in Holland, until about 1850. Since then a more decided movement of free thought has begun in the university of Leyden. Up to that time the venerable Van Hengel remained there, the example of the old philological orthodoxy of Holland. Two professors have now created an independent movement, more nearly resembling that of the Tübingen school; J. H. Scholten, in dogma; and, with rather more advanced views, the orientalist H. Kuenen in philology. (A list of some of Scholten's publications may be seen in the *Westminster Review* for July, 1862, page 43, note. His *Hist. comparée de la Philos. et de la Relig.* was translated by Reville, in the *Nouvelle Rev. de la Theologie*, April 1860.) Busker Huet has asserted still more advanced views than these, apparently simple naturalism. The Positivist philosophy has found an advocate in Opzoomer, one of the professors at Utrecht.

The sources of this account are chiefly found in Ullmann's paper in the *Studien und Kritiken*, 1840, part iii. translated by professor Edwards, with additions, in the American *Bibliotheca Sacra* for 1845; and in an interesting article by A. Reville of Rotterdam, himself one of the liberal school of the French protestant church, in the *Revue des Deux Mondes* for June 15, 1860. Chautepie de la Saussure, pastor of the Walloon church at Leyden, formerly of the Groningen school, has also written in French, *La Crise Religieuse en Hollande*, 1859; but it is chiefly devoted to personal questions. A sketch of the Dutch universities and their intellectual characteristics was given by Esquiros in the *Revue des Deux Mondes*, 1856, vol. iii.

Note 44. p. 297.

THE ECLECTIC SCHOOL OF FRANCE.

The Eclectic School is sketched in Morell's *History of Philosophy*, vol. ii. c. viii; Damiron's *Essai sur l'Histoire de la Philosophie en France au 19ème siècle*, 1828, pp. 280–385; Nettement's *Histoire de la Litt. Franç. sous la Restoration*, 1853, vol. i. b. ii. p. 127 seq.; vol. ii. b. viii. p. 290 seq.; and *Hist. de la Litt. Franç. sous le Gouvernement de Juillet*, vol. i. b. vi: also in Taine's *Philosophie Française du 19ème siècle.* The last writer is wholly unfavourable to the school, on the ground of the uselessness of metaphysical philosophy.

The eclectic school was the means of uniting together the philosophy of Scotland and Germany, which had previously been running in separate streams. The leading minds of the school have been four,—Royer Collard, Maine de Biran, Cousin, and Jouffroy.

The founder of it, R. Collard (1763–1845), was a disciple of the Scotch school, who about 1812 commenced an attack on the philosophy of Condillac, very similar to that of Reid on Hume. He devoted himself to the analysis of the intellectual and moral parts of men, in order to assert the existence of a world within, independent of sensational impressions. The next writer, Maine de Biran (1766–1824), devoted himself especially to the examination of the will and the notion of cause, and reproduced the ideas of Leibnitz. The third, Cousin (born 1792), succeeded Collard in 1815 as professor at Paris; and in his early lectures followed the Scotch school. When the conservative reaction occurred in 1822, consequent on the assassination of the duke de Berri, the constitutional party was thrown into disgrace; and Cousin therefore retired into Germany, and there imbibed the spirit of the great schools of philosophy, especially of Schelling and Jacobi. He has given his own history in the preface to *Fragments Philosophiques*, vol. ii. Lastly came Jouffroy, the translator of Dugald Stewart, who improved upon the Scotch school. See Sainte-Beuve's criticism on Jouffroy. (*Crit. Litt.* vol. i.)

Damiron was an admirable exponent of the eclectic school; Benjamin Constant, Degerando, and Lerminier, partially belonged to the same school. Its effects are ably stated in Morell. The delicate hand of E. Renan also has sketched the influence of *Cousin et l'école Spiritualiste*, in the *Revue des Deux Mondes*, April. 1858; reprinted in his *Essais de Morale et de Critique.*

Note 45. p. 300.

THE CATHOLIC REACTIONARY SCHOOL OF FRANCE.

Concerning this school, see Morell's *History of Philosophy*, vol. ii. pp. 274–318; Damiron (as in the last note), pp. 105–197; Nettement (second work), vol. i. b. v.

The members of this school all agree in reposing upon the principle of *authority;* but differ in the source in which they place it. Their philosophy accordingly does not aim at discovering truth, but only the authority on which we may rely as the oracle of truth.

The founder of the movement was De Maistre (1753–1821), the bitter opponent of the Baconian philosophy, whose doctrine, about the time of his death, was absolute submission to the catholic church. See concerning him C. Rémusat in the *Revue des Deux Mondes*, May 1857; and E. Scherer's *Mélanges de la Critique Religieuse.* Lamennais belonged to the same movement. In his early manner, as expressed in his *Essai sur l'Indifference*, 1821, he found the test of truth in primitive revelations transmitted by testimony; in his later, he abandoned this school, and strove to work out philosophy, in part independently of authority. The next writer, De Bonald, sought for truth in the same source, viz. fragments of divinely communicated knowledge, transmitted in the languages of mankind. On Bonald see C. Rémusat (*Revue*, as quoted above). The Abbé Bautain improved upon this system by placing the ground of certitude in the authority of Revelation, and considered the office of philosophy to end when it has shown the necessity of a revelation. Next to him came D'Eckstein, who sought the test of truth in authority based on researches into the catholic beliefs of mankind. The two latter views, it will be perceived, are far nobler than the former. Maret, whose writings have been before cited, also belongs to this reactionary school.

Note 46. p. 304.

THE MODERN SCHOOL OF FREE THOUGHT IN THE PROTESTANT CHURCH OF FRANCE.

The object of this note is to enumerate some of the chief of those theologians to whom allusion is made in the text, and to exhibit their relations to each other.

One of the best known is Colani, a pastor at Strasburg, the able editor of the *Nouvelle Revue de la Theologie*, and author of several volumes of sermons: also A. Reville, pastor of the Walloon church at Rotterdam, a frequent writer in the same Review, and in the *Revue des Deux Mondes;* Reuss, a professor at Strasburg, author of a history of the early church, in French, and *Beiträge zu den Theologischen Wissenschaften*, in German; Scherer, the friend of Vinet, once professor at Geneva, author of *Mélanges de Critique Religieuse*, reprinted mostly from Colani's Review, of which the first four papers give his theological views on Inspiration, the Bible, and Sin.[18]

The able critic, Michel Nicholas, professor at Montauban, author of *Etudes Critiques sur la Bible*, and *Des Doctrines Religieuses des Juifs pendant les deux siècles antérieurs à l'ère Chrétienne*, probably may be classed with the same; but he has not written on doctrine. A. Cocquerel *fils*, pastor at Paris, also is connected with Colani's Review, and is considered to possess the same sympathies.

The difference of the point of view of these writers from that of the Eclectic school would be, that while the latter would regard the human race as able to pass beyond Christianity, the former would only wish to get rid of the dogmas which they think have been superadded in the course of ages, and to return to the simple teaching of the sermon on the mount.

One writer more has been reckoned with the same party by

[18] His work on *Dogmatique* is in his earlier manner.

the English public, E. De Pressensé, a pastor in the free Protestant church at Paris, author of the Church History so often referred to in this volume, and of sermons on the *Sauveur*, and editor of the *Revue Chrétienne;* but he appears to possess an evangelical and more orthodox tone than some of the above.

In truth there are two distinct parties in the movement which we are describing, each of which stands in a different relation to the older parties of the protestant church. At the beginning of the century the French protestant church held an unpietistic kind of supernaturalism, not very unlike that of Reinhard in Germany, of which the best living type is the eloquent and learned A. Cocquerel *père.* About 1820 an awakening of the spiritual life of the church took place, under the action of the Spirit of God primarily, and through the agency of such ministrations as those of Adolphe Monod instrumentally. From the former school has arisen the movement seen in Colani and Reville; from the latter, that seen in Vinet and Pressensé. The former is a change which has passed over the old Latitudinarian school, much like those which in Germany have taken the place of the teaching of such men as Reinhard and Bretschneider. Of the pastors named above, who belong to this class, A. Cocquerel *fils* is the least removed from the ordinary creed. His stand-point may be compared to that of Schleiermacher, or of the school of Groningen. (See Note 41.) Reville and Colani advance very much farther. The other movement, of which Vinet of Lausanne was the cause, has sprung from the application of science to the newly-spreading views of evangelical religion. Vinet tried to harmonize religion and knowledge, by presenting Christianity on the ground of its internal rather than its external evidence, and proclaimed it as ethics built on doctrine; which doctrine he held to be built on historic fact. His position may be best compared with Neander's in Germany, or perhaps in some respects with that of Tholuck. Nearly the same position is assumed by Pressensé at Paris, and Astié at Lausanne. Pressensé rests upon the Bible as the "formal principle" of theology, and the work of Christ as the "material."

The writer feels much hesitation in venturing to classify these authors, which nevertheless seemed desirable on account of the spread of their writings in England. The above description, founded on personal study of their works, is confirmed by two criticisms on them; one by C. Rémusat, in the *Revue des Deux Mondes*, Jan. 1862; the other in the *British Quarterly Review*, Oct. 1862. But care ought to be used in describing the actors in a movement which is not complete; and in making the attempt, to distinguish especially those who are conceived to deviate from vital truth in doctrine, from those who may differ in questions of literature or criticism. It is due to these writers to express admiration for their genuine love of intellectual and political liberty, much as we may be compelled to differ from their theological opinions.

LECTURE VIII.

Note 47. p. 320.

MODERN OPINIONS WITH RESPECT TO MYTHOLOGY.

In the last century the opinions on the nature of mythology were two. That which taught that myths are distortions of traditions derived from the early Hebrew literature, was put forward in the seventeenth century, as early as philosophy was applied to the subject, by Huet and Bossuet, and retained its hold throughout the last century, and is advocated in the present by Mr. Gladstone (Work on Homer, vol. ii. ch. ii). The opposite theory interpreted myths by an Euhemeristic process, or allegorized them by regarding them as originally descriptions of the physical processes of nature. In the present century Creuzer (*Symbolik*, 1810) applied the method of comparison, and, studying Greek mythology in correlation with that of other countries, taught in a Neo-Platonic sense that myths are a second language, the echo of nature in the consciousness. Creuzer's system was opposed by Lobeck about 1824, Voss, and G. Hermann, who objected to the excess of symbolism and the sacerdotal ideas implied in it; and by Ottfried Müller, and Welcker, on the narrower ground of asserting the independence of Greek mythology from foreign influence. More recently the careful study of the Sanskrit language and early literature by Max Müller, Kuhn, &c. has thrown new light upon the subject; and the solution of the problem is now approached from the side of language, and not merely from that of tradition or monuments. The distinction of myth and legend is now clear; the family relationship between the myths of different nations is made apparent; the date in human history of their creation; and the cause of them is sought in the attempt to express abstract ideas by means of the extension of concrete terms. See the Essay on *Comparative Mythology* by Max Müller, in the Oxford Essays for 1856. See also the Journal for Comp. Phil. of Kuhn and Aufrecht. And for a criticism on Creuzer, see E. Renan's *Etudes d'Histoire Religieuse* (Ess. i).

Note 48. p. 363.

THE EXTERNAL AND INTERNAL BRANCHES OF EVIDENCE.

It may be almost superfluous to name that the evidences are usually divided into 1. external, and 2. internal. Each of these requires a subdivision into (α) the divine, and (β) the human.

The *external divine* are miracles and prophecy; the *external human* are the historical proof as to the authenticity and genuineness of the literature which contains the narrative of the miracles and the prophecy. The *internal divine* are sought in the accordance of the materials of the Revelation, the character of Christ, the scheme of Redemption, &c. with the moral sense of man, and with the expectations which we should form antecedently of the contents of a revelation; the *internal human*, in the critical evidence of undesigned coincidence. Looked at logically, the second is like the corroboration of the testimony of a witness; the fourth, like cross-examining him. The first two may amount almost to demonstration, being what Aristotle (*Rhet.* i. 2.) would call τεκμήρια: the two latter have only the force of probability; the third being antecedent probability, εἰκός; the fourth, the ἀνώνυμον σημεῖον, or circumstantial evidence. The argument of analogy used by Butler, which may be regarded as almost[19] one form of Aristotle's παράδειγμα (*Rhet.* ii. 20), (if looked at on its positive side, and not merely its negative, as disproof of objections,) comes under the third, inasmuch as it offers a series of principles obtained by generalization from the natural and moral world, which furnish an antecedent presumption of the character of any revealed scheme. The remarks in the text relate to the comparative weight to be given to the first and third of the four classes named above. The advantage of Butler's argument over the other cases of internal *à priori* evidence is, that it is founded on previous careful induction; the other kinds of anticipations are founded only on hasty empirical generalizations. For this view of the evidences, see Hampden's *Introduction to the Philosophical Evidences of Christianity;* Davidson's *Lectures on Prophecy* (Introductory Lecture); and W. D. Conybeare's *Lectures on Theology*, ch. i.

Note 49. p. 366.

THE HISTORY OF THE CHRISTIAN EVIDENCES.

As frequent references have been made to the subject of apologetic in connexion with the history of free thought, it seems

[19] The strict difference would be, that analogy is the resemblance of ratios, where the objects, in which the ratios are perceived, are not known to be referable to the same general class; παράδειγμα on the contrary where they are so.

desirable to give a brief literary history of the Evidences, and to indicate the works where further information may be obtained with regard to them.

There are two methods of studying the subject; either to classify the Evidences in the manner of the last Note,[20] and proceed to notice the ages in which, and the authors by whom, each portion of them has been developed, together with the causes which have called them forth; or else, to adopt the historic plan, and trace their gradual growth through the course of ages. By the latter method (if we exclude all that strictly belongs to the province of polemic as distinct from apologetic), we find the following controversies:—in the early centuries, the double contest against the Jews and against the Pagans; in the early middle ages, against the Mahometans without, and Freethinkers within, the limits of Christendom; at the Renaissance, against unbelief within the church: in more modern times, whilst the argument against the Jew has been called forth by contact with the Jewish denizens scattered through Europe, and the Mahometan has been occasionally excited by missionary labours; there has been the contemporaneous struggle within the church, against deism, atheism, and rationalism.

This history, it will be observed, is so complex, that it would be necessary to study each branch of the contest separately. Accordingly, we have treated in distinct notes the contests with the Jew (Note 4), and the Mahometan (Note 5); and there remain for study those which existed with the Pagan in the early ages, and with the various forms of scepticism in the later.

It will be convenient to classify the inquiry, under the four epochs according to which we have studied the history of unbelief in the preceding lectures; viz. (1) the contest of Christianity with Paganism; (2) with the incipient free thought of the middle ages; (3) with the unbelief of the Renaissance; and (4) with the subsequent forms of unbelief, which it may be useful to classify according to the countries where they have respectively appeared,—England, France, and Germany.

I. The apology or defence of Christianity against Pagans commences with the apostolic age.[21] Its first form is seen in the missionary speech of St. Paul at Athens. The first chapter of his Epistle to the Romans also may be regarded as expressing the same ideas. The defence consisted in an appeal to the heart as well as to fact; to show the heathen the need of Christianity before presenting the statement of its nature, and the evidence of its divine character. In the second century, when it became gradually understood that Christianity was not a mere Jewish sect; and when the attack consisted in calumnies and persecutions, as stated in Lect. II. pp. 48, 54, the apologies especially were direct-

[20] A plan of arrangement of this kind is used by Mr. Bolton in the Hulsean Prize Essay for 1852, *The Evidences of Christianity, as exhibited in the writings of the Apologists down to Augustine.*

[21] Cfr. Gerard, *Compendium of Evidences*, 1828, part ii. ch. i.

ed to repel the charges, or to demand toleration: (see Note 15.) In the third and fourth centuries the attack was more intelligent, and the statement of objections more definite; and the character of the apologies altered correspondingly.

There is some difficulty in arranging the early Apologies. A recent writer, Pressensé, who has made a special study of them, has used, as his fundamental principle of classification, the view which the authors took of the relation of the soul of man to Christianity; according to which he makes three classes; the first, comprising those who thought that the soul of man was fitted for truth, and acknowledged the heathen religions as a preparation for Christianity; the second, those who, taking the same view of human nature, regarded the heathen religions as corruptions, and wholly injurious; and the third, those who took such a desponding view of human nature as to regard it as possessing no truth without revelation (*Hist.* vol. ii. ser. ii. p. 164–5.) As examples of the first class, he cites Origen and most of the earlier fathers; of the second, Tertullian; of the third, Arnobius. He thinks, but perhaps hardly rightly, that the chronological order in which the three views occurred, coincides also with this mode of arrangement. It will be evident that the first two classes show an attempt to approach Christianity *à priori*, by arousing the sense of want; the last by "crushing the human soul" by authority: the first of the three trying to open the way for the reception of Christianity, by describing it as the highest philosophy and religion; the second as the substitute for both; but both schools agreeing in describing it as the satisfaction of the world's yearnings. It will be also apparent why the presentation of the *à priori* internal Evidences should precede the external. When the world had been impressed with the necessity of a new religion, then the opportunity came for employing the cogent power of the external and historic evidence which authenticates Christianity.

A less artificial manner however of studying the Apologies would be to view them in time, and in space; i. e. according to their date, and the churches from which they emanate, whether Syrian, Alexandrian, Roman, or African; with the view of witnessing at once the alteration in the attack and the character of the apology which existed in different countries at one and the same time.

It appears worthy of notice however, that the attempt to find difference of treatment according to difference of country almost entirely fails. If applied as a principle of classifying manuscripts, or modes of exegesis, or liturgical uses, sufficient variety is exhibited to prove that the Christian church was a collection of provincial churches, each possessing its national peculiarity, each contributing to swell the general harmony by uttering its own appropriate note; but, when applied to the subject of apologetic, the method fails to show a difference in the method of defence which was simultaneously used in the great Christian army; which forms a proof of the facility of intercourse between different churches, and of the uniformity in the character of the attack directed simultaneously on the church in different lands. The change in the character of the Evidences with the growth of time, according to the alteration of attack described above, is apparent, but not the variation at the same date in different parts of the world. We shall therefore merely present a list, in which the apologists are arranged according to place and date, without attempting to draw inferences which cannot be supported.

The recent publication of Pressensé's work, where the spirit of the apologies is given, together with an analysis of their contents, renders it unnecessary to offer here a full analysis of them, as had been intended. Other works indeed partially supplied the need previous to his. Such, for example, were Houtteville's Introduction to *La Religion Chrétienne prouvée par des Faits*, containing an account of the authors for and against Christianity (translated 1739); Schramm's *Analysis Patrum*, 1780; Scultetus's *Medullæ. Patr. Syntagma*, 1631; and for the Apostolic Fathers, the Introduction to Mr. Woodham's edition of Tertullian's *Apology*.

It will be sufficient accordingly to give a list of the writers, with a very brief mention of the object of their treatises,[22] and to enumerate the literary sources from which further information may be obtained in respect to them.

[22] Notes 14, 15, 17, 19, afford illustrations bearing upon the same subject.

Table of the Early Apologists, according to Date and Place.

A. D.	Rome and Western Provinces.	Africa.	Athens.	Alexandria.	Syria.	Heathen Assailants.
150			[Aristides 130] [Quadratus] [*Justin ?* 150] *Tatian* *Athenagoras* *Hermias ?*			
200		*Tertullian* *Minucius Felix ?* 230		Clement 190	*Theophilus* 180	Celsus: answered by Origen.
		Cyprian Commodian		Origen 240		Porphyry: answered by Methodius, Jerome, Eusebius, & Augustin.
300		*Arnobius* *Lactantius*			[Methodius] *Eusebius*	Hierocles: answered by Eusebius
	Jul. Firmicus Ambrose Prudentius			Athanasius	Chrysostom	Julian: answered by Apollinaris and Cyril.
400	Orosius Salvian	*Augustin*		*Cyril*	Jerome ? Theodoret	

N. B. The names in brackets are of authors whose apologies are almost wholly lost; those in italics are the ones which alone are usually mentioned in a list of apologists. To the above ought perhaps to have been added for completeness, Maternus, A. D. 350; Ephraim the Syrian; and Apollinaris of Asia Minor, who replied to Julian. The names marked with a note of interrogation denote those in reference to which the reader may demur to the classification. Justin Martyr wrote at Rome; but he wrote in Greek, and was a Greek philosopher in spirit. Of Hermias little is known. Jerome lived much in Syria, and leaned to the Syrian school of exegesis, so that he has been classed with the Syrian church, though his intimacy with Augustin and his writing in Latin might rather have caused him to be classed with the western. Also Minucius Felix ought perhaps rather to be classed with the Roman than the African church.

We shall next state the purpose of the treatises of those Apologists, whose names are printed in italics in the table.

The first group consists of Justin, Tatian, Athenagoras, Hermias, and Theophilus; the first three of whom may be considered to express the defence of Christian philosophers, who were striving to explain the nature of Christianity, partly with a view to plead for toleration, partly to make converts.

Justin has left two apologies; one against the Jews, the other against the heathens; (a second against the heathens is a fragment.) In both he adopted the same plan, of first repelling prejudices, and then assaulting his opponent. That which is directed against the Jews is analysed in Kaye's *Justin*, c. xi. In that which was directed against the heathens, he first repelled the charges made against Christians, such as atheism, Thyestean banquets, and treason against the state; and next, those made against Christianity, especially those which related to its late introduction, the person of Christ, and the doctrine of the resurrection. In proceeding to assault heathenism, he endeavoured to show that it did not possess religious truth, and claimed that the points of agreement with Christian truth were borrowed; and after having thus shown the superiority of Christianity to heathenism, he endeavoured to show its divinity, by the internal evidence of its doctrines and effects, and by the external evidence of miracles and prophecies.

Tatian's treatise in substance was an invective against the pagans, on the absurdity and iniquity of the pagan theology and its recent origin, with a running comparison between it and Christianity.

The object of Athenagoras was to plead for toleration; and consequently he employed himself in vindicating the Christians from various charges, such as incest, Thyestean banquets; and retaliated the charges on the heathen.

The little work of Hermias, the date of which is uncertain,

(see Lardner, *Cred.* ch. xxv. and Cave, *Hist. Lit.* lxxxi. is a kind of sermon on St. Paul's words, "The wisdom of this world is foolishness with God." In an amusing manner, not unlike Lucian, he criticised the heathen philosophy, arguing its falsehood from the contradictory opinions held in it.

The form of Theophilus's work *Ad Autolycum* is not unlike some of those which have preceded. Indeed the form was suggested by circumstances; being a defence of Christianity against particular charges, and the retaliation of similar ones on the heathens. He drew out the attributes of the true God, b. i; and afterwards exhibited the falsehood of the heathen religion and history, b. ii; defending Christians from the absurd charges made against them; and attempting to show the originality and antiquity of the Hebrew history aud chronology, b. iii.

The next group of Apologists, which comprises the writers of the Africau church, Tertullian and Minucius Felix, differs from the last in spirit, though resembling them in purpose. It is the defence made by rhetoricians instead of philosophers. The purpose too, like that of the preceding Apologists, is partly to effect conviction, partly to obtain toleration; but there is a consciousness of the presence of danger, hardly perceivable in the former writers. We feel, as we read these early African writers, that they write like men who felt themselves in the presence of persecution, and who were brought more nearly than the former writers into the face of their foe.

Tertullian's Tract, which is analysed both by Mr. Woodham in his edition of it, and by Mr. T. Chevallier in his translation of it, is chiefly defensive. He claims toleration, ch. i–vii; refutes the miscellaneous charges against Christianity, ch. x–xxvii; and the charge of treason (xxviii–xxxvii); explains the nature of Christianity (xvii–xxiii); and compares it with philosophy, ch. xlv–xlvii.

The work of Minucius Felix is a dialogue between a heathen, Cæcilius, and a Christian, Octavius. The heathen opens by denying a Providence; next inveighs against the Christians, by a series of charges such as were named in Note 15; and then attacks the Christian doctrines and condition. The Christian Octavius is made to answer each point successively.

In passing now from the African school of Apologists to the Alexandrian, we leave the rhetoricians, and meet with the philosophers, Clement and Origen. Clement precedes Tertullian by a few years; Origen succeeds Minucius Felix.

Clement, in part of his *Stromata*, and in his *Cohortatio*, has expressed the spirit of his apologetic; which resembles those of the first group, in admitting the value of heathen philosophy as a preparation for Christianity, and claims that the Hebrews are the source of philosophy, and that Christianity is the full satisfaction for those who sought knowledge.

The spirit and details of Origen's defence have been so fully given in Lecture II. and Note 14, that it is unnecessary to enlarge upon the subject. His apology marks a further step. Tertullian replied to the prejudices of the vulgar, and M. Felix to the scepticism of the educated, which formed two elements in the heathen reaction of the second century. Origen furnished the reply to the attack made by the heathen philosophy. It is in reply to Celsus, who possessed a competent knowledge of Christianity; and who, though writing earlier than the time when the charges which Tertullian afterwards refuted were common, was too well informed to have believed them, and opposed Christianity on deeper grounds. Celsus stands later logically, though not chronologically, than the authors of those frivolous charges, and midway between them and the educated assailants of Christianity of the third century, such as Porphyry. Origen's defence too marks a similar advance, and, by exhibiting sympathy with the very philosophy which Porphyry and others adopted, shows the kind of defence which was thought likely to attract philosophic minds.

The chronology compels us to return to the African church, and introduces us to two Apologists;—Arnobius and Lactantius; one of whom seems to have written a little before Christianity had become a tolerated religion; the latter a little afterwards.

The work of Arnobius is taken up, partly in repelling charges made against the Christians, such as that the Christians do not worship, which are no longer charges of the absurd kind made a century before; partly in comparing Christianity and heathenism; and partly in offering the evidence for Christianity. It is in this point that we find the peculiarity which belongs to Arnobius. He is the first writer who lays firm stress on the demonstrative character of the evidence of fact. In previous writers Christianity had been proved by probability: he makes it to rest on the evidence of certainty; and considers the fact of the revelation to guarantee the contents of it.

The large work of Lactantius, the *Institutiones Divinæ*, is a work of ethics as well as of defence. Christians have obtained protection, and defence is becoming didactic: apology is expiring in instruction: all that is now needed for the spread of Christianity is, that its nature should be understood. The work is partly a work of religion, partly of philosophy, partly of ethics; the object in each case being to show that Christianity supplies the only true form in each department of thought.

The remaining Apologists may be grouped together, though they have no point of union, except that their arguments are directed to the special condition of heathenism; when, being no longer triumphant, it was standing on the defensive, and, at the time of the two latter of the group, was fast declining. They are, Eusebius, Cyril of Alexandria, and Augustin.

If Origen is the metaphysical philosopher of the early Apologists; if Augustin is the political; Eusebius is the man of erudition. He has left, besides the small work against Hierocles (see Note 17), two works of defence; the first the *Evangelica Præparatio*, against the Gentiles; the second the *Evangelica Demonstratio*, more suited for the Jews. The former work is to show that Christianity has not been accepted without just cause; which he attempts to prove by a very elaborate discussion (valuable to us in a literary point of view, on account of the quotations which he has preserved) of the various religions, Egyptian, Phœnician, Greek, and of the various types of Greek thought and belief; and, by a comparison of them with the Hebrew, he shows the superiority of the last. The other work, the *Evangelica Demonstratio*, is designed to prove that Christ and Christianity fulfil the ancient prophecies. His apology marks the transitionary time when Christianity was becoming the religion of the Roman world, and men hesitated as to its truth, looking back with regret to the past, with uneasiness to the future.

The other two Apologists are nearly a century later; when Christianity had been long established.

Cyril has already come before us as the respondent to Julian. It is enough to refer to Lecture II. and Note 19, in relation to him. It is worthy of observation, that the circumstance that he should consider it necessary to reply to Julian's work, at so long a period after the death of the author, and the frustration of his schemes, seems to show the continued existence of a wavering in the faith of Christians, of which we seldom have the opportunity of finding the traces at so late a period.

If Cyril marks the apology of the Alexandrian church at the commencement of the fifth century, Augustin similarly exhibits that of the African in presence of the new woes which were bursting upon the world. Christianity had long lived down the charges made against it by prejudice, and shown itself to be the philosophy which the educated craved. The charges of treason too had ceased, for it had become the established religion; but one prejudice still remained. Victorious with man; triumphant over the prejudices of the vulgar, the opinions of the philosophers, and the power of the state; it still was not, it seemed, victorious in heaven; and at last the heathen gods were arousing themselves to take vengeance on the earth for the overthrow of their worship, by a series of terrible calamities. Apprehensions like these haunted the imagination; and it was the object of Augustin, in his work, *De Civitate Dei*, to remove them. That work was a philosophy of society; it was the history of the church and of the world, viewed in presence of the dissolution, social and political, which seemed impending.

These brief remarks will suffice to give a faint idea of the line of argument adopted by the early Apologists. Further information in regard to them may be found in the following sources:—

In a history of this period written by Tzchirner, *Geschichte der Apologetik*, 1805; also another by Van Senden, 1831, translated into German from the Dutch, 1841; Clausen, *Apologetæ Ecc. Chr. ante-Theodosiani*, 1817; and a brief account in Stein, *Die Apologetik des Christenthum*, § 6. p. 13. Other references may be found in Hase's *Church History*, E. T. § 52; Hagenbach's *Dogmengeschichte*, § 29, 117; and in J. A. Fabricius, *Delectus Argument*, ch. i. In the same work (ch. ii–v.) is an account of the chief Apologists, and of the fragments of their lost writings. In reference to the character of the apologetic works of the early fathers, information may also be obtained in Walch's *Biblioth. Patristic.* (ed. Danz. 1834.) § 97–100. ch. x; and concerning some of them in P. G. Lumper's *Hist. Theol.-Crit. de Sanct. Patr.* 1785; Moehler's *Patrologie*, 1840; Ritter's *Chr. Phil.* i and ii; Neander's *Kirchengeschichte*, i. 242 seq.; ii. 411 seq.; Kaye's works on Justin, Clement, and Tertullian; and Dr. A. Clarke's *Succession of Ecclesiastical Literature*, 1832.

On a review of these early apologies, some peculiarities are observable.

First, with the exception of Origen's treatise, and some parts of Eusebius, they are inferior as works of mind to many of modern times.[23] This was to be expected from the character of the age; the literature of that period being poor in tone, compared with the earlier and with the modern. In works of encyclopædic history and geography, and in a reconsideration of philosophy by the light of the past, it had indeed some excellences; but the literature as a whole, not only the Latin, but even the Greek, was debased by the substitution of rhetoric for the healthy freshness of thought and poetry of older times: and the apologetic literature partakes of the tone of its age. The Christian writers, when looked at in a literary point of view, must be compared with authors of their own times. The Alexandrian apologies rise sometimes to philosophy; but those of the Greek nation sink to rhetoric. In later times, men who were giants in mind and learning have written on behalf of Christianity; and it would be unfair to the apologetic fathers to compare them with these.

Secondly, we cannot fail to remark the abundant use of what is now called the philosophical argument for Christianity, the conviction that prejudice must be removed, and antecedent probabil-

[23] This remark is only intended to apply to the apologetic writings, which are not the best works, of the fathers. In the fourth century we meet with a group of fathers of a higher type of mind than those of the first three; e. g. Eusebius Athanasius, Basil, the Gregories, Ambrose, and Jerome. Speaking generally, however, the three writers, Origen, Chrysostom, and Augustin, are probably the only ones who had minds of the highest class, and who thoroughly exceed the contemporary heathen writers of their day in mental penetration, freshness, and compass, respectively. If we have compared Origen in mind with Hugo St. Victor, and Schleiermacher, as a Christian philosopher (Lect. VI.), we might also venture to compare Augustin with Aquinas or Calvin, in power to grasp systematic truth; and Chrysostom with Bernard, and in some respects with Bossuet, in eloquence, learning, and vigour. Eusebius perhaps almost demands a place with these three; but he was a man of knowledge rather than originality.

ities be suggested, before the hearer could be expected to submit to Christianity. The just inference from this is not that which some would draw, the depreciation of the argument from external evidence, but rather a corroboration of the importance of the emotional element, as an ingredient in the judgment formed on religion. The only practical inference that can be drawn in reference to ourselves is, that if it be true that our age resembles theirs, as has been suggested by Pressensé (see Lecture VIII. p. 356), we must adopt the same plan; not because we admit that the external evidence is uncertain or unreal, but because the other kind of evidence is best adapted, from philosophical reasons, to such a state of society as ours.

Several centuries pass before we again meet with works of evidence. In the dark ages, the public mind and thought were nominally Christian; and at least were not sufficiently educated to admit of the generation of doubts which might create a demand for apologetic works. Accordingly we pass over this interval, and proceed at once to the middle ages.

II. The scepticism of the second period of free thought possessed so largely the character of a tendency rather than an attitude of fixed antagonism, that it gave no opportunity for direct works of refutation. But the spirit of apologetic is seen in two respects; in the special refutation of particular points of teaching, as in Bernard's controversy with Abelard, and more especially in the works of the scholastic theology.

This theology, especially as seen in the works of the great realist Aquinas, and of others who took their method from him, was essentially, as has been before said (pp. 11 and 92), a work of defence. In the two centuries before his time we already find the spirit of reverent inquiry working. Anselm's two celebrated works, the *Monologium* and *Proslogium*, a kind of soliloquy on the Trinity, and the *Cur Deus Homo*, or theory of the Atonement, are the work of a mind that was reconsidering its own beliefs, and restating the grounds of the immemorial doctrines of the church. (See J. A. Hasse, *Anselm*, 1843, 52.) In the following century (viz. the twelfth), the work of Peter Lombard, called the *Sententiæ*, marks an age when inquiry was active; and the material was supplied for its satisfaction by means of searching amid the opinions of the past for the witness of authority. But in the thirteenth century, the grand advance made by Aquinas in his *Summa*, is no less than the result of the conviction that religion admitted of a philosophy; that theological truth was a science; and so, commencing with the plan of first discussing God; then man; then redemption; then ethics; he created a method, which had been indeed suggested by his predecessors, but was more fully displayed by him, for arranging the truths of theology in a systematic form, in which their reasonableness might appear, and through which they might commend themselves to the judgment of a philosophical age.

The most successful mode of replying to objections is not to refute the error contained in them, but to grasp the truth and build it into a system, where the doubter finds his mind and heart satisfied with the possession of that for which he was craving. If the twelfth century had not had its Abelards, its spirit of inquiry, of analysis, and of doubt; the church would never have had its champion philosopher Aquinas: but if it had not had its Aquinas, the succeeding ages would probably have produced many more Abelards. The scholastic theology accordingly must be regarded as the true rationalism, the true use of reason in defence. Like as the mind goes through the process of perceiving facts, then of classifying and generalizing, next of defining and tracing principles to practical results; so the church, in forming its theology, receives its facts as they were once for all apprehended by inspired men of old, and are corroborated by the experience of the Christian consciousness from age to age: but, after so receiving them, it exercises its office in creating a theology, by classifying and arranging them, and generalizing from them; and when new doubts or objections arise, it recompares its teaching with the faith once delivered to the saints; defines and prescribes the limits of truth and error; and thus absorbs into its own system whatever is true in the newly-presented doubts or objections. This is really the action of the church in moments of peril; and is that which was effected by the scholastic theologians,—Anselm, the two Victors, Aquinas, Bonaventura, and others. It is sufficient to refer to Ritter's *Christliche Philosophie*, iii. 502 seq.; iv. 257 seq.; Neander's *Kirchengeschichte*, vol. viii; Stein's *Die Apologetic*, § 7 and 8; Hagenbach's *Dogmengesch.* § 150; and Hase's *Church History*, § 218, 277, 278; for information concerning these writers and their position.

III. At the time of the Renaissance, in the fifteenth century, which was the third period at which the Christian faith was in peril from doubt, we begin to meet with works of evidence of a more directly controversial kind. Defence is no longer a spirit, but a fact. Apologetic theology is severed from Dogmatic.

One work remains, written in the fourteenth century by Petrarch (*Opp. de Otio Religiosor*), which defends the truth of Christianity against Philosophers, Mahometans, and Jews; partly on the evidence of miracles, but mainly on the internal evidence of the purity and godliness of Christianity. In the early part of the fifteenth century, Raimond de Sebonde, professor of medicine at Barcelona, wrote his *Theologia Naturalis*, which was afterwards translated into French by Montaigne. It was charged with deism, but really was in spirit, as previously observed (p. 104), only like Locke's *Reasonableness of Christianity*. See Hallam's *History of Literature*, i. 138; Ritter's *Christliche Philosophie*, iv.

658 seq. Another exists by Æneas Sylvius; another by Ficinus, 1450, *De Relig. Christianâ*, in which the evidence of prophecy and miracles is adduced; the arguments from the moral character of the apostles and martyrs, the wonderful spread of Christianity, and the wisdom of the Bible, are used; and a comparison is drawn between Christianity and other creeds.

In the close of the same century, as soon as printing became common, several similar treatises occur. One exists by Alphonso de Spina, *Fortalitium Fidei contra Judæos, &c.* 1487; also by Savonarola, *Triumphus Crucis, sive de Vera Fide*, 1497; also by Pico di Mirandola; and by Ludovicus Vives, *De Veritate Christianâ*, 1551. A carefully written account of all these is given by Staüdlin, in Eichhorn's *Geschichte der Literatur*, vol. vi. p. 24 seq. See also Fabricius, *Delect. Argument.* ch. xxx.

The preceding works were mostly directed against the first of the two species of unbelief which belonged to this period, viz. the literary tendency (see Lecture III. p. 93, 94). A few however exist which were directed against the second species, which was connected with the philosophy of Padua. They are not so much general treatises, as works written against particular opinions, of Pomponatius, Bruno, or Vanini. An account of them may be found in the memoirs respectively published concerning these writers; the references to which are given in the notes to Lecture III. (See pp. 101–103.) The work of Mornæus, *De Veritate Religionis Christianæ adv. Atheistas, Epicureos, &c.* 1580, was probably suggested by this species of philosophy.

IV. The fourth great period, marked by the unbelief connected with the activity of modern speculation and the influence of modern discovery, commenced in the sixteenth century. The works of defence are so numerous that we can only give a brief notice of the principal writers and writings. A list may be collected, down to the respective dates of their publication, from J. A. Fabricius's *De Veritate Rel. Christ.* c. 30; Pfaff's *Hist. Litt. Theol.* ii. § 2; Buddeus's *Isagoge*, pp. 856–1237; Walch's *Biblioth. Theol. Select.* vol. i. ch. v. § 5–7: and the principal arguments are summed up in Stapfer's *Instit. Theol. Polem.* 1744, vol. i. ch. iii. and vol. ii. Tholuck also has written a history of modern apologetic, *Ueber Apologetik und ihre Litteratur* (Vermischte Schriften, i. pp. 150–376), and the Abbe Migne has published a most important collection of the principal treatises on apologetic in all ages, arranged in chronological order. It is contained in twenty vols. 4to. 1843. The title of the work is given below.[24]

[24] *Dèmonstrations Evangeliques*: (tome 1.) *de Tertullien*, *Origène*, *Eusèbe* (Præp. Ev.); (2.) *Eusèbe* (Dem. Ev.), *S. Augustin*, *Montaigne*, *Bacon*, *Grotius*, *Descartes*; (3.) *Richclieu*, *Arnauld*, *De Choiseul du Plessis-Praslin*, *Pascal*, *Pélisson*, *Nicole*; (4.) *Boyle*, *Bossuet*, *Bourdaloue*, *Locke*, *Lami*, *Burnet*, *Malebranche*, *Lesley*, *Leibnitz*, *La Bruyère*, *Fénelon*; (5.) *Huet*, *Clarke*; (6.) *Duguet*, *Stanhope*, *Bayle*, *Leclerc*, *Du Pin*; (7.) *Jacquelot*, *Tillotson*, *De Haller*, *Sherlock*, *Le Moine*, *Pope*, *Leland*; (8.) *L. Racine*, *Massillon*, *Ditton*, *Derham*, *D'Aguesseau*, *De Polignac*;

The work of Grotius, *De Veritate Religionis Christianæ*, is the one which opens the period of evidences which we are now considering; of which a notice may be found in Hallam's *History of Literature*, ii. 364, and in Tholuck, *Verm. Schr.* i. 158; but no very definite cause can be pointed out why it was written. It was merely indeed one of the class of treatises already described (Notes 4 and 5), which devoted a portion of space to the controversy with the Jews and Mahometans. It is when a new standpoint had been assumed by scepticism, and the causes, intellectual or moral, which have been pointed out in these lectures, had begun to create a real peril, that writings on the evidences begin to derive a new value and assume a new form.

We shall give an account of them according to countries.

THE ENGLISH WORKS OF EVIDENCE.—Those which were called forth in England by Deism were of several kinds. Perhaps they may be arranged under four heads.

The first class consists of specific answers to certain books, published from time to time; of which kind are most of those which are named in the foot-notes to Lecture IV. Waterland's reply to Tindal is a type of this class. Occupied with tracking the opponent from point to point of his work, such replies, though important while the sceptical book is operating for evil, become obsolete along with the war of which they are a part, and henceforth are only valuable in literary history, unless, as in the special instance of Bentley's *Phileleutherus Lipsiensis* in reply to Collins, they are such marvellous instances of dialectical ability and literary acuteness that they possess a philosophical value as works of power, when their instructiveness has ceased.

A second kind consisted of homilies rather than arguments; sermons to Christian people, warning them against forms of un-

(9.) *Saurin, Buffier, Warburton, Tournemine, Bentley, Littleton, Seed, Fabricius, Addison, De Bernis, J. J. Rousseau*; (10.) *Para du Phanjas, Le roi Stanislas, Turgot, Stattler, West, Beauzée*; (11.) *Bergier; Gerdil, Thomas, Bonnet, De Crillon, Euler, Delamarre, Caraccioli, Jennings*; (12.) *Duhamel, S. Liguori, Butler, Bullet, Vauvenargues, Guénard, Blair, De Pompignan, De Luc, Porteus, Gérard*; (13.) *Diessbach, Jacques, Lamourette, Laharpe, Le Coz, Du Voisin, De la Luzerne, Schmitt, Pointer*; (14.) *Moore, Silvio Pellico, Lingard, Brunati, Manzoni, Paley, Perrone, Lambruschini, Dorléans, Campien, Fr. Pérennès*; (15.) *Wiseman, Buckland, Marcel de Serres, Keith, Chalmers*; (16.) *Dupin Ainé, Grégoire XVI*; (17.) *Cattet, Milner, Sabatier*; (18.) *Bolgeni, Morris, Chassay, Lombroso et Consoni*—*contenant les apologies de* 117 *auteurs, répandues dans* 180 vol.; *traduites pour la plupart des diverses langues dans lesquelles elles avaient été écrites; reproduites* integralement *non par extraits. Ouvrage également nécessaire à ceux qui ne croient pas, à ceux qui doutent, et a ceux qui croient*, 20 vol. in 4to. Prix : 120 fr. Chaque volume se vend séparément, 7 fr. The references in the above title are to the volumes of the work.

There is an important article on the literature of Apologetics in the *North British Review*, No. 30, August 1851, the writer of which says that the claim that the above works are translated "integralement" is not literally correct; passages which assault the church of Rome being omitted. He considers that among the works of the above-named series which are not known in England, the most important are, Stattler, *Certitude de la Religion révélée par Jesus Christ*; Beauzée, *Exposition des Preuves Historiques de la Religion Chrétienne*; Abbé Para du Phanjas, *Les Principes de la Sainte Philosophie conciliés avec ceux de la Religion*; Cardinal de Vernis, *La Religion Vengée*; Cardinal Polignac, *Anti-Lucretius*.

belief, and regarding unbelief from a practical point of view rather than a speculative; and discussing, as would appropriately belong to such an object, the moral to the exclusion of the intellectual causes of doubt. Some of Tillotson's sermons are an example of the highest of this kind of works. The value of this class is two-fold: in a purely pastoral point of view, the suggestions which they contain concerning the moral causes of doubt being founded on the real facts of the human heart, and on the declarations of scripture, have a lasting value; and in a literary point of view, these works contribute to the knowledge of the state of public feeling of the time. This is seen in this instance. Until about the end of the seventeenth century, there is no clear perception, except among the very highest of this class of writers, of the particular character of the forms of doubt against which their remarks are directed. The general name, *Atheism*, is used vaguely, to describe every form of unbelief. This fact tells its tale. It witnesses to the consciousness that they lived in an age of restlessness, when change of creed was going on, and doubt was prevalent; but when unbelief had not shaped itself into form, and found as yet few organs of expression. We are reminded of the works before named of the fifteenth century (p. 93 seq. 104.) At that time doubt and restlessness prevailed, as we learn from the frequent references to it; yet the works which transmit the knowledge of it to us are few, and the allusions to it vague: while the works of evidence then written are directed against antiquated forms of it,—Mahometan, Jewish, or philosophical. In like manner, in the seventeenth age, we see, as we look back, that the Christian sermons were mostly directed against older forms of unbelief,—the atheism of the ancients, or of the Paduan school; and that the contemporary unbelief had not become definite enough to enable the Christian writers to apprehend its nature. This fact too explains another circumstance. The preachers evince a bitterness, which is not merely the rudeness common in that age on all subjects, nor the indignation which arises from solicitude for souls, common in all ages on a subject so momentous as salvation; but it is the bitterness of alarm. There is a margin in their expression of vituperation, which is only to be explained by the fact, that the absence of a clear statement of the grounds of doubt, such as was subsequently given in the eighteenth century, deprived the preachers of the means of understanding the alleged excuse for the prevailing doubt. They appear not to be conscious of the causes which could create in the minds of others a restlessness which they did not feel themselves. They seem like persons living in a state of political society, who are conscious of a vast amount of general dissatisfaction, and a suspicion of a plot against society, the authors of which are unknown, as well as the causes of their supposed grievances; and where the danger is necessarily heightened from the very absence of knowledge as to its precise amount.

A third class of the English apologies consists of works which have neither the speciality of the first class, nor the vagueness of the second. They were directed against special writers and particular books; but instead of being adapted as a detailed reply, chapter by chapter, to the special work, the authors of them seized hold of the central errors of the unbeliever, or the central truths by which he was to be refuted. The works of the two Chandlers against Collins, and Leland's work on the deists, rise into this tone at times. Bishop Gibson's later Pastorals against Woolston are a good type of it; and still better, many of the courses of Boyle Lectures; and above all, Warburton's *Divine Legation of Moses.*

There is a fourth class of works, of a grander type, which resemble the one just named, in discussing subjects rather than books; but differ in that they are not directed against particular books or men, but take the largest and loftiest view of the evidences of Christianity. The first of this class, though a small one, is Locke's *Reasonableness of Christianity.* The best examples are, *Things Divine and Human conceived of by Analogy*, by Dr. Peter Browne, 1733; and the *Analogy* of Bishop Butler, in reference to the Philosophical Evidence of Christianity; with the works of Lardner and Paley in reference to the Historical. Books of this class are elevated above what is local or national, and are in some sense a *κτῆμα ἐς ἀεί.*

After this description of the different classes of works of evidence, it remains to give a brief notice of a few of the more important writers, especially of the two latter classes, in chronological order.

Omitting the repetition of those books named in the foot-notes of Lect. IV. which were directed against Herbert, Hobbes, and Blount, and which, as already remarked, belonged to the first of the four classes just named, and also the enumeration of the various sermons which belong to the second, we meet with the following writers:—Robert Boyle (1626–1691), an intelligent philosopher and devout Christian, who wrote works to reconcile reason and religion, suggested by the growth of new sciences; and with Ray, who first supplied materials for the argument for natural religion, drawn from final causes, 1691; and Stillingfleet, who investigated religion from the literary side, as the two just named from the scientific. Boyle not only wrote himself on the Evidences, but founded the Boyle Lectures,[25] a series which was

[25] In naming the *Boyle Lectures*, it may be permitted to the writer of these lectures to express the regret which he has often felt, that there is no history written of the various apologetic Lectures, and of the works which they called forth; such, e. g. as the Boyle (1692), Lady Moyer (1719), Warburton (1772), Bampton (1780), Donnellan (1794), and Hulsean Lectures (1820), in the Church; and the Lime Street (1730), Berry Street (1733), Coward (1739), and Congregational Lectures (1833), among the Dissenters; and more generally that there is no history of English theology and of English theological literature. Much as we need a fair account of the English Church, viewed in its external and its constitutional history, we still more need a history which would enter into the inner life, and give its intellectual and spiritual history. Such a work would not only give a detailed account of the various works on evidence and of the other literature, but would enter into the

mainly composed of works written by men of real ability, and contains several treatises of value, as works of mind, as well as instruction. Among the series may be named those of Bentley (1692); Kidder, 1694; Bp. Williams, 1695; Gastrell, 1697; Dean Stanhope, 1701; Dr. Clarke, 1704, 5; Derham, 1711; Ibbot, 1713; Gurdon, 1721; Berriman, 1730; Worthington, 1766; Owen, 1769: all of which belong to the third of the classes named above, while one or two approach to the grandeur of the fourth.

Among separate treatises, the popular ones by the Non-juror Charles Leslie (†1722), *Short Method with the Deists;* Jenkins's *Reasonableness of Christianity*, 1721; Foster's *Usefulness and Truth of Christianity*, against Tindal; and Bp. Sherlock's *Trial of the Witnesses*, against Woolston; Lyttelton on *St. Paul's Conversion;* Conybeare's *Defence of Revelation*, 1732; Warburton's *Divine Legation of Moses;* are the best known. A complete list of the respective replies to deist writers may be found under the criticism of each writer, in Leland's *Deists*, and Lechler's *Gesch. des Engl. Deismus*. The great work of Bishop Butler, which appeared in 1736, has been sufficiently discussed in Lect. IV. p. 157 seq. It was the recapitulation and condensation of all the arguments that had been previously used; but possessed the largeness of treatment and originality of combination of a mind which had not so much borrowed the thoughts of others as been educated by them. Balguy's works also, though brief, are scarcely inferior. (See his *Discourse on Reason and Faith*, vol. i. serm. i–vii; vol. ii. serm. ii, iii, iv; vol. iv. serm. ii. and iii.)

We have already pointed out (p. 207), that in the latter half of the century, the historical rather than the moral evidences were developed. The philosophical argument preceded in time, as in logic. First, the religion of nature was proved: at this point the deist halted; the Christian advanced farther. The chasm between it and revealed religion was bridged at first by probability; next by Butler's argument from analogy, put as a dilem-

causes and character of the various schools of thought which have existed in each age,—e. g. of the struggle of semi-Romanist and Calvinistic principles in Elizabeth's reign:—in the next age, the reproduction of the teaching of the Greek as distinct from the Latin Fathers in Andrewes and Laud; the Arminianism of Hales and Chillingworth; the Calvinism of the Puritans: again, later, the rise of the philosophical latitudinarianism of Whichcote, More, and Cudworth; the theological position of the non-jurors; the Arian tendencies of Clarke and Whiston; the cold want of spirituality of divines of the type of Hoadley; the reasoning school of Butler, the evangelical revival of Wesley and Simeon; and, in the nineteenth century, the philosophical revival under Coleridge, and the ecclesiastical in the Tracts for the Times. Subjects like these, if treated not only in a literary manner, but in connection with their philosophical relations, would lift the history above a merely national purpose, and make it a lasting contribution to the history of the human mind. If executed worthily, such a work might take a rank along with the grand works on literature of Hallam. Much as the present taste for documentary history is to be commended, and the publication of ancient historic documents to be desired, it is to be hoped that it will not lead to the divorce of history from philosophy. History becomes mere antiquarianism, if the philosopher is not at hand to build its parts into the general history of humanity. Philosophy becomes an hypothesis, if it is disconnected from the actual exemplification of its principles on the theatre of the world.

ma to silence those who objected to revelation, but capable, as shown in Lect. IV. of being used as a direct argument to lead the mind to revelation; thirdly, by the historic method, which asserted that miracles attested a revelation, even without other evidence. The argument in all cases however, whether philosophical or historical, was an appeal to reason; either evidence of probability or of fact; and was in no case an appeal to the authority of the church.

Accordingly, the probability of revelation having been shown, and the attacks on its moral character parried, the question became in a great degree historical, and resolved itself into an examination either of the external evidence arising from early testimonies, which could be gathered, to corroborate the facts, and to vindicate the honesty of the writers, or of the internal critical evidence of undesigned coincidences in their writings. (See Note 48.) The first of these occupied the attention of Lardner (1684–1768). His *Credibility* was published 1727–57. The *Collection of Ancient Jewish and Heathen Testimonies* (1764–7.) The second and third branches occupied the attention of Paley; the one in the Evidences, the other in the Horæ Paulinæ.[26]

Before the close of the century the real danger from deism had passed, and the natural demand for evidences had therefore in a great degree ceased. Consequently the works which appeared were generally a recapitulation or summary of the whole arguments, often neat and judicious, (as is seen at a later time in Van Mildert's *Boyle Lectures*, vol. ii. 1805; and in a grander manner in Chalmers's works, vol. i–iv.); or in developments of particular subjects, as in Bishop Watson's replies to Gibbon and to Paine; (See p. 198, 199, note); or in Dean Graves's work on the Pentateuch, 1807.

It is only in recent years that a new phase of unbelief, a species of eclecticism rather than positive unbelief, has arisen in England, which is not the legitimate successor of the old deism, but of the speculative thought of the Continent; and only within recent years that writers on evidences have directed their attention to it. In the line of the Bampton Lectures, for example, which, as one of the classes of annually recurring volumes of evidences, is supposed to keep pace with contemporary forms of doubt, and may therefore be taken as one means of measuring dates in the corresponding history of unbelief; it is not until about 1852 that the writers showed an acquaintance with these forms of doubt derived from foreign literature. The first course[27] which touched upon them was that of Mr. Riddle, 1852, on the *Natural History of Infidelity;* and the first especially directed to them was that in

[26] Paley's argument has been extended to the Gospels and other parts of Scripture by the lamented Professor Blunt. (Cfr. also his Essay on Paley, reprinted from the *Quarterly Review*, Oct. 1828.)

[27] The course for 1849, on the Evidences, by Mr. Michell, marked the commencement of the consciousness of the spread of free thought; but was not directed to the novel foreign forms of it.

1853 by Dr. Thomson, on the *Atoning Work of Christ;* since which time only two courses, those of Mr. Mansel, 1858, on *The Limits of Religious Thought;* and of Mr. Rawlinson, in 1859,[28] on *The Historical Evidences of the Truth of Scripture,* have been directed to the subject, the one to the philosophy of religion studied on its psychological side, the other to the historical evidences.

Among isolated works on evidences not forming parts of a general series, it is hard to make a selection without unfairness. We can only cite a few, premising that silence in reference to the rest is not to be considered to be censure, nor to mark the want of a cordial and grateful acknowledgment of the utility of many smaller works of evidences in the present day, dictated by deep love for Christ; whose authors, though omitted in this humble record, have their reward in being instruments of religious usefulness by means of their works, and are doubtless not unnoticed by a merciful Saviour, who looks down with love on all who strive to spread his truth.

The following seem to merit notice. First, the arguments in favour of natural religion, drawn from physical science, stated in the Bridgewater Treatises, analogous to the earlier works of Derham and Paley; the connection of science with revelation, in Cardinal Wiseman's Lectures delivered in Rome, 2d ed. 1842, (which are a little obsolete, but very masterly;) several works by Dr. M'Cosh, *Divine Government,—Typical Forms,* &c. in which the author takes a large view of the world, and of the province of revealed religion in the scheme of general truth, founded mainly on Butler; also a work of Dr. Buchanan, *Modern Atheism,* valuable for its literary materials as much as for its argument; and of T. Erskine on the Internal Evidences, 1821. The Bampton Lectures of Mr. Miller in 1817 also deserve to be singled out as a thoughtful and original exhibition of the argument in one branch of the internal evidence; *The Divine Authority of Scripture asserted from its adaptation to the real state of human nature;* also Mr. Davison's *Warburton Lectures on Prophecy,* 1825. Among works directed to special subjects, we ought to specify, *The Restoration of Belief,* by Mr. Isaac Taylor, intended indirectly against speculations such as those of the Tübingen school; and an able and thoughtful work on the subject of the superhuman character of Christ, *The Christ of History,* by Mr. Young; also E. Miall's *Bases of Belief;* with the two Burnett Prize Essays by Thompson and Tullock; and a reply to Mr. Newman's Phases of Faith, viz. *The Eclipse of Faith,* and *Letters of E. H. Greyson,* by H. Rogers, constructed however partly on the argument of the dilemma.[29] The replies written to *Essays and Reviews,* especially *Aids to Faith,* ought to be added.

We have reserved for separate mention one work, which as-

[28] The Lectures however of Dr. Hessey in 1860, though directed to a different subject, evince a knowledge of the literary studies of foreign theologians.

[29] The writer hopes that the note on p. 374 will not be considered an ungenerous censure of Mr. Rogers, who is selected because he is the ablest and wisest of those writers who have used this argument.

cends to the philosophy of the religious question, Mr. Mansel's Bampton Lectures, 1858, *The Limits of Religious Thought*, because it is a work which is valuable for its method, even if the reader differs (as the author of these lectures does in some respects) from the philosophical principles maintained, or occasionally even from the results attained.[30] It is an attempt to reconstruct the argument of Butler from the subjective side. As Butler showed that the difficulties which are in revealed religion are equally applicable to natural; so Mr. Mansel wishes to show that the difficulties which the mind feels in reference to religion are parallel to those which are felt by it in reference to philosophy. Since the time of Kant a subjective tone has passed over philosophy. The phenomena are now studied in the mind, not in nature; in our mode of viewing, not in the object viewed. And hence Butler's argument needed reconstructing on its psychological side. Mr. Mansel has attempted to effect this; and the book must always in this respect have a value, even to the minds of those who are diametrically opposed to its principles and results. Even if the details were wrong, the method would be correct, of studying psychology before ontology; of finding the philosophy of religion, not, as Leibnitz attempted, objectively in a theodicée, but subjectively, by the analysis of the religious faculties; learning the length of the sounding-line before attempting to fathom the ocean.

These remarks must suffice in reference to the history of Evidences in England. We shall now give an account of those which existed in France; which will be still more brief, because the works are considered to be of small general value, at least they have not a general reputation.

2. THE FRENCH WORKS OF EVIDENCE.—In the middle of the seventeenth century we meet with Pascal and Huet; both of them, metaphysically speaking, sceptics, who disbelieved in the possibility of finding truth apart from revelation;[31] and with whom therefore the object of evidences was to silence doubt rather than to remove it. (On Pascal, see Rogers's *Essays*, Essay reprinted from the *Edinburgh Review*, January 1847; and on Huet, an article in the *Quarterly Review*, No. 194, September 1855, and the reference given p. 19. Also see Houtteville, introduction to *La Religion Chrétienne prouvée par des Faits*, 1722.)

Among the Roman catholics, at the close of the same century, were the following: Le Vassor († 1718); the two Lamy † 1710 and 15, and Denyse; and in the eighteenth century, Houtteville, whose preface to his own work, an historical view of evidences and attacks to his own time, has been just named; Bonnet; D'Aguesseau, † 1751; and Bergier † 1790: and among the Protestants,—Abbadie, † 1727; and Jacquelot, † 1708; nearly all of whom are treated of by Tho-

[30] It is hardly necessary to state, that Mr Maurice and Mr. Goldwin Smith, besides others, have criticised this work in distinct publications.

[31] Ellis's work on *The Knowledge of Divine Things*, 1811, breathes a similar spirit in modern times. Cfr. Note 44.

luck (*Verm. Schr.* i. p. 28) and Walch (*Bibl. Theol. Sel.* ch. v. sect. 6). Several more will be found in the *Demonstrations Evangeliques;* among which are Choiseul du Plessis, Praslin, Polignac, De Bernis, Buffier, Tournemine, and Gerdil; the Lives of several of whom are in the *Biographie Universelle.*

Though some of these were men whose works were of ordinary respectability, they were by no means a match in greatness for the intellectual giants who prostituted their powers on behalf of unbelief; and on one occasion, when a prize essay had been offered for a work in behalf of Christianity, no work was deemed worthy of it. (Alison, *History of Europe*, i. 180.) Since the beginning of the present century, however, there has been a change. Whatever may be thought of the line of argument adopted, the skill with which it has been put forward, and the ability of the minds that have given expression to it, is undoubted. Chateaubriand may be considered as the first who, with a full appreciation of the tastes and wants of modern society, tried to show not only the compatibility of Christianity with them, but that the perfection of society was only realized in it. The work of the Christian labourers who had to bring back France to Christianity was hard. It was not the apologist, acting, as in England, from the vantage ground of a powerful church against the Deist, who was making an attack on it; but it was a weak and feeble minority acting against a powerful mass of educated intellect. The apologists were indirectly aided by philosophy. The philosophers did not aim primarily at religious truth, and we have had reason to take exception to many of their views; yet they rekindled in France the elements of natural religion, on which the Christians then proceeded to base revealed. The works of Jules Simon are the highest expression of it. (See Note 44.)

The school of evidences that has existed, has been the church school of De Maistre, already described. (See Note 45, and the references given there.) With somewhat of the spirit of the writers of the fifteenth age, they have directed their efforts to re-establish the catholic church as the condition of re-establishing the Christian religion. To this we have already taken exception, Lecture VII. p. 300; and the remarks there given may suffice in reference to the movement. Yet the literary appreciation of the line of argument used by the older apologists, is perceptible in the large publication of Migne, already named.

The other attempt in France to re-establish Christianity by Protestant apologists, noticed in Lecture VII. p. 304, of which the ablest was Vinet, is rather directed against rationalism than against full unbelief; and aims to turn the flank of the rationalist argument, and, while accepting its premises, deny its conclusions. (On Vinet, see Note 46.) The problem which is now before the apologists is, not to show that Christianity is not imposture, but rather that it is not merely philosophy. (Compare the remarks of Strauss, at the close of his work on Reimarus, alluded to in Note 29. p. 427).

There now only remains the history of Apologetic in Germany.

3. THE GERMAN WORKS OF EVIDENCE.—As early as the end of the seventeenth century, we find the attention of Kortholt directed to Spinoza; and in the early part of the eighteenth we see, in the grand attempt of Leibnitz to find a philosophy of religion; in Haller, 1705–77; in Euler, 1747, (for which see Tholuck, *V. Schr.* ii. 311--362, together with a list of others there given,) a proof of the attention which the Evidences received. The existence of works like J. A. Fabricius's *Delectus Argumentorum*, 1725; Reimannus, *Historia Atheismi*, 1725; Buddeus, *De Atheismo*, 1737; Stapfer, *Inst. Theol. Polem.* 1752; as well as the attention shown by the bibliographers, Pfaff, Walch, Fabricius, to the literature of Evidences, is a proof of the same fact.

The replies were still directed against Deism, as in England or France. It is not till later in the century that rationalism appears. When however it arose, writers were not wanting who opposed it. The history of the German theology has been treated so largely in Lectures VI. and VII. that it is only necessary to indicate the steps. The early deistic rationalism of Reimarus and Lessing met its opponents in contemporary writers named in the notes to Lecture VI. The critical rationalism of Eichhorn and Paulus was really answered by the later critics, as was shown when we noticed that criticism gradually abandoned their view, and rescued itself from their extravagant opinions (p. 257 seq.), while the dogmatic rationalism which was connected with it was dispersed by the discussion on the province of the supernatural already described (p. 418). In the present century the aspect of the attack and of the defence has changed. The question had been as to the existence of the supernatural.

In the present the question has been, If the supernatural be admitted, what is the capacity of man to discover it by the light of feeling or reason respectively, without revelation? Therefore, while in the last century it was important to show that the supernatural exists, and that the religion that taught it was not deception; in the present the endeavonr has been, to bring men from the supernatural to the biblical, and to make them feel that the Christian religion is not a mere mistake. Thus they have been led from the natural to the supernatural; from the supernatural to the revealed; from the ideal to the historic.[32] The steps of this process in the present century have been twofold:—the philosophical Christianity of Schleiermacher, and the revival of biblical religion. Neander has been already adduced (p. 364) as the type of the Christian movement which sought to unite the two: wishing to appropriate that which he believed, he strove to present Christianity as the highest form of the religious life; as a life based on a doctrine; the doctrine itself being based on a revealed

[32] The anti-Straussian Literature described in Note 38 is an illustration of the German apologetic.

history. It must suffice thus to have indicated, without tracing into detail, the apologetic literature which has been partly named in the Notes of the lectures, and may be found by consulting the references there given.

In all ages the purpose of Evidences has been conviction; to offer the means of proof either by philosophy or by fact. In arguing with the heathen in the first age, the former plan was adopted; the school of Alexandria trying to lead men to Christianity as the highest philosophy: in the middle ages the same method was adopted under the garb of philosophy, but with the alteration that the philosophy was one of form, not matter. In the later middle ages the appeal was to the Church: in the early contests with the Deists to the authority of reason, and to the Bible reached by means of this process; in the later, to the Bible reached through history and fact: in opposing the French infidelity the appeal was chiefly to authority; in the early German the appeal was the same as in England; in the later German it has been a return in spirit to that of the early fathers, or of the English apologists of the eighteenth century, but based on a deeper philosophy; an appeal to feeling or intuition, and not to reflective reason; and through these ultimately to the Bible.

Note 50. p. 373.

ON THE HISTORY OF THE DOCTRINE OF INSPIRATION.

The subject of the history of inspiration has been named both in Lect. III. and VIII. It may be useful therefore to point out the sources for the study of it.

The history of it is briefly sketched in Hagenbach's *Dogmengeschichte*, § 32, 121, 161, 243, 292. A valuable catena of passages relative to the primitive doctrine of inspiration is given in Mr. Westcott's *Introduction to the Gospels*, Appendix B. second edition, 1860; and a continuation of the history to more recent periods in Dr. Lee's important work on Inspiration, especially in Appendices C and G; and in Tholuck's Doctrine of Inspiration, translated in the *Journal of Sacred Literature*, July 1854.

It appears that the theories held respecting inspiration in different ages may be arranged under three classes:

1. The belief in a full inspiration was held from the earliest times, with the few exceptions observable in occasional remarks of Origen, Jerome, Theodore of Mopsuestia, and Euthymius Zigabenus (in the twelfth century).

2. Traces after a time begin to appear of a disposition, (*a*) to admit that the inspiration ought to be regarded as appertaining to the proper material of the revelation, viz. religion; but at the same time to maintain firmly the full inspiration of the religious

elements of scripture. This view occurs in the allusions of the writers just named, and existed in the seventeenth century in the Helmstadt school of Calixt in Germany, and the Saumur school of Amyrault, Cameron, and Placæus, in France; and is stated decidedly by a series of writers in the English church. Some of the latter go so far as to avow, (β) that the value of the religious element in the revelation would not be lessened if errors were admitted in the scientific and miscellaneous matter which accompanies it. This admission increased after the speculations of Spinoza and the pressure of the Deist objections.

3. A third theory was suggested by Maimonides, which was revived by Spinoza, and has been held among many of the rationalists in Germany, and has lately appeared in English literature: this theory is, that the book does not, even in its religious element, differ in kind from other books, but only in degree. It will be observed that a wide chasm separates this view from either of those named under the second head; the only point in common being, that in all alike the writers agree that the nature of inspiration must be learned from experience, and not be determined antecedently by our own notions of optimism, without examining the real contents of revelation. Coleridge would by many be considered to give expression to this third theory in his *Confessions of an Inquiring Spirit.* Perhaps however he hovered between it and the one previously named; being anxious rather to identify inspiration psychologically with one form of the Νοῦς or "Reason," than theologically to confound the material of revelation with truth acquired by natural means.

It is not the purpose of this note to discuss the true view of inspiration; but merely to state the historic facts. The writer may however be allowed to repeat what has been already implied in the preface, that he dissents entirely from the third of these views. To him there seems evidence for believing that the dogmatic teaching implied on religious subjects in holy scripture is a communication of supernatural truth, miraculously revealed from the world invisible. Cfr. p. 29.

On the subject of inspiration, in addition to the works above named, instruction will be derived from the sources indicated in the Essay on Inspiration in Bp. Watson's Tracts, 1785, vol. iv. pp. 5 and 469; and from Dean Harvey Goodwin's Hulsean Lectures, first course, lectures vii. and viii. The first of the above-named views is stated in Gaussen's work on *Theopneustie*, and on the Canon; the third in Morell's *Philosophy of Religion*, c. iv; and in the first three essays of Scherer's *Mélanges de Crit. Religieuse.*

A list of those theologians who have held the second class of views above named, together with the extracts from their writings, is given by Dr. S. Davidson in his *Facts, Statements, &c. concerning* vol. ii. of ed. x. *of Horne's Introduction*, 1857; and Mr. Stephen, in his defence of Dr. R. Williams, 1862, has quoted some of the same passages, and added a few more (*Def.* pp. 127–160.[33]) As the reader was referred hither from Lecture III. p. 114. for the proof of the assertion there made, that this theory had been largely held in the last century in England, it seems fair here to add the references. At the same time this list is not given with the view of endorsing the views of these writers, but merely to prove the accuracy of the assertion in the text of Lectures III. and VIII.

Among English divines, those who have asserted the form of the theory named above as No. 2 *a*, are, Howe (*Div. Author. of Scripture*, lecture viii. and ix.); Bishop Williams (*Boyle Lect.* serm. iv. pp. 133, 4); Burnet (Article vi. p. 157. Oxford ed. 1814); Lowth (*Vind. of Div. Auth. and Inspir. of Old and New Testament*, p. 45 seq.); Hey (*Theol. Lect.* i. 90); Watson (*Tracts*, iv. 446); Bishop Law (*Theory of Religion*); Tomline (*Theology*, i. 21); Dr. J. Barrow (*Dissertations*, 1819, fourth Diss.); Dean Conybeare (*Theolog. Lect.* p. 186); Bishop Hinds (*Inspir. of Script.* pp. 151, 2); Bishop Daniel Wilson (lect. xiii. on *Evidences*, i. 509); Parry (*Inq. into Nat. of Insp. of Apost.* pp. 26, 27); Bishop Blomfield (*Lect. on Acts* v. 88–90).

Among those who have gone so far as to hold the form of the theory above given as No. 2 *b*, are, Baxter (*Method. Theol. Chr.* part iii. ch. xii. 9. 4.; Tillotson (*Works*, fol. iii. p. 449. serm. 168); Doddridge (*on Inspir.*); Warburton (*Doctr. of Grace*, book i. ch. vii; Bishop Horsley (serm. 39 on Ecc. xii. 7. vol. iii. p. 175); Bishop Randolph (*Rem. on Michaelis Introd.* pp. 15, 16); Paley (*Evidences of Christianity*, part iii. ch. ii); Whately (*Ess. on Diff. in St. Paul*, Ess. i. and ix; *Sermons on Festivals*, p. 90; *Pecul. of Christianity*, p. 233); Hampden (*Bampton Lect.* pp. 301, 2); Thirlwall (Schleiermacher's *Luke*, Introd. p. 15); Bishop Heber (*Bampt. Lect.* viii. p. 577); Thomas Scott (*Essay on Inspir.* p. 3); Dr. Pye Smith (*Script. and Geol.* 276, 237. third ed.); Dean Alford (*Proleg. to Gosp.* ed. 1859) vol. i. ch. i. § 22.[34]

It will be observed however, that both these classes of writers are separated by a chasm from those which belong to the third class above named; inasmuch as they hold inspiration to be not only miraculous in origin, but different in kind from even the highest forms of unassisted human intelligence.

[33] Dr. Pusey also, in his *Hist. Inq. on German Theol.* p. 2. ch. v, quoted many passages illustrative of the history of the same fact. He has, however, subsequently disavowed all concurrence in the opinions of the writers cited.

[34] Among writers who lived earlier than the periods alluded to in the passages of Lectures III. and VIII., the following are also cited in the works before named: Origen (*Comm. in Joan.* ii. 151. ed. Huet); Jerome (*Comm. in Gal* iii. vol. iv); Augustin (*in Joan.* iv. 1); Zuinglius (*Schrift.-von Usteri*, ii. 247); Calvin (*Comm. on Hebr.* ii. 21. Rom. iii. 4. Rom. ii. 8); Bullinger (on 1 Cor. x. 8), Castellio (*Dial.* ii. *de Elect.* on Rom. ix), Erasmus (on Matt. ii); Grotius (*Vot pro Pac. art. de Can. Script.*); Episcopius (*Inst. Theol.* iv. § 1). Passages of Hooker and Chillingworth were also cited by Mr. Stephen.

INDEX.

The figures refer to the pages, without distinction of text from foot-notes.

C.

D.

E.

Aids to Faith:

A SERIES OF THEOLOGICAL ESSAYS.

BY VARIOUS WRITERS.

Being a Reply to "ESSAYS AND REVIEWS."

1 vol., 12mo, cloth, 538 pages, $1.50.

CONTENTS.

I.	*On Miracles as Evidences of Christianity.*	H. L. MANSEL, B. D., Waynflete Professor of Moral and Metaphysical Philosophy, Oxford; late Tutor and Fellow of St. John's Coll.
II.	*On the Study of the Evidences of Christianity.*	WILLIAM FITZGERALD, D. D., Lord Bishop of Killaloe.
III.	*Prophecy*	A. M'CAUL, D.D., Professor of Hebrew and Old Testament Exegesis, King's College, London, and Prebendary of St. Paul's.
IV.	*Ideology and Subscription*	F. C. COOKE, M.A., Chaplain in Ordinary to the Queen, one of H. M. Inspectors of Schools, Prebendary of St. Paul's, and Examining Chaplain to the Bishop of Lincoln.
V.	*The Mosaic Record of Creation*	A. M'CAUL, D.D., Professor of Hebrew and Old Testament Exegesis, King's College, London, and Prebendary of St. Paul's.
VI.	*On the Genuineness and Authenticity of the Pentateuch.*	GEORGE RAWLINSON, M.A., Camden Professor of Ancient History, Oxford; and late Fellow and Tutor of Exeter Coll.
VII.	*Inspiration*	EDWARD HAROLD BROWNE, B. D., Norrisian Professor of Divinity at Cambridge, and Canon Residentiary of Exeter Cathedral.
VIII.	*The Death of Christ*	WILLIAM THOMSON, D. D., Lord Bishop of Gloucester and Bristol.
IX.	*Scripture and its Interpretation*	CHARLES JOHN ELLICOTT, B. D., Dean of Exeter, and Professor of Divinity, King's College, London.

EXTRACT FROM PREFACE.

This volume is humbly offered to the great Head of the Church, as one attempt among many to keep men true to Him in a time of much doubt and trial. Under His protection, His people need not be afraid. The old difficulties and objections are revived, but they will meet in one way or another the old defeat. While the world lasts skeptical books will be written and answered, and the books, perhaps, and the answers alike forgotten. But the Rock of Ages shall stand unchangeable; and men, worn with a sense of sin, shall still find rest under the shadow of a great rock in a weary land.

HISTORY
OF
CIVILIZATION IN ENGLAND.

By HENRY THOMAS BUCKLE.

2 Vols. 8vo, Cloth. $6.

(*From the Boston Journal.*)

"Singularly acute, possessed of rare analytical power, imaginative but not fanciful, unwearied in research, and gifted with wonderful talent in arranging and moulding his material, the author is as fascinating as he is learned. His erudition is immense—so immense as not to be cumbersome. It is the result of a long and steady growth—a part of himself.

(*From the Chicago Home Journal.*)

"The master-stroke of the first volume is the author's skill and success in delineating the train of causes which resulted in the early French Revolution (1793). These causes, with their combinations, are so arranged that the mind of the reader is prepared for results not very unlike such as actually occurred, horrible as they were.

(*From the Boston Transcript.*)

"His first volume evinces a clear head, an intrepid heart, and an honest purpose. A true kind of induction characterizes it. Indeed it is almost a new revelation, comprising the fidelity of Gibbon, the comprehensiveness of Humboldt, and the fascination of Macaulay."

(*From the N. Y. Daily Times.*)

"We have read Mr. Buckle's volumes with the deepest interest. We owe him a profound debt of gratitude. His influence on the thought of the present age cannot but be enormous, and if he gives us no more than we already have in the two volumes of the *magnus opus*, he will still be classed among the fathers and founders of the Science of History."

(*From the Newark Daily Advertiser.*)

"The book is a treat, and even 'mid the din of battle it will be extensively read, for it bears no little upon our own selves, our country, and its future existence and progress."

THE

TWO GREAT ANSWERS

TO THE

RECENT ATTACK ON THE BIBLE.

I.—REPLIES TO "ESSAYS AND REVIEWS."

With a Preface by the Lord Bishop of Oxford. 1 *Vol.*, 12*mo*, *Cloth*, $1.50.

CONTENTS.

I.—THE EDUCATION OF THE WORLD. By the Rev. E. M. GOULBURN.

II.—BUNSEN, the CRITICAL SCHOOL, and Dr. WILLIAMS. By the Rev. J. H. ROSE.

III.—MIRACLES. By the Rev. C. A. HEURTLEY, D.D.

IV.—THE IDEA OF THE NATIONAL CHURCH. By the Rev. W. J. IRONS, D.D.

V.—THE CREATIVE WEEK. By the Rev. G. ROBINSON, M.A.

VI.—RATIONALISM. By the Rev. A. W. HADDAN.

VII.—ON THE INTERPRETATION OF SCRIPTURE. By the Rev. CHR. WORDSWORTH, D.D.

APPENDIX:

I.—LETTER FROM THE REV. ROBERT MAIN, M.A., Pembroke College, Radcliffe Observer.

II.—LETTER FROM JOHN PHILLIPS, M.A., Magdalen College, Reader in Geology in the University of Oxford.

II.—AIDS TO FAITH.

A Series of Theological Essays by Various Writers. 1 *Volume*, 12*mo*, 539 *pages*, $1.50.

CONTENTS.

I.—ON MIRACLES AS EVIDENCES OF CHRISTIANITY. By H. D. MANSEL, B.D.

II.—ON THE STUDY OF THE EVIDENCES OF CHRISTIANITY. By WILLIARD FITZGERALD, D.D.

III.—PROPHECY. By A. MCCAUL, D.D.

IV.—IDEOLOGY AND SUBSCRIPTION. By F. C. CROOKE, M.A.

V.—THE MOSAIC RECORD OF CREATION. By A. MCCAUL, D.D.

VI.—ON THE GENUINENESS AND AUTHENTICITY OF THE PENTATEUCH. By GEO. RAWLINSON, M.A.

VII.—INSPIRATION. By EDWARD HAROLD BROWNE, B.D.

VIII.—THE DEATH OF CHRIST. By WM. THOMSON, Bishop of Gloucester and Bristol.

IX.—SCRIPTURE AND ITS INTERPRETATION. By CHAS. JOHN ELLICOTT, B.D.

ON

THE ORIGIN OF SPECIES

BY

Means of Natural Selection;

OR,

THE PRESERVATION OF FAVORED RACES

IN THE

STRUGGLE FOR LIFE.

BY

CHARLES DARWIN, A. M.

One Volume. 12*mo.* *Cloth,* $1.50.

"His first point is to show that species are in many cases not well defined, and that the whole order of natural history seems to be in a state of mutation, by reason of constant variations. Thus even under domestication, important changes may be introduced by intercrossing, by selection of the best individuals for propagation, by crossing parents marked by however slight, but favorable peculiarities.

"His second point is what he terms the universal and necessary struggle for existence. This follows from the high geometrical ratio of increase common to all beings. If there were no catastrophes, any one of the existing species would be sufficiently numerous in a few thousand years to cover the whole earth, to the exclusion of everything else.

"His third point is to prove that this struggle is directed by the law of natural selection. Even the races of domestic animals may be constantly improved and modified by choosing the best individuals for propagation. Nature brings the same discipline to bear upon the whole domain of animal and vegetable life. She seizes at once upon any slight variation that is favorable, and perpetuates it; in the universal pressure, any variation that is injurious is immediately extinguished."

www.ingramcontent.com/pod-product-compliance
Lightning Source LLC
LaVergne TN
LVHW021303110826
845150LV00003B/467

* 9 7 8 1 4 2 5 5 6 0 1 9 5 *